THE NAKSHATRA PERSPECTIVE

Om Gam Ganpataye Namaha

Harleen Kokri

The Nakshatra Perspective

Copyright © *Harleen Kokri*, 2025
All Rights Reserved

This book is subject to the condition that no part of this book is to be reproduced, transmitted in any form or means; electronic or mechanical, stored in a retrieval system, photocopied, recorded, scanned, or otherwise. Any of these actions require the proper written permission of the author.

Table of Contents

Disclaimer i
About the Author iii
Acknowledgements iv
Introduction v
Part 1 Prelude to the Nakshatras 1
   Chapter 1 The Cosmic Beginning 2
   Chapter 2 The 5 Elements 5
   Chapter 3 Layers of Astrology 12
   Chapter 4 The Cycles of Time 18
   Chapter 5 Planets - The Base Layer 22
      1 Sun 24
      2 Moon 37
      3 Mars 52
      4 Mercury 61
      5 Jupiter 71
      6 Venus 80
      7 Saturn 91
      8 Rahu 108
      9 Ketu 117
Part 2 The 27 Nakshatras 126
   1 Ashwini 127
   2 Bharani 156
   3 Krittika 178
   4 Rohini 203
   5 Mrigashira 225
   6 Ardra 257
   7 Punarvasu 280
   8 Pushya 311
   9 Ashlesha 339
   10 Magha 367

11 Purva Phalguni	390
12 Uttara Phalguni	404
13 Hasta	421
14 Chitra	435
15 Swati	449
16 Vishakha	464
17 Anuradha	482
18 Vishakha	499
19 Anuradha	517
20 Jyeshtha	534
21 Mula	552
22 Purva Ashadha	568
23 Uttara Ashadha	581
24 Shravana	602
25 Dhanishta	616
26 Shatabhishak	632
27 Purva Bhadrapada	647
28 Uttara Bhadrapada	663
29 Revati	676
Part 3 Application of the Nakshatras	688
Nakshatra Application	689
An Afterthought	702
Bibliography	705

Disclaimer

The planetary combinations and predictions described in this book are only an indication of the tendencies and are in no way the complete truth of life situations. To make precise predictions the whole birth chart should be looked at before coming to any probable conclusions.

The examples given in this book are of friends and relatives whom I know personally and whose consent has been taken before disclosing their birth data information or writing about any of their life experiences. However, their real names have not been revealed in order to protect and respect their privacy. The other examples given are from internet research of famous personalities who are still alive or have passed away. This has been done because the nature of the content of this book is research-oriented, whereby the examples help us to better understand the effect of the movement of the planets and nakshatras (constellations) from an astrological perspective.

This book is dedicated to the loving memory of my mum.

About the Author

The author, a dedicated teacher by profession, has nurtured a lifelong fascination with astrology since childhood. However, the demands of an active teaching career left little opportunity to explore this passion in depth. The creation of this book took shape during the COVID-19 pandemic years of 2020–2022, a period when circumstances necessitated a homebound lifestyle, providing the author with a unique opportunity for reflection and study.

Through extensive research into yoga, Ayurveda, astrology, and astronomy, alongside the analysis of numerous birth charts, the author has gained profound insights into the complexities of life. This journey of discovery has been both enriching and transformative, marking a significant learning experience.

The author found particular joy in creating the illustrations for this book, viewing the artistic process as a meditative endeavour. Each carefully crafted image serves as a powerful and elegant means of conveying intricate concepts with clarity and beauty.

The author extends gratitude to readers for engaging with this comprehensive exploration of Nakshatras, presented through the lens of Vedic wisdom. This work aims to bridge ancient knowledge with its modern applications, and it is hoped that readers find the astrological journey as rewarding as the author found in its creation.

Harleen Kokri

12.08.2022

Acknowledgements

The writing of a book, or any significant effort, cannot happen without the conducive ambience of the homely environment. I sincerely thank my husband for his incredible patience and cooperation, my son and daughter for their loving encouragement, my sister for her jovial motivation and my granddaughter for the innocent words of joy which worked like an inspiration for me.

Special thanks to all my friends, relatives and acquaintances who kindly allowed me to write about some of their life situations for explaining various concepts of birth chart readings.

Introduction

Life is a fantastic journey of a colourful kaleidoscope of experiences which we gather from the first inhalation to the last exhalation. This book is written as a humble attempt to understand the mysteries of life through the functioning of the horoscope. The effect of the planets, constellations - nakshatras and zodiac signs as arranged in individual horoscopes. To get deeper insights into the cause and effect principle behind our actions in terms of thoughts, feelings, words and actions.

As a part of that quest to understand the profound wisdom of Vedic Astrology, I started writing this book in the summer of 2020 and completed it in the summer of 2021. It was during the tumultuous time of the COVID-19 pandemic, which proved to be a blessing in disguise, because it gave me a lot of tranquil time to write this book. For me, it has been a way of paying homage and honouring the 9 planets (Navgraha) - an inner yajna of gathering relevant information, of thoughts, contemplation, reasoning, logic, understanding and insights.

In order to understand the nakshatras, we have to first delve into the basics of Vedic astrology because once we know the basic layers, we can build a beautiful multi-layered and colourful tapestry of astrological knowledge, insights and wisdom.

The word Veda literally means knowledge. The roots of Vedic astrology can be traced back to Rig Veda. This ancient text is considered to be at least 5000 years old. Vedic Astrology is one of the branches of Vedanta. The ancient texts of Vedas are a science of the body, mind and soul. Yoga, Ayurveda and Astrology are all sister sciences and complement each other beautifully.

Just as the ancient texts in all cultures across the world hold wisdom and give us insights into the profound aspects of life and death. Similarly, a long time ago, the ancient Vedic texts were narrated by our Rishis and Sidhas (the enlightened beings). The historians say that these renditions were initially passed on from one generation to the next through oral recitations and were later written down around 1500 - 1200 BC.

The knowledge of astrology is based on the keen observations, deep insights and scholarly research of ancient Rishis (seers). They derived their calculations by observing the synchronicity and meaningful coincidences between themselves and the other life forms that they experienced around them. The natural curiosity of man and the keen study of heavenly bodies, as seen in the sky, led to the birth of astrology.

Astrology

Astrology is the study of the movement of the celestial bodies - the planets and star constellations, and their relative position as seen from Earth. Based on these keen observations, interpretations are made by looking at the natural and cyclical patterns and the influence these changes have on the human psyche.

Although, in recent times, astrology has been reduced to a mere predictive tool, its real purpose is much deeper, which, when applied with greater understanding, can lead to the realisation of our true nature. Astrology helps us to understand destiny or fate with more clarity and create our future the way we want.

Sadhguru Jaggi Vasudev, the founder of the Isha foundation. An enlightened being and a well-known yogi of our times. According to him -

> *"Destiny is not a fixed destination, it's what you create."*

Carl Jung, a famous Swiss psychiatrist, who lived from 1875 -1961, was the founder of analytical psychology, had said that -

> *"What is not brought to consciousness, comes to us as fate."*

The ultimate purpose of studying any Vedic subject is to know our true self, and astrology is one such branch where we get to understand our true nature through the study of stars and planets and its influence on all life forms on Earth. In order to grasp the basics of Vedic astrology, let's first briefly look at the concepts of Karma, Jeeva Atma and Consciousness, destiny, and the story of our creation since this is where the human version of the story of life begins.

Karma

The word karma means action. It is the cause-and-effect principle of our actions and its consequences. This philosophy helps to explain the cycle of reincarnation. The karmic body is like a conditioned soul, which becomes the cause of the next birth. Vedic astrology connects the dots of birth and death and all the life events that happen between these 2 crucial junctures.

Karma can be broadly categorised into 2 parts -

- Sanchit karma - the storehouse of all previous karma of many lifetimes.
- Prarabd karma - the allotted karma for this lifetime.

In his book 'Karma,' Sadhguru explains that -

The word karma literally means action. It simply means we have created a blueprint for our lives. We are the makers of our own fate. In shifting the responsibility from heaven to oneself, one becomes the maker of one's own destiny. Karma is the natural basis of all existence and does not allow us to hold anyone else responsible for our own actions. It is an existential and ceaseless mechanism.

> "Do not think of karma in terms of lifetimes. Think of it in terms of this living moment. What is past cannot be fixed, what is now can only be experienced, what is next can be created."
> – Sadhguru
>
> "The less you understand life, the more you think it is accidental. Life is not accidental, everything happens between cause and effect."
> – Sadhguru
>
> "Punarapi jananam punarapi maranam."
> – Adi shankaracharya

He was an 8th-century Indian Philosopher who consolidated the doctrine of Advaita - non-duality.

Over and over again, we come into the cycle of life and death. Why does a soul choose to take birth again and again? The simple answer is to experience life. When a soul leaves the body, it is a crucial point and becomes the deciding factor for which womb the soul will choose to come into for the next birth. For instance, If in previous life one had a short life span, then in this life, the soul will be born with the desire for a longer life. Then, all the planetary arrangements will be such that they facilitate this desire.

Jeeva Atma -

Until we reach that final truth and experience it for ourselves, the journey of the soul continues. The ancient Vedic texts describe an individual soul is called <u>Jeeva Atma</u> - the individual soul that is conditioned by experiences of various lifetimes.

There are 2 kinds of lineages -

- <u>Ancestral lineage</u> - This is the lineage of our grandparents and great grandparents and further back...It is the lineage of the physical body which decides our physical and personality attributes.

- <u>Personal lineage</u> - The other is the subtle lineage of our soul. This is our very personal lineage, which is encapsulated in Jeeva atma (jeeva is the conditioned consciousness, and atma is the pure unconditioned non-physical dimension, which has no boundaries).

Based on the previous tendencies and patterns that the soul has gathered over time, through repeated cycles of life and death, it chooses the womb to be born into. And so the play of karma continues life after life.

Consciousness

The word consciousness, in simple terms, can be stated as pure awareness.

<u>Dr Deepak Chopra</u> is an endocrinologist, settled in California USA. He is the author of many books on a holistic approach to medicine, which combines the concepts of Ayurveda and Modern medicine. He is the founder of Chopra Well, which offers programmes on healthy living, wellness and spirituality. He says that -

> *"Consciousness can be described as a place inside us that is perfectly healthy, never dies, and is never stressed. Our real body is not physical - our real body is the body of bliss. Perfect health is a blissful body."*

The Story of the Beginning of the Creation

Taittiriya Upanishad, one of the Vedic texts, interestingly describes the scientific basis of creation in this chant. It gives a sequential description - of how consciousness manifests itself into the 5 basic elements.

> *"Tasmadva etasmadatmana akash sambhutah,*
> *Akasadvayuh, Vayoragnih, Agnerapah,*
> *Adbhyah prithvi, Prithivya osadhayah,*
> *Osadhibhyosnam, Annat purusah."*
>
> <u>Meaning</u> -
> From that which is atman (soul) - space came into being,
> From the space - came the wind,
> From the wind - came fire,
> From the fire - came water,
> From the water - came earth,
> And from the earth - came the plants,
> From the plants - came food,

The nature of the human mind is such that it's curious to know unknown things. This quest takes us to various places and to meet different people in order to explore the outer world. However, to explore the mystical dimensions which are beyond the stars and the inner world, which is beyond our daily perceptual experience - one has to pay keen attention to the inner depths of the body and mind.

> *"Yatha pinde tatha brahmande, yatha brahmande tatha pinde."*
> - *Yajur Veda.*
>
> <u>Meaning</u>:
>
> As is the individual, so is the universe, as is the universe so us the individual.
>
> <u>Pinde - microcosm - the atomic level.</u>
> <u>Brahmande - macrocosm - the cosmos.</u>

This famous verse of Vedic texts states that -

This scientific and philosophical statement - *"As is the microcosm - so is the microcosm"* stands true literally. Because the universal laws of physics that operate in the solar system and the entire cosmos also stand true at the atomic level. When we go deep enough into any subject, we discover that what we know is very limited and what is unknown is limitless. Now, scientists are saying that everything comes from nothingness. Yogis call it the Shoonya, the stillness, the purusha from which emerges the whole creation - which is called Prakriti - the manifest form.

Practising Vedic mantras systematically, diligently, and with total concentration helps us to come to a state of complete ease, and this allows the physical, mental, and energy body to regain its natural state. The transformative power of the Vedic mantras is based on the scientific fact that all forms of sound are nothing but a particular form of vibrational energy that allows us to connect to that specific frequency.

<u>Albert Einstein</u>, who has been the greatest physicist of all time, is world famous for giving us the theory of relativity and for his contribution to the development of quantum mechanics. His genius gave us the universal formula, $E=mc^2$. This means energy and matter are interchangeable, or in other words everything is the same energy expressed in different forms. Energy is never lost; only its form changes.

> *" Science without religion is lame, religion without science is blind."*
> — *Albert Einstein*

Nature of the Soul

Isha Upnishad, states that the soul is the unbounded energy that is never lost, it just changes forms. It's beautifully said in this famous hymn of the Vedas. This mantra is commonly chanted as a prayer before the study of any Vedic subject begins.

ॐ पूर्णमदः पूर्णमिदं पूर्णात्पूर्णमुदच्यते ।
पूर्णस्य पूर्णमादाय पूर्णमेवावशिष्यते ॥
ॐ शान्तिः शान्तिः शान्तिः ॥

"Om Puurnnam-Adah Puurnnam-Idam, Puur Naat-Puurnnam-Udacyate,
Puurnnasya Puurnnam-Aadaaya Puurnnam-Eva-Avashissyate,
Om Shaantih Shaantih Shaantih."

<u>Meaning-</u>
Om - omnipresence, Purna -complete , full
Adah - that , outer , supreme soul, infinite
Idam - this , inner ,individual soul

Udachayate- manifested, has come out, Adaya - giving away to Eva- thus, this way, Vashishyate- what remains, remainder, essence, pure - As said by Rishi Vashishta.

That, which is outside, the infinite self is complete .
This, which is the inner self, is complete.
From that complete unmanifest has manifested the form.
When the manifest is merged back into the unmanifest ,
What remains is complete.

Part 1
Prelude to the Nakshatras

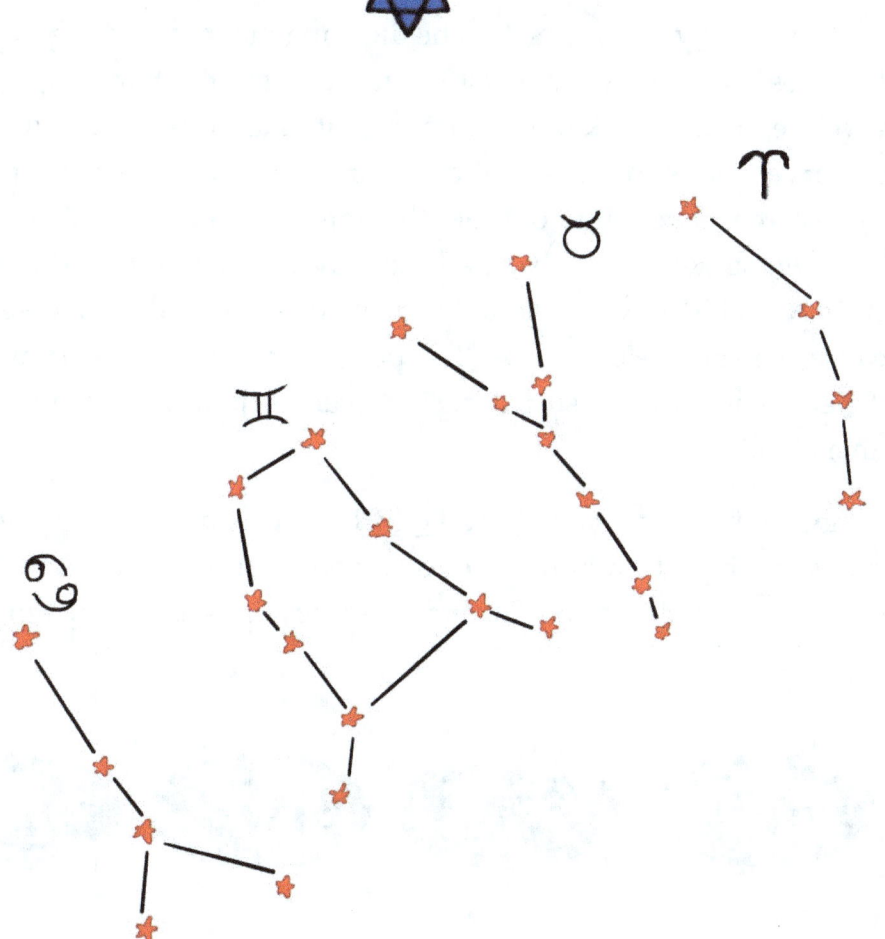

Chapter 1
The Cosmic Beginning

<u>Please note -</u> The explanations given here are very simplistic views of concepts. Of course the intricate nuances of science and mathematics have not been looked at. Because the author is not an expert in any of these subjects, the writing is purely based on the personal understanding of the concepts as seen, heard or read from various sources.

Before diving into Nakshatras, let's understand the basic concepts. It's like learning a whole new language, whether one is learning music, dance, yogic practices, or studying medicine, science or mathematics. We have to start from the basics and build it up in layers of understanding and cognising the concepts.

<u>Nasim Harem the astrophysicist,</u> says that the Big Bang theory was a big step in understanding the evolution of the cosmos. He says we can't be sure that the Big Bang happened. But when we look at the stars we are looking back in time. Because it takes a very long time for the light from distant stars to arrive, it could be a billion years ago. Astronomers, through their keen observations and research, have found out that the universe is expanding. If that is so, then if we rewind time, the universe will shrink back all the way to a single tiny dot. For the creation to happen, this tiny dot would have exploded into space-time reality. However, it's a massive assumption because we can't really locate that point in the universe from where the play of creation began. Science can only measure things to a certain point, and beyond that, it becomes a non-physical dimension.

Imagine the whole universe contained in a <u>POINT</u> - it will surely be a point of infinite density. This point is very, very tiny. It's a billion times smaller than an atom. The Big Bang explosion happened from that very tiny point. Through physics, this point of singularity cannot be calculated.

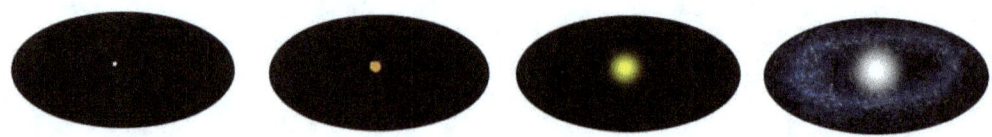

Origin of Elements

Let's start the story from the Big Bang. As the universe expanded and then began to cool down over billions of years. The first protons were formed. Nucleosynthesis is the process that creates new atoms. According to the current theory, the first nucleus was formed 3 minutes after the Big

Bang. After 20 minutes, the universe expanded, and the rest of the elements were formed in this order.

In the first few minutes, the 1st element formed was 75% Hydrogen, followed by 24% Helium. The rest were traces of other elements - lithium and hydrogen isotopes.

This was the beginning of the formation of stars, around which galaxies would spin, and over time, one of them (our Sun) would become the centre of their own solar system. Within the Milky Way galaxy, Our Sun (one of the lucky stars) is placed on the outer spiral arm of the galaxy. It was destined to become the source of life energy around which the planets would revolve, and life would happen on the 3rd planet called Earth (our home).

Later, over many aeons rest of the elements were born from supernova nucleosynthesis within the exploding stars. From Oxygen to rubidium, and all the aspects between them, like nitrogen, calcium, Magnesium, iron, copper and many more were formed. These elements make up the composition of all living and nonliving creatures on Earth. Scientists very famously say that - "*We are made of stardust.*"

This is the story of the outer cosmos; amazingly, our inner cosmos also functions in a similar pattern and on the same laws of physics. An atom is made of a nucleus in the middle, which has positively charged protons and neutrally charged neutrons. Around the nucleus, negatively charged electrons revolve in an elliptical circle, just the way planets revolve around the Sun. The much-heard statement - "*As the macrocosm, so the microcosm,*" literally stands true.

Vedic Perspective

Rigveda mentions hiranyagarbha *(hirnya - golden, radiant and garbha - filled, womb)* as the source of creation. It's like a cosmic egg. Hiranya garbha is our galactic centre, and our solar universe moves around it in the Milky Way galaxy.

Hiranyagarbha is described to be in the shape of a lingam. Sadhguru explains that when the unmanifest begins to manifest, the first form it takes is the shape of an ellipsoid *(the 3-dimensional shape of an eclipse)*. This cosmic lingam (the galactic centre) contains the seed *(purusha - masculine aspect)* and the spiral galaxies are the yoni *(prakruti - feminine aspect)*. Like our Milky Way galaxy, there are trillions of galaxies in the vast infinite cosmic space. Each galaxy has its own centre *(the purusha)* and stars, asteroids and planets revolving around it are the prakruti - the feminine energy.

Purusha is the unmanifest form, the masculine principle, beyond the cause and effect, beyond space and time, it's pure existence. Prakruti is the feminine aspect, the creative force, the manifested attributes of nature. From the union of masculine and feminine, Mahad the cosmic intelligence is born. Which gives rise to the sense of self, Ahankar - ego. From ahankar the 3 gunas - sattva, rajas and tamas are born, which are the result of the interplay of 5 elements. These 5 elements are called <u>Pancha mahabhutas</u> - which means the 5 great elements. These are - space, air, fire, water and earth.

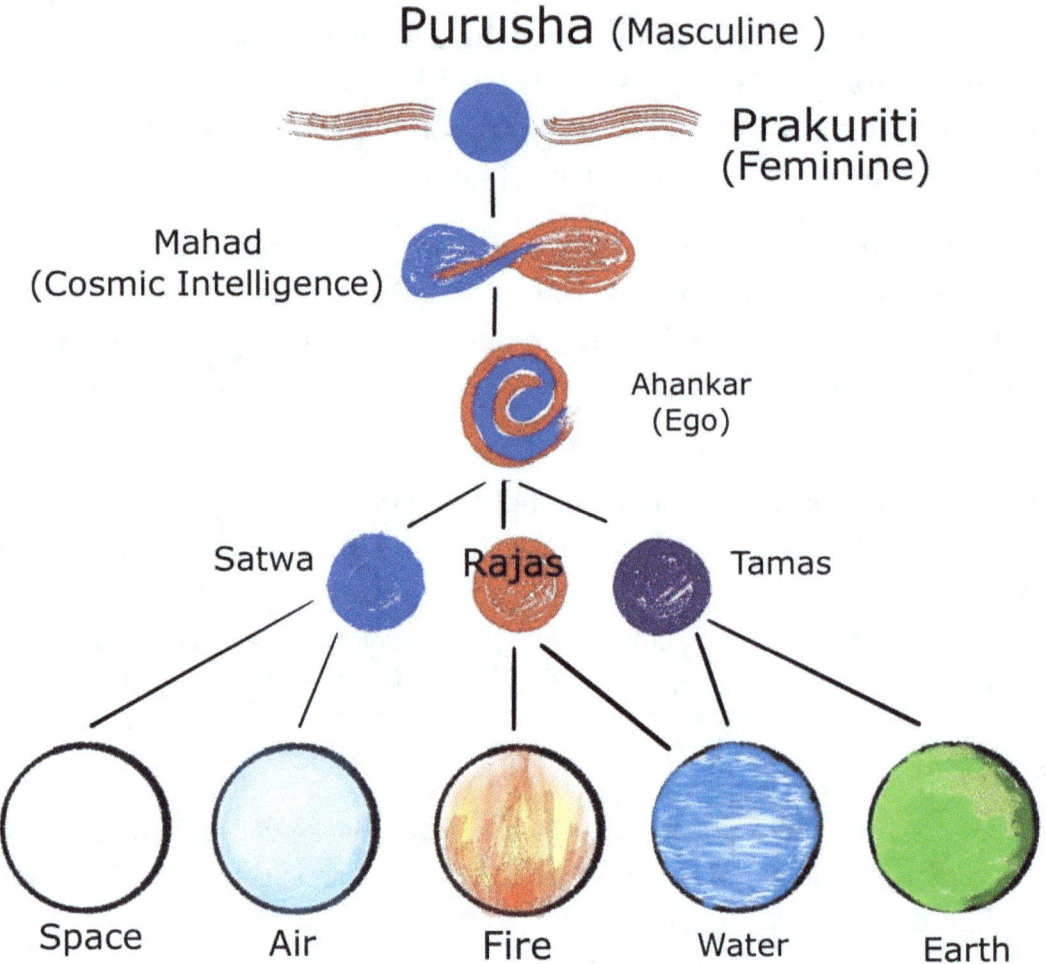

Chapter 2
The 5 Elements

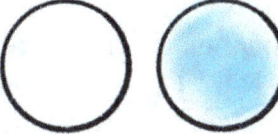

In this chapter we will look at how the basic elements are the foundational ingredients for our individual attributes as -Tamas, Rajwa and Satwa and our constitution as Vata, Pitta and Kapha. And how these qualities are related to the zodiac signs.

The ancient sages called these basic elements as <u>Pancha Mahabhutas</u> - the 5 great elements, because they form the basis of the whole creation. These 5 elements become the foundation or the main ingredients of everything that exists in the universe.

N	Element	Sanskrit name	Qualities
1	Space	Akasha	Etheric, omnipresent, subtle, backdrop of all visible creation.
2	Air	Vayu	air, wind, movement, breath, prana
3	Fire	Agni	heat, warmth, transformative energy.
4	Water	Apah	Fluid, liquid, chemical base.
5	Earth	Bhumi	mass, inertia, solid, tangible, gross

These 5 elements are further associated with 5 sense perceptions, as shown in the table.

Elements related to the sense perceptions -

Elements	Sense perceptions
Space	Beyond the sense perceptions, it is the spatial dimension that accommodates the other 4 active elements.
Air	Is associated with the sense of <u>hearing</u> and is responsible for all movement.
Fire	Gives the sense of <u>sight</u> and is the heat energy that has the ability to transform.
Water	Gives the sense of <u>taste</u> and forms the chemical basis of all matter.
Earth	Gives the sense of <u>smell</u> and <u>touch,</u> and gives solidity and shape to all forms.

Vedic astrology has assigned these elements to particular zodiac signs, which sets their tone and quality. The 5th element of space has not been included because it's not an element as such but a backdrop landscape on which the play of the 4 elements happens - <u>fire, air, water and earth.</u>

For example, Aries carries the energy of fire because fire has transformative energy. Our Sun, which is the source of all life on this planet, is a ball of fire. The heat aspect of fire is needed for any life form to exist. For instance, in the dark crevices of the ocean, where no sunlight reaches, there are hydrothermal vents, which expel extremely hot fluid which seeps through the earth's crust due to the shifting of the tectonic plates. This makes the surrounding environment a perfect habitat for a range of organisms to survive and thrive even in the cold, dark depths of the ocean floor.

The ancient sages assigned the first sign - Aries, to the fire element because without the warmth of the fire, life cannot exist. Even our body has a normal core temperature of 37 degrees centigrade. Similarly, other astrological signs have been assigned an element based on its foundational quality.

We will look at the nature of these elements a little more in detail later while describing the nakshatras. Here is the table of the elements, signs and houses assigned to them in a standard horoscope.

Element	Sign	House
Fire	Aries Leo Sagitarius	1 5 9
Earth	Taurus Virgo Capricorn	2 6 10
Air	Gemini Libra Aquarius	3 7 11
Water	Cancer Scorpio Pisces	4 8 12

Based on this basic concept of elements, the signs – rashi(s), have been further assigned particular trigunas and tri doshas, which define the character of that zodiac sign. Before we look at the classification, let's briefly understand what are trigunas and tridoshas.

<u>Trigunas</u>

In Sanskrit, the word tri means 3, and gunas means qualities.

Ayurveda looks at life from the perspective of 3 main qualities - trigunas - Rajas, Tamas and Sattva. These are the universal energies that are present in all life forms - animate and inanimate. In every individual, there is a mixture of all 3 qualities in different proportions. These 3 gunas can also be looked at from the perspective of the body, mind and soul.

- The gross physical body that we can touch and feel - has the quality of tamas.
- The mind - that is ever active in the process of thinking - has the quality of rajas.
- The soul - that is the silent witness to everything we do feel or think - has the quality of Satwa.

These trigunas resonate with the 3 functional principles of existence - creation, maintenance and destruction. In the Hindu philosophy, these laws of nature are personified in the form of deities.

- Satwa is the quality of Lord Brahma - the principle of creation.
- Rajas is the quality of Lord Vishnu - it is the principle of maintenance.
- Tamas is the quality of Lord Shiva - is the principle of destruction.

All these 3 aspects are needed for any physical form to manifest, and the wheel of karma recycles again and again the process of life, death and rebirth.

Rajas signifies activity, ambition, passion, change and transformation.

Tamas signifies stability, strength, grounding, inertia, and rest.

Sattva signifies goodness, truth, clarity, and love. It brings joy, health and healing.

This table lists the triguna, element, sign, deity and its characteristics.

Guna	Element	Deity	Characteristics
Rajas	Air Fire Water	Vishnu Maintenance Sustainable	activity, passion, drive, dynamism.
Tamas	Water Earth	Mahesh Destruction Devolution	inactivity, restfulness, sleep, dullness, inertia, ignorance.
Satwa	Space Air	Brahma Creative aspect	balance, harmony, purity, creativity.

Tridoshas

According to Ayurvedic philosophy the entire cosmos is an interplay of the energies of the five elements - Space, Air, Fire, Water and Earth. Giving rise to 3 basic gunas - Rajas, Satwa and Tamas.

Stemming from the 5 basic elements and the 3 gunas are the <u>tridoshas - Vata, Pitta and Kapha.</u>

Ayurveda is a Vedic science of healing and rejuvenation, which originated in India about 5,000 years ago. The word Ayurveda means 'The Science of Life.' Just as everyone has a unique fingerprint, each person has a particular pattern of energy - an individual combination of physical, mental and emotional characteristics which make up their own constitution.

The tridoshas manifest as patterns which are present in all physical creation. In the physical body, vata is the subtle energy of movement, pitta is the energy of digestion and metabolism, and kapha is the energy that forms the body's structure.

Guna	Elements	Quality	Pure essence
Vata	Air + Ether	movement, creativity, spontaneity.	Prana - vital life force or energy
Pitta	Fire + water	focused, ambition, passion, activity, leadership.	Tejas - metabolic fire and transformative energy
Kapha	Water + Earth	calm, nurturing, stable, grounded.	Ojas - maintains cellular and metabolic activity

According to Ayurveda, body, mind and consciousness work together in maintaining balance. They are viewed as different facets of one's being. To learn how to balance the body, mind, and consciousness requires an understanding of how vata, pitta and kapha work together.

<u>Vata</u> is the subtle energy associated with movement - composed of Space and Air. It governs breathing, blinking, muscle and tissue movement, pulsation of the heart, and all movements in

the cytoplasm and cell membranes. When in balance, vata promotes creativity and flexibility. Out of balance, vata produces fear and anxiety.

Pitta expresses the body's metabolic system- made up of Fire and Water. It governs digestion, absorption, assimilation, nutrition, metabolism and body temperature. When in balance, pitta promotes understanding and intelligence. Out of balance, pitta arouses anger, hatred and jealousy.

Kapha is the energy that forms the body's structure- bones, muscles, tendons and provides the 'glue' that holds the cells together, formed from Earth and Water. Kapha supplies the water for all bodily parts and systems. It lubricates joints, moisturises the skin, and maintains immunity. When in balance, kapha is expressed as love, calmness and forgiveness. Out of balance, it leads to attachment, greed and envy.

All people have the qualities of vata, pitta and kapha, but one of them is the primary tridosha. The cause of disease in Ayurveda is viewed as a lack of proper cellular function due to an excess or deficiency of vata, pitta or kapha. The disease can also be caused by the presence of toxins. To maintain balance and health, it is essential to pay attention to the choices we make- diet and lifestyle appropriate to one's individual constitution strengthen the body, mind and consciousness.

Prakriti - is our natural constitution, which is determined at the time of conception by a number of factors and remains the same throughout one's life.

Vikriti - is the altered state of the constitution, the change that happens in our natural constitution over time because of various factors like - change of environment, frequent travel, change of diet, change of climate, change of season, stressful relationships, financial anxiety, exhaustion, not getting ample rest and age.

Once these factors are understood, one can take appropriate actions to minimise or even nullify their effects by working on the causes of imbalance and re-establishing one's original constitution. Balance is the natural order, and imbalance is disorder. Health is order, and disease is disorder.

The knowledge of Ayurveda helps us to understand how to create the homeostatic balance of body, mind and consciousness by bringing our altered state of constitution as close as possible to our natural state of constitution. This can be done by making lifestyle changes. Ayurveda places great emphasis on prevention and encourages the maintenance of health by paying close attention to our body type or natural constitution. By detecting the imbalance of the doshas, preventive steps can be taken before the manifestation of a disease.

Ayurveda defines perfect health as not mere absence of disease but a state of perfect balance. When the body, mind and consciousness are in sync. Which is indicated by

- Proper digestion of food - we should feel light and energised after eating.

- Good appetite - we should feel hungry at regular meal times.

- Sound sleep - falling asleep easily and naturally at bedtime at night.

- Waking up fresh - every morning, feeling awake and ready to start the day with invigorated energy levels.

- Elert sense perceptions - our 5 sense perceptions of hearing, seeing, touch, smell and taste should not diminish.

- Regular elimination - daily bowel movements and comfortable elimination of faeces, urine, sweat and monthly menstruation of women.

- Healthy ratio - we should not be overweight or emaciated, there should be a healthy ratio of bone, muscle and fat tissues.

- Good immunity - we should have the natural ability to fight against the disease.

- Healthy skin - the lustre, colour, tone and texture of the skin should be natural and even.

- Contentment - the mind should be peaceful and content.

The holistic approach to perfect health is attained by - modulating our body and mind. Ayurveda looks at the body through the concept of 5 koshas (layers or sheaths), packed one inside the other, like layers of an onion.

1. <u>Annamaya kosha</u> - the food body - the outermost layer of the physical body as we see it. This is the sheath of recycled food.

2. <u>Manomaya kosha</u> - the mental body - is not just the thought process that happens in the brain but the intelligence present in each and every cell of the body. For example, there is more memory and intelligence in each molecule of DNA than our brain can decipher. We usually live and experience life in these 2 outer layers of the body-mind phenomenon.

3. <u>Pranamaya kosha</u> - the energy body - that provides vitality, nourishment and sustenance to the physical and mental body of thoughts and emotions. This layer of energy comes into experience when we walk the spiritual path.

4. <u>Vignayanamaya kosha</u> - the extraordinary knowledge body - is a transitory layer when the physical body is fading into a non-physical dimension. Through regular spiritual practices, one can experience glimpses of this inner sheath where the inner awakening, self-realisation, or knowledge about the ultimate truth unfolds.

5. <u>Anandamaya kosha</u> - the bliss body - is the innermost layer, which is totally non-physical in nature. When one comes in touch with his or her innermost core, one becomes blissful.

That's why Vedas define the soul or consciousness as - <u>Sat, Chita, Ananda</u> - eternal, aware and blissful. To what extent one experiences it varies on their level of spiritual depth. One may experience it as a drizzle of rain or get drenched in it if there is heavy rainfall of blissful drops.

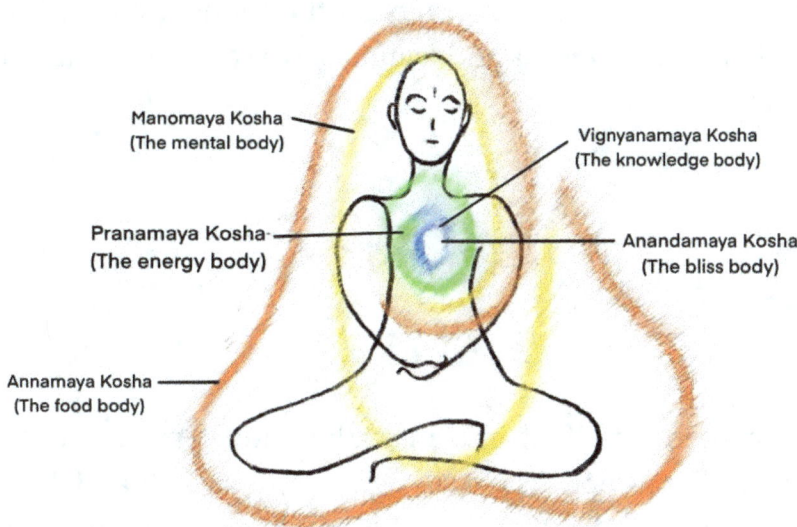

As we go through each nakshatra, we will look at the qualities of each one from the perspective of the elements, trigunas, and tridoshas. This will help to hone in and fine-tune the energy pattern of each nakshatra. This table lists the element, primary triguna and tridosha assigned to each zodiac sign.

Element	Sign	Triguna	Tridosha
Fire	Aries Leo Sagitarius	Rajas Tamas Satwa	Pitta Pitta Pitta
Earth	Taurus Virgo Capricorn	Tamas Satwa Rajas	Kapha Kapha Kapha
Air	Gemini Libra Aquarius	Satwa Rajas Tamas	Vata Vata Vata
Water	Cancer Scorpio Pisces	Rajas Tamas Satwa	Kapha Kapha Kapha

Chapter 3
Layers of Astrology

The concept of astrology is built on multiple layers, which keeps getting complicated as we add more layers to it. This is why we need to establish the foundation well. Once we get a basic understanding of the elements, tridoshas and trigunas, we can slowly build the characteristics of each sign and nakshatra.

Masculine and feminine

The signs have also been classified into masculine and feminine traits according to their placement in the original horoscope. The odd signs - 1, 3, 5, 7, 9 and 11 have been named as masculine and the even signs - 2, 4, 6, 8, 10 and 12 have been called feminine. This tells us more about the quality of that sign. The masculine signs will be more extroverted, ambitious, outward-focused and go-getters. While the feminine signs will be more introverted, receptive, creative and inward drawn.

Motivation

The next aspect of the basic description of the signs is their motivation - the intention behind their actions. The desire that motivates one to think or act in a certain way helps us to get a deeper understanding of human nature.

According to Hindu philosophy, there are 4 primary motivations for life.

Dharma, Artha, Kama and Moksha. Vedic Astrology considers these as the major milestones of human life. The purpose of going through all good and bad experiences, the joys and sorrows, the challenges and learning experiences, is ultimately to attain Moksha - liberation.

Dharma - the word dharma literally means duty. Therefore, all actions that are righteous, not selfish, and lead to our well-being and the well-being of others are dharmic.

Artha - means to gather resources. This desire emerges from the instinct of survival to live well and not to face any shortages.

Kama - means the wish to fulfil our desires. The soul takes birth in order to achieve its desires and go through different experiences.

Moksha - means liberation. After having passed through many varied experiences, life after life, the ultimate desire of every soul is to attain freedom from the cycle of birth and death.

In the standard birth chart, particular signs are assigned to these motivational desires.

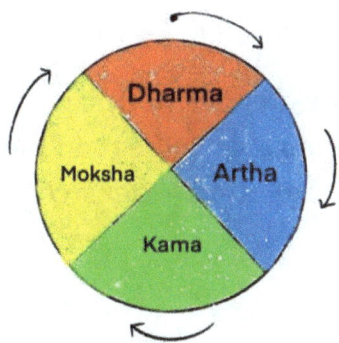

The 3 modes of action

In astrology, each sign is further looked at from the perspective of - what kind of action will be performed based on the type of energy the sign carries. The 3 modes are assigned according to the triguna quality of the zodiac sign.

- Rajas guna is <u>Cardinal - Chara - movable -</u> has the quality of initiating and starting things, is dynamic and action-oriented.

- Tamas guna is <u>Fixed - Sthira -</u> is stable, determined and unyielding.

- Satwa guna is <u>Mutable - Dwi - Dual–</u> it is flexible, communicative, balanced and harmonious.

Here is the table of the characteristics of each sign based on their motivation, gender and mode of action modes of action.

Motivation	Sign	Mode of action	Gender
Dharma	Aries Leo Sagittarius	Rajas - Chara - movable Tamas - Sthira - fixed Satwa - Dwi - dual	1- Masculine 5- Masculine 9- Masculine
Artha	Taurus Virgo Capricorn	Tamas - Sthira - fixed Satwa - Dwi - dual Rajas - Chara - movable	2- Feminine 6- Feminine 10- Feminine
Kama	Gemini Libra Aquarius	Satwa - Dwi - dual Rajas - Chara - movable Tamas - Sthira - fixed	3- Masculine 7- Masculine 11- Masculine
Moksha	Cancer Scorpio Pisces	Rajas - Chara - movable Tamas - Sthira - fixed Satwa - Dwi - dual	4- Feminine 8- Feminine 12- Feminine

Ashta Dikpala

The Sanskrit word Ashta dikpala means - Ashta is 8, dik is direction, and pala is the one who looks after. In Hinduism, there are 8 guardians for the 8 directions, and each direction is ruled by a deity. It is called Kālacakra, or Dasha Dikpala, which means the wheel of time, covering the 10 directions, including the top and bottom.

The 2 more deities represent the Zenith (top) and Nadir (bottom). This ancient Vedic information about the cardinal directions, the deities and mantras helps in the remedial measures in astrology. These directions are also used extensively in Vastu, which is the science of architectural and spatial geometry.

Here is a table of the 10 directions -

Direction	Deity	Planet	Element	Consort	Weapon	Mantra
North	Kubera	Budha Mercury	Water	Bhadra	Gadha Mace	Om Sham Kuberaya Namah
South	Yama	Mangal Mars	Earth	Urmila	Pasam Rope	Om Mam Yamaya Namah
East	Indra	Surya Sun	Earth	Sachi	Vajra Thunderbolt	Om Lam Indaraya Namah
West	Varuna	Shani Saturn	Water	Varuni	Pasha Noose	Om Vam Varunaya Namah
North East	Ishana	Brihaspati Jupiter	Space	Parvati	Trishul Trident	Om Ham Ishanaya Namah
South East	Agni	Shukra Venus	Fire	Svaha	Danda Staff	Om Aam Agniaya Namah
North West	Vayu	Chandra Moon	Air	Lehari	Ankush Goad	Om Yam Vayave Namah
South West	Nirriti	Rahu	Space	Shiva	Khadga Sword	Om Ksham Rakshasaya Namah
Zenith top	Brahma	Ketu	No element	Saraswati	Padma Lotus	Om Hreem Brahmane Namah
Nadir Bottom	Vishnu	Lagna Ascendent	No element	Lakshmi	Chakra Discuss	Om Kleem Vishnave Namah

Vastu directions

Direction	Significance
North	Gain of wealth
North east	Good health
East	Social benefits
South east	Cash flow, security
South	Fame
South west	Relationships
West	Fulfillment of desires
North west	Government and bank support

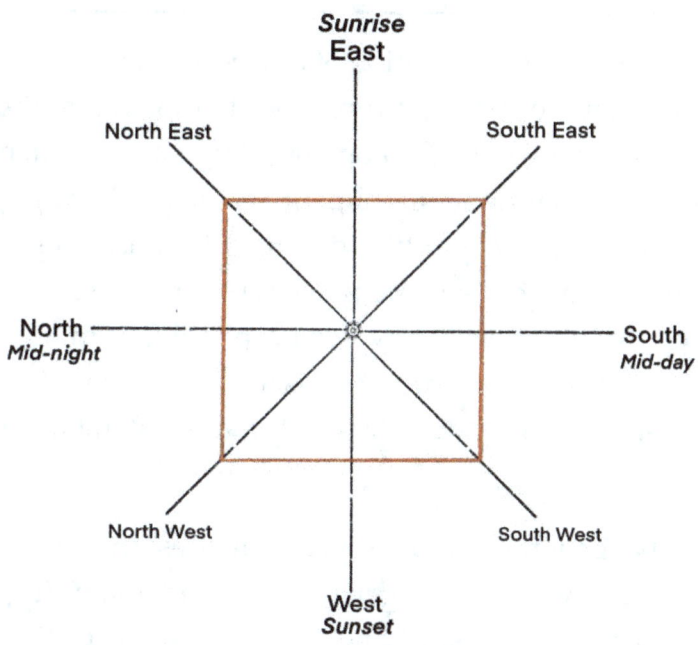

Later, we will look at each nakshatra in the light of these qualities.

The popular zodiac signs -

Most of us are familiar with our zodiac sign, also called sun sign or star sign, according to the date and month we were born in, which is a simple and easy guide. Here is the list of zodiac signs as we know them from a beginner's perspective -

N	Sun sign	Dates
1	Aries	21st March - 19th April
2	Taurus	20th April - 20th May
3	Gemini	21st May - 20th June
4	Cancer	21st June - 22nd July
5	Leo	23rd July - 22nd August
6	Virgo	23rd August - 22nd September
7	Libra	23rd September - 22nd October
8	Scorpio	23rd October - 21st November
9	Sagittarius	22nd November - 21st December
10	Capricorn	22nd December - 19th January
11	Aquarius	20th January - 18th February
12	Pisces	19th February - 20th March

These signs give quite an accurate description of our personality, only that it's too generalised, though it gives us some pointers in the right direction. For example, the sign of Leo runs from 23rd July - to 22nd August. If a person is born on 10th August 2021, then he or she is a Leo. The native will come across as - confident, intelligent, creative, honest, determined, generous, dignified and proud. These are very Sun-like qualities because the Lord of Leo is the Sun. However, all Leo born will not have the same personality, body physiology, mental attributes, likes or dislikes. Moreover, the situations every Leo born will face in life will be very unique and individual for each person. In a way, the horoscope is a tailor-made - destiny map for each one of us. This is where the fine-tuning of Nakshatras helps us understand each Zodiac Sign more deeply.

Basically, looking at the general characteristics satisfies the curiosity of anyone who is intrigued about astrology. But if you want to get a deeper understanding of the subject, you need to give more time and attention. It's like studying any other subject - the more you learn and put the learnt concepts into practice, the easier it gets. Still, one can never fully master it because Vedic Astrology is such a vast subject - it's like an ocean of knowledge. One can only explore one tiny fragment of it and give predictions or advice based on that limited knowledge.

Original horoscope

The standard birth chart is called the Naisargik Kundali, which means the natural placement of houses, signs and their lords. In Vedic astrology the most popular styles of horoscope used are the North Indian and the South Indian style. Here is the diagram of both these styles.

North Indian (anti clockwise zodiac cycle) and South Indian (clockwise zodiac cycle) style birth charts.

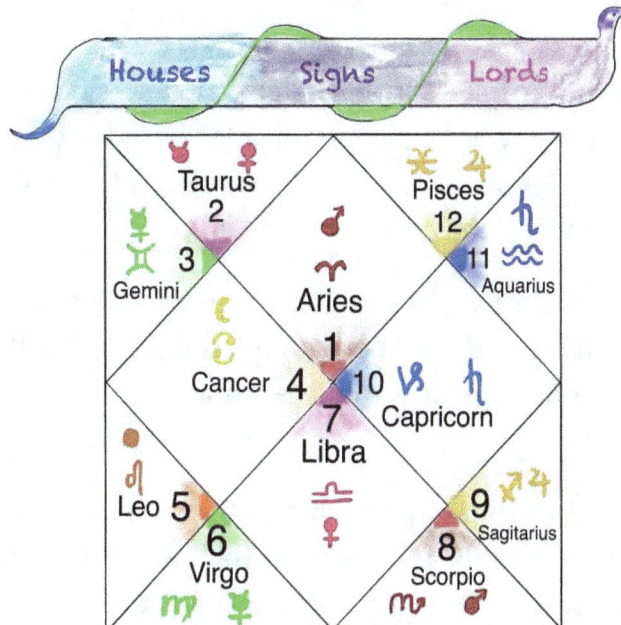

Chapter 4
The Cycles of Time

The word Jyotish means celestial light - it's the study of stars and planets and their impact on Earth and all life on Earth. The science of Vedic astrology is far deeper and far broader than just making predictions, which is only one essential part of Jyotish. To grasp the basics of this mystical and practical subject we need to start with understanding the concept of time.

The ancient seers and sages started measuring time by observing the repetitive patterns in nature. The most obvious cycle is - day and night. At the most basic level, time in itself is a consequence of the cyclical nature of existence. Vedas refer to time as - samaya or Kala (time) chakra, which means a cyclical movement.

At the cosmic scale, the 3 most critical cyclical events that have the maximum impact on us are the Earth's rotation on its tilted axis, causing days and nights and seasons; the moon's revolution around the Earth, causing waxing and waning phases. Earth's revolution around the Sun causes yearly cycles. These 3 cycles together give rise to a - day (vasara), month (masah) and year (varshah).

These cycles affect the functioning of every living creature on planet Earth. As human beings, these cycles of time can be experienced at a deeper level, and intelligent inferences can be drawn from them, which can help us ride the cycles of time. By staying in tune with Mother Nature we enhance our well-being and the well-being of all life that exists on earth.

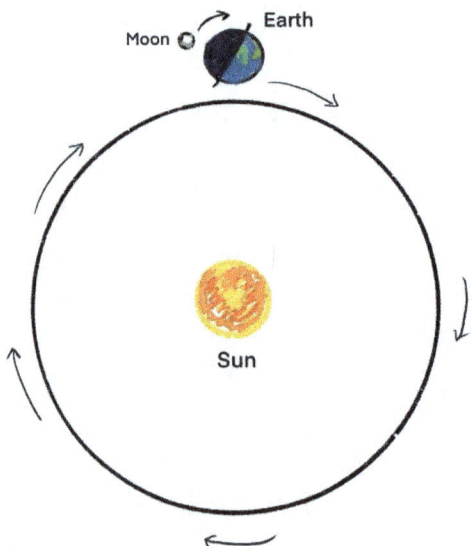

How sensitive one's perception is decides how keenly one can observe both the minutest and the largest cycles of existence.

In these tables, we can see the terminology used by the ancient Vedic scholars for cycles of time - bringing it down to the minutest unit of time (atomic level) - and taking it up to the largest units of time (cosmic level) that can be possibly derived through numerological inference.

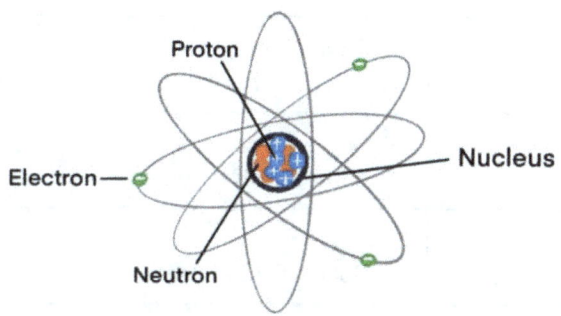

Microcosmic units of time

Units of time	Vedic units of time
1 cycle of day and night 24 hours 12 hours - day 12 hours - night	1 Ahoratra (aho- day, ratri- night) 8 -Prahar (1 prahar = 3 hours) 4 Prahar - day 4 Prahar - night
24 hours	30 mahurats (inauguration) 1 muhurat = 48 minutes
48 minutes	1 muhurat - 2 ghatis 1 ghati = 24 minutes
24 minutes	1 ghati - 30 kalas 1 Kala = 0.80 minutes
0.80 min= 48 seconds	1 Kala - 30 kaastha 1 kaastha = 1.6 seconds
1.6 seconds	1 Kaastha - 18 nimesh 1 nimesh = 0.8 second
0.08 second	1 Nimesh - 30 tatpara 1 tatpara = 0.296 second
0.00296 second	1 tatpara - 100 trutti 1 trutti = 0.0296 second
29.6 microsecond (about half a second)	1 Trutti

Macrocosmic units of time

Units of time	Vedic units of time
1 year on earth	1 Dev ahoratra 1 celestial day
360 earth years	1 Dev varsha 1 celestial year
1728000 earth years	Satya yuga 4800 celestial years
1296000 earth years	Treta yuga 3600 celestial years
864000 earth years	Dwapar yuga 2400 celestial years
432000 earth years	Kali yuga 1200 celestial years
4320000 earth years	Chatur yuga 12000 celestial years
4320000000 earth years	Kalpa yuga 1000 celestial years
8640000000 earth years	1 Brahma ahoratra 2 celestial years
3110400000000 earth years	1 Brahma varsha 360 celestial years

Breath cycles

Normally, we take 12 - 15 breaths/minute.

15 x 60 = 900 breaths/hour. In 24 hours, we breathe -

900 x 60 = 21,600 breaths / 1 day and night.

A nautical mile is the unit of measurement used in marine, air and space navigation. It's interesting to note that there are 21,600 nautical miles around the equator, which is the usual number of breaths a human being takes in 24 hours.

On keen observation, it can be noticed that there are many cyclical patterns in life, from solar cycles, to lunar cycles, from seasons to annual cycles. Our solar system and our galaxy move in a cyclical pattern. Electrons revolve around the nucleus in a cyclical pattern, too. From the outer to the inner cosmos- life moves in a cyclical pattern. Even reincarnation of the soul itself is cyclical. It is just the time frame that varies. Electrons move at supersonic speed, and the planets move at a larger time scale of years, according to our sense of time.

It is very insightful to notice that everything that has manifested in the creation follows a specific pattern. From the sprouting of a seed, which develops its roots and shoots, to the cell division, DNA strands, beating of the heart, to growing and ageing, all work like a divine computer program. This intelligent design is so perfect and gives birth to such complicated life forms that lead to the biodiversity and richness of life.

For instance, the growth of trees in the forest seems random, but nature has an ingenious creative intelligence behind it, otherwise, life in such diverse forms would not have survived on planet Earth for millions of years and continues to do so. Our limited brain power cannot fathom the intricacies of nature but can enjoy the creator's creation by being in tune with all life forms around us.

There is a certain sense of fulfilment and liberation when we understand a concept in depth, and the profoundness of it makes us bow down in humility from the sheer immensity of how much we don't know, and so much more we cannot know. But whatever little we understand helps us appreciate the bounty and the magnificence of the creator.

<u>Inference</u>

Astrology is the science of patterns and numbers derived from paying close attention to everything in nature - solar and lunar cycles, patterns of the stars seen in different constellations, movement of the planets, phases of the moon, equinox times, sunrise and sunset times, change of seasons, observation of plant life, animals and birds. All the knowledge and wisdom we gain from observing nature can be related to health patterns, emotional patterns and human psychology. This is how the ancient sages made possible predictions in astrology based on precise calculations and keen observations.

Chapter 5
Planets - The Base Layer

In Sanskrit, a planet is called a graha, which means - to catch hold of or grasp. In this context, the planets are placed in our horoscope according to our karmic patterns and tendencies, which, in a way, learn us and make us go through certain life situations. This emphasises the significance of the planets and the role they play in our birth charts.

The astrological mechanics, calculations and derivations are layers built up on the base layer of planets. The signs, nakshatras, weekdays, lunar days, deities, colours and sounds have all been assigned a planet. The planets are personified, and the deities assigned to them show their formidable qualities.

Planet	Personification	Deity
Sun Surya	The King	Surya Dev, Agni Dev, Lord Rama
Moon Chandra	The queen	Soma, Chandra Dev, Lord Krishna, Lord Shiva, Devi Parvati
Mars Mangal	The soldier, administrator	Narsimha avatar, Lord Hanuman, Skanda, Kartikeya
Mercury Budha	The prince, student	Vamana Avatar, Lord Vishnu, Devi Saraswati
Jupiter Guru	The teacher, spouse	Brahma, Guru Brihaspati
Venus Shukra	The spouse, feminine	Guru Shukracharya, Devi Lakshmi
Saturn Shani	The worker	Lord Shani, Yama, Bhairav Dev, Devi Kali
Rahu	The head of the serpent	Devi Durga
Ketu	The tail of the serpent	Lord Ganesha

Planets

Let's first look at the qualities of the 9 planets, which will later help us understand fundamental aspects of the nakshatras.

1
Sun

Om hram hreem hraum saha Suraya namah

Sanskrit names	Surya, Ra, Ravi, Aditya, Bhanu, Dinekar, Bhaskar, Arun Grahapati, Arka, Savitr, Pushan, Martanda, Mitra, Prabhakara and Vivasvan.
Lord	of Leo - Simha
Deities	Shiva, Rudra, Vishnu, Indra
Rides on	A chariot pulled by 7 horses - representing the 7 colours of the rainbow.
House	5th house - bhava
Weekday	Sunday
Numbers	1, 10, 19, and 28
Friends	Moon, Mars, Mercury and Jupiter
Enemies	Saturn, Venus, Rahu and Ketu
Neutral	Mercury
Exalted	Aries
Debilitated	Libra
Aspects	the opposite - 7th house from where it sits.
Mulatrikona	Leo
Solar cycle	12 years
Vimshotari dasha	6 years
Matures	at 22 years

Nakshatras	Kritika, Uttara phalguni and Uttara Ashadha
Lunar days	1st tithi - pratipad and 9th tithi - navami
Das Maha Vidya	Matangi
Gender	Male
Cast	Kshatriya - warrior
Element	Fire
Colour	Orange
Motivation	dharma - righteous action
Sounds	All vowels - a, aa, e, ee, u, uo, o, ou
Chakra	Manipura
Tridosha	Pitta
Direction	East
Guna	Satwa
Represents	vegetation - mula
Vehicles	cars, luxury vehicles, caravans, aeroplanes, rockets and spaceships.
Animals	Lions, tiger, bull, goat, horse and mouse.
Birds	Peacock, goose and eagle
Metal	Gold
Gemstones	Ruby
Organs	Heart, teeth, bones, stomach, right eye, spine and chest.
Body part	Ring finger on the hand.
Spices	Black pepper, cardamom, cinnamon and saffron.
Taste	Bitter and pungent
Food	Wheat, gur - jaggery and honey
Plants	Oak tree, wheat, bilva, sunflower, rudraksha tree and thorny plants.
Season	Summer
Places	Forest, mountains, deserts, open fields, temples and mountains.
Objects	Lamps and windows
Signifies	King, father, soul - atma, health, power, authority, name, fame, government, wool, wood and medicine.

Relatives	Father and paternal side relatives.
Diseases	Headaches, loss of appetite, diarrhoea, heart problems, eye, bone, teeth problems, increased bile, fever, increased heat and sun rash.
Yogic practice	Pranayama and hatha yoga.
Chant	Aditya hridyam and Surya gyatri mantra "Om bhur bhuvah svaha, tat savitur varenyam, Bhargo devasya dhimahi, dhiyo yonah prachodayat." Meaning - Om, O earth, sky and heaven, May we place within ourselves the radiance of the divine Savitur, The Sun god, who shall then awaken our insight.
Physical appearance	Average height, sparse hair, reddish brown skin colour and honey coloured eyes.
Qualities	<u>Positive -</u> Dignified, creative, intelligent, generous, royal, regal, independent, proud, confident, active, energetic, enthusiastic, helpful, appreciative, good vitality, pure and powerful. <u>Negative -</u> Mildly cruel, authoritative, egoistic, aloof, irritable, agitated, selfish, restless, forceful and controlling.
Careers	All positions of authority, government job, politician, banking manager, leader, I T consultants, photographer, jeweller, designer, doctor and lawyer.

Astronomical perspective

The Sun and the rest of the solar system formed from a giant, rotating cloud of gas and dust known as the solar nebula. As the nebula collapsed because of its gravity, it spun faster and flattened into a disk. Most of the material was pulled toward the centre to form the sun.

The visible part of the sun is about 10,000 degrees Fahrenheit, while temperatures in the core reach more than 27 million, driven by nuclear reactions. The sun was born about 4.6 billion years ago, and our home planet Earth, was formed about 4.5 billion years ago, as dated by scientists.

Our solar system is located on the outer spiral of the Milky Way galaxy called the Orion arm. It is about 26,000 light years away from the centre of the galaxy. The Sun is the centre of our solar system, and the Earth orbits 93 million miles away from it.

In comparison to other stars in the universe, our Sun is described as a yellow dwarf star, a hot ball of glowing gas. The Sun's magnetic field spreads throughout the solar system and is twice as strong as the Earth's field. The Chemical composition of the Sun shows that the Sun is mainly made of Hydrogen and Helium. Hydrogen is the lightest of all gasses, followed by Helium.

Solar cycle

NASA astronomers have observed over many years that the number of Sunspots increases and decreases because of the Sun's magnetic activity. In about 11 years, the cluster of Sunspots changes from a minimum of none to a maximum of 250, and then back again to a minimum, this cycle is known as one complete solar cycle. At the end of every solar cycle, the magnetic field rapidly reverses its polarity.

The wise sages in ancient cultures often built stone monuments to mark the motion of the Sun and moon, charting seasons, creating calendars and monitoring eclipses. They believed that the Sun revolves around the Earth.

Nicolaus Copernicus, a Polish mathematician and an astronomer, was the first one to formulate the model of the Sun centric solar system in around 1514. In 1608, a telescope was invented by a Dutch spectacle maker, Hans Luppershey. Later, in 1609, Galileo Galilei made an updated version of this telescope, which had 3 times more magnification, in order to study distant stars. He mainly became well known for his findings that -

- The Sun was the centre of the universe.
- Earth was not flat.
- Jupiter had 4 moons.
- The surface of the moon and earth had similar geological make-up.

Deities of the Sun

Since the Sun is the source of life on Earth, he is personified as the king and our soul, in Vedic astrology. Sun worship can be found throughout most of recorded history in different cultures across the world. A Sun god or goddess is invoked for its power and strength. The various forms of solar deities represent a certain aspect of the Sun.

Here is a list of Sun deities in different cultures around the world.

Country	Solar Deity
Egypt Egyptian	Ra- Sun god Horus - god of sky whose right eye is Sun and the left eye is moon. Hathor- Sun goddess mother of Ra and Horus. Khepri - the rising sun Atum- the setting Sun Aten - the visible Sun Sopdu- the summer sun
Mexico Aztec	Nanahuatzin- Sun god Tonatiuh- Sun god and ruler of heavens.
USA Mayan	Ah Kin- Sun god, protects against evil and darkness. Kinich Ahau- Sun god. Hunahpu- Hero twins - sun and moon.
Arab Arabian	Malakbel- Sun god Shams- Solar Goddess

China Chinese	Marici or Doumu- Sun Goddess Xihe- Sun Goddess, mother of 10 suns.
Greece Greek	Helios - Sun god who drives a chariot. Apollo - God of sun and light. Hemera- Goddess of day. Eos- Goddess of dawn.
Germany Germanic	Sol- Sun Goddess with a horse drawn chariot.
Rome Roman	Sol- Sun God riding a horse chariot. Aurora- Goddess of dawn.
Australia Abroginial	Wala-Solar Goddess Yhi or Karur- Goddess of sun, light and creation. Bila- Cannibal sun goddess. Gnowee- Solar goddess who searches for her lost son, her torch is the sun.
Africa Zulu	Umvelinqangi- God of Sun and sky. Magec- Goddess of sun and light. Mawu-Goddess of sun and moon.
India Buddhist	Marici- Goddess of sun and light. Surya- Sun God
Hindu	Surya- Sun God Aruna- Charioteer of Sun God Savitur- God of sunrise and sunset. Aryaman- God of midday. Tapti - Sun Goddess.

The Vedic mythology

The Vedic texts refer to the Sun as the king or soul because he is the initiator of life on earth and the source of light and heat.

Sun god is depicted riding a chariot with 7 horses, which represent the 7 colours of the visible light, and 7 days in a week.

The mythological stories state that Surya was the son of Sage Kashyapa and his wife Aditi. When he grew up he married Sanjana, who was the daughter of Visvakarma. From their marriage, they had 3 children, Vaivasvata (one of the 14 men who were the first to start the human race), Yama (god of the dead), and Yami (goddess of the river Yamuna).

Over time, Samjna could not bear the proximity of her husband, Surya, because of his extreme heat and light. One day, she decided to leave him and left her clone Chaya (Shadow) behind to look after him in her absence. She transformed herself into a mare and went into the forest in order to stay incognito. Surya however, soon found out that Chaya was not his real wife, and he went in search of Samjhana. On finding her disguised as a mare, he transformed himself into a stallion and mated with her. From their union, the Ashwins were born. They are the youthful twin sons who have a horse head.

Meanwhile, Vishvakarma chipped off some of Surya's brilliance, to try and dim his light and heat and make it bearable and easier for his daughter to live with him. From these blazing fragments, various weapons were made for the gods - Vishnu's discus, Shiva's trident, Kubera's club, and Karttikeya's lance.

Mahabharata connection

In the epic of Mahabharata, Karna was the firstborn Son of Kunti and Sun god. Because he was born before marriage, Kunti had to keep it a secret to avoid a scandal. In spite of being a Prince, Karna was brought up by a Charioteer and his wife. For this, Karna suffered immense pain and bitterness in his heart for being called a charioteer's son and faced prejudice in spite of his excellent archery skills.

Karna was known for his generosity, being the son of the Sun god, he inherited his quality of magnanimity. Throughout his life, he followed a disciplinary code of never refusing anyone who came to ask for help just after finishing his morning worship. Indra dev had taken advantage of this and had asked for his Kavach (a protective shield), so that his son Arjun could defeat him in the war. Karna had the special blessing of being given the Kavach (which was attached to his skin right from birth) by his father- Surya Dev. To provide this Kavach to Indra, he had to tear it away from his chest, which literally made him bleed.

Karna was an invincible warrior, skilled at archery just like Arjuna and was the only one who could defeat Arjuna. So, during the Mahabharata war, Kunti had come to ask him for a boon that he would not kill any of the Pandavas in the war. By then, Lord Krishna had told Karna who his real parents were. Karna was hurt deeply by his mother's request and said, "I cannot promise that, but because it's my principle not to refuse anyone who comes to me for help, I assure you that by the end of the war, you will have your 5 sons alive, which ones they will be I cannot say."

Sun-like qualities-

The attributes of the Sun played out in Karna's life very prominently, he was very generous, proud, honest, dignified, brave and feared for his excellent archery skills, which were second to none.

The 12 Adityas -

Bhagavata Purana states that Aditi Devi (Goddess), who was the wife of Rishi (sage) Kashyspa, gave birth to 12 Adityas. These are the 12 qualities of the Sun.

N	Adityas	Sign	Qualities
1	Dhata	Aries	Creativite power Intelligence, idealistic, active, excellence, leadership, radiance, starts new projects and confidence.
2	Aryaman	Taurus	Power of the wind Noble, family oriented, lineage, good resources, family values and tradition, distinguished, determined, convert ideas into reality.
3	Mitra	Gemini	Friend of all Friendly, easy going, knowledgeable, fair, intelligent, liberal, appreciative, affinity to the moon and oceans, forms alliances, contracts and agreements.
4	Varun	Cancer	Lord of the oceans - Emotional, has attachments, follows laws and moral behaviour, works tirelessly on a job, takes responsibility, nurtures, needs the comfort zone and has affinity to water.
5	Indra	Leo	Destroys enemies - Ultimate reality, likes to lead, destroys enemies, is generous, intelligent, creative, learned, holds positions of power, has self control and likes to control situations, can take harsh decisions, and has political interests.
6	Vivasvan	Virgo	Lord of the fire - Bright, radiant, energetic, looks for perfection, purity, likes to serve, spiritually inclined, interested in medicine and likes cooking.
7	Tvashtar	Libra	Lord of the trees and herbs - Material desires, creativity, comforts, thinks more and acts less, seeks balance, likes travelling, meeting people, likes animals and countryside.
8	Vishnu	Scorpio	Destroys enemies - Gives secret knowledge, purifies, infinite resources, emotional depth, explorer, researcher, surgeon, healer, spiritual and psychological interests, transformation and determination.
9	Anshuman	Sagittarius	Lord of the wind - knowledgeable, radiancece, philosophical, optimistism, spiritual, religious, clarity, intelligence, liberal, fights for justice, humanitarian, confidence and bravery.
10	Bhaga	Capricorn	Present in all living beings -

			Reliable, disciplined, hard working, likes luxury, benefits from inheritance, intelligent, practical, detail oriented, devoted, serves people, cares for all, leader, responsible and unyielding.
11	Pushya	Aquarius	<u>Lord of food - makes grains grow-</u> Nourisher, increases the resources, builder, designer, social service, grows food, is involved in agriculture, food business, provider, diplomat, works with large organisations.
12	Prajanya	Pisces	<u>Resides as prana in the offsprings-</u> Spiritual seekers who seek the dimensions of the beyond, calm, intelligent, showers rain, affinity to water, dreamy, imaginative and escapism.

<u>The placement of Sun</u>

The strength or weakness of the planet can be determined by its placement and its degrees. When a planet has the highest degree in the natal chart (atmakaraka) and when it is close to the Ascendant degrees, it will be strong. For example, suppose the Ascendant is at 12 degrees, and Sun is placed in the 10th house at 12 degrees (or in the range of 1 degree before or after 12). In that case, it will be very strong and will be capable of delivering excellent results during its dasha.

The first and the last degrees of any sign are very crucial. For example, when a planet is at 0 degrees, it is in a shoonya state of death or stillness, which can become a powerful possibility for spiritual growth. However, on the materialistic side, the planet will not be able to give results with conviction or assurance. At 1 degree, the planet is still at a very young age and lacks the strength and maturity to deliver results fully during its dasha. Similarly, at 29 degrees, the planet, although it has the wisdom, lacks the energy to give strong and sure results during its dasha.

This table shows the influence of the Sun in the birth chart and its effect.

Influence	Placement	Effect
Sun is strong when placed in	Leo - moolatrikona and own house. Aries - exalted Sun nakshatras - Krittika, Uttara Phalguni and Uttara Ashadha. Directional strength - 10th house. Atmakaraka - highest degree. Near to the Ascendant degree.	Good health, success, confidence, intelligence, creativity, motivation and determination.
Sun is weak when placed in	Libra - debilitated 7th house - no directional strength. At 0, 1 and 29 degrees.	Lack of confidence and low energy.

Inference

Those who have a strong influence of the Sun in their birth chart will have light-coloured eyes with a yellowish tinge, a broad chin and an oval to square-shaped face. It's easy to spot a sun-ruled person by their unmistakably charming and sunny smile that lights up their face.

Usually they have a medium height and are physically fit. Their chest has an expanded and healthy look and is generally more prominent than their lower body. They have a very confident persona and a dignified personality. They have luxurious and shiny hair but tend to have a receding hairline as they get older.

For example, a Leo ascendant person will be very conscious of their physical appearance and gait and like to always dress up smartly. They love being the centre of attention and easily draw attention from other people, not by intent, but through their inherent charm and exuberant personality. They have a pitta-predominant constitution, which makes them very ambitious and active, and they don't like to sit around and waste time.

They are usually very warm-hearted, magnanimous, liberal, joyful, high spirited people and direct and honest in their dealings. But you will also come across quiet and serious-minded introverts if their natal moon is in Krishna paksha (dark cycle), or the moon is conjunct Saturn or the Sun is placed in the Saturn signs of Capricorn and Aquarius, or the Sun is sitting in the nakshatras of Saturn - Pushya, Anuradha or Uttara Bhadrapada.

They are very good at motivating others because they are very enthusiastic and passionate about life. Their creative ideas and exuberant zeal easily rub on to others. They love leading, and because of their confidence, they are able to easily convince others.

For example, the Sun in Punarvasu Pada 1 in Gemini in the 2nd house will be very communicative about their feelings and will love to spend time with their family. Just as a just king never betrays the honour and trust of his kingdom, they will be very loyal towards their family. They will be protective of their loved ones and will always be looked up to for advice because they can confidently handle any kind of crisis in the family.

The beneficence of Jupiter will give them the opportunity and interest to do everything at a grand scale. Very often, they will find themselves in situations where they have to invite many friends at home or attend large social functions. Their family will have a specialised skill of hands in some form of art or craft.

On the other side, they can come across as self centred and elusive. They can be extravagant, and their sensitive ego can easily feel hurt when not appreciated or recognised for their generous actions. When out of their element, they can become irritable, demanding and bossy. For example, the Sun in Swati in Libra in the 6th house can make them very impatient, and they can end up making wrong decisions or making enemies because of their impulsive behaviour. Because the sun is debilitated in Libra and Venus, the Lord of Libra is Sun's enemy. Moreover, Rahu, the Lord of Swati, magnifies this quality, which makes the natives lose their confidence and doubt their creative capabilities.

When the Sun is placed in Aries, it gives good results because it's exalted in this sign. Sun is friends with Moon, Mars and Jupiter and, therefore, does well in their signs of Cancer, Aries, Scorpio, Sagittarius and Pisces. For example, Sun in Scorpio in the 9th house, the natives will have an interest in the occult, spirituality and mysticism. Their father will be their guide and teacher, and they will do a master's degree or research on any of the above subjects. Their research will be motivated by the thought of discovering hidden knowledge or exploring the secrets of the past. They will not be the loud extrovert types but the quiet, intense introverts who go to the depth of exploring any subject, situation, person or relationship. They will not be frivolous but focused, dedicated, honest and loyal to their cause or purpose of life.

The position of the Sun, Moon and Ascendant and the placement of their lords play an important role in deciphering the natal birth chart accurately. Since the Sun is the centre of the solar system, it represents the soul, the initiator of life. In the Jaimini fixed Karkas, the Sun is the Atmakaraka (significator of the soul), and for each individual, the planet with the highest degree is taken as the personalised Atmakarka. Sun as Atmakarka sets the tone of life in terms of the soul desire of a person.

For example, if the Sun is the atma karaka for a Libra Ascendent person, and the Sun is sitting in Capricorn in the 4th house in Shravana, which is the nakshatra ruled by the moon. The native's soul desire is to be loved by the mother and to have an ambience of respect and admiration at home. The native's mother will be an excellent listener (the effect of Shravana) and will have the beautiful quality of being able to pay close attention to his or her likes and dislikes, and will happily do whatever is needed for the wellbeing of her children (Capricorn influence). Therefore, this person will have a very good relationship with his or her mother, and she will be a great influence in the native's life.

Please note - The examples given for each planet have been looked at from the perspective of the Ascendant, because it's the most crucial and important aspect of any birth chart.

Example

Leo Ascendant - ruled by Sun

Paramahansa Yogananda - Spiritual Guru.

Born on 5th January 1893 at 8:30 pm in Gorakhpur, India - left his body on 7th March 1952 in Los Angeles, USA, at the age of 59.

Paramahansa Yogananda was an Indian monk, yogi and guru who introduced millions to the teachings of meditation and Kriya Yoga through his organisation- Self-Realisation Fellowship (SRF) and Yogoda Satsanga Society (YSS) of India. He lived the last 32 years of his life in the USA.

He was the chief disciple of the Bengali yoga guru Swami Sri Yukteswar Giri and was sent by his lineage to spread the teachings of yoga to the West. He is often referred to as the "Father of Yoga" in the West.

Yogananda was born in Gorakhpur, Uttar Pradesh, India, to a Hindu family of Bengali origin. According to his younger brother, Sananda, from his earliest years, young Mukunda's awareness and experience of the spiritual was far beyond the ordinary. His father, Bhagabati Charan Ghosh, was a Vice-President of the Bengal-Nagpur Railway, the travelling nature of his job would move his family to several cities during Yogananda's childhood. When he was 11 years old, his mother passed away, which had a profound effect on him.

After finishing high school, Yogananda formally left home and joined a Mahamandal Hermitage in Varanasi. His spiritual yearning led him to his Guru, Swami Sri Yukteswar Giri, whom he met at the age of 17. He would go on to train under Sri Yukteswar as his disciple for the next 10 years (1910–1920) at his hermitages in Serampore and Puri. Later on, Sri Yukteswar informed Yogananda that he had been sent to him by the great guru of their lineage, Mahavatar Babaji, for a special purpose, to spread yoga throughout the world.

In July 1914, several weeks after graduating from college, he took formal vows into the monastic Swami order. Sri Yukteswar allowed him to choose his own name, Swami Yogananda Giri. In 1917, Yogananda founded a school for boys in Dihika, West Bengal, that combined modern educational techniques with yoga training and spiritual ideals. A year later, the school relocated to Ranchi.

One of the school's first batch of pupils was his youngest brother, Bishnu Charan Ghosh, who learnt yoga asanas there and, in turn, taught asanas to Bikram Choudhury (the famous yoga teacher). This school would later become the Yogoda Satsanga Society of India, the Indian branch of Yogananda's American organisation, Self-Realisation Fellowship.

In 1920, while in meditation one day at his Ranchi school, Yogananda received a vision. He saw the faces of a multitude of Americans, which passed before his mind's eye, intimating to him that he would soon go to America. Seeking out his guru's advice, Sri Yukteswar advised him to go. Later, while in deep prayer in his room, he received a surprise visit from Mahavatar Babaji, the Great Guru of his lineage, who told him directly that he was the one chosen by the Masters to spread Kriya Yoga to the West. Reassured and uplifted, Yogananda soon afterwards accepted the offer to go to Boston.

In August 1920, he left for the United States aboard the ship "The City of Sparta," on a two-month voyage that landed near Boston by late September. In 1925, he established an international centre for Self-Realisation Fellowship in Los Angeles, California, which became the spiritual and administrative heart of his growing work. Yogananda was the first Hindu teacher of yoga to spend a significant portion of his life in the USA.

The last 4 years of his life were spent primarily in seclusion with some of his inner circle of disciples at his desert retreat in 29 Palms, California, to finish his writings. In the days leading up to his death, Yogananda began hinting to his disciples that it was time for him to leave the world. On 7th March 1952, he attended a dinner for the visiting Indian Ambassador to the US, Binay Ranjan Sen, and his wife at the Biltmore Hotel in Los Angeles. At the conclusion of the banquet, Yogananda spoke of India and America and their contributions to world peace. According to an eyewitness – Daya Mata, a direct disciple of Yogananda (who was head of the Self-Realisation Fellowship from 1955 to 2010) – as Yogananda ended his speech, he read from his poem *My India*, concluding with the words "*Where Ganges, woods, Himalayan caves, and men dream God – I am hallowed, my body touched that sod.*" As he uttered these words, he lifted his eyes to the Ajna Chakra, and his body slumped to the floor. His followers said that he had entered mahasamadhi. The cause of death was diagnosed as heart failure.

Analysis

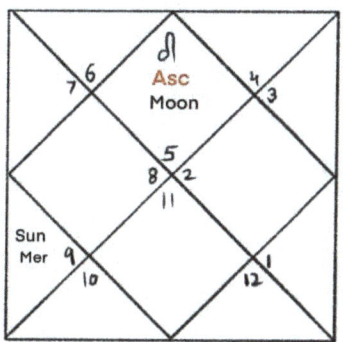 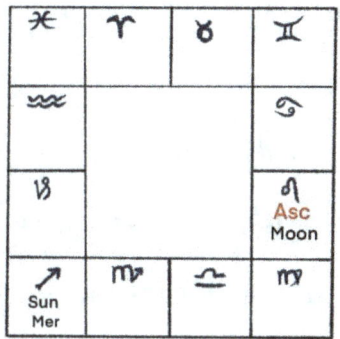

Moon and Ascendant in Leo in Magha.

Paramhansa Yogananda ji has a very strong influence on Leo because both his Ascendant and Moon are in Magha, which is the nakshatra placed in Leo.

The Ascendant and moon in the same house gave him clarity, confidence and steadfastness in his purpose of life. His physical actions were aligned with his thoughts and feelings, and what he pursued with passion manifested in his life. Very prominent Leo qualities can be seen in him - he was intelligent, creative, confident, and took pride in his lineage of Gurus. Leos are idealistic, generous, honest, aloof and proud. Leo is a masculine sign which exudes determination and will power.

It's also a fixed sign which makes them very organised and stubborn about what they want to achieve in life. Here, the soul seeks to blossom with a wild, unleashed beauty and spread its radiance of the bright sunshine across the world.

Sun, the lord of Leo, is sitting with mercury in the 5th house of Sagittarius. The lord of Sagittarius is Jupiter, so it's a fantastic placement because Sun and Jupiter are good friends. Therefore, the dashas and transits of the Sun and Jupiter will give excellent results. He travelled to the USA for the first time in 1920 to spread yoga in the West. He soon founded the Self-Realisation Fellowship in Los Angeles, California. During that time, he was running his <u>Sun Mahadasha</u>.

Moreover, Sun, the Lord of his Ascendant, sitting with mercury in the 5th house, forms a Budha Aditya yoga, which makes him highly intelligent and creative and brings him many students and followers. Just as the Sun is considered the king of the solar system, Yogananda was the master and guru in his field of Kriya yoga.

Sun, the poet

Sun - the day maker, the giver of light,

In his eyes, the spirit of life.

The creative intelligence, an exuberance alive,

On Motivation he thrives.

Sun - the generous, proud and royal king,

Honours his word, love is not a one-day fling.

The confidence that can win hearts - with a Sunny smile,

And gracefully takes all - good and bad in his stride.

2
Moon

Om shram shreem shraum saha Chandraya namah

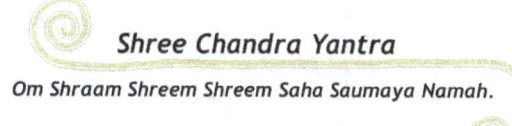

Shree Chandra Yantra

Om Shraam Shreem Shreem Saha Saumaya Namah.

Sanskrit names	Chandra - shining, Indu - bright drop, Shashi - swift, Atrista - son of sage Atri, Sachin - marked by a hare, Tar Adhipati - Lord of stars, Soma - Nectar and Nishakara - the night maker.
Lord	Of Cancer
Deities	Chandra Dev and Devis - Durga, Parvati and Gauri.
Rides on	Antelope and Reindeer
Personification	Queen and mother
House	4th house
Weekday	Monday
Numbers	2, 11, 20 and 29
Friends	With all planets
Enemies	With none
Neutral	With all planets
Exalted	Taurus
Debilitated	Scorpio
Aspects	The opposite aspect - 7th place from where it's sitting.
Mulatrikona	Taurus
Lunar cycle	28 years

Vimshotari dasha	10 years
Matures	At 24 years
Nakshatras	Rohini, Hasta and Shravana
Lunar days	2nd tithi (dwitya) and 10th tithi (dashami)
Gender	Female
Element	Water
Colour	White
Motivation	Moksha
Sounds	ya, ra , la, va, ha , sa, sh
Chakra	Anhatta
Tridosha	Kapha
Direction	North and north east
Guna	Satwa
Represents	Fluids - blood, plasma and spinal fluid.
Vehicles	Cars, boats and ships.
Animals	Male cobra, fish, aquatic animals, creepy animals, hare, antelope , white horse and deer.
Bird	Swan
Metal	Silver
Gemstones	Pearl
Organs	Lungs, stomach, bladder, breasts, left eye, nerves and heart.
Body part	Hand - the mount of the palm above the wrist opposite the thumb, is called the mount of the moon.
Spices	Salt
Taste	Salty and pungent
Food	Milk and rice
Plants	Water lily, Moringa tree, banana tree, drumsticks, sugarcane, sandalwood, rice, vegetables, crops, herbs
Season	Rainy season
Places	Kailash mountain, mansarovar lake, rivers, canals and swimming pools.
At home	Kitchen, bathroom and toilet, and left side window.

Objects	Washing machine, cooking pots, water storage containers, ice box and water tap.
Signifies	Emotions, water, mind, home and travel
Relatives	Mother, elder sister and maternal relatives.
Diseases	Cold, cough, phlegm, spleen and liver issues, mental illness, epilepsy, smallpox, measles, skin and venereal issues, sinus problems, influenza, blood issues and thyroid problems.
Yogic practice	Pranayama, alternate breathing and breath watch.
Chant	Chandra Gayatri mantra "Om padma dwajaya vidmahe hema roopaya dheemahi, Tanno Chandra pracho dayat." Meaning - I bow down to Lord Chandra, who has a lotus flag, He shines with cool white brilliance, illuminates my intellect and lights my path.
Physical appearance	Round face and beautiful eyes.
Qualities	Artistic, caring, nurturing, musical, good singer, good cook, good knowledge of herbs and liquid concoctions, emotional, calm, cheater, adultery, charitable, helpful, kind, harmonious, refined, sleeps deeply and tends to gain weight easily.
Careers	All professions that involve - art, music, poetry, medicine. businessman, chemist, hotel manager, travel agent, driver, environmentalist, writer, clothes business, tailor, fashion designer, milk man, dairy owner, cook, farmer, grocery shop owner, pharmacist, astrologer, studying or teaching vedas, bank manager, accountant, midwife, nurse, boatman, dry cleaner, sailor, postman, navigator, pearl merchant, cargo shipping agents, oil merchant , priest, journalist and nursery worker or owner.

The moon has great significance in Vedic astrology because it's through the window of the mind that we perceive the world around us.

<u>The Influence of the Moon</u>

The 24-hour biological clock sets the rhythm for all organisms living on Earth. While the solar cycles regulate the metabolism, hunger, seasons, harvest and migration. The lunar cycles regulate sleep, mating and reproduction.

The pull between the earth and the moon sets our biological rhythms.

Mother Nature has set the <u>biological clock</u> to the cycles of the moon. It is very fascinating to observe how - many birds, animals and sea creatures, like an automatic clockwork, mate and reproduce at the same time every few months or every year. They don't wear watches or, look at a clock or follow any calendar with dates written on it. How do they know when the time is right? They have their inner biological clock to refer to.

The journey of female red crabs

As the moon is coming to its fullness, the sound of waves striking against the rocky shores of Christmas Island, which is about 200 miles south of Java in the Indian Ocean, triggers the annual journey of the female red crabs. Towards the end of November, when the moon is in the last quarter, a few days before the full moon (which will be on the 11th day, ekadashi, or 12th-day dwadashi tithi of waxing phase, shukla paksha in the lunar month of end of Kartik).

The stretch of about 5 miles from land to the ocean coastline is a marathon journey for millions of female red crabs. As it nears midnight, triggered by the wet season and rains. The adult female crabs travel to the ocean for annual spawning to lay their eggs. They pick the moment when the tide is at its highest so that they have the shortest distance to travel, the astronomical number of their eggs turns the clear ocean water into a black turbid soup. As dawn approaches, the tide recedes, eggs are swept out to the sea, and female crabs return to land.

The eggs hatch on contact with water, and in about a month, millions of tiny crabs walk out of the water onto the sandy shores. The females had made this hazardous journey to give birth to the next generation, and their triumph is commendable.

The lunar clock

Scientists have conducted various experiments, and through observation of many land and sea creatures, it has been seen that the Moon transforms ecosystems. A full moon is 100 times brighter than a no moon. For many species, the moon's glow is crucial to their survival.

Frogs

A full moon is excellent for predators who can see their hunt, which helps them to forge and navigate better. On the other hand, Moonlight can be risky for the prey animals. Some frog species don't croak during the full moon because it makes them vulnerable to predators. In today's world of light and electricity, artificial light is seen everywhere at night, which can throw the ecosystems out of whack. Antelopes, coral, fish, wildebeest and other animals, their phases of life are also set by phases of the moon.

Marine bristles

Scientists observed the behaviour of marine bristles, which live underwater and rise to the surface under the darkness of the new moon nights. They come together in huge masses and swirl around, releasing their gametes in sync, this mating dance increases the chances of the number of worms surviving into the next generation. Some eels also reproduce at the same time on new moon nights. They chose this as a safe time to avoid predators and the low tide helps the egg and larva to survive.

Marine worms

Another interesting study was conducted by a scientist who wanted to know what actually triggers their peculiar mating dance. They studied the marine worms in the laboratory. It was observed that the marine worms did not reproduce in artificial light or darkness, but when the darkroom was combined with new moon days, the worms did their mesmerising mating dance. They found that there are special neurons in the worm's brain which respond to moonlight and are linked to tiny genes that control the lunar behaviour. Moon activates the signal that supercharges the desire to mate. The scientists concluded that the worms have an inner moon clock set in place for the survival of their species.

Grunion fish

In another close observation, it has been seen that Grunion fish lay eggs on high elevations during high tides; the sand protects the eggs, and the next cycle of high tide washes them into the sea.

Impalas

In the study of land mammals, observational data shows that impalas follow their biological clock to attract their mates.

The Male impalas roar on the whole moon night which stimulates ovulation in the female impalas. The glow of the moon initiates the timing for mating, which is a crucial signal for the survival of their species.

Badgers

Researchers have observed that European badgers tend to raise one of their hind legs up when they pee more often during the new moon than on the full moon. The badgers use this move to mark territory, especially when they are getting ready to mate because increased darkness provides the badger couple protection from lurking predators. So, while the pee pattern may seem to be a loony habit, it appears to have a practical root in self-defence.

Coral

On a particularly moonlit night each December, corals off the coast of Australia synchronise the most massive release of egg and sperm on Earth. While a variety of environmental factors likely work together to trigger the event — including temperature, salinity and food availability — researchers have found that levels of moonlight seem to play a major role. The event always occurs on or near a full moon.

Cats and dogs

Cats and dogs seem to find more mischief and get injured more often during the full moon. It was noticed by veterinarians and other workers in animal care that a 23% increase in cat visits and a 28% per cent increase in dog visits to emergency rooms was there on nights when the moon was fuller.

Doodlebugs

Doodlebugs scurry around sandy environments in search of places to catch prey, leaving winding doodles in their paths. Once they find their spot in the sand, they dig funnel-shaped holes in which they sit and wait for prey to fall in. Doodlebugs dig new traps every day, and researchers have found that these holes get bigger during full moons. This surge in hole size may be the result of their insect prey becoming more active under the light of the full moon, making the extra effort of digging larger holes pay off. However, researchers have found that this habit persists even within the complete darkness of a laboratory, suggesting that other components of the lunar cycle play a role as well.

Scorpions

The UV rays of moonlight react with a protein in scorpions that makes them glow in the dark. These arachnids seem to react to glowing the way that people respond to blushing. The brighter the signal, the deeper they try to retreat. They tend to be more active during the new moon and seek shelter later in the lunar cycle. Researchers are still not quite sure why this is, but some suggest prey may be more available during darker nights. And with less prey roaming about during the full moon, the scorpions shy away from the spotlight.

Sparrows

The light of the moon even influences animals that are active by day. That's what behavioural ecologist Jenny York learned while studying small birds in South Africa's Kalahari Desert. These white-browed sparrow weavers live in family groups. Year-round, they sing as a chorus to defend their territory. But during the breeding season, males also perform dawn solos. She discovered over a 7-month period that when a full moon was visible in the sky, males started singing an average of about 10 minutes earlier than when there was a new moon.

Lions

Lions hunt best at night but will sometimes kill during the day, especially after a full moon. Research has shown that lions consume less food during moonlit nights, possibly because prey is less active during these times. To make up for a slow night's hunt, the lions must find extra fuel during the day following a particularly well-lit full moon night.

Plants

Similarly, plants respond to energies differently from day to day, the knowledge of which is crucial for successful cultivation, tending and harvesting of crops. It has been observed that the herbs gathered at certain times contain more active agents than at other times.

Dr Vasant Lad, an Ayurvedic practitioner, is well known for his exceptional skill of reading the pulse on both right and left hands and giving accurate diagnoses and treatment through the knowledge of Ayurveda. He explains that even plants have feminine and masculine qualities. The top of the leaf that faces the sun and has a darker, waxy and shiny surface is the solar side (which helps it absorb the sun's energy and reduce water evaporation). The bottom side (which helps with gas exchange) is darker and has a rough texture - it is the lunar side of the leaf. The middle ridge of the leaf is the sushumna nadi, the left side ridges or veins are the Ida and the veins on the right side are Pingala. If we count all the veins on both the right and left side we can know whether the plant is masculine or feminine. If the total number of veins on a leaf is an odd number -1,3,5 …it's a male plant, and if the total number of veins is an even number - 2,4,6 … it's a female plant.

The tidal waves

Unlike a 24-hour solar day, a lunar day lasts 24 hours and 50 minutes. This occurs because the moon revolves around the Earth in the same direction that the Earth is rotating on its axis. Therefore, it takes the Earth an extra 50 minutes to "catch up" to the moon. Since the Earth rotates through two tidal "bulges" every lunar day, we experience two high and two low tides every 24 hours and 50 minutes. The gravitational pull of the earth on the Moon influences the ocean tides, which rise and fall during full moon and new moon days.

These observations show that the behaviour of many animals and birds depends on the phases and position of the moon in the sky.

Similarly, the phases of the moon have a subtle effect on countless everyday activities like - travelling, cooking, eating, cutting hair, gardening, doing laundry, taking medicines, performing surgical operations, and many other things that can be enhanced by aligning our actions to the rhythms in nature.

According to Hindu tradition, the farmers would not plough their fields on these 6 days of the month - one day before and after the full moon (3 days) and after the new moon (3 days). This was based on keen observation of how fast or slow the seeds sprout after the plantation. In other words, the success of an action depends not only on the skills and resources but also on the timing of the action.

Circadian clock

In 2013, a study conducted at Basal University in Switzerland found that on full moon days and 2 days before and after - people took 5 minutes longer to fall asleep and slept for 20 minutes less, on average, around a full moon night, as compared to the rest of the month – even though they weren't exposed to any moonlight. The study shows that circular lunar rhythm is connected to how long we take to fall asleep and how long we sleep.

Humans

In human beings, a healthy adult woman's reproductive cycle of 28 - 30 days is about the same length as the lunar cycle. This shows that the rotation of the moon around the earth has a very crucial role to play in the reproductive process of many species on earth and on plant life, as has been observed by scientists.

Human behaviour

As we have seen, life on Earth is closely related to the moon cycles. On full moon days, ocean tides are high, and so are our emotions, likes or dislikes. For centuries, people have believed that the Moon affects human behaviour. The word lunacy comes from the Latin word lunaticus, which means moonstruck.

Mental health science in the USA states that certain bipolar mood swings are influenced by the phases of the moon. Small numbers of statistical studies have suggested that violence among psychiatric patients or prison inmates and outdoor criminal activity – incidents occurring on streets or beaches may be higher when there is more moonlight.

Mystical significance

Sadhguru explains that it is not by coincidence that many spiritual beings realise their ultimate nature on the full moon day or night. The most famous example is of Budha - he got enlightened on the full moon night, which is now celebrated as, *'Bhudha Purnima.'*

Technically, the Moon is not a planet but a satellite revolving around the Earth and has a big influence on us because of its closeness to earth. It guides our birth and life and can determine our death.

It's not that the moon instigates madness, but when the moon is in certain phases, it heightens the emotions. For example, if you are loving, you become more loving. If you are joyful, you become more joyful. If you are meditative, you become more meditative on full moon days. It enhances everything that you are. A full moon gives an outward expression, and a new moon brings an inner awareness. Moon does not make us mad or meditative, but it just enhances our inherent quality.

Moon also has an influence on our gut, that's why, on certain days, we tend to feel less hungry. The ancient sages have recommended certain days for fasting based on the keen observation of the phases of the moon. For example, Ekadashi (11th lunar day) is considered very conducive for fasting and doing spiritual practises.

Today, most of us don't consciously know what phase of the moon is, but if we pay attention, we can start noticing it through our eating habits and emotional feelings and can use the heightened energy on full moon days in a positive way.

The 16 kalas of the moon

The astrological Vedic texts describe the moon as having 16 kalas (qualities). During the waxing phase, these qualities expand, and in the waning phase, they shrink. The 15 kalas are the phases of the moon from the new moon to the full moon - while the 16th Kala is of the beyond, or an enlightened being who would have all the 16 attributes. <u>Lord Krishna</u> is mentioned as a 16 Kala Avatar in Mahabharata. He was an enlightened being and had all 16 qualities of a whole, complete being.

N	Kala	Meaning
1	Amrita	nectar, elixir of life.
2	Manada	pride, self respect.
3	Pusha	nourishment
4	Tushti	contentment
5	Pushti	comfort
6	Rati	passion
7	Dhriti	courage
8	Shashini	Swiftness
9	Chandrika	moonlight
10	Kanti	beauty
11	Jyotshna	the halo of light
12	Shree	wealth, wellbeing, auspicious
13	Preeti	Love
14	Angada	penance to gain mastery
15	Purna	fullness
16	Purnamrita	nectar of fullness, beyond physical dimension.

Phases of the moon -

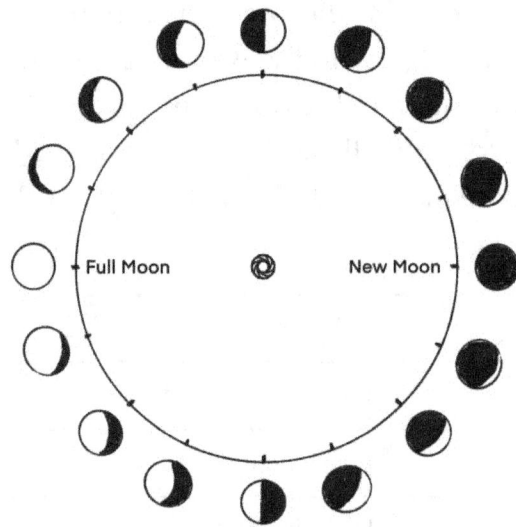

The Lagna - Ascendent describes the external factors, physical attributes, life situations, material gains and physical effort. The placement of the moon represents how we deal with situations through our thoughts and feelings. Therefore, the strength of the moon holds great importance in deciding whether we will succumb to the difficulties and challenges or will emerge a winner - stronger and wiser than before. On close observation, you will notice that whatever activity the body does - sit, stand, walk, sleep, eat, listen to music, take a shower, drive, work, relax ... or whatever else, is driven by our thoughts and feelings. For example, if I am thinking of a concept and want to note it down, I will open my laptop, iPad or notebook and write it down. If I am feeling hungry, I will get up and eat something ... and so on. Throughout the day and night, the body moves according to where the mind wants to go or what the mind wants to do.

For this reason, huge importance is given to the placement and strength of the moon. Wherever the moon is placed in the chart, the mind will be focused on that area of life, and the opposite house will directly impact the thoughts and feelings of the native. For example, if the moon is placed in the 11th house, they will always be thinking of how to get easy or speculative gains, increase their profits, work less and earn more. They will most probably have a well-paid job and other sources of income, too. Opposite to 11th is the 5th house of education, creativity, entertainment, and children. The natives will find that whenever they pay attention to their children or do something creative their gains are increased.

On the other hand, if there are fluctuations in their gains, they will not be able to connect to their creativity, or their children might feel the impact of their frustrations. There will be a direct link and a vice versa effect of the 5th and 11th house - to their thoughts and emotions because of the placement of the moon.

The placement of Moon

This table shows the influence of the Moon in the birth chart and its effect.

Influence	Placement	Effect
Moon is strong when placed in	Taurus - moolatrikona and exalted Cancer - own house Moon nakshatras - Rohini, Hasta and Shravana. Directional strength - 4th house. Full moon Atmakaraka - highest degree. Near to the Ascendant degree.	Kind, caring, intuitive, receptive, imaginative, calm, peaceful.
Moon is weak when placed in	Scorpio - debilitated 10th house - no directional strength. New moon At 0, 1 and 29 degrees.	Emotionally sensitive, too attached, aloof or detached.

Inference

Those who have a strong influence on the Moon in their birth chart will have a very feminine and gentle look. They will have a round face and big eyes with fuller features. On the whole, they will have a plump look.

One of the names of the Moon is Soma, which means nectar or the elixir of life. It nourishes our thoughts and emotions and represents all body fluids. In the birth chart, when the moon is in the waxing phase (Shukla Paksha) the person will be more outgoing and emotionally well-balanced. When the native moon is in the waning phase (Krishna paksha), he or she will be more inwardly drawn and will not express emotions openly.

The bright cycle of the moon is considered beneficial because it's better able to provide opportunities and nourish desires in terms of making resources available. The dark side of the moon supports inner growth, and therefore, it is considered malefic in terms of providing opportunities for worldly success. Here, the moon directs its energy and nourishment inward. For any struggle faced outside, one has to turn inward to find the answers. In this process, one matures and evolves mentally and spiritually.

Those who are born with the Moon or Ascendent in Cancer have a strong influence on the moon because the moon rules Cancer.

For example, a Cancer Ascendent person has a moon in the 3rd house of Virgo in Hasta, which is a moon ruled by nakshatra. The native will be emotionally attached to his or her siblings, friends or neighbours. He or she will get along well with them, and they will spend a lot of time together. Their focus will be on doing something with their hands. They will be skilled in some form of art that involves the use of hands. It could be art, painting, handicrafts, pottery, or IT skills. Life will provide opportunities and resources that enhance their special talent.

Moon is exalted in Taurus and debilitated in Scorpio. Taking on from the above example, for a Cancer Ascendant person, if the moon is placed in Rohini in Taurus in the 11th house. Rohini, again, is a moon nakshatra, this will nourish all the desires and bring easy gains for the native. He or she will benefit greatly from the elder siblings and from large organisations. They will find great fulfilment in taking care of people in need, either through volunteering, through a job, or through attending huge social functions and gatherings. Life will bring such opportunities where they have to take care of a large group of people.

With the same Cancer Ascendent, if the moon is placed in the 5th house of Scorpio in Jyeshtha, which is a Mercury-ruled nakshatra, the native will be very creative-minded. He or she will be respected like an elder in his or her family, friends circle or community at large. Here, the debilitation of the moon makes them confused about their options, so they might end up wasting time or missing opportunities. The moon will make them work hard at their project quietly behind the scenes and ultimately create something brilliant for which they will be recognised.

Let's look at another example with a different Ascendent and see how the quality and energy of the moon change. A Sagittarius Ascendant person who has a moon in Shravana in the 2nd house of Capricorn. Shravana is also a moon ruled by Nakshatra. Since Sagittarius is ruled by Jupiter, and its element is fire, the native will be very idealistic, religious and spiritual and his emotions and thoughts will be focused on providing resources for the family. He or she will not like to sit idle because the fire gives the drive and passion, which will be directed towards listening and paying attention to family and home matters.

Example

Cancer Ascendant - ruled by Moon

Raj Kapoor - Famous Hindi film director and actor.

Born on 14th December 1924 at 10 pm in Peshawar, Pakistan.

Died on 2nd June 1988 in Delhi, India, at the age of 63.

Raj Kapoor is an Indian actor, film producer and film director. He received multiple awards - 3 National Film Awards and 11 Filmfare Awards in India. The Filmfare Lifetime Achievement Award is named after him. His films attracted worldwide audiences, particularly in Asia and Europe. He was honoured with the Padma Bhushan in 1971 for his contributions to the arts. India's highest award in cinema, the Dadasaheb Phalke Award, was bestowed on him in 1987 by the Government of India.

Raj was born in a Punjabi Hindu family in 1924 at Kapoor Haveli in Peshawar, which is now in Pakistan. His father was the famous actor of 1930 - 1950's - Prithviraj Kapoor, and his mother,

Ramsarni Devi Kapoor, was a housewife. He was the eldest sibling of 6 children in the family. They later moved from Peshawar to India for children's education and better prospects.

At the age of 10, Raj appeared in a Hindi film for the first time in 1935's Inquilab. Raj Kapoor's big break came with the lead role in Neel Kamal (1947) opposite Madhubala in her first role as a leading lady. In 1948, at the age of 24, he established his own studio, R. K. Films. He became the youngest film director of his time, making his directorial debut with Aag, starring himself, Nargis, Kamini Kaushal and Premnath.

In May 1946, Raj Kapoor married Krishna Malhotra, who was his cousin. It was a match arranged by their families, and it lasted all their lives. The news of Raj Kapoor's marriage was reported in the cine-magazine Filmindia June 1946 issue as, "Raj Kapoor, the talented and versatile son of Prithviraj Kapoor, ended his career of wild oats by marrying Miss Krishna Malhotra." Raj and Krishna Kapoor had 5 children - 3 sons and 2 daughters.

In 1970, he produced, directed and starred in his ambitious film Mera Naam Joker, which took more than 6 years to complete. His son Rishi Kapoor made his debut in this film, playing the younger version of his character. When released in 1970, it was a box office disaster and put Kapoor and his family into a financial crisis. In later years, the film was acknowledged as a cult classic.

He launched his 2nd son Rishi Kapoor's career in 1973 when he produced and directed Bobby which was a huge box office success and introduced actress Dimple Kapadia, who later became a popular actress. The story was based on a teen romance.

Raj suffered from asthma in his later years. He died of complications related to the disease in 1988 at the age of 63. He collapsed at the event where he was to receive the Dadasaheb Phalke Award and was taken to the All India Institute of Medical Sciences (AIIMS) for treatment. He was hospitalised for about a month before he succumbed to complications arising from his asthma.

Raj is appreciated both by film critics and movie fans. Film historians speak of him as the "Charlie Chaplin of Indian cinema" since he often portrayed a tramp-like figure - who, despite adversity, was still cheerful and honest.

Analysis -

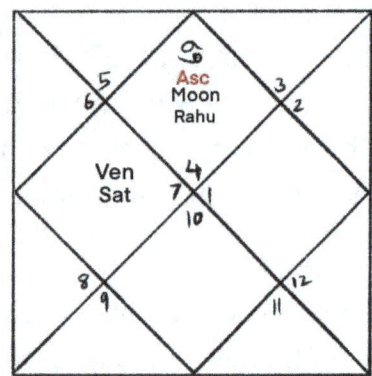 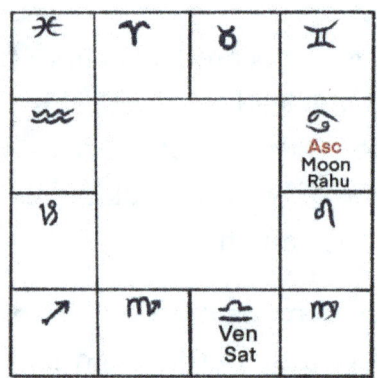

Raj is a Cancer Ascendant, and Moon, the lord of Cancer, is sitting in the Ascendant with Rahu. This placement strongly amplifies all the Cancerian qualities in him. It's a feminine sign which reflects the superb nourishing quality of the night. His sensitive, creative and imaginative aspect can be seen in his exceptional talent for acting, producing and directing films.

In 1970 he produced, directed and starred in his ambitious film Mera Naam Joker. Although this film was not a box office success, it was a film closest to his heart and his Cancerian character. It had a very philosophical message about life. We can see the lunar sensitivity of Cancer expressed beautifully in this film. The combination of tragedy and comedy was brought alive on the screen through this film. During the making of this film he was running his Venus mahadasha. Venus represents creativity, beauty and harmony. In his birth chart, Venus is happily sitting in its own house of Libra with Saturn in the 4th house of home. At the young age of 24, he established his own studio- R. K. Films, which was his home production and did all his creative projects through this studio (the effect of the 4th house Venus). It took 6 long years to finish making the film Mera Naam Joker (effect of Saturn). It was hard work but a very fulfilling project for him in terms of expressing his talent and creativity.

Here are some of the quotes from Raj Kapoor -

"What do you mean, you have no dreams, the truth is you have no courage."

"Light comes from the moon and not the stars. You can be friends with one and not with thousands."

"A woman always has her man, but the man unconsciously leans on his roots, his heritage. He feels like an orphan without his parents."

"I have struggled a lot for what I have today."

The poetry of Moon

Imaginative, caring and emotional moon,
Wavers like the tidal waves often and soon.
The window of the mind unfolds and reveals,
Fascinating life as the time wheels.

The love affair of day and night,
Are there wrongs and rights?
Experience is the garden
Blossoming of flowers - the Eden.

3
Mars

Om kram kreem kraum saha Bhumiaya namah

Sanskrit names	Mangala - auspicious, Bhumija - son of Earth and Angrakha - hot as burning coal and Kuja.
Other names	Roman God of war.
Lord	Aries and Scorpio
Deities	Kartikeya - son of Lord Shiva
Rides on	Ram - the mountain goat
House	1st and 8th
Weekday	Tuesday
Numbers	9, 18 and 27
Friends	Jupiter, Moon, Sun and Ketu
Enemies	Mercury and Rahu
Neutral	Saturn
Exalted	Capricorn
Debilitated	Cancer
Aspects	4th, 7th and 8th from itself.
Mulatrikona	Aries
Vimshotari dasha	7 years

Matures	At 28 years old.
Transit	Stays in one sign for about 45 days.
Nakshatras	Mrigashira, Chitra and Dhanishta.
Lunar days	Ekadashi - 11th lunar day
Gender	Male
Element	Fire
Colour	Red
Motivation	Dharma
Sounds	ka, kha, ga, gha and nga.
Chakra	Muladhara
Tridosha	Pitta
Direction	South
Guna	Rajas
Represents	Kshatriya - warrior
Vehicles	Trucks and heavy-duty vehicles.
Animals	Deer, horse, goat and sheep
Bird	Eagle
Metal	Copper
Gemstones	Red coral
Organs	Neck, Blood, bone marrow and veins
Body parts	Bone marrow and red blood cells
Spices	Chillies
Taste	Bitter and spicy
Food	Red gram, chillies, red peppers, onion, garlic and bitter gourd (Karela).
Plants	Neem trees and thorny cactus plants.
Season	Summer
Places	Deserts and tropical places.
At home	Kitchen
Objects	Fireplace, oven and heaters, explosives, iron and steel, and corals.
Signifies	Brothers, land, property, action, aggression, energy and strength.

Relatives	Brothers
Diseases	Injuries, surgeries, headaches, blood pressure, sores and itching.
Yogic practice	Hatha yoga practises and surya namaskar.
Chant	*"Om Angarkaya vidmahe, bhoomipalaya dhimahi, tanno Kujah prachodayat."*
Physical appearance	Medium height, well built and red eyes.
Qualities	Malefic, cruel, aggressive, anger, energy, fierce, thorns, spikes, cut, retaliate, revolt, destroy, conquer, fight, win, war, command, dominate, ego, sudden burst of energy, discipline, strict, accidents, trained, technical, get things done, promotes non living things, likes to progress, logical, skilful, my way or highway, act first and think later and are easily flattered.
Careers	Army commanders, emergency doctors, surgeons, dentists, surgeons, farmers, property dealers, army officers, fire fighters, ambulance staff, race car drivers, truck, train and taxi drivers, weapon dealers, police staff, sports players, security personnel, mechanics, garage owners, automobile salesman, mining and technical jobs.

Mars as a physical planet

It is called the red planet because of rich iron oxide deposits on the surface of Mars. It is the 4th planet from the sun, earth (being the 3rd). It has 2 moons and a rocky, rugged desert-like surface and is half the diameter of Earth. Formed around the same time as Earth. It has a fragile atmosphere.

Mars is about 56 million km away from Earth. It revolves around the Sun in 687 days. Mars turns retrograde (appears to move backwards as seen from Earth) for about 60 to 80 days every 26 months. It stays for about 45 days in each sign and takes nearly two years to complete the circle of the whole zodiac.

Mythology of Mars

The word Mars has a Germanic origin and has been derived from the word *'marrren,'* which means to hinder or damage. The word *'mar'* in many Indian languages like Punjabi and Hindi literally means to *'hit.'* This signifies the inherent quality of Mars.

In Roman mythology, Mars has been described as the god of war and also an agricultural guardian. He was the son of Jupiter and Juno and was the most prominent of the military gods in the religion of the Roman army. Most of his festivals were held in March, the month named for him (Latin Martius), and in October, which began the season for military campaigning and ended the season for farming. In Greek religion, Ares is the God of war and the spirit of battle. The word Aries has been given to the 1st sign of the zodiac, whose ruler is Mars. This signifies the burst of Martian energy needed to kick start life, from a state of inactivity to activity.

In <u>Vedic mythology,</u> Mars is called Mangala, which means auspicious. Mars is said to have this quality because, without the needed energy, one cannot perform any action or acquire things to their fullest potential. But the malefic quality of Mars does remain. For example a strong Mars in the chart can bring injuries or accidents during its dasha but also gives tremendous energy to achieve goals.

He is said to be the son of Mother Earth and called *Bhumija*. The other names of Mars are *Lohit*, which means iron and red rusty colour; *Angrakha*, which means red hot coal, and *Kuja*, which means an earthen pot used as a mould.

Deity of Mars

<u>Kartikeya</u> is one of the deities associated with Mars, the planet of war and aggression. The mythological story of Kartikeya, who was the 2nd born son of Shiva and Parvati, has been assigned the nakshatra of Kritika.

Kartikeya, from a very young age, had fought many battles against the demons to restore dharma (righteousness) in society. He killed the seemingly invincible demon Taraka and released the Devas from Taraka's oppression. These myths depict his valour, strength and courage, and most fittingly, the protective quality of Mars. Therefore, a strong Mars in the birth chart gives a high moral code, the one who becomes the protector of dharma.

Later, as Kartikeya grew older, the anguish and pain of seeing so much bloodshed made him renounce the aggressive way of life. He washed his sword in the river and never touched it again. He is known as the God of war and victory, there are many temples built in South India to honour him.

Kartikeya is the god of anger and aggression. He is also called Skanda - the one who was born with 6 heads, and Kumara - the youthful one. Vedas state that he was a celibate. Therefore, Mangal dosha occurs in the horoscope when Mars is placed in the 2nd, 4th, 7th, 8th or 12th house in the birth horoscope, which can cause separation between the couple. But it gets cancelled when Mars is placed in the movable (chara) signs of Aries, Cancer, Libra and Capricorn. There are certain other conditions like - if both the boy and girl have mangal dosha in their birth chart, this dosha gets cancelled.

The placement of Mars

This table shows the influence of Mars in the birth chart and its effect.

Influence	Placement	Effect
Mars is strong when placed in	Aries - moolatrikona. Scorpio - own house Capricorn - exalted Mars nakshatras - Mrigashira, Chitra and Dhanishta.	Good health, vitality, strength, energy, high moral code, honesty, determination and courage.

	Directional strength - 10th house. Atmakaraka - highest degree. Near to the Ascendant degree.	
Mars is weak when placed in	Cancer - debilitated 4th house - no directional strength. At 0, 1 and 29 degrees.	Short tempered, aggressive behaviour, overly dominating, cowardice and low energy.

Inference

Those who have a strong influence of Mars in their birth chart will have a masculine and youthful look. They tend to have medium to large eyes, fuller lips and full roundish nose. Their hair colour is usually dark, and they have a good set of hair.

Mars is a masculine planet, signifying strength and supremacy. The positive influences of this fiery planet are courage, enthusiasm, activity, youth, vitality, dynamism, confidence, initiation, innovation, and originality. Its negative influence can give arrogance, ego, anger, short tempered, stubbornness, selfish temperament, and recklessness.

Depending upon its placement in the birth chart, with strong directional strength and in a friendly sign, Mars can help overcome challenges, face competitions, and win over enemies. On the other hand, its energy can be self-destructive, can cause harm, injury, wounds, and accidents, and give excessive sexual urges when - Mars has a low Shabala score of less than 250 out of 500.

Mars signifies our desire, energy, drive, motivation, ambition and action. Martian energy represents physical, mental and sexual action and gives us the courage to face challenges. It gives the drive to win and become the best. Mars is also the significator of brothers, assertion, aggressiveness, soldiers and military endeavours, mechanical ability, engineers and surgeons, commanders and rulers, accidents, violence and war, ambition, strength, arguments and conflict, passion and desire.

Mars is our energy, but aggression or violence is the misuse of that energy. Since energy can be used both constructively or destructively, depending upon how strong is the person's will power to withstand opposition and where Mars is placed in the birth chart.

Wherever Mars is placed in the chart one will have to spend a lot of energy and attention towards those matters. For example, Mars in the 5th house - signifies creative projects, speculations, romance, children, education and learning new skills. One will be naturally inclined to spend time and will have to put more effort into these areas of life.

Mars has a pitta or fiery quality, which makes the natives very adventurous and enthusiastic. They are always ready to take on new projects. They are not the types who will sit around passively and wait for things to happen. They go ahead and create situations for people to join them. They are motivational and inspirational leaders.

Aries and Scorpio are ruled by Mars, and it is exalted in Capricorn.

Whenever Mars is placed in any of these signs, it gives good results during its dasha, for example, for a Capricorn Ascendent Mars placed in the 1st house, in Dhanishta Pada 1. Here, Mars is exalted, sitting in the sign of Saturn (Capricorn) and in the nakshatra of Mars (Dhanishta). This will make the natives very masculine in their looks, very determined, fearless and ambitious. They will have a richness of strength and physical stamina and will have great interest and talent in sports or athletics. They will choose a career in the army, police or sports. They will be very outgoing and straightforward in their dealings. Since the 4th house of Aries and the 11th house of Scorpio will also be ruled by Mars, their home environment will be active and full of energy. They will gain through property, and will either run a large organisation or will be employed by one. Their mum or a mother-like figure and an elder sibling will be motivational in helping them in their chosen career. Since they have a powerful streak of Martian energy, they need to have a regular exercise or gym routine to work out their excessive energy, otherwise, it can manifest in cruel ways.

Looking at the same Capricorn Ascendant as the above example, if Mars is sitting in the 7th house of Cancer in Pushya, it will be debilitated. Here, Mars will share the influence of the Moon and Saturn. The native will not have Mangala dosha because Mars is sitting in the movable (chara) sign of cancer. Still, it will have its malefic effect, which can bring delay in marriage, no marriage, or an incompatible marriage partner. Here, the birth chart and navamsa chart will have to be looked at carefully before making any predictions or giving remedies.

Mars also gives good results when it's placed in the friendly signs ruled by - Sun, moon and Jupiter - Leo, Cancer, Sagittarius and Pisces. Just like the Sun, Mars' most powerful position is in the 10th House, where it brings success and fame during its dasha.

Example

Aries Ascendant - ruled by Mars

Neil Armstrong - Famous Astronaut - The first man to step on the moon. Born on 5th August 1930 at 12:31 am, in Wapakoneta, USA.

Died on 25th August 2012 in Ohio, USA, at the age of 82.

Neil Alden Armstrong was an American astronaut and aeronautical engineer and the first person to walk on the Moon. He was also a naval aviator, test pilot, and university professor.

Neil was born near Wapakoneta, Ohio, and was the son of Viola Louise and Stephen Armstrong. He was of German and Scottish descent. He had a younger sister and a younger brother. His father was an auditor for the Ohio state government, and the family moved around the state repeatedly, living in 16 towns over the next 14 years. His love for flying grew during this time, having started at the age of 2 when his father took him to the Cleveland Air Races. When he was 6 years old, he experienced his first aeroplane flight in Warren, Ohio, when he and his father took a ride in a Ford Trimotor.

The family's last move was in 1944 which took them back to Wapakoneta, where he attended Blume High School and took flying lessons at the Wapakoneta airfield. He earned a student flight certificate on his 16th birthday, then soloed in August, all before he had a driver's license.

Following his graduation from Purdue, Neil became an experimental research test pilot. In June 1958, he was selected for the U.S. Air Force's Man in Space Soonest program. Collins wrote that Neil was by far the most experienced test pilot in the Astronaut Corps.

Voyage to the Moon - A Saturn V rocket launched Apollo 11 from the Kennedy Space Centre on July 16th July, 1969, at 13:32. While flying toward the Moon on 18th July 1969, he sent his regards to attendees at the National Scout jamboree in Idaho. Among the few personal items that he carried with him to the Moon and back was a World Scout Badge. His wife, Janet and his 2 sons watched from a yacht moored on the Banana River. He went smiling in his space suit with the helmet off, and his eyes looked slightly watery.

During the launch, Neil's heart rate peaked at 110 beats per minute. Apollo 11's objective was to land safely on the Moon. He landed the Lunar Module Eagle on the Moon on 20th July 1969. When he noticed they were heading toward a landing area that seemed unsafe, he took manual control of the LM and attempted to find a safer location. This took longer than expected and longer than most simulations had taken. For this reason, Mission Control was concerned that the LM was running low on fuel. On landing, Aldrin and Armstrong believed they had 40 seconds of fuel left, including 20 seconds' worth, which had to be saved in the event of an abort. During training, Neil had, on several occasions, landed with fewer than 15 seconds of fuel. He was also confident the LM could survive a fall of up to 50 feet.

The landing on the surface of the Moon occurred several seconds after 20:17 on 20th July 1969. As Neil made his way down the ladder, he turned and set his left boot on the lunar surface at 02:56 on 21st July 1969, and then said, "That's one small step for a man, one giant leap for mankind."

Shortly after Apollo 11, Neil announced that he did not plan to fly in space again. He was appointed Deputy Associate Administrator for Aeronautics for the Office of Advanced Research and Technology at ARPA, served in the position for a year, then resigned from it and NASA in 1971. After he resigned from NASA in 1971, Neil taught in the Department of Aerospace Engineering at the University of Cincinnati until 1979.

In 1985, professional expedition leader Mike Dunn organised a trip to take men he deemed the "greatest explorers" to the North Pole. The group included Neil Armstrong, Edmund Hillary, Hillary's son Peter, Steve Fossett, and Patrick Morrow. They arrived at the Pole on 6th April 1985. He said he was curious to see what it looked like from the ground, as he had seen it only from the Moon. He did not inform the media of the trip, preferring to keep it private.

Neil's family described him as a "reluctant American hero". He kept a low profile later in his life, leading to the belief that he was a recluse. He turned down most requests for interviews and public appearances. Recalling his humility, John Glenn, the first American to orbit Earth, told CNN, "Armstrong didn't feel that he should be out huckstering himself. He was a humble person, and that's the way he remained after his lunar flight, as well as before."

Neil underwent bypass surgery on 7th August 2012 to relieve coronary artery disease. Although he was reportedly recovering well, he developed complications in the hospital and died on 25th August in Ohio, aged 82.

Analysis

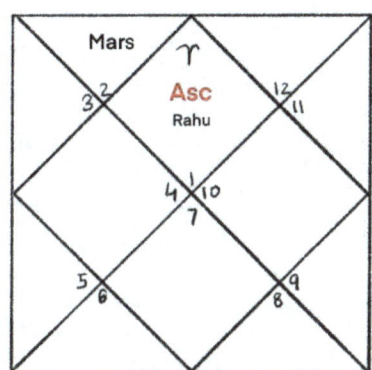

Neil has his Ascendant in Aries, and Rahu is sitting in the Ascendant. Mars, the lord of Aries, is sitting in the 2nd house of Taurus. Mars has the highest degree (21 degrees) in the birth chart, which makes him the Atma Karka. When the Ascendant lord sits in the house 2nd from it - it becomes it's gain. Mars provided an abundance of energy and timely resources needed for the fruition of the desired results.

His life has been an excellent example of Martian bravery, determination, energy, motivation and enthusiasm. The fire of Mars has been amplified by Rahu giving it the thrust of positivity and vitality. Mars becomes a functional benefic for an Aries Ascendant because it's the lord of the Ascendant and the 9th house of fortune. Moreover, when Aries is the Ascendant, it's a very balanced horoscope because all the signs are placed in their original houses as per naisargik Kundali (original birth chart). Which gives it the natural goodness, grace and blessings.

On 21st July 1969, when he set foot on the Moon (a historical moment for all mankind), he was running his <u>Moon Mercury Jupiter Rahu Mars dasha.</u> His sukshma and prana dasha were of Rahu and Mars, which are directly connected with his Ascendant. On his death, The White House released a statement in which President Obama described Armstrong as "among the greatest of American heroes—not just of his time, but of all time." It went on to say that Armstrong had carried the aspirations of the United States citizens and had delivered "<u>a moment of human achievement that will never be forgotten.</u>"

<u>Here are some quotes by Neil Armstrong -</u>

"Mastery creates wonder, and wonder is the basis of man's desire to understand."

About his landing on the moon and coming back to Earth safely, he said - *"I was elated, ecstatic and extremely surprised that we were successful."*

"One thing I regret was that my work required an enormous amount of my time and a lot of travel."

"Science has not yet mastered prophecy."

Mars the poet

Mars is the fearless soldier,

The protector and upholder.

Martian spirit is the motivational drive,

Keep you going until you arrive.

The courageous one - faces all strife,

With a brave smile - in the rigmarole of life.

An adventurous spirit - and intensity of purpose,

Enriches every experience through absolute focus.

4
Mercury

Om bram breem braum saha Bhudhaya namah

Sanskrit names	Budha - intellect, Induputa - son of moon and Jna - knowledge.
Lord	Lord of - Gemini and Virgo
Deities	Vishnu, Narayana, Vamana avatar
Sound	tt, th, d, dh, n
House	3rd and 6th house
Weekday	Wednesday
Rides on	a Lion
Personification	Prince, younger siblings, friends and neighbours.
Friends	Sun and Venus
Enemies	Moon
Neutral	Mars, Jupiter and Saturn
Exalted	Virgo
Debilitated	Pisces
Aspects	7th from where it sits.
Vimshotari dasha	17 years cycle
Matures	at 32 years
Transit	Varies- stays in 1 house from 15- 60 days, and is never more than 2 houses away from the sun.

Retrograde	Goes retrograde 4 times /year
Nakshatras	Ashlesha, Jeyshtha and Revati
Lunar days	4th lunar day - chaturthi and 12th lunar day - dwadashi.
Motivation	Kama
Gender	Eunuch
Element	Air
Colour	Green
Chakra	Ajna
Tridosha	Vata
Direction	North
Guna	Rajas
Represents	Jiva - living creatures
Vehicles	All 2 wheelers , 4 wheelers and aeroplanes.
Animals	Male cat and jackal
Birds	Parrot and sparrows
Metal	Mercury
Gemstones	Emerald
Numbers	5, 14, 23 - all numbers that add up to 5.
Organs	Nervous system and skin
Body parts	Forehead, neck , tongue, throat, arms, shoulders, hands, lungs, hand - little finger.
Spices	Cumin and cinnamon
Taste	Sweet, pungent, sour and salty
Food	Green lentils - moong dal
Plants	Green creepers, flowers, foliage plants
Season	Autumn and spring
Time of the day	Sunrise and sunset
Places	Vishnu temple, schools, colleges, universities, shops, libraries, recreation centres, theatres, printing press, stationary shops, halls for social functions, clubs and bars.
At home	Study room

Objects	Books, book shelf paper, stationary, computers, phones, photos and study desk.
Diseases	Skin ailments, eczema, itchiness, stomach and intestinal issues, sore throat, baldness, leucoderma and tonsils,
Yogic practice	Breath watch, alternate nose breathing pranayama and mindfulness.
Chant	Budha Gyatri chant - '*Om Gajadhwajaaya vidmahae,* *Sukha hastaya dheemahi* *Tanno budhaya prachodayat.*'
Physical appearance	Short or medium height, well built body and thin lips.
Signifies	Intelect, communication, education, curiosity and speech.
Qualities	Talkative, witty, quick thinker, quick swift actions, analytical, great sense of humour, will question a lot, curious, intelligent, ready to learn new things, flexible, adaptable, friendly, studious, romantic, cunning, diplomatic, soft spoken, well mannered, discriminative, opportunist, trickster and a light sleeper.
Careers	IT jobs, accountant, journalist, public relations manager, mathematician, scientist, banker, teacher, public speaker, actor, dancer, writer, poet, businessman, publisher, librarian, lawyer, comedian, painter, astrologer, lecturer, researcher, engineer, stock market broker, business shareholder, magician, gambler, news broadcaster, clerk, inspector, examiner, auditor, import export business, advisor, agent, commissioner, advertising job and fashion designer.

The Vedic name of Mercury is <u>Budha -</u> which represents the discriminating intellect. The famous example of Prince Sidhart who was called Budha after his enlightenment, because he realised his true self and reached the peak of his intelligence. The other name of Mercury is <u>Saumya</u> because he is the son of the moon, "Saumya" also means calm, gentle, and unruffled. The predominating qualities of Mercury are curiosity, intelligence, speed - -quickness and communication - speech.

<u>Astronomical perspective</u>

Like the other planets in the solar system, Mercury was born about 4.5 billion years ago, condensing from the swirling ring of dust and gas left over from the sun's formation. Mercury became a terrestrial planet with a dense metallic core, a rocky mantle, and a solid crust.

Despite its proximity to our star, Mercury is not the hottest planet in the solar system. This is because there is no atmosphere to trap heat, and the surface temperatures on Mercury can swing from 800 degrees Fahrenheit during the day to -290 degrees Fahrenheit at night. Mercury may even have reservoirs of ice sitting deep inside permanently shadowed craters at its poles. By contrast, the surface of hazy Venus sits at a sweltering 880 degrees Fahrenheit all the year-round, making it the hottest planet in our solar system.

Mercury is the closest planet to the sun, zipping around our parent star at an average of 36 million miles away. However, Mercury's orbit is not a perfect circle. The planet can pass as close as 29 million miles and as far away as 43 million miles. Living up to its name, Mercury is the fastest planet in the solar system, speeding along at about 29 miles per second and completing each orbit around the sun in just 88 Earth days. Mercury is also the smallest planet in the solar system, measuring just 3,032 miles wide at its equator. That makes it only slightly larger than Earth's moon.

Because Mercury is so small and so close to the sun, it is the most elusive of the five planets that are visible to the naked eye. You can only catch Mercury at dawn and dusk, and it usually does not rise far above the horizon. Mercury passes between Earth and the sun 13 times each century (100 years) in an event known as a transit. During a transit of Mercury, observers on Earth can see the planet in silhouette as it seems to sweep across the sun's disk.

Since ancient times, people observing the heavens have noticed that the naked-eye planets sometimes appear to move backwards, briefly shifting from their usual eastward motion to a westward path across the sky. This retrograde motion is an illusion created when one planet moves faster in its orbit than another, so it catches up to and passes the slower-moving planet. For observers on Earth, Mercury is in retrograde about 3 to 4 times a year.

If you could watch the skies from the surface of Mercury, you would sometimes catch the rare sight of the sun in retrograde. As Mercury makes its closest approach to our smouldering star, its orbital speed exceeds its rate of rotation on its axis. That means someone standing on Mercury would see the sun start to rise, then briefly set, and then rise again all within the same day.

Mythology of Mercury

Roman mythology

Mercury is named after the Roman messenger god Mercurius, who is a major god in Roman religion and mythology. He is the god of financial gain, commerce, eloquence, messages, communication (including divination), travellers, boundaries, luck, trickery and thieves. He also serves as the guide of souls to the underworld.

He was considered the son of Maia, one of the 7 daughters of the Titan Atlas and Jupiter in Roman mythology. The name Mercury comes from the Latin word merx, which means merchandise, merchant, commerce, trade and wages.

Vedic mythology

Vedic stories state that Budha was the son of Chandra (moon) and Tara (star). Tara was the wife of Brihaspati (Jupiter), with whom Chandra had eloped. The story goes like this - Sage Brihaspati was the Guru of the Devas, and he was always busy performing rituals and reading scriptures. Therefore, he ended up spending very little time with his wife Tara, who felt sad and ignored. The Sage never showed any interest in being proximate with his wife. Tara was disillusioned and fell in love with Chandra when he approached her, they both eloped together.

As time passed, Indra, the king of Devas, decided to conduct a yajna (fire ritual) to gain strength to defeat the Asuras or demons.

Sage Brihaspati used this as an opportunity and said that he could only perform the yajna with his wife by his side. The Devas were divided in opinion on the issue. Some saw no reason in Tara to return to a husband who only needed her for rituals. They argued that Tara should remain with Chandra, who valued her as a living being.

But the Devas could not stop the yajna, so Indra decided that Tara should return to Brihaspati. Tara returned reluctantly, and the yajna was completed successfully. But soon it was discovered that Tara was pregnant. Both Chandra and Brihaspati claimed to be the father. Tara kept quiet. But as the debate raged, the unborn child cried out – and wanted to know who his father was? All who were gathered there were amazed by the desire of the child. The gods declared that he would be <u>Budh</u> – the lord that rules the intellect, because of his exceptional intelligence.

Tara answered to Budh that Chandra was his father. Sage Brihaspati could not tolerate the events, and he cursed the child that Chandra fathered - that he would be neither male nor female but a neuter gender. Tara, in due course, gave birth to Budh (Mercury). As the young Budh grew, his eagerness to learn and ability to grasp new subjects was excellent. Seeing this, Sage Brihaspati became more appreciative of Budh. Over time, he proudly accepted him as his son and taught him vast knowledge of the scriptures.

<u>The Placement of Mercury</u>

This table shows the influence of Mercury in the birth chart and its effect.

Influence	Placement	Effect
Mercury is strong when placed in	Virgo - moolatrikona and exalted. Gemini - own house Mercury nakshatras - Ashlesha, Jyeshtha and Revati Directional strength - 1st house. Atmakaraka - highest degree. Near to the Ascendant degree.	Intelligent, excellent communication and writing skills, very good in accounts, very good at negotiations, good business sense and financial wisdom.
Mercury is weak when placed in	Pisces - debilitated 7th house - no directional strength At 0, 1 and 29 degrees.	Impatient, distracted, can cheat others, misunderstandings, arguments and lack of focus.

<u>Inference</u>

Those who have a strong influence of Mercury in their birth chart will have a youthful look, thin lips, medium-sized eyes, medium height and quick movements and gestures. Just by looking at them, one may not be able to figure out straight away if they are male or female because they will not look overly feminine or overly masculine.

They will have a very friendly, easy-going persona who are quick to adjust to any kind of changing situation. Mercury is the planet of speed. Therefore, mercury-ruled people are fast thinkers, get bored easily, have a perfect sense of humour, are curious and intelligent, and are very good with mimicry, accounts, finance and communication.

The story of the birth of Budha gives suggestions regarding the nature of Budh. Just as Brihaspati was impressed by Budh's cognitive abilities, those who have a strong influence of Mercury in their birth chart are very intelligent. People around them are impressed by their intellectual prowess. This is because their inherent interest is to learn. They grasp new concepts very quickly and are able to articulate their thoughts very well, which makes them successful businessmen, negotiators, accountants and writers.

Mercury is also personified as a Prince who doesn't have to struggle hard. Usually, things are laid out for Mercury-ruled natives, all the facilities are provided for them, they just have to walk the path, and their life tends to follow the path of accumulating knowledge.

In the mythological story of Budh, he was cursed by Brihaspati to be a neuter gender. This gives the mercury-ruled natives the ability to handle both the feminine and masculine sides of their personalities with ease. They are not really interested in having children. They may not have any children or may choose to adopt a child. Physically, they will not have an ultra-feminine or an ultra-masculine look. Their physical persona fits into the middle of both genders.

Mercury is friendly with the Sun and Venus; therefore, it gives good results in signs and nakshatras ruled by these planets. For example, a Taurus Ascendent person who has mercury in Leo in Purva Phalguni in the 4th house, here mercury will have the influence of the Sun and Venus. The native's mum will be very creative, intelligent, and confident and will be a source of motivation and inspiration. His or her home environment will be such that it facilitates and promotes the artistic talent of writing, creating and communication.

Gemini and Virgo are ruled by Mercury, which is the natural 3rd and 6th house in the horoscope. Those who have the moon or Ascendent in these signs will have a strong influence of mercury. For example, the Moon in Gemini in Ardra, sitting in the 7th house, will make the natives very skilled communicators, and they will meet like-minded partners in their lives. Their spouse will love talking things over and discussing endlessly about things that bother them or please them, and they both enjoy long-winded discussions.

Because of mercury being influenced by Rahu in Ardra, they will be very shrewd with their money, very good at negotiations and would make excellent lawyers or businessmen. Since Gemini is a dual sign, they can switch roles very easily from being a fun-loving family man to a professional hard-core businessman. Gemini is also a masculine sign which makes the natives go-getters, and it's a Kama house, which makes them desire many things, chase goals and accomplish them.

The same mercury will behave differently when sitting in Virgo. Mercury is exalted in Virgo, so it feels very comfortable and gives excellent intellectual abilities. For example, a Virgo Ascendent person with mercury is sitting in Hasta. Here, the mercury will have the influence of the moon, which will make the natives very communicative about their emotions. They will be very particular about their routines and will have the skill of paying attention to detail. This quality makes them want to do things perfectly. They like things to be immaculate and tidy. If they are working on a project, they will make sure the finished product is up to the mark, with no faults. Because of this habit of perfection, they can become very critical and conscious of themselves, their work, their looks, and of others, too. Mercury in Hasta will also make them skilled in IT and keyboard skills. They can become excellent writers of fiction stories because of their ability to spin and weave tails of imagination and articulate their thoughts with the richness of vocabulary.

Virgo is an Artha sign; therefore, it supports and facilitates the accumulation of resources and a comfortable home and career. Moreover, Hasta is ruled by the moon, which nourishes physical health and overall personality. Virgo is a feminine sign, which makes them receptive and very easygoing people, they approach and achieve things through patience. They go by the wisdom of waiting for conducive situations rather than running after pushing their way through and creating friction or tension. They will always have a business-like approach to life.

Mercury is debilitated in Pisces, so it's not a comfortable placement for Mercury. For example, the Sun and Mercury in conjunction with a Pisces Ascendant. This conjunction is quite common because Mercury is never more than 2 houses away from the sun on the zodiac wheel.

Here the calculative and logical inference of mercury gets confused, because of the intuition of Pisces. They can make excellent astrologers, where they can combine the skills of both logical thought processes and intuition. For debilitated and exalted planets, look at the navamsha, too, to see how the earth will behave in the later years of life.

Example

Virgo Ascendant - ruled by Mercury

William Henry Davies - An English poet.

Born on 3rd July 1871 in Newport, UK, at 12 pm (estimated time of birth). Died on 26th September 1940 in Nailsworth, UK, at the age of 69.

William Henry Davies was a Welsh poet and writer of the 19th century, and his poems, which are grounded in realism, have been very popular. One of his popular poems has been shared in Uttara Phalguni.

"What is this life if, full of care,

We have no time to stand and stare." - W.H Davies.

William Henry Davies spent much of his life as a tramp in the United Kingdom and the United States but still became one of the most popular poets of his time. His main themes are observations about life's hardships, the ways the human condition is reflected in nature, his tramping adventures, and the characters he meets.

He was the son of an iron moulder and had one older brother and a younger sister. In November 1874, when William was only 3 years old, his father died. The following year, his mother, Mary Anne Davies, remarried as Mrs Joseph Hill. She agreed that care of the 3 children should pass to their paternal grandparents, Francis and Lydia Davies, who ran the nearby Church House Inn. His grandfather Francis Davies, had been a sea captain.

In 1883 he moved to Alexandra Road School and the following year was arrested, as one of a gang of 5 schoolmates and charged with stealing handbags. He was given 12 strokes of the birch. In 1885, Davies wrote his first poem entitled "Death".

In Poet's Pilgrimage, Davies recalls that at the age of 14, he was left with orders to sit with his dying grandfather. He missed the final moments of his grandfather's death as he was too engrossed in reading "an exciting book of wild adventure."

After school, Davies worked as an ironmonger. His grandmother in November 1886, signed papers for Davies to begin a five-year apprenticeship to a local picture-frame maker. Davies never enjoyed the craft. He left Newport, took casual work, and began his travels.

He became the most painted literary man of his day.

On 5th February 1923, Davies married 23-year-old Helen Matilda Payne. Davies's book Young Emma was a frank, often disturbing account of his life before and after picking Helen up at a bus stop on Edgware Road near Marble Arch. He had caught sight of her just getting off the bus and described her wearing a "saucy-looking little velvet cap with tassels." His last home was the small roadside cottage Glendower in the hamlet of Watledge. The couple had no children.

About 3 months before he died, Davies was visited by Osbert Sitwell, who noted that Davies looked very ill. His health continued to deteriorate, and he died in September 1940 at the age of 69.

Analysis

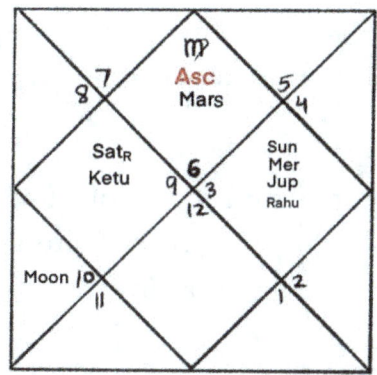
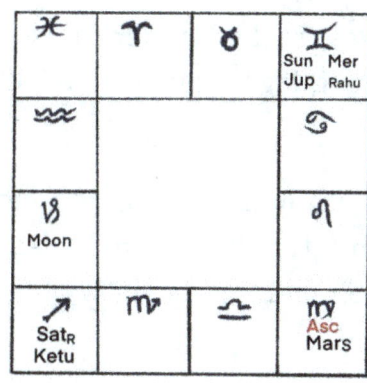

He is a Virgo Ascendant, and Mars is sitting in the Ascendant. Mercury, the lord of Virgo, is sitting in the 10th house of Gemini with Sun, Jupiter and Rahu.

This placement of planets gave him very strong Mercurian attributes - he was full of curiosity, he loved meeting people, love of learning, love of adventure and travelling. He had the gift of stringing words into poetic rhythms, a wonderful expression of words and articulation.

Oswald Sitwell, in his introduction to the 1943 Collected Poems of W. H. Davies, recalled Davies telling him that in addition to his grandparents and himself, his home consisted of "an imbecile brother, a sister, a maidservant, a dog, a cat, a parrot, a dove and a canary bird." This shows his love for life. He was surrounded by people and pets which made his experience very enriching. Especially a parrot that is associated with Mercury, it's interesting to see that he had him as a pet in his childhood.

Moreover, Moon sitting in Capricorn, in the 5th house of creativity, made him imaginative and intuitive, and he went on to become an exceptional fiction writer and a poet. Since Capricorn is the original sign of ambition and profession it helped him to get his poems and stories published in spite of financial hardships.

The Autobiography of a Super-Tramp (1908) covers his life in the United States from 1893 to 1899, including many adventures and characters from his travels as a drifter. During this period, he crossed the Atlantic Ocean at least 7 times on cattle ships.

Virgo is the original 6th house of challenges. We can see that his life was full of financial difficulties. Virgo is governed by the earth element, William was a very down to earth person. He travelled through many states doing seasonal work. His extensive travels contributed greatly towards his creative writings which is reflected beautifully in his simple and heart touching stories and poems.

The 10th house signifies career and public image. He has 4 planets sitting in the 10th house which brought him recognition and fame, but with a painful assurity. The turning point in Davies's life came after a week of rambling in London. He spotted a newspaper story about the riches to be made in the Klondike and set off to make his fortune in Canada. Attempting with a fellow tramp, to jump a freight train at Renfrew, Ontario on 20th March 1899, he lost his footing and his right foot was crushed under the wheels of the train. The leg was amputated below the knee and he wore a peg-leg thereafter. On 20th March 1899 he was running his <u>Rahu Saturn Mars dasha.</u>

Rahu is sitting with Mercury, Jupiter and Sun in the 10th house of public image. Saturn is retrograde sitting with Ketu in the 4th house of Sagittarius, and Mars is sitting in the Ascendant. In Vedic Astrology Shani Dev, the deity of Saturn is depicted as a slow mover who walks with a limp.

Davies writes, "I bore this accident with an outward fortitude that was far from the true state of my feelings. Thinking of my present helplessness caused me many bitter moments, but I managed to impress all comers with a false indifference. I was soon home again, away for less than 4 months, but all the wildness was taken out of me, and my adventures after this were not of my seeking, but the result of circumstances." Davies took an ambivalent view of his disability. In his poem "The Fog", published in the 1913 Foliage, a blind man leads the poet through the fog, showing the reader how someone handicapped in one domain may have a big advantage in another.

Davies' biographers agree the accident was crucial, although Davies played down the story. Moult begins his biography with the incident, and Stonesifer suggests this event, more than any other, led Davies to become a professional poet.

"I love thee for a heart that's kind - not for the knowledge in the mind." - W H Davies

Mercury the poet

Mercury, the Prince, talks you into a fun filled ride,

A sharp intellect to discern and decide.

The intellectual prowess and financial wisdom,

Helps to build a friendly kingdom.

A skilled negotiator,

Curiosity- the motivator.

The quest for learning,

Is a lifelong yearning.

5
Jupiter

Om gram greem graum saha Gurave namah

Sanskrit names	Guru - teacher - 'Gu' means darkness, and 'ru' means light, Guru is the one who takes us from the darkness of ignorance to the light of knowledge. Brihaspati - lord of vegetation, Vachaspati - lord of speech, Indraprohit - priest of Indra and Devapati - lord of devas.
Lord	Sagittarius and Pisces.
Deities	Vamana avatar
Sound	t, th, d, dh, n
House	9th and 12th
Weekday	Thursday
Rides on	an elephant
Personification	Teacher, mentor, guide and advisor.
Friends	Sun, moon and mars.
Enemies	Mercury and Venus.
Neutral	Saturn
Exalted	Cancer
Debilitated	Capricorn
Aspects	5th, 7th and 9th
Vimshotari dasha	16 years
Matures	At 16 years

Transit	Stays in 1 sign for 1 year.
Nakshatras	Punarvasu, Vishakha and Purva bhadrapada.
Lunar days	5th (panchami) and 13th tithi (trayodashi)
Motivation	Dharma
Gender	Male
Element	Ether - space
Colour	Yellow
Chakra	Ajna
Tridosha	Vata
Direction	North east (Ishana)
Guna	Satwa
Represents	Jiva - living creatures
Signifies	Growth and expansion
Vehicles	Reliable Cars
Animals	Domestic animals, horse, elephant and stag.
Bird	Eagle
Metal	Gold
Gemstones	Yellow sapphire
Organs	Kidneys, liver, lungs, spleen, fat and brain.
Body parts	Knees, tongue, ears, thighs and index finger.
Spices	Turmeric - haldi
Taste	Sweet
Food	All sweets and yellow coloured foods.
Plants	Peepal tree and jasmine flowers
Season	Spring time
Places	Temples and places of pilgrimage.
At home	Prayer room
Objects	Prayer items used for rituals.
Diseases	Cough, phlegm and congestion,
Yogic practice	Pranayam, hatha yoga and meditation.

Chant	Gayatri Guru mantra *"Om Gurudevaay Vidhmahe Parbrahmaay Dheemahi Tanno Guru Prachodayat."*
Physical appearance	Obese, fair and tendency to put in weight.
Qualities	Optimistic, strategist, beneficent, knowledgeable, wise, extravagant, adventurous, religious, spiritual, respectable, philosophical and humane.
Careers	Gurus, mentors, astrologers, spiritual leaders. saints, spiritual seekers, yogis, teachers, consultants, philosophers, financial advisors, managers, storytellers, script writers and directors.

Astronomical perspective

Jupiter is the largest planet in our solar system and is 5th from the Sun. It is a gas giant with a mass one-thousandth that of the Sun. It is one of the 3rd brightest objects visible to the naked eye, after the moon and Venus, in the night sky. It has been known to ancient civilizations since before recorded history and has been named after the Roman god Jupiter.

Jupiter is primarily composed of hydrogen, with a quarter of its mass being helium and lacks a well-defined solid surface. Jupiter's rotation is the fastest of all the Solar System's planets, this creates an equatorial bulge, which means that the diameter across its equator is longer than the diameter measured between its poles.

Storms are common within the turbulent atmospheres of Jupiter.

It has 79 known moons, including the four large Galilean moons discovered by Galileo in 1610. Ganymede, the largest of these, has a diameter greater than that of the planet Mercury. Future targets for exploration in the Jupiter system include the probable ice-covered liquid ocean of one of its moons, Europa.

Interesting facts

- Jupiter's magnetic field is 14 times stronger than Earth.

- It completes an orbit around the sun every 11.86 years.

- It completes a rotation on its axis in slightly less than ten hours.

- The Great Red Spot seen on Jupiter is large enough to accommodate Earth.

- Jupiter appears to undergo retrograde motion with respect to the background stars. Earth overtakes Jupiter every 398.9 days as it orbits the Sun, a duration called the synodic period. As it does so, Jupiter seems to move backwards in the night sky, performing a looping motion.

- NASA scientists say that Jupiter shrinks by about 2cm each year. When it was first formed, it was much hotter and was about twice its current diameter.

- Jupiter has been called the Solar System's vacuum cleaner because it protects Earth from numerous asteroids. It experiences about 200 times more asteroid, and comet impacts than Earth.

Mythology

In ancient Greek religion, the chief deity of the pantheon, the sky god, is called Zeus, who was identified with the planet Jupiter. Zeus was regarded as the sender of thunder and lightning, rain and winds, and his traditional weapon was the thunderbolt. He was called the father, the ruler and protector of both gods and men.

In German mythology, Jupiter is identified with Thor, the god with a heavy hammer in his hand, who sends lightning, thunder, and storms and represents the strength in the trees, giving fertility and protection. The name Thursday has been given after Thor.

Guru Brihaspati

The word Briha in Sanskrit means the spirit of vastness. In the Vedic era, sage Brihaspati was the counsellor of Devas (gods). In Vedic astrology, Jupiter has been named Guru Brihaspati, the teacher of the gods (devas). The word Guru means the heavy one. It is considered the Guru of all the gods and planets in astrology and the most sacred and holy because of its huge influence. In the epic of Mahabharata, it is said that Brihaspati had taught Bhishma Pitamah the duties of a king, and Bhishma had later taught it to Vidura.

In Rig Veda, he is described as a sage born from the first great light, the one who drove away darkness. He is bright and pure and carries a special bow whose string is Rta or cosmic order, which forms the basis of dharma. His wife is Tara, the goddess who personifies the stars in the sky.

As we have seen in the story of the birth of Budh, Tara ran away with Chandra, with whom she bore a son, Budha (planet Mercury).

This signifies Guru Brihaspati's disinterest in mundane family matters and sexual pleasures. His natural inclination is towards religion, philosophy, spirituality, astrology and esoteric subjects.

His knowledge and character are revered. Brihaspati as Jupiter is part of the Navagraha (the 9 planets) in the Hindu zodiac system and is considered auspicious and benevolent.

The placement of Jupiter

This table shows the influence of Jupiter on the birth chart and its effect.

Influence	Placement	Effect
Jupiter is strong when placed in	Sagittarius - moolatrikona. Cancer - exalted Pisces - own house Jupiter nakshatras -Punarvasu, Vishakha and Purva Bhadrapada. Directional strength - 1st house. Atmakaraka - highest degree. Near to the Ascendant degree.	Wisdom, knowledge, positive thinking and optimism.
Jupiter is weak when placed in	Capricorn - debilitated 7th house - no directional strength. At 0, 1 and 29 degrees.	Manipulative and dogmatic.

Inference

Jupiter is a benefic planet and supports growth and expansion, the natives born with a strong Jupiter influence will tend to be on the chubby side. They will have a plumpy face, will tend to put on weight easily and will love eating sweets.

Basically, Jupiter is a teacher, so people born with a strong influence of Jupiter will be in a teaching or counselling profession, priests, preachers, philosophers, guides, advisors, spiritual leaders, astrologers, psychologists, consultants, scholars and advocates.

Even if they are not officially working as a consultant, they will love advising others on any topic that interests them, and people also perceive them as a go-to person.

Jupiter is a very optimistic planet. Those who have a strong influence of Jupiter, or Jupiter is their Atma Karka, always look at the positive side of things. Even amidst a difficult situation, they will find a ray of hope. Because at the soul level, they feel that things will work out, they always come out of difficulties without much harm, except for the lessons learnt.

Jupiter represents good luck, fortune, expansion, self-development, higher learning, wisdom and spiritual intelligence. It is the most generous planet which gives abundant resources. When it's well placed in the horoscope, it grants happiness, good health, prosperity, spiritual inclination and success.

Jupiter is friends with the Sun, Moon and Mars. Therefore, it gives good results when placed in any of the signs ruled by these planets. For example, Jupiter in Cancer is exalted. Its optimism, growth and benefic nature of Jupiter provide great opportunities for the emotional and empathetic moon to spread its love and nourishment. The wisdom of Jupiter and the nourishment of the moon is a wonderful combination that supports harmonious relationships, trust and abundance. The natives will be caring, kind and loyal, and people around them will feel their genuine support. Jupiter is also well known for the stern ways of teaching, but despite all hardships, struggles, trials and tribulations, one comes out as a winner, who is wiser and more mature than before.

Jupiter is the Lord of Sagittarius and Pisces, the original 9th house of dharma (righteousness) and the 12th house of moksha (liberation). This shows that Jupiter ruled people like to do things correctly and ethically, and they understand the transitory nature of all that we see and experience in this world. Therefore, they view life from a very philosophical perspective.

Jupiter is exalted in Cancer and debilitated in Capricorn. This represents Jupiter's more gentle, idealistic, philosophical, optimistic and dreamy approach to life. In the natural horoscope, Cancer is in the 4th house of home and comfort, and directly opposite to it is - Capricorn, where Jupiter is debilitated. The 10th house of Job and career requires working away from home. This shows that Jupiter-ruled natives prefer to be in their comfort zone, read scriptures, contemplate the truth and untruth, philosophise, give advice, have intellectual discussions, counsel others, gain knowledge and walk the spiritual path. If they have to go out and earn money, then it has to be an easy academic job of teaching or counselling. Their delicate and sensitive constitution cannot withstand hard physical labour. The beneficence of Jupiter usually grants them these needed comforts. If there is a malefic influence of Saturn, then the natives may have to face delays and restrictions, in obtaining the desired comforts.

As seen earlier in the story of Budh Graha's birth, Guru Brihaspati was not interested in sexual intimacy; therefore, his wife Tara ran away with Chandra. Those who have a strong influence of Jupiter in their birth chart, for example, Sagittarius or Pisces Ascendent or moon sign, or Jupiter Sitting in the Ascendent or the 7th house, these people have all the success and comforts. Still, their marriage life always has something missing, or they may choose not to get married. This is because their inherent interest does not lie in earthly pleasures. They are more of spiritual seekers.

<u>Sage Bhrigu</u>

Maharishi Bhrigu was one of the 7 great sages, the Saptarishis. He was the first compiler of predictive astrology and also the author of Bhrigu Samhita, the astrological (Jyotish) classic. Bhrigu is considered a Manasa Putra - mind-born son of Brahma. He states that Jupiter signifies not just the blessings but also the curses.

In other words, he is saying that Jupiter, the Guru, teaches us the lessons of life, if needed, life after life, until we learn to overcome our limitations and follow the path of dharma - righteousness, or the path of the divine and until we realise our true self, our consciousness.

This is the reason why, in spite of Jupiter being a benefic planet, it's dasha can be very challenging in some way because it wants us to learn our lessons and overcome our limitations.

Example

Pisces Ascendant - ruled by Jupiter

Linda Goodman - Famous American Astrologer and poet.

Born on 9th April 1925 in Morgantown, USA at 6:05 am.

Passed away on 21st October 1995 at the age of 70.

Mary Alice Kemery, popularly known as Linda Goodman, is famous for her first Astrology book - "Linda Goodman's Sun Signs" (1968). Some have suggested that Linda was responsible for accelerating the growth of the New Age movement through the unprecedented success of her first astrology book. This was the first astrology book ever to earn a spot on the New York Times Best Seller list. Which was followed by "Linda Goodman's love signs" (1978) and was also the best seller that set a record with $2.3 million being paid for paperback rights.

Linda Goodman was born in Morgantown, West Virginia. Although she never revealed her year of birth, swearing even her father to silence, it emerged posthumously that she was born in 1925. Her father's name was Robert Stratton Kemery, and her mother's maiden name was Mazie McBee. By her own account, Goodman was born in her maternal grandparents' house. She attended and graduated from Parkersburg High School in 1943 at the age of 18.

She assumed the name 'Linda' during World War II for a popular WCOM radio show in Parkersburg that she hosted called Love Letters from Linda. Each show consisted of her reading letters written between soldiers and their loved ones. Each letter was punctuated with a popular song of the day. While working in radio, she met her second husband, Sam O. Goodman, and took his last name. She had 4 children, 2 children were from her 1st marriage and 2 were from her 2nd marriage.

She began writing for newspapers in the eastern and southeastern United States. Also, she wrote speeches for black American civil rights leader Whitney Young, who served for several years as president of the National Urban League. Linda retired in Colorado and died there on 21st October 1995, at the age of 70, from complications of diabetes.

Analysis

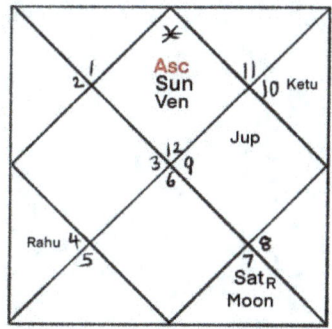

Linda is a <u>Pisces Ascendant,</u> Jupiter, the lord of Pisces is confidently sitting in the 10th house of career and public image in his own house of Sagittarius. Jupiter is also her Atma karka at 28 degrees - the planet with the highest degree in her birth chart.

The Jupitarian optimism, expansion and wisdom can be seen in her writings. The Pisces natives are naturally more inclined towards the spiritual and philosophical side of life. Having passed through the long experiential journey of all zodiac signs, in the last sign of Pisces, the soul becomes more sympathetic and humbler. In the final vibration of the water element, the receptivity and femininity come forth with a new vulnerability and urgency to discard the negative and master the positive aspects of life.

Linda has beautifully articulated through her poetry and astrological narrative the mystical dimensions of here and beyond. When her 2nd book, "Linda Goodman's Love Signs," was published in 1978 - which was an even bigger success, she was running her <u>Saturn Rahu Venus dasha.</u> Her Saturn is retrograde, sitting with the Moon in Libra in the 8th house of research and depth. Rahu is in the 5th house of Cancer - which represents creativity and followers. Her Venus is exalted in the Ascendant, sitting in Pisces with the Sun.

Saturn made her work patiently and enduringly for 5 long years - she started writing this book in 1973 and published it in 1978. Rahu amplified and exaggerated the success of her book beyond her imagination, and Venus exalted in the Ascendant, bringing the abundance of creativity and fortune.

<u>Here are some of Linda Goodman's quotes -</u>

"For all those who believe, expect a miracle."

"By learning to use the wisdom of the planets, our co - creators' code the universal truth."

"We may each create a fragment of the rainbow spectrum - a message of peace on earth to men and women."

"In the neverland mathematics of metaphysics, you see-

The more miracles we give away to others, the more we have left for you and me."

Jupiter, the poet

Jupiter the Guru, his beneficent generosity,

The giver of luck and prosperity.

The wisdom that comes from an inner knowing,

Grants abundance and success, playing and winning.

Beware, though, of the tough tests - that come your way,

A Jupitarian way of not letting you go astray.

The cosmic coach, the ultimate

Guides your fate.

6
Venus

Om dram dreem draum saha Shukraya namah

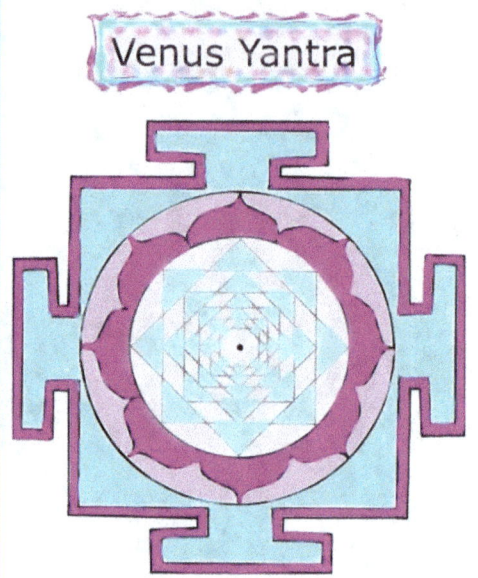

Lord	of Taurus - Rishabh and Libra - Tula
Deity	Indrani, Lakshmi and Sachi
Other names of Venus	Shukra, Asura Guru, Brigu Suta, Bhargave, Kavya, Ushana, and Roman Goddess of love and beauty.
Friends	Saturn and Mercury
Enemy	Sun and Moon
Neutral	Mars and Jupiter
Exalted	Pisces
Debilitated	Virgo
Guru	of demons - Shukracharya
Matures	at 25 years
Sounds	ch, csh, j , jh, gna
Chakra	Heart chakra - Anahata
Tridosha	Kapha
Animal	Jackal
Bird	Swan

Taste	Sour taste
Season	Spring time
Direction	South east
Colour	All pastel colours
Qualities	Fragrance, luxury, comfort, beauty, art, music, harmony, enjoyment, wealth, bhoga, mrit sanjeevani vidya - knowledge of rejuvenation, love, romance, passion, intoxication, cars, charm, sweet, female, seminal fluid reproduction, spouse, partner, silver, brahmin, jyotish, occult knowledge, worldly, versatile, splendour, light, culture, fashion, design and literature.
Careers	Poets, fiction story writers, musicians, actors, dancers, cinema, show biz, designers, artists, advisors, teachers, councillors, financial advisors, hotel managers and IT professionals.

<u>Astronomical perspective</u> - Venus is the 2nd planet from the Sun, has a rocky surface and has no moons. It goes retrograde every 18 months for 48 days. Its surface has been shaped by volcanic activity and has a dense atmosphere, which constitutes 96% carbon dioxide, and the clouds are mostly made of sulphuric acid. Researchers have recently discovered about 37 active volcanoes on Venus, which were earlier thought to be dormant, and the surface temperature is 900 degrees Fahrenheit.

It is seen as the brightest star in the sky and is called the evening and morning star. Venus is bright because its hot, dense atmosphere is covered by clouds that reflect the light. The clouds are made mostly of droplets of sulphuric acid, this makes the sunlight bounce off the smooth crystals that doubly make Venus appear very bright.

Venus as a physical planet is called the earth's twin, because it's almost the same size as the earth. However, they are not identical twins in any way, in fact they are radically apart. Because Venus has yellowish clouds of mostly sulphuric acid that trap heat and create a runaway greenhouse effect, for this reason Venus is the hottest planet in our solar system, although Mercury is the closest planet to the Sun. Apart from this Venus has a crushing air pressure at its surface, similar to the pressure one would feel a mile below the ocean on earth.

<u>Interesting facts about Venus -</u>

- Earth and Venus are almost the same size.
- Venus is the 2nd closest planet to the Sun and is the hottest.
- One day on Venus is 243 earth days long.
- On Venus, the Sun rises in the west and sets in the east.
- The solid surface of Venus is a volcanic landscape.

- Venus has no moons and no rings.
- The atmosphere of Venus is so hot that even lead can melt.
- Venus has yellowish clouds mostly made of sulphuric acid.
- The winds on Venus blow with a hurricane force.
- The rotation of Venus is slower than the Earth, and it revolves around the Sun in the opposite direction than the Earth.

Devi Lakshmi

Venus is associated with wealth, beauty, harmony and abundance, all these qualities are personified in Devi Lakshmi. The word Lakshmi means wealth, and Devi Ma Lakshmi is the Goddess of abundance, prosperity and wealth. The word Lakshmi is derived from the root word Laksha, which means goal. Therefore, Lakshmi is the one who provides the resources to help us achieve our goals.

Lakshmi is venerated as a principle aspect of the Mother goddess. She is both the wife and divine energy (shakti) of the Hindu god Vishnu. She helps Lord Vishnu maintain the universe and sustain all beings who stay on earth. Whenever Vishnu chose to descend on earth as an avatar, Lakshmi accompanied him as his wife. She was his wife, Sita, when he came as Rama, and his lover, Radha, when he came as Krishna.

There are 8 prominent manifestations of Lakshmi, called Ashtalakshmi, and they symbolise the 8 sources of wealth.

N	Lakshmi	Meaning
1	Adi Maha Lakshmi	The first goddess.
2	Dhana Lakshmi	Goddess of wealth.
3	Dhanya Lakshmi	Goddess of agriculture, food.
4	Gaja Lakshmi	The elephant Goddess - of animals.
5	Vidya Lakshmi	Goddess of knowledge.
6	Santana Lakshmi	Goddess of children.
7	Veerya Lakshmi	Goddess of valour.
8	Vijaya Lakshmi	Goddess of victory.

Goddess Lakshmi is also addressed with other names, which describe her attributes.

Names of Lakshmi	Meaning
Kamal	Lotus
Padma	Lotus
Padmakshi	Beautiful lotus shaped eyes
Padma sundari	Beautiful face like a lotus
Padma Hasta	Who has lotus in her hand
Padma Priya	Who loves lotus
Shree	Radiance, wealth and splendour
Vishnu Priya	Beloved of Vishnu

In Indian traditions, it's often said that "Wealth *and abundance come because of the females in the house, especially the wife."*

It makes logical sense because without the support of the wife, even if the wealth comes, contentment and true joy are not felt.

As the prevalent saying goes, "Behind *every successful man, there is a woman." this* has come about from years of wisdom and experience and, in a way, stands true. In Vedic culture, honouring the feminine is an essential part of many ritual practices. Numerous ancient Stotras of Hinduism recite hymns dedicated to Goddess Lakshmi. Kamala Stotram, verse 10, states that all women are the embodiments of Devi Lakshmi.

"Balya Cha Balika tvam hi Yauvane Yuvati Cha,
Sthavire vtudh rupa Cha, Prassana bhava sundari."

– Shree Kamala Strotam

<u>Meaning</u>

Every woman is an embodiment of you,

You exist as little girls in their childhood,

As young women in their youth,

And as elderly women in their old age,

You are always joyous.

Lakshmi Beej Mantra - *Shreem*

It can be chanted as *Om Shreem* 108 times to enhance the energy of abundance. Lakshmi Beej Mantra is considered the origin of all powers of Goddess Lakshmi. The intense vibratory energy produced by repetitive chanting produces an energy field which attracts abundance and fortune.

Shukracharya

The deity of Venus is Guru Shukracharya, who is the Guru of asuras - demons. His father was Sage Bhrigu, and mother was Kavyamata. He had 2 wives named Urjja Svati (Jayanti) and Sataparva and had one daughter named Devayani and 4 sons named - Tvasthadhar, Ara, Shand and Amark.

The mantra for Venus is - *Om Shri Shukra devaaaye namah.*

The ancient Puranas state that Shukra had worshipped Lord Shiva with devotion who blessed him with Sanjeevni Vidhya - knowledge of reviving the dead. Guru Shukracharya used this special knowledge to bring his disciples and Asuras back to life.

In the epic of Mahabharata, Shukra is mentioned as one of the mentors of Bhishma. In a particularly sensitive situation, where Shukracharya wanted to be fair to both parties, he had divided himself into 2, one half becoming the knowledge source for the Devas (gods) and the other half being the knowledge source for the Asuras (demons).

Venus the Goddess of beauty

Venus is the Roman goddess of love, beauty, prosperity, fertility, and victory. She was so important to Romans that they claimed her as their ancestress. According to mythology, her son Aeneas fled from Troy to Italy. He became the ancestor of Remus and Romulus, who founded Rome. Venus personifies the receptive beauty of the feminine. Julius Caesar, the Roman general, claimed her as his ancestor.

The mythical stories about Venus state that she was married to Vulcan, the god of fire and the forge. Vulcan was notoriously ugly – one of the ugliest of the gods. But he loved her so much that he created a golden carriage to pull her around. This carriage was drawn by doves to match Venus's own beauty. It is said that Venus was also the mother of CUPID, the god of love.

Because she was the goddess of love, Venus was very important to new brides. They made offerings to her before they got married. Some people also say that they gave their childhood toys to her when they left home to get married. The planet Venus is named after the goddess. It was visible in the ancient night sky at certain times of the year and looked like a very bright star. Because it was so bright and beautiful, it was named Venus.

The other names for the Goddess of beauty, which describe her attributes are -

Names of Venus	Meaning
Venus Cloacina	The Purifier
Venus Felix	Lucky, Brings good luck
Venus Genetrix	The mother
Venus Murcia	Myrtle Herb
Venus Verticordia	Changer of hearts, attractive
Venus Victrix	Victorious

Ayurvedic perspective -

The Vedic name for Venus is Shukra. The word shukra means the reproductive fluid. Shukra in Sanskrit means pure, bright and radiant. In Ayurveda, the word Shukra is used for both the male semen and the female egg.

The reproductive fluid contains the essence of all of the other dhatus (tissues) of the body. Shukra is the 7th and final dhatu in the dhatus formation cycle. A person who has a healthy shukra has a youthful lustre in the eyes and skin and is confident.

Ojus is the energy essence of the tissues that provide immunity and vitality. From shukra are formed the ojas, which then become a part of every dhatu, giving strength and stability. The journey from rasa to ojas is a cycle that takes 1 month, according to vaidya Sushruta.

In order to produce shukra dhatu, the primary element that must be consumed is water. Water is the primary nourishment of the body and of the dhatus, and shukra is its most refined form. The fluid of shukra dhatu is the essence of other body fluids. Only the most highly nourishing foods contain the essence of water, and only proper digestion liberates it as shukra. Foods that have a high shukra potential are unctuous (slimy), like milk, meat, juice, ghee, and nuts.

On a psychological level, shukra dhatu is related to the ability to sustain creativity. When the dhatu is healthy, there is a natural creative instinct and an ability to complete all projects. When the dhatu is deficient, there may still be a creative instinct, but the ability to follow it through to completion lessens.

Whenever any of the tridoshas are imbalanced, it affects the virality and quality of shukra dhatu. In such a situation, lifestyle changes in terms of diet and exercise must be made, which will help to bring back the balance. Steady routines help to balance all doshas. Vata dosha is the king among them that can cause all reproductive disorders. When vata dosha is imbalanced, one should eat warm cooked meals and rest more often. When pitta dosha is imbalanced, one should refrain from eating spicy and oily foods and should avoid getting into intense or competitive activities.

When kapha dosha is out of balance, one should eat more fresh and raw fruits and vegetables, and increase their exercise routine and activity level.

For those who are on the path of family life, sexual expression is a natural and healthy part of a relationship. However, excessive indulgence in sexual activity can make the person weak. For those who are on the spiritual path, building up one's shukra is necessary for its transformation into healthy ojas. High levels of ojas are needed for performing intense spiritual practises and thereby building it up towards enlightenment.

The placement of Venus

This table shows the influence of Venus in the birth chart and its effect.

Influence	Placement	Effect
Venus is strong when placed in	Libra - moolatrikona. Pisces - exalted Taurus - own house Venus nakshatras - Bharani, Purva Phalguni and Purva Ashadha. Directional strength - 4th house. Atmakaraka - highest degree. Near to the Ascendant degree.	Creative, passionate, artistic, charming, attractive, well mannered, friendly, popular and spontaneous.
Venus is weak when placed in	Virgo - debilitated 10th house - no directional strength. At 0, 1 and 29 degrees.	Selfish, hot tempered, impatient, irresponsible, and inconsiderate.

Inference

The Venusian beauty lies in the harmonious and balanced features of the face and body, which makes the natives irresistibly attractive.

They have medium-sized eyes, wavy to curly hair, and medium height.

They dress up in a simple way and don't overly dress up or apply makeup on their face. They are naturally attractive. This means others are drawn to them, not necessarily because of their looks, but because of their qualities. They have a very fine sense of aesthetics and have the talent of appreciating and creating beauty in all art forms - through acting, directing films, singing, painting, drawing, architecture, writing, poetry, graphic designing, cooking, tailoring, gardening, and decorating. One of the many names of Shukra is also Kavya, which means poetry. They have an intrinsic sense of harmony and rhythm and can, therefore, be wonderful poets.

Shukra is the reproductive fluid, which signifies that they have a sexual appeal and the opposite sex is naturally attracted to them. Their attractiveness may not be immediately apparent and may look very simple, but they understand love and beauty at a deeper level, which is projected by their sparkling eyes.

Venus, as a planet, has active volcanoes on its surface, which makes the atmosphere hot and dense, and it's the 2nd planet from the sun. This makes Venus shine as bright as the evening and the morning stars. This shows that Venus is inwardly corrosive and volatile but outwardly bright and beautiful. In fact, its beauty comes from the intense activity within. Similarly, Venus ruled natives are outwardly soft and polite, but inwardly they are fiery and fierce. They always want to create something and create the best.

They love beauty and truth and are very tuned to their senses. They enjoy all forms of pleasurable indulgence, whether it's through food, sex, art or music, it fuels their passion - they love to create beauty and to please beauty.

Venus involves indulgence of the senses - they love looking at, creating and surrounding themselves with beautiful things. However, at a deeper level they understand that true beauty lies in nature and in its natural form. They inherently know that nature responds best to things that make it and shape it. For this reason, they like to use things in its natural form, which is a good and healthy choice for the body and mind. For example, they will prefer eating fresh fruits that are more nutritious than canned fruits.

Since Venus ruled, people have a very keen sense of form and balance, they don't like to overdo things. For instance, they want to dress up in clothes that are simple and comfortable, for them, their luxury and fashion statement is comfort. At home they will prefer to have a flower arrangement with real flowers rather than with artificial flowers, or they will love spending time in the garden or going for holidays where they can be close to nature.

The beneficence of Venus provides material comforts. For example, the Moon in Bharani in the 2nd house gives the natives the comfort of resources and good family earnings.

Shukracharya is said to be the Guru of asuras. Rig Veda describes asuras as a class of beings who oppose the devas or suras. In Sanskrit language, the word 'sur' means to be in tune, and 'asura' means to be out of tune. This signifies those qualities in us that create chaos or disharmony. In other words, it's the opposite force, like - positive and negative. Asuras is the counter force - the negative force. We are able to recognise and appreciate the positive only because of the negative side. Both are equally needed for the play of creation to happen. In existence, there is nothing good or bad, it's more a matter of our perspective.

In that sense, Guru Shukracharya teaches the art of indulging the senses, and Venus provides the material luxuries and comforts needed for enjoying relationships. Both suras and asuras have a purpose. Venus, as a significator of harmony, helps us to harmonise and balance worldly and spiritual desires.

Venus is friendly with Mercury and Saturn; therefore, when Venus is placed in Mercury-ruled signs of Gemini and Virgo and Saturn-ruled signs of Capricorn and Aquarius, it gives good results.

Venus is the Lord and benefic provider of the 2nd house of accumulating resources and wealth and of the 7th house of relationships, which give a sense of pleasure, fulfilment and happiness. In the 12th house of Pisces, Venus is exalted, this is the house of losses of the material world - but signifies gains of the psychic and spiritual realms.

This shows that Venus is not only the giver of worldly comforts, enjoyments and pleasures - but its ultimate intention is to help us experience the highest level of pleasure, enjoyment, ease and relaxation by letting go of the transitory worldly desires and seeking the eternity of our divine self, which is - 'Sat Chit Ananda,' - the eternal truth, which is fully aware and is always in a state of bliss.

For example, suppose an exalted Venus is sitting in Pisces in the Ascendent. In that case, it will grant facial beauty, a good body, an intense sexual energy, and the opposite sex will be attracted to the native. The native will be very creative and artistic and could do well in the field of acting, art or music. They will also have the resources and knowledge to keep their body well and healthy. This is a general prediction, if there are any malefic planets like Saturn, Mars, Rahu or Ketu sitting with Venus or aspecting it, the results will alter accordingly. The effect of the exalted Venus will still be there, but there will be a lack of opportunities because of other planetary influences.

Example

Taurus Ascendent ruled by Venus

Nina Simone- An American singer, songwriter, musician and civil rights activist.

Born on 21st February 1933 in Tryon, N Carolina, USA at 12 pm (estimated time of birth) and died on 21st April 2003 in Carry le rouet in France at the age of 70.

Eunice Kathleen Waymon was professionally known as Nina Simone.

She was the 6th born child of the 8 children born to a poor family in Tryon, North Carolina.

Simone began playing piano at a very early age of 3. The first song she learned was "God Be With You, Till We Meet Again". Her concert debut was given to her when she was 12 years old. Simone later said that during this performance, her parents, who had taken seats in the front row, were forced to move to the back of the hall to make way for white people. She said that she refused to play until her parents were moved back to the front and that the incident contributed to her later involvement in the civil rights movement.

In order to fund her private lessons, Simone performed at the Midtown Bar & Grill on Pacific Avenue in Atlantic City, New Jersey, whose owner insisted that she sing as well as play the piano, which increased her income to $90 a week. In 1954, she adopted the stage name "Nina Simone". Knowing her mother would disapprove of playing "the Devil's music," she used her new stage name to remain undetected. Simone's mixture of jazz, blues, and classical music in her performances at the bar earned her a small but loyal fan base.

In 2003, just days before her death, the same Music Institute which had denied her admission in 1950 due to racial discrimination awarded her an honorary degree.

Analysis

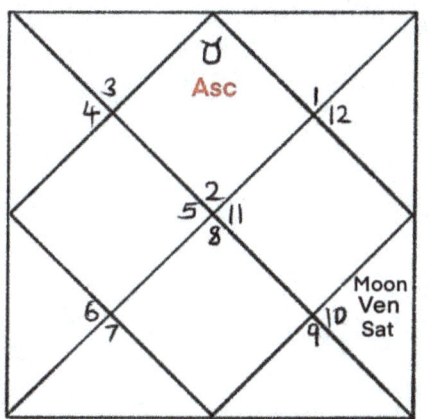 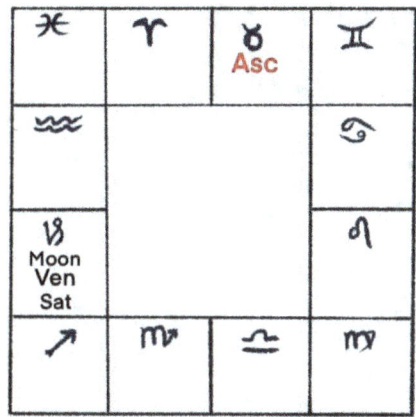

She is a Taurus Ascendant, Venus, the lord of Taurus is sitting in the 9th house of Capricorn with Moon and Saturn. We can see prominent Venusian qualities in her - she was hugely talented in singing and was also a songwriter, musician and civil rights activist.

Taurus, being an earth sign, also gave her steadfastness, patience, conviction and strength of purpose to face the challenges she had to face in the early part of her singing career.

After her graduation, Simone spent the summer of 1950 at the Juilliard School as a student of Carl Friedberg, preparing for an audition at the Curtis Institute of Music in Philadelphia. Despite a well-received audition, she was denied admission due to racial discrimination.

She was in her Rahu Saturn Saturn dasha in 1958 when she started the successful phase of her career. She went on to record more than 40 albums between 1958 and 1974, making her debut with Little Girl Blue. She had a hit single in the United States in 1958 with "I Love You, Porgy." She received the Grammy Hall of Fame Award in 2000 for her interpretation of this song.

Both Saturn and Rahu are in young and awake avastha (state) and, therefore, are capable of giving results during their dashas and transits. The Moon is with Saturn and Venus in the 9th house of Capricorn. Saturn and Venus are good friends, and Saturn is strong and comfortable sitting in his own house of Capricorn. Moreover, Saturn, being the Lord of the 9th and 10th house, is a yogakaraka planet and becomes a functional beneficial for her.

Venus, the poet

Venus, the bright Goddess of beauty personified,

Tempts and attracts in ways that mystify.

The fragrance of creativity and essence of art,

Fills the air with love and romance.

The evening star shining bright,

Inspires creativity through the night.

And at dawn - her beauty serene,

Spreads into a spectacular scene.

7
Saturn

Om pram preem praum saha Shanicharaya namah

Sanskrit names	Shani, Shanishchara, mandaya - the one who moves slowly, Sanjana ja - son of Sanjana, Surya chaya - shadow of the Sun.
Lord	Capricorn and Aquarius
Deities	Shani Dev and Hanuman
Sound	pa, fa, ba, bh, ma
House	10th and 11th
Weekday	Saturday
Rides on	a crow
Personification	Worker
Friends	Mercury and Venus
Enemies	Sun and Moon
Neutral	Mars and Jupiter
Exalted	Libra
Debilitated	Aries
Aspects	3rd, 7th and 10th from itself.
Vimshotari dasha	19 years cycle
Matures	at 35th year

Transit	Stays in 1 sign for 2 years and 6 months.
Retrograde	Once a year it goes retrograde for 4 months.
Nakshatras	Pushya, Anuradha and Uttara bhadrapada.
Lunar days	Saptami tithi - 7th lunar day
Motivation	Artha - material well-being
Gender	Feminine
Element	Air - Vayu
Colour	Blue and black
Chakra	Vishuddhi
Tridosha	Vata
Direction	West
Guna	Tamas
Represents	the 8th house, occult, mysticism and death.
Vehicles	Old model vehicles
Animals	Buffalo, donkey, bear, pig and goat.
Birds	Crow, cuckoo and vulture.
Metal	Iron
Gemstones	Blue sapphire
Organs	Urinary bladder and anus.
Body parts	Middle finger of the hand, chin, feet, knees and buttocks.
Spices	Black pepper
Taste	Pungent
Food	Mustard seeds, black sesame seeds, coffee, tobacco and sunflower oil.
Plants	Bilva tree
Season	Winter and stormy weather.
Places	Remote places, forests, deserts and construction sites and garbage sites.
At home	Toilet
Objects	Antiques, old clothes and objects, leather and coal.
Diseases	Can experience problems in digestion and constipation, joint pains, toothache, ulcers, asthma and phlegm.

Yogic practice	Meditation, breath watch, Surya namaskar and pranayama.
Chant	Shani gyatri mantra *"Om Kaakadhwajaaya Vidmahe, Khadga Hastaaya Dheemahi, Tanno Mandah Prachodayat."*
Physical appearance	Tall, slim, dark complexion, long limbed, small reddish-brown eyes, large teeth, large nails, rough thick hair, and rough textured skin.
Saturn is strong	Saturn's most powerful place in the chart is in the 7th House or in Libra where it's exalted. It also gives good results in the Kendra houses (1st, 4th, 7th and 10th). He is a particularly beneficial planet for Taurus and Libra Ascendents.
Signifies	Saturn is a karaka, or indicator, of longevity, misery, sorrow, old age and death, discipline, restriction, responsibility, delays, ambition, leadership and authority, humility, integrity, and wisdom born of experience. It is also the karka of asceticism, denial, non-attachment, spirituality, hard work, organisation, reality and time itself.
Qualities	Wise, old, patient, fearful, sad, secretive, rebel, limps, poverty, delays, frustrations, restrictions, elderly, orthodox, slow, disciplined, long-lived, can be lazy or hard-working, endurance, cold, can be scruffy appearance, adversity, responsibility and obligations.
Careers	Workers, farmers, miners, estate agents, security personnel, archaeologists, lawyers, social workers, cleaners, regular jobs, jailers, managers, caretakers, undertakers, butchers, plumbers, builders and jobs requiring physical or mental endurance.

Shani's image

He rides a crow and is also often seen with black dogs. Both signify the play of time and the eventual death of all beings.

Astronomical perspective -

Saturn is the 6th planet from our Sun and the farthest planet seen without a telescope. It is unique because of its spectacular and dazzling icy rings. Like Jupiter, Saturn is mainly made of hydrogen and helium, the same two main components that make up the Sun.

It is surrounded by 53 known moons and has some of the most fascinating landscapes in our solar system. One day on Saturn is 10.7 hours long, the time it takes to rotate around once. Its axis is tilted, which means that, like Earth, Saturn experiences seasons. It makes a complete orbit around the Sun in about 29.4 Earth years.

Saturn, the gas giant

Saturn is the only planet in our solar system whose average density is less than water. The giant gas planet could float in a bathtub if such a colossal thing existed. Saturn took shape when the rest of the solar system formed about 4.5 billion years ago when gravity pulled the swirling gas and dust in to become this gas giant. About 4 billion years ago, Saturn settled into its current position in the outer solar system.

As a gas giant, Saturn doesn't have a solid surface. The planet is mostly swirling gases and liquids deeper down. While a spacecraft would have nowhere to land on Saturn, it wouldn't be able to fly through unscathed either. The extreme pressures and temperatures deep inside the planet would melt and evaporate any spacecraft trying to fly into the Earth. Saturn is blanketed with clouds that appear as faint stripes, jet streams and storms. The planet has many different shades of yellow, brown and grey. The pressure on Saturn is the same kind you feel when you dive deep underwater. It's so powerful that it squeezes gas into liquid.

Saturn's magnetic field

Saturn's north pole has an interesting atmospheric feature, a six-sided jet stream with a massive, rotating storm at the centre. There is no weather feature like this anywhere else in the solar system. Saturn's magnetic field is smaller than Jupiter's but is 578 times more powerful than the Earth's magnetic field.

Rings of Saturn

Saturn's rings are thought to be pieces of comets, asteroids or shattered moons that broke up before they reached the planet, torn apart by Saturn's powerful gravity. They are made of billions of small chunks of ice and rock. The ring particles mostly range from tiny, dust-sized icy grains to chunks as big as a house, and a few particles are as large as mountains.

Saturn's moons

Saturn is home to a vast array of intriguing and unique worlds. From the haze-shrouded surface of Titan to crater-riddled Phoebe, each of Saturn's moons tells another story surrounding the Saturn system. Currently, Saturn has 53 confirmed moons. Cassini images from 2012 showed that Titan and Saturn's environment is not conducive to life as we know it.

Interesting facts

- 1 day of Saturn is 10.7 hours long.
- 1 year of Saturn is 29 Earth years.
- Saturn has 53 confirmed moons.
- Saturn is sometimes called, 'the jewel of the solar system.'
- 9 earths can fit across Saturn.
- It is very windy on Saturn. Around the equator, winds can blow at 1,800 kilometres per hour.

- Saturn's beautiful rings are not solid. They are made up of bits of ice, dust and rock and are the only ones that can be seen from earth through a telescope.

- Saturn is so light that it can float in water.

- Saturn was named after the Roman god of farming.

Roman Mythology

Saturn is named after the Roman god of agriculture and wealth, who was also the father of Jupiter. He was described as a god of generation, dissolution, plenty, wealth, agriculture, periodic renewal and liberation. Saturn was also known as a god of time. His consort was his sister Ops, with whom he fathered Jupiter, Neptune, Pluto, Juno, Ceres and Vesta.

Image of Saturn

Saturn is depicted with his head protected by a winter cloak, holding a sickle in his right hand, and is also sometimes shown as veiled and winged.

Festivals of Saturnalia

Saturn was especially celebrated during the festival of Saturnalia each December, perhaps the most famous of the Roman festivals, a time of feasting, role reversals, free speech, gift-giving and revelry. The Temple of Saturn holds the treasury and archives of the early Roman Empire. The planets Saturn and Saturday are both named after the Roman God.

His nature becomes evident in his mastership over the annual time of crisis around the winter solstice, the social order and its rules. It signifies the power of annihilation present in the feminine Goddess Lua and Opa, the Goddess of plenty and bounty, who brings annual fertility and renewal.

The 2 wives of Saturn

Saturn had two wives, Ops and Lua. Ops, the Roman equivalent of Greek Rhea, signifies wealth, abundance and resources, while Lua represents destruction, dissolution, death and losses. She was the goddess who received the bloodied weapons of enemies destroyed in war.

Saturn and the cycle of time

Saturn is seen as the God of a timeless era - before the concept of time was perceived as day and night. He is believed to reinstate renewal during the winter solstice, which usually comes around 20th December, marking the shortest day of the year and the start of winter in the northern hemisphere. Saturn's festival in the Roman calendar led to his association with the concept of time. Cronus-Saturn's aged appearance represents the waning of the old year and the birth of the new.

Saturn as the God of time

Since time consumes all things, Saturn is believed to grant justice through the relentless arrow of time. Under Saturn's rule, humans were punished or rewarded according to their deeds. People enjoyed the spontaneous bounty of the earth without labour in the *'golden age,'* he was known as the God of time during the ancient Roman era.

Saturn, the God of agriculture

The word Saturn is derived from the Latin word satis, which means filled or satiated by all things or all generations. The other meaning of Saturn, with reference to land and farming, comes from the root word stercus, which means dung or manure. This signifies the re-emergence from death to life. In this interpretation, the agricultural aspect of Saturn would be secondary to his primary relation with time and seasons. Since agriculture is so closely linked to seasons. Therefore, an understanding of the cyclical passage of time, weather patterns and seasons was associated with Saturn being the God of agriculture.

Temple of Saturn

The temple of Saturn was located at the base of the Capitoline Hill. According to tradition, it was known as Saturnius Mons. As a remnant of this ancient building, a row of columns still stands. This temple was consecrated in 497 BC, and the area around it was called Saturni, which was built by King Tullus Hostilius.

Saturn, the politician

Around 104 BC, Saturninus was a popular politician who proposed reduced-price grain distribution to the poor people of Rome. He intended to alter the social hierarchy to his advantage by giving his political support to the ordinary people rather than the senatorial elite.

Interesting facts

- Jupiter is the son of Saturn.
- Saturn's name was derived from status, which means to show.
- Saturn was named after the Roman God of agriculture.
- Saturn has 2 wives, Opa (Goddess of bounty) and Lua (Goddess of destruction).
- Saturn was a well-loved politician, a helper of the poor.

Vedic mythology

In Vedic astrology, Saturn is called *'Shani,'* which comes from the Sanskrit word Shanishchara, which means the slow mover. When Shani was born, the Sun went into an eclipse. This shows the impact of Shani in Vedic astrology. He was born on Vaishak Vadya Chaturdasi Amavasya, which is observed as Shani Amavasya or Shani Jayanti.

Birth of Saturn

According to Vedic mythology, Shani is the son of the Sun god and his wife Chaya (shadow). It is said that Surya Dev was initially married to Sandhya. Still, because of his unbearable heat and brightness, she left him and went away for penance, leaving her shadow Chaya behind. From their union, Yama, Shani and Tapti were born. For this reason, Shani dev is also called Chayaputra, which means the son of Chaya. While his mother was pregnant with him, she went through severe penance, and Lord Shiva therefore blessed her son Shani with a dark complexion, symbolising the power of extreme penance and the eternal quality of darkness.

Shani's elder brother Yama is also known as Dharma Raja, or God of death, who dispenses justice and gives rewards or punishment for one's deeds after death. While Shani is known to give the fruits of one's Karma (deeds) in this life itself.

As soon as Shani was born, his gaze fell on his father and caused him vitiligo (a skin disease where the natural pigmentation and colour of the skin are lost). Next, his gaze fell on the Sun's charioteer. He fell and broke his thigh. When he looked at the 7 horses next, they all went blind. The Sun tried many remedies, but nothing worked. It was only when Shani's gaze left them that the Sun's skin got back its original colour, his charioteer's leg healed, and his horses regained their sight. Saturn was given the position of a Deva after performing penance in Benaras and praying to Lord Shiva.

Saturn delivers justice through time.

Saturn is the lord of longevity, death, justice and time. Even King Indra and all the gods panic when Saturn is nearby, for over the ages, many thousands of Indras have been overtaken by the power of time.

Saturn, the slow mover

It is believed that Shani had kicked his mother because of her biased approach towards her other son. In her anger and retaliation, Sandhya cursed Shani that his leg may become invalid, and because of this Shani limps and strolls.

Qualities of Saturn

Saturn's vata influence

Shani's elemental constitution is *'air'* which represents the Vata Dosha in Ayurveda, and its qualities are dry, light, cold, subtle and mobile. From 50 years onwards, it's called the vata age because as we age, the vata in our constitution increases, which causes physical and mental changes. It can bring problems of dry skin, greying of hair, constipation, stiffness of joints, pains and aches, decline in cognitive abilities and also brings wisdom.

Over the years, stress, environmental toxins, unsuitable foods and unbalanced lifestyle habits have taken their toll on our bodies. Ayurveda, the oldest system of natural medicine, offers strategies for better health and reversing the effects of ageing.

Ayurveda tips for the over 50s -

- Vata is cold, rough, dry and irregular, which is balanced by the opposite qualities of staying warm, avoiding raw food and soaked dry nuts.
- Don't overdo things.
- Maintain a regular daily routine.
- Get plenty of rest, and go to bed by 10pm.
- Meditate for at least 5 - 15 minutes every day.
- Eat freshly cooked warm meals.
- Have the main meal of the day at lunchtime.
- Eat Vata-pacifying foods like carrots, tomatoes, broccoli, and spinach, and use Vata-pacifying spices like turmeric, cumin, fenugreek, and asafoetida.
- Take herbal supplements as recommended by the Ayurvedic practitioner.
- A daily sesame oil mini massage of the head, hands and feet.
- Exercise regularly, according to your capacity.
- Keep your mind sharp and engaged.

We must acknowledge and revere good health because the most significant asset in our lives is our health, and the most significant suffering is caused by physical, emotional, mental, and social ill health.

Special transits

Saturn, being a slow-moving planet, stays in one sign for 2 and a half years. Special transits of Saturn have an impact in terms of delays or difficulties faced during that period. These effects will be felt more keenly if the natives are going through the Saturn dasha or sub dasha during the time of these transits.

Sade sati- This is a 7-and-a-half-year transit over the natal moon (2 and a half years times 3 - representing the transit signs before and after- the sign in which the moon sits). For example, if the moon is in Capricorn, Saturn's transit over Sagittarius, Capricorn, and Aquarius will and this will be the period of Sade sati. This can bring difficult situations, setbacks and delays.

Dhaiya - It is 2 and a half year when Saturn is transiting exactly in the opposite sign in which the natal moon is placed. For example, if the moon is in Cancer, when Saturn transits in Capricorn, the native will go through the dhaiya period. This period can bring delays and frustration.

Wisdom

Symbolically, Saturn is the planet of wisdom gained through many incarnations of tests and trials. They can be bossy employers, grandparents, government officers or anyone in authority. Their wisdom lies in having a very practical and cautious approach to life. Saturn being the restriction, they represent all those people who enjoy saying 'NO,' 'yes' seems to be a typically foreign word to them. Ironically, you will find that those natives who have a strong influence of Saturn will avoid saying 'yes' directly and will substitute it with words like - ok, we will see, I suppose so, it depends, etc.

Restriction

Saturn also represents limitation and restriction. It confines and demands discipline during its dasha. In the long run, it supports our growth and development. Saturn's incredible wisdom and patience are focused on long-term goals and support those activities that bring meaning and structure to our lives. It demands commitment and responsibility, which by nature seem restrictive. If we want to succeed in life safely and surely, endurance and self-control are definitely needed. Saturn is famous for delivering results slowly but surely. Without dedication and discipline, nothing substantial can be achieved in life.

Responsibility

Since Saturn rules the 10th house of career and 11th house of desires, it gives ambition and the ability to work hard towards our desired goals. Those who have a strong influence of Saturn in their birth chart, with good strength and ashtakavarga score, will be serving the public in a responsible position of authority.

Saturn teaches the lessons of life through challenges and trials, restrictions and delays, frustration and fears. This relentless drill gives the gifts and needed virtues of patience, perseverance, stability, hard work, reliability and dependability. Saturn also signifies old traditions and values. The natives who have a strong influence of Saturn will have great interest in history and will like collecting antiques.

Justice

Saturn is also known for its cold and cruel approach because it believes in perfect justice and does not give leeway for any faults - a reward for the hard work and punishment for the lapses.

This makes the natives practical and conservative, disciplined and hardworking, lazy or disillusioned.

Those who have Saturn placed in the ascendant, or their Ascendent sign is Capricorn or Aquarius, or they are born in the Saturn-ruled nakshatras- Pushya, Anuradha, or Uttara Bhadrapada- will find that their life situations will be such that they will have to serve one person, or many people either through social work, voluntary work, or through a position of responsibility at some point in their life.

Patience

The popular phrase - *"slow and steady wins the race"* stands true for Saturn. It gives a very cool, calm and patient approach to situations. This is a beautiful and enduring quality that helps to climb the ladder to success. Especially those who have their moon in Capricorn or Aquarius, or their moon is in Pushya, Anuradha or Uttara Bhadrapada, will not get into a rage of anger, they will be cool and patient, may seem slow to others, they will be dedicated, disciplined and will patiently work towards their goals.

Saturn, the karmic planet

Shani has been given the responsibility of delivering karmic justice, the giver of rewards and punishment based on our deeds.

Kabir, the famous mystic, saint and poet of the 15th century, has written many spiritually inspiring poems. Here is a verse on Karma from one of his poems.

"Sabhi karma hamara kiya, hum karman se nyare ho." - Kabir

This means I am totally responsible for all my actions, in thought, words, and deeds, of the past and present, yet my true being, 'I', is not in any way influenced or tarnished by these actions. My consciousness is free.

Lord Saturn cannot be ignored since ignorance, pride, and ego are the central vices he wishes to remove. Such is the blessing of his timeless wisdom and teaching of Karma, samsara and reincarnation. Saturn need not be feared but honoured, the best way to please him is to be disciplined and humble, patient and faithful.

Karma Karka

Saturn is called the karma karka, which means it defines our profession, career, or the kind of work we will do in our lives. For example, suppose Saturn is placed in the 4th house. In that case, the natives will work from home, will feel responsible for their mother, will work towards building a new house or buying properties, might work as estate agents, will follow a disciplined and strict routine at home, and will work hard to provide a comfortable home for their family.

Saturn and Karma

This popular verse of the Bhagavad Gita offers a deep insight into how we should perform our duties.

In Bhagavad Gita, chapter 2, verse 47, Lord Krishna says-

"Karmaṇy-evādhikāras te mā phaleṣhu kadāchana

mā karma-phala-hetur bhūr mā te saṅgo 'stvakarmaṇi."

Meaning of the Sanskrit words -

karmaṇi—in prescribed duties, eva—only, adhikāraḥ—right, te—your, mā—not, phaleṣhu—in the fruits, kadāchana—at any time, mā—never, karma-phala—results of the activities, hetuḥ—cause, bhūḥ—be, mā—not, te—your, saṅgaḥ—attachment, astu—must be, akarmaṇi—in inaction.

Meaning

We must do our duties and perform action as needed, but we don't have any control over its results. Because we are not the cause of the results, therefore shouldn't be attached to action or inaction (our intention).

Do your duty, but do not concern yourself with the results. We have the right to do our duty, but the results are not dependent only upon our efforts. A number of factors come into play in determining the results—our efforts, destiny, our past karmas, the will of God, the efforts of others, the cumulative karmas of the people involved, the place and situation, luck, etc.

If we become anxious about the results, we will experience anxiety if they are not according to our expectations. On the other hand, when we are focused and totally involved, we are able to give our best. Sincere effort never goes unrewarded, even if it does not bring success in the material world or as compared to someone else. The fulfilment of having given our best can never be taken away. It's a beautiful recipe for a stress-free work ethic. When we do anything wholeheartedly, the result will anyway be good without having to worry too much about it.

Karma and intention

The word Karma literally means action, not just physical action, but also at the level of thoughts, emotions and energy - all of it is Karma done at the gross level and at the subtle level.

Sadhguru explains the concept of Karma beautifully. He says,

"Karma lies in the intention." The intention behind the action is what matters. For example, Sue is taking a walk in the countryside and steps on an ant and it dies. This is the Karma of an accident; her intention was not to kill, but it died, or she steps on the ant to kill it because she doesn't like ants. This is the Karma of hate. Or she is scared of ants, and she kills them and runs away. This is the Karma of fear, or she did not kill the ant but lifted it and put it under the bush in a safe place to ensure that it does not get killed accidentally. This is the Karma of love or compassion.

In all these scenarios, it was the same action of reacting to the ant with different intentions. Accordingly, our Karma gets stored in the file of accident, hate, fear, or love. Sadhguru further explains the yogic perspective of Karma. We are made of 5 sheaths or layers called -

N	Sheaths	Meaning
1	Anna Maya kosha	The physical body is nourished from the food we eat.
2	Gyan Maya kosha	The mental body of thoughts and emotions.
3	Prana Maya kosha	The energy body is sustained by the air we breathe.
4	Vigyan Maya kosha	The body of inner knowing and wisdom, transitory layer.
5	Ananda Maya kosha	The blissful body is non-physical.

Sadhguru explains further that Karma only operates at the first 3 layers of the body, mind and energy. Beyond that, the 4th and 5th layers of inner knowledge and bliss are not affected by any karma. This is because they are non-physical in nature, and the laws of Karma only operate at the physical level, just as the laws of physics and gravity are applicable only to tangible, physical forms.

In this context, when people pray, meditate, chant mantras or do any kind of spiritual practises, they are trying to touch that dimension within themselves which is non-physical. Once one gets to experience the truth within, even if it's very brief, it takes one beyond the impact of *Karma or Saturn*.

This is easier said than done. The karmic patterns are so resilient that they outlive the body. Even when the body dies, the karmic patterns tendencies (vasanas) don't die. The soul moves on to find another womb.

It is driven by subtle inclinations and dispositions based on its previous input or software....and the cycle of Karma continues to build up, like a domino effect. The only way to lighten this karmic debt is by performing selfless action with no personal agenda attached. This is a wonderful technique given in the Vedic shastras, which changes Karma (selfish action) into dharma (selfless action).

<u>Saturn, the spiritual guide</u>

He can be seen as the karmic teacher because, through turbulence and trials, he makes us look at life from a deeper perspective. In a way we get panel belated into the correct habits and lifestyle that will enhance our wellbeing. Saturn also has an ascetic quality, disillusioned and disinterested in the materialistic ways of the world and rich with inner spirituality.

The placement of Saturn

This table shows the influence of Saturn in the birth chart and its effect.

Influence	Placement	Effect
Saturn is strong when placed in	Aquarius - moolatrikona. Libra - exalted Capricorn - own house Saturn nakshatras - Pushya, Anuradha and Uttara Bhadrapada. Directional strength - 7th house. Atmakaraka - highest degree. Near to the Ascendant degree.	Patient, disciplined, ambitious, committed, practical, calm, mature and wise.
Saturn is weak when placed in	Aries - debilitated 1st house - no directional strength. At 0, 1 and 29 degrees.	Rigid, scheming, stingy, lazy, slow, fearful and melancholic.

Inference

Saturn ruled natives will have a darker skin colour, and will be slim and tall. They will have medium sized eyes which are deeply set and have a piercing look. Their lips are medium-sized, and they have large, prominent teeth and sharp features set on a thin face. Overall, they have a sober and serious look on their face. They also tend to have prominent ears and a long neck, with an Adam's apple that protrudes in the neck. Saturn is farthest from the Sun and is a cold and airy planet. Therefore, it gives a vata-type constitution.

The natives may have some or all of these attributes, depending on how strong the influence of Saturn is in the birth chart. If Saturn is sitting in the 1st house of physical features and overall personality, these attributes will manifest. For example, if the moon is in Anuradha, the natives will have an oval face because of the influence of the moon and Saturn.

In the birth chart, in whichever house the Saturn moon conjunction happens will show the karmic influence, the duty that cannot be escaped. Saturn stands for restraint, limitation and submission- these are the limitations we put on ourselves because of our ego. A strong Saturn influence in the birth chart shows that the native tends to obey, serve and submit to traditional values. Wherever Saturn is placed in the chart it submits to that area of life.

For example, Saturn in the 7th house, the native submits to the partner until it has overcome the limitation of false identity or the ego. The karmic accumulation is such that the lessons in life have to be learnt through partnerships and relationships. This is also the area where they have to put in more effort for relationships to work.

Saturn is also called the rebel, just like Shani rebelled against his stepmother's mistreatment. The natives who have a strong Saturn influence may face such a situation in the early years of their lives, where they have to rebel against the unfair or partial treatment rendered to them.

Saturn also likes the wild, unrestricted freedom because it's an airy planet. This draws them to open, spacious places. This is the reason why they like having a house in the countryside, in a calm, open and serene environment. They also love gardening or farming.

The natives tend to have vata dosha problems because the air element rules Saturn. They have to take care to eat more warm cooked foods and less raw and dry foods. After the age of 50, when vata age sets in, they tend to have issues with constipation, joint pains and gastric problems. Warm climates and warm foods agree better with their natural constitution.

The ultimate goal of Saturn is to overcome all limitations and restrictions. They usually tend to rebel when they are young, but as they get older, they learn to submit and follow rules. Because with experience they understand the wisdom of following tradition, which helps to liberate their time and energy. The calm nature of Saturn prefers to wait for the opportune time rather than create stress by resisting. This allows them to sail smoothly through all kinds of rough circumstances.

They will find that - the more they follow the routine of discipline, the easier their life becomes. The mature Saturn natives who have learnt their lessons through life's challenging experiences become more down-to-earth, humble, and non-competitive.

Saturn is also a very spiritual planet, it gives great interest and talent in psychic, occult and spiritual capabilities. Many spiritual seekers who go through severe austerities in order to go beyond the limitations of the body have a strong influence of Saturn in their birth chart. They will either be born in a Saturn nakshatra, or their moon will be conjunct Saturn. These natives seem to have a 6th sense, a way of receiving and interpreting messages from the spirits or ghosts. Saturn is a very passive planet and likes to follow rather than lead. That's why many Saturn natives end up dedicatedly following a large organisation, cult, or religion.

Many famous psychics and mediums have their Ascendent in a Saturn nakshatra. For example, Carl Jung, the famous philosopher, has his Sun in Pushya, firmly placed in the 11th house. The Lord of Pushya is Saturn, which is placed in Cancer whose lord is the moon. The Saturn-moon combination gives great psychic interest and capabilities.

Saturn tends to give a lack of confidence, making one fearful, uncertain and indecisive. This is because it's sensitivity can feel the subtle vibrations of the other realms. It also gives the steely willpower and great endurance to go through hardships and eventually overcome them.

Aspects of Saturn

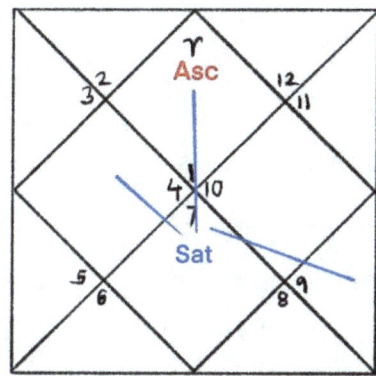 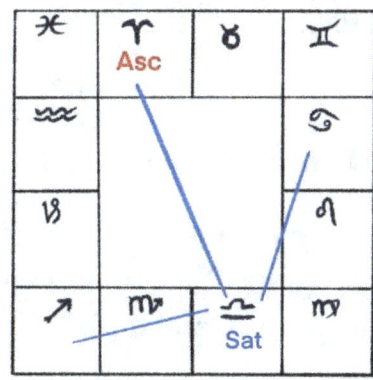

In the horoscope, where Saturn sits, shows the karmic duty to be performed in this life, it also restricts you most to that area of life. Saturn's 3rd aspect shows the area where most effort has to be put, and the opposite -7th aspect shows the direct impact of Saturn on that area of life. The 10th aspect will show the kind of work the native will do.

For example, for an Aries Ascendant, if Saturn is in the 7th house of Libra, it shows that the native will have to work hard to keep the marriage or relationship going. Although the native wants to break away from the bondage responsibilities and restrictions that come with marriage or partnership, he or she is not able to break free easily or quickly. Saturn makes you go through your karmic duties. However, Saturn is exalted in the 7th house, so the responsibilities one has to go through will not seem burdensome because the native will naturally like to do things for his or her partner. Moreover, because of its slow and steady nature, it delays both good and bad results.

The 3rd aspect will be in the 9th house of Sagittarius, which shows that the native will have to put in a lot of effort towards getting a higher qualification, and it will be delayed. From the 7th house, the opposite aspect of Saturn is on the Ascendent. This shows that the native feels restricted. The 10th aspect will be on the 4th house of Cancer, which shows that the native will have to work from home, at home and for the mum in some way, or they may have to serve someone at home.

Saturn rules Capricorn and Aquarius. Capricorn is the 10th house of the original horoscope, which signifies our career or job, and Saturn befittingly rules this house being a karma karka. The 11th house of Aquarius is ruled by Saturn and co-ruled by Rahu, this is the house of fulfilling desires, the house of expansion and gains. Saturn and Rahu expand the gains to the maximum and give much more than expected.

If Saturn is weak in the birth chart with a low ashtakavarga score, then it restricts and disciplines you in a painful way. If Saturn is strong with a good ashtakavarga score it restricts you in a good way, which helps to enhance your growth.

Example

Capricorn Ascendant - ruled by Saturn

Zeenat Aman - A popular Indian film actress 1970 - 1990.

Born on 19th November 1951, at 12pm in Mumbai, India (estimated time of birth).

Zeenat Aman is a popular Indian actress from 1970- 1990. She first received recognition for her modelling work at the age of 19, and then went on to participate in beauty pageants, winning both the Femina Miss India pageant and the Miss Asia Pacific pageant in 1970 and began acting in films in the same year.

Her father was a Muslim, and her mother was a Hindu. Her father, Amanullah Khan, was a scriptwriter and had written dialogues for famous classical Hindi movies like - Mughal-e-Azam and Pakeezah.

Her parents got divorced when she was young. At the age of 13, her father passed away. She did her schooling in Panchgani and went to the University of Southern California in Los Angeles for further studies on student aid, but she could not complete her graduation. She married actor Mazhar Khan in 1985, who died in 1998. She has 2 sons. In 2014, in her interview with the Times of India, she said that she was not happy in her marriage.

Analysis -

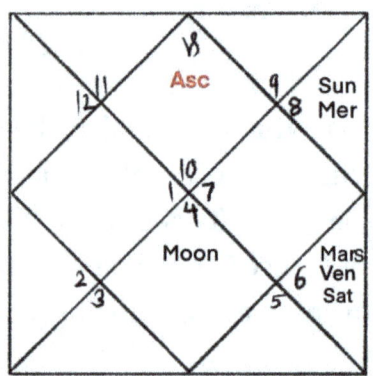

She is a Capricorn Ascendent. Saturn, the ruler of Capricorn, is sitting in the 9th house of Virgo with Mars and Venus. Saturn, being the ruler of the Ascendant, gives her a calm and practical approach to life. Zeenat has always been known as a professional who was disciplined and punctual during her film shootings.

Her Moon is in the Saturn-ruled nakshatra (Pushya) in the 7th house of Cancer, which gives her a tall body frame with a well-curved bodily feminine beauty. Moon in the 7th house also has a lot of association with other people. As an actress, she was a popular public figure. In a way, she served the people through her acting talent because Saturn is the planet of service.

Her Capricorn Ascendent is in Shravana - the nakshatra ruled the moon, which gives her a tall physique (Saturnian attribute) and a beautiful round face with full features (moon-like looks). The moon is in the 7th house of Cancer. In Pushya, it is said to be the most nurturing nakshatra that grants all good things in life.

Capricorn being the original 10th house of the profession makes one very ambitious. It can be seen in her successful career as an actress from 1970 to 1980. When she was at the peak of her career she was running her <u>Mercury Mahadasha.</u> Mercury is sitting with Sun in the 11th house of gains in Scorpio.

<u>Saturn</u> also brings its share of karmic debts, the difficulties one has to face, and the lessons to be learnt. Zeenat has enjoyed a fabulous and successful career in films, but did not have a happy married life. She married her co-actor in 1985, who died in 1998 from an illness. About her marriage she had said, "Mazhar never wanted me to grow as an individual or as an artist. He always wanted me to be with the kids and be at home. During the very first year of marriage, I realised I had made a huge mistake, but I decided to live by it and make it work. I tried to make it work for another 12 years. There was no light at the end of the tunnel for me. There was not a single moment of happiness or joy during those 12 years. But I still tried making it work."

Saturn, the poet

Saturn the karmic Lord and the keeper of time,

Testing in ways cruel and kind.

Cool and calm, slow and steady,

To charter the path, makes us ready.

Effortful are his ways,

Message of discipline he conveys.

The zig zag maze of life,

The ups and downs and strife.

All is not in vain,

In the end, there is a sure gain.

8
Rahu

Om bhram bhreem bhraum saha Rahave namah

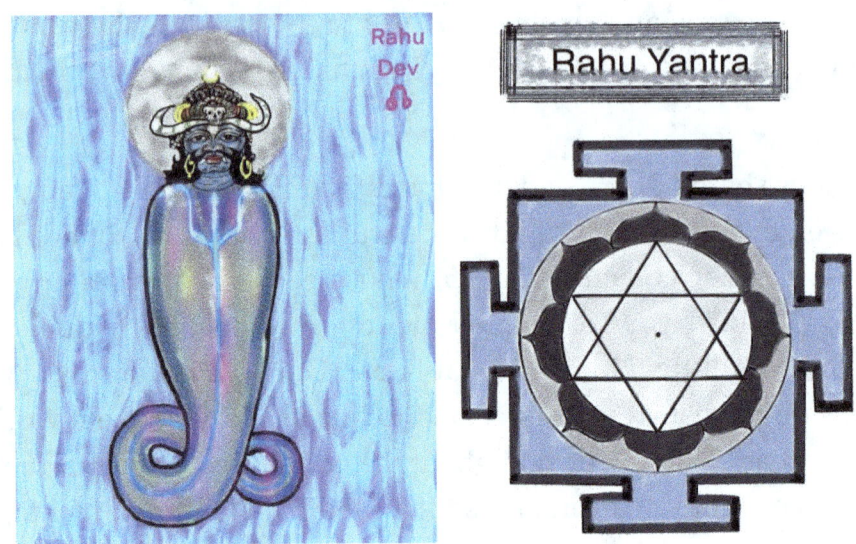

Sanskrit names	Swarbhanu - sound of the Sun and Shanivata Rahu - Saturn like
Other names	North lunar node- shadow planet
Lord	Behaves like the lord of the sign it's placed in.
Deities	Naga deva, Devi Durga or Kali and Devi Saraswati.
Rides on	a Lion
House	2nd and 3rd house
Weekday	Saturday (as co lord with Saturn in Aquarius)
Friends	Mercury, Saturn and Venus
Enemies	Sun, Moon and Mars
Neutral	Jupiter
Exalted	Taurus
Debilitated	Scorpio
Aspects	7th from itself - opposite to it.
Mulatrikona	Gemini
Vimshotari dasha	18 years
Transit	Stays in one sign for 18 months.

Matures	at 41 years
Transit	Stays in one sign for about 1 year and 8 months.
Nakshatras	Adra, Swati and Satabhishak
Lunar days	Panchami (5th lunar day) and Ashtami (8th lunar day) and Amavasya
Element	Air
Colour	Grey, ultra violet and electric blue
Chakra	Anhatta
Tridosha	Vata
Direction	Always moves retrograde
Guna	Rajas
Vehicles	Big black cars
Animals	Horse, elephant, wolf, snake and donkey
Bird	Owl
Metal	Lead
Gemstones	Hessonite (Gomed)
Organs	Lungs
Body parts	Neck, chest and legs
Spices	Cumin and fennel
Taste	Spicy and pungent
Food	Garlic
Plants	Tobacco
Season	Winter - cold and dry
Places	Foriegn lands, graveyards, snake holes and anthills, tombs and caves
At home	TV room
Objects	IT and electronic gadgets, ivory, leather, trident, sword and horse shoe.
Signifies	Expansion, illusion, magnify, smoke and endless desires.
Represents	Foreigners and in-laws
Diseases	Fever, leprosy, snake bite, pains, blisters, sores, cancer, phobias, paranormal illusionary experiences and restlessness.
Yogic practice	Meditation and Pranayama - alternative nose breathing.

Chant	"Om Shiro Rupaay Vidhmahe Amrateshaay Dheemahi Tanno Rahu Prachodayat."
Physical appearance	Good complexion and hypnotic eyes.
Qualities	Prosperity, materialistic ambitions, mindless expansion, greed, sudden events, addictions, sense of mastery, wealth, fame, good position, arrogance, deception, illusion, does not feel satisfied or satiated diplomacy and fraud.
Careers	Speculations, magicians, jugglers, detectives, stock brokers, diplomats, politicians, physiotherapists, doctors, pharmacists, engineers, electricians, research workers, scientists, homoeopaths, ayurvedic doctors, IT consultants, actors, pilots, detectives, conmen, cyber fraud hackers, winemakers or wine sellers, ayurvedic doctors and film directors.

"Reality is merely an <u>illusion</u>, albeit a very persistent one."

- Einstein

In Vedic astrology, Rahu and Ketu are the 2 invisible astronomical points in the sky called the north and south lunar nodes. They are not physical planets like the other 7 planets. Instead, they are areas of churned-up energy, pregnant with mysticism and significance. Astronomically, the lunar nodes are the 2 points where the moon's orbital path crosses the ecliptic. Ecliptic is the Sun's apparent yearly path on the celestial sphere. This creates 2 intense points of electromagnetic vibration, which are directly opposite each other and have come to be known as the Moon's north and south Nodes or, in Vedic terms, Rahu (northern node) and Ketu (southern node).

<u>Samudra Manthan -</u> churning of the ocean.

In Hindu mythology, there is an interesting story of how Rahu and Ketu came into existence. Once both the gods (devas) and the demons (asuras) agreed to form an alliance to produce nectar.

(amrita) that could give them immortality.

Mount mandara was the churning rod, and Vasuki the snake was the rope used for churning. Lord Vishnu, in the form of a huge turtle, provided the base for the churning process to happen. It was agreed that devas would hold the mouth and rakshasas would hold the tail of the snake. It is believed that the process of churning produced many items. Here is the list of those precious items-

N	Products of churning	Meaning
1	Halhala	The first item released was the poison. Lord Shiva agreed to consume the poison when he was approached to help, and that's why he is also called neelakantha - the one with blue throat.
2	Herbs	All kinds of healing herbs came next.
3	Gems	14 precious gems were produced.

4	Lakshmi	The Goddess of wealth chose Lord Vishnu as her consort.
5	Apsaras	The celestial nymphs - Rambha and Meneka chose Gandharvas as their companions.
6	Varuni	The Goddess of intoxication was taken by the asuras.
7	Kamadhenu	The wish-granting cow was taken by Lord Brahma.
8	Airavata	The white coloured elephant with many tusks was taken by Indira.
9	Uchaishravas	The divine 7 headed horse was given to Bali.
10	Kaustubha	The most valuable jewel was worn by Lord Vishnu.
11	Parijata	The divine flowering tree whose flowers never wilt was planted in Indraloka.
12	Sharanga	A powerful bow was given to Lord Vishnu.
13	Chandra	The moon adorned Lord Shiva's head.
14	Shankh	Lord Vishnu's conch.
15	Alakshmi	Goddess of misfortune would always be seen as leaving Lord Vishnu.
16	Amrit	And finally, the nectar came out.

Dhanvantri, the heavenly physician, came with the pot of nectar of immortality. Devas and Asuras started fighting over the nectar while Garuda - the divine falcon, flew away with the pot. Devas then asked Vishnu for help. Lord Vishnu then took the pot of nectar and disguised himself as a beautiful maiden called Mohini. Carrying the pot of nectar, she enchantingly distributed it to all the Devas.

The Asuras were feeling left out and were not happy about it. One of the clever asura names Swarabhanu, disguised as one of the Devas and, drank some drops of nectar. However, the luminosity of the Sun and Moon noticed this disguise quickly. It informed Lord Vishnu, who cut Swarbhanu's head immediately with the Sudarshana Chakra before the nectar could reach the body. From that day, Rahu is personified as the cut-off head, and Ketu is the body.

Now that Rahu drank the nectar, it has given him immortality, and he cannot die. So Rahu - Ketu axis is a very powerful force that operates in our lives, it influences the karmic patterns. Rahu and Ketu are always directly opposite each other, 180 degrees apart, in the birth chart.

The other astronomical inference is that - the lunar eclipse symbolises the moon being swallowed by Rahu, and the release of the eclipse is represented by Ketu.

The placement of Rahu

This table shows the influence of Rahu in the birth chart and its effect.

Influence	Placement	Effect
Rahu is strong when placed in	Taurus - exalted Aquarius - co Lord with Saturn Rahu nakshatras - Ardra, Swati and Shatabhishak. Directional strength - according to the house and its lord - will amplify the effect. Atmakaraka - highest degree. Near to the Ascendant degree.	Intelligent, clever and progressive.
Rahu is weak when placed in	Scorpio - debilitated At 0, 1 and 29 degrees.	Manipulative, obsessive, greedy and unsatisfied.

Inference

The nakshatras ruled by Rahu will take on the attributes of the sign they sit in. For example, Ardra is in Gemini. Therefore, the natives will have amplified mercurian traits of logical thinking and intellectualising everything. The Moon Rahu conjunction will bring out the qualities of Rahu very strongly, because the moon represents our mind.

The natives may have some or all of these attributes, depending on how strong the influence of Rahu is in the birth chart. Suppose Rahu is positioned in the 1st house, which governs physical features and overall personality. In that case, the native will likely have light-coloured eyes — such as grey, blue, green, or light brown — because the dominant colours associated with Rahu are grey and electric blue. They will have lighter colour skin, too. Since Rahu amplifies everything, it gives the natives an exceptional facial beauty that easily stands out in a group of people.

The facial look will modify depending on the influence of other planets on the Ascendant, or the moon. For example, if Sun is sitting in the Ascendent of a Shatabhishak (Rahu ruled nakshatra) they will have a square jaw bone, broader lips, small but bright honey-coloured eyes (Sun-like quality), light-coloured skin (Rahu- like characteristic), and Saturn-like attribute of a sober look.

Rahu is the boss, the head without a body, which means it has very intellectual energy and likes to lead and not follow. Rahu can be described as a rule breaker, a revolutionary, an entrepreneur, and a new-age thinker. Rahu ruled natives will make their own rules to their own advantage and break rules set by others.

Whichever house Rahu is sitting in, the natives are not clear about how to deal with that area of life, because it creates an illusion they tend to make wrong decisions and make blunders. For example, in Rahu in the 3rd house, the natives will have an exaggerated sense of friendliness or rivalry with the siblings or the neighbours. They may get on extremely well, but they will feel cheated by them, or the natives themselves might manipulate their siblings or neighbours into doing things for them.

Everything scientific, logical and intellectual attracts them. They understand everything through the magnifying lens of the intellect. This makes them miss the beauty of emotions and feelings unless Rahu is conjunct with the moon. With the Rahu Moon combination, the natives will be very imaginative and tend to live in their own fairyland.

The head of Rahu makes the natives consume everything, yet not feel contentment or satisfaction no matter how much they accomplish. Because the head without a body cannot digest or assimilate things, it ends up accumulating quantity but not necessarily quality.

Rahu is interested in all worldly matters and will encourage the natives to seek gratification, success and power in that area of life where it's placed. In its quest to fulfil its ambitions, it can become manipulative and deceptive. Rahu leads us to experience many different situations and sensations in a heightened and magnified way, like the expansion of smoke. Since Rahu is the head only, with no body - it consumes but does not feel satiated. It's more of thoughts and less of feelings. Wherever Rahu is placed - Intellect dominates and overrides the feelings.

A strong Rahu influence has been seen in the chart of many successful people. It has been seen favourably by politicians, actors or businessmen - or any significant position because it brings great opportunities during its dasha. It gives sudden wealth and fame, makes the natives rise and succeed through fair or unfair means.

Rahu also signifies foreigners and foreign lands, so natives are more likely to succeed in a place away from their birthplace, and when they deal with people from another culture. Rahu dasha also gives marriage. During the Rahu transit or Mahadasha, natives can fall prey to black magic, fraud, deception or situations which are ambiguous. If placed negatively in a horoscope, it can create confusion or stress, but the whole chart has to be studied carefully before making any such predictions.

The alignment of Rahu with different planets creates different types of bondages (problems). Rahu can not discriminate between good and evil, and so it works against the standards of righteousness (Dharma). Rahu is said to be ignorant about the authentic self and falls for Illusion (Maya).

Rahu, because of its illusionary nature, constantly lures the natives to make changes in their lifestyle - thereby causing changes in residence, friends, desires and goals in life. Rahu provides information through IT technology, and gives interest in exploring the mysteries of life. He is an intellectual and likes to know all that is mystical and scientific through logic and reason.

"Shanivat Rahu kujavat ketu" is a phrase often used in Vedic astrological texts to describe the nature of Rahu and Ketu. Which means Rahu is like Saturn and Ketu is like Mars. Ketu is like a fire with intense heat, and Rahu is smoke and expansion. The influence of Rahu is expansive. It

will make situations seem bigger than they really are but will have the calm practical approach of Saturn.

Rahu is well placed in the 3rd, 6th and 11th house of the birth chart and gives good results in these houses. Rahu is exalted in Taurus because he enjoys the worldly pursuits of gathering resources and having a comfortable family and home life. Rahu is also very comfortable in Aquarius. During the Rahu dasha, it can bring gains which create the illusion of being more than they really are. Natives could open their own company or work for a large organisation that can give fame and recognition.

In Scorpio, Rahu is debilitated because he is not happy in the hidden depths. For example, if Rahu is placed with the moon in Scorpio, whose Lord is Mars. This is a very uncomfortable and frustrating placement for Rahu, it can make the natives impatient and emotionally and mentally aggressive and frustrated over trivial issues which seem insurmountable. Their thought process will be such that they end up making wrong choices and thereby suffering the consequences. As always, the whole chart should be studied closely to see any beneficial aspects from Jupiter and how the placement of planets pans out in divisional charts (Vargas), especially in Navamsha -D9, before drawing any conclusions.

Example

Aquarius Ascendant - ruled by Saturn and Rahu

Arundhati Roy - An Indian Author

Born on 24th November 1961 in Shillong, India, at 12 pm (estimated time of birth).

Suzanna Arundhati Roy is an Indian author who is best known for her novel, 'The God of Small Things,' for which she won the Booker Prize in 1997. It became the best-selling book by a non-expatriate Indian author. She is also a political activist involved in human rights and environmental causes. Currently, she is settled in Delhi.

Her mother, Mary Roy, is a women's rights activist from Kerala, and her dad, Rajib Roy, is a tea plantation manager from Calcutta. When she was 2 years old, her parents divorced, and she returned to Kerala with her mother and brother. For some time, the family lived with their maternal grandfather in Ooty, Tamil Nadu. When she was 5 years old, the family moved back to Kerala, where her mother started a school.

After finishing her schooling in Karela, she studied architecture in Delhi. Here, she met her boyfriend, Gerard. They lived together in Delhi and then in Goa before they separated. In 1984, she returned to Delhi and met Pradip Krishen, who offered her a role in his award-winning movie Massey Sahib. Later, they got married.

Disenchanted with the film world, she experimented with various fields, including running aerobics classes. Roy and Krishen eventually separated. She became financially secure with the success of her novel The God of Small Things, published in 1997. She attracted attention in 1994 when she criticised Shekhar Kapur's film Bandit Queen, which was based on the life of Phoolan Devi - the female dacoit in north India. In her film review titled "The Great Indian Rape Trick," she questioned the right to "restage the rape of a living woman without her permission" and charged Kapur with exploiting Phoolan Devi and misrepresenting both her life and its meaning.

She began writing her first novel, The God of Small Things, in 1992, completing it in 1996. The book is semi-autobiographical, and a major part captures her childhood experiences in Aymanam. The publication of The God of Small Things catapulted her to international fame.

Since publishing The God of Small Things in 1997, she has spent most of her time on political activism and nonfiction. She was awarded the Sydney Peace Prize in May 2004 for her work in social campaigns and her advocacy of non-violence. In November 2011, she was awarded the Norman Mailer Prize for Distinguished Writing. She was featured in the 2014 list of Time 100, the 100 most influential people in the world.

Analysis -

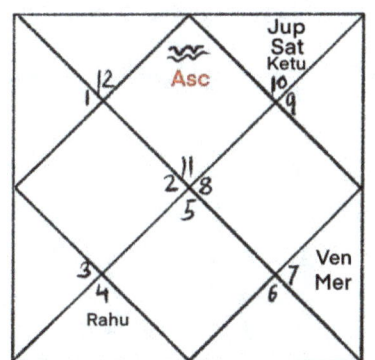

Arundati has her <u>Ascendant in Aquarius</u>, whose ruler, Saturn, is placed in the 12th house of Capricorn with Jupiter and Ketu. Rahu, the co-lord of Aquarius, is placed in the 6th house of Cancer.

Saturn is sitting strong in his own house of Capricorn in the 12th house. This shows that her Karma or her duty will have to be done in isolation. Writers need a lot of time by themselves in order to pen their thoughts. As an Aquarian water bearer, she has poured her knowledge through her writings. Aquarius is the sign of serving the community at large. She has served people through her writing. The Jupitarian and Saturn wisdom is reflected in her talks and writings.

She was not afraid of taking risks, leaving her old job and trying something new, or breaking off a strained relationship and moving on in life. Moon, the Lord of the 6th house, is sitting in the 5th house of creativity. When a planet is placed 12th from the sign it rules, it becomes the loss of it. The 6th house signifies opposition, competition, debts or diseases. An emotional pain would have brought out the creativity in her, which she expressed beautifully through her writing.

She became famous in her <u>Jupiter Rahu Mercury</u> dasha for her book - <u>'God of Small Things,'</u> - Jupiter sitting with Saturn and Ketu in the 12th house of Capricorn, which made her work hard and spend many long hours contemplating and writing in a quiet room. Rahu in the 6th house of Cancer amplifies the emotions, which might have caused an emotional wound that led to the therapy of healing through writing.

Mercury with Venus in the 9th house of Libra shows that a female teacher or guide would have motivated or inspired her. Mercury is the communicator so it culminated into a fictional tale of imaginative writing based on personal experiences.

Rahu, the poet

Rahu, the illusion of Maya,

Spreads its intellectual aura.

Like the genie that expands,

Granting wishes tall and grand.

Reason and logic, wit and thought,

ambition that seems well wrought.

One wish - leading to the next,

Leaving one perplexed.

9
Ketu

Om sram sreem sraum saha Ketve namah

Quality	Like Mars - flag, conquer, separate, break, pierce and cut.
Co Lord	Scorpio
Significator	8th house, sudden events, ancestors and past life.
Astronomically	South lunar node, lunar eclipse
Symbol	Body of the snake
Friend	Mercury, Venus, Saturn
Enemy	Sun and Moon
Neutral	Jupiter
Exalted	Scorpio
Debilitated	Taurus
Element	Fire
Colour	Brown
Animal	Dog
Weapon	Bhaala - spear
Rides on	Eagle

Karka	Moksha karka
Nakshatras	Ashwini, Magha and Mula.
Matures at	48 years
Vimshotari dasha	7 years

Positive side	Spiritual progress, renunciation, asceticism, profound transformation, liberation
Negative side	Malefic, difficulties, material losses, detachment, impatience, confusion, mindless choices.

Astronomically, the lunar nodes are the 2 points where the moon's orbital path crosses the ecliptic. Ecliptic is the Sun's apparent yearly path on the celestial sphere. The ascending (north node) is where the moon moves into the northern ecliptic hemisphere, also called the dragon's head or Rahu. The descending (south node) is where the moon moves into the southern eleptic hemisphere, also called the dragon's tail or Ketu. In Kalachakra tantra (an ancient text), the south node is named Kalagni, which means the fire of time.

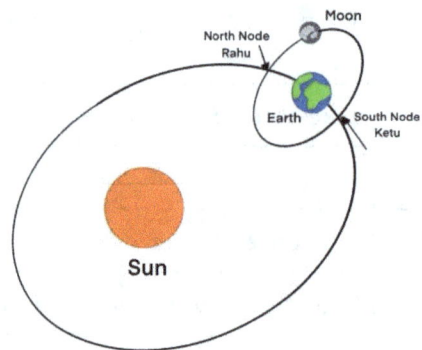

Ketu is a moksha Karka (promotes liberation), which makes one detached. Metaphorically, it can be seen as the umbilical cord being cut as the baby comes out of the womb. Ketu, as the nakshatra Lord, needs to be looked at carefully. It tells us about the ancestral connection and past life skills or talents.

Ketu has the same fiery energy as Mars but is more subtle and more intense. The energy of fire is needed for one to be born into this world. That's why in Rig Veda, the hymns start with salutations to Agni Dev (the fire God). More than half of the hymns are dedicated to Agni Dev. Because the transformative energy of fire is needed for life to happen in any form. The Vedas state that devas (Divine beings) receive the offerings through Agni (fire). Because the fire burns the physical form and transforms it into a subtler form of gas, air, smell, and fragrance.

Scientific perspective -

Ketu is the infrared light. It's the electromagnetic invisible light that has a longer wavelength than the visible light. Our thermal body temperature can be seen under infrared light images. At the cosmic level, it has been studied that more than half of the Sun's energy comes to the Earth as infrared rays. This has a critical effect on the Earth's climate.

At the body level, infrared rays are absorbed by the molecules only when they change their vibrational movements. This helps in studying the energy states of the molecules. Infrared radiation is used in industrial, scientific, military, law enforcement, medical, wireless communication, surveillance, weather forecast and astronomy applications. Infrared light helps to detect planets and stars (redshift effect) from the early days of the universe.

The genius of Ramanujan

Ramanujan was the genius who gave the mathematical calculations of black holes. He has been one of the most extraordinary figures in the history of mathematics. Some psychologists would say that Ramanujan could harness a process in his brain that gave him deep insights into infinities and more without the use of analytical reasoning. His visceral insights enabled him to excel in pure mathematics.

Ramanujan credited his profound insights to the Hindu goddess, he said he received these insights in his dreams. This wellspring of creativity and flashes of insight came through Namagiri, a local incarnation of Lakshmi, the Hindu goddess of good fortune. We all use our intuition in the beginning and then try to look for a logical explanation for that instinctive feeling.

Scientific research on intuition

(These clips are taken from the article published by Philip Perry in January 2018).

You just know - when that gut feeling tells you something.

Scientists are now starting to zero in on the origin of that feeling. And yes, you should trust it. Previous research has shown that when it comes to decision-making, going with our gut usually makes for a better outcome than if we go with intellect alone.

In this latest study, scientists at the University of Exeter in the UK looked at how a basic drive, such as hunger, could influence the decision-making process. It seems that our gut can actually store memories and that hunger can trigger a sophisticated series of calculations that make us arrive at a decision using our intuition or gut — in the literal sense.

This study surrounds computer models set up to see how well an animal could survive in an environment dotted with predators and where food availability fluctuates. Those animals who searched using their cognitive abilities had about the same chance of survival as those who went on gut feeling alone. Prof. John McNamara explained that it costs a lot of resources to be so clever. As a result, natural selection found a cheaper way to make decisions. A rabbit in the wild, for instance, might be motivated by hunger to eat some clover. But noticing a patch of grass near a wolf, hidden in the tall grass next to the clover, could indicate not only to steer clear but also help the bunny realise that there hasn't been a lot of food in this area, lately anyway. This would cause it to move on to an entirely new territory. Hunger actually jars the memory, which causes the rabbit to be more careful.

"This doesn't just lend insight into animal behaviour but ours as well," according to the study led by Dr Andrew Higginson. He added, "The usefulness of such memory means that animals, including humans, may appear to be processing a great deal of information in the brain when, in fact, they are just following their gut."

The placement of Ketu

This table shows the influence of Ketu in the birth chart and its effect.

Influence	Placement	Effect
Ketu is strong when placed in	Scorpio - exalted and co Lord with Mars. Ketu nakshatras - Ashwini, Magha and Mula. Directional strength - according to the house and its lord - it will detach and seperate. Atmakaraka - highest degree. Near to the Ascendant degree.	Spiritual inclination, intuition, inner knowing, intense, focused and detached.
Ketu is weak when placed in	Taurus - debilitated At 0, 1 and 29 degrees.	Losses, sorrow and separation.

Inference

The natives may have some or all of these attributes, depending on how strong the influence of Ketu is in the birth chart. If Ketu is sitting in the 1st house of physical features and overall personality, these attributes will manifest. For example, if Venus is sitting in the Ascendent of a Magha (ketu ruled nakshatra), these features will be modified by Venusian looks of symmetrical facial features.

A strong Ketu influence in the birth chart gives a dusky, dark, mysterious, intriguing beauty. They will have dark eyes, a good set of dark hair, a longer pointy chin, an oval face and fuller lips. They will have large teeth, and there could be a gap in the front teeth. A very distinguished shape of the nose, a fuller-shaped nose with raised nostrils, adds to their Halloween-like beauty. A prominent forehead, with high cheekbones and a larger or longer pointed chin, makes their face look oval.

Ketu makes their body frame thinner, with narrow shoulders and long thin waist, narrow rib cage, with curved hips and breasts.

Their voice will have the quality of cutting through, which can range from a high-pitched tone to a deeper, mellow voice.

The influence of Ketu shows the past life connection and mastery of a certain skill. The house and sign in which Ketu is placed will specify the natural talent a native has. For example, if a person is a Leo Ascendent (in Magha), and Ketu is sitting in the 3rd house of Libra, he or she will have a past life connection with the younger sibling, they will have a deeper bond of sharing, understanding and empathy. The native will prefer to communicate in fewer words with neighbours and friends. He or she will be very talented with using the skill of hands, could be a very good artist, painter, very good with knitting, embroidery, craft work, graphic designer, IT technician, electrician, tailor, surgeon, boxer, tennis player, billiards player, or a jewelsmith.

Ketu can be understood as the intense energy that builds up before the manifestation. Just like the dark grey clouds in the sky when pregnant with the fullness of the water droplets before the rain showers. Ketu energy is the stillness just before the dynamic action.

Ketu also signifies a past life connection. For example, moon ketu conjunction in the 9th house of Scorpio shows a past life connection with a Guru who would have been the master of the occult, tantra and mantra. So, in this life, the native will have an inherent knowledge and deeper understanding of occult subjects like astrology. He or she will naturally be drawn to spiritual and religious practises and will find a female Guru or a Male Guru who will guide like a mother, or their mother will be their guide and teacher.

The prominent quality of ketu is the extreme heat and darkness that absorbs light, like a black hole effect. Therefore, the natives have a mysterious and elusive side to them that cannot be grasped in totality. A huge part of them is a mystery to others, and even to themselves, therefore life for them becomes a spiritual seeking. They look for answers in scriptures, in religious discourses, and in philosophy but feel that it's the other person's truth. Then they turn towards science, art, and music and seek to find the answers themselves - in all life's good and bad experiences, and ultimately turn inwards to find their own truth.

This makes them elusive and unpredictable. Ketu has the effect of ecliptic darkness, where the light gets blocked but holds intense heat that can cut through all bondages and deliver one to freedom. Therefore, the natives feel engulfed in their own solitude, which they begin to cherish, and over time, they slowly uncover the hidden layers of possibilities of boundless freedom within them.

If the moon and Ketu are conjunct, the natives will feel a disconnect to emotions, and can feel numb or blank towards the display of emotional responses, which can make them come across as cold or unsympathetic. This is because they don't identify with anything very strongly.

Especially if Ketu is in the Ascendant, they will seek to find some stable foundation in the person who is in front of them. In a way they start reflecting the attributes of their partner or anyone whom they are close to. For this reason, many actors have ketu in the Ascendent because they easily take on the roles and become that personality that they are portraying on stage or on screen because their own identity and ego are not in their way.

You will come across Ashwinis, Maghas and Mulas (Ketu ruled nakshatras) who are seemingly loud and expressive in public, but they love and need their quiet moments to replenish their energy. They obscure themselves and reveal very little of themselves because they are still struggling to understand themselves.

Ketu people often feel misplaced in the material world. They feel disconnected from the material things, and like to contemplate on the nature of sorrow, joy, life and death. They feel an internal void, a vacuum, and a mystery that seems to make them do impulsive and self-destructive things. They are not strongly identified with any object, person, relationship, or position. They realise the impermanence and transitory nature of everything, so they don't invest much energy into anything materialistic. It's not that they don't enjoy material things, but they don't feel connected to partying and shopping. They never really get attached to materialistic enjoyments of life.

They like to spend a lot of time alone and keep things to themselves. For this reason, they have very few close friends and usually get along well, only with those who are also Ketu or Rahu people. If they don't channel their energies into spiritual practises, they can become a source of worry for their loved ones. On the negative side, they could be drawn towards self-destructive acts like smoking, consuming drugs or alcohol, or engaging in compulsive or risky impulsive behaviour. The dark energy is like an obsession that absorbs them. They tend to have their interim periods of tamasic energy that pull them in.

They feel drawn towards the past and love reading, watching films or listening to mythological or historical stories, fiction novels, religious scriptures and books on the occult, dream interpretations, spiritual discourses, psychology and philosophy. They can sit for hours at a stretch and research or read on a topic of their interest. It's like getting absorbed into the adventurous and intriguing black hole of information, an endless tunnel that can consume their attention for hours on end.

With their loved ones, they may not be the most nurturing or comforting people because they are so detached and hard to reach. But they are great to go to for advice because they are far removed and unbiased and never take sides because they can see both sides of the situation. When combined with their intuition, they can see clearly the result of the situation, and are very good at detecting the true intentions of people, yet without judging them.

They have strong intuition, astral and psychic abilities, and an uncanny way of seeing things ahead of time through visions or dreams. They also have a unique ability to understand the deeper meanings behind religious teachings because they are very intuitive and receptive to subtle energies.

Since they are sensitive to subtle energies around them, their open auras easily internalise the influences that they come across. Therefore, they should be careful because they imbibe both positive and negative energies around them. For them, keeping up their spiritual and religious practices is of vital importance because it helps to cleanse their aura and keeps them physically and mentally healthy and balanced.

The image of ketu is seen as a snake without a head. This shows when they have to make choices, they mostly go by their gut feeling or intuition and do not analyse too much with their mind. Our intuition arises as a feeling within our body that is purely experiential. Ketu is a different level of intelligence which we are not usually aware of.

The headless nature of ketu also makes them very spiritual, and they don't care much about following the social norms and often prefer to follow their own intuition. Life situations keep separating them from the things, people or situations they love or are attached to, and this makes them disillusioned with the uncertainty of life. They tend to become reclusive or go on spiritual retreats in an attempt to find who they really are.

The inner search for their true identity makes them change their hobbies or professions a few times in an attempt to find who they really are. Their lack of ego identity makes them great artists because they can channel divine inspiration into any creative talent. Since they are not bridled with ego or faulty misconceptions of oneself, they can become conduits for accurate creative channelling.

Ketu natives can seclude themselves in a room for a week and channel an entire script, write a book, or create an entire album, even without studying, training or preparing for it. They just have to let themselves be in a closed environment where they can let the channelling take place.

They see mundane life as an obstacle to their spiritual pursuits. Routine is highly recommended for Ketu people because a daily routine will help them ground and bring stability. When the external situation is calm and stable, it will make the internal environment less chaotic too.

They will be light sleepers or can have sleep or behavioural disorders because of internal instability. Ketu ultimately represents the evil that we rise above and stand upon, like Devi Mahisasur Mardini, who stands on the buffalo because she has mastered the negative forces within her.

Ketu is exalted in Scorpio because here, Ketu is happy dealing with hidden aspects, which is its domain. In Taurus, Ketu is debilitated because his nature is more inwardly drawn and he doesn't feel comfortable dealing with external aspects of home and family.

The nature of the intense energy of Ketu is such that it separates and detaches in order to liberate the soul from the bondage of endless desire.

Example

Scorpio Ascendant - ruled by Mars and Ketu

Dhyan Chand - Legendary Indian Hockey Player.

Born on 29th August 1905, in Allahabad, India, at 12 pm (estimated time of birth). Died on 3rd December 1979 in Delhi, India, at the age of 74.

Dhyan Chand was an Indian field hockey player widely regarded as the greatest in the history of this sport. He was popularly known as the Wizard of Hockey for his superb ball control and his complete mastery over the skill of using the hockey stick and never missing a goal.

Among the many interesting and inspiring incidents that occurred during his successful career as the captain of the Indian hockey team, one stands out in particular. One of them states that once when their team was playing with Germany in the 1936 Berlin Olympics, the spectators thought he had a special magic hockey stick with which he could stick the ball to his hockey. They broke his hockey stick to examine it and even changed his hockey a few times. In the same series of matches, a lady came up to him and asked him to play with her umbrella and use it like a hockey stick. On her repeated insistence, he did so and still scored 3 goals. All over the world, in every country that they played, the spectators were always spellbound and enthralled to see him play hockey and score goals.

He was known for his extraordinary goal-scoring feats, in addition to earning 3 Olympic gold medals in 1928, 1932 and 1936, during an era when India dominated field hockey. His influence extended beyond these victories, as India won the field hockey event in 7 out of 8 Olympics from 1928 to 1964. By profession, he was a major in the Indian army.

Dhyan played internationally from 1926 to 1949. During his time in the game, he scored 570 goals in 185 matches. The Government of India awarded Dhyan India's 3rd highest civilian honour, Padma Bhushan, in 1956. His birthday, 29th August, is celebrated as National Sports Day in India every year.

Analysis -

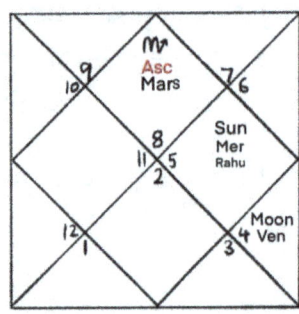

He was a Scorpio Ascendant, Mars the lord of Scorpio is sitting in the Ascendant. This makes him a very brave, fearless, determined, full of energy and a motivated sportsman. He was exceptionally good with his hockey and ball dribbling skills and was popularly called the <u>Wizard of hockey.</u>

As a Scorpio Ascendant - we can see his depth, integrity and intensity in his passion towards the game of hockey. In his early days he used to practice hockey every night in an open field outside his house, under the coolness of moonlight, while others were asleep. Seeing his utmost devotion his mentor changed his name from Dhyan Singh to Dhyan Chand and said, "just as the moon lights up the sky and earth at night, your fame will spread like the moonlight through the world."

In 1928 when he won his first Olympic medal he was running his <u>Venus Rahu Mars dasha</u>. Venus is with the moon in the 9th house

(Cancer) of fortune and higher learning, Rahu is with Sun and mercury in the 10th house of Leo, of career and public image. Mars is in the Scorpio Ascendent, which gave him the interest, opportunity, strength, determination and courage to pursue athletics, and made him dedicate his life towards representing India in hockey and athletics.

Ketu the poet

As Ketu, I connect you to the past archives,

Having experienced many lives,

Draw in from the richness of experience,

Allow me to unfold the genius.

An intuitive ability,

That can truly give a sense of reality.

The infinite possibilities,

Lie hidden in the void of probabilities.

Part 2
The 27 Nakshatras

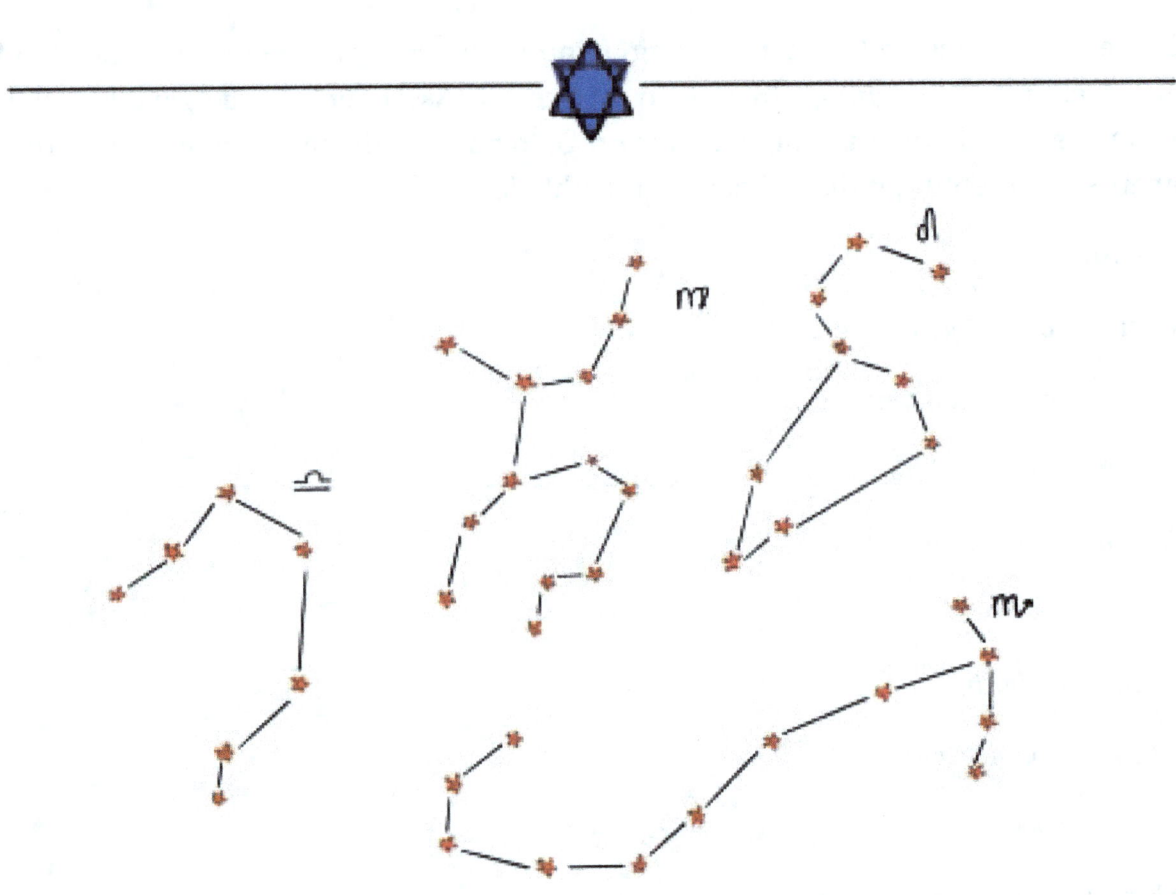

1
Ashwini

Om am aam Ashwini nakshatraye namah

Zodiac degrees	0-13.20-degree Aries
Ruling planet	Aries - Mars Ashwini - Ketu
Sanskrit name	Asvayujau- means she who yokes horses.
Astronomical name	Alpha Arietes and Beta Arietis. They can be seen just below Andromeda in the night sky, which is close to the planetary eleptic.
Symbol	Aries - Ram, the mountain bighorn sheep Ashwini - Horse
Element	Fire - Aries
Deity	Ashwini Kumaras - The twin brothers with horse heads.
Quality	Laghu - light and swift, Kshipra - quick Moveable - chara - Aries
Shakti and desire	Shidravyapana Shakti - power to give quick results.
Cast	Vaishya - trader
Gender	Male- Aries
Motivation	Dharma - righteousness - Aries
Triguna	Rajas - Aries
Tridosha	Pitta - Aries
Body parts	Head, knees and top of the feet.

Direction	East, south and north west.
Month	1st half of **Ashwin** lunar month - mid September
Bird	Swan - Hamsa and eagle
Sound	Chu, che, cho, la
Tree	Nux Vomica, poison nut tree
Chakra	Muladhara -Mars and Ketu
Das Maha Vidya	Devi Bagalamukhi - Mars and Devi Dhumavati - Ketu

Special degrees -

Yoga Tara	10 deg Aries It's a point where the planet will show the strongest and sure results during its dasha.
Exaltation	10 deg Aries - Maximum exaltation of Sun. When the Sun is placed at this degree, it will give excellent results during its dasha.
Vargottama	Pada 1 This Pada stays in Ashwini in the navamsa chart, which gives good steady results, and is considered auspicious.
Mulatrikona	0 - 12 deg - Mulatrikona of Mars. When Mars is placed at these degrees it feels confident in its own territory and therefore gives good results, especially during its dasha.
Amrit nadi	9.20-10.30 deg Aries Planets placed here give good results like the nectar that nourishes.
Visha nadi	11.06- 12 deg Aries This brings situations which one does not like dealing with.
Gandanta	0 - 1 deg Aries The gandanta zone Pada brings challenging situations because this is the junction point where a karmic knot is formed.

Auspicious and inauspicious activities -

The energy of each nakshatra makes it favourable or unfavourable for certain days and activities. The activities mentioned in the table will be auspicious or inauspicious on the days when the Ascendant or the moon is in a particular nakshatra.

Auspicious and inauspicious days-

On particular days when the moon or the ascendant is in particular nakshatra, and it matches the weekdays and lunar days as mentioned in the table above, they become auspicious or inauspicious.

For example, if it's a Tuesday and the 1st lunar day (pratipada tithi) of any month and the moon or the ascendant is in Ashwini. You are planning to start working on your new project, it's a good day to go ahead with it because this particular day supports such activity. The project will go smoothly and will get done in good time.

Shukla and Krishna paksha-

The waxing lunar phase (Shukla paksha) is suitable for any physical and outward-bound activities that need to be done for worldly survival. The Waning lunar phase (Krishna paksha) is suitable for mental and inward-drawn activities like spiritual practises needed for inner progress.

Auspicious and inauspicious table -

Auspicious	Inauspicious
Activities Good for starting any new projects, inaugurations and initiations, healing, taking medicine and rejuvenation, self improvement, exercise, yoga, meditation, gardening and planting seeds, buying or selling things, taking care of the horses, or going for a horse ride, traveling and repairing vehicles, wearing new clothes or jewellery, learning new subjects- medicine, spiritual or occult, installing sacred items or an altar for prayer and naming the new born baby. Take care - If the ascendant or moon is in 1st Pada, avoid starting any new activity or projects, because it's a gandanta zone.	Activities Not good for marriage and sexual activities, for any kind of endings or finishing projects, for getting intoxicated or high emotions and for planning long term projects.
Days Tuesdays - only when it falls on the 1st, 3rd, 5th, 6th, 7th, 8th, 11th or 13th lunar day. Wednesdays- only when it falls on the 5th or 7th lunar day. Thursdays - only when it falls on the 4th, 5th, 6th, 7th, 9th, 13th or 14th lunar day. Fridays - only when it falls on the 1st, 2nd, 6th, 7th, 11th or 12th lunar day.	Days Wednesdays - only when it falls on the 2nd, 3rd, 8th or 9th lunar day.

Compatibility table -

Ashwini	Compatible with
Sexual compatibility Yoni animal	Ashwini - Male horse - compatible with - Female horse - Shatabhishak
Sign compatibility	Aries - Leo and Sagittarius.
Nakshatra compatibility	Magha and Mula.
Lunar day compatibility	Pratipad - 1st lunar day

Day compatibility	Sunday and Tuesday
Colour compatibility	Red, orange and brown.
Numerological compatibility	1 and 9 and all numbers that add up to make 1 and 9.
Sound compatibility	Sun - all vowels - a, aa, e, ee, u, oo, ey, aye, o, ou, am, ah

Sign Lord and Nakshatra lord - Mars and Ketu

Ashwini is placed in the sign of Aries, whose Lord is Mars, and the Lord of Ashwini is Ketu; therefore, the 1st nakshatra exudes the energy of Mars and Ketu.

Mars is a masculine planet, signifying strength and supremacy. The positive influence of this fiery planet includes courage, enthusiasm, activity, youth, vitality, dynamism, confidence, initiation, innovation, and originality. Its negative influence can give arrogance, ego, anger, stubbornness, selfish temperament, and recklessness.

Ketu is not a physical planet; it is the south node of the moon and is symbolised by the body of the snake or a snake without a head. This shows that Ketu is more about feeling the sensations in the body rather than thinking of the mind. Ketu is said to be Mars-like in its quality. The prominent quality of ketu is the extreme heat and darkness that absorbs light, like a black hole effect.

Therefore, the natives have a mysterious and elusive side to them that cannot be grasped in totality. A considerable part of them is a mystery to others, and even to themselves, therefore life for them becomes a spiritual seeking. They first turn towards science, art, and music and try to find answers to life's mysteries. Later, they become spiritual seekers and look for answers in the scriptures, religious discourses, and philosophy. However, they feel that it's still the other person's truth and ultimately turn inward to find their own truth.

Ketu has the effect of ecliptic darkness, where the light gets blocked. Still, it holds tremendous and intense heat that can cut through all bondages and deliver one to freedom. Therefore, the natives feel engulfed in their own solitude, which they begin to cherish. Over time, they slowly uncover the hidden layers of possibilities of boundless freedom within them.

Inference

Mars is a very fiery planet, and when combined with Ketu becomes more fiery, determined and full of youthful energy. In Ashwini, the Mars - Ketu effect makes them energetic, enthusiastic, adventurous, active, alert, quick-witted, determined, quick body movements, short-tempered, impatient, detached, quick to initiate new projects, and quick to lose interest.

Quality -

<u>Laghu - light and swift, Kshipra - quick</u>

The energy of Ashwini natives is light, swift and quick, and so are their thoughts and actions. Nothing bogs them down for long. They are always cheerful, enthusiastic and optimistic. The speedy energy helps them to come out of ailments quickly. They almost never fall prey to any lingering illness and are blessed with good health.

On the negative side, they easily get bored. They are impatient, and because of this, they start many projects with great enthusiasm but leave them halfway, when something else which is more interesting catches their attention. In terms of life situations, they move quickly in and out of good or bad circumstances; nothing sticks to them for long. They are likely to change a few jobs and a few residences before they settle down. They have many friends but do not have a deep or binding bond with anyone.

<u>Chara - movable</u>

Ashwini placed in chara rashi (Aries sign) shows that natives like travelling, need a change of scenery very often, and are most happy when they are on the move. Both mentally and physically they need to be actively involved in some or the other project. Also, they will not have a load of heavy karma backlog, and life patterns will be quick moving. It will not take them long to snap out of a melancholic mood. They cannot stay depressed for too long. On the other hand, they will quickly get bored of good things as well.

Element- Fire

Rig Veda starts with hymns dedicated to Agni Dev - the fire god. The scriptures have described fire as a transformative energy that is a vital ingredient for life to happen in all forms and at all levels.

<u>Agni, the fire God</u>

Rig Veda begins with hymns dedicated to Agni Dev.

"To thee dispeller of the night, O Agni,

Day by day, with prayer bringing thee reverence, we come.

Ruler of sacrifices, guard of law eternal,

Radiant one, increasing in thy own abode.

Be to us easy of approach, even as a father to his son

Agni, be with us for our weal."

The significance

Agni is worshipped in many forms - as transformative energy, the digestive fire of the stomach, fire of cooking, the sacrificial fire, fire of the cremation ground, fire of rebirth, fire in the wood, atmospheric fire, the lightning in the sky, the solar fire and the light in the distant stars.

Agni represents all Gods and permeates the entire universe in the form of energy. The Upanishads describe it as knowledge that dispels darkness, transforms or procreates and brings forth an enlightened state. Agni is conceived as the original force of creation and pervades in maintenance and destruction.

Agni, the fire god in the Vedic scriptures, is personified as having a ruddy complexion, and his hair stands on ends like the flames. He has 2 faces, 7 tongues, 3 legs and 7 arms. He rides the ram (mountain goat). He is also associated with Rudra (the fierce form of Shiva). He is the guardian of the southeast direction, and his presence is invoked during fire rituals.

The Ayurvedic perspective

Ayurvedic texts state that the presence of Agni (the fire element) is in every cell of the body. The tridosha of Pitta is the heat energy in the body. According to its function and site of action there are 13 types of fire in our body. Types of Pitta are-

Pitta - Agni	Type of fire
1 Jathar Agni	The digestive fire.
5 Bhuta Agnis	The elemental fire.
7 Dhatu Agnis	The 7 types of tissues have a certain kind of fire.

The scientific perspective

Fire is the visual effect of a chemical reaction called combustion. When the fuel and oxygen react with one another, the transformation happens within the atoms, and they rearrange themselves irreversibly. Scientists describe it as a fire triangle. Where there is oxygen (air), heat (ignition) and the fuel (the object that burns).

The colour that the fire emits depends on the temperature and the composition of the atoms of the material that is being burnt. Here is a table that shows how stars vary in their colour according to the intensity of heat they are emitting.

Colour and quality of the star	Intensity of heat
White -Very short wavelength	Pure, bright, highly intense - consumes all colours.
Blue - Very hot and young stars. Shortest wavelength	High oxygen fire

<u>Yellow</u> (our Sun) - Stable and warm, supports life.	Low oxygen fire
<u>Red</u> - Betelgeuse is a red giant, the second brightest star in the Orion constellation.	Lesser intensity, an old star on the verge of exploding into a supernova.

<u>Interesting facts -</u>

- The human eye has evolved to see yellow and green radiation because our sun emits those wavelengths.

- Our Sun emits a lot of green light, but our eyes see it as white light.

- Our eyes cannot see purple-coloured stars because we are sensitive to blue light.

<u>Inference</u>

As there is the energy of fire in the larger universe, so also in our bodies and all living creatures at the atomic level. The white light contains all the colours but is visible to us only when the phenomenon of the rainbow occurs. A rainbow is formed when the light from the sun gets retracted and bent while passing through the droplets of rain in the atmosphere. It's the play of water and fire that helps us see the magic of a rainbow.

Similarly, the 7 chakras (the energy vortices) in our body emit the wavelengths of light as seen in the colours of the rainbow. This now has been seen through capturing the aura of a person by Kirlin photography. These colours of the aura of any person or a creature are not visible to the naked eye. Our aura is not constant, but fluctuates according to our thoughts, emotions and play of energy within us.

<u>The 3 levels</u>

- At the gross physical level - it's the fire of digestion which is needed for the survival of the body.

- At the psychological level - it's the fire of motivation, ambition and passion, without which we lose all purpose to do any activity.

- At the subtle or soul level - it's the fire of being, our consciousness, the basic form of energy at play, which is eternally present.

Motivation - <u>Dharma - righteousness.</u>

Those who are born with an Ascendant, Sun or the moon in Ashwini's actions will be motivated by the desire to do the right thing as the situation demands. Their choices and decisions will be aligned to the social norms, the ethics, the moral code, the legal law of the society they live in, and to their own beliefs and principles. Which means they will never do anything unethical through fraud or deceit.

Triguna - Rajas

The triguna of Rajas signifies motion and activity. It is the dynamic pursuit of our needs and desires. The element of air and the tridosha of Vata is associated with Rajas, because it has the quality of movement, agility, activity and creativity.

Rajasic food is the food required for athletes, warriors, administrators, and leaders of the world who are constantly in action and need to take decisive action, those who work hard with their bodies and minds and love to enjoy the pleasures of life. For example, tea coffee, food that has spicy, sharp and pungent taste, all vegetables, meats, seafood, and lentils. This type of food raises Pitta, which provides the energy and stimulation needed for vigorous activity.

This table shows the positive and negative traits of Rajasic qualities.

Rajas	
Positive traits	Negative traits
Energetic, intelligent, creative, passionate, adventurous, active, ambitious, achievers, motivated, motivational speakers, inspire others, brave, go getters, rise to the occasion and problem solvers.	Selfish, can be rude, impatient, irritable, easily bored, short tempered, indulgence, prone to skin rashes, pitta imbalance, and can get blood pressure.

Inference

Ashwini, being the first nakshatra of the zodiac, is full of energy and is the most active. Their enthusiasm, passion, freshness and buoyancy for life are remarkable. It's like the energy that gives the strength to the little seedling to sprout out of the seed, the energy that helps the egg to hatch, and the energy that allows the foetus to come out of the womb.

Similarly, those who are born with an Ashwini Ascendent, or Sun or Moon in Ashwini, will have a fresh, raw energy that is exuberant and ready to explore life. They will be very active and will not like to sit around and do nothing. They easily get bored and need some mental or physical activity to keep them occupied. They want to lead and take initiative; they cannot wait for things to happen but will go get them. Their enthusiasm can be motivating and inspiring for others. Yet, at times, their endless passion and excitement can exhaust their own energy and the energy of others around them. They will only stop to rest when they are fatigued.

To channel their fiery and youthful energy positively and constructively, they should keep themselves physically active by playing sports or doing regular exercise and mentally active by playing indoor or online games, solving puzzles, or working on some challenging project. Being active and involved gives them the greatest joy. Ashwini natives love being busy and active. They easily get bored if there is nothing for them to do. You will rarely find an Ashwini sitting idle; they will always have something to do.

They will not have just one, but several projects running side by side which keeps them engaged 24/7. Even in their restful hours, they will be thinking of something new to start. They sleep only when their body and mind are sufficiently exhausted and need rest. A short stretch of sound sleep is enough for them to be rejuvenated, and they feel ready and refreshed to get back to activity.

Their actions are not motivated by a particular thought of gaining something; just being active and being passionately involved gives them the greatest joy and fulfilment. They don't think too much about the future or become anxious about it, and they don't brood too much over the past as well. Nothing drags them down because they love being in the moment; the sheer joy of being active and playing the game well is their most excellent satisfaction.

Tridosha - Pitta

In Ayurveda, the individual constitution is seen from the proportion of the 3 doshas; when the 3 doshas are in equal balance, it's a state of absolute health, which is rare. The predominant dosha of Ashwini natives is pitta, which makes them very ambitious, motivated, intelligent and energetic. They are born leaders, and love being outdoors, and are always brimming with energy and strength. Physical exercise is good for them, which helps to let out their burst of energy, but they should avoid extreme sports. They need a good stretch of uninterrupted sleep, regular holidays and time to relax, which will help to balance their activity.

This table shows how Piita will manifest when it's in balance or out of balance, and the diet and recommendations related to pitta.

In balance	Passionate, enthusiastic, motivated, determined, love challenges, active, athletic, fiery, self confident, leaders, quick learners, love intellectual discussions, focused, organised and charismatic.
Out of balance	Impatience, irritability, anger, workaholics, can be aggressive and bossy. Physically they can feel - heartburn, stomach ache, diarrhoea, acidity, headaches, skin problems, alopecia, gallbladder issues, fevers and inflammation.
Diet	They need to drink water regularly, eat more often and in smaller amounts because they perspire more and their food gets digested quickly. Sweet fruits are good for them. Avoid oily, spicy, pungent and sour foods because they tend to increase pitta.
Recommendations	Avoid extreme heat or extreme cold. Well ventilated spaces help to cool the excessive heat in the system. Open shady places and being near water calms the pitta as well.

Chakra - Muladhara - Mars and Ketu

The tremendous Martian power and the fiery intensity of Ketu are needed to initiate life into action. That's why Muladhara, the foundation chakra, is ruled by Mars and Ketu.

Chakra	Planets	Symbol	Element	Sound	Colour	Petals	Glands
Muladhara	Mars Ketu	Square and Downward facing triangle	Earth	Lam	Red	4	Adrenal gland

Mula means the root, and adhara means the support. This is the foundation chakra, when it is stable and balanced, it gives good health. It is located between the anal and the genital outlet. Sadhguru explains that - When the energies are overly dominant in the root chakra - food and sleep will be the guiding factors of life. Chanting the mantra – "*lam*" can activate the Muladhara. When this chakra is well balanced, it gives good health, and one can have mastery over the earth element.

It has 4 petals, which signify a solid, square, stable and grounded base as a foundation layer on which the interplay of energy happens. It also represents the 4 cardinal directions - north, south, east and west. This sets the stage for pursuing the 4 goals of life - dharma - righteous action, artha - wealth and resources, Kama - desires and moksha - liberation.

The symbol of a square and a downward-facing triangle shows the downward movement of energy needed for grounding and stabilising, nourishing and sustaining the body. Vedic texts describe Muladhara to be the abode of Ganapati; he is also the deity of Ketu, worshipping Ganapati helps to gain the knowledge and wisdom of Lord Brahma and removes obstacles.

Muladhara is located 2 fingers above the external genital organs, which is a very sensitive point. When Muladhara is balanced, one feels grounded, secure, and stable and feels well connected to one's own body and to the environment. When out of balance, it can cause ill health and chronic problems.

Laziness, inertia, lack of exercise, eating or sleeping too much and excessive indulgence in bodily pleasures can cause an imbalance in the energy of this chakra. There are many ways to balance the Muladhara - through regular exercise, conscious and mindful eating, various yogic practices - hatha yoga asanas and pranayama, meditation - breath watch and mantra chanting. This will help to activate the latent Kundalini energy and will help to overcome the natural tendency and temptations of food and sex. It is best to take guidance from an experienced yoga teacher or a guru because these subtle yogic practices have a powerful effect on our body and mind, so one needs to take care to follow the instructions and do them correctly.

Dr Deepak Chopra, an endocrinologist and a preacher of the holistic approach to medicine, gives excellent guidelines for perfect health; he calls it the 5 pillars of good health. Which will work for balancing all aspects of the body and mind holistically. He says that research has shown - that only 5% of diseases are related to gene mutations and cannot be stopped. That means 95% of what happens to our health is in our control. To help prevent illness and inflammation in our bodies that can lead to chronic diseases, here are 5 simple things we all can do to lead a healthier life. He says, "If you have these 5 things in your mind, you set the stage for self-regulation and healing."

The 5 pillars of good health	
1	Restful sleep - get enough sleep.
2	Meditate daily - start your day with meditation.
3	Healthy emotions - be aware of your emotions, especially anger.
4	Exercise - stay active, move your body.
5	Eat a healthy balanced diet - eat freshly cooked meals, avoid frozen foods and include fresh fruits and salads in your regular diet.

Inference

Ashwini carries a strong Muladhara energy because it's the 1st nakshatra that's the initiator of life. This gives the natives a natural vitality and physical strength. Their basal and survival instincts are strong, which provides them with a very zestful approach to life.

Suppose the energies of Muladhara are out of balance. In that case, they can suffer from ill health and lack of vitality because of overindulgence or excessive activity. A balanced state of the Muladhara chakra forms the basis for good health and vitality. Only when the foundation is stable and strong, then one can dare to climb the heights without the fear of falling. Ashwini natives can channel this tremendous root energy positively by keeping themselves physically and mentally active.

Shakti -

This shows our exceptional inner strength that we are blessed with, which we should make use of in times of need, it will guide us into the easiest and best way out of challenging circumstances.

If you feel confused about which remedy will work for you. Then look at the Shakti (energy) of your moon and ascendant nakshatra. It's best to take both into account because the body and mind are one entity. For example, if one is experiencing stress, it will affect the physical health inevitably, and any physical ailment will become the cause of underlying stress and anxiety.

Shakti of the nakshatra represents our inherent capability and talent that can pull us out of situations when life seems in peril. Even if one does not look into astrology for answers, they will naturally discover their inner strength during difficult times, and that will pull them out of seemingly black holes of hopelessness.

<u>Shidravyapana Shakti - the power to give quick results.</u>

For Ashwini people, their exceptional strength lies in giving quick results. So whenever in life they are faced with a 'stuck in the mud' situation, they will recover best by doing activities that can give quick results. On observing closely, they will see that whenever they do things spontaneously, like - going for short family trips or a bike ride, or when they help someone without any hesitation - their situations improve.

Symbolic signification

<u>Aries - Ram and Ashwini - Horse</u>

In astrology, the zodiac signs and nakshatras are given a particular symbol which literally represents its quality. Therefore, understanding these symbols will significantly help us understand the nature of that sign or nakshatra.

<u>Ram</u>

Rams are mountain sheep that have big, strong, curved horns. They live in the mountains and often settle arguments by ramming their heads into each other. They have split hooves that have a rough bottom, which helps them with traction and grip. They have a fantastic balance and can stand on narrow ledges, jump up to 6 metres and go up a mountain very briskly. They also have excellent eyesight, which allows them to judge distances accurately when jumping. They are related to antelopes, bison, buffalo, cattle and goats.

They live in the Rocky Mountain regions of North America. Male and female Rams live in separate herds. Rams are herbivores and get most of their water from eating plants to survive. They will rechew the food and swallow it again; this is part of their digestion process. Rams typically don't mate until they are around 7 years old. They can live from 10 to 19 years in the wild.

<u>Horse</u>

Early humans domesticated them mainly for transportation because of their strength and speed. Research shows that man started domesticating the horse around 3000 BC. Horses have long necks, long legs, and singular solid hooves. Only horses, ostriches, whales, and seals have large eyes. The horse skeleton averages 205 bones. A significant difference between the horse skeleton and that of a human is the lack of a collarbone. The horse-hoofs are of vital importance. The sole of the hoof is made of keratin, the same material as a human fingernail.

As herbivores, they feed exclusively on grass and graze throughout the day. An average-sized Horse is capable of consuming more than 20 pounds of food per day. They need a large field to graze around and like staying in open green meadows. They are social animals and like to live in herds. Their gestation period is 11 months. A newly born foal is able to stand and walk shortly after birth and is usually born in springtime. They do not mate until about 3 years old, and their average lifespan is 25 to 30 years.

Interesting facts-

- Their sense of smell is much better than humans, but not as good as dogs.

- Their ears can rotate up to 180 degrees, which makes them sensitive to noise. Research shows that they get nervous and even develop ulcers with loud noises and jazz music.

- Because their eyes are on either side of their heads, they can see nearly everything around them. They have 350° vision, with blind spots directly in front of and behind.

- They have a great sense of balance because of their high ability to feel their footing and their gait.

- They are prey animals and, therefore, have a strong sense of fight or flight response. Their first response is to flee.

- They are social animals with a clear sense of hierarchy, led by a dominant male.

- They are animals of habit and respond well to consistent routines.

- They can sleep, both standing and lying down and sleep in short periods of rest, primarily for about 15 minutes each. However, they need to lie down in a deep sleep for an hour or two every 2 to 3 days otherwise, they may suddenly collapse.

Inference

Ashwini natives will be headstrong and like to argue or debate to settle things. They are happiest when they are heading a project or leading a group. They love fast racing cars, bikes or motorbikes and can handle speed with a great sense of balance. They will have lovely luxurious hair and like to leave it loose like the horse's mane. Feeling the wind through their hair when speeding on their favourite bike is the most exhilarating feeling. 'Born *to be free,*' this is their soul desire.

They are very easygoing by nature and get along with everyone. They will not impose restrictions and neither will welcome anyone curtailing their sense of freedom. They will not hold strong opinions against or for anyone to the point where it becomes unpleasant. Light-hearted differences and jokes, they are up for it anytime. They love being in nature. That's when they feel truly in their element. When they are roaming the open grasslands, countryside fields, meadows or mountain peaks, they feel at home.

Their vitality and strength are naturally good. They are light sleepers and feel fresh and rejuvenated even with a short nap. They are not afraid to face things head-on, but if the situation seems dangerous, they will be quick to respond and escape it with lightning swiftness.

They are joyful and spontaneous, and their enthusiasm is contagious to those around them. They live more in the moment and do not have the anxiety of long-term plans or carry the burden of past actions. For this reason, they are very aware of what's happening now. This approach to life keeps them youthful and lively, no matter what their age is. They prefer light, calm, serene places to relax; too much noise disturbs their inner sensitivity.

They love socialising with family and friends. There is never a dull moment in their life because they will always have an exciting venture up their sleeve. They are not the type who will dig deep into research and spend their whole day in a dreary laboratory or on a computer desk. They need to be out and about exploring life, meeting people, experiencing the exuberance of life. Daily routines may seem binding, but they plan to finish the job quickly and then enjoy the freedom of being in the landscapes where they can see and explore up to the horizon's end.

The symbolism of Ram, the mountain sheep, shows their prowess in reaching the heights, their sure-footed confidence and the feeling of being comfortable at the top. It also shows that they like head-butting, arguing, debating, and confronting head-on. They particularly enjoy taking up all kinds of mental challenges, which brings out the best in them.

The horse signifies tremendous strength and speed. They have plenty of horsepower energy in them. Just like the horse they can gallop ahead and reach targets quickly, ahead of everyone else. But they can utilise their strength efficiently, only in quick, short bursts. They will need plenty of rest after that before going for another galloping expedition.

Mythology

"God always speaks mythologically." - Carl Jung

Deity - Ashwini Kumaras

Looking at the deity of each Nakshatra will help us understand the inner functioning and fundamentals of the natives born in that Nakshatra.

Story of Ashwins

As mentioned in rig Veda, the story of Ashwini Kumars goes back to 1001 BC during the time of the Bronze Age and Mesopotamian civilisation. More than 50 hymns are dedicated to Ashwin Kumars in Rig Veda. The word Ashwin in Vedic Sanskrit means dual horse possessors. Ashwini Kumaras are twin Vedic Gods of medicine, described as youthful and divine travelling in a chariot drawn by horses.

Birth of Ashwins

It is said that Sanjana (meaning consciousness), the wife of Surya (Sun God), could not bear the heat and radiance of the sun. Hence, she made her duplicate chaya (means shadow) and left her with her husband. She went to stay at her father's home, who was the celestial architect, Vishwakarma.

Meanwhile, Surya Dev, oblivious to the replacement of his wife with a clone, had 3 children with Chaya. Shani (Saturn) and twins Manu and Tapti. While Sanjana's children, Yama and Yami were neglected and not well looked after by Chaya. Disturbed by his Mum's favouritism for Shani, Manu and Tapti, Yama kicked her. Chaya cursed him that his leg may be infected with worms. When Surya came to know about this incident, he thought about it deeply and concluded that no mother can curse her own child. He questioned Chaya, and she revealed the truth about her being a duplicate of Sanjana.

Surya decided to go and find Sanjana, leaving the kingdom of ancestors to Yama. He went to Vishwakarma to ask if he knew where his wife was. Vishwakarma tells Surya that she left because his radiance was too bright for her to bear. Vishwakarma helped him to reduce his radiance by taking off one ray of sunlight and making it into sudarshana chakra. Surya Dev then went to the earth and found Sanjana in the form of a horse. He, too, assumed the form of a horse to mate with her and twins were born, named Dasra and Nastya. It is said that twin Ashwin Kumaras were born from her nostrils.

Inference

Sun refers to sunlight, the source of all energy on Earth. Sanjana is consciousness. Chaya is the shadow cast on Earth during solar eclipses. Vishwakarma is the celestial cosmic design of planets and star constellations.

Healing abilities of the ashwins

Ashwini Kumaras are said to be the gods of medicine. Those who are born with the Ascendant, Sun or Moon in Ashwini will have an inherent ability to know about the Ayurvedic herbs, to heal, and will be very good at repairing and fixing cuts and wounds. They will naturally be drawn to a career in medicine or veterinary doctors. Even if they are not doctors by profession they will have the knack of administering medicine to anyone.

Whenever they give medicine to anyone, the healing is fast since they are the divine physicians of the zodiac.

Qualities of Ashwins

They were the master healers, experts in Ayurveda, had knowledge of herbs, knew madhu vidya (understanding of how to use honey), surgeons, quick, young and energetic, pranksters, child-like innocence, naive, straightforward, honest, have a great sense of humour, are lively and enthusiastic explorers.

Ashwini padas

0 - 13.20 degrees Aries

Padas	Degrees
1	0 - 3.20
2	3.20 - 6.40
3	6.40 - 10
4	10 - 13.20

Please note -

The brief descriptions given for each Pada will be more noticeable or seen prominently when the native has their <u>Ascendant, Sun or Moon</u> placed in that Pada. For example, those who have their Ascendant in the 1st Pada of Ashwini in the birth chart will be determined, fearless and adventurous. Suppose When Sun is placed in the 1st Pada of Ashwini in the 10th house, the same qualities will manifest in their chosen career. In that case, they will be very ambitious and will follow their professional goals with confidence and intelligence. Suppose the Moon is placed in the 1st Pada of Ashwini in the 9th house. In that case, they will manifest the same quality of determination and aggressive approach to pursuing their higher education to improve their skills or talent. They will be well supported by their father and teachers.

The qualities and attributes described below for each planet and house, will be modified according to other planetary placements, aspects and conjunctions. It's the qualities assigned to the planets as per astrological inferences that set the baseline for all interpretations. For accurate readings and predictions, the placement of other planets and the birth chart needs to be looked at as a whole.

Pada 1

0 - 3.20 deg Aries, Navamsha - Aries (Lord - Mars)

Rashi Lord - Mars and Nakshatra Lord - Ketu

Mars Ketu energy is predominant in this Pada. People born in this quarter can be recognised by their goat-like slim faces, small pairs of eyes, small noses, ordinary features, skinny bodies and heavy voices. They will have red eyes and very focused attention. Their fiery side is very distinguished - the need to win arguments, clashing of ideas, headstrong nature and very motivated and enthusiastic. Because of this, they may often clash with their friends or colleagues, not because of any intended malice but to prove their point, they end up hurting others' feelings. They will be quick to snap and quick to apologise. These qualities will be seen in those who are born with their Ascendant, Sun or Moon in the 1st Pada of Ashwini.

On the positive side, their aggressive, forceful approach will enable them to push their way through any situation fearlessly. They will have sudden outbursts of energy and then a period of lull to re-energise. The 1st Pada is vargottama, which gives the natives good, steady results and success in their endeavours. For example, the 1st Pada of Ashwini in the 2nd house, will have a constant flow of income and will always have a backup resource.

They will have a high moral code, will not be afraid to take responsibility and will not step back in situations that demand courage. To protect and provide security for their family and friends will be their desired role. They will be able to accomplish things quickly and swiftly. They can be impatient and find shortcuts to finish things off, which may result in an unsatisfactory outcome for them and for others.

They will have a logical and technical approach to things. They can be self-centred and oblivious to others' feelings. The word ash-win is very appropriate because their main priority is to win and win quickly. Because of this, they can come across as abrupt and unsympathetic.

Though their intention is never to hurt anyone, they end up doing so because of their direct and impatient approach. Natives born in this Pada will face situations (during Ketu or Mars dasha). Where they feel that they have been thrown into the deep end of the pool suddenly, cut from the familiar warm surroundings of their comfort zone. Since they have the Mars energy to back them up, they will face all challenges with great courage and overcome difficulties swiftly and quickly. Saturn placed here can bring challenges in terms of delays, loss of interest and motivation.

Careers -

Firefighters, athletes, mechanical engineers, emergency doctors, soldiers, police officers, truck drivers, working in a factory, working at the farm, shopkeepers, truck drivers, horse trainers, veterinary doctors, emergency doctors, gym trainers, surgeons, stunt performers, circus gymnasts, hatha yoga practitioners, racing, adventure sports, explorers, mountain climbers, sherpas, hiking and trekking tourists, contractors, builders and IT professionals.

Pada 2

3.20- 6.40 deg Aries, Navamsha - Taurus (Lord - Venus)

Rashi Lord - Mars and Nakshatra Lord - ketu

Mars Ketu Venus energy scenario will play here. Since Pada 2 falls in the Taurus Navamsa governed by Venus, the natives will be more practical and resourceful here. The influence of Mars will give them motivation, energy and determination to pursue goals. They will be able to manifest ideas and be graceful, indulgent and materialistic. Mars Venus Ketu energy will bring more passion and can have a series of quick romances.

Mars, the planet of war and aggression, and Venus, the planet of love and beauty, make a heady concoction of passion and indulgence. Moreover, Ketu is also Mars-like in nature, adding to the intensity, which is invisible, like the infrared waves. So those born with their Ascendant, Sun or Moon in Pada 2 can feel the inner drive, the fire in them which makes them compulsive. They will anyway go ahead and take action headlessly without thinking, riding on the heat of the moment. This can later lead to total detachment from the relationship or from a certain situation because ketu will lead to such a scenario of separation - moksha.

They will be enthusiastic, passionate, creative and resourceful. For example, in Ashwini Pada 2 in the 3rd house, natives will be very skilful and talented in IT and communication. They will not be stage-shy and could be good public speakers. They will have multiple communication devices like phones, laptops and iPads and will use them efficiently.

Careers-

Doctors, athletes, goldsmiths, jewellers, selling clothes, councillors, therapists, dancers, hatha yoga and pranayama practitioners, teachers, gardeners, ayurveda doctors, a career in holistic medicine, pioneers, strategy consultants, beauticians, interior designers, fashion designers and tailors.

Pada 3

6.40- 10 deg Aries, Navamsha - Gemini (Lord - Mercury)

Rashi Lord - Mars and Nakshatra Lord - Ketu

Mars Ketu Mercury will give the natives a lot of energy, fire, drive and a perfect sense of humour. The 3rd Pada falls in Gemini Navamsha, whose ruler is Mercury. Natives will be intelligent, have good decision-making ability and will have strong communication skills. They will express their thoughts and feelings with ease, will be very informative about various subjects and good conversationalists. These qualities will be seen in those who are born with their Ascendant, Sun or Moon in the 3rd Pada. However, suppose this Pada is placed in any other house. In that case, it will take on the signification of that house, even if no planets are sitting in that house. For example, the 3rd Pada of Ashwini in the 5th house will be quick and skilled in IT communication and can produce a lot of creative IT products.

They will be quick in replying, witty, fast thinker, and can keep their friends enthralled by their mimicry. This natural gift makes them confident and comfortable with live performances. They will also have the reckless impulse of Mars and Ketu and an eternal curiosity of Mercury that will keep them engaged in many different projects at the same time. They will start something with great enthusiasm, then leave it halfway because something more interesting has caught their attention.

Of course, too much mental and emotional freedom can bring confusion about choices; they can get caught in their own web of distractions. They can multitask and will be the jack of all trades and masters of none.

Careers-

Physiotherapists, marriage counsellors, computer engineers,

IT consultants, athletes, promotional jobs and campaign advertisers, public relations coordinators, actors, comedians, teachers, ayurveda doctors, gardeners, farmers, bankers, business people, industrialists, tour guides and travel agents.

Pada 4

10- 13.20 deg Aries, Navamsha - Cancer (Lord - Moon)

Rashi Lord - Mars and Nakshatra Lord - Ketu

Mars ketu moon effect will make the natives born in this Pada receptive and empathetic. They will make excellent doctors and surgeons because they have a tremendous interest in the science of the body and will have the skill and dexterity. These qualities will be prominent for those who have their Ascendant, Sun or Moon in the 4th Pada of Ashwini.

Ashwini Kumaras are said to have nimble hands.

"Ye Ashwins, rich in treasure, Lords of splendour, having nimble hands, accept the sacrificial food." - *Rig Veda*

The friendly effect of the moon gives them a motherly and caring nature in this Pada. They will be often seen in the medical field.

This is an excellent placement for a leader, social worker or writer. They will have an intrinsic knack for understanding people and relationships at a deeper level and respond to them accordingly. The technicality of Mars and the sharp cutting quality of ketu will not allow them to articulate fully what they feel or want to express. They will tend to explain things in a brief synopsis. The effect of the moon can cause fluctuations and can make them frustrated at times because they feel misunderstood. They may think that even when they constantly endeavour to do things in the best interest of others, it is often not appreciated or noticed.

They will be very knowledgeable and technically minded and do very well in the field of science. For example, the 4th Pada of Ashwini placed in the 10th house can make them excellent and successful doctors.

Careers-

Doctors, athletes, scientists, herbalists, councillors, cooks, public relations jobs, veterinary doctors, property agents, car salesmen, travel agents, game ranchers, selling pets, nurses and midwives.

The effect of planets

The house placement of certain planets can make them functional benefics or functional malefic for each Ascendant. Please note - the changed effect of these planets is only applicable from the Ascendant and not from the placement of the Moon.

Ashwini is placed in the sign of Aries. For an Aries Ascendant, Venus becomes a functional malefic because it has the Kendra Adi Pati dosha - it is the lord of the 2nd and the 7th house, which are Maraka houses. For example, Venus, a benefic planet placed in the 6th house, can cause problems in marriage or relationships during the Venus Maha dasha, antar dasha and transits.

Mars, Jupiter and the sun give good results here because they become lords of the trine houses - 1, 5 and 9. The moon is neutral.

Venus is a killer, being the Lord of both maraka houses, and Saturn and Mercury are obstacles, as lords of 3, 6, 10 and 11. Rahu and Ketu will behave like the rashi they are sitting in, Rahu will exemplify, and Ketu will detach.

Please note - The malefic effect of Venus will be seen only for an Aries Ascendant. For all other Ascendants, Venus remains a benefic.

This table gives the effect of certain planets, for an Aries Ascendant.

Ashwini - Aries	Planets that get affected
Functional Benefic - give good results during their dasha.	Sun, Moon and Mars
Functional Malefic - can give problems during their dasha.	Mercury, Rahu and Ketu
Functional Neutral	Moon, Jupiter and Saturn
Kendra -Adi pati dosha - can give problems in relationships.	Venus

Please note -

Although the placement of all planets should be looked at carefully for a complete and full analysis of any birth chart. In this book (in order to keep it concise) - each nakshatra will be looked at from 3 critical aspects, which are crucial points to be noted - The Ascendant, the placement of the Sun and the placement of the moon. Even though only 3 placements are being looked at, it will give you a good idea about how to approach and study any horoscope.

Most importantly it will help you to understand how the planets form the base layer of all astrological inferences and predictions. Therefore, knowing the planets well is of absolute importance in order to create a good foundation on which other layers can be added. Just as practice and experience can help us master any skill, over time - through studying various horoscopes, one can become an excellent astrologer.

Ashwini Ascendant

Aries is the 1st house in the naisargik kundali (original horoscope) Therefore, those who are born with an Ashwini Ascendant will have the natural benefit of being a very balanced personality. Mars Ketu effect will be seen here. The natives will be well-mannered, polite and charming and will have a good physical appearance. They will be skilled, knowledgeable, adventurous and intelligent.

They can get into the habit of starting projects with great enthusiasm and then leaving them halfway because of a loss of interest. They can be impulsive and short-tempered because of the Mars ketu effect.

They will almost always be in a lively mood, will be bold and courageous, adventurous and youthful, motivated, intuitive and helpful. They will be very straightforward and direct in their approach, and will be competent workers, and will be natural healers. Even if they are not in the medical profession, they will inherently know what herbs or supplements to take if they are not feeling well.

They are very self-conscious and are ultra concerned about how they look because in the original placement of signs (naisargik kundalini) Aries is the 1st house, which rules the physical appearance, especially the head. They simply don't like anyone messing about with their heads- physically or mentally - and for this reason, they are very particular about their hairstylist or would much rather prefer to style their own hair. In fact, they are sensitive about their whole face and don't like sitting in the dentist's chair or in a beauty parlour, where someone else is messing about with their face, hair, nose, eyes or ears. Mentally, too, they are very headstrong and love fighting, arguing, or reasoning it out, which means they don't mess with their opinions either.

The 1st house is the most crucial house in the birth chart. It sets the tone of the whole chart. It's called the tanu bhava - means physical body and bhava means feeling or emotion. Therefore, the planets placed here will manifest their results on the body during its dasha.

It's the bhavat bhavam of 7th house (7th from 7th), which means how one relates to others is directly influenced by the type of personality he or she is. The native will be a go-getter, can not wait around for things to happen, and will get along very well with people who have a similar outlook on life.

Ashwini natives will always look youthful no matter how old they are. This is because the nature of their energy is light and swift and moves quickly, nothing sticks to them for long - low or high moods, emotions, situations, relationships, attachments, friendships - everything moves fast. Their thoughts, speech and actions, and the result of their actions, are also quick. This means they usually do not have to wait around too long for things to progress because of the effect of the fast moving energy.

They are more receptive and aligned to the adventurous and passionate side of life - something that keeps them on their toes. Their lifestyle and life situations are such that there is no time and no chance of getting bored. Their underlying motivation is righteousness. They like to deal with all situations in a straightforward, honest and ethical manner. Being a trader by nature, they are very good at negotiating business deals. They are inspired by causes that deal with higher knowledge or philosophy.

The element of fire gives them energy, passion and zest. Ashwini, being in the masculine sign of Aries is more outgoing and extroverted. They are good talkers but not good listeners. That's why their inherent desire is to listen well because this is the quality they need to work on. Their sight is always looking straight, or level means their focus is always straight ahead on the target, aiming towards their goal. There is no room for distractions while they are at it, although the span of their focus is not long.

Ashwini carries the planetary effects of Sun, Mars and Ketu - this gives them a fiery, enthusiastic and passionate approach to life. The impact of Ketu detaches them from what they have achieved, and even what they could not achieve - and they are able to move on to the next exploration without brooding too much over it.

The dharma triangle - Ashwani is in Aries - the 1st sign of the zodiac. The trine of the 1st, 5th and 9th house from the dharma triangle. It's the trine of fire signs - Aries, Leo and Sagittarius - whose lords are - Mars, Sun and Jupiter. Mars represents energy and drive, the Sun represents authority, generosity, creativity and confidence, and Jupiter represents knowledge and wisdom. All these qualities inspire and motivate the Ashwini natives to do something good and meaningful. Even if no planets sitting in these houses, the natives will have such situations in their lives where they are inspired to do good.

The 1st house is also 5th from the 9th house of Guru, Dad, religion and higher education. It shows that the native's father will be a very energetic and enthusiastic personality and will be a huge influence in shaping the native's personality and physical skills. Natives will have strong vitality and good digestion. Because of good, strong Pitta (digestive fire), they will be able to eat any kind of food and not put on weight. They will be adventurous and fearless and will have a sudden wave of enthusiasm and then a downward wave of rest to recapitulate their energy. This is the natural rhythm of nature. After a high wave, a low wave has to follow to balance the flow of life.

Sun in Ashwini

Those who are born with the Sun placed in Ashwini, will have the effect of the Sun, Mars and Ketu. This will give them a very aggressive approach to life - they will have the do or die kind of spirit, enthusiasm and determination. Sun will provide them with confidence, Mars will make them determined and fearless, and Ketu can make them impulsive and short tempered.

Since the Sun, Mars and Ketu all have a very fiery quality, they will have a pitta-predominant constitution. They should take care not to eat too much spice as it aggravates Pitta. It's also better for them to do their physical exercise in a cool place. They will be easily angered and quick to cool down as well. They may say something rude at the spur of the moment but regret it later and are always willing to apologise. They don't have any malice in their hearts and are very straightforward and honest.

They will be authoritative and generous and will love adventure and sports. Sun is exalted at 10 deg Aries. It will give fame and position but can make one egoistic and self-centred. Their Dad will be very brave, dominating and generous. The native will speak with authority and confidence and will not be shy of speaking on a public platform. He or she has the capability of holding a leadership position in politics, business or sports.

They will be headstrong and independent and will not have the patience or inclination to sit through the nitty-gritty of things. They will prefer to delegate the detail-oriented jobs to others.

They will like to give orders rather than take orders from anyone. Therefore, they will do well running their own business or working in a managerial position.

They will thrive on appreciation, it's fuel for their motivation. If they feel their efforts are not acknowledged, they will be deeply hurt. But their pride will not allow them to show their disappointment or hurt. They would rather leave with grace and respect than be caught crying or asking for help in any way. They are willing to survive on less, but their honour cannot be compromised. For them, their honour and self-respect are the most valuable asset and cannot be sacrificed for any amount of money or wealth of any kind.

For example, when the Sun in Ashwini is in the 1st house. Ascendant being the 10th from the 4th house of mum, the native's mum would have a prestigious job as a manager or a political leader, or dad could be in a government job because the Sun signifies dad. Either way, the mum or dad will have a significant influence in shaping the personality of the Ashwani native.

Moon in Ashwini

The placement of the moon is considered very important in Vedic astrology because it's through the window of our mind we perceive life. It tells us about the natives' mental approach to things and situations.

Moon here will give a beautiful combination of courage and empathy because it will have the influence of Mars and Ketu. They will have a good balance of logical, practical approaches, will be receptive to others' emotions and will be intuitive. They will find happiness in doing things for others and can make wonderful doctors and nurses. They will be quick thinkers and will grasp any subject quickly.

They can be impatient and will like to drive fast. They will be very competitive and can do things like- enter into a relationship just to compete and win. They may have to deal with family emergencies and quarrels and will be very protective of their family and siblings.

Their mum could be a doctor or have a career in the medical field, and she will be an inspiration towards their chosen career.

For example, the moon in the 7th house of Ashwini, the native's partner, will be emotional and passionate about outdoor sports, spending time in nature, and doing physical activities. They will be attracted to people who are adventurous and enthusiastic. They will initiate projects that bring people together and do some fun activities, play games, go for holidays and spend time in nature.

Here, we must look at the waxing and waning phases of the moon.

The waxing phase (shukla paksha) will give the native more of an extroverted quality, where the natives will be more vocal about their feelings and thoughts. While the waning phase (Krishna paksha) will give an introverted quality of keeping more to oneself and reflecting on things. Their expression will come more through writing, art, singing, dancing, going to the gym, or sports activities.

Moon also represents the mum, so she will be a great influence in the native's life. Since it's the 10th house from the original home of the mother (4th house), the career chosen by the native, and his or her public image will be hugely influenced by their mum, she will be a great support in the native's career. The decisions about the career will be emotional, and they can experience ups and downs in career and health.

If there is a malefic planet like Saturn sitting with the moon, then their own emotions or mum could be an obstruction in their career. They can experience anxiety and stress because of these fluctuations in their career. A benefic planet like Jupiter, with the moon, will enhance the sound auspicious effects and the lifeof natives will be more easygoing. However, the chart should be seen as a whole to give accurate predictions.

Venus and Moon's conjunction is not considered good because it will make the native pleasure-seeking. Running after immediate senseof gratification can lead to many relationship problems in life, especially during Venus Moon dasha.

Ash-win the poet -

Ash is to usher the light of dawn,

Win is a win-win game.

Ketu and Mars- give the fiery energy,

For the soul to manifest in human synergy.

Horse power is my strength,

Speedy hoofs and elegant,

Ramming the horns with thoughts and words,

To settle the win and winner of herds.

If I win, I gain; if I lose, I learn.

Brave are the ones,

Who hail through life untouched

By scathing heat or biting cold.

Quick is my pace,

And at the finishing line____

To say - "I never was bored."

Is a life well lived?

Remedies

Please note - The remedies given for all nakshatras are recommended for those who have their Ascendant, Sun or Moon in that nakshatra. For example, Devi Bhairavi mantras will provide positive support for those who have their Ascendant, Sun or Moon in Ashwini.

Das Maha Vidya

Bhairavi Devi rules the Ascendant because she controls the effect of 9 planets on Earth. She is said to control all electro-magnetic or atomic radiations that come from outer space. She is also the time factor, which fructifies our karma, dissolves everything and re-creates again.

Bhairavi Devi Mantras-

'Om Bhairavi Saham.'

'Om Hreem Bhairavi Klaum Hreem Swaha.'

When the Ascendant is afflicted by malefics like Saturn, Mars, Rahu or Ketu, or has a low shadbala score, the person can have a weak constitution. Worshipping Bhairavi will help to prevent untimely death, reduce the effect of premature ageing, prevent infections, and protect from bites of poisonous insects or animals. In the human body, she represents the Kundalini energy that spreads in all the organs and chakras. It is believed that only the accomplished yogis can understand her functioning.

Remedies for a weak Ascendant -

- Give time and attention to your body, thoughts and feelings.
- Follow a wholesome routine of healthy diet and exercise.
- Meditation and yogic practice will enhance the strength of the body and mind in a big way.
- Chant Devi Bhairavi Mantras 108 times on the days when the moon is transiting in Ashwini. Keep her yantra and image with her mantra written in front of you. This will help to stabilise and energise the body and mind from within.

Devi Dhumavati - Ketu

Devi Dhumavati is ruled by Ketu and controls its effects in the birth chart. She reveals the nature of ultimate knowledge which is beyond name and form and beyond human divisions. Married couples are advised not to worship Dhumavati. It is said that her worship creates a distaste of worldly things and a feeling of solitude, which is considered as the highest characteristics of a spiritual seeker. Chanting her mantra can give spiritual guidance, and help one to go through the suffering, or difficult period gracefully and smoothly.

For those who have ketu in the Ascendant or moon with Ketu, or have Kala Sarpa dosha, or are running ketu dasha, can feel the effect of Ketu through illness, viral infections, separation from the family, or spending time in a remote, isolated place.

Remedies -

- The best remedy is to practice detachment as much as possible. Her worship is among the most difficult; only those who have reached their peak of spiritual growth can truly connect with her energy. She grants the highest knowledge, the state of samadhi (equanimity), and liberation.
- Her mantra is believed to create a protective aura of smoke, shielding the devotee from negativity and even death. Chanting her mantra 108 times with her yantra and image helps

one gain spiritual strength and overcome enemies. It is recommended to chant her mantra on the 4th lunar day of the dark fortnight (Krishna Paksha).

Mantras of Devi Dhumavati -

'Dhum Dhum Dhumavati Swaha,' and 'Om Dhum'

Devi Bagalamukhi - Mars

'Om Hleem Sarva Dusthaanaam Vacham Mukham Paadam stambhaya jihvyam kilaya buddhim vinaashaya Hleem Om Swaha.'

'Om Hleem'

Devi Bagalamukhi is associated with Mars. She is said to be the Goddess who paralyses her enemies because of her Mars-like fearlessness and determination. She symbolises the potent female primaeval force. She is said to smash the delusions and misconceptions.

Remedies -

- The best remedy is to have control over your speech and not speak without thinking.

- Being truthful and not speaking unkind, harsh, or abusive words that can hurt others' feelings will greatly please Devi Bagalamukhi and her grace will help to keep the enemies at bay and help you become successful in all your endeavours.

- If someone has debilitated Mars, a Mars-Saturn, Mars-Rahu combination in the chart, or problems in the south-east corner according to Vastu, they should worship her by wearing yellow clothes and offering yellow-coloured flowers. Chanting her mantra 108 times with her yantra and image will help to overcome issues of lack of confidence. Her mantra can be chanted for 9 consecutive Tuesdays to reap the benefits.

- She has the power to change the course of action into the opposite direction.

Mantras of Devi Bagalamukhi -

'Om Hleem Sarva Dusthaanaam Vacham Mukham Paadam stambhaya jihvyam kilaya buddhim vinaashaya Hleem Om Swaha.' and 'Om Hleem'

Other Remedies

- Chant the Ashwini mantra 108 times on the day when the moon is transiting Ashwini. This will help to speed up things that have been stuck. *'Om am aam Ashwani nakshatraye namah.'*

- Start taking medicine on the day when the moon is in Ashwini. This will speed up the recovery and the healing process.

- Doing spiritual practises and practising detachment is the best way to be in tune with the energy of Ashwini. This will give one the ability to stay equanimous in all kinds of situations.

- The best remedy will be pranayama. It's a practice of breath regulation. In Sanskrit, prana means life energy, and Yama means control. Being aware of the inhalation and exhalation and taking deeper breaths helps to relax the body and mind. Alternative nose breathing - (alom vilom) through right and left nostrils is an excellent practice which balances the right and left energy channels.

- Doing hatha yoga practises like Surya namaskar and yoga asanas will help greatly in enhancing body flexibility and bringing ease to the whole system.

Scientists have now done extensive research on this and found that yogic practises have various benefits- reduce stress, improve sleep quality, improve lung function, enhance cognitive performance, reduce cravings, and enhance perception and awareness.

Please note - Learn the yogic practises from qualified yoga teachers because these have a powerful impact on our inner system and bring changes at a deeper level. So great care has to be taken to do the practises correctly as instructed.

Example

Ashwini Ascendent 1 Pada

Born on 7th January 1978, Jalandhar, Punjab, India, 12:30 pm.

Luke is a male, 42 yrs in 2020.

The Ashwini theme plays out very strongly in his life because they are twin brothers. He is the younger twin; his elder twin brother does not have the same Ascendant because he was born half an hour after him. They are my cousins, and we feel fortunate to have twins in the family. The best part is that they look remarkably similar, like identical twins, and it takes a while to decipher who is the younger twin and who is the older one!! Especially if they are wearing the same type of clothes and the same colour. We often have many hilarious conversations when they are both together.

In one such very factual and filmi situation - after they both got married, they actually managed to confuse their newly wedded wives. It was so amusing and entertaining for everyone - but the wives did eventually pick their right husband because the elder twin was slightly more heavily built than the younger one.

The younger twin - who is an Ashwini Ascendant, works for a catering company to supply food to the air crafts. After marriage, he moved to a foreign country and is happily settled there with his wife. They now have 2 children. He loves riding his bike and spending time with friends and family.

Analysis -

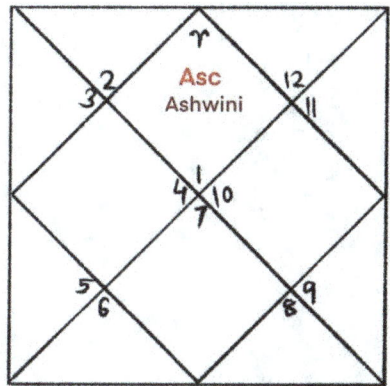 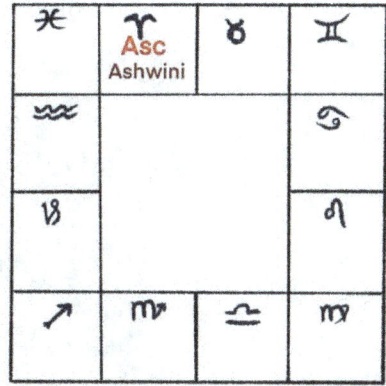

His Ascendant is in the 1st Pada of Ashwini. The pranks and lighthearted jokes of Ashwini are very prominent in his jovial personality. He takes things in a very light-hearted way and is always cheerful. He has a great sense of humour, is always ready to help and will never say no when asked. He is very religious, kind and generous. He has a healing touch in his hand. Whenever he gives medicine to the children or anyone else, they recover very quickly. His mum has great knowledge about plants and herbs and has her own vegetable garden.

Please note - The examples of those whom I know personally have been given, by their consent. Only their names have been changed to maintain privacy.

2
Bharani

Om eem Bharani nakshatraye namah

Zodiac degrees	13.20 - 26.40-degree Aries
Ruling planet	Aries - Mars Bharani - Venus
Sanskrit name	Bharani means she who bears, who is full.
Astronomical name	3 faint stars - seen as an inverted triangle, which represents a yoni (womb). They can be seen between Alpha Arietes (the bright star) and the Pleiades cluster of stars.
Symbol	Aries - Ram, the mountain sheep Bharani - Yoni - the womb and an elephant.
Element	Fire - Aries
Deity	Yamraj (God of death)
Quality	Ugra- fierce Movable - chara - Aries
Shakti	Apabharani Shakti - power to take things away with water.
Cast	Malecha - outcast
Gender	Male - Aries
Motivation	Dharma - righteousness - Aries
Triguna	Rajas - Aries

Tridosha	Pitta - Aries
Body parts	Head, waist and soles of the feet.
Direction	East, south and southeast.
Month	2nd half of Ashwin - October
Bird	Crow
Sound	Lee, lu, lay and lo
Tree	Amla
Chakras	Muladhara - Mars Swadhisthana - Venus
Das Maha Vidya	Devi Bagalamukhi - Mars Devi Kamala - Venus

Special degrees -

Yoga Tara	24.20 deg Aries It is a point where the planet will show the strongest and sure results during its dasha.
Debilitation	20 deg Aries - Maximum debilitation of Saturn. This will bring in situations which demand hard work and discipline, which the native will not feel comfortable with.
Pushkar bhaga	21 deg Aries Planets placed here will fruitify results like the blossoming of a flower.
Amrit nadi	24 - 24.53 deg Aries Planets placed here give good results like the nectar that nourishes.
Visha nadi	18.40 - 19.33 deg Aries Planets placed here can bring situations which one does not like dealing with.

Auspicious and inauspicious table -

Auspicious	Inauspicious
<u>Activities</u> Good for all creative activities, procreation, endings and finishing projects, gardening, serving others, dealing with children and self-discipline and fasting.	<u>Activities</u> Not good for travel or starting any new projects.

Days	Days
Fridays - only when it falls on the 1st, 2nd, 6th, 7th, 11th or 12th lunar day.	Sundays - only when it falls on the 3rd, 4th, 8th, 9th, 13th or 14th lunar day. Mondays - only when it falls on the 6th, 7th or 11th lunar day. Wednesdays- only when it falls on the 2nd, 3rd, 7th, 8th, or 9th lunar day. Saturdays - only when it falls on the 3rd, 7th, 9th, or 11th lunar day.

Compatibility table -

Bharani	Compatible with
Sexual compatibility Yoni animal	Bharani - Female elephant - compatible with - Male elephant - Revati
Sign compatibility	Aries - Pada 1 - Leo and Sagittarius.
Nakshatra compatibility	Purva Phalguni and Purva Ashadha.
Lunar day compatibility	Chaturthi - 4th lunar day
Day compatibility	Tuesday and Friday
Colour compatibility	Red and all pastel colours.
Numerological compatibility	6 and 9 - and all numbers that add up to make 6 and 9.
Sound compatibility	Mars - guttural sounds - ka, kha, ga, gha, kna Venus - palatal sounds - cha, ccha, ja, jha, nga

Sign Lord and Nakshatra Lord - Mars and Venus.

Mars - as described earlier.

Venus - The Venusian beauty lies in the harmonious and balanced features of the face and body that make the natives irresistibly attractive. They have a very fine sense of aesthetics and have the talent of appreciating and creating beauty in all art forms - through acting, directing films, singing, painting, drawing, architecture, writing, poetry, graphic designing, cooking, tailoring, gardening, and decorating.

They love beauty and truth and are very tuned to their senses. They enjoy all forms of pleasurable indulgence, whether it's through food, sex, art or music, it fuels their passion to create beauty and to please beauty. Venus involves indulgence of the senses, and they like surrounding themselves with beautiful things. However, at a deeper level, they understand that true beauty lies in the harmonious quality and not the outer covering.

Venus-ruled people have a very keen sense of form and balance. They don't like to overdo things. For instance, they like to dress up in clothes that are simple and comfortable. For them, their luxury and fashion statement is comfort. At home they will prefer to have a flower arrangement with real flowers rather than with artificial flowers, or they will love spending time in the garden or going for holidays where they can be close to nature. The beneficence of Venus provides material comforts, enjoyments and pleasures. Its ultimate intention is to help you experience the highest level of pleasure, enjoyment, ease and relaxation by letting go of the transitory worldly desires and seeking the eternity of our divine self, which is - *'Sat Chit Ananda,'* - the eternal truth, which is fully aware and is always in a state of bliss.

Inference

In Bharani, the energy of masculine Mars and feminine Venus form a very well-balanced combination which makes them very complete in their approach to life. They have the determination and ambition to follow their dreams and the aesthetic sense and receptivity to understand deeper philosophies.

Quality - Chara - as described earlier and Ugra.

Ugra - fierce

The ugra quality signifies the rising of energy. For the energy to rise, it needs to have a strong, fierce and volatile nature. This becomes a tremendous possibility and choice - either to rise above the difficulties or to be defeated or crushed by them.

Those who are born with Bharani as an Ascendent, or Sun or Moon in Bharani, have a fierce and upward rising energy that can pierce through all odds. Just as a firecracker shoots out a lightning blaze as soon as it is lit by a matchstick, similarly, they can erupt into a volcano of activity when they are motivated or inspired by someone or some cause.

On the negative side, they could let out their anger or frustration in the form of physical aggression or abusive language. That's why it's very important for them to channel the storehouse of excessive energy within them in a positive way by keeping themselves physically active - like going to the gym regularly, bicycle riding, jogging, outdoor games, swimming and yogic exercises. This will help them to stay healthy and balanced.

Element, motivation, triguna and tridosha - as described earlier.

Chakras - Muladhara - as described earlier.

Swadhisthana

The energy of Bharani resonates with the Swadhisthana chakra.

Venus, the lord of Bharani, signifies love, harmony, balance and beauty. The Vedic name for Venus is Shukra. In Ayurveda, Shukra means both the male semen and the female egg, as they contain the essence of all of the other dhatus (tissues) of the body. Shukra is the 7th and final dhatu and contains the essence of all other dhatus. The word Shukra means - the essence of something, bright, pure, and radiant.

Chakra	Planets	Symbol	Element	Sound	Colour	Petals	Glands
Swadhisthana	Venus	Downward facing triangle	Water	Vam	Orange	6	Ovaries and prostate gland

Swa means self, and adhishtana means to be established. It's also called the sacral chakra and is located 2 inches above Muladhara.

Sadhguru explains that when the energies are dominant here, one will be a pleasure seeker. This does not necessarily mean sex, but someone who wants to enjoy the world. This person lives a little more intensely than the one who is living just for food and sleep. This chakra gets blocked by fear and opening this chakra gives desire, creativity and confidence.

It has 6 petals, which represent the 6 basic qualities on the emotional level - that arise from the ego - desire, pride, anger, hatred, jealousy and cruelty. Physically, it represents the shata rasa - the 6 tastes - sweet, sour, pungent, astringent and bitter.

As described earlier, the symbol of a downward-facing triangle shows the downward movement of energy.

In a standing posture, the centre of gravity is normally located in front of your sacrum, which is where swadhisthana- the sacral chakra is located. The sacral bone region is the lower spine - the pelvic area, where the reproductive organs are located. It is considered the centre of our private self and the centre of pleasure.

When this chakra is balanced, the person radiates warmth and is able to speak openly about emotions. A healthy Swadhisthana brings a powerful and natural feeling of intimacy. One will be joyful, passionate, sensual, connected to their feelings and emotionally stable.

On the other hand, misuse of sexual energy or overindulgence can block the energies and cause health issues. One can feel out of balance, experience emotional instability, lack of confidence, fear of change, sexual dysfunction, depression, or addictions.

Healing -

The energies blocked at swadhisthana can be released by -

- Chanting the mantra Vam while visualising a bright orange colour at the point of swadhisthana chakra in the pelvic region.

- Doing Surya Namaskar - sun salutations for at least 12 cycles. The yogic practises should be done only after learning properly from a hatha yoga teacher.

- Doing fun activities like dancing, cycling, walking or any outdoor activities.

- Meditation - <u>breath watch</u> helps to ease the whole mind-body system and balance the chakras. You can practice this simple yet very effective technique by following these steps - sit comfortably, close your eyes, be aware of your incoming and outgoing breath, just let it flow naturally, and simply become aware of your breath and the thoughts that are passing by. Every time you get carried away by a thought, bring your attention back to your breath. Slowly, you will begin to relax into the zone of comfort and ease, where the mind and body begin to heal.

- Ayurveda recommends <u>abdominal breathing</u> which helps to increase the flow of oxygen and nutrients to all the cells in the body. It also relaxes the muscle spasms, tension and stress in the body. Initially you can start by placing one hand on your chest and the other on the abdomen. When you take a deep breath, you should feel the hand on your abdomen rise higher than the hand on your chest. With practice, you can breathe deeply without placing your hands on the chest and the abdomen. Practising abdominal breathing for 5 to 10 at least once a day on a somewhat empty stomach will help you to relax and feel more energised.

- In order to have healthy shukra dhatu, the primary element that must be consumed is water. Water is the primary nourishment of the body and of the dhatus, and shukra is its most refined form. Foods that have a high shukra potential are unctuous (slimy) - and include milk, meat juice, ghee, and nuts.

- Practising yogic asanas, pranayama meditation, and less sexual activity helps to enhance the Shukra in our body because excessive indulgence in sexual pleasures drains vital energy since it requires high levels of Shukra energy.

<u>Inference</u>

Bharani is placed in Aries, and the nakshatra Lord is Venus. Therefore, it carries the energies of both Mars and Venus. Muladhara and Swadhisthana chakras resonate with the intense quality of Bharani.

Muladhara, the root energy gives the Bharani natives a strong and healthy physical constitution, and Swadhisthana gives them the passionate vigour of both masculine and feminine aspects.

This makes them passionate lovers, adventurous romantics, fearless opponents, defenders of justice, tough administrators, courageous comrades, determined individuals, magnetic personalities and benevolent friends. When the chakras are balanced, they have fantastic health and enjoy everything they do in life, but when the energies are imbalanced, there can be a lack of vitality and ill health because of overindulgence.

Shakti - <u>Apabharani Shakti - the power to take things away with water.</u>

Bharani natives will always benefit from falling back on their inner strength during times of trouble. They have immense emotional strength and can contain a lot in them, more than they ever have realised. But they need to find an outlet for these intense emotions, and need to channel them into a creative process.

The best remedy for them would then be to pen their thoughts and feelings or paint, draw, sing, dance, go for long walks, be emotional support for others, help children and women in need, help someone who needs a water source, or offer water to the thirsty. You already have this special and enduring innate quality in you to take care and bear the pain of the other, to help them sail through a difficult time. Bharani natives will be able to do this very easily and naturally because they have a deep, profound understanding of their own pain. You will find that whenever you make time to share the pain of another, your own situations improve.

Symbolic Signification

Aries - Ram - as described earlier.

Bharani - Yoni - womb and an elephant.

Yoni

The womb is a noble organ in the female body that houses and nourishes a human being in it's most crucial, transformative, vulnerable and sacred time in the development of the body - when the soul comes into the physical form.

From the time the chosen sperm (seed) has reached the egg and through the entire time of 9 months in the womb. The foetus is dependent on the mother for nutrition, which comes through the umbilical cord. The umbilical fluid (apa - Sanskrit name for water) keeps the foetus safe, protected and cushioned. When the baby is born after enduring the labour pains, the umbilical cord is cut. For the next cycle of life to happen, the previous one has to be cut. These huge transformations are engineered and guided by nature for a being to be born into a physical form.

Inference

The symbol of Bharani is the yoni (womb). Bharani natives feel pain more deeply than others. Just as a pregnant woman has been gifted with endurance and courage to go through the period of pregnancy and labour pains to deliver a baby, but on seeing the face of the baby, she forgets all her pain. Likewise, they have tremendous tolerance hidden in them to go through the tough times in life. They also have it in them to create something beautiful out of the intense pain that they might have to endure at some point in their lives.

This also signifies that to create something truly significant or to achieve success in any of their endeavours, they have to go into the cocoon of hard work for a substantial amount of time. It could involve sitting in the office or at home in one room and working on the computer or any other project for a long period of time at a stretch.

Women who are born with Ascendant, Sun or Moon in Bharani might have a difficult pregnancy if the 5th house is afflicted with Saturn, Mars, Rahu or Ketu conjunction or aspect. Praying to Maha Kali Devi or Goddess Durga will be a helpful remedy. However, the placement of other planets should also be seen, which could reduce or nullify the negative impact, also D 7 should be looked at for children and D 9 for the influence of these planets after the age of 30.

Elephant

Elephants are the largest existing land animals, descendants of the mammoths from the time of the ice age. They are found in tropical climates of Asia and Africa. Distinctive features of all elephants are their long trunk, tusks, large ear flaps and massive legs. They have thick, tough skin. Mud baths and mud spray acts like sunscreen protection for their skin and keeps them cool.

An elephant's trunk is the fusion of the nose and upper lip and is used for multiple purposes - breathing, bringing food and water to the mouth, grasping objects, spraying water or mud on their bodies, and making trumpet sounds. When underwater they use their trunk as a snorkel, for taking in air from the surface.

Their tusks serve both as weapons and as tools for moving objects and digging. The large ear flaps assist in maintaining a constant body temperature as well as in communication. The pillar-like legs carry their great weight. They are herbivores and coexist peacefully with other animals unless threatened.

They are considered to be keystone species due to their impact on their environments. Other animals tend to keep their distance from elephants, except for their predators, lions, tigers, hyenas, and wild dogs, which usually target only young elephant calves.

Elephants are a matriarchal society which has multiple family groups. They come together to socialise. Female elephants tend to live in family groups, which can consist of one female with her calves or several related females with their offspring. These groups do not include the male elephant bulls and are usually led by the oldest female elephant. Calves are the centre of attention in their family groups and rely on their mothers for about 3 years. Male elephants leave their family groups when they reach puberty and may live alone or with other males. Adult bulls mostly interact with family groups when looking for a mate.

Elephants can live up to 70 years in the wild. They communicate by touch, sight, smell, and sound. They use infrasound waves to communicate over long distances. Elephants appear to have self-awareness and empathy for dying and dead family members.

Interesting facts

- An elephant never forgets, their long memory recall power is an evolutionary gift that has helped them to survive.

- Elephants see better in dim light but not in bright light.

- They can, like all mammals, raise or lower their core body temperature by a few degrees in response to extreme environmental conditions.

- They take mud baths to stay cool in the tropical heat.

- They fan their large ear flaps to cool down in the tropical heat.

- They can hear very low frequencies (subsonic waves) from long distances, which are inaudible to the human ear.

- They use their tusks for digging for - water, salt and roots, for marking trees and clearing paths. When attacked, the tusks are used to defend and protect the vitally important trunk.

- They can stand still for long periods of time without using much energy.

- They cannot rotate their front legs. That's why they can only move forward or backwards but cannot jump or gallop. They can only walk or walk faster (it appears like running).

- Their circular feet have cushion pads which help to distribute their body weight. When they walk, the cushion pads expand and contract, reducing the pain and noise of the heavy body.

- Elephants have good stamina, walk for long hours, and swim for up to 6 hours.

- An elephant has a pouch in his or her throat where it can store water.

- <u>Smart elephants -</u> A study conducted in 2006 reported that besides humans, elephants, dolphins and apes are the only mammals that can recognise their reflection in the mirror.

<u>Inference</u>

Bharani natives will have the qualities of both - the agility of a Ram and the sturdiness of an elephant. Physically, they will have a heavier physique, good height, with strong stout limbs. They will have long noses and a good set of teeth, which will last longer into ripe old age. They will have smaller eyes and will wear glasses at some point in their life, especially for reading. They feel more comfortable in the coolness of the dim light whereas bright light dazzles and compromises their vision.

They have a special gift of listening to the unheard sounds, the unspoken words, the unstruck music on the strings of the guitar and the sound of the silence. They can tap into this special sense if they pay a little attention and listen to their inner rhythm.

To cool down in the heat of the tropical weather, they need to take showers and baths more often than others. Ayurvedic mud therapies will greatly enhance the texture and tone of their skin. They have a special ability to dig out the right Ayurvedic roots and salts as needed for their health. They know exactly where to find the right source of food or drinks they need and will instinctively know and select the right food at the grocery store.

They are also very good at surviving through long periods of fasting and will prefer to be vegetarians. They are good at multitasking, have great stamina and can stand for long hours to finish the job on hand. The feminine instinct of protecting their young, their family, and their clan is very strong in both male and female Bharani natives.

The famous statement - *'An elephant never forgets,'* holds true.

They never forget - this is a great asset for them, and they can recall things even after many years, while others around them would have long forgotten about a particular incident. They are also very good at remembering faces. Once they have seen someone, they will not forget that face (provided they have paid attention to that person).

When they lose their near or dear ones, the pain goes deep, and they genuinely grieve for them. During times of crisis, they will take on the role and responsibility of the head of the family even though they might be the youngest born.

They can lead their family to greener pastures of wealth and comfort, of sustenance and well-being, with the same ease - as a female elephant would lead its herd. The others in the family may doubt or become apprehensive in challenging times, but they will prod along with trust in their strength and love in their heart. Therefore, tough times will never deter them. They may appear anxious on the surface, but within themselves, they know they are capable of handling the situation. They know how to clear the obstructions in the path during times of trouble. They should rely on their own memory, how they dealt with a similar kind of situation in the past. That is the key to their survival now and again or even again. They usually live up to a good old age because they never fail to learn from their mistakes. They are not likely to make the same blunder twice. They charter their path to success through endurance and strength and never forget what they have once learnt.

Mythology

Deity - Yama

Yamraj, the God of death.

The story of Yamraj is narrated in Vishnu Purana, as previously seen in the story of Ashwini; Yama and Yami were the firstborn children of Surya Dev (sun God) and his wife Sanjana. Yami, the sister, was attracted to her brother Yama and wanted to have children with him, but Yama refused. He became the first mortal to die. After he died, Yami was very sad and wouldn't stop crying. Gods then created the darkness of the night so that Yami could rest and sleep. She was able to let go of the pain and flowed as river Yamuna on earth.

This shows that Yama had a great sense of discipline and would not do anything wrong, no matter how great the temptation was or what consequence he would have to face. His father

Surya, was very pleased and appreciative about his son and appointed him as the God of death and justice.

Yama and Shani

Shani (Saturn) and Yama (God of death) do not get along. Shani feels that Chaya, his mum, had to leave because of Yama. While Yama is righteous and law-abiding, Shani is a rebel who stands up for the weak. Yama looks at the scales of justice after death, while Shani balances the scales of justice while we are living. He does this by bringing forth the challenges in this life. Both Shani and Yama are sons of Surya Dev (Sun God) and stand for justice.

Other names of Yamraj are,

Dharma raja - The lord of justice, lokapala - the guardian of all directions. He rules the south direction in particular. Pitri raja - the lord of ancestors and Kala - time. Yamraj has an assistant called Chitragupt, which means the hidden picture. His job is to keep a record of all the good and bad deeds done. This shows that we are our own witness to all we think, feel or do. He rides a water buffalo and holds a stick. Which represents the steady flow of time and the lessons we have to learn in life.

The gayatri mantra

ॐ सूर्यपुत्राय विद्महे महाकालय धीमहि तन्नो यमः प्रचोदयात्

"Om Surya putraya Vidmahe Maha Kalaya Dheemahi Thanno Yamaha Prachodayath."

Meaning -

Om, Let me meditate on the son of the Sun God, Oh, great Lord of time, give me higher intellect, And let the God of death illuminate my mind.

Chanting this mantra can give courage and bring clarity to Bharani natives during times of distress.

From the yogic perspective, life and death are the play of time (Kala). They are 2 sides of the same coin, are intertwined. In life, death exists, and from death sprouts new life. Every inhalation is life, and every exhalation is death.

Living beyond death

Long ago, in the forest, there lived Rishi Mrikandu (seer) and his wife Marudhvati. For many years, they did not have any children, so they Prayed to Lord Shiva. After 18 long years, Lord Shiva was pleased with their austerities and asked them to choose between a dull-witted son who would live long or a very intelligent son who would only live up to 16 years. Without hesitation, they chose a clever son. They were blessed with a son whom they named Markandeya. He mastered the Vedas and scriptures in a very short time and was a devotee of Shiva. However, time seemed to be going very fast and soon their son would be 16 years old. This thought worried the parents a lot. When his parents told him the story of his birth, Markandeya smiled and said, "Don't worry, I will not die so soon. I will win over death."

Markandeya started his penance and prayed to Shiva and Shakti. When the time of death came near, he hugged the Shiva lingam and chanted the mrityunjaya mantra. Yama could not take his soul away because he was being protected by Shiva and Shakti. He later went on to write Markandeya Purana, one of the 18 major texts of Hinduism. It talks about Shiva, Vishnu and Devi Shakti. Shiva is the unmanifest, and Shakti is the manifested creation. This is the space-time concept at play.

Nachiketa and Yamraj

This is a story from Kuto Upanishad (an Ancient text from the 9th century BC). It's a story of a young boy who went to the gate of death and waited there for 3 days.

There was once a young 12-year-old Brahmin boy called Nachiketa, son of Sage Vajashravas. His father loved doing rituals and giving offerings for materialistic gains. Nachiketa questioned his father and asked why he was giving old cows as a donation. We are supposed to offer the best of what we have. He further asked his father if he loved him the most. Vajashravas said, "Of course, my son, you are the most dear to me." Nachiketa said then it would be most appropriate to offer me as a sacrifice in the yagna (sacred fire ritual). His father did not know how to best answer his son's righteous question, so he kept quiet. When Nachiketa repeatedly asked the same question, in his annoyance, he said, "I offer you Yamarāja (the Lord of death)."

Nachiketa died and went to the gates of heaven only to find that Yamaraja was not there. After 3 days, Yamarāja came and found the little boy waiting at the gate. The little boy had not had food or water for 3 days. On seeing Nachiketa, Yamarāja said, "I was not expecting you since it is not yet your time to come." Nachiketa explained the whole sequence of events. Yamarāja was pleased with the child's understanding of the righteous way of living. So he granted Nachiketa 3 boons, and he could ask for any 3 things. These were his 3 wishes -

<u>1st wish</u> - He asked that when he goes back, his father should not be angry and should receive him lovingly. Yamarāja happily granted his first wish.

<u>2nd wish</u> - He asked about the yagna (fire rituals) that would open the gates to heaven. Because he didn't want to have to wait again the next time he came. Yamarāja readily fulfilled his second wish as well.

<u>3rd wish</u> - He asked about knowing the secret of immortality.

Yamarāja was very reluctant to grant his 3rd wish. He tempted Nachiketa into having all the comforts of an earthly plane. This was also a test for Nachiketa, if he was really worthy of receiving the higher knowledge. Nachiketa stood unwavering, and Yamarāja began to explain.

The secret of immortality -

Doing good is one thing, and doing pleasant things is another. Both these desires may prompt the same action, but the consequence or the result is based on the intent behind the action. For example, offering a donation, if done with the intention of getting more wealth, becomes an action done to get pleasant results, which then tangles one in more karmic bondage - and a series of desires that follow this action. On the other hand a selfless offering done for the well-being of another, without expecting anything in return, becomes a liberating action and not an action of bondage. The same action of donation - karma (action) becomes dharma (righteous action) because of the chosen intention.

Therefore, the wise will choose righteous actions over selfish actions and thus untangle their karmic bondages. Because it's through these bondages that we continue to come back again and again into the cycle of birth and death. Birth and death are only of the physical body. The consciousness is never born and, therefore, never dies. It's omnipresent, all-pervading and eternal.

This pure consciousness is the immortal aspect, which is the essence of all beings. When we can become capable of experiencing the divine source within at a conscious level, we have touched the immortal aspect that lies within us. Nachiketa thanked Yamaraja for this profound wisdom and came back to earth and lived many happy years.

Inference

In Sanskrit, the word <u>yam</u> means to restrain or stop, that's why the Lord of death is named yamraj, because he ends the cycle of breath. In this context, Bharani is called the <u>star of restraint</u>. In Sanskrit language, the word Kala signifies both death and time. At the subconscious level, Bharani natives have the desire to stay connected to the energy of the other dimensions, because they come from the realm of the ancestors.

The deity of Bharani is Lord Yamraj - who is also called Dharamraja. He is the god of death and justice and is responsible for dispensing the law of reward and punishment. In Bharani natives, the sense of justice is very strong because here the sense of righteousness is being reinforced by the law-abiding Yama -the god of death.

They will actively stand up for causes that fight for justice like - racism, discrimination, cruelty against animals, equality and equal job opportunities for women, or religious or social equality issues.

Not all Bharani natives will join a big movement or an organisation to fight for justice. Essentially, their sense of righteousness is so strong that even in their daily routine, they will not put up with any kind of injustice done to them or to anyone around them.

Bharani natives feel strongly for justice. They can come across as harsh or rude, especially if they see injustice being done and will not be afraid of exposing the person if something wrong is being done. They have a very practical approach, will be disciplined, and know how to restrain themselves where needed.

Bharani natives have the inherent know-how of rejuvenation and can bounce back from death-like situations. They may not be consciously aware of it, but they can access this hidden capability through meditation and spiritual practices. At some point in their life, they have to deal with the death of their close family member or their friend, which will have a deep impact on them. They come out stronger from every situation where they have to give up everything and start again from scratch. It's like dying to the previous way of life and being born again into a new lifestyle.

Bharani padas

13.20 - 26.40 degrees Aries

Padas	Degrees
1	13.20 - 16.40
2	16.40 - 20
3	20 - 23.20
4	23.20 - 26.40

Pada 1

13.20 - 16.40 deg Aries , Navamsha -Leo (Lord - Sun)

Rashi Lord - Mars and Nakshatra Lord - Venus

Those who are born with their Ascendant, Sun or Moon in this Pada will have the energy of Mars, Venus and Sun. They will be honest, fearless, courageous, straightforward, creative, intelligent, passionate and generous. On the other hand, they can also be proud and self-centred and will not be afraid to say things straight in the face. They will face challenges head-on.

They will be ambitious about gaining respect in society. Honour and prestige will be their underlying motivation behind all actions. They can be stubborn, my way or highway attitude. They will not like taking orders from anyone but will order everyone around. They can be controlling and authoritative. They will have a pitta constitution and may have red eyes. Physical exercises, swimming or hatha yoga, will help them greatly to work out their active energy.

For example, the 1st Pada of Bharani in the 3rd house, their sibling will be courageous and intelligent and might have a good, prestigious job in the government.

Careers-

Government jobs, judges, gynaecologists, builders, managers, politicians, graphic designers, IT consultants, actors, dancers, mortuary owners, hatha yoga teachers or practitioners, firefighters, lifeguards, athletes, gym trainers, sportsmen or sportswomen, horse trainers, garage owners, motorbike racers and businessmen.

Pada 2

16.40 - 20 deg Aries, Navamsha - Virgo (Lord - Mercury)

Rashi Lord - Mars and Nakshatra Lord - Venus

Mars, Venus and Mercury's energy will play in the 2nd Pada. They will be most happy and will be able to offer their best when they are leading or giving instructions to others. Since Saturn is debilitated here, they will not be the ones who can work under someone or be subservient in their job. Being their own boss will be the best career choice for them. This combination will also make them impatient and would like to invest their time and energy where they can get a quick turn over. Perseverance, endurance and patience are definitely not their strong points.

They will be courageous and hard-working and will do the job diligently. They will be talkative and will love interacting with the opposite sex. This pada will bring wealth and materialistic comforts.

For example, the 2nd Pada of Bharani in the 5th house will be very creative and romantic. Their children, students or followers will be motivated by their ingenuity and words of encouragement.

Careers

IT professionals, supervisors, managers, judges, salesmen or women, actors, dancers, singers, teachers, lawyers, athletes, sportsmen or sportswomen and writers.

Pada 3

20 - 20.23 deg Aries, Navamsha - Libra (Lord- Venus)

Rashi Lord - Mars and Nakshatra Lord - Venus

Mars and double Venus energy here will make the natives very artistic and they will have a wonderful sense of aesthetics. It's a Pushkar navamsa, which means desires will be fulfilled. Natives will be attracted to the opposite sex and can have more than one partner.

They will have a comfortable and luxurious lifestyle because of the beneficial effect of Venus and the ambition and drive of Mars.

This is a good combination that gives results and brings comfort and conveniences especially during Venus dasha. They will have the willpower of Mars and the sweetness of Venus which is a great combination for steering their way to success. On the negative side, it can make them proud, which can affect their relationships, especially after the age of 30, because Venus can become a functional malefic only if one becomes careless or indulgent. For example, the 3rd Pada of Bharani in the 2nd house will have a good source of income. However, as they get older, they may face some relationship problems because of their way of speaking.

Careers

Florists, fashion designers, interior designers, architects, tailors, film directors, actors, artists, dancers, musicians, IT professionals, YouTubers, supervisors, managers and writers.

Pada 4

20.23 - 26.40 deg Aries, Navamsha - Scorpio (Lord - Mars)

Rashi Lord - Mars and Nakshatra Lord - Venus

Venus and the double effect of Mars will give an explosive and intense energy. It's a Pushkar bhaga, and Yoga Tara Pada - any planets placed here will give good and strong results during its dasha. Natives will have tremendous drive and energy to get things done. They will be interested in exploring, adventure sports, mountain climbing, martial arts, hatha yoga and athletics. Basically, all activities that require physical stamina will be their forte. The martial energy will be fired by the passionate Venus, which will make them very ambitious and motivated.

They will direct their passion and energy towards pursuits of beauty and harmony. They need to calm down the dynamic Mars energies through physical and mental activities. A good physical workout at the gym brings ease and relaxation to the mind and body. They need to follow their exercise routine more diligently than others. Otherwise, the danger lies in sudden volcanic eruptions of anger or frustration that can make them lose their placid mystique. If they feel overwhelmed by aggression - active physical workout is the best and expedient remedy for them.

For example, in the 4th Pada of Bharani in the 7th house, they will seek a partner or a spouse who is intelligent, dedicated, focused, intense and secretive - because these are the qualities that reflect their inner need.

Careers-

Engineers, researchers, archaeologists, scientists, doctors, surgeons, army officers, policemen, lawyers, detectives, judges, midwives, managers, athletes, sportsmen or sportswomen, gym trainers, coast guards and firefighters.

The effect of planets

Bharani - Aries	Planets that get affected
Functional Benefic - give good results during their dasha.	Sun, Moon and Mars
Functional Malefic - can give problems during their dasha.	Mercury, Rahu and Ketu

Functional Neutral	Moon, Jupiter and Saturn
Kendra -Adi pati dosha - can give problems in relationships.	Venus

Bharani Ascendant

Bharani natives will usually have smaller or medium-sized eyes, long noses and long straight hair. They will be tall, slim and well-built and will have an erect and straight posture. They will have a big, built and well-formed body. They will have a prominent forehead and an intoxicating smile.

They will feel things at a deeper level and will be hard-working and disciplined. They are deeply spiritual and sexually intense. They will go through situations that bring intense transformations in their life. They will always stand up for any injustice happening around them. They have tremendous courage and strength to go through tough times with grace. They will have tolerance and self-restraint.

Bharani natives will experience transformations in relationships.

Meditating and reflecting on things and situations will help to heal. They can get stuck with the emotions of past events, having long baths and showers, letting go of the past pain and flowing with the present will help them greatly. Drinking water and staying hydrated will be a great healing therapy for them as well.

Bharani natives have the power to take things away just as the strong flow of water washes away or destroys everything that comes in its path, it's unstoppable.

The nature of this fierce energy enables them to bear and nourish another life in its womb. This means that both men and women born in this nakshatra have a tremendous ability to stay strong in the face of any hardships. They have an exceptional ability and strength to bear the joys, sorrows and pain of others within them.

Sun in Bharani

The Sun placed in Bharani will have the flair of Mars and Venus.

It will make the native confident, generous, passionate and proud.

They will be positive, enthusiastic and straightforward about things. They don't mind going through the extra trouble for themselves or for the other if they are convinced it's for a just cause. They will give more than needed of their love, money, time, loyalty and everything. When it comes to themselves, they tend to bring on extra trouble that brings on problems where none would exist if the situation was left alone. *'Leave it alone'* seems like silly advice to them. For them, it's not good enough when a little more effort can give excellent results. But they sometimes don't realise that 'well enough' could have been made worse by their over-enthusiasm!!

For example, the Sun in Bharani in the 1st house (Ascendent), makes a raja yoga and Pancha mahapurusha yoga (great human being), which means they will have the strength and ability to overcome obstacles and rise above the difficulties through their determination. They will have an authoritative look, will have brown eyes and will be prone to baldness.

Sun is exalted in the 1st house, especially between 8 - 12 deg. It will give strong and best results. During the dasha of the Sun, the natives will rise to a position of authority. Sun being the 5th lord in the 1st house, the qualities of the 5th house will be prominent in the natives. They will be intelligent creative, will have a good education and will love children.

However if the sun is aspected or conjunct Saturn, Mars, Rahu or Ketu, this will dilute the effect of the yogas formed. When situations don't happen as planned, they can become short-tempered, impatient, arrogant, demanding and aggressive.

Moon in Bharani

This is a good combination which brings the energy of the Moon, Mars and Venus. One will be emotionally passionate and will have a love for fine things in life. Every nakshatra and rashi has a strength that can be turned into a weakness. Both possibilities always exist. We must always bear in mind that it's about how we deal with situations that determine the outcome and not the situation alone.

"I am not what happened to me, I am what I choose to become." - Carl Jung

The positive side of Mars will be courage, and the negative will be impulsiveness. The lunar effect of the moon in Bharani can turn from nurturing and caring into attachment and possessiveness.

The sensitivity of the moon makes them very receptive, and for them, love is the basis of all existence, and they do not know any other way to be. With time Bharani natives will mature into handling their emotions well. On the negative side, they can become selfish and egoistic. The positive side is their heart-tugging innocence, wonder, faith and raw courage.

For example, the Moon in Bharani in the 12th house will travel to foreign lands many times for work or holidays because the moon represents emotions, fluctuations and travel. Their younger sibling will find success in a foreign land because the moon is the lord of the 3rd house of Cancer - sitting in the 12th house of foreign lands.

The poetry of Bha- Rani

Bha - the fullness of the womb

Rani - the queen of creation, a boon

Venus and Mars, my passion and strength,

Granted an enduring bequeath,

Yama- the Lord of justice and death,

No loss, no fear hath,

My guiding deity - the giver and taker of my life breath.

Ram, the mountain sheep,

Shure footed on the slope steep.

On the heights dizzy, seemingly risky,

There I stand, confident, not fuzzy.

Fiery heat and waters cool

Together the tangible they rule.

Responsibility and care

With ancestral flare

Courage and integrity rare

Of strife or dare

Mars and Venus - a pair of intensity

Can help cross bridges, relentlessly

In love and war - is it all fair!

Remedies

- <u>Das Maha Vidya -</u> Devi Bagalamukhi - as described earlier.

<u>Devi Kamala -</u> Venus

Goddess Kamala is said to be the most benign and benevolent form of Devi Kali because she is the tantric form of Goddess Lakshmi, who is the giver of all kinds of physical and spiritual wealth and prosperity.

She is associated with Venus and is the giver of all comforts, luxuries and vehicles, and helps to have harmonious relationships.

It is believed that worshipping Kamala Devi grants divine blessings, which help to destroy poverty in every form. Her grace can also eradicate sorrow, failure, childlessness, misfortune and the malefic effects of planet Venus.

If Venus is weak in the birth chart, has a low Shadbala score, is very old, nearing 30 degrees, or an infant in the early 0-1 degree, or is inflicted by Mars, Saturn, Rahu or Ketu, it can cause problems in relationships or physical issues related to the reproductive system. If Venus is placed in Cancer, Leo or Virgo, can also give these problems. Men may have a low sperm count, and women may have menstrual problems. However, the D 7 chart for children and the

D 9 chart for adulthood should also be checked carefully before making any such predictions.

Remedies -

- The best remedy is to have harmonious relationships and create things of beauty that give joy to all.

- Offering her lotus flowers or white hibiscus flowers, lilies, or Pomegranate fruit on Fridays or days when the Moon is transiting over natal Venus will help to get the beneficence of Venus.

- Chanting her mantra 108 times, keeping her yantra and image in front, can help to reduce the negative effects of afflicted Venus. It is recommended to chant her mantra for 6 consecutive Fridays to reap the effects. Mantras of Devi Kamala - "*Hasauh Jagatprayutai Swaha*" and "*Om Shreem.*"

Other remedies

- The best remedy is to create something unique and new with your personal touch because it will activate the energies of Venus, which is a planet that gives abundance.

- Worship Devi Kali or Kalabhairava (a fierce form of Shiva), who is the lord of time and space.

- Can donate white clothes on Friday (Venus Day).

- Connecting to Mother Earth, gardening, grounding- walking barefoot or sitting on the ground will help to balance and stabilise the panchabhuta (5 elements) in the body and bring good health.

- Wearing a 6 mukhi rudraksha will help to improve relationships.

- Dark colours are good for Bharani natives.

- The best remedy is to do yogic practises, meditation, pranayama and hatha yoga. This will calm the turbulent emotions.

- Chant the Mrityunjaya mantra 108 times on a Tuesday or a Friday. It helps to tune into the healing force that is always there within us.

    "Om tryambkam yajamahe, sugandhim pushti vardhanam,

    urvarukamiva bandhanan, mrityu mukshiya mamritat."

- Chant Bharani nakshatra mantra 108 times when the moon is transiting Bharani nakshatra. This will help to tune into the nakshatra energy.

    "Om im iem Bharani nakshatraye namah."

- Colour an elephant in the colour of the planet placed in Bharani and place it in the direction of the desired result.

Here is the table of the Vastu directions. This remedy can be used for any planet that is afflicted in the birth chart. For example, suppose Jupiter has Low degrees and is placed in Aries in Bharani. In that case, you can colour a yellow elephant and place it in the west direction if you are looking for fulfilment of a certain desire. You can place it on a Thursday for 3 days in the west because Jupiter rules number 3.

Vastu directions

Direction	Significance
North	Gain of wealth
North east	Good health
East	Social benefits
South east	Cash flow, security
South	Fame
South west	Relationships
West	Fulfilment of desires
North west	Government and bank support

Example

Bharani Ascendant

Anita - My sister's friend.

Born on 6th May 1977, 5;25 am, Ludhiana, Punjab, India.

She works as a supervisor at a clothes manufacturing factory. They stay upstairs, and on the ground floor, they make T-shirts wholesale. She is a very hard-working and practical person, ready to work and get things sorted quickly and efficiently. She has a little temple at home and is religious-minded. She goes out of her way to make time for her friends and never shies away from work.

Analysis -

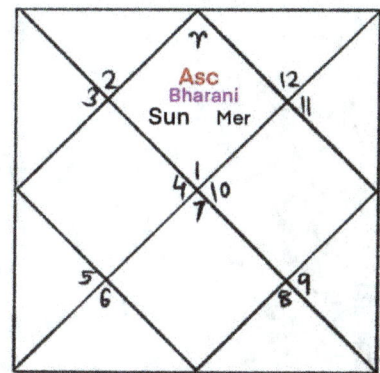 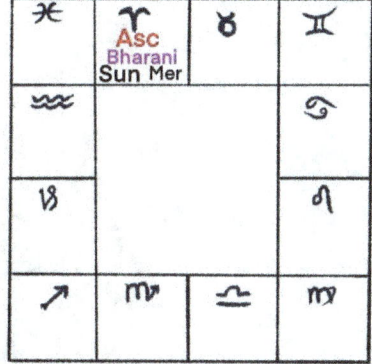

She is an Aries Ascendent in Bharani - Mercury is in Bharani Pada 1 and Sun in Pada 3. This makes Bhuda Aditya yoga - she is an intelligent, creative and confident person and has fantastic management skills.

The Lord of Bharani is Venus, which gives her feminine beauty.

She is tall and slim and has lovely expressive eyes and a long nose. Her hair is lovely, thick and long, which she usually braids into a plait.

The deity of Bharani is Yama. At a young age, her mum passed away. Those were the tough years of her life. She has one younger brother. She is now married and has 2 lovely daughters. Her mother-in-law is a great support to her, and because of her support, she can go and work. She always says, "I have found my mum in my mum-in-law." It is very heartwarming to know such a lovely person and to see that she is settled well and happy in her family.

3
Krittika

Om aym oo u Krittika nakshatraye namah

Zodiac degrees	26.40 Aries to 10-degree Taurus Aries - 1st Pada Taurus - 2nd, 3rd and 4th padas.
Ruling planet	Aries - Mars and Taurus - Venus Kritika - Sun
Sanskrit name	Kritika means the one who cuts.
Astronomical name	Seen as 7 bright stars as clusters in the constellation of Pleiades.
Symbol	Aries - Ram, the mountain sheep and Taurus - Bull Kritika - Sword, razor, blade, or a knife
Element	Fire - Aries and Earth - Taurus
Deity	Agni Dev (fire God) Kartikeya (Son of Lord Shiva)
Quality	Chara - movable- Aries and Sthira - fixed- Taurus
Shakti	Dahana Shakti - power to burn and purify.
Cast	Brahmin (priest)
Gender	Male - Aries and Female - Taurus
Motivation	Dharma - righteousness - Aries Artha - to gather resources - Taurus
Triguna	Rajas - Aries and Tamas - Taurus

Tridosha	Pitta - Aries and Kapha - Taurus
Body parts	Head, hips and loins.
Direction	East and North
Month	2nd half of Ashwini month - till mid-October.
Bird	Peacock
Sound	a, ee, oo, aye
Tree	Cluster fig
Chakras	Muladhara - Mars, Swadhisthana - Venus and Manipura - Sun
Das Maha Vidya	Devi Bagalamukhi - Mars, Devi Kamala - Venus And Devi Matangi - Sun

Special degrees -

Yoga Tara	6 deg Taurus It's a point where the planet will show the strongest and sure results during its dasha.
Mulatrikona	4 - 20 deg Taurus -Mulatrikona of Moon When the Moon is placed at these degrees, it is happy and comfortable and gives good results and brings emotional fulfilment, especially during its dasha.
Exaltation	3 deg Taurus - Maximum exaltation of Moon. When the Moon is placed here, it will give wonderful results, the native will be very good-natured, friendly, kind and fortunate.
Pushkar amsha	1st and 4th pada Planets placed here will fruitify results like the blossoming of a flower.
Amrit nadi	8.40 - 9.33 deg Taurus Gives good results like the nectar that nourishes.
Visha nadi	3.20 - 4.13 deg Brings situations which one does not like dealing with.

Auspicious and inauspicious table -

Auspicious	Inauspicious
Activities Good for all purification activities and fire rituals, giving up old habits, for initiations, activities that require courage, leadership and executive activities, military activities, debates, cooking, cutting, chopping, sewing and shaving.	Activities Not good for socialising and diplomatic meetings, for relaxing and sailing.
Days Mondays - only when it falls on the 1st, 2nd, 3rd, 5th, 6th, 7th, 8th, 10th, 11th, 12th or 13th lunar day or full moon day of the waxing moon phase. Wednesdays - only when it falls on the 1st, 2nd, 3rd, 5th, 6th, 7th, 8th, 10th, 11th, 12th or 13th lunar day or full moon day of the waxing moon phase.	Days Sundays - only when it falls on the 5th lunar day. Mondays - only when it falls on the 6th, 7th or 11th lunar day. Thursdays - only when it falls on the 6th, 8th, 9th, 12th or 13th lunar day.

Compatibility table -

Kritika	Compatible with
Sexual compatibility Yoni animal	Kritika - Female goat - compatible with - Male goat - Ashwini
Sign compatibility	Aries - Leo and Sagittarius. Taurus - Virgo and Capricorn.
Nakshatra compatibility	Uttara Phalguni and Uttara Ashadha.
Lunar day compatibility	6th Lunar day, sashti tithi
Day compatibility	Sunday, Tuesday and Friday
Colour compatibility	Red, orange and all pastel colours.
Numerological compatibility	1, 6 and 9 - and all numbers that add up to make 1, 6 and 9.
Sound compatibility	Sun - all vowels - a, aa, e, ee, u, oo, ey, aye, o, ou, am, ah Mars - guttural sounds - ka, kha, ga, gha, kna Venus - palatal sounds - cha, ccha, ja, jha, nga

Sign Lord and Nakshatra Lord - <u>Mars, Venus and Sun.</u>

Mars and Venus - as described earlier.

Sun

Sun is the Lord of Kritika. Just as the Sun is the centre of our solar system and the source of all life on Earth. Vedic astrology considers the Sun as the king, father or soul of the zodiac because it's the initiator of life. The position of the Sun, Moon and Ascendant and the placement of their lords plays an important role in deciphering the natal birth chart accurately.

Sun signifies authority, confidence, generosity, honesty, intelligence, creativity, passion, royalty, nobility, pride, commanding persona, dominance and aloofness. It is also considered mildly cruel because of its unbearable heat.

Those who have a strong influence on the Sun in their birth chart are very warm-hearted, magnanimous, liberal, joyful, high-spirited people and are direct and honest in their dealings. They are very good at motivating others because they themselves are very enthusiastic and passionate about life. Their creative ideas and exuberant zeal easily rub on to others. They love leading, and because of their confidence, they are able to easily convince others.

Just as a just king never betrays the honour and trust of his kingdom, they will be very loyal towards their family. They will be protective of their loved ones and will always be looked up to for advice because they can confidently handle any kind of crisis in the family. On the other side, they can come across as self centred and elusive. They can be extravagant, and their sensitive ego can easily feel hurt when not appreciated or recognised for their generous actions. When out of their element, they can become irritable, demanding and bossy.

Inference

In the 1st Pada of Kritika, the influence of the Sun is combined with Mars, which makes them very confident, energetic, dominating, bossy, intelligent, creative, honest, straightforward, quick-tempered, proud and generous. In the 2nd, 3rd and 4th padas, the energies of the Sun and Venus make them more artistic and creative, and they have a very fine sense of balance and harmony. Their actions will be motivated by the desire to provide family comfort and security, and enough backup resources.

Quality - Chara - As described earlier and Sthira.

Sthira - fixed -

When born in Pada 2, 3 and 4 - Kritika natives will have more endurance and perseverance, a steady flow of resources, good health and grounding. They also are stubborn, determined, structured, fixed and practical in their approach. This helps them to achieve goals and succeed in their endeavours.

Elements -

Fire - As described earlier.

Earth -

Padas 2, 3 and 4 of Kritika fall in Taurus, which is governed by the earth element. In Sanskrit, the earth is called Prithvi. It is the 5th and the grossest of the 5 great elements (pancha mahabhutas). This is so because it has evolved out of the other 4 elements (ether, air, fire and water), containing the essence of these elements within itself.

The Earth element represents solid matter and the structure of the universe, it gives form and structure to the human body and to all things in the creation. The structure provided by the earth is the conduit through which the other elements flow. All elements are born of ether and contained within the earth.

Earth and the sense of smell

The origin of the earth element is the tanmatra of smell called gandha. The state of the earth element in the body and the capacity to smell are deeply connected. Gandha is the primordial cause of the experience of smell. It is the seed energy, or the potential emerging from the causal body, that sprouts into the earth element. The earth then builds the potential for the experience of smell in the subtle body through which smell can be experienced in the physical body. Thus, the gandha is not the smell itself, but the smell is dependent upon it. Disorders of the ability to smell reflect an imbalance of the earth element.

The nose is the vehicle through which the gandha manifests. Through the nose, we take in the scents of the creation. These impressions enter the body, mind and consciousness, deeply affecting us physically and emotionally. The Vedas describe that the soul takes birth again and again because of its vasanas. The word vasana literally means smell, which shows that our sense of smell is deeply rooted in our consciousness.

Ayurvedic perspective

Just as the consumption of food is important for the survival of the body, defecation is also equally important for the balance of the earth element in the body. The rectum is the organ of excretion. If too much earth is released, as it occurs in diarrhoea, the body structure weakens. If too little earth is released, as it occurs in constipation, the body remains strong for a while but becomes more and more toxic. Because the earth element and smell are intimately connected, both diarrhoea and constipation negatively impact the ability to smell. Excess of this element can obstruct the sense of smell, while it's deficiency can weaken the structures responsible for the smell. Thus, healthy elimination is essential for the balance of the earth element, the sense of smell and the overall well-being of the body are connected at a deeper level.

Quality of earth

We can understand any element through its qualities. Earth is cool, stable, heavy, dry, rough, gross, dense, dull, clear, and hard. The earth element is the antidote to symptoms that have the opposite qualities in the body. It is important to take in the qualities of the earth when you are feeling too hot, ungrounded, chaotic, emaciated, lacking in self-esteem, feeling insignificant, irritable, vulnerable, or can't withstand stress.

Staying connected to the earth by walking barefoot, gardening, and spending time outdoors helps to balance the kapha dosha, which is made of earth and water. Earth enters the body through the foods we consume and provides the chemical balance for all physical forms (stones, plants, animals, birds and humans).

This table shows the amount of earth elements found in different foods. If one feels weak, one should consume foods which have a high amount of this element, and if one is overweight then eat foods that have a lesser amount of it.

Amount of earth element	Foods
Largest	grains, nuts, legumes and meats.
Moderate	dairy products.
Least	fruits, vegetables, and spices.

Inference

The earth element gives stability, grounding and good physical health to those who have their Ascendant, Sun or Moon in the 2nd, 3rd and 4th padas of Kritika. This also blesses them with a steady flow of resources ability to take on a lot of physical activity and work hard for a long stretch of time. They have good stamina to work hard and achieve goals, which helps them to succeed in their plans and projects.

Motivation -

Dharma - As described earlier.

Artha - to gather resources (for the 2nd, 3rd and 4th padas).

Kritika natives' actions and thoughts will be driven by the desire to have enough resources available for the rainy day when the need arises. They are competent enough to take responsibility for their family and are good providers. They will work towards building a good bank balance and will maintain a healthy financial backup. Their pantry will be well stocked up with all the necessary ingredients needed in the kitchen for cooking, their wardrobe will have all the seasonal clothes kept ready for the change of weather, their bathroom will be well stocked with the needed accessories, the dressing table or the dressing room will have the elegant jewellery and makeup ready for use according to the occasion, and their garage or store will be well stocked up with all the necessary tools needed for their chosen profession or trade. The drive to keep their needed resources well stocked does not come from the sense of greed but from the sense of convenience of use.

Inference

They are ambitious and enthusiastic and are passionate about achieving the goals they set for themselves. Their hopes, aspirations and ambitions are for both worldly and spiritual pursuits. The fulfilment of desires is a basic need for them. Until their object of desire is achieved, they will carry on relentlessly. The path can be easy or tough but their determined effort ultimately makes them reach their desired destination.

Triguna - Rajas- As described earlier.

Tamas

The triguna of Tamas is the gross or the material quality of any substance. The physical quality of tamas gives structure and solidity to all forms, and the subtle quality of tamas gives stability and stamina. This table lists the main characteristics of people who have Tamas as the predominant guna.

Tamas	
Positive traits	Negative traits
Capacity to work hard, endurance, persistence, cautious, good stability, grounded, practical, determined, organised, trustworthy, reliable, dependable, always there in time of need, patient, kind, and empathetic.	Lazy, tend to put on weight, lack of exercise, eating junk food, feeling of heaviness, sluggishness, apprehensive, materialistic, stubborn, attachment, and possessiveness.

Inference

The 2nd, 3rd and 4th padas of Kritika are placed in Taurus, which gives it the Tamasic quality. Kritika natives have a great capacity to work hard and accomplish goals. However, they have to consciously overcome their desire to laze around too often or for too long. They need plenty of rest before and after getting into activity. They often tend to say - "not today, or not now. You should have told me earlier I need to plan and organise, or give me time, I will let you know or get back to you about this." They love being busy and actively involved but need time to organise and plan.

They like to have a regular routine and are quite set in their habits, thought patterns and behaviour. They have the stability and endurance to deal with situations patiently. They can appear stubborn, but a determined approach is a positive quality and are reliable and dependable friends. They are stubborn enough to follow their dreams and bring them to reality. It also shows that their thoughts and actions are motivated by previous karmic baggage, because of which they feel a strong need to follow their vision or ideas.

The fixed nature of Taurus makes them fixed in their thought patterns and habits. They prefer to make others adapt and follow their ideology or thought process rather than follow them. On the positive side, it's a good help because, from an early age, they will have clarity of purpose, and there will be no confusion about what they want to pursue or achieve in life. Life situations will arrange themselves in such a way that they are left with little or no choice but to follow the path that life is guiding them towards.

On the negative side it can make them follow their ambition ruthlessly, without caring for others sentiments or emotions. They don't like to be rushed into anything, but once they get into the job, they do it well. They are the ones who can carry on working even after others have given up because they are blessed with tremendous strength and endurance. However, after they are done with the job on hand, they need their well-deserved rest, and time to relax in order to get back their energy.

Tridosha - Pitta - as described earlier.

Kapha - Those who are born with their Ascendant, Sun or Moon in the 2nd, 3rd or 4th Pada of Kritika will have the predominant quality of Kapha. They are blessed with strength, endurance and stamina, have sweet and loving disposition and are stable and grounded.

The qualities of Kapha are- heavy, slow, steady, solid, cold, soft and oily. Kapha lends structure, solidity, and cohesiveness to all things and is therefore associated primarily with the earth and water elements. Kapha also embodies the watery energies of love and compassion. This dosha hydrates all cells and systems, lubricates the joints, moisturises the skin, maintains immunity, and protects the tissues.

Kapha types have a strong build and excellent stamina. They have large, soft eyes, smooth and radiant skin, and thick hair. They sleep soundly and have good regular digestion. Kapha types are naturally calm, thoughtful, caring and loving. They have an inherent ability to enjoy life and are comfortable with routines. When in balance, Kaphas are strong, loyal, patient, steady, and supportive. When out of balance, kapha triggers emotions of attachment, greed, and possessiveness and can also create stubbornness, lethargy, and resistance to change.

Physically, kapha tends to invite stagnation and congestion in organs and tissues throughout the body—including the mind.

Excess of Kapha on an emotional level can be seen as - too much attachment, holding on to things, jobs, and relationships long after they are no longer nourishing or necessary. When Kapha is in excess, there will be weight gain, fluid retention, and allergies that can manifest in the body.

Out of balance, Kapha symptoms can develop into - overweight, excessive sleep, asthma, hay fever, diabetes, and depression. For Kapha types - bitter, astringent and pungent tastes are good. Fresh salads and fruits are recommended, especially ginger and black pepper are particularly good for reducing kapha. They actually need foods that will invigorate their minds while limiting their overall consumption of food.

To balance Kapha -

- Eat - apples, apricots, cranberries, mangoes, peaches and pears, a light dry diet, more fresh fruits and salads, green leafy vegetables, baked, roasted and boiled food, lentils, grains, raw honey is good; fresh and dry ginger, ginger turmeric and lemon herbal tea.

- Avoid eating - root vegetables like potatoes and sweet potatoes, sour fruits, oily fried foods, dairy products, sweets, chocolates, frozen foods and ice cold drinks.

- Bring variation into your routine, go for outdoor trips, exercise regularly, keep yourself physically active and do no day time naps.

- Bring change into your diet and exercise routine gradually in small steps.

This table shows the signs and symptoms of Kapha in balance and out of balance, the good markers that help us stay in touch with our natural physiology and habits that can help us make the right choices as needed for our perfect health.

Kapha	
Signs of balanced Kapha	Good digestion, very good stamina, can overcome cravings for fatty foods, healthy lustrous skin, sparkling eyes, happy disposition, active, friendly, kind and caring.
Signs of imbalanced Kapha	Cold, congestion, runny nose, seasonal allergies, a feeling of heaviness in the stomach, sluggish digestion, lack of appetite, weight gain, water retention, feeling lazy, attachment, greed, hoarding, stubbornness, dullness, feeling unmotivated, boredom and sadness.
Gets out of balance	Eating heavy, dense, thick, oily, sticky and cold foods (refrigerated), getting stuck in routines, waking up late, sleeping in the daytime, sedentary lifestyle, no physical exercise. Cold and wet weather makes one more susceptible to Kapha imbalance.
Comes back in balance	Make changes in small steps, change the choice of food, build up an exercise routine, go for walks and cycling, meet friends, spend time outdoors, avoid cold drinks in cold weather, body massage with sesame oil, and have warm herbal tea with ginger, lemon and honey. Practice hatha yoga and meditation.

Chakras - <u>Muladhara, Swadhisthana and Manipura</u>

Muladhara and Swadhisthana - as described earlier.

Manipura

Chakra	Planets	Symbol	Element	Sound	Colour	Petals	Glands
Manipura	Sun	Downward facing triangle	Fire	Vam	Yellow	10	Pancreas

Manipura is also called the solar plexus because it is the seat of the sun, the metabolic fire. The lord of Kritika is the Sun which resonates with the energy of Manipura chakra. When Manipura chakra is balanced, the person will have very good health, will overcome any illness very quickly and will have a very good digestion. This chakra regulates the function of the Pancreas and digestive organs, any blockage in Manipura can cause health problems like - digestive disorders, circulatory disease, diabetes and fluctuations in blood pressure. When the energy of this Chakra flows freely - it's like being connected to the power station, constantly supplying vitality, balance and strength to the body.

Mani means precious gems and pura means a city. This chakra is located 2 fingers below the navel, also called the solar plexus. Sadhguru explains - If the energies become dominant in this chakra, the person is a doer in the world. He or she will be very active and energetic. The instinct of survival and self-preservation are in the lower 3 chakras.

The symbol of the Manipura is a downward-facing triangle, which indicates the downward flow of energy needed for sustenance and stability. Activation of the Manipura Chakra frees one from negative energies purifies and strengthens one's vitality. The deities of this Chakra are Vishnu and Lakshmi. Lord Vishnu is the sustainer, and Goddess Lakshmi represents material and spiritual prosperity.

It has 10 petals, which represent the 10 vayus (pranas) - 5 inner vayus and 5 outer vayus. The 10 pranas are -

N	Main Pranas	Upa (sub) Pranas
1	Prana - The vital life force.	Naga - Responsible for burping.
2	Apana - Downward moving energy.	Kurma - Responsible for blinking.
3	Udana - Upward moving energy.	Devadutta - Responsible for yawning.
4	Vyana - Energy that moves through the nerves (nadis).	Krikala - Responsible for sneezing.
5	Samana - The energy of Jathar Agni, the digestive fire - distributes nutrition to the body.	Dhananjaya - Responsible for opening and closing of the heart valves.

On an emotional level, it represents the 10 positive emotions that can enhance the flow of energy and 10 negative emotions that can block the flow of energy.

N	Positive emotions	Negative emotions
1	Love	Sadness
2	Compassion	Fear
3	Devotion	Anger
4	Kindness	Hatred
5	Selflessness	Disgust - unpleasantness
6	Trust - faith	Shame - guilt
7	Calmness - peaceful	Treachery - cheating others
8	Contentment	Jealousy
9	Equanimity - not perturbed by difficulties.	Attachment - possessiveness
10	Awareness - of your true nature.	Ignorance - about the nature of your true self.

All Nadis meet and redistribute -

Sadhguru explains that, at the Manipura chakra, 3600 Nadis from the left side and 3600 Nadis from the right side, all 72000 Nadis meet and redistribute themselves throughout the entire body.

This chakra is also the point where the foetus in the womb is connected to the mother through the umbilicus - which provides the nourishment and support for the survival of the foetus during the most crucial part of it's making. In other words, it is our maintenance chakra.

Throughout the body - these energy channels meet at 114 major junction points, but out of these, only 7 chakras are important or significant in terms of spiritual evolution. Sushumna is the central nadi that runs through the centre of the spine, all the way from the Muladhara to the sahasrara chakra. Ida (left) and Pingala (right) energy channels go only up to Ajna chakra.

Inference

Kritika has the quality of the first 3 chakras- Muladhara, Swadhishtana and Manipura. This is because the 1st Pada of Krittika lies in Aries, which is ruled by Mars. The 2nd, 3rd and 4th Pada of Kritika are placed in Taurus, which is ruled by Venus, and the Lord of this nakshatra is the Sun. This shows that Kritika natives are blessed with the fiery determination of Mars, the intelligence of the Sun and the passion, beauty, and romanticism of Venus.

The first 3 chakras have downward-flowing energy, which gives them a good stable constitution. When the chakras are well balanced, Muladhara gives good health and a stable grounding, Swadhisthana provides the passion and the desire to enjoy all the pleasures of life, and Manipura makes them ambitious, strong, determined and confident. On the other hand, if the energy is out of balance in any of the chakras, they can suffer from ill health, lack of vitality, excessive indulgence and ruthless ambition.

Shakti - Dahana Shakti - the power to burn and purify.

Kritika natives have the special power to burn and purify. This means that they will face situations which require them to burn their old habits, patterns, connections or relations with the strength of sheer fire of determination, motivation or inspiration. They have the inner strength to cut clean and start fresh. For them, the remedy lies not in burning bridges in the sense that they destroy all possibility of going back or revisiting. Which can happen in the literal sense. But they have to learn to look at life from a fresh perspective. The same people, the same relations, and same situations they have to be dealt with from a deeper inner knowing. They will find that any kind of fire ritual or even lighting a lamp helps improve their circumstances in a big way.

Symbolic signification

Ram - as described earlier, Taurus - Bull

Kritika - A knife, sword or a sharp blade.

A knife

The symbol of Kritika is a sharp blade, knife or sword. This means Kritika natives will have a very sharp intellect that can cut and dissect things, situations, and relationships neatly and clearly. This may sound cruel, but as always, each nakshatra's energy can operate both ways, negatively or positively, depending on other planetary placements and combinations. These kinds of situations can arise where they have to make a clear choice of yes or no. There is no in-between path. It is like a trade-off, to gain something, you have to give up another thing, cannot have both.

They will have clarity of thought and will not get tangled up with emotions when the situation demands immediate and quick action.

They will be good at editing scripts, cutting out the extra material that is not needed and will not be confused about making decisions. They can be critical of themselves and of others. They can become wonderful surgeons and army officers.

Bull

A bull is an adult male of the Bos taurus species. Bulls are much more muscular and aggressive than cows, with thicker bones, larger feet, a very muscular neck, and a large, bony head with protective ridges over the eyes. They have a hump on their back, where they store water, and this helps them to survive in hot arid conditions.

These features assist the bulls in fighting for domination over a herd, giving the winner superior access to cows for reproduction.

It's a common misconception that bulls are angered by the red colour, which incites them to charge. In fact, like most mammals, cattle are red-green colour-blind. In bullfighting, it's the movement of the cape and not the colour, that provokes a reaction in the bull.

Adult bulls may weigh between 500 - 1000 Kg. Most bulls are capable of aggressive behaviour and require careful handling. They are controlled by nose rings. A bull is brought near a cow only to mate and is usually kept away from cows in bachelor herds or alone. It has been observed that bulls kept alone are more aggressive than the ones kept with the cows.

Bulls have held a place of significance in human culture since before the beginning of recorded history. They appear in cave paintings estimated to be up to 17000 years old. In mythology, it is often associated with fertility. In Hinduism, a bull named <u>Nandi</u> is seen seated with and is the vehicle of Lord Shiva.

<u>Inference</u>

We have to turn to the Rocky Mountain goat and the earthy Bull's nature to really understand their perspective towards life. Kritika natives of Pada 1 will have the qualities of the Ram. They will have well-built shoulders and an elegant stride and will have a sure-footed confidence that does not waver with challenges. They like to look presentable and prim all the time. Their faces will exude the charm that's very attractive and pleasing to people. They will be very particular to follow their exercise routine of walking, jogging, going to the gym, or yoga and meditation, because they are aware that beauty happens from within. You will rarely see a Kritika native out of shape or sloppily dressed.

They are far-sighted and quick to spot trouble when it's coming. They will be fiercely defensive about their children and family and will take swift action to combat any danger. They are most comfortable when at the top or leading and guiding others comes naturally to them. In a literal sense they love the heights, trekking mountain peaks is the most exhilarating experience for them. When they are in deep thought, they lower their heads and scratch the ground with their fingers or toes.

Yes, they are competitive and don't like to lose an argument or a game, and this motivation drives them to reach the top. You may come across a Kritika who seems docile, but wait, you don't really know them yet until you have had a full-fledged heated conversation, and then they will battle it out head-on.

Their driving motivation is to reach the top in whichever field of work they are in. Of course, they are very headstrong individuals. When they set a goal, they follow it with all honesty and passion. Their amazing sense of balance when climbing the dizzy heights gives them a leeway to stay ahead of others.

They are competent and courageous when it involves dealing with situations the way they can understand. If the other person refuses to compete, it will bewilder them at first, but with experience, they will grow emotionally and will be able to look at the situations not just from a logically correct perspective but from feelings, emotions and empathy.

Kritika natives born in Pada 2, 3, and 4 will have the qualities of a bull. Here, the natives will have more determination and stubbornness to stick it out, no matter what. They will have bushy eyebrows, a lot of hair, a heavier physique and a steady gait. With the earthy bull, one cannot jump to hasty conclusions.

They are tough and can withstand challenges without flinching an eyelid. They truly have the bull's eye focus, not distracted by trivial matters that might be happening around them. Here lies the key to their success. They will hit it bang on - on target, with dogged determination. They will approach challenges with immovable obstinacy. Winning the controversy and getting one's way is all that counts.

Remember Nandi, Lord Shiva's patient companion and vehicle.

When it comes to patience, they most certainly have an abundance of it. They can endure and tolerate things for a long time, but even a Bull, when driven too far, can attack, for they do not lack strength or courage. If it comes to action that is needed to defend their loved ones or their beliefs and principles, they will do so fiercely. And you better believe it! - it will be most wise then not to be anywhere near them when they are getting into their attack mode. However, they absolutely see no point in stirring up the muddy waters or risking violent agitation just to prove a minor point. Only if the situation has driven them to such a tight corner where there is no other option left will they take such a drastic step of aggressive display.

They prefer action rather than words. Listening to empty talk or endless discussions can wear them out or exhaust them more than running a mile-long marathon. For them, constant arguments are most futile and wasteful. Their mode of action is just do what you please, but once you have decided your course of action then do not budge from it.

They are capable of lazing around for days and then spring into action. For the amount of energy that goes into their aggressive approach, they need ample time out to relax. They are the most dependable people around and the best ones available to deal with long term projects that need patience and resilience. Whether it's marriage or business partnership they will stick it out through thick and thin, be sure of that.

Mythology

Deity - Kartikeya

The story of Kartikeya's birth

Kartikeya is also known as Skanda, Kumara, Murugan and Subramanya. Kartikeya wished to be born to kill the demon called Tarakasura. Since Tarakasur was blessed with a boon he could only be killed by Shiva's son. Tarakasur was clever to ask for this boon from Shiva after his long penance, for he knew that Shiva was an ascetic and there was no chance of him getting married and having a son. Devas then came up with a plan to induce Parvati to marry Shiva.

Shiva, however, was totally absorbed in meditation and was not interested in any worldly matters. Even the carefully planned act of asking Kamadeva (the god of desire) to help with this situation had failed. For Shiva had burned Kamadeva to ashes when he was disturbed by his arrow of (desire) made of flowers that hit him in his heart.

After many years of waiting, serving and perseverance, Parvati won Shiva's heart and he agreed to get married. Shiva's seed was so strong that Parvati could not contain it, so Agni Dev received it and dropped it in the river Ganga, from there emerged a beautiful baby- this is how Kartike was born. He had 6 faces and was looked after by 6 mothers; therefore, he was called Skanda. He was a very strong boy, and at a very young age, he killed Tarakasur. He was a very brave, youthful warrior and protector of the people. His vehicle was a peacock.

He is described as a youthful god whose body glows like the rising sun from the emerald sea. He represents victory over evil, and many temples situated on the hills of south India are dedicated to him.

Inference

The Krittika nakshatra has been named after Katikaye, which shows a strong influence on his qualities. Those who are born with Ascendant, Sun or Moon in Krittika will have the courage, determination, willpower, and fiery ambition and will be fierce protectors of their people, ideology or faith - just like Kartikeya. They will be spiritually inclined and will follow their dreams with great passion.

Kritika padas 26.40 deg Aries - 10 deg Taurus

Padas	Degrees
1	26.40 - 30 deg Aries
2	0 - 3.20 deg Taurus
3	3.20 - 6.40 deg Taurus
4	6.40 - 10 deg Taurus

Pada 1

26.40 - 30 deg Aries, Navamsha - Sagittarius Lord - Jupiter

Rashi Lord - Mars and Nakshatra Lord - Sun

Since the first Pada falls in the navamsha of Sagittarius, the natives will be very idealistic about their approach to life. The play of the Sun, Mars and Jupiter's energy makes them very creative, intelligent, ambitious, righteous, generous and proud. They will have a very high moral code and a sense of discipline. Because of these wonderful qualities, they will be successful and have leadership roles in the community and their workplace. This Pada is a Pushkar amsha, which shows that any planets placed here will blossom and be fruitful in terms of giving results during their dasha period. If you want to know the precise time, then look at the current transits along with the dasha. For example, the sun placed in Pada 1, during the maha dasha of the sun and the transit of the sun in Aries will bring dominance, confidence, creativity, rise in position and success.

They are somewhat bossy and insist on getting their own way and are eternally sentimental and romantic. Jupiter's idealism can get clogged with overly technical martian ways of thinking. They are blunt and straightforward in their speech and can lack consideration for others' sensitivities. They can be clumsy when it comes to expressing their emotions. They cannot put up a show of false humility. Showing their talent and capabilities is their favourite pastime. Whether it's in family gatherings, friends circle, or a large crowd, they will not be shy of performing in front of them. Sun's confidence, martian passion and Jupitarian's fondness for expanding things is a perfect combo for a politician, leader, manager, spokesperson, actor, singer or stage performer.

Careers-

All positions of authority - managers, leaders, consultants, military and police officers, critics, editors, teachers, priests, doing fire rituals, lawyers, judges, surgeons, doctors, artists, painters, fashion designers, jewellers, firefighters, running foster care homes and rehabilitation centres, astrologers and politicians.

Pada 2

0 - 3.20 deg Taurus, Navamsha - Capricorn (Lord - Saturn)

Rashi Lord - Venus and Nakshatra Lord - Sun

Sun, Venus and Saturn's energy will set the ambience for this Pada. The natives will be career oriented and will achieve success through endurance and dedication towards their profession. Will become well-established in their profession.

Sun here can make one feel that they need a lot of compliments and admiration to be motivated, while Venus appreciates the beauty and harmony in all they do or see. Saturn brings practicality and discipline into life. It will also give the lessons of delays and dedication to achieve anything substantial and worthwhile. Moon exalted at 3 deg Taurus in this Pada. For example, Moon placed in the 2nd Pada of Kritika in the 2nd house, will make the native very caring, who will love to support and sustain his or her family and will have the resources to do so.

Saturn being the stern and wise master, considers money as an essential commodity to elevate human suffering. Having savings is an absolute must. Their family status, community, reputation, and status matter to them. As they get older, they will feel Saturn's restrictive influence, which can frustrate the kingly Sun.

Careers-

Consultants, managers, social workers, government jobs, lawyers, doctors, engineers, builders, drivers, teachers, IT professionals, interior designers, tailors, fashion designers, boutique owners, and running recruitment agencies.

Pada 3

3.20 - 6.40 deg Taurus, Navamsha - Aquarius (Lord - Saturn)

Rashi Lord - Venus and Nakshatra Lord - Sun

The Sun, Venus and Saturn effect will be seen here. This is a wonderful placement for achieving gains for which you don't have to work too hard. They will have a good source of income, and gains will come more easily to them. In other words, at some point in life, you will get the gains in income, salary or profits in business, large organisations, and friends circle - which you were not particularly chasing. They just come and fall in your lap. Whether you want it or not, you will be pulled into it and will have to take the responsibility of that role. You may feel reluctant to accept it in the beginning simply because you have not yet realised your true potential.

If destiny brings you to such a point where situations are falling in place for a certain event to happen, then it's a clear sign, given by life, that you were destined to fulfil this role in this lifetime. The natives will be more inclined towards humanitarian causes and helping the people at large.

In navamsha, this Pada falls in Aquarius, which is a fixed sign. This shows that as they get older, they will become more stubborn about their beliefs and will follow them through with conviction. They will be interested in finding new innovative and scientific ways through which they and everybody else can benefit. This also indicates that they will have fixed karma (drira karma) that is sure to give results during the dasha of Saturn.

In this Pada Yoga, Tara point is at 6 degrees Taurus. Any planets placed at this degree will give positive results during its dasha. For example, Saturn, sitting in the 10th house in the 3rd Pada of Kritika, will bring a rise in career and more responsibility.

Careers-

Managers or an employee of a large company, entrepreneurs, government jobs, teachers, priests, astrologers, engineers, doctors, lawyers, running a social service or working on one, IT professionals, community workers, socialists and activists.

Pada 4

6.40 - 10 deg Taurus, Navamsha - Pisces (Lord - Jupiter)

Rashi Lord - Venus and Nakshatra Lord - Sun

The energies of the Sun, Venus and Jupiter are at play here. It also falls in Pushkar navamsa, which means any planets placed here will surely be fruitful and give results during its dasha. Sun Venus effect going into Pisces navamsha will make them very philosophical and spiritual as they get older. They are more passive and laid back about everything and would rather walk out than get into a wasteful argument. Moreover, it's genuinely not worth spoiling the mood over trivial matters. For they have the wisdom of having been through the whole zodiac cycle, and nothing baffles them inwardly. They are always equanimous.

Since they are very idealistic, they seem to come across as dreamy and unambitious. They are also very sensitive to others' feelings and aspire to experience things which are beyond the limits of earthly knowledge. They will be humble, and sympathetic and can be good listeners. For example, in the 4th Pada of Kritika in the 4th house, their mother will be a very spiritual and religious-minded person. Their home environment will be a guiding light which will influence their way of thinking, philosophy and faith in a positive way.

They may have all the comforts in life, but their inner self will always be drawn to the ultimate epitome of pure love, which is without boundaries and conditions.

"Where love rules, there is no will to power, and where power predominates, love is lacking. One is the shadow of the other." - Carl Jung

Careers-

Actors, artists, painters, dancers, musicians, yoga and meditation practitioners or teachers, doctors, counsellors, writers, poets, IT designers, illustrators, florists, pet shop owners, scriptwriters, fashion or interior designers, astrologists and priests.

The effect of planets

Bharani - Aries	Planets that get affected
Functional Benefic - give good results during their dasha.	Sun, Moon and Mars
Functional Malefic - can give problems during their dasha.	Mercury, Rahu and Ketu
Functional Neutral	Moon, Jupiter and Saturn
Kendra -Adi pati dosha - can give problems in relationships.	Venus

Kritika - Taurus Padas - 2, 3 and 4	Planets that get affected
Yoga Karka - the most benefic planet.	Saturn
Functional Benefic - give good results during their dasha.	Sun and Mercury
Functional Neutral	Moon, Venus, Jupiter and Mars
Functional Malefic - can give problems during their dasha.	Rahu and Ketu

Kritika Ascendant

Persons born with Kritika lagna will have a Sun, Mars or Venus energy scenario. This nakshatra transits from Aries to Taurus. Those who are born in the 1st Pada will have more Mars energy at play. They will deal with situations in a more straightforward and upfront manner. They will be put into leadership positions in whichever field of work they have chosen. Since this Pada falls in the dharma rashi of Aries, they will love to take action for the wellbeing and protection of others, and this also gives them Mars-like determination and fearlessness.

Those who are born in the 2nd, 3rd and 4th padas of Kritika will have a bull-like stubbornness. This helps them to prod along and achieve their goals and gate crash through all hurdles by the sheer strength of purpose. They face challenges head-on, through intellectual debates or physical strength, depending on how the other planets are placed in their birth chart. In the face of danger, they take appropriate action and will not recede, for they are brave souls. They will determinedly dig their hoofs deeper and refuse to budge if they feel pushed around. Just like a charging bull, their wrath of anger can crush everything in its way, even if they themselves get injured or destroyed in the process. They have the capacity to come charging at you if provoked beyond the threshold of tolerance. However, the bar of tolerance level will vary, depending on the feel of the whole chart. Some will be as calm as the still waters of a lake, while others can be blazing like the sun, but both will be ambitious and firm.

They are like a Bull in the pasture enjoying the grazing, and have a cool but determined approach to everything. Sometimes, their stubbornness may appear cold and cruel, but they are the ones whom you can always count on. Even after the next fiery emotional farewell, they will still be there waiting for you. They have this passive quality of steadfastness and quiescent receptivity that will always give them a slight edge over all situations.

In the later padas, there will be more of Sun and Venus qualities because these padas fall in Taurus, which is an artha rashi.

Their actions will be motivated by the desire to build resources for themselves and their family. This also brings the stability of the earth element, which provides grounding and availability of resources to follow their ambitions.

They are born homemakers unless the lagna is afflicted by malefic aspects or conjunction of Saturn, Mars, Rahu or Ketu. Even if they are tempted to spend their adolescent years exploring sensual pleasures, their basic desire, nevertheless, is to create a comfortable home filled with fine furnishings, good food, pets, babies and music. With beds all nicely made, laundry folded and put away, bills paid, and, of course, a flower garden in the backyard for sunny barbecue days. And to top it all, they can be good listeners when they want to! And when they are not too busy.

Kritika natives have the fiery energy of intense heat, the fire that can both burn and purify. Just as a forest fire can consume everything that comes in its way, their intense passion towards a certain goal consumes their attention and time fully because of this endearing quality, they are able to achieve even the unattainable. Their razor-sharp attention and focus cut clean through all sticky or unsurmountable situations.

The element of fire is also associated with vision. They are artistic and can be lucid dreamers, have clear visions, remember things through visual representations, and are good at capturing images through video and photography. The influence of the Sun makes them very creative and intelligent, and they are able to tackle tricky situations with tact and efficacy.

This also shows that when they are pursuing a goal, they will not let emotions get in their way. This quality makes them ruthlessly determined and ambitious, which works both ways. It's a positive asset if their goals are more inclusive and can bring well-being to many, or negative if their ambition is based on selfishness or greed for power.

Their actions are motivated by the fulfilment of desires, which keeps them active, and they like being busy. Inactivity or nothing to do makes them feel out of their element. They like performing rituals, learning scriptures, or reciting mantras because Kritika is a priestly class.

This nakshatra has the Shiva energy, which means power of dissolution, this shows they are not afraid of new beginnings. They are able and willing to destroy old habit patterns which hinder their growth, in order to improve themselves. The downward-facing quality shows that they are careful with where they place their foot. They do not ignore the immediate to chase fancy ideas.

Sun in Kritika

For those who are born in 1st pada will have sun, sun and mars energy. This will make the natives very confident, energetic, determined and even harsh. For this reason, ancient astrologers warned that if these qualities are not carefully balanced, they can result in cruelty. They need to expend their energy through regular physical exercise. When the determination of Mars is combined with the Sun's confidence, it gives an immense amount of power. The natives will love outdoor and adventurous sports and will do very well in careers like - the army, police and sports.

If one is born in padas 2, 3 or 4, there will be sun, sun and Venus energy. Sun and Venus don't get along well because they are both immensely hot, which can make natives short-tempered. However, on the positive side, they will be highly intelligent and creative and can become excellent managers and coordinators. It will be particularly promising in giving results if Sun is placed at 6 deg of yoga Tara or in the 4th pada of Pushkar amsha.

This placement can make the natives stubborn and silently expect absolute obedience from others. Or they might be in situations where commitment is needed from them, especially if there is a Saturn aspect. They will be very generous with their gifts and with words of appreciation. Feeling neglected - that's one thing they will not stand for. They would rather leave the project, the job, or the person than put themselves through such indignation. They will be very ego-sensitive.

Moon in Kritika

Here, the energy of the Sun, Mars and Moon will be there for those born in the 1st pada. It will be good to check here, whose energy is stronger in the chart, the sun or the moon's. The planet closest to Lagna's degree will be stronger. This can also be checked through the Shadbala or bhava bal of the planets or the houses, and results will alter accordingly. Moon's maximum exaltation is at 3 degrees Taurus. Natives who have the moon placed at this degree will benefit from the nourishing and friendly aspect of the moon. Moon dasha and transits of the moon over the Ascendant, the natal moon and Saturn will bring strong results, both positive or negative, depending on the placement of other planets.

If the moon has good strength, the natives can become like mountain goats who are confident of their path. Moon placed in the sun nakshatras will imbibe the sun's energy and will behave like the sun and mars (Lord of Aries), which will give a more aggressive and determined approach. Despite the surface gentleness and apparent reticence, they will always be in a rush to get things done and will be looking for shortcuts. The karmic lessons to be learnt here are patience, tenacity, persistence and perseverance to eventually achieve what they set for. For example, the Moon placed in the 4th Pada of Kritika in the 11th house will bring many easy gains and promotions in their career. Moreover, the 4th pada is a Pushkar navamsha. The results are likely to blossom in the moon dasha.

If the Sun is stronger they will be like a confident bull. It will then be good to heed the advice of not confronting them when they are in the mood of achieving their target, they will be going for it, no matter what! Like a siege of subtle but determined strategy, their unusually strong-willed personality will deliver results. However, there are lessons to be learnt here because of the sun's authority. You may unconsciously try to overpower others around you. This can make them distant from you, and a strong sense of pride can set forth the karma into a dreary chain of future incarnations. This realisation can go a long way to help us. Learning to acknowledge that our actions or words can hurt others makes us more aware of what we say and how we say it. Kritika natives will never hurt others out of malice but rather due to their intense focus on achieving goals, which can make them oblivious to others' feelings.

Kri-tika, the poet

Kri - full of action, both outer and inner

Tika- adorns the forehead, a mark of knowledge, a winner.

Sun, Moon and Mars- King, Queen and commander in chief.

Making sure, all is in order and there's no mischief.

Transition from Mountains to landscapes,

From tough Ram horns to strong bull capes.

From fiery Aries to earthy Taurus,

Hold the possibilities enormous.

The fiery passion, drive and zest,

The earthly conquest at its best.

Sharp as a razor cutting across,

Through thorny weeds and clearing the moss.

After the darkest clouds, merges a brave fighter,

The glory of the Sun - shines brighter.

A Visionary aspirant, as the light spreads - clearly sees,

the inner and outer realms with ease.

Remedies

- <u>Das Maha Vidya -</u> Devi Bagalamukhi and Devi Kamala -as described earlier.

<u>Devi Matangi</u> - Sun

Goddess Matangi is also called Tantric Saraswati because her energy resonates with the Sun, which is the source of all knowledge and creativity. She is also associated with Mercury, which is why she is said to have a green complexion, which is the colour assigned to the planet Mercury.

She is the goddess of music and learning. Like Sarasvati, Matangi governs speech, music, knowledge and the arts. Her worship is prescribed to acquire supernatural powers, especially gaining control over enemies, attracting people to oneself, acquiring mastery over the arts and gaining supreme knowledge. She controls all areas of politics and government administration, and also the overall body constitution and physical health.

Remedies for weak Sun -

In the birth chart, if the sun is weak, it will manifest with skin problems, blood pressure, or weakness of the heart if it's associated with the ascendant. Or it can show up as difficulties with the boss or government officials, ego-related status problems, or lack of confidence. If connected to the moon, during the Sun dasha and transit, these effects can be seen. If the sun is afflicted with Saturn, Mars, Rahu or Ketu or has a low shadbala score, worshipping her can bring some relief.

Remedies -

- The best remedy is to overcome the aversion towards what we consider impure. To be able to see everything as an essential part of the creation, because without one, the other cannot exist in the physical existence.

- Offering red hibiscus flowers and reciting her mantra or ashtothram is said to be beneficial.

- Chanting her mantras 108 times, along with her yantra and image, is recommended. This will help the native to become confident and have clarity. It is recommended to chant her mantra on 10 consecutive Sundays to reap the benefits.

Devi Matangi is often worshipped with the mantra syllable - *Aym*, which is associated with Saraswati and is the seed-syllable of knowledge, learning, and teaching. A longer mantra is also used -

"Om Hreem Aym Shreem Namo Bhagavati Ucchishtachandali Shri Matangeswari Sarvajanavasankari Swaha."

Meaning -

Reverence to adorable Matangi, the outcast and residue, who gives control over all creatures.

Other mantras -

"Om Hreem Kleem Hum Matangyai Phat Svaha."

"Om Hreem Aim Shreem Namo Bhagavati Ucchishta Chandali Sri Matangeshwari Sarvagya Navashamkari Swaha."

Other remedies

- Doing fire rituals or lighting a lamp will improve the energies of Kritika.

- Wear a 1, 11 or 12 mukhi (faced) rudraksha, which has 108 beads. This will protect and aid in spiritual progress.

- Wear bright fiery colours which resonate with the energy of Kritika.

- Colour a peacock in the colour of the planet placed in Kritika for fulfilment of desire.

- The best remedy will be to go to the gym regularly or do hatha yoga, which will help to maintain good physical and mental health and enhance spiritual growth.

- Chant the Kritika nakshatra mantra 108 times to improve the energies of this nakshatra. The chanting can be done on a Sunday or when the Moon is transiting Kritika.

"Om aym oo u Krittika nakshatraye namah."

Example

Moon in Krittika Pada 2 in the 8th house

Here is an example of one of my sister's friends, Sangita.

Born on 5th February 1979, 1:20 am, Pathankot India.

She was born and brought up in India. After marriage, they moved to Italy and stayed there for a couple of years and had 2 children. They later moved to Canada.

Analysis -

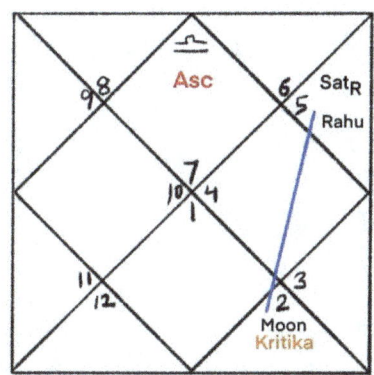 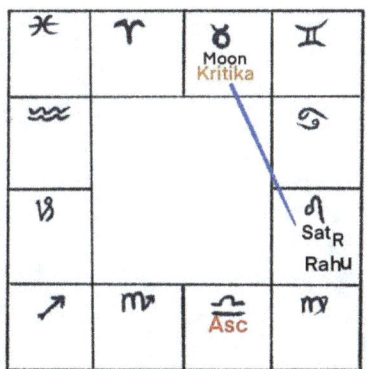

Her moon being in Kritika Pada 2 in the 8th house has brought many sudden changes in her life. Moon is exalted here and therefore accentuates the fluctuations, but also gives the beautiful quality of nourishment.

During her Jupiter Saturn Saturn dasha, she went through a rough period of health and financial issues. Her Saturn is retrograde and Conjunct with Rahu in the 11th house of Leo - From there Saturn has the 10th aspect on the Moon. This shows that she will go through frustrations and delays and will have to put in effort towards getting to the bottom of a problem regarding her career.

She said, "It's like all the problems have come pouring down on her and her family at the same time, mercilessly with no respite."

Kritika pada 2 carries the Sun, Venus and Saturn's energy, which makes it a challenging placement because Saturn considers the Sun his enemy. Saturn's 10th aspect on the 8th house brings sudden changes in jobs, resources and finance. She is very hard-working and does not like to take time off from her job, even if she is feeling under the weather.

4
Rohini

Om rm rrm lrm lrrm Rohini nakshatraye namah

Zodiac degrees	10 - 23.20 degrees Taurus
Ruling planet	Taurus - Venus Rohini - Moon
Sanskrit name	Rohini means the reddish one, growing one, and Ruh means to grow.
Astronomical name	Aldebaran is a bright rose star which can be spotted in the evening sky. Also called the abode of Brahma (the creator). It is seen as a group of 5 stars representing the head of a bull or Hyades - a Greek mythological name.
Symbol	Taurus - Bull Rohini - Ox cart and Cobra
Element	Earth
Deity	Brahma (Prajapati)
Quality	Sthira - fixed
Shakti	Rohana Shakti - power to make things grow.
Cast	Shudra - worker
Gender	Female
Motivation	Artha - to gather resources.
Triguna	Tamas

Tridosha	Kapha
Body parts	Forehead, ankles, skin and legs calves.
Direction	East, south and northwest.
Month	2nd half of Kritika - November.
Week day	Monday and Friday
Bird	Swan, Heron
Sound	o, va, ve, vu
Tree	Jamun
Chakras	Swadhisthana - Venus and Anhatta - Moon
Das Maha Vidya	Devi Kamala - Venus Devi Bhuveneshwari - Moon

Special degrees -

Yoga Tara	16 deg Taurus It's a point where the planet will show the strongest and sure results during its dasha.
Mulatrikona	4 - 20 deg Taurus - Mulatrikona of Moon. It is the placement where the planet is happy and comfortable and gives good results.
Vargottama	Pada 2 Planets placed in this Pada will give a good, steady foundation and results.
Exaltation	15 deg Taurus - maximum exaltation of Rahu. When Rahu is placed at this degree, it will bring wonderful opportunities, especially during its dasha.
Pushkar amsha	Pada 2 Planets placed here will fruitify results like the blossoming of a flower.
Amrit nadi	21.33 - 22.26 deg Taurus Gives good results like the nectar that nourishes.
Visha nadi	18.53 - 19.46 deg Taurus Brings situations which one does not like dealing with.

Auspicious and inauspicious table -

Auspicious	Inauspicious
Activities Very good for all initiations and starting new projects, for marriage and romance, making financial and business deals, buying and selling, for planting, healing, travelling, all building projects and spiritual practices.	Activities Not suitable for all kinds of endings, destruction or death rituals.
Days Mondays - only when it falls on the 2nd, 4th, 7th or 12th lunar day. Tuesdays- only when it falls on the 5th or 7th lunar day. Wednesdays - only when it falls on the 2nd, 3rd, 7th, 8th, 12th and 13th lunar day. Saturdays - only when it falls on the 2nd, 4th, 7th or 12th lunar day.	Days Tuesdays- only when it falls on the full moon day (Purnima). Thursdays - only when it falls on the 2nd, 3rd, 6th, 8th, 9th, 10th, 11th, 12th or 13th lunar day. Fridays only when it falls on the 2nd, 3rd, 6th, 8th, 9th, 10th, 11th, 12th or 13th lunar day.

Compatibility table -

Rohini	Compatible with
Sexual compatibility Yoni animal	Rohini - Male serpent, cobra - compatible with - Female serpent, cobra - Mrigashira
Sign compatibility	Taurus - Padas 1 and 2 - Virgo and Capricorn.
Nakshatra compatibility	Hasta and Shravana.
Lunar day compatibility	2nd Lunar day, Dwitya tithi.
Day compatibility	Monday and Friday
Colour compatibility	White and all pastel colours.
Numerological compatibility	2 and 6 - and all numbers that add up to make 2 and 6.
Sound compatibility	Moon - semi vowels - ya, ra, la, va, sa, sha, ssa, ha, lr, rr Venus - palatal sounds - cha, ccha, ja, jha, nga

Sign Lord and Nakshatra Lord - Venus and Moon.

Venus - as described earlier.

Moon - Lord of Rohini.

In Vedic astrology, the placement of the moon is of great importance because it represents the mind, and through the window of our mind, we perceive life, make choices and handle situations. Ascendent gives us a preview of the possible life events and circumstances. At the same time, the placement of the moon shows how the person will handle these situations, what impact it can have on him or her and what are the possible precautions, remedies or solutions that can work.

One of the names for the Moon is Soma, which means nectar or the elixir of life. It nourishes our thoughts and emotions and represents all body fluids. In the birth chart, when the moon is in the waxing phase (Shukla Paksha), the person will be more outgoing and emotionally well-balanced. When the native moon is in the waning phase (Krishna paksha), he or she will be more inwardly drawn and will not express emotions openly.

The bright cycle of the Moon is considered beneficial because it's better able to provide opportunities and nourish desires in terms of making resources available. The dark side of the moon supports inner growth, and therefore, it is considered malefic in terms of providing opportunities for worldly success. Here, the Moon directs its energy and nourishment inward. For any struggle faced outside, one must turn inward to find the answers. In this process, one matures and evolves mentally and spiritually.

Moon is friendly, feminine and receptive and gets along well with all planets. Moon signifies mother, thoughts, imagination, emotions, feelings, compassion, kindness, care, love, devotion, quickness, changeable, fluctuations, moody - feeling high and feeling low, and attachments.

Inference -

In Rohini, the influence of the Moon and Venus makes them very feminine, receptive, laid back, content, happy, gentle, caring, kind, devotional, dreamy, moody, sensitive, intuitive, imaginative, loved by the family and friends, artistic, creative, possessive and attached to their comfort zone. The beneficence of Venus usually provides them with a good source of income.

Quality, element, motivation, triguna and tridosha - as described earlier.

Chakras - Svadhisthana and Anahata

Swadhisthana - as described earlier.

Anahata

Moon is the ruler of Rohini, and it signifies emotions. Therefore, it resonates with the energy of Anhatta. This chakra is located in the middle of the chest- at the point where the rib cage meets.

Chakra	Planets	Symbol	Element	Sound	Colour	Petals	Glands
Anhatta	Moon	6-pointed star - upward and downward facing triangle.	Water	Yam	Green	12	Thymus gland

Anahata means the unstruck sound. In the Devi Linga Bhairavi chant, the energy of Anahata chakra is described as the shape of an ellipsoid.

Sadhguru explains when energies move into Anhata, the person becomes very creative. He or she will become very artistic and poetic and will want to create something unique and original. One will be able to tap into the infinite field of creative expression. At a deeper level, one will be able to hear the unstruck sound, the sound of silence, the melody from within. This is a meeting point between the downward and upward-moving energies, like the Star of David, which symbolises balance. This chakra is the creative centre that supports both - worldly and spiritual desires. It expresses both the survival instinct and a longing to go beyond. Up to Anhata, the energies rise easily through meditation and yogic practises. But after this one needs dedication and devotion towards pursuing the spiritual path and experiencing the ultimate truth.

The 12 petals signify a specific sound and the emotion -

Petals	Sound	Emotion
1	Kam	Bliss
2	Kham	Peace
3	Gam	Harmony
4	Gham	Love
5	Ngam	Understanding
6	Cham	Empathy
7	Chham	Clarity
8	Jam	Purity
9	Jham	Unity
10	Nyam	Compassion
11	Tam	Kindness
12	Tham	Forgiveness

The 12 gunas or qualities are also viewed as vrittis, which arise from the fluctuations or deviations from the prakruti, which is nature in its most fundamental or purest form.

N	Vrittis	Meaning
1	Ahamkara	Egoism and self-identity.
2	Asha	Hopes, wishes and desires.
3	Mamta	Attachments and possessiveness.
4	Cheshta	Effort
5	Chinta	Worries, anxiety, stress and tension.
6	Viveka	Discrimination
7	Vikalata	Languor, lethargy, fatigue and weariness.
8	Vitarka	Debates and arguments.
9	Lolata	Covertness, hidden actions, selfishness and greed.
10	Dhamba	Vanity, arrogance, conceit and false pretence.
11	Kapata	Hypocrisy and deceit.
12	Anutapa	Regret, guilt, depression and misery.

Some of these vrittis are positive, which promote growth, and some are negative, which inhibit growth. For any game to take place, you need an opposition. Similarly, nature has the intelligent design of opposite qualities for the game of life to happen. When Anhata is balanced, it will radiate the positive attributes of creativity, love and compassion. But when the energies are blocked, or out of balance, the negativity of selfishness, greed and depression can seep in.

Anahata is also considered to be the seat of the Jivatman -the conditioned or individual soul, and Parashakti- the first primordial form of energy or power which can be felt or experienced. In the Vedic texts, Upanishads describe jeevatman as a tiny flame inside the heart. Anahata is believed to have been named by the sages and mystics who had heard the unstruck sound within themselves. Anahata is also associated with qualities of the other dimension like, intuition and psychic powers.

The energies in this chakra can be awakened and balanced by asanas, pranayama, meditation, chanting the Bija sound yam and mantras related to Shiva and Parvati.

Healing

- The feelings of sadness, grief and depression can block the energies of Anhatta. All activities that make you joyful and lift you out of a melancholic mood will balance the energies of this chakra. Listening to classical music and spending time in nature will be particularly beneficial.

- Meditation and pranayama are an excellent way to bring balance to our emotions, which in turn will help to bring balance to our actions.

Inference

Rohini is placed in Taurus, whose Lord is Venus, and the nakshatra Lord is the moon. Therefore, the energies of both Swadhisthana and Anhata resonate with Rohini. Both Venus and the moon have a benefic, gentle and feminine influence, this makes the natives fortunate, beautiful, kind, loving, caring, well mannered and friendly. They also have a very fine sense of aesthetics and harmony.

Swadhisthana energy makes them very fertile, which means they will have healthy children. They are passionate about food, sex, and comforts of life. The influence of Anahata makes them emotional, imaginative and empathetic. When the energies in the chakras are balanced, they are the most loving, friendly and kind individuals, while imbalanced energies can make them overly attached, fearful and possessive.

Shakti - Rohana Shakti - to make things grow.

Lord of Rohini is the moon, which gives it a nurturing quality. Moon God (Soma) liked Rohini the best and stayed longest in this nakshatra, because of its wonderful nourishing quality. The natives will naturally find great satisfaction in providing - food for others that nourishes the body, emotional support that nourishes the feelings, positive thoughts that nourish the mind, and nourishing spiritually through meditation and prayer. Rohini natives will feel healed from within when they help others. Whenever they are in their motherly mode, they are at their best because this is their natural way of being.

Symbolic signification

Taurus - Bull - as described earlier.

Rohini - Cobra and Ox cart.

Ox cart

The symbol of Rohini is an ox cart. This shows that Rohini natives are blessed with an easy ride through life. Even if they face obstacles, in their experience, they will not be so drastic that they are insurmountable. They will be equanimous in all circumstances. Nothing will throw them off balance. Their inherent nature is to go with the slow, steady pace of life. They don't feel rushed about anything and have enduring patience. They are certainly not city people and are the happiest in the countryside when they are close to nature. They may come to a city to do a certain job when needed, but their desire is always to be away from the noisy cities in the tranquillity of the pastures or fields.

Cobra

Fossil evidence suggests that snakes may have evolved from burrowing lizards. The forest cobra is a species of venomous snake family and is commonly found in Africa and India. It likes lowland forests, moist savanna habitats and dry climates. It is a competent swimmer and is often considered to be semi-aquatic. The forest cobra is classified in the genus Naja of the family Elapidae.

The Sanskrit word naga means cobra. Indian cobras are named Naga and Nagaina, the Hindi words for male and female snakes.

They vary tremendously in colour and pattern, are medium in size and are heavy-bodied. A cobra can easily be identified by its relatively large and quite impressive hood, which it expands when threatened. They have medium-sized eyes and round pupils. Their length ranges from 1 to 2 metres. A Cobra breathes very slowly and exhales only once in 7 - 9 min, or in 12 min if it's a large snake.

The Indian cobra inhabits a wide range of habitats and can be found in dense or open forests, meadows, plains, rice fields, wheat crops, rocky terrain, wetlands, wells, under the sea, in lakes and springs, rivers, oceans, on the mountains, on the trees, in the borrows, shrines and temples, and can even be found in heavily populated urban areas, villages and city outskirts. Their preferred hiding locations are holes in embankments, tree hollows, termite mounds, rock piles and small mammal dens.

Cobra has a highly varied diet, it eats anything from large insects to small mammals and other reptiles. Indian cobras lay their eggs between April and July. The female snake usually lays between 10 and 30 eggs in rat holes or termite mounds and the eggs hatch in 48 to 69 days. The baby snakes are independent from birth and have fully functional venom glands. Bites to humans are less common but are life-threatening emergencies. The Indian cobra's venom is powerful and acts on the synaptic gaps of the nerves, thereby paralysing muscles and, in severe bites, leading to respiratory failure or cardiac arrest.

It moves swiftly in a mysterious gliding motion, and the power of its unblinking, mesmerising eyes holds one spellbound. The other characteristic features of a snake are its forked tongue and the periodical casting of its skin, rejuvenating itself each time.

The deadly venom they hold and inject causes the whole species to be looked upon as dreaded beings that are to be feared, respected and worshipped.

There is always an aura of mystery surrounding the snakes. They are said to be greatly attracted by the strong fragrance of the Champaka flowers (Michelia champaca). The hood of the cobra is also called Phana, Phata, Sphata, Phuta and Dravi (like a ladle or a spoon). A snake is often referred to as Phani or Dravi. There is also a belief that some serpents can grow to such a huge size as to be able to devour goats, and hence are called Ajagara.

Snake habitat -

Snakes, like all reptiles, are cold-blooded, which means they regulate their body temperature by lying in the sun to warm up or moving into the shade to cool down. Snakes play an important role in our ecosystems. They are both predator and prey. By feeding on frogs, mice and other small animals, snakes help to maintain healthy ecosystems and keep the populations of certain animals in check. Snakes are also an important source of food and energy for birds and other larger animals.

Snakes and the environment -

There is a belief that when the snake inhales, it also sucks in the poisonous elements in the air. Thus, the snakes help to purify the atmosphere. They also protect the environment and the crops from the menace of the rodents. An indiscriminate killing of snakes will surely lead to severe ecological imbalance.

Trees and snakes -

In the ancient Indian symbolisms, the tree and the snakes are considered twin spirits. The two have a close association with the mountains. The big trees that populate the hills are the natural abode of the serpents that move around freely amidst the branches and the foliage of the giant trees.

The seals of the Indus Valley excavated from the sites in Harappa and Mohenjo-Daro also depict the close association of trees with the serpents.

Mythology -

There are numerous myths about cobras, and they have a deep religious significance in India. It is greatly respected and feared and even has its own place in Hindu mythology as a powerful deity. Lord Shiva is often depicted with a cobra called Vasuki, coiled around his neck, symbolizing his mastery over Maya - illusion. Lord Vishnu is usually portrayed as reclining on the coiled body of Adishesha, a giant snake deity with multiple cobra heads. Cobras are also worshipped during the Hindu festival of Nag Panchami.

Ancient Indians both feared and revered the snakes, as they were seen to be associated with power, fear and deference. They are considered to be the embodiments and custodians of terrestrial waters. They are creatures of abundant power who defend the underworld and confer fertility and prosperity upon those who connect with them.

The Snakes are always looked upon as mysterious and dangerous, and yet there has always been a strange kind of fascination towards them. The serpent lore in India is not only vast and varied but is also very old and persisting. After the cow, the snake was perhaps the most revered animal of ancient India. Even as early as the 1st century, Huvishka, the emperor of Kushan, had erected a stone sculpture of a hooded serpent with the inscription - propitiation to the worshipful

Naga. That was to mark the consecration of a tank and a garden dedicated to Bhagavat Bhumi Naga.

There was also the practice of erecting a Naga-kastha, a pole with a snake-shaped logo at the top to mark the occasion. There are plenty of references to snake worship in the Hindu and Buddhist mythologies. That tradition still continues. Hindus worship snakes in temples as well as in their natural habitats, offering them milk, incense, and prayers.

Snakes cannot hear -

The snakes are mesmerised by the flute (called pungi) of the snake charmer and sway their heads to the tune of the pungi. It is a common scene of a small town street in India or in a Hindi movie. But can a snake really hear the sound?

Snakes do not have external ears and, therefore, cannot hear like us. They have a hearing organ inside their head, which is connected with their jaw bones. Snakes can detect the vibrations of any sound by this hearing organ. Their jawbones can move up, down, left and right independently. As they crawl on the ground, they can detect the location or direction of a sound by the movement of their jaws. There is a belief that snakes can hear through their eyes; hence, they are called Chakshu-shravana (hearing-by-sight).

They also have highly sensitive sensory nerves throughout their skin, and these are connected with their spinal cord. These nerves enable the snakes to sense even the slightest sound vibration, which is not audible to the human ear. The vibrations of the sound pass from the skin to muscles and from muscles to the jaw bones, which are connected with the inner ears. Thus, sound vibration reaches the inner ears, and snakes can hear the sound. But they don't hear in the same way as we hear. They can hear low-frequency sounds.

Sadhguru explains that when a person becomes still and meditative, the snakes will naturally sense the vibration and gather around him or her. Snakes are stone-deaf and find their way around by literally putting their *'ear to the ground,'* they can sense the vibrations from miles away. Which is not in human perception.

Even Satya Sai Baba, an Indian mystic, had said that when he was young, there would always be snakes coiled up in the corner of his room, but they would never harm him, and he would let them be. There are many such stories in India. In Indian culture, they will never kill a snake. It is worshipped and considered a special blessing when they see a cobra. Offering milk to a snake is always considered auspicious. Snake and mysticism are always connected. Where there is a powerfully vibrant spiritual space, snakes will always be around.

Scientific perspective

Nature's ingenious design of spirals can be seen everywhere, from seashells and whirlpoolsto atoms and embryos and in planets and galaxies. It is a timeless glyph of energy moving in a spiral form.

Thermals the spiral currents

Thermals are updrafts of warm air that rise from the ground into the sky. By flying a spiralling circular path within these columns of rising air, birds are able to ride the air currents and climb to higher altitudes while expending very little energy. Migratory birds and large birds of prey use warm, rising currents of air to gain height. In doing so, they use little energy to fly over long distances. Once they are up high, they glide towards their destination on the wind, just like hang-gliders. Without thermals, many large birds could never get across seas and deserts.

This phenomena of thermals can also be seen on Mars, they are often seen in the form of dust devils, viewed from the Martian rovers and orbiters. Our Milky Way galaxy, which includes Earth and our solar system, is an example of a spiral galaxy.

The Tesla coil

Nikola Tesla was working on a way to supply power without using wires. He almost accomplished his goal when his experiment led him to the creation of the Tesla coil. His invention completely transformed the way electricity was comprehended and used. Radios and televisions still use variations of the Tesla coil today. The power is transferred through the plastic cases using magnetic induction. By using the same principle of Tesla coil, which creates magnetic fields, at some point in the future, electric vehicles are expected to be refuelled within 3 feet of the charging station.

The DNA helix

Deoxyribonucleic acid (DNA) is a molecule that contains the biological instructions that make each species unique. DNA contains the hereditary material which is passed from an adult to their offspring during reproduction. This packaged form of the DNA is called a chromosome, which lies within a cell's nucleus.

DNA is a tightly coiled, threadlike molecule. Each cell is very small because organisms have many DNA molecules per cell; therefore, each DNA molecule must be tightly packaged. DNA's chemical makeup, along with the actions of proteins, twist DNA's two outer edges into a spiral shape, or helix, that helps DNA fit into a tiny nucleus.

So we can see that it is a universal phenomenon that energy moves in a spiral form at an atomic level and the cosmic level.

Yogic perspective

Cobra or the snake also signifies the movement of the kundalini energy because energy always moves in the form of a curvy wave. Kundalini is the life force within us. This energy remains coiled at the base of our spine and spirals upwards through the chakras with yogic practises and meditation. The word kundalini comes from the root word kundal, which means a curl-like shape. The spiralling movement of kundalini energy through the body is one of the reasons why it has been referred to as a snake-like energy.

Inference

Rohini natives will have the steadiness of the bull and receptivity of the snake. They will have good vitality and strong, robust bodies. They will be healthily slim and agile. They are capable of unwavering devotion and dedication and can be highly evolved spiritually, which can be beyond our common understanding.

When they listen, they truly listen, and the advice they give is genuine and to the point. They will hit it on the nail, the perfect solution needed for the many things that you might be anxious about. They are not frivolous about relationships. When they commit themselves to a marriage or a partnership, they will stick it out. They can equally be materialistic and stubbornly ambitious.

Mythology

Deity - Brahma

Brahma and Rohini

The Vedas state that in the beginning, when Brahma (the creator) was planning on populating the earth with humans, he created a woman and named her Rohini. She was so immensely beautiful that he fell in love with her. She ran away, but he chased after her. Eventually, the situation was saved by Lord Shiva, who cut off one of Lord Brahma's head and then in that direction, he could not see or chase Rohini. (To start with, Brahma had 4 heads representing 4 directions). Brahma now has 3 heads. He was also cursed that because of his unreasonable desire he would not be worshipped on earth. That's why Brahma is not popularly worshipped in India.

Rohini and Chandra

Since Rohini was so pretty and charming that, even Moon God fell in love with her and would spend more time with her than with any of his other 26 wives (the 27 nakshatras). Jyeshtha, the eldest sister, complained about this to their father, King Daksha. He cursed Chandra that you will lose your charm, beauty and luminosity. This made Chandra very worried. He asked Lord Shiva for help, who lowered the effect of the curse by granting him 14 14-day cycles towards the full moon, the brighter half (waxing phase) and a 14-day cycle towards the new moon, the darker half (waning phase). The lunar calendar is based on this cycle of waxing and waning phases of the moon.

Hymns dedicated to Soma

In rig Veda there are many hymns dedicated to the Moon God

(Soma), the nourishing aspect of the moon.

Hymn 91

"Thou, Soma, art preeminent for wisdom, along the straightest path thou art our leader.

O royal Soma, our oblations, And Soma let it be thy wish that we may live and may not die.

Be, Soma, a good Friend to us, these herbs, these milch-kine, and these running waters, all these, O Soma, thou hast generated."

In the above verses, Soma, the moon God, is referred to as the giver of wisdom, wealth, guidance, water, cool light, treasures, riches, vitality, health and happiness. He grows the plants, is the healer and protects us against disease and distress.

The Lunar dynasty

According to the Shatapatha Brahmana, Budha (the son of Soma) and a gender-switching deity, Ila (the daughter of Manu), were married and gave birth to a son called Pururavas.

Pururavas's great-grandson was Yayati, who had 5 sons named Yadu, Turvasu, Druhyu, Anu, and Puru. These were the 5 Indo-Aryan tribes as described in the Vedas.

Chandravanshi King Yayati was suffering from a curse he had received from Shukra and had lost his youth. Because King Yayati had married Shukra's daughter Devayani and then married another woman called Sharmishtha. After many years of suffering he requested his sons to help relieve him from that curse. His son Puru agreed to help by giving him his youth. Yayati rewarded him by making him the king. His lineage was King Dushyant, Bharata, Kauravas and Pandavas. Later, Yadu also agreed to help King Yayati, who was very pleased with his son and gave him a boon that Lord Narayana himself would be born in his dynasty. The descendants of Yadu were Sahasrabahu, Kartavirya, Vasudeva and Lord Krishna.

Inference

The Moon's changing phases are closely related to our emotions, moods and feelings. Rohini natives will feel the effect of the Moon more keenly. They will usually follow the lunar astrological calendar closely and observe the auspicious, inauspicious days, good days to travel, or fast, or start any project. Even if they don't follow it on the app, they will be intuitively tuned to the phases of the moon and will instinctively choose a good time or a day to do a certain activity because they will feel it from within.

At the subconscious level, Rohini natives will be very much in tune with the lunar cycles. For example, on full moon days, they will feel the fullness of emotions and strongly feel their likes and dislikes. While on new moon days they will feel the need to spend time on their inner spiritual growth and reflect on things.

Rohini padas

10 deg - 23.20 deg Taurus

Padas	Degrees
1	10 - 13.20 deg Taurus
2	13.20 - 16.40 deg Taurus
3	16.40 - 20 deg Taurus
4	20 - 23.20 deg Taurus

Pada 1

26.40 - 30 deg Aries, Navamsha - Aries (Lord - Mars)

Rashi lord - Venus and Nakshatra Lord - Moon

The first Pada falls in the Navamsha of Aries, where the energies of Venus, the Moon and Mars will be at play. The natives will be fearless and will have a technical approach to things. The play of the Moon, Venus and Mars's energy makes them passionate, indulgent and extravagant. They will have materialistic aspirations combined with spiritual wisdom, which is a wonderful balance. The determination of Mars initiates, the Moon nourishes, and Venus maintains with grace, thoughtful wisdom and a warm sense of affection.

They are pragmatic and pursue stability. Being in a fixed sign of Taurus their determination and steadiness of walking the path bears fruit. They are not frivolous about what they say and do. If they promise to do something, they will deliver it. Whichever project, job, relationship, or belief they follow, they will sincerely devote their time and energy towards that. For example, the 1st Pada of Rohini in the 5th house will be very creative, energetic, artistic and romantic and will do well in the field of entertainment.

It has an earthy quality which helps manifest the desires and is, therefore, a fortunate Pada. The deity of this nakshatra is Brahma so they will have the artistic talent of creating their own product.

From simple activities to big products - they will prefer making their own flower arrangement to buying a ready-made one, or designing their own clothes, making their own new brand and selling it rather than buying an established product. They can do so, but how far it can manifest depends on their effort, determination and planetary placements.

Careers-

Farmers, botanists, herbalists, doctors, pharmacists and nurses, engineers, bankers, accountants, musicians, artists, actors, industrialists, factory owners, grocery store owners, professionals connected to the food industry, hotel managers, shipping business, sports careers, interior decorators, architects, designers, jewellers, business, property dealers, lawyers and builders.

Pada 2

13.20 - 16.40 deg Taurus, Navamsha - Taurus (Lord - Venus)

Rashi lord - Venus and Nakshatra Lord - Moon

This Pada gives the best abundance because of the Yoga Tara 16-degree point. Yoga Tara shows the brightest star of that constellation. So, any planet placed at this degree or within 1-degree orb will give excellent results. It is also a vargottama and Pushkar amsha pada, which shows its auspicious and fortunate effects. Any planets placed in this Pada will give good and excellent results during their dasha and transits. For example, 2nd Pada of Rohini in the 3rd house will have great support and great bonding with their siblings.

This Pada gives good stability in life. There will not be very turbulent, stormy, sudden, life-transforming events in their life. (unless other planetary placements like Rahu, Ketu, Saturn or Mars indicate that). These factors make this the Pada of manifesting desires, actualisation of plans, and fulfilment of dreams.

Double Venus and Moon energies show that natives born in this Pada will have materialistic comforts and resources. They will be expressive about their feelings and thoughts and will have empathy towards others. Since it's a Pada that brings comforts and conveniences, there is a possibility that natives might get carried away by the materialism and luxuries that life offers and totally miss out on the spiritual essence of life.

Careers-

Businessmen, artists, actors, singers, dancers, musicians, designers, florists, beauticians, wedding planners, party venue hirers, gardeners, farmers, dairy owners, hotel managers, cooks, restaurant owners, writers, poets, leaders, gurus, mystics, saints, IT professionals, salesmen, journalists, lawyers, consultants, teachers, doctors, pharmacist, nurses, psychologists, yoga teachers, ayurveda doctors, architects, interior decorators, priests, astrologers, accountants and bankers.

Pada 3

16.40 - 20 deg Taurus, Navamsha - Gemini (Lord - Mercury)

Rashi lord - Venus and Nakshatra Lord - Moon

This Pada has the energies of Venus, Moon and Mercury. Natives born in this Pada will be fortunate and clever. The beneficence of Venus, nurturing of the Moon and intelligence of Mercury is a wonderful combination for a career in arts, science and business. They will be versatile, talented, clever and can literally do well in any profession they choose to follow. For example, the 3rd Pada of Rohini in the 9th house will travel away from home to pursue their higher education, will have an excellent teacher or guide, and will do very well in their studies.

The creativity of Brahma, the steadiness of the Bull and the receptivity of a cobra are exotic ingredients to make a successful soup and have it too. The wonderful news is that they will love to share this treasure of talent and capability with their friends and family. This is the inherent nature of natives born in this Pada.

If there are other malefic influences in the chart it can alter the results by giving struggles and obstacles. But remember, these hurdles are only transitory and are meant to be crossed. There is nothing that can deny the inherent talent to blossom when the time is right. When time is conducive, everything falls in place, and the wheel of destiny rolls smoothly.

Careers-

All careers that require creativity, art, IT professionals, writers, poets, businessmen, lawyers, artists, actors, singers, dancers, musicians, designers, florists, beauticians, wedding planners, party venue hirers, gardeners, farmers, dairy owners, hotel managers, cooks, restaurant owners, writers, poets, leaders, gurus, mystics, saints, salesmen, journalists, consultants, teachers, doctors, pharmacists, nurses, psychologists, yoga teachers, ayurveda doctors, architects, interior decorators, priests, astrologers, accountants and bankers.

Pada 4

20 - 23.20 deg Taurus, Navamsha - Cancer (Lord - Moon)

Rashi lord - Venus and Nakshatra Lord - Moon

Moon Venus Moon is a fantastic combination that gives the goodness of abundance and nurturing. They will have attractive, beautiful, round faces, and large expressive eyes. They tend to easily put on weight and are on the plumpier side. They will have materialistic comforts, but the danger lies in becoming hoarders. They will love travelling and will get a lot of opportunities to go on short and long journeys. For example, the 4th Pada of Rohini in the 4th house will be very attached to their mother and their home, and their mother will be a great support for them.

They love talking about babies, food, money, good clothes, shopping, and are gentle, homely and motherly. Because of their sensitive nature, they easily get hurt by others' opinions or remarks and will withdraw into their secure shell for solace. They are moody. Their moods will fluctuate with the changing phases of the moon, even though they may not consciously realise this. At times they will be serious and concerned or worried, and other times humorous and funny, and of course, they are very imaginative.

Even if there is no cause for concern, they can imagine and make up one. It's not that they seek self-pity, but they do like to know that others sympathise with them. From their perspective, they are not complaining or exaggerating situations, or making them sound like tragedies. They are just being cautious. They need their comfort zone, and for this reason, they will be very security conscious and will always save up for a rainy day.

Careers -

Insurance consultants, hotel managers, cooks, restaurant owners, dietitians, cake and sweet shop owners, grocery store owners, working at a clothes shop - salesman or saleswoman, accountants, bankers, child caretakers, nursery owners, writers, poets, businessmen, artists, singers, dancers, musicians, designers, florists, beauticians, wedding planners, party venue hirers, gardeners, farmers, dairy owners, journalists, teachers, architects, interior decorators, priests, astrologers, doctors, pharmacist, nurses, psychologists, yoga teachers and ayurvedic doctors.

The effect of planets

Rohini - Taurus	Planets that get affected
Yoga Karka - the most benefic planet.	Saturn
Functional Benefic - give good results during their dasha.	Sun and Mercury
Functional Neutral	Moon, Venus, Jupiter and Mars
Functional Malefic - can give problems during their dasha.	Rahu and Ketu

Rohini Ascendant

Rohini lagna natives will have the energy of Venus (sign lord) and Moon (nakshatra lord). They will have a strong vitality and good physique. They have a fantastic appetite and love to try different recipes and enjoy eating delicious meals with friends and family. They are not the types to jump into impulsive action but will look at various possible outcomes and carefully consider them before taking it up. They also have bull-like stubbornness in them, but are more calm and composed, not as fiery in their expression as the bull of Kritika.

They have the blessing or energy that makes things grow, to create new things because Lord Brahma is the ruling deity. Devi Lakshmi is also the co-deity of Rohini which gives them the talent of maintaining and sustaining projects that they or anyone else has started or created. This means whatever assignment or work they take up, it will grow well and they will be able to nourish themselves and others from it. They have the natural good luck and auspiciousness on their side, and specially do well in their own enterprises or businesses.

They are very artistic and imaginative because both Venus and Moon have feminine qualities. The coolness and friendliness of the moon and the beauty and talent of Venus can win over anyone; unknowingly, others find their beauty in thought, word and action irresistible. This makes them very attractive to the opposite sex, and they can please people easily with their charming manners. Their inherent desire is to attract a lover, unite and procreate. For this reason, nature has blessed them with sweet amiability and winsome nature, which is a great asset for them.

The symbol of an ox cart shows their leisurely and laid-back approach to life. Situations change at a steady pace in their life, and they don't feel rushed into any change of circumstances. The fixed nature of this nakshatra doubly grants them a good, steady grounding and guards them against abrupt or disruptive changes. They may come across as stubborn or fixed in their lifestyle or habits, but this stability acts as a fortunate blessing because a steady platform helps them to nourish and grow things.

A serpent signifies their grounded but determined approach to life; they may look vulnerable, but they know very well how to defend themselves if attacked. Just as a cobra's raised hood is enough to warn the potential attacker to stay away, they are very efficient at warding off danger quietly but assertively.

They are determined and firm in their convictions and can be stubborn but do not easily get angry. They do not appreciate abrupt changes, and need time to prepare, think and plan events before taking action. They are on guard against quick reforms and like the familiarity of their comfort zone. They like the steady pace of life and fixed way of doing things. If it's needed they can do peace protests but not aggressive demonstrations.

They would stand up for a genuine cause because they are sincerely and deeply concerned about the financial security and well-being of their family, community or the country. They are musically gifted and have a beautiful voice. They are born singers. Whether they sing professionally or just for the joy of it, they simply love to sing.

A typical Rohini native would rather- embrace and not reject, build and not destroy, nourish and not starve, peace and not war, gentle and not aggression, kind and not cruel, patient and not impatient, quiet and not chatty, content and not needy, provide and not snatch, love and not hate.

Sun in Rohini

When the Sun is placed in Rohini, it will share the influence of Venus and Moon. The natives will have a good personality and a confident, authoritative look. They are loyal, affectionate, generous and love to be appreciated, admired, cherished and complimented. And they will generously shower the well-deserved compliments on others, too. Their language will be dramatic and aristocratic, with a blend of regality and sophistication. They can be arrogant and proud, which can distance people from them.

For example, Sun in Rohini in the 2nd house will give the natives good earning capacity, a good source of income and family resources will be steady because of their father being in a good government job. It will also show that the native will be authoritative at home, proud of his or her family lineage and expect appreciation and respect from the family members. It can bring separation from the family because of having to take on responsibilities of earning money and being the provider, particularly during the dasha of the Sun. They are very creative and imaginative and have a fine sense of aesthetics. Their home and workplace will be well decorated, exuding warmth and affection.

They are very good organisers and are capable of handling large projects, heading a large organisation and taking on a position of responsibility. Their priorities are- to have financial security and a steady source of income for their family and loved ones. They are honest and will honour their promises. They will never back off in times of need when asked, and all they expect in return is appreciation and recognition for their sincere efforts.

Moon in Rohini

The Moon in Rohini will also have the flavour of Venus and Moon again. So, the double influence of the moon makes the natives very imaginative, moody, unpredictable, emotional, changeable and erratic. This fluctuating and wavy influence can bring instability in the moods, but the steadiness of the bull and the earthen influence will be a good stabiliser.

Mukatrikona of the moon lies in 10- 20-degree Taurus, which shows that the moon in Rohini is very happy, comfortable and well placed, and therefore gives good, benefic and nourishing results.

For example, if the Moon in Rohini is placed in the 3rd house, the natives — or their siblings — may possess talents such as singing, cooking exquisite meals, writing fiction or poetry, painting, drawing, sculpting, or designing other forms of art, including IT design. They will also travel a lot, especially short trips for work or enjoyment. They will be passionate about visiting assorted holiday destinations, meeting people and trying exotic recipes from diverse cultures and traditions.

They love to mother or be mothered. They get along very well with their mums, and she always holds a very special place in their hearts, no matter how old they are or how far away they might live from her. Similarly, they share a beautiful bonding with their children too.

They feel emotions very deeply, and therefore, both joy and pain affect them seriously. They are natural nurturers and love to take care and look after others, but are equally receptive to the love or pain they might receive. Since they are very responsive to their environment, unpleasant circumstances can depress them more quickly than others, and pleasant situations can lift them out of it as easily. Just like the phases of the moon change so quickly, so do their moods and emotions. Their moods seem to ride the tides of moon literatim.

The poetry of Rohini

As Chandra moves at a ox cart pace,

Wishing a longer stay in grace.

Rohini, the beauty that attracts the moon,

And creativity that unfolds a special boon.

Through the beauty of Venus untold.

The friendly moon guides and destiny unfolds,

Go, grow and glow.

Waxing on to fullness, Waning into darkness.

The cool poetic moonlight, inspires many more,

Nourishing the hearts with the ambience of love.

The eternal romance of earth and moon,

Can fulfil dreams richly, when aligned to nature's tune.

Sharing the most wonderful gift of life,

In the harmonious play of day and night.

Remedies

- <u>Das Maha Vidyas</u> -Devi Kamala - as described earlier.

<u>Devi Bhuvaneshwari</u> - Moon

According to the legend stated in Shaktism, Bhuvaneshwari Devi is the queen of all worlds. She controls all processes of the mind - thoughts, memory and emotions. She is worshipped for peace of mind, sound sleep, good relationships and harmonious marriage. She is said to give relief from stress, lack of concentration, frequent distractions of the mind, mental diseases, bad dreams, wet dreams, sleepwalking, hysteria, sexual perversions, cough, cold and asthma.

She can control the bad effects of South-West and North-West corners in Vastu, so keeping her image and yantra, with the mantra written on it, in these directions will negate any inauspicious vibes.

Remedies for the weak moon -

- Taking care of your mother or a mother-like figure is the best remedy.

- Wearing white-coloured clothes resonates with the energy of the moon.

- Looking at the full moon and visualising the nourishing moon rays healing the body and mind will help to enhance positive thinking.

- Those who have a moon with low shadbala score, or moon is conjunct or direct aspect of Rahu, Ketu, Saturn, or Mars, chanting her Mantra 108 times on Mondays will help to strengthen the moon. While chanting, keeping her yantra and image in front is recommended. This will help the native to have peace of mind, a sound sleep, and harmonious relationships. It is recommended to chant her mantra for 11 consecutive Mondays to reap the benefits.

Mantras of Devi Bhuvaneshwari -

"Om Hreem Bhuvaneshwaraye Hreem Namah," and "Om Hreem."

Other remedies

- Reverence to Mother Nature and cows is a wonderful remedy.

- Worshipping Brahma, the creator, or honouring his energy by creating anything new.

- Offering milk on Mondays or Fridays at a temple.

- Wearing white or light colours.

- Plant a Jamun tree if possible.

- Wearing a 2 mushing rudraksh will help to balance the shiva and Shakti energy (feminine and masculine). This will help improve relationships and any mental health issues.

- Chanting the Rohini nakshatra mantra 108 times regularly for 40 days will enhance the benefic aspects of Rohini.

'Om rm rrm lrm lrrm Rohini nakshatraye namah.'

Example

Moon in Rohini Pada 2 in the 11th house

This is the example of my friend Aruna.

Born 11th May 1967, 12 pm Ludhiana Punjab

Exact time of birth not known.

She has a very attractive round face and beautiful long wavy black hair. She comes from a business family, and they are very well off financially. She had a love marriage and is very well settled. Her interest was not so much in studies or academics. She has always had a lot of material comforts. She always looks for reassurance from friends and appreciates their support. She is feminine, homely, warm, caring, and gentle and loves children, loves well designed clothes, cooking, and music.

Analysis-

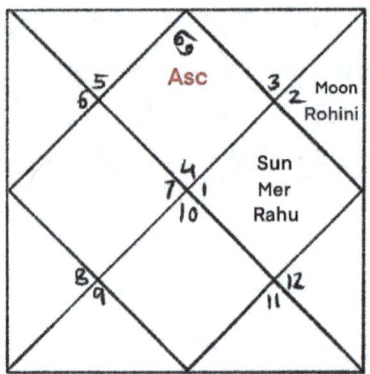

She has her moon in Rohini in Pada 2, which brings the beneficence of resources, wealth, comforts and beauty. Moon is sitting in Rohini in her 11th house of Taurus. It has given a lot of easy gains and fulfilment of desires. She got married in 1989 when she was running her <u>Rahu Mercury Moon</u> dasha. Rahu, Mercury and Sun are in Aries in the 10th house and Moon in the 11th house. Moon is the lord of her Ascendant - Cancer. We can see that this time period fulfilled her desires because the moon is sitting in the 11th house. While Mercury is the lord of the 3rd house and 12th house. Which made her move away from home, and Rahu amplified the effect of the desired results, in terms of having a grand wedding.

5
Mrigashira

Om em Mrigashira nakshatraye namah

Zodiac degrees	23.20 deg Taurus - 6.40 deg Gemini Taurus - 1st and 2nd padas Gemini - 3rd and 4th padas
Ruling planet	Taurus - Venus and Gemini - Mercury Mrigashira - Mars
Sanskrit name	Mrigashira means a deer's head -Mriga - deer, Shira - head. Other names are - Saumya meaning benevolent and Soma - the divine nectar.
Astronomical name	Bellatrix, along with 3 other stars, is seen as a bright star in the Orion constellation, which represents Mrigashirsha. The ancient seers saw it as a deer head shape in the sky.
Symbol	Taurus - Bull and Gemini - Twins Rohini - Deer's head and pot full of Soma (nectar).
Element	Earth - Taurus and Air - Gemini
Deity	Chandra (Moon God) and Devi Parvati (wife of Lord Shiva).
Quality	Mridu - mild - Mrigashira and Sthira - fixed - Taurus Dwi - dual - Gemini
Shakti	Piranha Shakti - Power to give fulfilment and joy.
Cast	Farmer
Gender	Female - Taurus and Male - Gemini
Motivation	Artha - to gather resources - Taurus Kama - to fulfil desires - Gemini
Triguna	Tamas - Taurus and Satwa - Gemini

Tridosha	Kapha Vata
Body parts	Eyes and eyebrows
Direction	South, west and northwest.
Month	1st half of Mrigashira - December.
Bird	Pigeon
Sound	ve, vo, ka, kee
Tree	Khedira
Chakras	Muladhara - Mars, Swadhishtana - Venus and Ajna - Mercury.
Das Maha Vidya	Devi Kamala - Venus, Devi Tripura Sundari - Mercury And Devi Bagalamukhi - Mars

Special degrees -

Yoga Tara	29.45 deg Taurus It's a point where the planet will show the strongest and sure results during its dasha.
Amrit nadi	1.42 - 2.36 deg Gemini Gives good results like the nectar that nourishes.
Visha nadi	26.26 - 27.20 deg Taurus Brings situations which one does not like dealing with.

Auspicious and inauspicious table -

Auspicious	Inauspicious
Activities Good for all learning and light-hearted activities, artistic and creative projects, singing, drama, dance, acting, and for learning IT skills, enrolling for any new degree or diploma courses, healing and rejuvenation, spiritual initiations, travelling, all social events, taking a new name, or naming a newborn child, for advertising, sales and all promotional activities which involve dealing with people.	Activities Not good for marriage because Mars, being the lord of Mrigashira, gives it plenty of energy and an aggressive streak, too, which may not be conducive for marital bliss. For any confrontations and making long term plans.
Days Mondays - only when it falls on the 2nd, 5th, 7th or 12th lunar day. Wednesdays - only when it falls on the 2nd, 3rd, 7th, 8th, 12th or 13th lunar day.	Days Sundays - only when it falls on the 3rd, 4th, 8th, 9th, 13th or 14th lunar day. Thursdays - only when it falls on the 6th, 8th, 9th, 12th or 13th lunar day.

Compatibility table -

Mrigashira	Compatible with
Sexual compatibility Yoni animal	Mrigashira- Female serpent, cobra - compatible with- Male serpent, cobra - Rohini.
Sign compatibility	Taurus - Padas 1 and 2 - Virgo and Capricorn. Gemini - Padas 3 and 4 - Libra and Aquarius.
Nakshatra compatibility	Chitra and Dhanishta.
Lunar day compatibility	5th Lunar day - panchami tithi.
Day compatibility	Tuesday and Wednesday
Colour compatibility	Red, green and pastel colours.
Numerological compatibility	2, 5 and 9 - and all numbers that add up to make 2, 5 and 9.
Sound compatibility	Mars - guttural sounds - ka, kha, ga, gha, kna Venus - palatal sounds - cha, ccha, ja, jha, nga Mercury - lingual sounds - ta, tha, da, dha, na

Sign Lord and Nakshatra Lord - <u>Venus, Mercury and Mars.</u>

Venus and Mars - as described earlier.

<u>Mercury - Lord of Gemini.</u>

The Vedic name of Mercury is <u>Budha -</u> which represents the discriminating intellect. The famous example of Prince Sidhart who was called Budha after his enlightenment, because he realised his true self and reached the peak of his intelligence. The other name of Mercury is <u>Saumya</u> because he is the son of the moon. Saumya also means calm, gentle, and unruffled. The predominating qualities of Mercury are curiosity, intelligence, speed - -quickness and communication - speech.

They will have a very friendly, easygoing persona and are quick to adjust to any kind of changing situation. Mercury is the planet of speed. Therefore, mercury-ruled people are fast thinkers, get bored easily, have a very good sense of humour, are curious and intelligent, and are very good with mimicry, accounts, finance and communication.

People around them are impressed by their intellectual prowess. This is because their inherent interest is to learn. They grasp new concepts very quickly and are able to articulate their thoughts very well, which makes them successful businessmen, negotiators, accountants and writers. Mercury is also personified as the Prince who doesn't have to struggle hard, usually, things are laid out for Mercury-ruled natives. All the facilities are provided for them; they just have to walk the path, and their life pattern tends to follow the path of accumulating knowledge.

Inference

The 3rd and 4th padas of Mrigashira are placed in Gemini, which is ruled by Mercury here the influence of Mars (lord of Mrigashira) and Mercury makes them very quick-witted, intelligent, brave, courageous, outspoken, and will always stand up for a rightful cause.

Quality -

Sthira - as described earlier.

Natives born in the 1st and 2nd Pada will have a fixed or stubborn quality towards their thought patterns and actions. Even the karmic patterns are not so easily washed away by doing a superficial remedy. They have to go through the transformative process of experiencing the joys, the pain, success and failures. All signs and nakshatras falling in fixed signs have this relentless repetition of the same cyclical patterns showing up every few years until they come to a deeper understanding of why it is happening and what lessons need to be learnt. Once a deeper insight into the problem dawns on them, the solutions can be seen as clear as daylight.

Dual -dwi -Gemini

Natives born in the 3rd and 4th Pada of Mrigashira will have a dual nature. It's almost like 2 personalities residing in one body. One masked version is for the people, and another hidden version is for themselves.

The need for duality arises only for 2 reasons - either when the outer circumstances do not allow us the freedom to express fully - who we are or would like to be. Or we might get entangled with thoughts or activities that we feel need to be hidden for personal, social, spiritual, religious, political, financial, legal, or ethical reasons.

It's not that they are choosing these tricky situations. Still, as the drama of life unfolds, they find themselves caught up in these circumstances - willingly or unwillingly, they get caught up in moral or ethical dilemmas! For this reason, the initial hesitation or seeming uncertainty about making decisions can be there. This quality will be there for all signs and nakshatras classified as dual.

Mridu - Mild

Mrigashira natives will be gentle-natured, sensitive, intuitive, artistic, imaginative, empathetic and emotional. For them, relationships and friendships are more important than being ruthlessly ambitious. Sharing and communicating brings them the greatest joy.

Their happiest moments are spent with their friends or family, exchanging ideas with their colleagues, sharing their new project plan with their partner, designing a new surprise gift for their loved ones, planning a family holiday, or walking in the park with their neighbour. All activities that involve human interaction, being close to nature, acts of kindness towards animals, playing with the children, and creating something new give them great happiness.

They don't like confrontations, fights or arguments. Any acts of violence or harsh words disturb their sensitive and delicate constitution.

Most of their life situations are such that they don't have to deal with rough, aggressive or harsh actions or abusive language. They usually don't have to go fight a war or face a war-like situation. Generally, their daily life routines are smooth and easygoing. It is said that destiny dishes out only as much pain as much as we can handle, so all those who are born in the mild nakshatras are generally given mild, protected and gentle scenarios to deal with.

Elements -

Earth - as described earlier.

Air

The element of air is most crucial and an immediate need for an organism to stay alive. The lack of air can kill us faster than the lack of any other element. Thus, the concept of Vayu (air) is synonymous with that of prana (life energy). The ancient rishis have described air in 5 forms according to its direction of movement. These 5 types of movements are called the 5 vayus or pranas.

N	Vayu (prana)	Function
1	Prana	Inward breath
2	Udana	Upward movement
3	Apana	Downward movement
4	Vyana	Outward movement
5	Samana	Balanced and stabilizes these movements, a force that pulls toward the centre.

By understanding the quality of the element, we can know it's functioning and utility. Air is mobile, cool, light, dry, rough, subtle, flowing, sharp, clear, and hard. Although air is subtle, its effects are observable, and so we have a sense of what it is. Air makes the empty space become active and alive. The element of air represents the capacity for motion or kinetic energy.

Air and the sense of touch -

Ayurveda describes Sparsha as the sense of touch in its most subtle form. Touch and air are inseparable because through the skin, we experience the sense of touch, and skin is associated with the element of air. Touch which is the sense organ associated with the air element. Especially through our hands, we reach out, touch and feel things. Hence, disorders of tactile perception are the result of disturbances in the functions of the air element in the body.

<u>Air and movement</u>

Air is the energy behind all motion. It is the energy that allows blood to circulate, breath to move, nerve impulses to glide, thoughts to flow, and joints to propel our movement. Disturbances in the functions of air result in an erratic motion. Air may move too fast, too slow, or become obstructed and blocked. Each occurrence produces different effects depending upon the location of the air that has been disturbed.

This table shows the effect of the disturbed flow of air on different systems in our body.

Body system	Excessive flow of air	Deficient flow of air	Blocked flow of air
Nervous system	Restlessness and hyperactivity	Sluggishness and dullness	Loss of motion.
Digestive system	Diarrhoea	Sluggish digestion and heaviness	Constipation or obstruction.
Circulatory system	Increased heart rate and blood pressure.	Slower heart rate and poor circulation.	Death of the tissue.
Joints	Hyper uncontrolled mobility	Slower movement	Frozen joints.

<u>Air and Vata</u>

The vata dosha contains both air and ether. Any vitiation of air will ultimately result in a vitiation of vata. Vata remains healthy when the flow of air is regulated and is able to flow without obstruction. The balance between activity and rest is the key to healthy vata.

<u>Balanced flow of air -</u>

A smooth flow of air helps to keep the Vata balanced and the body and mind healthy. This can be done by -

- Having steady routines.

- Eating heavier foods - cereals, pulses, grains and milk will also support and stabilise the light, cold and dry qualities of the air element.

- Practising yoga and meditation will help to keep calm and deal with stressful situations with ease. Any kind of tension blocks the flow of air, and over time, it builds up into chronic ailments like joint aches and pains. Therefore, it's very important to make time for spiritual and yogic practises.

Air element and bitter foods -

In our diet, the bitter taste contains the most air. The bitter taste is composed of both air and ether; it is the air that provides the uniqueness of the taste. Consuming bitter foods is an excellent way to increase the influence of the air element. This is wonderful if a person is feeling sluggish or lazy. However, an excess of air in the diet, especially in the diet of an individual with a vata constitution, can result in too much hyperactivity which can lead to a loss of stability and cause dryness. Therefore, to balance the vata, one should eat warm cooked meals, soaked nuts and more grains and cereals. Keeping a proper balance in accordance with a person's constitution and the current state of health is very important.

Air season - Autumn -

Autumn is the season of the air element. As the leaves begin to fall, the weather becomes cooler, and there is a sense of transition or movement in the weather. It represents the gradual transition of nature from its full bloom towards the dormancy of winter. Excessive travelling at this time of the year can cause anxiety and restlessness. While it is natural to feel lighter at this time, excess lightness can cause depletion of energy. Therefore, keeping the balance between activity and rest is very important.

Air and transitional phase of life-

In the cycle of life and death, air represents the transitional period between the most productive years of adulthood and the last years of our life in old age.

Women go through the transition of menopause at this time, while men find themselves desiring retirement. The idea of motion is reflected in the transition. To live in harmony with this time it is necessary to spend some time in meditation and prayer. Excessive activity during the later years of life can cause anxiety, restlessness and sleeplessness.

Inference

Those who are born with their Ascendant, Sun or Moon in the 3rd and 4th padas of Mrigashira, which are placed in Gemini, will have the influence of the air element. So, they should take precautions as needed for a Vata-predominant tridosha. Steady regular routines, eating warm meals, meditation and yogic practises will help to balance the vata. Basically, if they pay close attention to their body type and stay in tune with the seasons and cycles of Mother Nature they will be able to keep their air element in balance and stay healthy.

Motivation- <u>Artha</u> - as described earlier.

Kama

Kama can be described as harmonious experiences that arise from a good relationship between the self and the world. The word Kama literally means desire. The Vedic texts do not look at Kama only from the perspective of sensual pleasures but in a broader context of all human desires. It signifies desires, wishes, passion, emotions, the pleasure of the senses, the aesthetic enjoyment of life, affection, and love - with or without sexual connotations. Kama has been defined as love without violating dharma - the personal duties.

Kama Deva is personified by the deity of love, sensory pleasures and sexual union. The ancient Vedic texts narrate a story of how Lord Brahma had told Narada to send Kamadeva to influence Lord Shiva so that the marriage between Shiva and Parvati could be felicitated. It is said that Kama Deva was reduced to ashes, when he had come to entice Lord Shiva.

In Vedic astrology, the 3rd sign of the zodiac - Gemini, is called Mithuna, which means union of the male and female, sexual union, mating, pairing, or a couple. Very aptly the sign of Gemini is represented by twins, and it's also classified as a dual sign.

The famous epic of Mahabharata is a wonderful example of the cycle of Kama - the human relationships - the pains, joys, pursuits, triumphs and defeats that human beings are capable of facing because of their endless pursuit of desires.

Inference

For those who are born in the 3rd and 4th padas of Mrigashira, their actions and thoughts will be driven by desires, hopes, aspirations and ambitions, for both worldly and spiritual pursuits. They are ambitious and enthusiastic and are passionate about achieving the goals they set for themselves. The fulfilment of desires is a basic need for them. The path can be easy or tough but their determined effort ultimately makes them reach their desired destination.

On close observation, they will realise that the vicious circle of desires is a never-ending process. At some point in their life, they will begin to feel the illusory nature of their desires and will want to turn away from chasing worldly dreams and seek the inner truth that will lead them to the ultimate freedom.

Triguna - Tamas - as described earlier.

Satwa

The word Satwa is derived from the root word Sat, which means truth. Therefore, all activities (in thought, word and action) that connect to the ultimate truth, the inner reality, or our consciousness become sattvic qualities. Satwa is the quality of goodness, positivity, truth, intelligence, awareness, serenity, balance, harmony, peacefulness, and virtuousness that guides us towards dharma (righteousness).

Sattvic qualities -

Joy, delight, happiness, peace, wellness, freedom, love, compassion, equanimity, empathy, friendliness, focus, self-control, satisfaction, trust, fulfilment, calmness, bliss, cheerfulness, gratitude, fearlessness and unselfishness.

"Sattva Guna, being pure, is illuminating, and it frees one from all reactions of bad karma. Those situated in that mode become conditioned by a sense of happiness and knowledge." – Bhagavad Gita

The ancient text of Shrimad Bhagavatam describes the Satwic qualities as - Control of the mind and control over the senses, tolerance, discrimination, sticking to one's prescribed duty, truthfulness, kindness, discretion between the right and wrong, contemplation, contentment, generosity, renunciation of selfishness, faith in the guru, being aware improper thought and action, charity, simplicity and humbleness.

The activities that support and enhance the Sattvic qualities are -

- Having a regular routine.
- Going to bed early and waking up early in the morning.
- Have an exercise routine.
- Spend time on your own - contemplate and meditate.
- Stay away from intoxication
- Regulate your sex life.
- Work-life balance.
- Take time away from electronic gadgets.
- Spend time in nature.
- Vegetarian diet.

If one chooses to consume sattvic food, perform sattvic activities, and cultivate a sattvic mindset, the consciousness will gradually be raised to sattva guna. A person situated in sattva can make better decisions, will be content and fulfilled, will be calm and at ease even in difficult situations, and can lead a happy and healthy life.

Inference

The 3rd and 4th padas of Mrigashira are placed in Gemini, which has Satwic energy because it's governed by the air element. They will be active towards actions that promote spirituality, religion, or any ethical or righteous acts that are done for the wellbeing of all. Their actions will be motivated by the desire to know the ultimate truth, and will have a lot of zeal, fire and enthusiasm to pursue such goals. They like to be actively involved, and through their actions they are able to make a difference for themselves and for others. Their thoughts and actions are not selfish.

Tridosha - Kapha - as described earlier.

Those who are born with their Ascendant, Sun or moon in Mrigasira padas 1 and 2 will have the tridosha of Kapha because the first 2 padas fall in Taurus, which is an earth sign. Those who are born in padas 3 and 4 will have the tridosha of Vata because these padas are placed in Gemini, which is an air sign.

Vata -

The qualities of Vata are - dry, light, cold, rough, subtle, mobile and clear. Those who have the predominant tridosha of Vata are usually slim with bony limbs and a straight body shape. Their skin is fine and dry, and they feel the cold more than others. They tend to have an irregular and erratic appetite. Their digestive system is sensitive, and they are prone to constipation or stomach upset if they feel stressed, have a hectic routine, or have constant travel.

They are very creative, because the quality of air does not restrict to boundaries. They are very friendly, adaptable, enthusiastic, active and alert. When Vata is out of balance they can become restless and jumpy and can lose their focus.

Vata types are quick to learn, are often very chatty, spiritually perceptive and are the happiest when in contact with nature and are outdoors. They have a heightened sense of touch and an appreciation for beauty.

Vata foods are pungent, bitter and astringent in taste. Therefore, choosing the foods that have the opposite quality of heaviness - for example, warm food and drinks, milk and dairy products, grains and cereals, sweet and salty foods.

This table shows the qualities when Vata is in balance, out of balance, and the recommended diet and seasons that are conducive.

In balance	Good health, motivated, energetic, active, flexible, friendly, ambitious, joyful, friendly, open-minded, free in spirit, embrace change and learn easily, clear and alert, sleep long and lightly, have balanced digestion, good circulation and an even body temperature.
Out of balance	Digestive disorders, sleep disorders, anxiety, irritability, nervous, hyperactive, dry skin, constipation, tiredness, fatigue, forgetful, spaced-out, anxious, lack of focus, difficulty in falling asleep, and poor circulation.
Diet	Cooked foods, warm meals, seasonal fruits and vegetables, soaked dried fruits, oats, rice, wheat, eggs, fish, chicken, honey, jaggery, milk, ghee, and warm drinks.
Seasons	Spring and summer

Chakras - Muladhara, Swadhishtana and Ajna

Muladhara and Swadhisthana - as described earlier.

Ajna

Ajna means the command centre. This chakra is located between the eyebrows. If the energies move into Ajna chakra. One is intellectually realised. He or she can see things clearly. That's why we call them seers, saints or rishis. One can see everything the way it is and is absolutely at peace. That's why it's called the 3rd eye (trinetra)- the inner wisdom.

Jupiter is the planet of wisdom and higher knowledge, and Mercury is our intelligence and the power to discern. Both these qualities are essential for one to be intellectually realised or to know their true nature through Jnana marga - the path of knowledge. Therefore, it makes logical sense for these 2 planets to represent the Ajna chakra, which is the seat of inner knowing and gives clarity of thought and the ability to envision things.

"Ajna sthanam shanti dayani." - Linga Bhairavi

In the Devi Linga Bhairavi chant, Ajna chakra is described as the giver of peace.

Chakra	Planets	Symbol	Element	Sound	Colour	Petals	Glands
Ajna	Jupiter Mercury Rahu	Upward facing triangle.	Air and space	Aum	Purple	2	Pineal and Pituitary glands

It has 2 petals, which represent the last remaining duality of self and God. It also shows that the energy is more concentrated and diverges only at 2 points - left and right. The symbol of upward-facing triangles shows the upward-moving energy that is capable of piercing through the veil of false illusions and seeing the truth clearly as it is. This focused energy helps to break through the veil of illusion and perceive images of the beyond.

Ajna means command. It is the command centre for our bodily functions and is located between the eyebrows. The brain in the frontal area of the forehead coordinates the activity of the pituitary gland and the cerebellum. In medical terms, it is called hypophysis and has a vital role. Together with the hypothalamus, it constitutes the command system of the rest of the endocrine glands. Ajna chakra is also the location of the pineal gland. On a psychic level, it is responsible for superior intuition, clairvoyance, the capacity to anticipate certain events, and extra-sensorial perceptions. When the Ajna chakra - the 3rd eye gets activated, one will have an excellent photographic memory.

Ajna Chakra represents the superior mental consciousness, which allows the direct perception of the invisible worlds and the direct perception of the subtler aspects of the manifested universe. Ajna Chakra is considered the centre of spiritual perception. It is a focal point of sending and receiving energies, ideas, thoughts, and mental structure through which we can conceive and understand the subtle mental universe - our inner universe. The one who manages to raise the energies to Ajna chakra can visualise life with a deeper and more profound perspective.

In yogic traditions, a healthy Ajna chakra enables us to step beyond the mind into the realm of universal knowledge and wisdom. When Ajna's chakra is balanced, one is able to see things as they truly are and can make choices based on intuition and clarity of perception.

If Ajna's chakra is overactive, then we may feel overwhelmed with intuitive interaction and hypersensitivity and can feel disconnected. On the other hand, if it is blocked, one is unable to experience subtle aspects of life, will have a narrow-minded approach, feel self-doubt, indecision and lack of clarity. Physical symptoms can represent eye problems, headaches, migraines, sleep disorders, endocrine imbalances, and issues with the pituitary gland, the pineal gland and the hypothalamus.

Healing

Ajna's chakra can get blocked with anxiety and stress. Pranayama practises and meditation will help to keep the mind calm, bring balance to the thoughts and harmonise the emotions. Pranayama- alternate nose breathing, Om chanting, Beeja mantra chanting - *Aum* and *Ksham*, and meditation can help to balance this chakra.

Inference

Mrigashira has the Muladhara energy because it's Lord is Mars. The 1st and 2nd padas of Mrigashira are placed in Taurus - ruled by Venus. Therefore, they have the quality of Swadhisthana, and the 3rd and 4th padas are in Gemini - ruled by Mercury, which carries the energy of Ajna chakra.

The Muladhara energy gives them good vitality, Swadhisthana makes them passionate, and Ajna gives them a spiritual inclination. When the energies in the chakras are balanced, they are in good health, enjoy everything thoroughly and have a high level of awareness because of the upward movement of energy. If the energies are not balanced, they can feel a lack of vitality, low moods and disinterest.

Shakti - Prinana Shakti - the power to give fulfilment and joy.

Mrigashira natives have the inherent quality of being joyful and spreading that joy to others. Whenever they feel stressed the best remedy for them will be to do something that makes them happy or others happy. In other words, they can bounce out of low moods very easily because of their special power to attract joy. Our subconscious and unconscious levels have a more powerful influence than our conscious thoughts and actions.

Sadhguru has said this many times - *"whatever our consciousness is focused on is what will manifest in our lives and around us."*

Symbolic signification

<u>Taurus</u> - as described earlier, <u>Gemini</u> - Twins

<u>Mrigashira</u> - Deer - Deer's head and Soma- a pot of nectar.

Twins -

The sign of Gemini is associated with twins because by joining the dots together of the stars that are seen in the constellation of Gemini, they form the shape of 2 individuals standing together. This image literally describes the prominent characteristics of Gemini natives.

Those who are born with their Ascendant, Sun or Moon in Gemini will be friendly, very good communicators, and will almost always have a best friend, partner, sister, brother, or someone with whom they get along very well and get to share their life's experiences, their joys and sorrows, just like having a twin.

They are very good actors and can live as 2 personalities in one person. At work, they can behave completely differently compared to how they are at home, and they are capable of playing both roles with ease. This also shows that having someone to share ideas with is their basic need and ultimate joy, too. Life grants them this special blessing and talent to be able to articulate their thoughts so well that others are naturally attracted and impressed by what they have to say.

Moreover, being friendly is their inherent nature. You will never find a Gemini without a friend, they will either be talking, messaging or emailing someone. If there is no one to talk to they always have their imaginary twin to give them company. They are equally efficient at communicating through words, speech, thoughts, images, art or music. To put it simply, they are multi-talented, skilful in gathering and sharing information, and excellent at all kinds of online and offline communication.

Deer

There are about 60 species of deer. They originally lived in the northern hemisphere. Deer are even-toed hoofed mammals, and most deer have antlers on their head (deer horns). Female deer have smaller antlers or no antlers. Deer are a very diverse family, and their characteristics vary in size of the deer, skin colour, patterns on the skin, shape and size of the antlers.

They do not make dens. When they want to rest, they just find a safe, comfortable spot under the low-hanging tree branches and do not store food for winter. During the cold season, they dig under the snow for food with their hooves. During spring time, the doe will give birth to 1 or 2 fawns and the group stays together until the fawns are 4-5 months old. They are excellent jumpers and swimmers and prefer mixed grassland areas. They mostly eat a low-fibre diet - fresh grass, leaves, fruits, fungi and lichen.

Musk deer

Musk deer are a species which make moschus and do not have antlers. They look different from the other deer and are found in forest areas of Asia and in the Himalayan regions of India. The musk gland is found in the male adults. It's a sac located between the genitals and the umbilicus. The Male deer uses these fragrant secretions to attract the female deer.

Interesting facts

- Deer have 4 chambered stomachs, which help them digest a variety of plant food.
- The Chinese water deer sheds and grows new antlers every year.
- Reindeer have the largest and heaviest antlers.
- Male deer Antlers are intended for selecting mate through combat and to define their hierarchical position in the group.
- The doe (female deer) will hide each fawn (baby deer) in a different spot.
- Deer have been used as a mythical symbol in many cultures -

    Rudolf the reindeer stories from the bible.

    Ramayana story - Sita's desire for the golden deer.

- They have many predators (wolves, lions and humans) and are therefore always aware of imminent danger and are on guard. They can listen and smell danger.
- By nature, Deer are social and like to live together, this ensures their safety.
- They warn the other deer through posture and sound.
- They are outstanding runners.
- Most of the year, Deer stay in single-sex groups.

Soma - the pot of nectar

Rig Veda hymn 91 Soma

" *Thou Soma art preeminent for wisdom along the straightest path thou art our leader. Praise–loving Lord of plants art thou.*

Enricher, healer of disease, wealth–finder, prospering our store,

Be Soma a good Friend to us."

Vedic texts describe Soma as the nectar of Gods. It is also another name for the Moon. Without this necessary beneficial, wholesome and nourishing aspect of the Moon - the plants would not have the herbal quality of rejuvenation, cows milk would not be able to nourish the calf, and even for the humans - the mothers would not have the blessing of soma in their milk to nourish their young infants.

The nourishing aspect of the moon comes alive in the coolness of the night. All the romantic poetry and scripts are inspired by the moon because it has the quality of nourishing the mind with - imaginative and creative thoughts and emotions with - feelings of love and romance. It has the caring qualities of a mother and is gentle and friendly to all.

In Rig Veda, Soma is said to be of many different types, and it exists in the plants. Somalata (Ephedra) is one of the plants found in Afghanistan and Iran and is used as a soma herb by the Persians. The vedas have named 5 plants which are rich in soma - darbha, marijuana, barley, kusha and kushta. All these herbs have a direct impact on the mind.

The Himalayan water taken from gomukh (the starting point of river Ganga) is also one kind of Soma, because of its richness and the purity of nutrients. In Ayurveda, herbal honey and ghee preparations are also called soma.

Shushrut (Ancient Ayurvedic doctor) has mentioned 24 soma plants growing in the Himalayas. Soma is an important part of Shamanic medicine as well.

In yogic philosophy - Soma (Amrita) is the sweet nectar secreted from the pineal gland. When one reaches that higher state with regular yogic practises, the sweetness of this nectar can be felt on the tongue. Soma, therefore, has a spiritual significance because of its quality of nourishment.

Inference

Deer

Mrigshira natives will have the alertness and awareness of the deer. They are surely seekers - for knowledge, money, love, friends, spirituality, or whatever is their currency of joy. They will either be searching for something, or someone will be searching for them. Most of the time, they don't have to go looking for people or situations, but the situations and people catch up with them. They are almost mystical, divine and enchanting, and others feel drawn to them - for this reason, they feel the need to guard themselves.

They can be timid wanderers always in search of something and weary of any looming danger. Thankfully they are elusive and know their escape route, and will be found only if they feel safe. They totally feel at home in nature, the greenery, the trees, the pastures and scenic landscapes. Their sense of smell and listening is excellent, and their stride is extraordinarily graceful. They are gentle and romantic, prefer calm environments and love to be with family and friends.

Soma

Mrigashirsha natives are blessed with the quality to nourish others and be nourished in all aspects of life - health, food, thoughts and emotions. They will have a knack for knowing and selecting the nourishing herbs that relax the mind. Soma - particularly refers to the nourishing and feminine quality of the moon. In scientific or logical terms, it would represent the liquids, fluids and juicy parts - of food, vital body fluids, emotions, feelings, sense of love, romance, caring, devotion, pleasure and intoxication. Mrigashira natives are blessed with the possibility to experience wholesome nourishment - physically, socially, psychologically and spiritually.

Mythology

Deity - Chandra - Moon God and Parvati, Lord Shiva's wife.

Chandra

In Atharva Veda, the moon God is described as a young, handsome and charming man who has a club and a lotus in his hands. He is the father of Buddha (Mercury). He wears white robes, and his chariot is driven by a reindeer or an antelope. He rides a chariot of 3 wheels driven by a reindeer. In his chariot, he visits his 27 wives in one month and repeats this cycle over and over again every month. Chandra is also called Soma - the nectar, Taradhipati - Lord of the stars, and Nishakara - the night maker.

Chandra, the moon God, met Tara, the wife of Brihaspati (Jupiter) and was captivated by her beauty. Tara was also attracted to him. From their union Budha (Mercury) was born. Brihaspati, being upset, declared war on Chandra, but the Devas intervened, and Tara was returned to Brihaspati. Eventually Brihaspati was impressed by the intelligence of Buddha (Mercury) and accepted him as his son.

After Tara returned to her husband Brihaspati, Chandra married Daksha's 27 daughters. Among them, Rohini is his favourite wife. So the other wives complained to Daksha who cursed Chandra. That he will lose his lustre and charm. Chandra prayed to Lord Shiva and asked for his help. His curse was then softened - to have waxing and waning phases and was thus partially released from the curse.

Parvati

The ancient Vedic texts state that Parvati is the reincarnation of Sati (Lord Shiva's first wife). She was born to the mountain king Himavat and Queen Menaka. She is also called Uma or Gauri.

From a young age she had nurtured the wish to marry Shiva.

But Lord Shiva was an ascetic who would not open his eyes for days on end, steeped in deep meditation and was not even remotely interested in marriage.

After many years of waiting and serving him with ceaseless devotion - Shiva, at last, pleased with her sincerity, agreed to marry her. They settled at Mount Kailash after marriage. As always, Shiva would be gone for many years at a stretch, lost in deep states of meditation. While Parvati felt very alone during his long absences, one day, she thought of creating her own baby to reduce her boredom. Parvati took the paste of mud and Chandan from her body and created a baby. One day, Parvati was going to take a bath and asked her Son to stand guard and not let anyone enter.

This was the time when Shiva came back after many years, oblivious to what had happened while he was away. As instructed, Shiva was stopped at the entrance by a young boy. Even after revealing his identity, the young boy would not let him enter. This enraged Shiva, and he cut off his head. When Parvati came out, she was devastated and told Shiva the story about her Son's birth and asked him to bring her son back to life. Lord Shiva realised his mistake and asked one of the ganas (his devotees) to give him his head, whose head looked like an elephant. So the boy's head was replaced by a Gana's head - that's why he was named Ganapati - Lord of the ganas.

Lord Ganesha

Since the Ganas were not beings from this earth, but were celestial beings who were very close to Lord Shiva and always used to hang around with him. They even spoke in a cacophony of sounds that no one could understand. Ganesha's head looks like an elephant, but it was not an elephant head that was put on him, but a Gana's head - that's why he is called Ganapati and not Gajapati (Gaja means an elephant).

For this reason Ganesha is incredibly intelligent because he has celestial knowledge. Lord Ganesha is appointed as the god of learning and wisdom and removal of obstacles. He has been given special power to initiate all actions.

Many years later, Kartikeya was born. His birth happened for a special reason, to kill the demon Tarakasur and fight against evil. Kartikeya, the leader of celestial armies, is also known as Skanda and Murugan, the story about his birth has been described in the 3rd nakshatra of Kartikeya.

<u>Ardhanarishwara</u> - Shiva and Parvati are also represented as half of the other (image of half woman and half man). This symbolises Shiva-Shakti and the same principle is also represented by the linga and the yoni.

Inference

These are the masculine and feminine energies, depicting interdependence and harmony. This also signifies that - a path of an ascetic and family life, spirituality and materialistic needs co-exist. They are not contradictory but complementary. One half completes the other half.

The Ramayana connection

The golden deer

Ramayana, the ancient Indian epic, was composed around the 5th century BC by Rishi Valmiki. The incident of the golden deer happened when Lord Rama, Sita and his younger brother Lakshman were in exile. Towards the end of their time in exile, one day, Sita saw a beautiful golden deer and asked Lord Rama to get it for her. Before going, Rama instructed Lakshman to look after Sita.

Rama followed the deer and shot it. As soon as he shot the deer, he knew that someone had played a trick on them because, at that point, his true form of demon Marichi was exposed. Marichi, on getting injured, had shouted for Lakshman to get him away from Sita. On hearing the shout and a cry for help, Sita got worried and requested Lakshman to go help Rama because he might have been injured. On her insistence, Lakshman reluctantly agreed to go, but for her safety, he drew a circular line around the hut and asked her to stay within that boundary (known as Lakshman rekha).

This was how Ravana planned and got the chance to abduct her.

On seeing her alone, he disguised himself as an ascetic (sadhu) and asked for alms. When Sita came to offer food, he refused to accept until she stepped out of the Lakshman rekha. As soon as she stepped out, he grabbed her and, put her in his flying chariot and took her to his Kingdom in Srilanka.

Rudolf the Reindeer

Although there are many myths and legends connected to the deer. The most famous one is the story of Santa Claus - his sleigh is pulled by a flying reindeer, and Rudolf is the head deer. This tradition started in the 19th century, and Rudolf became famous in 1939 after a poem written for children by Clement C Moore, commonly known as the *night before Christmas.* The poem is a mix of European legends, Norse mythology and aspects of the story of the Christian Saint Nicholas.

Santa Claus, otherwise known as Saint Nicholas or Kris Kringle— has a long history steeped in Christmas traditions. Today, he is thought of mainly as the jolly man in red who brings toys to good children on Christmas Eve, but his story stretches all the way back to the 3rd century when Saint Nicholas walked the earth and became the patron saint of children. It is believed that St Nicholas was born sometime around 280 A.D. in Patara, near Myra in modern-day Turkey. He was admired for his piety and kindness, and over the years, he became the subject of many legends.

He gave away all of his inherited wealth and travelled the countryside, helping the poor and sick. One of the best-known St. Nicholas stories is the time he saved 3 poor sisters from being sold into slavery or prostitution by their father - by providing them with a dowry so that they could be married. Over time, St Nicholas's popularity spread, and he became known as the protector of children and sailors. His feast day is celebrated on the anniversary of his death, <u>December 6.</u> This was traditionally considered a lucky day to make large purchases or to get married.

<u>Going back to Rudolf</u>

Seeing Rudolf's shiny red nose, Santa asks for his help in leading the sleigh safely through the dense fog, after which he says to him - "*By You, last night's journey was actually bossed. Without you, I am certain we would all have been lost."*

The present-day tradition of Santa Claus and his sleigh, pulled by 9 reindeer with Rudolf the red-nose reindeer in the lead, brings presents to children all over the world on Christmas Night.

Here are the lyrics to the song -

<u>*Rudolph the Red-Nosed Reindeer.*</u>

"Rudolph the Red-Nosed Reindeer

Had a very shiny nose,

And if you ever saw it,

You would even say it glows.

All of the other reindeer

Used to laugh and call him names,

They never let poor Rudolph

Join in any reindeer games.

Then one foggy Christmas Eve,

Santa came to say,

Rudolph with your nose so bright,

Won't you guide my sleigh tonight?

Then how the reindeer loved him

As they shouted out with glee,

Rudolph the Red-Nosed Reindeer,

You'll go down in history.

You know Dasher and Dancer and Prancer and Vixen,

Comet and Cupid and Donner and Blitzen.

But do you recall?

The most famous reindeer of all?

Rudolph the Red-Nosed Reindeer."

Inference

Deer have been connected with mythical stories in many cultures - European, American, Mongolian and Indian. Their elegance, grace and beauty represent our inner sense of harmony, aesthetics, love and compassion.

Mrigashira natives accompass all of these qualities. They are very alert to their surroundings and are sensitive to any changes that happen within them and around them. With experience and maturity, they begin to understand that self-awareness is the key to personal and spiritual growth. By knowing their own strengths and weaknesses, they are able to tap into their competence with efficiency and grace.

Mrigashira Padas

23.20 deg Taurus - 6.40 deg Gemini

Padas	Degrees
1	23.20 - 26.40 deg Taurus
2	26.40 - 30 deg Taurus
3	0 - 3.20 deg Gemini
4	3.20 - 6.40 deg Gemini

Pada 1

23.20 - 26.40 deg Taurus, Navamsha - Leo (Lord Sun)

Rashi Lord - Venus and Nakshatra Lord- Mars

This Pada will have the energy of Venus, Mars and Sun. The natives will be passionate, energetic, intelligent and dominating. They will be creative, artistic, very organised, and determined and will have the ability to lead others and manage projects. They are generous with both - their money and compliments. Their greatest joy comes from buying extravagant gifts for themselves and their loved ones. And yes, appreciation is what keeps them inspired and motivated. They will be very straightforward and honest about their opinions, beliefs, ideas, aspirations and expectations. They will talk without mincing words and will respect those who are direct and forthright in their dealings.

Creativity and passion are the 2 ingredients that are essential for them to function. They will never commit themselves to projects or situations which are too long winded, boring and have no scope of creating anything new and exciting. For example, in the 1st Pada of Mrigashira in the 6th house, they will win over their opposition, debts or disease with sheer willpower and confidence.

When it comes to relationships, once they commit themselves, they will see it through, no matter what, because of the fixed quality of Taurus. Of Course, they will, together with their spouse, be constantly exploring life, going on adventurous holidays and planning and promoting grand ideas. Obstacles, for them, are not impediments but a welcome opportunity to polish their skills and win the battle. Their motto would be - *"something is worth doing only if it's done well."*

Careers

Managers, leaders, politicians, actors, artists, dancers, singers, fashion designers, architects, yoga teachers, gurus, priests, computer professionals, engineers, army commanders, police officers, bankers, teachers, professors, psychologists, astrologers, doctors, surgeons, dentists, gynaecologists, paediatricians, consultants' specialists and emergency doctors.

Pada 2

26.40 - 30 deg Taurus, Navamsha - Virgo (Lord Mercury)

Rashi Lord - Venus and Nakshatra Lord- Mars

This Pada will have the qualities of Venus, Mars and Mercury. Natives born in this Pada will be passionate, determined, practical, analytical, perfectionist, detail oriented and communicative.

They will love to learn new things and gather information about various subjects. Yoga Tara point is at 29.45 deg Taurus, any planets placed at this degree will give good and sure results during its dasha, and will trigger specific events during its transit. For example, the 2nd Pada of Mrigashira in the 12th house can bring foreign travel during the dasha and transits of Mars over the Ascendant, natal Sun and natal Moon, or the 12th house.

Their life will be oriented towards doing their daily duties and following routines meticulously. There is a nagging voice in them that keeps reminding them that wasting time is somehow sinful. Being in Taurus gives them the strength of purpose and perfectionism of Virgo (in the navamsha), especially as they get older. They need to keep their bright minds constantly busy with something. They can remember every fault, or a crack in the wall, or a flaw in a design. They may helplessly cling to old memories as if they have been engraved in stone. This can create unnecessary fears. With time, some will gain the wisdom of realising that wasting time on memories of the past that cause anxiety is a greater sin done unto oneself.

They are passive, receptive and cautious because both Taurus and Virgo are feminine signs. Music for them is a therapy for everything - from low moods to entertainment, holidays, relaxation, driving, cooking, eating, exercising, yoga, and meditation - for any activity, the solace of background music is a need. They are great singers or can play a musical instrument if they take the time to practice and nurture that talent.

Careers-

IT professionals, teachers, doctors, nurses, writers, poets, editors, data analysts, accountants, bankers, artists, singers, actors, dancers, yoga and meditation teachers, ayurveda doctors, dress designers, interior decorators, florists, beauticians, psychologists, astrologers, media reporters, farmers, gardeners, and public relations professionals.

Pada 3

0 - 3.20 deg Gemini, Navamsha - Libra (Lord Venus)

Rashi Lord - Mercury and Nakshatra Lord- Mars

The energies of Mercury, Mars and Venus will be manifested in this Pada. In the 3rd Pada, Mrigashira moves to Gemini and Navamsha is in Libra. With the influence of Gemini - they tend to change their minds quite often, because their interests are varied and many, and Librans too cannot make their minds - because they are constantly striving to get the right balance. Mars being the nakshatra lord- helps to manifest these qualities energetically.

The natives will love having long discussions on intellectual subjects and will not give up until they have proven their point. These talks may not always be harmonious, but they will always be thought-provoking. Because silence for them is impossible, they love to talk - not necessarily listen.

The inconsistency of decisions is there because when they think of anything, the contradictory viewpoint pops into their head straight away. Their thoughts have to go through the filter of analysis before they can be acted upon. For their sense of balance and peace of mind, whatever situation happens, the opposite has to be looked into. With the impact of Mars their thoughts and actions will have a more prompt and direct approach.

For example, the 3rd Pada of Mrigashira in the 9th house will make them very brave and determined and will not mind going through the extra trouble to travel away from home or to far-off lands in order to achieve academic excellence, and will meet a very motivational teacher who will guide them well. They will always be ready to stand for justice, fight for their rights or others' rights, do the right thing according to the law, and in times of need they will be there like brave heroes saving the situation with their battle of words.

Careers- army officers, police officers, politicians, stage performers, actors, comedians, magicians, insurance brokers, salesmen or women, IT professionals, public relations coordinators, doctors, engineers, teachers, writers, blog writers, scriptwriters, poets, news reporters, artists, YouTubers, accountants, bankers, businessmen, factory owners, entrepreneurs, sportsmen or sportswomen, forest officers and tourists guides.

Pada 4

3.20 - 6.40 deg Gemini, Navamsha - Scorpio (Lord Mars)

Rashi Lord - Mercury and Nakshatra Lord- Mars

The energies of Mercury, Mars and Mars will be seen in this Pada. The 4th Pada being in the sign of Gemini and going into Scorpio in the navamsha shows that natives will have a very determined and intense approach to situations, they will get into intellectual arguments, and their speech can be direct and rough.

Mars considers Mercury it's enemy because when these 2 come together, it gives a very strong, direct communication. Their speech can come across as harsh if there are other malefic aspects of Saturn, Rahu or Ketu. It also gives quickness of speech and action, which can lead to unpleasant consequences. The natives may find themselves in situations where they have to deal with people who are aggressive in their behaviour - in words, thoughts, emotions or actions.

They will tend to be secretive about certain things for their own safety and security. There can also be situations that can give rise to feelings of jealousy because the other person is being favoured due to prejudices that exist in the social structure. They can make wonderful detectives, lawyers and researchers because they love diving deep into things and exploring the hidden mysteries.

It's almost like 2 personalities wrapped into one individual. The Gemini sign gives the desire for communication, socialising, meeting people and exploring different cultures. They make excellent communicators and their words are like bubbles of joy. On the other hand, the Scorpio sign (in navamsha) is looking for deeper esoteric meanings of life. Their relationships are not superficial. When they know the person, they know them totally - mind, body, soul connection - that kind of deep understanding is there. They are usually very reserved, and talking for the sake of entertainment is not their piece of cake. Most of the time, they prefer to be seen and not heard, and sometimes not even heard. If they have gone deep into their well of exploration, especially as they get older they will feel more - the need to be on their own.

For example, the 4th Pada of Mrigashira in the 3rd house, they are very good at keeping their siblings or neighbours enthralled and engaged in their interesting conversations - yet never or seldom discuss anything truly personal. They have the knack to get the secrets out of you, but not tell their own.

Gemini, being the air sign and Scorpio, the deep waters, bring in the misty air with the heat of Mars. Yes, they almost become like the mythical reindeer, who is elusive and needs to be so for its protection and for the kind of job it has been assigned - to bring the much-awaited Santa at the end of each year. The smiles on the children's innocent faces and the pure joy in their hearts lift the spirits of Mrigashira natives and keep them motivated to go through this specific duty all over again. This Pada is placed in Gemini, which gives the Mrigashira natives in this Pada the ability to balance these 2 seemingly opposite qualities - of being mysterious yet communicative, with elegance and grace.

Careers-

Engineers, technicians, sportsmen and women, athletes, yoga teachers, surgeons, doctors, veterinary doctors, managers, army and police officers, firefighters, circus artists, stuntmen, race car drivers, truck and taxi drivers, businessmen, property dealers, psychiatrists, psychologists, researchers, archaeologists, lab technicians, phlebotomist, IT technicians, builders, judges, lawyers and detectives.

The effect of planets

Mrigashira - Taurus Padas 1 and 2	Planets that get affected
Yoga Karka - the most benefic planet.	Saturn
Functional Benefic - give good results during their dasha.	Sun and Mercury
Functional Neutral	Moon, Venus, Jupiter and Mars
Functional Malefic - can give problems during their dasha.	Rahu and Ketu
Mrigashira - Gemini Padas 3 and 4	Planets that get affected
Functional Benefic - give good results during their dasha.	Mercury
Functional Malefic - can give problems during their dasha.	Mars, Rahu and Ketu
Functional Neutral	Sun, Moon, Venus and Saturn
Kendra Adi Pati dosha - can be malefic	Jupiter

Mrigashira Ascendant

Natives born in the 1st and 2nd Pada of Mrigashira will have the qualities of Venus and Mars. The influence of Venus in Taurus will make them steadfast, quiescent, receptive and passive, while the nakshatra lord Mars is aggressive and independent. This makes them intense, passionate and determined with a wonderful sense of knowing when to step back and be cautious.

In the 1st and 2nd Pada, the natives will have the courage of Mars, and the elegance of Venus in the earthy sign gives good grounding and the ability to follow their ambitions and manifest their desires. The position of Mars and Venus in the horoscope will show in which area these qualities will manifest.

For example, Mars in the 1st Pada of Mrigashira, in the 1st house and Venus in the 2nd house will give them a youthful look and determination to achieve their goals. They will have a practical approach to situations and will follow rules and regulations. They will have a steady flow of income, and their home will be well-decorated.

Those born in the 3rd and 4th Pada of Mrigashira will have the influence of Mercury (the lord of Gemini) and Mars (the lord of Mrigashira). Mars gives the energy and Mercury the intelligence. They will be idealistic and persistent and will love speaking up for causes that grab their attention - liberty and justice are the causes they feel genuinely for. They will pour their energy into anything that interests them - for that moment. They are fiercely independent and cannot be confined in a morass of convention.

They have a very good sense of salesmanship because of their ability to convince others. Mars gives them the energy, while Mercury gives them the ability to look into the details. They can reflect on the pros and cons, sort out the calculations and look into possible conclusions with ease. Mars will be the fuel, the energy for any project and Mercury will calculate, reason out, and see it logically in the impersonal light of analysis. They are clever and intelligent, especially in the fields of - business, accounts and IT.

The placement of Mars and Mercury will give more understanding of how their energies will play out. For example Mars in 3rd house and Mercury in 4th house, the natives have great courage and determination to follow their talent and skills, they can be very good athletes or in any other field of sports. They will be creative, will have leadership skills and will be proud of their capabilities. They will change their residence many times or can have multiple homes. They love inviting their friends at home or talking to them over the phone. They love to have long discussions about their favourite topics - which can be many and varied.

The nature of the energy in Mrigashira has the power to bring fulfilment and joy. Furthermore, the desire of this nakshatra is to spread joy, which doubly supports their friendly nature. They have the ability to talk their way out of confrontations with ease and grace. Bringing a smile on someone's face gives them the greatest joy, and they are most hurt or saddened when friends don't reciprocate or respond to their feelings.

Chandra, being the deity, and soma (nectar), being the symbol, gives them the ability to make the right choices in terms of food that will nourish them. They have a special talent for knowing and picking the right herbs and can become fantastic Ayurvedic doctors or dieticians because Chandra (moon) is responsible for dispensing nourishing quality to the plants.

Farmer is the cast, which shows they are very good at growing herbs and gardening, because of their natural affinity with Mother Earth. Those born in padas 1 and 2 have the fixed and earthen quality, which makes them more set in their habits, and gives stability and grounding in life. This also grants them a natural talent and great interest in gardening, being in nature, walking barefoot and being in touch with Mother Earth. Those who are born in Padas 3 and 4 will have the quality of air and duality, which makes them very creative and flexible. They don't take long to adjust to a new environment and are very good at acting, pretending or masking their emotions.

The quality of Mrigashira is mild and gentle, which shows their approach to situations is not aggressive. They are more passive and like to think before they act. However, they are assertive and determined because of the influence of Mars. There can be those Mrigashiras who, like the musk deer, might not realise their inner fragrance of endearing qualities and keep mistaking it as an outside influence. This wisdom may or may not come to them. With time, as they go through the rigmarole of life, the ones who tap into their inner strength will discover these riches within.

Sun in Mrigashira

When the Sun is placed in Mrigashira, it will share the qualities of Venus and Mars in the 1st and 2nd Pada. The natives will be strong-willed, self-centred, creative, intelligent, confident and arrogant. They need a lot of compliments and appreciation to show that they are admired and loved, and they will be generous in giving compliments, too.

They are very passionate, stubborn, hot-tempered, straightforward and honest. Because the Sun, Mars and Venus - are all hot planets placed in the earthy and fixed sign of Taurus. For this reason, they will tend to have high pitta, and people around them may find them dominating and obstinate. They cannot take orders or work under anyone, so they do well running their own business where they are their own bosses.

On the positive side, it gives tremendous courage to face challenges, stand their ground, and win against all odds. They are very dependable, genuine, honest, intelligent, creative, good managers and capable of leading others. They will have high energy levels and will love going on adventurous trips like mountain climbing, hiking, trekking and going to game reserves. For example, Sun in Mrigashira in the 10th house in 1st Pada is an excellent placement, which will put them in leadership and managing roles in their chosen profession or a high post in a government job or a success in career will manifest during the sun dasha.

In the 3rd and 4th Pada Sun will have the influence of Mercury and Mars. This combination gives the natives excellent communication skills. They will be very good at articulating their thoughts, will be confident speakers, honest and direct in their talk, and will be able to put their views forward with reason and logic. For example, the Sun placed in the 3rd Pada of Mrigashira in the 11th house will bring a lot of gains during the dasha of the Sun. They will head large organisations and have a large friends circle, or will be well known in his or her community. Depending on the strength of the Sun — if it has a good Shadbala score and is well dignified — the native can become an excellent public speaker and a popular politician, known for their motivational speaking abilities.

Moon in Mrigashira

Moon (Soma) being the deity of Mrigashira in the form of a nourishing elixir of life. The placement of the moon has a very profound and major influence on our personality and our way of thinking. In the 1st and 2nd Pada, the Moon will imbibe the qualities of Venus and Mars. This combination will make the natives strongly emotional, physically active and passionate. They will have a beautiful, charming, attractive and youthful face.

They cannot avoid getting emotionally hurt or hurting others because of misunderstandings. If the moon is not afflicted by any malefic aspects of Rahu, Ketu, Mars or Saturn, they will be able to nourish and heal themselves and others more easily and more quickly. On the other hand, if there are any malefic aspects on the moon from Saturn or Rahu they can even cheat or lie for their own benefit or to escape situations. The whole chart should be taken into consideration before making any concrete conclusions.

They will have wonderful insight into making herbal drinks and various concoctions that enhance physical and mental health. They will be empathetic towards others and this makes them sensitive to spoken and unspoken words. They are so sensitive to the feelings of others that they can sense what they are feeling, even without anything being said. Therefore, they are usually compassionate. They will intuitively sense the energies of the place, and it's negative or positive influence. Like the phases of the moon, their moods swing high and low, making them unpredictable. For example, the moon in Mrigashira in the 4th house, the natives will be attached to their home and to their mother. They simply love being at home, cooking delicious meals, eating with the family, listening to music, watching TV in the cosy sitting room and many more usual comforts.

The Moon in the 3rd and 4th Pada of Mrigashira will share the energies of Mercury and Mars. Moon and mercury are both fast-moving planets and, backed by Martian energy, will make the natives fast talkers. They will be quick thinkers and quick in answering any questions and will put their viewpoints across, forcefully with conviction. They will be good with all kinds of communication, writing, online or talking - they have the wonderful knack of saying the same thing in many different ways, spinning the web of words in most imaginative stories. They can keep the other person engaged for hours in listening to their interesting tales which are usually spiced up with gossip and humour. They are never short of words to express their realistic and fairy tale ideas.

However, if mercury is retrograde then they can be forgetful about what they have said or done, or may have to repeat the same process 2 or 3 times to get it tight. They can also get into the habit of repeating the same tales over and over again or going into a detailed explanation. For this reason, they will hear this often -

"get to the point, or you have said this before."

The poetic Mriga-shira

Mriga- the deer, free spirited and elegant,

Shira-the head, aware and intelligent.

Mars the energy and drive,

Taurus to Gemini, a deer stride.

Chandra the cool nourisher of emotions and herbs

Soma the nectar, elixir of life superb

As the fragrance of musk motivates the seeking

A life of wonder unfolds, the joy of giving and receiving

Mars the determined soldier, resolute and knew

Aspirants are many, but determined are few.

Who respect time, and discipline the mind,

The dreams they wove, become a reality that slowly unwinds,

Such is the nature of a deer, strong and sublime

Strides with confidence through the scapes of time.

Remedies

- <u>Das Maha Vidya -</u> Devi Kamala and Devi Bagalamukhi - as described earlier.

<u>Devi Tripura Sundari -</u> Mercury

Goddess Tripura Sundari is also called Shodashi, Lalita or tantric Parvati. The word Tripura means the 3 cities, and Sundari means the beautiful one. She is, therefore, referred to as the most beautiful of the 3 worlds. She has a calm, serene face, beautiful lotus petal-shaped eyes and the

3rd eye of wisdom. She dispels the fear of her devotees and, is the embodiment of peace knowledge (vidya) and grants all kinds of wealth.

The Vedic story narrates that Devi Tara had assumed the form of Goddess Shodashi to provide greenery to all plants. Devi Shodashi then placed a bamboo in the earth and poured one drop of water from her waterpot. This gave birth to all plant life, and then all forests, trees, and plants in nature grew.

If Mercury is afflicted by Mars, Saturn, Rahu or Ketu, or it's debilitated or retrograde - these remedies can bring some relief.

Remedies for weak Mercury in the birth chart -

- Sponsoring the education of a child or a young adult in need would be the best remedy.
- Worshipping Devi Tripura Sundari, wearing white or green clothes during sunrise time, with red hibiscus flowers and making any sweet dish with rice is beneficiary for those who have mercury conjunct moon, Saturn, Rahu or Ketu.
- She is related to the planet Mercury, and her yantra is the Shree Yantra. Her beneficent energy can be invoked by chanting her mantra with her image and Yantra in front. Any of her mantras can be chanted 108 times on a Wednesday.

Mantras of Devi Tripura Sundari -

"Om Aim Hreem Shreem Sri Lalita Tripurasundari Padukam Poojayami Namah," " Aym sauh Kleem" and

"Ka Ey Ee La Hreem – Ha Sa Ka Ha La Hreem – Sa Ka La Hreem"

Other remedies

- The best remedy is to volunteer - get actively involved in social causes that can help others in need - and bring a smile to sad faces. In doing so, a lot of the karmic baggage will be shed, and the hurdles in life will be automatically removed.
- Red, white and green are good colours to wear.
- Worship the deities - Chandra and Parvati or chant their mantras 108 times for 40 days.

Beej mantra for Chandra -

"Om Shram Shreem Shraum Saha Chandraye namah."

- <u>Mantra for Devi Parvati</u> - chanting her mantra on Tuesdays 108 times will give strength and love and increase productivity.

"Sarva Mangala Mangalye, Shive Sarvartha Sadhike,

Sharanye Tryambke Gauri, Narayani Namostute."

<u>Meaning</u> - Goddess Parvati is the auspiciousness of all that is auspicious. (another name for Mars is mangal, which means auspicious). She is the consort of Lord Shiva and grants all desires of those who are making sincere efforts. (sarvartha means all and sadhike means the ones who do their practises regularly to master a certain skill). I take refuge in Devi Parvati.

- Chanting the Mrigashira nakshatra mantra 108 times for 40 days will help to align with the energies of Mrigashira and bring stability and good health.

"Om em Mrigashira nakshatrae namah."

Example

<u>Mrigashira Ascendant</u>

<u>Sahir Ludhianvi - Famous Indian poet</u>

Born on 8th March 1921, in Ludhiana, Punjab, India, at 12 pm (estimated time of birth). Died in Mumbai at the young age of 59, on 25th October 1980.

Sahir Ludhianvi was an Indian poet, and film song lyricist who wrote in the Hindi and Urdu languages. Sahir won Filmfare Awards for Best Lyricist for Taj Mahal (1963) and for Kabhie Kabhie (1976). He was awarded the Padma Shri in 1971.

Sahir was born on 8th March 1921, in Ludhiana, Punjab, India, into a Gujjar Muslim landlord family. That's why he added the suffix Ludhianvi after his name. His mother, Sardar Begum, left her husband, thus forfeiting any claim to financial assets from the marriage. In 1934, Sahir's father remarried and unsuccessfully asked for custody of his son. In his biography, written by Surinder Deol, the author summarises Sahir's life story in a nutshell, *"In his entire life, Sahir loved once, and he nurtured one hate. He loved his mother, and he hated his father."* His mother required protection from his father and suffered financial deprivation.

Sahir was educated at the Khalsa High School in Ludhiana. He did his degree from the Government College, Ludhiana. The auditorium there is named after him. As a college student, Sahir was popular for his ghazals and nazms (poetry in Urdu) and impassioned speeches.

In 1943, he settled in Lahore. There, he published his first book in Urdu - Talkhiyan (restlessness) (1945). He was a member of the All India Students Federation, edited Urdu magazines, and became a member of the Progressive Writers' Association. However, when he made controversial statements promoting communism, a warrant for his arrest was issued by the Government of Pakistan. In 1949, after partition, Sahir fled from Lahore to Delhi. After 8 weeks, he moved to Bombay. In the 1970s, he built a bungalow, which he called Parchaiyaan (Shadows), after one of his works, and lived there till his death.

Sahir's work as a lyricist in the film industry gave him financial stability beyond his earnings as a poet. He made his debut with 4 songs performed in the film Azadi Ki Raah Par (1949). Both the film and its songs went unnoticed. He got his first major success with the songs he wrote for Baazi (1951) and the music was composed by S D Burman.

Sahir's image was controversial because he was artistically temperamental. He insisted that the film score should be composed for his lyrics and not the other way around. He also insisted on being paid one rupee more than Lata Mangeshkar, and this created a rift between them.

On 25th October 1980, at the age of 59, Sahir died of a sudden cardiac death. He died in the presence of his friend, Javed Akhtar. He was buried at the Juhu Muslim cemetery. In 2010, his tomb was demolished to make room for new interments.

Analysis

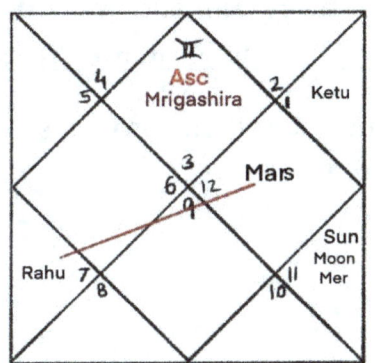

He is a <u>Gemini Ascendant in the 3rd Pada of Mrigashira</u>. Mercury, the lord of his Ascendant, is placed in the 9th house of Aquarius with the Sun and Moon. Mars, the lord of Mrigashira, is placed in the 10th house of Pisces. Moreover, he was born on a Tuesday, which shows that he had a <u>strong influence of Mars</u> in his birth chart.

Since his Sun and Moon are in the same house, he was born on Krishna Chaturthi - the 14th lunar day (waning phase), close to Amavasya.

All these influences contributed towards his difficult childhood and the emotional trauma that he had to go through because of the separation of his parents. His father had an aggressive personality, and because of this, his mother had to seek protection. His biographer sums it up - *"In his entire life, Sahir loved once, and he nurtured one hate. He loved his mother, and he hated his father."*

Father is signified by the 9th house - where his Sun, Moon and Mercury are placed. The Sun also represents the father, and the Moon represents the mother. Since the Moon was near to the new Moon (darkest night), the relationship between his mum and dad was difficult, which made his young and sensitive mind and emotions go through an inner turmoil and also lay the foundation of expressing his pain through poetry. His first book in Urdu - was titled Talkhiyan (restlessness).

In 1934, his father remarried and unsuccessfully asked for custody of his son. Sahir was running his <u>Rahu Sun Mars</u> dasha in 1934 when he and his mother were going through a rough patch in their life. For Gemini Ascendants, Mars becomes a functional malefic which can bring aggressive situations during its dasha.

<u>Mars,</u> sitting in the 10th house of career in Pisces (which signifies public image) - brought him fame and success and also made him a controversial figure. Those who knew him say that - he was artistically temperamental and often had some conflicts among his colleagues. From the 10th house, Mars is aspecting the 5th house of creativity (8th from the 10th house). Moreover, <u>Rahu</u> is sitting in the 5th house of Libra. This placement amplified his creativity and his connection with the entertainment industry.

<u>Mercury,</u> his Ascendant (Gemini) lord, is the most beneficial planet for him. His poetic nature comes from the intelligence of Mercury and the innate curiosity of Mrigashira. The sukshma dasha of Mercury brought him success and fame. He got his first major success with the songs he wrote for Baazi (1951). At that time, he was running his <u>Jupiter Rahu Rahu Mercury</u> dasha.

His birth chart shows how the placement of planets and their lordships play a crucial role in situational circumstances and the timing of events.

6
Ardra

Om aym Ardra akshatraye namah

Zodiac degrees	6.40 - 20 deg Gemini
Ruling planet	Gemini - Mercury and Ardra - Rahu
Sanskrit name	Rudra
Astronomical name	Betelgeuse - A bright red star in Orion constellation. It's called the red supergiant and is the largest star visible to the naked eye.
Symbol	Gemini - Twins and Ardra - Diamond and teardrop
Element	Air
Deity	Shiva
Quality	Tikshna - Sharp and dwi - dual.
Shakti	Yatna Shakti - power to make effort
Cast	Butcher
Gender	Male
Motivation	Kama - to fulfil desires
Triguna	Satwa
Tridosha	Vata
Body parts	Eyes, head and hair
Direction	South west, west and north

Month	Middle 9 days of Mrigashira (December)
Bird	Swan
Sound	ku, kha, nga, ccha
Tree	Agarwood (black ebony)
Chakra	Ajna - Mercury and Rahu
Das Maha Vidya	Devi Chinnamasta - Rahu Devi Tripura Sundari - Mercury

Special degrees -

Yoga Tara	5 deg Gemini- the yoga tara of Ardra lies in the 4th Pada of Mrigashira. It's a point where the planet will show the strongest and sure results during its dasha.
Pushkar bhaga	18 deg Gemini Planets placed here will fruitify results like the blossoming of a flower.
Pushkar amsha	4th pada Planets placed here will bear fruit and give good results, during its dasha.
Exaltation	15 deg Gemini - Maximum exaltation of Rahu. This will bring wonderful opportunities during its dasha.
Amrit nadi	14.26 - 15.20 deg Gemini Gives good results like the nectar that nourishes.
Visha nadi	11.20- 12.13 deg Gemini Brings situations which one does not like dealing with.

Astronomical perspective-

The stars which are considered old in astronomical age are seen as red giants, because they have expanded and are nearer to their explosion as supernovas. Ardra is represented by Betelgeuse- a red giant star seen in the Orion constellation. This star is about 700 light years away from our Sun and is likely to explode in about 100,000 years.

Auspicious and inauspicious table -

Auspicious	Inauspicious
Activities Ardra carries fierce energy therefore, it's good for demolishing buildings, clearing up unwanted things, or facing confrontations. Rahu, the lord of Ardra rules electricity and science, therefore it supports all scientific pursuits and online activities.	Activities Not good for starting any new projects or happy occasions and celebrations.

Days	Days
<u>Wednesdays</u> - only when it falls on the 2nd, 3rd, 7th, 8th, 12th or 13th lunar day. <u>Fridays</u> - only when it falls on the 1st, 2nd, 6th, 7th, 11th or 12th lunar day.	<u>Tuesdays-</u> only when it falls on the 1st, 2nd, 7th, 8th or 10th lunar day. <u>Thursdays-</u> only when it falls on the 6th, 8th, 9th, 12th or 13th lunar day.

Compatibility table -

Ardra	Compatible with
Sexual compatibility Yoni animal	Ardra- Male dog - compatible with - Female dog - Mula
Sign compatibility	Gemini - Libra and Aquarius.
Nakshatra compatibility	Swati and Shatbhishak.
Lunar day compatibility	11th lunar day (ekadashi)
Day compatibility	Wednesday
Colour compatibility	Grey and green
Numerological compatibility	5 all numbers that add up to make 5.
Sound compatibility	Mercury - lingual sounds - ta, tha, da, dha, na

Sign Lord and Nakshatra lord - <u>Mercury and Rahu Mercury</u> - as explained earlier.

<u>Rahu -</u> Lord of Ardra.

"Reality is merely an <u>illusion</u>, albeit a very persistent one." - Einstein

In Vedic astrology, Rahu and Ketu are the 2 invisible astronomical points in the sky called the north and south lunar nodes. They are not planets of physical substance like the other seven planets, instead, they are areas of churned-up energy at the north and south side of the Moon. They are the points where the Moon and Earth's orbits intersect. This creates two areas of electromagnetic disturbances, which are directly opposite each other and have come to be known as the Moon's Nodes or, in Vedic terms, Rahu and Ketu.

The main quality of Rahu is that it amplifies everything, Rahu is represented as the head of the snake, without a body, which shows that Rahu-ruled people are very intellectual. They understand and connect to things or relationships logically rather than feeling it emotionally. Everything scientific, logical and intellectual speaks to them. They understand everything through the magnifying lens of the intellect. This makes them miss the beauty of emotions and feelings.

Rahu is considered the boss, the head who likes to lead and not follow. Rahu can be described as a rule breaker, a revolutionary, an entrepreneur, and a new-age thinker. They will make their own rules to their own advantage and break rules set by others, and can manipulate or cheat others, or get cheated by them.

The head of Rahu makes the natives consume everything, yet not feel contentment or satisfaction no matter how much they accomplish. Because the head without a body has no capacity to digest or assimilate things, it ends up accumulating quantity, but not necessarily quality.

Rahu is interested in all worldly matters and will encourage the natives to seek gratification, success and power in a particular area of life. In its quest to fulfil its ambitions, it can be manipulative and deceptive. Rahu leads us to experience many different situations and sensations in a heightened and magnified way, like the expansion of smoke. Since Rahu is the head only, with no body - it consumes but does not feel satiated. It's more of thoughts and less of feelings. Wherever Rahu is placed - Intellect dominates and overrides the feelings.

Rahu is a powerful and malefic planet that is never completely satisfied, so it drives the natives to go for more and more gains. Therefore, a strong Rahu influence has been seen in the chart of many successful people. It has been seen as favourable for politicians, actors or businessmen - or any significant position because it brings great opportunities during its dasha. It gives sudden wealth and fame and makes the natives rise and succeed through fair or unfair means.

Rahu also signifies foreigners and foreign lands, so natives are more likely to succeed in a place away from their birthplace, and when they deal with people from another culture. Rahu magnifies sudden events and gives much more than expected. Rahu dasha can also give marriage.

Rahu, because of its illusionary nature, constantly lures the natives to make changes in their lifestyle - thereby causing change in residence, friends, desires and goals of life. Rahu provides information through IT technology, and gives interest in exploring the mysteries of life. He is an intellectual and likes to know all that is mystical and scientific through logic and reason.

"*Shanivat Rahu kujavat ketu,*" is a phrase often used in Vedic astrological texts to describe the nature of Rahu and Ketu. Which means Rahu is like Saturn and Ketu is like Mars. Ketu is like a fire with intense heat, and Rahu is smoke and expansion. The influence of Rahu is expansive. It will make situations seem bigger than they really are and will also have the cool practical approach of Saturn.

Inference

Ardra is placed in Gemini; therefore, the natives will have amplified mercurian traits of logical thinking and intellectualising everything. They will be very friendly, quick-witted and intelligent. They will, in a way, live a dual life, one personality for home and another for work - like the twins.

Quality - Dwi - as explained earlier.

Tikshna - sharp

Ardra natives have a fierce and sharp energy which makes them fearless in their actions. This is a ruthless, brutal, dreadful or violent force that can pierce through any tough situation. Their manner can be domineering or forceful. The intensity of the energy is such that it comes forth like a bolt of lightning that has a devastating effect on whatever or wherever it strikes. Ardra natives can face such intense situations in their lives where the pain and suffering are acute and sudden, which can leave a transformative and definitive impact on their perspective towards life. Or they can inflict pain on someone else, which may not be intended but circumstantial.

Basically, their way of reacting or responding to any challenging situation is sharp and razor-like which cuts and pierces through precisely and promptly. Just as the phenomena of lightning and thunderbolts happen when the huge, dense and grey clouds accumulate enough negative electric charge that spills over and comes in contact with the positive charge from the earth, which explodes in the form of heat, light and thunder. Similarly, the Ardra natives' reaction may seem sudden, but it was brewing up within them for quite some time until one day, it reaches the tipping point, which can be triggered by a difficult situation, and it explodes in the form of anger or frustration. They face such a life-transforming situation at least once in their life.

Element, motivation, triguna and tridosha - as described earlier.

Chakra - Ajna - as described earlier.

Ardra is placed in Gemini, whose ruler is Mercury, and the nakshatra Lord Rahu amplifies the effect. Ardra natives have a strong influence on the Ajna chakra energy. The energy of Ajna chakra is upward moving, which makes them intelligent, wise and highly spiritual.

Their interest lies in esoteric, religious, spiritual, scientific and philosophical subjects. They have a great potential to open their 3rd eye of inner knowing and becoming self-realised beings. If the energy is blocked at the Ajna chakra, they can have headaches and convulsions or feel stressed, tense, and anxious. When the Ajna chakra energy is balanced, they have heightened levels of awareness and consciousness and can become enlightened.

Shakti - Yatna Shakti - Power to make an effort.

Ardra natives have the blessing of pulling through harsh or difficult situations with amazing strength and resilience. They may have to face circumstances that cause pain or suffering, but their hidden strength lies in facing these situations bravely and coming out victorious and strong.

Their remedy lies in their strength to face situations and not to postpone or try to escape them. To their surprise, they will discover that they have the inner power of Rudra (fierce form of Lord Shiva) to face challenges. The situations are intense but not insurmountable.

This makes them even stronger, confident and clear about the ways of life and the deceit of people around them. They become better equipped, more mature, wiser and capable of handling such situations. They will find that when they face situations, they overcome them very easily. On the other hand, if they run away from their problems, they get more entangled.

Symbolic significance

<u>Gemini</u> - Twins - as described earlier.

<u>Ardra</u> - diamond and teardrops.

<u>Diamond</u>

Diamonds are made from carbon and are the hardest natural substance on earth. The word diamond comes from the Greek word - Adam, which means unconquerable or invincible. They are formed deep within the Earth, about 100 miles below, where it's very hot. Natural diamonds are formed by being underground for millions of years. Pure diamonds are incredibly rare. They are the purest form of carbon and are formed under tremendous pressure and depth. The combination of high temperature and high pressure helps to form diamond crystals. The diamonds that we see at the surface are ones that are brought to the surface by a very deep-seated volcanic eruption. They get transported to the earth through special volcanoes called kimberlites. It takes 10 - 20 years of searching if there are any diamond crystals in a volcanic eruption.

Diamonds are formed as carbon atoms bond together very strongly, where each carbon atom is bonded to four other carbon atoms that's why a diamond is such a hard material. Hope Diamonds found in India were brought to the surface at least a billion years ago or perhaps longer than that. The size and colour of this diamond make it very rare and precious. Only one diamond has ever been found that has a dark-blue colour and has the size and quality of the Hope Diamond.

<u>Kohinoor diamond</u> is a very rare and precious diamond and is one of the oldest and most famous diamonds in the world. Its history goes back more than 5000 years. The word Kohinoor means a mountain of light. It is believed that the diamond was first mentioned more than 5000 years ago in a Sanskrit script, where it was called the Syamantaka.

Up until 1304 AD the diamond was in the possession of the Kings - Rajas of Malwa, but was not named Kohinoor. After 1304, it belonged to the Emperor of Delhi, Allaudin Khilji. It is believed that this rare diamond brings misfortune to the men who wear it and is auspicious only for women.

Later the diamond was gifted to Sultan Ibrahim Lodi, one of the descendants of Babur. Later Aurangzeb protected the diamond diligently and passed it on to his heirs. The Persian general Nadir Shah went to India in 1739, took the diamond and named it Kohinoor. But Nadir Shah was assassinated in 1747, and the diamond was taken by his general, Ahmad Shah Durrani.

In 1813, a descendant of Ahmad Shah, Shah Shuja Durrani, brought the Koh-i-noor back to India and gifted it to Maharaja Ranjit Singh (the emperor of the Sikh Empire). In return Maharaja Ranjit Singh helped Shah Shuja get back the throne of Afghanistan. In 1849, after the conquest of the Punjab by the British forces, the properties of the Sikh Empire were confiscated. The Kohinoor diamond was taken to Britain in 1850 and gifted to Queen Victoria. In 1852, the Queen decided to reshape the diamond, and it was taken to a Dutch jeweller, Mr Cantor, who cut it to 108.93 carats.

Queen Victoria wore the diamond occasionally afterwards. She left in her will that the Koh-i-noor should only be worn by a female queen. If the head of state was a man, his wife would have to carry the diamond. After Queen Victoria's death, the Kohinoor became part of the Crown Jewels.

Inference

Ardra natives have the strength to endure difficulties in life and emerge strong - shining like the brilliance of a diamond. They can withstand immense pressure with amazing resilience and overcome challenges by sheer willpower and inner strength. The greater the challenge the more they shine with the brave, enduring qualities of strength that are unbeatable.

Just like diamonds, their friendship will be precious and valued by their friends and relatives. With time, their wonderful qualities will shine because of the challenges they have to face. They bravely endure it and come out victorious, not succumbing to the pressure, but in the process of dealing with the tough circumstances, they discover their inner brilliance- the shine of which cannot be hidden.

Teardrops

This also refers to the drops of rain; the word Ardra means moist, green and fresh. When clouds become heavy with moist rain droplets, they pour out in the form of rain. Rainfall is a climatic parameter of great importance, which transforms the landscape and allows crops to grow and river networks to refill.

Tear drops, being the other symbol for Ardra, are an idiographic sign for crying. It is a natural human response to profound emotions of sadness, grief, frustration and joy. Research shows that crying activates the parasympathetic nervous system and, therefore, helps us to relax.

Inference

Ardra natives can face situations of sorrow, pain, and sadness in life, which can bring tears in their eyes. This also indicates storm-like circumstances, where they can be swept by its intensity that leaves them transformed in a big way. They can face acutely challenging situations which come and go suddenly like a hurricane or a tornado, but leave them transformed and have a huge influence on the way they perceive life.

It completely changes their perspective of life- where nothing of the old pattern of thinking or lifestyle remains, they make a fresh start - a new beginning in their life - like they are born again, ready to take on life with new intensity and vigour. Like the coming of rain is a welcome sign of revitalisation, the welling up of tears is a much-needed outlet for pent-up emotions. It refreshes the inner being, where we become our own solace.

Mythology

Deity - Shiva in Rudra (fierce) form.

Rudra is a Rigvedic deity associated with wind (vayu) or storm and the hunt. Rudra has been praised as the *"mightiest of the mighty."* Rudra can be seen as the most severe roarer or howler, like a hurricane or tempest, or the most frightening one.

Rudra is also one of the names of Lord Vishnu in Vishnu Sahasranama and is described as the lord who does total destruction at the time of great dissolution. Vedic scriptures state that Lord Shiva, in the form of Rudra, fights against the demons. He wears lion skin, has matted hair and serpents around his neck, holds a trident and a skull, and has the crescent moon on his head.

Puranas describe the 11 forms of Rudra as - Aja, Ekapada, Ahirbudhnya, Tvasta, Rudra, Hara, Sambhu, Tryambaka, Aparajita, Ishana and Tribhuvana. It is also stated that Brahma gave the 11 Rudras the following positions- Heart, 5 sensory organs and 5 the five organs of action.

Rudra is also addressed as the Lord of Remedies (vaidyanatha), for he is believed to cure diseases and is said to have healing powers. A verse from Shree Rudram speaks of Rudra as Lord of the Universe. *"Jagatam pataye namaha."* In Another verse in Yajur Veda, Rudra is referred to as being present in the heart of the gods. *"Devanam hridaye bhyo namo."*

Mahamrityunjaya Mantra
is dedicated to the Rudra form of Lord Shiva, the one who is the giver of liberation (Moksha). It is said to be one of the most beneficial mantras because it restores health and happiness and brings calmness in the face of death.

"Om tryambakaṃ yajāmahe sugandhiṃ puṣṭivardhanam urvārukamiva bandhanān mṛtyormukṣīya mā'mṛtāt."

Meaning-

Om, we worship the Tryambaka - the three-eyed one,

Who is fragrant like the flower holding the spiritual essence,

Which increases the nourishment of our spiritual core,

Who releases us from the many bondages of Samsara - the worldly desires,

Which are similar to the cucumbers tied and tangled on the creepers,

May I be liberated from death - from the attachment to all that is perishable,

So that I am not separated from the perception of my real self, which is immortal and imperishable.

Rudra is also referred to as -

The eliminator of evil and the usher of peace, the cry at the time of dissolution, the one who destroys evil and kills the forces of darkness, roarer or loud cry, the wild or untamed, the lord of animals - Pashupatinath, fierce and terrible, ruddy - dark reddish colour, signifies the number 11 and rudraksh tree.

Rudraksha tree -

Mythological stories state that Rudraksha beads were formed from Lord Shiva's tear drops and, therefore, have a spiritual significance.

This is a huge evergreen tree with broad leaves, which grows abundantly at the foothills of the Himalayas in India. Blue-coloured berries grow on these trees. When they fall on the ground and are dry, they become brownish and are then strung together to make necklaces (malas). These prayer beads are worn by many, especially by those who are on the spiritual path. It is said to have the power of healing and gives protection. The Rudraksha beads are found in various sizes and shapes and accordingly have their specific significance.

Rudraksha beads vary between having 1 to 27 ridges on them, which are called faces (mukhi). Most commonly worn are the ones having 4, 5 or 6 faces. The 2 faced Rudraksha is called Gauri-Shankara, which supports positive vibes in relationships, and is therefore very conducive to be worn by couples. Single-faced Rudraksha bead is very rare and is worn only by those on the ascetic path and not by householders because it has a very powerful influence and would pull one away from worldly desires.

Inference

The word Rudra literally means - 'the roarer.' - like the roar of a lion, or the sound of the thundering bolt of lightning, the roar of the ocean waves, the downpour of heavy tropical rain, the trumpeting sound of the elephant, or the howl of a human being. All these are expressions of intense energy, the kind of energy needed to release immense power in a short time.

It refers to the wild, untamed and raw energy. This fierce form of energy deals with both dissolution and healing. This signifies the ruthless aspect of nature that is brought into action to bring about transformations, which would not be possible by a mild, regular flow of energy.

Explosions in space

For example, supernova explosions happen when a star explodes in space. Scientists believe that these explosions play a key role in distributing elements throughout the universe. Even in the beginning of the creation- for the universe to manifest in the form of stars, galaxies, constellations and planets - a series of big explosions happened, and through this huge amounts of energy were released, thereby forming new elements and compounds which became the basic building blocks of life in various forms.

Human emotions

In our lives, we are sometimes faced with situations which touch us very deeply - both pain and joy can bring tears to our eyes. These responses are the inner emotional explosions that signify a silent revolution within us, which is far more powerful than any outside situational change. This inner transformation may be triggered by an outside stimulus, but the process happens within. Ardra natives, at some point in their lives, may experience such profound transformation, which can bring the dissolution of a relationship, followed by the healing of emotions.

The storm within

Ardra represents Shiva in Rudra form, who carries the intensity of a storm that clears everything in its way and makes a fresh start. It's nature's way of sustaining the food chain - like being the hunter and also being hunted, the predators and the prey, the wild and the tame - all these seemingly opposite aspects are an integral and important part of the food chain. Everything in nature has its place and purpose. Being there, destruction is equally as important as creation and maintenance in order for life to happen and flourish.

Ardra natives will always feel the intensity of emotions, feelings and thoughts within, they somehow feel like an outcast and will not have many friends because they look at life from a different level. They will have more affinity to animals than humans. Their inner energies will match more with the intensity of Shiva, the wild esthetic, than with any other god who looks very docile and cultured.

When they are angry, it will come like a storm, breaking dishes, shoving everything on the table, even bending or crushing metallic objects, or verbally lashing out with a fury of abusive words. There can be those Ardras who will express their inner storm by buying a painting of a storm in the ocean, or high tidal waves, or online pictures of wild animals or wild art, or rock music, drum beats, or soul sufi music that expresses deep pain, intensity and philosophy of life.

Ardra Padas

6.40 - 20 deg Gemini

Padas	Degrees
1	6.40 - 10 deg Gemini
2	10 - 13.20 deg Gemini
3	13.20 - 16.40 deg Gemini
4	16.40 - 20 deg Gemini

Pada 1

6.40 - 10 deg Gemini, Navamsha - Sagittarius (Lord -Jupiter)

Rashi Lord - Mercury and Nakshatra Lord- Rahu

The 1st Pada will have the energies of Mercury, Rahu and Jupiter. They will be willing to support people in trouble, support social causes, and will have a sharp mind. The influence of Rahu can create turbulence in the mind, and natives may find it difficult to neatly bring things to a conclusion, especially during the Rahu dasha. Meditation, long walks in nature, keeping a pet, and playing a musical instrument would be great remedies to keep calm during the turbulent days of the passing storm of emotions, feelings and compulsive thoughts.

The natives will be intelligent, communicative, cheerful, optimistic and philosophical. They will be curious about everything in life, from science to creative arts, from IT to space crafts, farming to herbology, from astrology to yoga and meditation, journalism to law, to acting. Their talent and skills will be versatile, and they will be apt to give blunt, straightforward answers.

They are born learners and eternal students who love to learn and explore new concepts - and are looking for opportunities to learn and share their knowledge - through speech or writing. *"Once you stop learning, you start dying." - Einstein*

They love their freedom and will not break any laws because it's not worth risking their independence. They have more intellectual acumen than raw physical energy and make excellent politicians and lawyers. They would rather mastermind a project, make calculative decisions, and delegate jobs to others rather than waste their time and effort to do everything themselves. They know how to use time, resources and effort efficiently.

They may look placid and quiet on the surface but have active and fertile minds operating at high speed. Whatever they do, they would like to do it on a grand scale. For example - they will choose to live in a bigger, spacious house, have big parties - invite many friends, and have many clothes and shoes - more than they need. The expansiveness of Rahu magnifies everything they think or do. The intensity of the Ardra storm will be expressed through religious and spiritual philosophy, reading books or watching movies which depict the deeper aspects of life.

For example, if the 1st Pada of Ardra is in the 7th house, the natives will have many friends and acquaintances and can have multiple partners or business partners. Can face an explosive situation in relationships during Rahu or Jupiter dasha. After the age of 30, they are more likely to face problems regarding their ideology, faith, or some issues with their teachers or mentors, or they will put on weight that can bring some health issues because Jupiter has the Kendra Adi Pati dosha. The position of Jupiter should be checked in the birth chart and in navamsha. These are the areas of life that can be troublesome, especially during the dasha and transits of Jupiter over the Ascendant, natal Sun and natal Moon.

Careers-

Politicians, lawyers, detectives, actors, musicians, IT professionals, software developers, game designers, public relations managers, accountants, businessmen, news reporters, TV broadcasters, astrologers, astronauts, priests, teachers, doctors, pharmacists, engineers, electricians, scientists, philosophers and writers.

Pada 2

10 - 13.20 deg Gemini, Navamsha - Capricorn (Lord - Saturn)

Rashi Lord - Mercury and Nakshatra Lord- Rahu

The combination of Mercury, Rahu and Saturn can be seen in this Pada. The natives will be more career-oriented because the navamsha falls in Capricorn. The challenges and frustrations are felt more in this pada because of the influence of Saturn. However, this gives them a very practical and materialistic approach, which will help them to do well later in life after the initial struggle.

They will have the intelligence to choose the career of their choice and work towards it. They may have multiple and consecutive jobs, which can start with initial excitement and turn into a burden with time, because of the extra workload. They like to do things at their own pace, and frenetic activity can drain their mental and physical energy.

The influence of Saturn in this Pada can bring delays, frustrations, and storm-like situations, which can be deeply life-transforming during the Rahu or Saturn dasha. The inner storm of Ardra in the 2nd pada will be influenced by Saturn. The placement and aspects of Saturn will show the areas of life towards which they have to put effort. Since Saturn is the karma karka it represents the duty which cannot be escaped.

"You never fail until you stop trying." - Einstein

The biggest danger for natives in this Pada is if they give up or feel it's not worth trying because Saturn makes us go through the tests, and Rahu amplifies it, making the problem seem larger than it really is. For example, the 2nd Pada of Ardra in the 12th house can give foreign travel, and in a new place, the natives may have to face difficulties with initially settling in or getting an appropriate job.

Rahu amplifies the challenges, and Saturn gives delays but does not deny, it blesses with the rewards of hard work in its own time.

Careers-

Lawyers, social workers, politicians, detectives, working for an IT company, computer engineers, electricians, accountants, mathematicians, doctors, businessmen, industrialists, scientists, pharmacists, X-ray specialists, plumbers, shop and store workers, meteorologists, people working from home via online.

Pada 3

13.20 - 16.40 deg Gemini, Navamsha - Aquarius (Lord - Saturn)

Rashi Lord - Mercury and Nakshatra Lord- Rahu

This Pada has the energies of Mercury, Rahu and Saturn. Here Saturn comes in the navamsha of Aquarius, where Saturn and Rahu are the lords and give good results.

The natives born in this Pada will have a scientific inclination. They will be intrigued about how things work and will most probably have opened up many toys in their childhood to discover a small battery inside. And, of course, they would have tried inserting these tiny metallic objects in different toys and finally, one day would have opened up the battery itself by crushing it with a stone, only to be utterly confused and surprised to see the gluey and smelly chemical inside, or a little square with some shiny dots on it (which they were told was called a - CHIP !) that makes the toys dance and sing and the race cars run?? Surely, in high school, they might have found some helpful explanations in their physics textbook. In their adulthood, even if they become lawyers or accountants, the scientists in them will never die and they will keep up their quiet and intriguing hobby in their study or garage.

The 3rd Pada is aligned to fulfil desires and do humanitarian work through large organisations. Their interest will be in researching online about their million and one questions - what makes the clock tick? to why the grasshopper is green in colour?

With their knowledge and understanding they aspire to one day help others, even if it's in a small way, to enhance human life and the life of other living beings on our planet. The effect of mercury and Rahu gives the natives excellent IT skills, communicative- speaking and writing skills, and intelligence to articulate their ideas well. It also brings added responsibility of handling big projects - the effect of Saturn will give delays and achievements will come only through hard work. There is a possibility that the inner storm of Ardra could be expressed by giving up the responsibility and walking out because of repeated frustrations.

Aquarius, being a fixed sign, gives a steady sense of purpose. They are independent and follow their plans. They need plenty of alone time and like to be mentally active and stimulated. Their ideas may seem eccentric to others because their genius way of thinking is unique and ahead of their times. They will be interested in watching the latest sci-fi films and documentaries on the newest technology, scientific research in the chosen field, and upcoming IT gadgets and will put this equipment to good use.

"The greatest thing about big ideas is being able to share them." - Einstein.

Ardra natives in the 3rd Pada love to work on new ideas through the use of the latest technology and share it with the world. For example, the 3rd Pada of Ardra placed in the 11th house will give good results because this is the original house of Aquarius.

The natives will work for a large organisation or will have their own company and will do a lot of research work in the field of science or IT. This result will be more pronounced during the dasha of Saturn and Rahu.

Careers-

IT professionals working for a large organisation, social workers, researchers, scientists, pharmacists, doctors, electricians, engineers, photographers, musicians, graphic designers, software and game developers, philanthropists, writers, and businessmen.

Pada 4

16.40 - 20 deg Gemini, Navamsha -Pisces (Lord - Jupiter)

Rashi Lord - Mercury and Nakshatra Lord- Rahu

In the 4th Pada, the energies of Mercury, Rahu and Jupiter will be at play. In the navamsha, it will be placed in Pisces. Here, Jupiter is an imaginative dreamer and an optimist. With Mercury and Rahu encouraging them to communicate their inspirational thoughts and ideas, natives can become prolific writers of sci-fi, fiction, thrillers and philosophers. This Pada is Pushkar amsha and Pushkar bhaga point at 18 deg Gemini. Any planets placed in this Pada, especially at 18 deg, will do well and give sure results during its dasha.

Being in the navamsha of Pisces makes the natives sensitive and compassionate. They have a strong desire to help those less fortunate than themselves. Planets positioned here usually give beneficial and expansive results. Natives born in this pada are emotional and caring. They are charitable and will not hesitate to give any financial support to others when needed.

Ardra natives in the 4th Pada will be seen as more eccentric than others because of their out-of-the-box thinking. They also have the genius and unconventional perspective, but how motivated they feel to bring it out, put in the effort and express it in words will depend on various factors. They have the inborn talent to look at things from a place where wisdom comes from within, and it's not just the bookish knowledge or information gathered from outside.

They may not discover their hidden abilities until faced with a challenge and they have no choice left but to use their inner wisdom to come out of that particular confrontation or dispute. The inner storm of Ardra can attract them to fall into addiction as an escape route. However, they always have it in them - the wisdom to make the right choices and overcome any difficult circumstances.

For example, Ardra 4th Pada in the 4th house can bring challenging situations at home in terms of arguments and disagreements, change of residence, and misunderstanding with their mother. Jupiter causes a Kendra Adi Pati dosha for Gemini born Ascendants, so the position of Jupiter should be looked at carefully. These upheavals are more possible in Rahu or Jupiter dasha, but with time, the natives will develop insight and wisdom on how to deal with these situations.

"Be a loner, that gives you time to wonder, to search for truth. Have a holy curiosity, make your life worth living."

"The true sign of intelligence is not knowledge but imagination."

"I would rather be an optimist and a fool, than a pessimist and right." - Einstein

Careers-

IT professionals, novelists, blog writers, fiction story writers, teachers, philosophers, homemakers, gurus, priests,

scientists, doctors, pharmacists, psychologists, consultants, advisors, astrologers, ayurvedic doctors, homoeopaths,

healing therapists and working from home.

The effect of planets

Ardra - Gemini Padas 3 and 4	Planets that get affected
Functional Benefic - give good results during their dasha.	Mercury
Functional Malefic - can give problems during their dasha.	Mars, Rahu and Ketu
Functional Neutral	Sun, Moon, Venus and Saturn
Kendra Adi Pati dosha - can be malefic	Jupiter

Ardra Ascendant

Ardra lagna natives will have the energy of Mercury's analytical intelligence amplified by Rahu. Natives born in Ardra can be recognized by their fair complexion, large face and red eyes, they will tend to have thick limbs, large heads and protruding veins. They will also be very sensitive about their hairstyle. The twin effect of Gemini makes them good communicators, and they can make friends easily if they wish to.

On the positive side - they will be sweet talkers, very social, liked by many and pure-hearted. When they are feeling out of sorts or unhappy they can feel regretful, weak-hearted, unwell, and can do something immoral, can lie or cheat, because of aggressive or impulsive behaviour.

Ardra has a special affinity towards animals and will willingly donate towards animals that are abused or in captivity. They love pets, like living in remote places away from noisy cities, and need their alone time to calm their edgy thoughts and emotions. They like to be mentally active, but to do any physical activity, they have to put in the effort and make time to exercise regularly for health benefits.

Ardra is in Gemini, which is the 3rd house of the original birth chart. It signifies our talent, skills of the arms and hands, siblings, friends, neighbours, communication and short travels. It's also called the sehaj bhava, which means the place of our natural abilities and our capacity to adapt to change.

"It's not the strongest of the species that survive, nor the most intelligent, but it's the one that is most adaptable to change." - Charles Darwin.

Ardra falls in Gemini, which is an air sign. This makes the natives flexible, friendly, creative, easy to get on with and adjust to change more easily. Those who are born with Ardra Ascendent, they will have the ability to adjust to circumstances, no matter how difficult or challenging they might be.

However, if the lagna has low ashtakavarga points, natives can struggle to deal with challenges and will easily be stressed, tense, overwhelmed or influenced by others. (ashtakavarga points are based on 8 divisions. The maximum points for any house can be 56, and the average score is 28. If the points are lower than 20 in the lagna, then it will make it weak). How flexible we are in dealing with people around us depends on how much at ease we are within ourselves.

Rahu is exalted in the 1st, 2nd and 3rd Pada of Ardra. Those who are born in these padas will have exceptional communication skills and will be very good with IT and all communication gadgets. They will be very good at talking others into their deals, which they can use to their advantage. They have the knack of conning or manipulating people. They can make successful insurance agents, lawyers, accountants, IT consultants and actors.

Since Ardra is placed in the sign of Gemini, which is a dual sign and has air as the element. It makes the natives very creative and easily changeable. They will feel like they are living two separate lives, one for themselves and one for others. Their personality will be like a kaleidoscopic pattern, switching easily from one to the other - as the changing weather patterns around them and within them. They have their share of bright and hopeful moments and equally wistful, lost and lonely moments. They can easily get carried away by trying to follow the rainbow that forever eludes them. This can make them disoriented and inwardly insecure.

Ardra represents the power to make an effort. This gives them the strength and ability to stay strong amidst storms or hardships. This also shows that they usually have to pass through acute and painful circumstances in life, which leave a deep and transformative impact on them. Teardrop is one of the symbols of this nakshatra, which signifies that at least once in their lifetime, they will pass through a heart-wrenching situation that will make them cry. The other symbol is a diamond, which shows their resilience in passing through harsh circumstances. The penance and endurance of withstanding agony or distress make them strong like a diamond, which shines with priceless brilliance.

"In the middle of difficulty lies the opportunity." - Einstein

The quality of this nakshatra is sharp which gives them the ability to pierce through all difficult situations by the sheer strength of their conviction. This also means that their words or sarcastic remarks can cut through a person when they are unhappy. The deity is Shiva in his Rudra form, which signifies intensity and dissolution.

Ardra is a very intense nakshatra that makes the natives particularly good at all kinds of work that requires - endings, completions, destructions or renovations. This also shows that they will have to deal with death and destruction in some way. They could be scientists, technicians, criminal lawyers, surgeons, soldiers or policemen. This nakshatra is masculine in nature, and the cast is a butcher, which shows they like doing things in a structured and organised way and are not afraid of cutting off ties or relationships that become painful.

Their best remedy will be to balance their thoughts and emotions by grounding themselves into some stable routine or pattern. Which will not come easily to them because they are very free-spirited and cannot be bound by anything or anyone. But if they bring in some structured activity to stabilise their routine, it will, in turn, help to balance their thoughts and emotions. Even a simple start, like listening to their favourite music at a particular time every day, which they can then combine with their exercise routine, will do wonders. Slowly, they will be able to stay more focused on the job at hand without getting distracted by messages or phone calls.

"Peace cannot be kept by force, it can only be achieved through understanding." - Einstein

Sun in Ardra

Sun in Ardra will share the energies of Mercury and Rahu. This combination will magnify the confidence and authoritative quality of the Sun and the intrinsic intelligence and curiosity of mercury. The natives will be confident, bossy, generous with their time and money, intellectual, creative, fun-loving, strong, brave and organised.

They will often try to hide their extravagant need for respect and the feeling of superiority. They will be very ego-sensitive and will feel hurt by the slightest remarks even though they are unintended. They thrive on compliments and are generous in bestowing them on others, too. Even if they cannot afford it, their pride will not let them say no to their friend or their loved one, and they will willingly help them in whichever way they can.

The airy nonchalance of mercury will help to ignite the fiery temper of the Sun, which will be difficult to extinguish once it's aroused. They may use this motivational and inspirational fire towards achieving meaningful goals or may end up wasting their time and energy on insignificant quarrels - just to practice their syntax and sarcasm, which can cut sharply into others.

Sun is considered mildly cruel because it tends to keep others at a distance, like the king interacts with others very selectively, which can bring the feeling of being alienated. They are good organisers and have a strong sense of purpose, which can bring wonderful results during the Sun or Rahu dasha. For example, the Sun in Ardra, in the 9th house, will give a lot of support and benefits from the father and the government. This will manifest strongly if the Sun's degree is close to the Lagna degree. If there is a malefic aspect of Saturn or Mars, it can give confrontations and disputes with the father, teacher, advisor, authorities or the government. The whole chart must be considered before making any plausible predictions.

Moon in Ardra

When the moon is placed in Ardra, it will share the energies of Mercury and Rahu. Moon and mercury, being planets of quick movement and fluctuations, when amplified by Rahu, will make the natives very unstable in their emotions and thoughts. They will be easily swayed by others' opinions and will tend to do too much wool-gathering and not enough concrete action. Their vivid imagination can build sand castles from the colourful ether that are tall enough to reach the stars, but with no stable foundation, they keep crashing to the ground.

They will have the propensity to lie not because they want to, but because their friendly nature lures them to get along with all and they dislike arguments and will want to avoid these unpleasant scenarios at all costs.

There is a danger of either cheating others or being caught in deceitful situations where others may cheat on them, trick them or rob them. This is more likely to happen in the Rahu or moon dasha. They could face problems of anxiety, depression, or mood swings. However the whole chart has to be studied carefully before making any predictions. Going for long walks, watching the moon and stars at night, gardening, walking barefoot, sitting on the ground, all those activities which help in grounding and connecting to nature will be very beneficial in calming and stabilising the anxious mind.

If the moon is strong in the waxing phase, has a good ashtakavarga score, and has the benefic aspect of Venus, the effects will be positive and good. The natives will be very imaginative and empathetic, they can become prolific writers, poets, guides, gurus or philosophers. Because they will feel things very keenly and pick up the vibes of the place or people around them at a subtle level, they have the inborn talent of being in tune with their environment and can, therefore, guide others from a deeper dimension, which is, more profound than the superficial quick fixes.

They love to connect with the devastating or powerful side of nature and will enjoy watching wildlife documentaries. They will have an intrinsic knowledge of herbs, wines, liquid concoctions and home remedies that can be made and used for health benefits or intoxication. They will do well in the medical field or as holistic lifestyle consultants - it will be a very fulfilling career because their happiness comes from taking care of others and helping to relieve their pain and suffering.

For example, the moon in Ardra in the 3rd house will give a lot of short travel and good interaction with siblings, friends and neighbours. The natives will be very friendly, skilled in IT, engaging conversationalists, good writers, and will be very informative about varied subjects.

Ardra, the poet

Ardra is the zest for life- fully on,

Intensely vibrant like the roar of the storm,

Time to destroy the old, to transform.

Easy to bear- it certainly is not,

The cry, the howl, the pain - a lot!

Rahu the serpent head, fully aware,

Mercury the curious one, fans the air,

Together can know and share,

Twins, a great pair,

Can achieve all, though a tricky affair!

As the brave and fearless move on,

Not deterred, for they are spirited and strong.

The fossil that silently lay underground, securely store,

After the penance of centuries and more.

It's hibernation is not a waste,

The tears were not in wane.

For every experience has been an added drop of strength,

That now shines through at length.

The resolute diamond bright and gleaming,

Admired by all, yet cannot be stolen, a priceless quality unyielding.

Is an inspiration for many to come

For Melania and more.

Remedies

- <u>Das Maha Vidyas</u> - Devi Bagalamukhi - as described earlier.

<u>Devi Chinnamasta - Rahu</u>

In Sanskrit, Chinnamasta means the one whose head is severed.

She is a goddess of contradictions, she is both the food and the eater of food, thereby symbolising the whole world by this act of being devoured and the devourer.

The dichotomy of receiver and giver or object and subject collapses into one. She symbolises both aspects - a life-giver and a life-taker. She is considered both a symbol of sexual self-control and an embodiment of sexual energy, depending upon the interpretation. She represents immortality, recreation, death, life, and destruction. The goddess conveys spiritual self-realisation and the awakening of the kundalini – spiritual energy.

<u>Inference</u>

If one has to bring out the best in oneself, one has to sacrifice the immediate pleasures, the ego, and the false pride. Which is not always an easy choice to make. Only the genuine, brave, determined and fearless ones can take this step into the unknown and discover the other side of life, which is beyond the compulsions of the body and mind.

<u>Effects of Rahu</u>

She rules over Rahu and its effects and is said to represent that side of one's personality which brings one's downfall through one's own mistakes. All accentuated attributes of Rahu, like - sudden decisions, accidents, snake bites, thefts, robberies, attacks, treachery, gambling, share brokers, and unexpected sudden events signify her energy.

All professions which require dealing with blood, body fluids or chemicals are also controlled by her. Professions like - doctors, surgeons, chemists, making or selling alcohol, liquid gas dealers and petrol pump owners. Rahu is also associated with electrical energy. All professions related to electrical engineering, computers and new-age technology are therefore associated with Goddess Chinnamasta.

Rahu in the birth chart-

The effects of Rahu in the birth chart are seen by sudden events like - falling in love, marriage, foreign travel, job in a foreign country, overnight stardom, fame and money, or sudden loss of finance, reputation, position or accidents.

Those who have Rahu in 1st, 8th or 12th houses, or Rahu conjunct Mars or Saturn should worship Goddess Chinnamasta to stabilise the amplified effects which can otherwise create havoc, during the Rahu dasha, antardasha and transits over one's Ascendent and natal moon.

Rahu and Saturn are 100% karmic planets, and if they are conjunct in any house, they make us face the effects of past life karma forcefully and no other planet can save us from this effect.

Remedies -

- To help people in foreign lands or to help foreigners is a good way to please Rahu.

- Chant the mantra of Devi Chinnamasta 108 times on the day when Rahu is transiting over your Ascendant, natal sun or natal moon. Combine the chanting with her image, yantra and written mantra. Chanting the sacred mantras is said to grant beauty, light, spiritual fire, self-realisation, and destruction of delusion.

Mantras of Devi Chinnamasta -

"Om Shreem Hreem Hreem Aim Vajra Vairochaniye Shreem Hreem", "Hreem Phat Swaha." and

"Srim hrim klim aim Vajravairocaniye hum hum phat svaha."

Other remedies

- Ardra being the nakshatra of intense and fierce energy the best remedy will be to do some form of physical exercises, cycling, swimming, hatha yoga, pranayama and meditation. This will help to calm the storm within and give a focused and clear approach.

- Keep a pet dog, or donate towards animal causes.

- Go for a holiday to the Grand Canyon, game reserves or remote open landscapes which connect you to nature.

- Make a donation on Wednesday (Mercury's day) of green vegetables or green moong lentils.

- Worship Lord Shiva in his Rudra form on the days when the moon transits Ardra nakshatra.

- Wearing an 8-faced rudraksha mala will protect you from destructive energies.

- Green, grey and black colours are favourable because they resonate with the energy of Ardra.

- Chant the Ardra nakshatra mantra 108 times regularly for 40 days. *"Om aym Ardra nakshatrae namah."*

Example

Moon in Ardra

Amita Sharma - Born on Sunday, 12th September 1982, in Delhi, India. An all-rounder in the Indian women's cricket team.

Amita first played for India in 2002. She has played 5 test matches and took 14 wickets in the 2005 World Cup in South Africa and helped her team reach the finals. She plays domestic cricket for Northern Railways.

She says that right from her childhood, she was actively involved in sports and was in her school volleyball team. Later, she joined the women's cricket team in Bangalore when she was in 10th grade. She practised as a medium-pace bowler in the cricket team.

She remembers her first ball was bowled to a boy who was the batsman. She jokingly states that "he removed his helmet thinking, it's just a girl bowling. To his utter surprise and mine! the ball hit him straight on his nose." From there, her journey as a medium-pace bowler started.

She said she was very excited to play for the Indian team, and it was the 1st ever World Cup for women's cricket teams in 2005 in South Africa. Since then, her team has played 4 world test matches. Since 2017, she has become a cricket coach, she is now married and has a 4-year-old son.

Analysis -

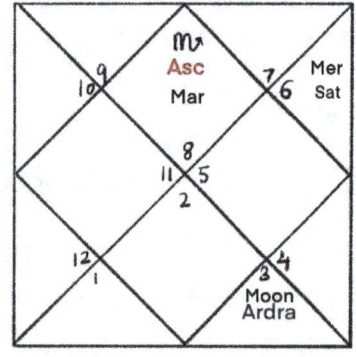

Amita's Moon is placed in Ardra Pada 3 and Rahu in Pada 4 in the 8th house of her horoscope (Gemini). This gives her intensity and fearlessness of action.

The 8th house represents sudden ups and downs and gains from insurance or ancestral property. We don't know anything about the financial gains, but from her career graph we can see many opportunities that suddenly came her way. She is very good with communication, and her sporting talent comes from her confidence. Mercury, the lord of Gemini, is sitting with Saturn in the 11th house (Virgo) of gains. This shows her language will be rough, straight forward, technical and practical, and she will get gains through large organisations. (cricket team and national railways).

Mars, the natural significator of the 8th house, is sitting in the lagna in Anuradha nakshatra, in Scorpio. Mars, being the lord of Scorpio, sitting in his own house is very comfortable and makes her very fearless and confident in her approach. She has an army-like discipline to practice and go through the tough training of an athlete.

Ardra represents the storm within, which is brought forth beautifully and efficiently by the vigorous and intense routine of being an international-level cricket team player. She has been referred to as a pioneer in the field of women's cricket. Doing something extraordinary is the possibility, quality and capability inherent in Ardra natives.

7
Punarvasu

Om aum Punarvasu nakshatraye namah

Zodiac degrees	20 deg Gemini - 3.20 deg Cancer Gemini - 1st, 2nd and 3rd padas Cancer - 4th Pada.
Ruling planet	Gemini - Mercury and Cancer - Moon Punarvasu - Jupiter
Sanskrit name	Punar means once again, and vasu means to reside. It can also be translated as good again or wealthy again. Because vasus are the gods who have the qualities of goodness, strength and prosperity.
Astronomical name	At the top left-hand corner of the Orion constellation in Gemini are seen 2 bright stars called the twin stars, which can be easily spotted in the night sky named Castor and Pollux, which represent the Punarvasu nakshatra. The ancient Vedic seers also saw them as a quiver of arrows.
Symbol	Gemini - Twins and Cancer - Crab Punarvasu - Quiver of arrows and return of light.
Element	Air and Water
Deity	Aditi, the mother of 12 adityas - 12 solar deities.
Quality	Dwi - dual - Gemini and Chara - movable - Cancer
Shakti	Vastuva prapana Shakti - the power to retrieve objects.
Cast	Vaishya - trader
Gender	Male - Gemini and Female - Cancer
Motivation	Kama - to fulfil desires - Gemini Moksha - liberation - Cancer
Triguna	Satwa - Gemini and Rajas - Cancer

Tridosha	Vata - Gemini and Kapha - Cancer
Body parts	Fingers and nose
Direction	West, north and north west.
Month	First half of Pushya lunar month - late December
Bird	Peacock
Sound	kay, ko, ha, hee
Tree	Bamboo
Chakras	Anhatta - Moon and Ajna - Jupiter and Mercury
Das Maha Vidya	Devi Tara - Jupiter, Devi Tripura Sundari - Mercury And Devu Bhuvaneswari - Moon

Special degrees -

Yoga Tara	29.30 deg Gemini It's a point where the planet will show the strongest and sure results during its dasha.
Amrit nadi	2 - 2.53 deg Cancer Gives good results like the nectar that nourishes.
Visha nadi	26.40 - 27.33 deg Gemini Brings situations which one does not like dealing with.

Auspicious and inauspicious table -

Auspicious	Inauspicious
<u>Activities</u> Good for activities which require harsh or decisive measures, filing lawsuits, strategic planning, sexual activity, making short-term plans and low-risk activities, yoga and meditation.	<u>Activities</u> Not good for any beginnings, auspicious activities, negotiations, making business deals, or borrowing or lending money.
<u>Days</u> <u>Mondays</u> - only when it falls on the 2nd, 7th, or 12th lunar day. <u>Thursdays</u> - only when it falls on the 4th, 5th, 7th, 9th, 13th or 14th lunar day.	<u>Days</u> <u>Tuesdays</u>- only when it falls on the 1st, 2nd, 7th, 8th or 10th lunar day. <u>Fridays</u> - only when it falls on the 2nd, 3rd, 6th, 8th,10th or 11th lunar day. <u>Saturdays</u> - only when it falls on the 3rd, 7th, 9th or 11th lunar day.

Compatibility table -

Punarvasu	Compatible with
Sexual compatibility Yoni animal	Punarvasu - Male cat - compatible with - Female cat - Ashlesha
Sign compatibility	Gemini - Padas 1, 2 and 3 - Libra and Aquarius. Cancer - Pada 4 - Scorpio and Pisces.
Nakshatra compatibility	Vishakha and Purva Bhadrapada.
Lunar day compatibility	8th lunar day (ashtami)
Day compatibility	Monday, Wednesday and Thursday
Colour compatibility	Yellow, white and green
Numerological compatibility	2, 3 and 5 are all numbers that add up to make 2, 3 and 5.
Sound compatibility	Moon - semi vowels - ya, ra, la, va, sa, sha, ssa, ha, lr, rr Mercury - lingual sounds - ta, tha, da, dha, na Jupiter - dental sounds - tta, ttha, da, dha, kna

Sign Lord and nakshatra lord - <u>Mercury, Moon and Jupiter.</u>

Moon and Mercury - as described earlier.

<u>Jupiter - lord of Punarvasu</u>

Jupiter is a benefic planet and supports growth and expansion. It represents good luck, fortune, expansion, self-development, higher learning, wisdom and spiritual intelligence. It is the most generous planet which gives abundant resources. When it's well placed in the horoscope, it grants happiness, good health, prosperity, spiritual inclination and success.

Basically, Jupiter is a teacher, so people born with a strong influence of Jupiter will be in a teaching or counselling profession, priests, preachers, philosophers, guides, advisors, spiritual leaders, astrologers, psychologists, consultants, scholars and advocates.

Even if they are not officially working as a consultant, they will love advising others on any topic that interests them, and people also perceive them as a go-to person.

Jupiter is a very optimistic planet and helps people to always look at the positive side of things even amidst a difficult situation, they will find a ray of hope. Because at the soul level, they feel that things will work out, they always come out of difficulties without much harm, except for the lessons learnt. Jupiter ruled people like to do things in a right and ethical manner, and they understand the transitory nature of all that we see and experience in this world, therefore, they view life with a very philosophical perspective.

A Jupiter-ruled native prefers to be in their comfort zone, read scriptures, contemplate on the truth and untruth, philosophise, give advice, have intellectual discussions, counsel others, gain knowledge and walk the spiritual path. If they have to go out and earn money, then it has to be an academic job of teaching or counselling. Their inherent interest does not lie in earthly pleasures. They are more of spiritual seekers.

Inference

The 1st, 2nd and 3rd padas of Punarvasu are placed in Gemini, whose ruler is Mercury, and the lord of Punarvasu is Jupiter. The influence of Mercury and Jupiter makes the natives very vocal and communicative about what they know and what they have learnt. They love intellectual discussions and love to advise and counsel others, especially on philosophical subjects.

The 4th Pada of Punarvasu falls in Cancer, which is ruled by the moon. Here, the energies of Jupiter and the moon make them very idealistic, kind, emotional, empathetic and receptive to others' feelings. Jupiter's moon combination is considered good and fortunate because it gives an abundance of beautiful humanistic qualities. People born in this Pada are fortunate and usually succeed in whatever they do because of their good intentions and genuine caring for others.

Quality - Dwi and Chara -as described earlier.

Element - Air - as described earlier.

Water

In the sequential order, water is the 4th of the 5 main elements (Pancha mahabhutas) because it evolves from ether, air, and fire and contains the qualities of the other 3 elements within it. The element of water represents fluidity, matter and the cohesive principle of physics. Water provides the body with its most basic nourishment and soothes all pain and inflammation in the body.

Water and sense of taste -

The origin of the water element is in the tanmatra of taste, rasa. Rasa is the chemical energy that provides the potential for the experience of taste to occur. Since the sense of taste depends upon the water element, the disorders of the ability to taste are due to an imbalance of the water element.

Water and the tongue -

The tongue is the sense organ of water. Through the tongue, we taste everything. It is interesting to note that the taste buds of the tongue only work when water or saliva is present. No water means no taste. Imbalances of the water element in the body can be observed by monitoring changes in a person's experience of taste as well as through alterations of urine or seminal fluid.

The qualities of Water-

Water is cool, stable, heavy, moist, smooth, gross, flowing, dull, cloudy, and soft. The water element is the antidote to symptoms that have the opposite qualities in the body. In order to stay healthy, it's important to keep yourself well hydrated by drinking enough water as needed for your body type, according to the climate and your health condition.

Water and diet -

In our diet, the sweet taste is the main source of water. Cooked grains, curries, soups, smoothies, milk, fresh fruits and salads and soaked nuts are foods with ample water element within them. The proper intake of these foods supports healthy water elements in the body.

Water and the seasons -

Spring is the season of water because, in springtime, the water that is stored within the snow begins to flow from the mountains into the rivers and streams. Water is the source of life and the container of prana. As the water begins to flow, life grows in its wake. Spring is sweet, and its sweetness nourishes all of life. During this time, the water element in our bodies naturally increases and flows. Therefore, eating too many sweets during spring can cause an excess of water element in the body.

Water and Kapha -

The kapha dosha contains both water and earth. It is water that is responsible for most of the protective and healing aspects of the kapha dosha. This table shows the effect of excess and deficient water in the dhatus (body tissues)

Water	Caused by	Effect	Balance
Excess	Oily fatty foods	Reduced digestive strength, reduced appetite, heaviness, sluggish digestion and imbalance of Kapha.	Eat less oily and fatty foods.
Deficient	Drinking less water and eating dry foods.	Dehydration, dryness, weakness, weight loss, constipation and decrease in urination	Drink more water.

Inference

Those who are born with their Ascendant, Sun or Moon in Punarvasu Pada 4 will have the influence of water because this Pada is placed in Cancer, which is ruled by the water element. Therefore, they will be more prone to put on weight, and will be fond of eating sweets and fatty foods. They will be sensitive, emotional, caring, kind and empathetic.

Motivation- <u>Kama-</u> as described earlier.

<u>Moksha - liberation</u>

The word Moksha means to be set free, release, liberation and enlightenment. The Vedic texts refer to it as the freedom from saṃsara - the cycle of death and rebirth, freedom from ignorance, self-realization and self-knowledge. In Hindu traditions, there are 4 Purusharthas - objects of human pursuit -

Purusharthas	Meaning
Dharma	Virtuous and moral life.
Artha	Material prosperity and income security.
Kama	Pleasures and emotional fulfilment.
Moksha	Liberation, freedom and enlightenment.

While moksha is a central concept and the ultimate aim of human life, it is attained by going through the previous paths of - dharma, artha and kama. Self-discipline is considered necessary to achieve dharma and moksha because doing the right thing is not always the easiest thing to do. It takes determination, willpower and effort to follow the path of dharma that leads to moksha.

In the legendary story of the young boy Naciketa and the lord of death - Yamaraj. <u>Nachiketa asks Yamraj</u> - "What causes samsara - worldly pursuits, what leads to liberation? And What causes sorrow?" <u>Yamaraj answers</u> - "That suffering and samsara result from a life that is lived absent-mindedly, with impurity, with neither the use of intelligence nor self-examination, where neither mind nor senses are guided by one's atma - soul or true self. Liberation comes from a life lived with inner purity, an alert mind, led by buddhi - reason and intelligence, and realization of the supreme self, who dwells in all beings. Inner knowing and wisdom liberate, and knowledge is the path to freedom."

The ancient Vedic text - Narada parivrajaka upanishad, describes the attributes of those who are on the path of moksha -

- They are not bothered by disrespect and can endure cruel words, not out of weakness but out of compassion.

- When faced with any confrontation he or she does not react in anger. Instead responds with awareness, calmness and maturity.

- They have a lot of integrity and keep their promises.

- Even in difficulties they choose to tell the truth.

- They do not crave rewards or expect praise from others.

- They never cause any physical harm (ahimsa) to any life or being.

- They are not selfish and do things for the well-being of all beings.

- They are as comfortable being alone as they are in the presence of others.

- They are equanimous in all extreme situations of joy or sorrow.

- They are not attracted or tempted to worldly pleasures. If they have the comforts of life they don't get attached to them, and don't despair when they don't have those comforts.

- Outer appearances and rituals do not matter to them. Only true knowledge matters.

- They do not hold strong opinions against or for anyone.

- They do not have strong likes or dislikes and easily adjust to changing situations, get along with everyone, and joyfully do whatever needs to be done.

- They are humble, high-spirited, and have clarity of thought and a steady mind.

- They are truthful, straightforward, joyful, compassionate, patient, calm and courageous.

- They speak clearly, firmly and gently. They are never rude or abusive.

- They have a sense of neutrality towards miseries. In the midst of suffering or any external influences, they can be in the experience of samadhi - the state of ease and one's own bliss.

In Kaivalya Pada, Patanjali gives a very scientific explanation about how our mind gets conditioned with the outer influences called impressions -

"The pure consciousness always settles into its own pure nature. Only the mind born of meditation is great and is free from all karmic impressions. These impressions are held together by cause and effect, which are the basis and support. Since the desire to live is eternal, impressions are also beginningless. These impressions disappear with the disappearance of these 4 - dharma, artha, Kama and Moksha." - Patanjali

Nirvana Shatakam is a chant written by Adi Shankaracharya - where he describes the nature of pure consciousness, our true self. In one of the verses, he says -

"Na dharmo, na chartho, na kamo, na moksha,

Chidanand rupa Shivo hum Shivo hum." - Adi Shankaracharya.

Meaning-

Where there is no concept of Dharma, Artha, Kama and Moksha,

Our true nature is - awareness and bliss, and we are eternal - Shiva.

Inference

The 4th Pada of Punarvasu is placed in Cancer, which is a moksha sign. The natives' actions and thoughts will be motivated by the desire to be free, to escape from certain situations or people. They do not like being bound by anyone or any circumstances. They will feel the need to escape into solitude to refresh and rejuvenate.

Whether they are pursuing materialistic or spiritual goals, their underlying desire is to be free from all worldly responsibilities and have the freedom to follow their heart, where they are not tied down by any routines.

Triguna and tridosha - as described earlier.

Chakras - Anhatta and Ajna - as described earlier.

The 4th Pada of Punarvasu is placed in Cancer (ruled by the moon) and, therefore, has the influence of Anhatta. The ruler of Punarvasu is Jupiter, so it's energies also resonate with the Ajna chakra. Those who are born in the 4th Pada have a wonderful combination of emotions and wisdom. All Punarvasus have the qualities of Ajna chakra, which makes them very religious, philosophical and spiritual. If the energy of the chakras is blocked, they can become very self-centred and selfish, and when the energy flows smoothly through the chakras, they are compassionate, kind, knowledgeable and wise.

Shakti - Vastuva prapana Shakti - the power to retrieve objects.

Punarvasu natives have the unique ability to start again after facing a setback or abandoning a project. The second time around, they will succeed because they will have learnt their lessons and will not repeat the same mistakes again. They are blessed with the capability of sustaining what they have re-started in life. Even in the literal sense, they will be good at finding objects that have been misplaced, stolen or forgotten.

The natives can face such situations in life where they fail the first time and succeed the 2nd time. They will find that situations automatically improve for them when they help others to rebuild or restart their projects, relationships, or careers.

Symbolic signification

Gemini - Twins, as described earlier, Cancer - Crab

Punarvasu - Quiver of arrows and return of light and cat.

The return of light

The calm after the storm, the light after the dark, the tranquillity after the thunder, the equanimity after the chaos

The stability after the upheaval, the understanding after the confusion - is Punarvasu.

The padas 1,2, and 3 fall in Gemini, and Pada 4 falls in Cancer. This shows the shift that happens between the energy of Gemini and Cancer, from air to water, from duality to movability, and from desire to liberation. Jupiter, being the lord of Punarvasu, brings healing and beneficial effects. The purpose of the previous nakshatra - Ardra, was to dissolve in order to set conditions for fresh life to flourish. In Punarvasu, the ambience is conducive for growth, nourishment, rejuvenation and making a new start once again.

Quiver of arrows

Arrows represent the straight direction, one-way path from point A to point B, to move forward, move directly without any confusion or delays. The natives will not take a roundabout approach or beat around the bush but will come straight to the point, and will have a direct approach to things and situations. They will move with a focus, straight on their chosen path, without any distractions until the arrow of their desire has hit the target.

Crab -

Crabs are very unique creatures, since they can live on both land and in water, yet they are not classified as amphibians. They are called crustaceans because they are semi-aquatic and have exoskeletons (a hard-outer cover) for protection. They are found mostly in tropical climates, in coastal areas of salty ocean waters and in freshwater lakes.

There are more than 4500 species of crabs, and they vary in size, ranging from microscopic to several feet in diameter. Regardless of their size, all crabs have 10 legs - 8 legs on the sides and 2 legs in front - which have claws that enable them to catch their prey and eat it.

Crab Diet

Crab claws, which are an excellent tool for their survival, they help them to grab their prey, eat it, defend themselves and attack when needed. Crabs are omnivores and feed primarily on algae, molluscs, worms, other crustaceans, fungi, bacteria, and detritus, depending on their availability and the crab species. For many crabs, a mixed diet of plant and animal matter results in the fastest growth and greatest fitness. However, some species are more specialised in their diets. Some eat plankton, some eat primarily shellfish such as clams, and some even catch fish.

Males and females

Male crabs often have larger claws and a narrow triangular-shaped belly at the bottom. While female crabs have a broader rounded abdomen, which is designed to keep their fertilised eggs. Male crabs attract the female mate by releasing a chemical, which has a certain smell, and by a visual signal of waving their large claws.

Crabs are known to work together to provide food and protection for their family and are mostly active and communicate by drumming or waving their pincers. Male crabs tend to be aggressive towards one another and often fight to gain access to females. During the mating season, males help to find a comfortable spot for the female to release her eggs.

Females carrying eggs are called berried, since the eggs resemble round berries. When development is complete, most species of terrestrial crabs make very extensive migrations from land to water. The female releases the newly hatched larvae into the water, where they become part of the plankton. The release is timed with the tidal waves and light and dark cycles of the moon.

Moulting

The young crabs still have to go through a difficult process of moulting many times to become adults. Since they are covered with a hard shell, which would otherwise prevent growth. The moult cycle is coordinated by hormones. When preparing for moult, the old shell is softened and partly eroded away, while the rudimentary beginnings of a new shell form under it.

At the time of moulting, the crab takes in a lot of water to expand and crack open the old shell at a line of weakness along the back edge of the carapace. The crab must then extract all of itself from the old shell. This is a difficult process that takes many hours, and if a crab gets stuck, it will die. After freeing itself from the old shell, the crab is extremely soft and hides until its new shell has hardened. While the new shell is still soft, the crab can expand it to make room for future growth.

The sideways walk

Most crabs walk sideways because it's easier and quicker since they have stiff jointed legs. Moreover, 4 legs on each side would get in each other's way, sidewalk assures that they don't trip over their feet. This crab behaviour gives us the word crabwise. However, some crabs walk forwards or backward.

Decorative crabs

Scientists have closely observed many crab species and have seen that crabs have evolved clever ways of avoiding predators.

The 7,000 species of crabs on earth have looks ranging from scary to cute to surreal. Some are fashionistas, and some make pretty strange fashion choices — like toxic wigs.

These observations have been made by Weis, the crab researcher. Sponge crabs of West Africa wear sponges on their heads and bodies, not to attract attention but to deflect it. The sponges camouflage the crabs from predators, and some sponge species emit toxic chemicals, making the crab unappealing to predators.

Decorator crabs have hooked hairs all over their shell that act like Velcro to hold any sort of decoration in place. They protect themselves from predators by using toxic algae, which, like sponges, can both disguise the crab and deter predators.

Moss crabs of the southwestern U.S. are the most extreme decorators. They carpet themselves with tiny moss animals that look plant-like and furry.

Carrier crabs of the Indo-Pacific and East Africa have specialised back legs that help them hold the weight of a protective sea urchin when they go out for a stroll.

Hermit crabs have a tough exoskeleton on their front half and protect their softer back half by finding discarded snail shells to live in. Their soft bodies are coiled to fit in the spiralling shells, though sadly, some find less-fitting homes—like humans' trash. As they grow, they need to find larger shells, just like growing children need bigger shoes.

Crabby behaviour

Crab mentality- *"If I can't get it, neither can you."*

The metaphor is derived from a pattern of behaviour noted in the crabs when they were trapped in a bucket. While any one crab could easily escape, its efforts were undermined by others, ensuring the group's collective demise. The analogy in human behaviour is claimed to be that members of a group will attempt to reduce the self-confidence of any member who achieves success beyond the others out of envy, resentment, spite, conspiracy, or competitive feelings to halt their progress.

Inference

Cancer is associated with the symbol of a crab because the constellation of stars is shaped like a crab. Astrological inferences show that Cancer natives exhibit crab-like qualities. They are caring, empathetic, kind, hilarious, cautious, emotionally sensitive, imaginative, sentimental and moody.

Just like a crab who can survive both on land and in water, Cancerians are very versatile, resilient and strong survivors. The crab claws are wonderful survival tools provided by nature. When Cancer natives feel out of sorts, they become crabby, cranky, and snappy and withdraw into their shells to heal and recover.

The physiology of the crabs is very finely tuned to the waning and waxing moon phases. Similarly, Cancer natives go through phases of lunar fears and insecurities, which makes them hoard materials, information or knowledge. Cancer natives are very family-oriented and love to take care of their partners and children, just as the male crabs help to find a secure place for female crabs, their fulfilment comes from caring for their loved ones.

Crab's special ability to walk sideways is very unique, which gives them agility, similarly, those who are born with Ascendent or Moon in Cancer are very graceful and quick in their movements. The crabs are very quick to respond to any danger, and so are the Cancerians. Their heightened sense of awareness makes them spiritually inclined and gives them psychic abilities. They can easily sense any imminent danger lurking around them, and this can make them feel insecure, which makes them pushy, possessive, protective, economical, secretive and cautious.

They are very good at camouflaging their appearance or emotions, just like the decorative crabs; it's a clever way of keeping predators or possible intruders at bay. Their inner sensitivity needs to be protected from inconsiderate outsiders. Their sensitivity can kindle both tears and giggles simultaneously in them. But their vulnerability is never exposed in public, only in the secure privacy of their home; their inner soft nature is seen when they are totally relaxed and can safely let their guard down.

When they are feeling low, sullen, or depressed, their crabby and snappy nature pulls down everyone who is around them. On the other hand, when they are feeling on top of the world, they are so funny and hilarious and can make you laugh to bits. It's a joy to have them around. Just as the moon makes the night romantic, Cancer-born people nurture and nourish others with their empathy, receptivity, imagination, dreams and inner beauty of love and emotions.

Cat

Cats are the domesticated species of small carnivorous mammals and like to roam freely. They are kept by humans for company and for their ability to hunt rodents. Cats have a strong flexible body, quick reflexes, sharp teeth and retractable claws adapted for killing small prey. Its night vision and sense of smell are well-developed.

Cats communicate by meowing, purring, trilling, hissing and growling. It can hear sounds that are too faint or too high in frequency for human ears. Their ears are designed to hear the sounds of mice and other small mammals.

Cats love their independence and know how to survive well in nature because of their small size, social nature, deliberate and cautious body language, love of play and relatively high intelligence. Female domestic cats can have kittens from spring to late autumn, with litter sizes often ranging from two to five kittens. Cats love sitting in high places or perching. It serves as a concealed site to survey the territory from which to hunt and strike prey by pouncing.

The timing of cats' activity is quite flexible, but they are more active during dawn and dusk. Cats conserve energy by sleeping more than most animals, especially as they grow older. The daily duration of sleep varies, usually between 12 and 16 hours. The average lifespan of a cat is 15 years.

Interesting facts

- Cats are solitary hunters but a social species, predators, and are most active at dawn and dusk.

- Cats have excellent night vision and can see at only one-sixth the light level required for human vision.

- They can detect an extremely broad range of frequencies which helps them to hear ultrasonic sounds made by rodent prey.

- Cats prefer food with a temperature around 38 °C, which is similar to that of a fresh kill and will reject eating food that is cold or refrigerated; it acts as a signal that the prey is long dead and has decomposed, eating it would be toxic.

- Cats' whiskers are highly sensitive to touch and they help to protect the eyes from damage.

- The term 'cat nap' comes from the cat's tendency to fall asleep briefly at any time during the day.

- When the cat wakes up from catnap sleep, it will always stretch to tone up the muscles for activity.

- Cats have a remarkable sense of balance. When they fall from an altitude, they usually land on all 4 paws. Slow motion photography has shown that cats always right themselves, turn their bodies around in the air before they touch the ground and land on all fours.

Inference

Independent

Just as cats are very independent and will come to you out of their own will. Similarly, Punarvasu natives don't like to be bound - they know how to escape situations that might bind them into a contract, relationship or responsibility if it's enforced on them.

Single pointed focus

Cats know how to hunt their prey with full attention on it. Punarvasu natives also set their eyes on the target they pursued. They will never lose focus of what they wish to achieve and will go for it with a single-track mind. They also know how to wait in the wings and to creep into situations when the time is right to strike, their inbuilt hunting skills will seldom let them down.

Solitary time

Domestic cats are trained and conditioned to be social, but when they hunt, they hunt alone. Punarvasu natives need time for themselves, without any disturbance, especially when they are chasing their dream project or working towards a deadline.

Catnap

Their periods of activity can be random, and there might not be a fixed time for sleep; therefore, to catch up on their sleep, catnap is needed to re-energise. Punarvasu natives are usually more active at dawn and dusk.

Freshly cooked food

They will be very particular about eating freshly cooked food since they have a keen sense of knowing if the food is stale. Cold refrigerated food will usually not agree with their physiology.

Stretching exercises -

Punarvasu natives will benefit greatly from stretching exercises or hatha yoga practises. The flexibility of their muscles will keep their body healthy and in tone.

Remarkable balance -

They will always bounce back from anything that throws them off balance, whether it's a sudden change of events, loss of a job, low mood, heartbreak or separation. Just like cats have an amazing ability to always land right, cancer-born natives will instinctively know what needs to be corrected when things go wrong. Their flexibility and agility of thought and action carry them intelligently through all situations.

Please note - The crab-like and cat-like qualities will be seen for all those who are born with their Ascendant, Sun or Moon in Cancer. Therefore, these attributes will be seen in all those who are born in the 4th Pada of Punarvasu, in Pushya and in Ashlesha, and not in the first 3 padas of Punarvasu, which fall in Gemini.

Mythology

The Ramayana connection

Lord Rama's Lagna (Ascendant) is Punarvasu. The epic Ramayana was originally written by rishi (sage) Vālmīki, where it's said that Lord Rama was born on Ram navami (the 9th lunar day of the waxing moon). Based on this, the astrological calculations show that he was born 7,122 years ago in Ayodhya, which is in the state of Uttar Pradesh in India.

The story of Lord Rama's birth

Thousands of years ago, there lived a King named Dashratha of the Ikshvaku dynasty ruling the kingdom in the beautiful city of Ayodhya, on the banks of river Sarayu. He was a generous and intelligent king who was well-loved by his people. He had 3 wives, Kaushalya, Kaikeyi and Sumitra, but had no children, which made him very worried and sad.

One day, the king went to see sage Vashishtha and expressed his concern and deep sadness. Vashishtha advised him to perform Ashwamedha Yagna. King Dasharatha followed the instructions and Vedic rituals precisely and religiously. After 12 months, in the month of Chaitra, on a day when it was neither hot nor cold, winds blew softly, and the forest was full of beautiful blossoms. When the rivers flowed swiftly and sang with joy, a divine being was born.

The eldest Queen Kausalya gave birth to a handsome son, whose bodily lustre had a greenish hue, like the fresh green grass. King Dashratha was overjoyed with the birth of his elder son, who was named Rama because of his divine attributes. It is said that Lord Rama is the 7th incarnation of Lord Vishnu. Soon after this, Queen Kaikeyi gave birth to Bharata, and Queen Sumitra gave birth to twins Lakshmana and Shatrughna. So King Dasharatha was now content and happy that he had 4 sons and a worthy heir to his kingdom.

Deity - Aditi

The Vedantic texts describe Aditi as the fundamental fabric of creation because she held the universe in her womb before the manifestation of creation happened. In this context, she is considered the female version of Lord Brahma, who is the God of creation. The story goes that Aditi and Diti were sisters, and both were married to sage Kashyap. While Aditi gave birth to virtuous sons who became the Devas, Diti's sons were the Daityas or Asuras.

Scientific perspective

Ancient mythological stories are a way of explaining scientific principles in a simple manner. The reference of Aditi and Diti is the 2 opposite forces of nature through which the game of creation happens. For example, if there were only good forces and no counter force, there would be no act of creation. 2 teams are needed for the game to happen, just as we need 2 hands to clap. Similarly, the 4 fingers on their own would not be able to hold anything with precision if there was no thumb placed opposite to them. The finer motor skills are only possible because of the thumb's unique and vital position on the hand.

Newton's 3rd law of physics states that' *for every action, there is an equal and opposite reaction.*' This law represents a certain symmetry in nature because forces always occur in pairs. One body cannot exert a force on another without experiencing a force itself. For example, helicopters can create a lift by pushing the air down, thereby experiencing an upward reaction force. Birds fly by exerting a force on the air; the wings of a bird force the air downward and backwards in order to get a lift and forward motion, which enables them to fly.

When we walk, the foot that is placed behind gives a push to bring the other foot in front. All movement is possible because of an opposite force exerted on it.

One of Patanjali's Yoga Sutra states, "*pratipaksha-bhavana*." Which means the opposite emotion. (e - motion is also a subtle form of motion). In other words, Patanjali is saying that to bring balance, we must do the opposite. For example, negative thoughts of anger or frustration can be balanced by peaceful and calming thoughts of love and compassion.

Aditi, as the Goddess

Vedas hold Aditi as one of the most auspicious and widely regarded divine powers. Aditi is normally depicted as a very graceful figure, riding a cock or a rooster, which stands for strength and honour. She also represents space, time, freedom, fortune, change and protection.

"Daksha sprang from Aditi and Aditi from Daksha." - Rig Veda.

This signifies the eternal cyclic pattern of death and rebirth. The ancient Puranic texts state that Aditi was the daughter of Daksha and Panchajani. Aditi's siblings were Diti, Kadru, Vinata, Sati, Swaha, Rohini, Revati, Danu and Muni. Aditi was the wife of sage Kashyapa and they had 33 sons, who were the - 12 Adityas, 11 Rudras and 8 Vasus.

The 12 Adityas

N	Adityas	Significance
1	Surya	our energy source.
2	Vivasan	social law
3	Aryaman	close friend, partner
4	Pushan	nourishment, prosperity
5	Tvastar	crafting skills
6	Savitar	the life-giving aspect
7	Bhaga	fortune, inheritance
8	Dhata	generous, kind
9	Varuna	Lord of the Oceans and the west direction.
10	Mitra	friendship
11	Shakra	whose other name is Indra - the leader, the eldest.
12	Vishnu	born as Vamana avatar in the dwarf form.

The 8 Vasus -

N	Vasus	Significance
1	Dhara	prithvi, earth
2	Anala	agni, fire
3	Anila	vayu, wind
4	Aha	antariksha, space

5	Aditya	pratyusha, Sun
6	Soma	chandrama, Moon
7	Dhruva	north Pole star
8	Prabhasa	dyaus, dawn

<u>The 11 Rudras -</u> have been listed in Ardra nakshatra.

<u>Qualities of Aditi</u>

As Aditi she is an unbound, free soul and is seen as the guardian of cosmic moral order and the supporter of creatures. Her weapons are a trishul and a sword. She represents truth, generosity, purity, beauty and regality. She has the power to give abundance and productivity. She is the protector of children and the mother and sustains life on earth.

<u>Inference</u>

Punarvasu natives are blessed with qualities that help to make a fresh start in life and sustain the resources needed for nourishment and productivity. Like a mother nourishes and protects her children, she looks after them until they are old enough to fend for themselves. The genuine care, love, understanding, empathy, and kindness - the motherly qualities, will be inherent in them.

Since Aditi is the mother of 33 gods which represents the basic ingredients and qualities needed for life to happen and flourish on earth. Punarvasu natives will have the ability and capability to tap into these wonderful virtues whenever they need them. Armed with all these gracious qualities, which are always with them like arrows in their quiver, there is nothing in life that they cannot accomplish or recover.

Punarvasu Padas

20 deg Gemini - 3.20 Cancer

Padas	Degrees
1	20 - 23.20 deg Gemini
2	23.20 - 26.40 deg Gemini
3	26.40 - 30 deg Gemini
4	0 - 3.20 deg Cancer

<u>Pada 1</u>

20 - 23.20 deg Gemini, Navamsha - Aries (Lord - Mars)

Rashi Lord - Mercury and Nakshatra Lord- Jupiter

The 1st Pada will have the energies of Mercury, Jupiter and Mars. The communication skills of Mercury, the wisdom of Jupiter and the determination of Mars make a wonderful backdrop, and the stage is set for the enactment of success. If there is no malefic aspect from Saturn, their ventures will succeed the second time round, because the punarvasu energy will create situations which will be more conducive when the same project is tried again with a different approach.

This can happen during Mercury, Jupiter or Mars dasha and transit. If the dasha and transits match in the birth chart, navamsha (D9) and dashamsha (D10) for career, it will ensure success. For example, Punarvasu Pada 1 in the 10th house will bring success in their profession the second time around, during Mercury, Jupiter or Mars dasha, even if there are no planets sitting there.

The natives may go through the rags to riches scenario, and although they have the inborn qualities of putting their point forward, intelligence, and determination, their efforts fructify only when the time is right.

Since this nakshatra is placed in Gemini going to Aries in navamsha, the natives will be energetic, enthusiastic and straightforward in their communication. They would like to initiate or lead projects or a conversation. They will be weary of any kind of binding through words, emotions or contracts because it will curb their freedom. Punarvasu, being in the masculine and movable sign of Gemini, the natives will have their own minds and will know how to change their approach and adjust to the changing times.

A bird flying in the direction of the wind flies effortlessly, but to fly in the opposite direction needs oodles of drive and energy. Since Pada 1 lands in the navamsha of Aries, which is ruled by Mars, they will energetically pursue their goals. Though they do not actively seek confrontation, if they are faced with an opposing situation, they will be able to push through and validate their reasoning and logic.

Careers-

Managers, instructors, consultants, teachers, politicians, lawyers, actors, musicians, IT professionals, blog writers, YouTubers, public relations managers, talent managers, accountants, businessmen, TV broadcasters, astrologers, priests, army doctors, pharmacists, surgeons, dentists, engineers, electricians, scientists, philosophers, writers, sportsmen and target shooters.

Pada 2

23.20 - 26.40 deg Gemini, Navamsha -Taurus (Lord - Venus)

Rashi Lord - Mercury and Nakshatra Lord- Jupiter

The combination of Mercury, Jupiter and Venus set the ambience of this Pada. This gives the natives an appreciation of aesthetics, art, beauty, harmony, music, romance, elegance, grace and poetry. This Pada also brings the love of comforts, luxury and pleasure, and the beneficence of granting these worldly desires.

The 2nd Pada pushkar amsha has the ability to support the blossoming of the desired results, which are more likely to happen on the 2nd attempt.

Venus represents relationships, Jupiter gives wisdom, and Mercury is the communicator. Although everyone has a story to tell, natives born in Pada 2 of Punarvasu will be very good at articulating their feelings and thoughts both in the form of poetry and fiction. They can enthral their readers or listeners with the magic of storytelling. They have the knack of weaving their experiences into compelling stories.

They tend to have a more laid-back and 'take it easy' approach to life. Since this Pada goes into Taurus navamsha, the natives will be motivated by the desire to have a good steady income and financial security. During the dasha of Venus, they will have a comfortable lifestyle. They will be more fixed in their habits and way of thinking, attached to their comfort zone, and will prefer to live in a quiet suburb rather than a noisy city.

They are usually very eloquent, logical and clear in their speech, and have a skilful way of persuading others. They may be cautious about getting themselves tangled up in the romantic poison ivy in the beginning but may slowly tip into moonlight talks, fragrant bokays and fragile promises. However, they will decide to commit themselves into a relationship only after scrutinising the fundamental needs of comfort and financial security being met.

Once their mind is made about something they will seldom change, the earthy Taurus gives stability and endurance to stick to their decisions and see them through. They are determined and don't like to be pushed. They will do things and complete tasks in their own way and in their own time.

For example, when the 2nd Pada of Punarvasu is in the 4th house, they will have a comfortable home with basic luxuries, multiple IT gadgets, and a good relationship with the mum. Their mum will be very supportive, they will have wonderful cooking skills, and they will enjoy learning the art of healthy cooking from their mum. They may have to shift home once before they settle and will love to be at home in their comfort zone. They will also have a talent for singing and an aesthetic sense of decoration.

Careers-

Actors, singers, fashion designers, consultants, advisors, mentors working for an IT company, online graphic designers, poets, fiction writers, dialogue and scriptwriters, film directors, artists, painters, stage performers, fashion designers, interior designers, florists, teachers, priests, philosophers, actors, singers, musicians, accountants, bank managers, working in the bank, doctors, nurses, pharmacists, opticians, businessmen, shop and store workers, salesmen and people working from home via online.

Pada 3

26.40 - 30 deg Gemini, Navamsha - Gemini (Lord - Mercury)

Rashi Lord - Mercury and Nakshatra Lord- Jupiter

This Pada has the energies of double Mercury and Jupiter. Natives born in this Pada will be very quick in their communication, quick to give answers and good at IT. They will love to give advice but will not take anyone else's advice, for they feel they know better than those who are offering unsolicited advice. Yoga Tara point is at 29.30 Gemini in this Pada; any planets placed at this degree will show sure and strong results during its dasha and transits.

They will be intelligent, swift, and smart at planning strategies, idealistic, philosophical, cheerful, optimistic, will like making honest comments cynically, and can be mercilessly frank. They will often ride the waves of invisible enthusiasm, dream the impossible, and find ways to implement their thoughts into action. To fall in love, they must be intellectually fascinated because if they don't feel mentally motivated, they easily get bored. They have a myriad of topics to talk about and share their dreams, ideas, visions, strategies, plans for the future and accomplishments.

Mercury, being a very receptive planet, imbibes the influence of the planet it's sitting with. Here, Mercury will teach higher learning, wisdom and philosophy in an analytical, logical and realistic way.

They tend to procrastinate a lot because of the effect of Jupiter's wisdom, which will make them observe and think things over before acting on them, while the quick pace of Mercury will want them to finish things fast and move on. Therefore, Punarvasu natives can feel this confusion at times. In this Pada, the natives will be very intelligent, will be able to pick up things and learn them very quickly, and will have wonderful writing and speaking skills.

They will be more intellectually inclined, even though they might have to do a mechanical job if there is an aspect of Mars or Saturn. Still, in their free time, they will always be reading books or learning through the internet because they simply love to learn new things and need intellectual stimulation to feel happy and fulfilled in life. They love to attain knowledge, and are brilliant at understanding new concepts or ancient philosophies, and therefore make very good teachers and guides.

Because of the double impact of Mercury, they will want to learn things quickly, teach it to others and make money from it. They will use the information and knowledge they learn more logically and realistically. For example, Punarvasu Pada 3 in the 6th house can make the natives brilliant accountants. They will be very good financial managers or a professor of economics or accounts. They will have a regular job and will change their job once before they settle into their chosen profession.

Careers-

Teachers, professors, yoga teachers, consultants, advisors, psychologists, philosophers, bank workers, managers, financial advisors, IT professionals, astrologers, priests, doctors, pharmacists, ayurvedic doctors, blog writers, scriptwriters, musicians, graphic designers, businessmen, travel guides, travel agents, working in the post office and telecommunication.

Pada 4

0 - 3.20 deg Cancer, Navamsha - Cancer (Lord - Moon)

Rashi Lord - Moon and Nakshatra Lord- Jupiter

The 4th Pada will share the energies of the double Moon and Jupiter because it falls in the sign of Cancer. This is the most beneficent Pada as it's both Pushkar navamsha and vargottama, which gives very positive and assured results. This brings forth the nourishing side of the Punarvasu nakshatra. They make good teachers and advisors, they are very caring, and have an optimistic approach to life.

They will always follow laws and regulations and will not do anything unethical, unless there is a malefic influence of Saturn or Rahu.

Jupiter is the lord of Punarvasu nakshatra and is exalted in Cancer. Here, the divine knowledge, wisdom, philosophy, upliftment for well-being and opportunities - all these Jupitarian qualities expand in a nourishing and motherly way. Jupiter also represents children and husbands- in a woman's chart. For example, females born with their Ascendant in Punarvasu Pada 4 will love children, and their husbands will have a philosophical approach to life and will like to advise others on religion and spirituality. Since this Pada is placed in Cancer, which represents mother, security and comfort. The natives will be attached to their comfort zone, will have a wonderful relationship with their mum, and will be compassionate mothers themselves.

Just as a crab has a protective outer shell and is quick to respond, natives will be sensitive and cautious, emotional and vulnerable, protective and empathetic. This is a beautiful human quality that radiates with kindness and love, but it makes the person vulnerable to harsh words spoken by others. They will be sensitive even to the unspoken thoughts and feelings of others and can actually feel unwell if they sense negativity around them. But thankfully the beneficial influence of Jupiter keeps them away from these potentially harmful situations. They will usually succeed the second time around in whatever they do. For example, in Punarvasu pada 4, in the 7th house, the native may get married twice, or the 2nd relationship will be more stable and long-lasting.

The sensitivity and sympathy of the moon, combined with the wisdom and farsightedness of Jupiter, is a favourable blend. Since Moon rules the emotions, they will be moody, will cry or laugh easily, and can get overly anxious over minor issues. They will love being near the ocean, and listening to the sound of the waves will be very therapeutic for them. They will also enjoy spending time in the coolness of the night, moonlight walks, watching the moon or star gazing will be one of their favourite hobbies. Philosophising about where we come from, where we go after we die, what our connection to the stars, and other deeper esoteric questions will come to their mind at some point in their life, for which they will seek answers.

Careers-

Teachers, professors, councillors, advisors, gurus, priests, philosophers, psychologists, homemakers, doctors, nurses, care workers, pharmacists, dentists, opticians, astrologers, ayurvedic doctors, homoeopaths, healing therapists, singers, actors, dancers, musicians, farmers, fishermen, beauticians, IT consultants and writers.

The effect of planets

Punarvasu -Gemini Padas 1,2 and 3	Planets that get affected
Functional Benefic - give good results during their dasha.	Mercury
Functional Malefic - can give problems during their dasha.	Mars, Rahu and Ketu
Functional Neutral	Sun, Moon, Venus and Saturn
Kendra Adi Pati Dosha - can be malefic	Jupiter
Punarvasu - Cancer Pada 4	**Planets that get affected**
Most Benefic - Yoga karka Removes the effect of Mangal dosha.	Mars
Functional Benefic - give good results during their dasha.	Moon
Functional Malefic - can give problems during their dasha.	Mercury, Rahu and Ketu
Functional Neutral	Sun, Jupiter and Saturn
Kendra Adi Pati Dosha - can be malefic	Venus

Punarvasu Ascendant

The energy in Punarvasu has the power to retrieve objects, which means they are good at finding lost objects, or what they think they have lost always comes back to them. Their life follows a repetitive pattern of having to go through a similar situation twice, and they are usually successful at the second attempt. Brahma is the deity, which shows their creative talent. They like producing something original that is designed by them. The symbolism of a quiver of arrows and their gaze - looking straight ahead, shows their ability to focus on targets and plan towards long-term goals. They will have the ability to walk the path, stay on track and finish the job on hand without getting distracted.

The cast of Punarvasu is a trader, which makes them good negotiators and businessmen, and their quality is divine, which makes them religiously and spiritually inclined. They like to actively participate in all religious or spiritual events, and are always motivated to follow the path that leads them to true knowledge. They will have a natural liking towards cats, or they may repel or dislike them. Either way, their feelings will be strong towards them.

Those who are born in Punarvasu lagna Pada 1, 2 and 3 will have the energy of Mercury and Jupiter. The Jupitarian optimism will be prevalent in them, and nothing can deter them, rain, clouds, storms, scorching heat, icy winter, or darkness of the still night. Whatever the situation, they will not lose hope. They will be quick-witted, spontaneous and open to new experiences.

Since Jupiter and Mercury are both intellectual planets, Punarvasu natives will not like doing physical or manual work. Their life situations will be such that they have to deal with things more on the level of the mind and will not have to do physical hard work. They will not particularly enjoy mundane daily responsibilities and will prefer to sit and learn something new or search the internet for topics of their interest. They like to self-study and explore various subjects that intrigue them.

They will adapt well to changing situations but not compromise their independence. Their exceptional communication skills will help them deal with all kinds of situations efficiently.

They will be particularly good with languages and may speak and write 2 or 3 different languages. They will also be clever and efficient in IT skills - they will be good at analysing data, logical reasoning, and understanding concepts.

Padas I, 2 and 3 of Punarvasu are in Gemini, which governs the air element. This makes the natives friendly and adaptable. Gemini is also a dual sign, which shows that they can switch between roles easily whenever needed, like having a duplicate twin. Those who are born in these padas will have a Vata predominance. They will have a lighter and thin frame of body, thinner skin, fuzzy hair, tooth irregularities, smaller eyes, quick body movements and a quick style of speech.

When Vata is in balance they will be creative, friendly and vibrant. If vata is out of balance, they can get restless and anxious, which can cause a skin rash. They may not find time to eat at regular times, and this can hurt their digestion because of frequent changes in diet patterns. Because of their active mind, it can bring anxiety and sleep disorders. Irregular lifestyles can bring joint problems and constipation in time as they get older. They should take care to eat at regular times, not to go on a strict diet routine to slim down, and not to do strenuous physical activities. Warm climate, cosy ambience, warm water baths or showers, warm food and hot beverages are conducive for them. Listening to calming soft music, having alone time, spending a relaxed day at home and meditation will bring emotional stability and calm their restless mind.

Punarvasu energy supports development and growth at all levels, physically keeping healthy and fit, mentally nourished by healthy and positive thoughts, emotionally keeping healthy by acknowledging gratitude, and spiritually being prayerful and practising yoga and meditation. All these abilities and talents lie inherent in them, but how aware they are about it and how well they use them depends on their situations, intentions, motivations and planetary placements.

In Pada 4 the natives will have the influence of the Moon and Jupiter. They will be more emotional, empathetic and sensitive. They will be compassionate, loving, warm-hearted and caring. Their friends and family will love being around them because of their genuine caring and positive feelings that support nourishment and growth.

Aditi, being the deity who is the mother of Devas, gives an added assurance and confirmation that in Pada 4, the natives will approach life and deal with situations in a very kind and compassionate manner.

They can also be very protective, overly anxious, have fluctuating moods and are sensitive to the environment around them. When faced with challenges, they will respond by withdrawing into their shell of a secure zone. The benefic influence of Jupiter will help them get over difficult situations through deeper understanding and insight. They have a tendency to hoard things because of their attachment to their comfort zone and fear of not having enough. Because of their empathetic nature, they will be very good at helping others come out of their shell of anxiety by genuinely listening to them and offering their attention, time and care.

The 4th Pada of Punarvasu is placed in Cancer, which is governed by the water element. They will have a vata kapha constitution, which will give them a good physique, a very attractive face, beautiful eyes, and a good set of hair. Their love for cooking and eating delicious meals, or insufficient exercise and excessive sleep, can make them overweight. Having a regular workout, eating consciously, and avoiding cat naps during the day will keep them healthy and fit.

When they give or receive affection, they feel emotionally nourished and fulfilled. Their need for love and respect is essential for the smooth functioning of their day-to-day life because they look at life through the lens of compassion and love, kindness and well-being for all. Any harsh words, feelings or situations will injure them deeply, and they will take a long to recover from emotional hurt. However, the Jupitarian grace is always protecting them.

"It will come alright in the end." - Ramana Maharishi

Sun in Punarvasu

Sun in Pada 1, 2 and 3 of Punarvasu will share the energies of Mercury and Jupiter. Sun, Mercury and Jupiter get along well with each other. Sun is the intelligence, and it brightens the wisdom of Jupiter and the communicative skills of mercury.

This also makes the natives egoistic about their knowledge. The heat of the sun burns away the humility and makes them fall for praise. Their pride gets in the way of true joy and fulfilment.

However, after 32 years, the Sun's heat cools down, and the natives become more appreciative of others' contributions.

They will be easily noticed by others because of their creativity, intelligence, confidence and magnanimity. Their speech will be authoritative and commanding. They will never back away from helping others in need and will give generous donations. Their father will be in a high government post and will be a well-respected person in society and they get the benefit of inheritance of all the values that their father stands for. They will take great pride in their family lineage and will be very dignified. They will make brilliant family lawyers, politicians, managers and financial advisors.

They are like the big cats who are very self-assured and confident, independent and fierce, and protective of their clan. They love to laze in their den, especially during the hot afternoons. Survival alone is not the driving force of their thoughts and actions. Prestige and honour are of greater importance. They will always honour their promises, keep their appointments and will be loyal friends. Their words may come across as rude or brutal, but they will be honest opinions; they will not put on an act to please someone. They are well-integrated personalities whose words and actions match unless there is a malefic influence of Saturn, Rahu or Ketu.

When the Sun is in Pada 4 of Punarvasu, it will be influenced by the Moon and Jupiter. Sun represents the soul, father and government; Moon represents the mind, mother and emotions; and Jupiter represents the teacher, divine knowledge and all living beings. This shows that natives will have the love, care and support of their mum and dad or guardians. They will learn the knowledge, morals and values of life from them. The natives in this Pada will be very family-oriented and will love to learn from their parents and discuss various topics with them because they will be the best teachers for them.

For example, if the sun in Punarvasu is in the 9th house, their father will be a priest or head of a community, and the natives will inherit the knowledge, values and profession from their father.

Or they will meet an advisor or a teacher in their life who will guide and help them like a father in their higher education. They might have to take a gap year before starting their post-graduation or will have to apply twice before getting admission into a prestigious university of their choice (because of the Punar Vasu effect). Eventually, they will be successful in their endeavours.

Moon in Punarvasu

When the moon is placed in Pada 1, 2 and 3 of Punarvasu, it will share the energies of Mercury and Jupiter. Both Moon and Mercury move fast and signify our emotions and analytical thinking. Both these aspects are very abstract and changeable, it's like a world of virtual reality that we build around us for our survival and progress. Jupiter, as the lord of Punarvasu, supports, guides and encourages all thoughts and emotions that are needed for well-being and growth.

Sage Prashra says the Moon, Mercury and Jupiter conjunction forms Saraswati Yoga, which makes the natives creative, intelligent and well-educated. Since Punarvasu Pada 1, 2 and 3 have the influence of the Moon, Mercury and Jupiter, the natives may not be very rich but will be well respected and will have a wealth of knowledge. They will be natural councillors and advisors, and can be prolific authors and speakers because of their skill of communication and good command of spoken and written language. This can also make them arrogant. They will love to give advice but do not like being told what they should do.

They will have the comforts and resources needed for their growth and development. Their natural curiosity about things and concepts will keep their minds occupied. No matter how old or how young they are, they will never stop learning.

Since Punarvasu Pada 1, 2 and 3 are in Gemini, which is a movable and masculine sign, natives will adapt easily to the changing circumstances. The airy signs also do not give a firm, stable platform, which means natives will go through situations like a change of job, career, house, or ideology, friends, and relationships many times in their lives. However, the influence of Jupiter will make it smooth, in the sense that they will have time to plan for the next change rather than abruptly being thrown into the deep end of the pool.

For example, if the Moon in the 1st Pada of Punarvasu is placed in the 9th house, the native will travel away from home for higher education. The heavy ideology of Jupiter as a Guru teaches lessons in a gentle but sure way. It is said in Vedanta that Guru, in the form of Vamana Avatar, has a stick in his hand, which signifies that the lessons will be learnt silently but surely and inwardly in a comfortable environment.

The 4th Pada of Punarvasu is in the sign of Cancer. In this Pada there will be a strong influence of the moon and Jupiter. This will make the natives sensitive, empathetic, imaginative and emotional. Their sensitivity can be hurt even by unspoken words or feelings, and it can be tough for them to cope with the apprehensions of feeling lonely. The need to be reminded that they are loved is more urgent and more real for the Punarvasu natives born in Pada 4.

Yesterday, or 20, or 100 years ago, is very surreal to the moon-ruled natives. That's why they are naturally good at history. They will love to travel and see ancient monuments and visit museums. One of their favourite hobbies will be to make their scrapbook or make an online album with captions that will help them revisit the memory lane. They will also love to collect souvenirs or antiques from places they have been to. Jupiter governs vata, and the moon signifies water; the natives will be prone to vata kapha imbalances like congestion, coughing, sneezing, or sinus.

Since the 4th Pada of Punarvasu has strong influence from the Moon and Jupiter, it will have the energy of Gaja Keshari Yoga. This yoga is formed with Jupiter and moon conjunction, or if the moon and Jupiter are placed 1st, 4th, 7th or 10th from each other. Gaja means elephant, and Keshari means lion, which means it gives the fierce confidence of a lion and the convenience of comfortable vehicles because, in the olden days, an elephant was considered a royal and grand vehicle on which the King would travel or fight battles.

This signifies that the natives will be bold, courageous and dignified and will have strong viewpoints about their ideologies, which they will defend with a vengeance that can create enemies, especially if there is an aspect of malefic planets like Mars, Saturn, Rahu or Ketu. On the other hand, they can be motivational speakers. When they speak, people will sit up and listen.

For example, when the moon is placed in Pada 4 of Punarvasu in the 4th house, their Mother will be their first teacher. They will grow up with the comfort and conveniences of vehicles. Their mother will be a strong positive influence in their upbringing. She will be religious, very good with her communication, a wonderful cook, and will be loving and caring. The natives will imbibe and also learn many marvellous skills and qualities from their mother. They will have a wonderful relationship with their mother or a mother-like figure and will be attached to her, especially during the Jupiter and moon dashas; these attributes will be highlighted.

The poetry of Punar-Vasu

Punar- once again, the cycle begins,

Vasu - the one who resides, within

retrieving stories and games to win.

The soul incarnates,

With the desire to recreate.

To fulfil that which was unfulfilled,

To do that which was left undone,

I have been there, met you and done it all before,

Where, though, is not clear!

But the feeling so strong cannot be missed,

The second round has just begun,

With Jupitarian grace, enjoy the game and have fun.

Moving from mercury to moon, the lunar ocean,

Intellect, curiosity and emotion.

The lessons learnt, and stories woven, both the old

And new have been told,

The friends and foes, quiet and noisy, easy and difficult,

Were all part of the game,

At the end of name and fame,

Happy to be home again.

Remedies

- <u>Das Maha Vidyas</u>

Devi Bhuvaneshwari and Devi Tripura Sundari - as described earlier.

<u>Devi Tara - Jupiter</u>

Goddess <u>Tara</u> is the second of the Dasa (ten) Mahavidyas or the great wisdom goddesses. She is associated with Ugra Tara, which shows that her Shakti (energy) is ascending in nature. She has the power of uplifting and is also seen as the Goddess who gives protection.

The word Tara means a star, so she is a star Goddess whose energy rises upwards. She guides and protects and offers the ultimate knowledge, which gives salvation.

According to the Puranas (ancient Hindu texts), Tara is the 2nd wife of Guru Brihaspati (deity of Jupiter). Tara was the mother of Budha (Mercury) through her union with Chandra (Moon), and she had a Son named Kacha through Brihaspati.

<u>Weak Jupiter</u>

If Jupiter is weak or afflicted- has a low Shadbala score, is conjunct with malefic like Saturn, Mars, Rahu or Ketu, or is sitting with the lords of the 6th, 8th or 12th house. Then, during its dasha and transit, the natives will face problems like - inability to have children, missed opportunities, pessimistic approach, no financial gains, not benefitting from their knowledge, eating junk food or unhealthy lifestyle, or not being spiritually inclined.

<u>Remedies -</u>

- Spiritual counselling, meditation and reading scriptures are the best remedies.

- Reciting Devi Tara's mantra 108 times on a Thursday, or when the moon is transiting the sign where your natal Jupiter is placed, combined with her image and yantra, will enhance your personal well-being. It can be done for 3 consecutive Thursdays because 3 is the numerological number for Jupiter.

Mantras of Devi Tara -

"Om Hreem Streem Hum Phat." Beeja mantra - *"Om Treem."*

Other remedies

- The best remedy will be to calm the mind through meditation and pranayama practises.

- Green, yellow and white colours are favourable because they resonate with the energy of Punarvasu.

- Giving milk to the cat, especially for the natives born in the 4th Pada of Punarvasu, will be good.

- Water the Babool (Gum Arabic tree) and Velu tree. Plant bamboo or keep the Chinese indoor bamboo that grows in water. It's considered as a lucky bamboo that increases feng shui, the positive energy.

- When the moon transits punarvasu nakshatra to worship Aditi (the mother of devas), she is said to grant protection and care like a mother. She is normally worshipped by lighting ghee lamps. It is believed that worshipping her will bring protection, and healing and will help to overcome challenges. Buddhists worship her by lighting 12 yellow candles, representing the 12 Adityas.

- Draw a cat with the colour of the planet sitting in the punarvasu nakshatra and keep it in the desired direction for one week.

- Chant the Punarvasu nakshatra mantra 108 times regularly for 40 days. *"Om aum punarvasu nakshatraye namah."* It will help to connect to the energy of Punarvasu which can help to enhance the positivity.

Example

Ascendent in Punarvasu

Bob Dylan was Born on 24th May 1941, 9:05 am, in Minnesota, USA.

Bob Dylan is an American musician, singer, artist and writer.

He has been an influential figure in popular music and culture for more than 5 decades. Much of his most celebrated work dates from the 1960s, when he was an informal chronicler and a seemingly reluctant figurehead of social unrest. In May 2012, Dylan received the Presidential Medal of Freedom from President Barack Obama.

In 2016, he was awarded the Nobel Prize in Literature.

Analysis-

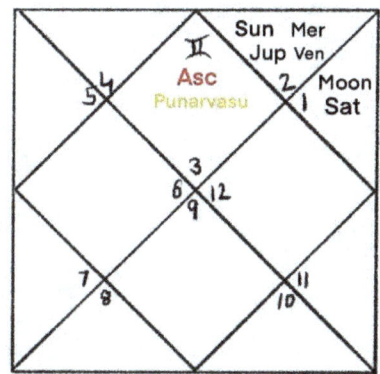 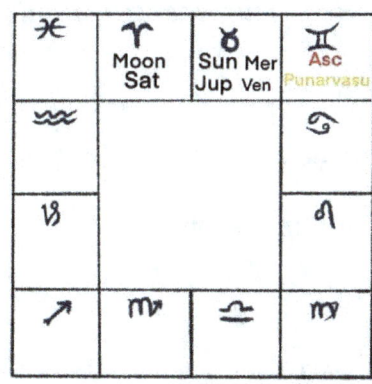

His Ascendant (Gemini) is in Punarvasu pada 3. The effect of double Mercury and Jupiter - is a beautiful combination of intelligence, philosophy and wisdom. It gives him excellent communicative abilities. The influence of Jupiter and Mercury enables him to look at the same situation from multiple viewpoints. In the 3rd Pada, there is the energy of Gemini, the airy sign which makes him flexible and creative, clever and enthusiastic, curious and light-spirited.

The lyrics of this song resonate beautifully with the energy of Punarvasu, the wind of Gemini fans, the creative play of words, and the simple articulation with a profound meaning that comes across - shows the bright intellect of Mercury. 'Blowin' in the Wind' was a song written by Bob Dylan in 1962. At that time, he was running his Moon Venus Venus dasha. His Moon is placed in the 11th house (Aries) of gains with Saturn, and Venus is placed in the 12th house (Taurus) of foreign lands with Sun, Mercury and Jupiter.

The Moon has a very receptive and feminine quality, and Venus is an epitome of beauty, harmony and artistic talent. One of the names of Venus is a poet. Bob has 4 planets placed in the 12th house, which shows that he had a very strong influence on the 12th house (of isolation) in his birth chart. Moreover, the Ascendant (Gemini) lord, Mercury, is placed in the 12th house. Although we don't know much about his life, the planetary placement shows that he would have spent a lot of time alone, all by himself, in the privacy of his home or in a remote place, and in this quiet and tranquil time, he came up with his poetic creativity.

It has been described as a protest song and poses a series of rhetorical questions about peace, war, and freedom. The lyrics of this song reveal that either the answer is so obvious it is right in your face, or the answer is as intangible as the wind. Here is his famously sung poem -

Blowing in the wind

"How many roads must a man walk down,

Before you call him a man?

How many seas must a white dove sail,

Before she sleeps in the sand?

Yes 'n' how many times must the cannonballs fly,

Before they're forever banned?

The answer, my friend, is blowin' in the wind,

The answer is blowin' in the wind.

Yes, 'n' how many years can a mountain exist,

Before it is washed to the sea?

Yes, 'n' how many years can some people exist,

Before they're allowed to be free?

Yes, 'n' how many times can a man turn his head,

And pretend that he just doesn't see?

The answer, my friend, is blowin' in the wind,

The answer is blowin' in the wind.

Yes, 'n' how many times must a man look up,

Before he can see the sky?

Yes, 'n' how many ears must one man have,

Before he can hear people cry?

Yes, 'n' how many deaths will it take 'till he knows,

That too many people have died?

The answer, my friend, is blowin' in the wind,

The answer is blowin' in the wind."

8
Pushya

Om kam Pushya nakshatraye namah

Zodiac degrees	3.20 - 16.40 deg Cancer
Ruling planet	Cancer - Moon and Pushya - Saturn
Sanskrit name	Pushya in Sanskrit means the nourisher, it signifies the benevolent nature of this nakshatra.
Astronomical name	Pushya is seen as 3 stars, which are not very bright in the constellation of Cancer. The ancient sages saw these 3 stars resembling the udder of a cow.
Symbol	Cancer - crab and Pushya - Udder of a cow
Element	Water
Deity	Brihaspati (the advisor of the gods)
Quality	Cancer - Chara - movable Pushya - Laghu and kshipra - light and swift.
Shakti	Brahma varchana Shakti - the power to harness creativity.
Cast	Kshatriya - warrior
Gender	Female
Motivation	Moksha - liberation
Triguna	Rajas
Tridosha	Kapha
Body parts	Mouth, face and lungs.

Direction	West and north
Month	January (the month of pausha)
Bird	Crow
Sound	hoo, hey, ho, dah
Tree	peepal tree and sacred fig
Chakras	Anhatta - Moon and Vishuddhi - Saturn
Das Maha Vidya	Devi Bhuvaneshwari - Moon and Devi Kali - Saturn.

Special degrees -

Yoga Tara	15 deg Cancer It's a point where the planet will show the strongest and sure results during its dasha.
Exaltation	5 deg Cancer - Maximum exaltation of Jupiter. When Jupiter is placed at this degree, it will bring good respect and appreciation, especially during its dasha.
Amrit nadi	13.60 - 14 deg Cancer Gives good results like the nectar that nourishes.
Visha nadi	7.46 - 8.40 deg Cancer Brings situations which one does not like dealing with.

Auspicious and inauspicious table -

Auspicious	Inauspicious
Activities It is one of the most auspicious Nakshatra, except for marriage, it is considered auspicious for starting any new activity. Good for all activities related to imagination and innovation, creative activities, music, dance, drama, and art, for starting building projects, buying a new vehicle or a new house, for financial transactions, starting education, re-starting things again, taking medication, gardening, travelling, all activities related to children, giving donations, teaching, doing spiritual practices and religious rituals, very good for worshipping the divine in feminine form- Devi.	Activities Not good for marriage, for activities related to law and settling disputes and for lending or borrowing money.
Days Sundays - only when it falls on the 1st, 4th, 5th, 6th, 7th or 12th lunar day. Thursdays - only when it falls on the 4th, 5th, 7th, 9th, 13th or 14th lunar day.	Days Wednesdays - only when it falls on the 2nd, 3rd, 8th or 9thlunar day. Saturdays - only when it falls on the 3rd, 7th, 9th or 11th lunar day.

Compatibility table -

Pushya	Compatible with
Sexual compatibility Yoni animal	Pushya- Female goat - compatible with - Male goat - Kritika
Sign compatibility	Cancer - Scorpio and Pisces.
Nakshatra compatibility	Anuradha and Uttara Bhadrapada.
Lunar day compatibility	Dashmi tithi (10th lunar day)
Day compatibility	Monday and Saturday
Colour compatibility	White and blue
Numerological compatibility	2 and 8 - and all numbers that add up to make 2 and 8.
Sound compatibility	Moon - semi vowels - ya, ra, la, va, sa, sha, ssa, ha, lr, rr Saturn - labial sounds - pa, pha, ba, bha, ma

Sign Lord and Nakshatra lord - <u>Moon and Saturn</u>

Moon - as described earlier.

<u>Saturn - lord of Pushya.</u>

Saturn is the farthest planet in our solar system and is called the slow mover. This quality of Saturn is very prominent in Vedic astrology. The Saturn period usually brings delays and restrictions in life. In the birth chart, in whichever house the Saturn moon conjunction happens will show the karmic influence and the duty that cannot be escaped. Saturn stands for restraint, limitation and submission- these are the limitations we put on ourselves because of our ego. A strong Saturn influence in the birth chart shows that the native tends to obey, serve and submit to traditional values. Wherever Saturn is placed in the chart, it submits to that area of life and shows the karmic duty to be performed in this life. It also restricts one to that area of life.

The natives tend to have vata dosha problems because the air element rules Saturn. They have to take care to eat more warm cooked foods and less raw and dry foods. After the age of 50, when vata age sets in, they tend to have issues with constipation, joint pains and gastric problems. Warm climates and warm foods agree better with their natural constitution.

Saturn is also called the rebel, just like Shani rebelled against his stepmother's mistreatment. The natives who have a strong Saturn influence may face such a situation in the early years of their lives, where they have to rebel against the unfair or partial treatment rendered to them.

Saturn tends to give a lack of confidence and makes one fearful, uncertain and indecisive. This is because it's sensitivity can feel the subtle vibrations of the other realms. It also gives the steely willpower and great endurance to go through hardships and eventually overcome them.

Saturn likes the wild, unrestricted freedom because it's an airy planet. This draws them to open, spacious places. This is the reason why they like having a house in the countryside, in a calm, open and serene environment. They also love gardening or farming.

The ultimate goal of Saturn is to overcome all limitations and restrictions. That's the reason they tend to rebel when they are young, but as they get older, they learn to submit and follow rules. Because with experience they understand the wisdom of following tradition, which helps to liberate their time and energy. The cool nature of Saturn prefers to wait for the opportune time rather than create stress and tension caused by friction or resistance towards situations which are not conducive. This helps them to sail smoothly through all kinds of rough circumstances.

They will find that - the more they follow the routine of discipline, the easier their life becomes. They can then find enough time to relax, develop their hobbies, do something for the community, be in nature, and do spiritual or religious practices. The mature Saturn natives who have learnt their lessons through life's tough experiences become more down-to-earth, humble, and non-competitive.

Saturn is also a very spiritual planet, it gives great interest and talent in psychic, occult and spiritual capabilities. Many spiritual seekers who go through severe austerities in order to go beyond the limitations of the body have a strong influence of Saturn in their birth chart. They will either be born in a Saturn nakshatra, or their moon will be conjunct Saturn. These natives seem to have a 6th sense, a way of receiving and interpreting messages from the spirits, ghosts, or goblins. Saturn is a very passive planet and likes to follow rather than lead. That's why many Saturn natives end up dedicatedly following a large organisation, cult, or religion.

Inference

Pushya is ruled by Saturn and it sits in Cancer, whose ruler is the moon. The Saturn-moon combination gives great psychic interest and capabilities. It also brings restrictions and delays in getting the mother's love and care and can cause childhood fears. However, with time as they get older, they overcome these feelings. They love to nurture, care for others, look after them, or mother them, and will always have children or pets around them.

Quality, element, motivation, triguna and tridosha - as described earlier.

Chakras - Anhatta-as described earlier.

Vishuddhi

Vishuddhi chakra is located at the pit of the throat and has a blue hue. It acts like a filter for the upward-moving energy, where only the subtle and purified form of the energy can move up to Ajna. In Vedic astrology, Saturn is said to be the karma karka. Therefore, it acts like a filter, as a gatekeeper, that allows only the purified emotional and intellectual energy to pass through

Vishuddhi to the higher realms of Ajna chakra. Moreover, the blue colour assigned to Saturn matches the bluish hue that the energy vortex at Vishuddhi chakra exudes.

It has 16 petals, which represent the 16 kalas, divine qualities or capabilities- compassion, patience, forgiveness, justice, impartiality, detachment, invincibility, spiritual prowess, beauty, beneficence, best dancer, best singer, honesty, knower of truth, controller of self and perfect master.

The symbol of upward-facing triangles shows the upward-moving energy that supports the rising of consciousness. This chakra can be activated by repeating the mantra - *ham* while focusing on the pit of the throat.

Sadhguru explains that Vishudhi chakra is the power centre for higher possibilities. If energies move into this chakra, one becomes very powerful. Not necessarily physical or financial power, but their presence has a strong influence on people and on other living creatures around them. One has to devote time and dedicatedly follow the spiritual practise under the guidance of a realised being to raise the energies to Vishuddhi.

Inference

Pushya is placed in Cancer, whose Lord is the moon. Therefore, it has the energy of Anhatta, and the Lord of Pushya is Saturn, so it has the quality of Vishuddhi as well.

The Anhatta energy makes them emotional and empathetic, and the Vishuddhi energy helps them to purify through hard work and endurance. They have the capability of facing all challenges, overcoming difficulties, breaking boundaries and limitations, and becoming powerful beings within themselves. When the chakras are balanced, they will be kind and compassionate and will fulfil their duties with diligence. But when the energies of the chakras are out of balance, they can become lazy and overly attached.

Shakti -<u>Brahma varchana Shakti, power to harness creativity.</u>

The word pushya means nourishment, blossoming or the best part of anything. Creativity means doing something new which is new to our way of thinking. The fact is that the only originality or creativity is life itself, the consciousness which is the source of all intelligence. We are creative when we create something we have not done or thought of before, whether we draw or write something, create a website online, create software, build a house, take a photo, cook a meal, sing a song, compose music, plant a tree, grow flowers, or a newborn baby is all an act of creation.

<u>Einstein</u> has been one of the most original thinkers and a genius of our century. Here are some of his insightful quotes -

"Imagination is more important than knowledge. Knowledge is limited."

"I very rarely think in words at all. A thought comes, and I may try to express it in words afterwards."

Pushya nakshatra natives have the blessing to be able to harness this intelligence of original and creative expression. Whenever they are being themselves, and create something that is entirely their idea, or they give a gift that they have made themselves and not just bought it from a shop, their difficulties will smoothen out more easily.

Symbolic signification

Cancer - crab - as described earlier.

Pushya - Cow and Cow's udder

Cow

Cows are gentle animals who are affectionate, emotional and intelligent. Mahatma Gandhi described a cow as *'a poem of compassion.'*

Cows have an excellent sense of smell and can detect odours up to 5 miles away. They can also hear both low and high-frequency sounds, which are beyond human capability. The cow eats by chewing on the grass and bringing it out again to help in digestion. A cow's stomach has 4 four chambers, which allows her to digest tough plant matter that would normally be indigestible, and they can drink the equivalent of a bathtub full of water in one day. They generally sleep only about 4 hours a day, and their average life span is 20 - 25 years. Cows can walk up a flight of stairs, but once there, they can't walk back down because their knees just don't bend the right way. They like to sleep close to their families, and sleeping arrangements are determined by their rank in the social hierarchy.

Interesting facts

- Cows are devotional mothers and are known to walk for miles to find their calves.
- A Cow's gestation period is 9 months, it lasts the same amount of time as human pregnancy.
- You can guess the age of the cow by counting the number of rings on her horns.
- Like humans, cows form close friendships and choose to spend much of their time with 2-4 preferred cows. And can also hold grudges for years and may dislike particular cows.

Reverence for the cow

The beauty of Vedic tradition lies in the appreciation and philosophy of respecting all that is in nature, plants and animals alike; all that nourishes us is respected and taken care of. It was a very eco-friendly way of functioning of the communities which provided a stable social and economic platform. In this context, the cow has been revered as sacred and is worshipped in many traditions across India during special festivals, where the cow is decorated and honoured. The Vedic Scriptures refer to the cow as our mother because it provides milk to humans.

Symbolic significance

Mother cow is seen as the symbol of Mother Earth because she is the nourisher, the ever-giving provider. She represents the sustenance of life, grace and abundance. She reminds humans about the virtues of gentleness, receptivity and connectedness with nature.

The special gifts

Milk is a unique food, containing the best the mother can offer. Cow milk is good for children as it has a good amount of calcium, which is vital for developing strong bones, teeth and muscle growth. It contains Vitamin D, which helps in the absorption of calcium in the body and also has a good amount of protein, which helps in their growth.

Ghee, in particular is an essential ingredient for wellbeing in Ayurveda. Ghee or clarified butter has healing benefits. It can fight inflammation, promote flexibility, enhance digestion and enhance the immune system. The Susruta Samhita, an Ayurvedic classic, claims that ghee is especially beneficial for skin ailments.

In many verses of Rig Veda, the reverence for the cows is seen.

"The cows have come and have brought us good fortune.

In our stalls, content, may they stay!

May they bring forth calves for us, many-coloured, giving milk for Indra each day."

Dr Vasant Lad -is an Ayurvedic doctor and the founder of the Ayurveda Institute in Santa Fe, USA. He has written many books on Ayurveda. He explains the advantages of ghee (made from unsalted butter). There is a tradition in south India where they keep the Ghee in an earthen pot, cover it well and bury it underground for many years. The pot of ghee which has been buried for 100 years is called - *Shata pranagritam* (shata means 100, prana is the life energy, and gritam us the ghee). This special ghee has tremendous healing powers; it helps the body to revitalise at the cellular level. It is particularly good for skin ailments like eczema and cirrhosis - when applied topically on the skin. When taken internally, it heals ulcers, irritable bowel syndrome and even autoimmune diseases.

Cow urine is used for treatment in Ayurveda for diabetes, blood pressure, asthma, psoriasis, eczema, heart attack, blockage in arteries, piles, prostrate, arthritis, migraine, thyroid, ulcer, acidity, constipation and gynaecological problems.

Cow dung is used in the rural areas of India and Pakistan as fuel, it is collected and used to produce biogas, which is rich in methane, to generate electricity and heat. Cow dung is also used to plaster the walls and the floor of the house, which acts as a coolant and keeps the house cool during the hot summers.

In tropical countries, in rural villages, cow dung and cow urine are also used as an additive for plastering because of their antifungal properties, which prevent the growth of harmful fungi within the house. Most villagers in India spray fresh cow dung mixed with water in front of their houses to repel insects. In central Africa, the Maasai villagers burn cow dung inside their homes to repel mosquitoes. It is also dried into cake-like shapes and used as a replacement for firewood.

Honouring the cow

The Yogic view is that when you honour the ever-giving cow, you also honour all creatures. According to the Vedic tradition, Cow's nature is very close to human nature. In rural areas, those who keep cows at home have seen that the cow develops a special bond with the one who takes care of her and milks her. She will not let anyone else milk her easily and is receptive to human emotions. She will empathise and share your sadness by shedding tears and show her affection by patiently waiting on you.

Kamadhenu - The wish-fulfilling cow

Cows are considered holy in India because they are the earthly embodiment of the Kamadhenu. She is an integral part of the Hindu culture and grants wishes and desires, fulfilling all that the human heart could possibly want. The Vedic texts describe Kamadhenu as the cow grants all desires. She is also called Surabhi who is the mother of all cows. The word Surabhi means - cow, earth, fragrant, charming and pleasing. Different texts provide diverse versions of the story of Kamadhenu's birth. One of them says that this Divine Cow emerged from the Ocean of milk or Kshira Sagar during the churning of the oceans.

Kamadhenu and Sage Jamadagni

The epic of Mahabharata narrates that Kamadhenu resided with sage Jamadagni. Having heard about the special powers of Kamadhenu, King Haihaya came with his soldiers to sage Jamadagni's hermitage and captured Kamadhenu and her calf.

To get them back, Jamadagni's son Parashurama slew the king, whose sons, in turn, killed Jamadagni. Parashurama then destroyed the entire kshatriyas (warriors) army.

Another version of this story states that another king, Kartavirya Arjuna, tried to capture Kamadhenu, and Kamadhenu, by her own power, defeated him and his army and flew off to heaven. The enraged king then killed Jamadagni.

Kamadhenu and Sage Vashishtha

In the epic of Ramayana, Kamadhenu is said to be staying with sage Vashishta. Once, King Vishwamitra came to visit sage Vashishta and was amazed at the unusual capabilities of the cow.

The sage had welcomed him and offered a grand meal to him and his men. When the king asked how he could make such elaborate arrangements in the forest? The sage replied that it was all done by Kamadhenu, his pet cow.

The king could not resist the temptation and opportunity to have the magical cow for himself that could provide everything he wished for. He asked the sage to let him have Kamadhenu, and in return, he offered 1000 cows, some elephants, horses and precious jewels. The sage refused the offer because she was not an object of trade but a being to be honoured.

When the king tried to take her forcefully, Kamadhenu produced warriors to fight his men. The King returned again and attacked with his full army. In this battle, the king lost his sons, which led to a great rivalry between Vashista and Vishwamitra.

Many years later, king Vishwamitra realised his mistake, that because of his greed, he had fallen into the vicious circle of revenge and war. He eventually renounced his kingdom and went into the forest. He went through various austerities and performed severe penance in order to win over his own vices. Later, he became a great sage and was known for his bravery and for winning over his own limitations.

There is a beautiful prayer song, which is quite well known, written by Gulzar; it was picturised for the film Guddi in 1971, which is a beautiful poetic expression of the strength of the mind and the ultimate win.

"Humko man ki shakti dena man vijay kare.

Doosron ki jai se pehle khud ko jai kare."

This means give us the strength of the mind to attain victory over ourselves before hailing the victory of others.

The cow's udder

It represents the cow that gives milk and signifies the nourishing side of Pushya nakshatra. Just as the cow provides milk to her calf and humans indiscriminately, it highlights the motherly instinct, the caring and nurturing side of human nature. Being a mother is a choice one makes every day to put someone else's well-being and happiness above our own. It can be both amazing and tough, challenging and fulfilling, which helps to bring out the strengths you didn't know you had or learn to deal with fears you never knew existed.

Inference

Pushya natives will be very caring and nurturing others will come naturally to them. They will find fulfilment in taking care of others, feeding them, looking after them, or doing something to help others when needed. They will be docile and gentle and, will approach situations non-aggressively and will prefer to eat a vegetarian diet. They will be family-oriented and attached to their comfort zone. They will not rush into things, but once they decide, they will follow it through with determination. They will follow their faith or religion with devotion and conviction.

Pushya nakshatra is blessed with abundance and can provide all the resources needed for the nourishment of the body, mind and soul, like the wish-fulfilling Kamadhenu cow who is capable of fulfilling all your wishes. Just like king Vishwamitra, Pushya natives' thoughts and actions can be motivated by the greed to expand their security and comfort zone at the cost of others being deficient. Fortunately, just like Vishwamitra, they will realise their limitation and will make an effort to correct them because their true happiness comes from nourishing and giving to others.

The days when the Ascendant, Sun or Moon is in Pushya nakshatra it's a very auspicious time for all activities of celebrations and for starting any new projects. The same stands true for those born with Pushya as their Ascendent or Sun or Moon in Pushya. Being a very fortunate nakshatra it can grant anything when asked in a rightful way and with gratitude, love and devotion.

It is said that on the days when the Ascendant, Sun or the Moon is in Pushya, it's not good for any marriage ceremonies because the moon Saturn combination brings a very psychic energy which may not be conducive to initiating family life for any newly wedded couples. Other than this, Pushya has a very nourishing quality. It encompasses all good things in life - good health, wealth, resources, security, education, intelligence and respect in society.

The scale of how much it will fructify and when the abundance will happen depends on various aspects, the planetary placements, the strength of the planets, the ashtakavarga score, dashas and transits. But it can be inferred that whatever path of life the natives chose, they will have it fairly easy going. Things will fall in place more easily and with less effort. In other words, the stage is set on a smooth platform, which ensures a fairly comfortable ride. Their calm nature will help them to sail through difficult times with patience, faith, devotion and endurance.

"No one succeeds without effort; those who succeed owe their success to perseverance."

- Ramana Maharishi

Mythology

Deity - Brihaspati

Vedic scriptures describe Brihaspati as manas putra, which means born from the mind of Brahmā, the creator. He comes from the lineage of sage Angiras, who was one of the sapta rishis - the first 7 disciples of lord Shiva. He is said to be born from the first light of the Sun, which is bright and pure and drives away the darkness. His knowledge and character are revered, and he is considered the Guru (teacher) of all devas. In jyotiṣa, there is a saying that when Jupiter protects, there is none that can destroy.

In Vedic paintings, Brihaspati is shown as sitting on a lotus and in his 4 hands, he holds a book, Kamaṇḍalu (container), a rosary and a Varada Mūdra for blessing. At other times he is also shown as riding a swan and rules the north-eastern direction. He has a yellow or golden colour hue and is the lord of Thursday (Guruvar) and represents the planet Jupiter. One of the 18 names of Jupiter is Bṛhaspati, according to the Bṛhaspati-kavacha-mantra. Brihaspati is the priest and is also known as the lord of sacred speech, the advisor of the gods, the master of sacred wisdom, and the counsellor of Indra in his war against the Asuras.

Brihaspati was the advisor and counsellor of the devas because he was skilled in arthashastra, the science of politics and governance.

The story goes that once he had gone to Inderlok to visit Lord Indra, who was in deep meditation and did not get up to greet the Guru. Brihaspati felt insulted and left the Indralok. In another story, Soma (Moon) woos away Tara, the wife of Brihaspati, and they have an illegitimate son, Budha (Mercury). Brihaspati later accepts him as his son because of his exceptional intelligence.

In the Mahabharata, the son of Brihaspati was named Bharadvaja and was the counsellor of the Pandavas. Brihaspati signifies the age from 35 - 42 years when the influence of Jupiter is strong. In the epic of Mahabharata, Brihaspati had taught Bhishma the duties of a righteous king which he had later taught Vidura.

Inference

Brihaspati, being the deity of pushya nakshatra, is described as born from the mind. This signifies the intellectual capabilities of human beings. It is through the mind that all creative ideas and concepts are born.

"What is called mind is a wondrous power existing in Self. It projects all thoughts. If we set aside all thoughts and see, there will be no such thing as the mind remaining separate; therefore, thought itself is the form of the mind. Other than thoughts, there is no such thing as the mind." - Ramana Maharishi

Pushya natives are very creative minded people and love giving advice. They have a keen sense of socio-political wisdom and are great at handling public relations. They are generally well known in their social circle because they always ingeniously come up with perfect strategic and ethical solutions to problems their family or friends might face. Just as Brihaspati was upset about being ignored by Indra. Pushya natives will also be very ego-sensitive because they expect their students to show respect and acknowledge their wisdom.

Since Brihaspati's wife was wooed away by Soma, there is a possibility of pushya natives' partners being attracted or seduced by another man or woman. Still, other combinations, transits and dashas should be looked into before making any such predictions. They will be interested in gaining knowledge about the occult, mysticism, spirituality, rituals, other cultures and their tradition, religion, philosophy, psychology, sociology, economics and politics.

Brihaspati, in his role as vachaspati makes him an exceptional public speaker. Pushya natives will not be stage shy once they have overcome the initial reluctance to face the crowd. They have an inherent talent for explaining concepts and techniques in a way that others can understand.

Pushya Padas

3.20 - 16.40 deg Cancer

Padas	Degrees
1	3.20 - 6.40 deg Cancer
2	6.40 - 10 deg Cancer
3	10 - 13.20 deg Cancer
4	13.20 - 16.40 deg Cancer

Pada 1

3. 20 - 6.40 deg Cancer, Navamsha - Leo (Lord - Sun)

Rashi Lord - Moon and Nakshatra Lord - Saturn

The 1st Pada will have the energies of the Sun, Moon and Saturn.

The dynamism, creativity and intelligence of the Sun and the caution of Saturn will influence the Moon. They will never shy away from responsibility and will take pride in taking care of their family and friends. Whenever needed they will generously donate towards humanitarian causes, but will like to do it in style and will most probably announce their charitable contribution in a grand function or an event. Their genuine caring and compassion will be appreciated and recognised by the people around them.

Although they prefer to have a structured and disciplined approach to situations when it comes to making crucial decisions, they will follow their heart and not the head.

The fiery Sun, the watery Moon and the airy Saturn make a warm and fuzzy mixture, a hot beverage which has to be handled with care if it has to be enjoyed fully. The sun can inspire and motivate the cautious and slow Saturn to take daring steps into the adventure of life, and with the support of the friendly and nurturing moon, there is nothing that natives born in the 1st Pada cannot achieve. The downside could be the imbalance caused by the pride of the Sun, which seeks recognition and appreciation for optimal functioning. At the same time, the fear and anxiety of Saturn can dampen the confidence of the Sun and hurt the emotions and sensitivity of the Moon.

A little respectful protocol will go a long way to win the hearts of Pushya natives born in the 1st Pada, which will be well worth the effort because they are very loyal and sincere friends. For them, friendships are for life, and they will honour them no matter what comes by. Their home will be like a palace. Even if it's a one-room house, it will be very exquisitely decorated and they will love to bring friends home and serve them delicious meals. They will be very creative and artistic in whatever they do and will make excellent politicians, managers, doctors and hotel owners.

For example, in the 1st Pada of Pushya in the 5th house, the natives will be very creative and can be excellent actors, singers, musicians, artists, dancers, fashion designers, online graphic designers and cooks. They will be very caring and loving parents and will love to spend time with their children and nourish them in every way- physically, emotionally, mentally and spiritually. Their greatest fulfilment will come from doing something for their children, their students or their followers. They will be well-loved and respected by their family and friends and can have a fan following because of their exceptional talent in their chosen field.

Careers-

Managers, councillors, owners or workers of charitable organisations, voluntary workers for humanitarian causes,

rotary club managers, professional cooks, politicians,

hotel owners, child care and nursery owners and workers,

kindergarten teachers, those working in the catering industry,

farmers, garden and landscape designers, actors, musicians, artists, IT professionals, public relations managers, talent managers, businessmen, astrologers, priests, nuns, ayurvedic doctors, doctors, nurses, physiotherapists, caretakers, pharmacists, opticians, dieticians and writers.

Pada 2

6.40 - 10 deg Cancer, Navamsha - Virgo (Lord - Mercury)

Rashi Lord - Moon and Nakshatra Lord- Saturn

The combination of Mercury, Moon and Saturn sets the ambience of this Pada. The natives born in the 2nd Pada will be more detail oriented and analytical in whatever they do because of the influence of Mercury. They will be very punctual, orderly, clean and tidy and will always do their duties diligently. They will follow their daily schedule with ease, but anything abrupt or a sudden change of plan will throw them off balance. Whenever such a situation arises, they will need to go back into the cocoon of their comfort zone, plan the details, and get their head around it in order to handle the change. Because they are perfectionists and like to do things in the right manner and to the best of their ability, they don't like to do anything half-heartedly just for the sake of it.

They are very genuine and sincere in their approach to work and like to plan things ahead of time in order to do their job well. The influence of Mercury can even make them self-critical and too harsh on themselves. In trying to perfect things, they will look into the minute details and can miss out on the bigger picture. They feel fulfilled when they can serve others and nourish them in some way. Their connection with others is more on an emotional level. The logical and analytical aspect of Mercury can make them weary of relationships because they will keep nitpicking on why things didn't work out and this can lead to emotional and mental stress.

Pushya natives generally enjoy being at home. With the influence of Mercury, this effect is accentuated because they would much rather be in their comfort zone where they can precisely follow their lifestyle in a measured way rather than go out and be in the strange environment of silly and impulsive behaviour of others, which can make them nervous and uncomfortable. They will be naturally shy and will feel more comfortable in their close group of family and friends because of the sensitivity of the Moon.

Since the Moon and Mercury are both fast-moving planets, those who are born in the 2nd Pada of Pushya will be able to jump in and out of moods and thoughts quickly. In other words, low moods will not depress them for long, and they will be able to snap out of it quickly. Their logical approach will give them the exceptional ability to analyse situations from different angles and arrive at a practical and reasonable solution for any problems they might face. All padas of Pushya are placed in the watery sign of cancer. The navamsha of the 2nd Pada comes into the earthy sign of Virgo. This is a good combination because the emotionally vulnerable Cancerians get a good, stable foundation with the earthy Virgo, which enriches their character and personality.

Water and earth are complementary to each other. Water nourishes and moisturises the earth, which makes it suitable for plant life. In this Pada Pushya natives will enjoy being close to Mother Earth and will have the inherent talent of growing their own herbs, vegetables or flowers in their back garden. They will love nourishing their family with fresh garden produce and cooking healthy meals. Their family and friends will love them for this and appreciate their special talent.

For example, the 2nd Pada of Pushya in the 3rd house, the natives will be very skilled in some kind of art or craft work, or gardening. They will also be very good with keyboard and IT skills and can be excellent editors and critics. They will be very caring towards their siblings and neighbours and will love going for short holidays with family and friends.

Careers-

Doctors, nurses, caretakers, pharmacists, opticians, dentists, dieticians, paediatricians, gynaecologists, ayurvedic doctors, healers, chiro practitioners, astrologers, priests, working for an IT company, working in the bank, working at a grocery store, chefs and waiters, hotel or restaurant owners, businessmen, working from home, writers and editors, accountants, financial advisors, farmers, dairy workers, teachers and blog writers.

Pada 3

10 - 13.20 deg Cancer, Navamsha - Libra (Lord - Venus)

Rashi Lord - Moon and Nakshatra Lord- Saturn

This Pada has the energies of Venus, Moon and Saturn. The natives will be feminine and emotional and will feel fulfilled when they take care of others, nourish them or help them. They will be selfless in giving, like a mother and will be willing to help others without any expectations. They are full of love and loveliness. Venus gives physical beauty and an enchanting smile that can melt away worries, like a yummy ice cream that melts in the mouth.

They are very artistic and creative, romantic and poetic. They have to feel emotionally connected to bring out their artistic talents. They can be the most wonderful actors because their face reflects their emotions like a mirror. The discipline of Saturn gives them the endurance to work steadily towards their goals.

Venus will bring many relationships in their life, which can be both painful and joyful. They usually have a cool, pleasant, caring and friendly approach towards life. The influence of the Moon makes them emotionally attached to people and things. For example, they will happily donate food or clothes to the needy but will not give away their mum's sari or scarf because they have fond memories attached to them that remind them of their mum.

They may be working for someone and doing a regular job, but it will be their dream to open a business where they can in some way serve the people, like opening a takeaway or a restaurant that provides affordable and healthy meals.

They are very good with business partnerships. Pushya, being in the sign of Cancer, gives the natives soft feminine qualities; they need comfort and security in great abundance, and this becomes their driving force to work hard, and they will make sure they have enough saved up for a rainy day. Saturn's invisible restrictions make them budget money carefully, but the Venusian side of them will make them spend money once in a while to pamper themselves and their loved ones.

Careers-

Actors, dancers, musicians, singers, artists, painters, poets, writers, fashion designers, farmers, dairy owners, cooks, restaurant owners, grocery store owners, financial advisors, bank workers, managers, graphic designers, IT professionals, teachers, professors, consultants, advisors, psychologists, philosophers, astrologers, priests, doctors, pharmacists, ayurvedic doctors, businessmen, social workers, voluntary workers, working for a charitable organisation and running a charity.

Pada 4

13.20 - 16.40 deg Cancer, Navamsha - Scorpio (Lord - Mars)

Rashi Lord - Moon and Nakshatra Lord- Saturn

The 4th Pada will share the energies of Mar, Moon and Saturn.

This Pada goes into Scorpio in navamsa. The natives will have an intense, deep and emotionally passionate nature. They will not be afraid of taking responsibility and will love to take care of others. There is an unearthly mystical sweetness, genuine caring for others and a dogged determination in their aura. The yogatara is at 15 degrees of Cancer in this Pada. Any planets placed at this point will give very good results during their dasha and transits. They have a profound understanding of human nature and can become wonderful psychologists and psychiatrists. They are brave and courageous and like to dig deep and get to the bottom of things. Therefore, they can make excellent surgeons, lawyers, detectives or firefighters.

They can experience sudden losses or gains, have affairs or breakups, minor injuries and miraculous recoveries. There is an air of mystery attached to them because they pass through such circumstances in life where something needs to be hidden or kept secret, which can be for good or bad reasons.

They can be suspicious and jealous about close relationships because they can easily feel let down or betrayed. When they give, they give fully and expect the same from others. They will never back away from challenges or from helping a friend in need and honour their promises.

They are drawn towards occult and spirituality and can make very good astrologers, or they will be strongly attracted to subjects that deal with the inner dimensions. They are good at keeping their own and others' secrets and are genuine friends. They will both - love and hate strongly because they feel things at a deeper level and cannot commit to relationships frivolously. When they commit, they stand by their friend or partner through thick and thin.

Since the waters of their emotions run deep and they are very sensitive, when their feelings are hurt or smashed in any way, they will make sure they teach the smasher a lesson. With emotional maturity and spiritual awareness, they can turn their hurt into a source of motivation to help others come out of similar pain or injustice. Their nourishing side ultimately finds fulfilment in helping others without expecting anything in return.

Careers-

Engineers, technicians, athletes, sports players, swimmers, firefighters, sportsmen and sportswomen, army officers, police officers, psychiatrists, psychologists, physiotherapists, doctors, surgeons, dentists, nurses, pharmacists, opticians, astrologers, ayurvedic doctors, homoeopaths, healing therapists, farmers, fishermen, butchers, lawyers, detectives, IT consultants, writers, social workers and businessmen.

The effect of planets

Pushya - Cancer	Planets that get affected
Most Benefic - Yoga karka Removes the effect of Mangal dosha.	Mars
Functional Benefic - give good results during their dasha.	Moon
Functional Malefic - can give problems during their dasha.	Mercury, Rahu and Ketu
Functional Neutral	Sun, Jupiter and Saturn
Kendra Adi Pati Dosha - can be malefic	Venus

Pushya Ascendent

When Pushya nakshatra is in the 1st house, it will carry the energies of Saturn and the moon, provided no planets are sitting in the Ascendant. This nakshatra supports the nourishment of the thoughts, emotions and the body. Pushya being in the emotional waters of cancer with a Saturnian influence gives a slow, relaxed, laid back, docile and steady pace of life. As the nakshatra lord, Saturn brings delays but supports hard work and assures steady gains and success.

Those who have Pushya as the Ascendent often tend to say,

"Why does everything in my life get delayed?" It is a genuine complaint because Saturn slows down everything. They finish their education later than their friends, get a steady job later in life, get married later in life, have children later, buy their own property much later, and are well settled much later in life. But the goodness about Saturn is that he gives slowly but surely, and there is no fear of it being taken away quickly or suddenly.

This assurance is a great boost because once the Pushya natives have achieved their desired goals, they can relax and enjoy the fruits of their hard work. This will be the usual life pattern unless some other malefic aspects of Mars, Saturn, Rahu or Ketu are there, or the Ascendent has low ashtakavarga points then the natives may have to face more struggle.

The symbol of Pushya is the cow's udder, which highlights their caring and motherly nature. The assuring promise of nourishment never fails them. In spite of the Satarian influence, of things getting delayed, they are well nourished and are able to look after others too, and are usually comfortably placed in life.

The symbol of Cancer is a crab. Therefore, Pushya natives represent crab-like qualities of caution, protection, defence and withdrawal. They can feel insecure about their finance, vehicles, home, mother, family, and relationships. They have a lingering fear of losing their comforts and, therefore, work hard to secure them. At some point during their childhood, they most likely had to be away from their mother for some time because of her work, sickness or some other compelling reason. The unreasonable fears from childhood can affect them in their adolescent years as they go through the sensitivity and insecurity of relationships. In their adulthood, they learn how to handle their emotions better and work towards securing their future financially and emotionally. Because of their deep need for receiving and giving nourishment, with time, slowly but surely, they grow into wonderfully loving individuals who are capable of supporting others and, in turn, feel supported.

Even if the natives don't get a higher academic degree, they will do well in their careers because this nakshatra supports growth. They like to do things methodically and carefully and are slow, cautious and logical in their approach. They do not like to rush into projects or situations without giving them ample thought, and once they commit themselves, they will see things through. They are not frivolous about anything. For them to feel connected, they have to be deeply and emotionally involved.

Pushya has the power to harness creativity- which gives the natives the ability to bring out the best in others to tap into their creative potential, which makes them very good leaders and managers. They are devoted towards serving others in whichever way possible. Therefore, they make excellent politicians, social leaders or managers of charitable organisations.

Despite their natural reluctance and cautiousness, they possess incredible tenacity of purpose. During the time of need they always rise to the occasion. They are law-abiding citizens, patriotic, and usually polite and well-mannered. They are fascinated by antiques and love visiting museums and historical sites. They usually get accused of collecting junk, as seen by others, but these are valuable possessions for them for many reasons.

Their sensitivity makes them laugh or cry easily, but they share their emotions only with their loved ones and don't display them openly for fear of getting hurt. Their moods can vary like the weather - one moment they are very chatty, then silent, sullen, depressed, impossibly cranky, sometimes pushy and at other times conservative, blushing, shy, timid, touchingly kind and hilariously funny. All these very human emotions are very transparently apparent in them.

You can also come across Pushya natives who are lazy daydreamers, engrossed in their luxurious comfort zone and listening to their favourite music, or watching their favourite TV programme. On the other hand, others combine work with mental relaxation through music. For instance, they might run a grocery store with their favourite music playing in the background. So they can be lazy and passive, or active with a slow paced life and comfortably running a business. Both Pushya types will be emotional, and music is their need because it nourishes their soul.

They are excellent homemakers and possessive parents and are very protective, sweet, gallant, soothing, kind and gentle towards their children and family. Money and food can seduce them into almost anything, and they are very sentimental at heart because their emotions are synchronised to the waxing and waning phases of the moon. Both men and women born with

Ascendant in Pushya will be very caring and motherly. Nourishing and caring for others brings them great joy and fulfilment.

Most of the time they have children, pets, their elderly parents, or someone to take care of- at home or in their workplace.

They are spiritually and religiously inclined because their desire is to create spiritual energy. Brihaspati is the deity of this nakshatra, which makes them good advisors, and they have a special talent for knowing and choosing the right vegetables, fruits, spices and herbs. They are also good at maintaining and sustaining long-term projects.

This beautiful song from the old classic musical children's movie - '*Chitty chitty bang bang,*' based on Ian Flemmings novel - 'The magical car,' directed by Ken Hughes, befits their caring nature.

"Someone to care for, to be there for,

I have you 2, you 2 have me…

Chitty chitty bang bang, chitty bang bang …"

Sun in Pushya

The Sun in Pushya will share the energies of the moon and Saturn. The fire of the sun, the waters of Cancer and the airy coolness of Saturn give a very wavering effect on emotions that can run high and low without much warning because there is no stabilising effect of the Earth element.

The heat of the Sun is opposed by the coldness of Saturn. Being a karmic planet, Saturn imposes restrictions as needed, which can be exasperating for the Sun. This is where the study of astrology helps when we come to terms with the cyclical pattern of karma, and are more in acceptance rather than defiance, situations begin to ease out. Because in acceptance, we are at ease with ourselves which helps to break the resistance and obstructions of the play of karma.

Sun and Saturn don't get along well with each other. The kingly and dynamic Sun will feel uncomfortable in the docile atmosphere of the Moon and Saturn. Although they will be very generous and kind and will never say no to anyone who genuinely needs their help. However, there will be situations where they feel that they are not being appreciated for their generous support, and this can break their heart.

A little appreciation will go a long way with natives who have Sun in Pushya. It is not much to ask for when you get their loyalty in return. Yes, they are very sincere, genuine and honest in their relationships and dealings and expect the same from others.

If the Sun is the King, the soul, and the source of energy, then the moon is the queen, the mind and the nourisher. Our thoughts and emotions decide the quality of our life, the way we think is the way we live our lives. Therefore, when the Sun and Moon's energy comes together in Pushya it gives confidence to the gentle moon and can be an excellent placement which brings intelligence and creativity to the imaginative and receptive moon. The discipline and endurance of Saturn will demand patience but not deny success.

For example, in Sun in Pushya in the 10th house, the natives will be very creative and intelligent and will do very well in leadership positions. They will rise and shine in their career, especially during the Sun dasha. They will make excellent politicians, managers, leaders, CEOs and businessmen.

Moon in Pushya

When the moon is in Pushya, it will have the quality of a double Moon and Saturn. Moon represents emotions, feelings, nurturing, caring, and receptivity, and Saturn represents practicality, logic, restrictions and discipline. The natives will make choices from the heart, based more on how they feel, not so much on how they think. At a subconscious level, they fear losing their comfort and therefore emotional and financial security will be the top priority for them.

Pushya being in the sign of cancer, and with a double moon effect, natives will have a very crab-like behaviour. Just as the life cycle of the crabs is tuned to the cycles of the moon, their thick shell acts like armour to protect their soft inner core. They will need and seek healing by withdrawing into their cocoon of comfort. For those who don't know them well, they may come across as snobbish, but this is a shield of protection needed for their tender and sensitive emotions.

The natives will tend to withdraw into their protective shells because the shallow waters of cancer make them emotionally attached and vulnerable to hurt. Their beautiful and expressive eyes will swell up in tears ever so often because of their sensitivity. However, they do not display their emotions openly because of the fear of getting hurt. Even the slightest hint of feeling neglected or ignored can wound them deeply, and they will withdraw into their shell for a long time in order to heal. They will find great solace in music, listening to spiritual masters or Gurus or in meditation and prayers.

Saturn signifies both logic, practicality and fears and anxiety. If the house in which Pushya sits has a good ashtakavarga score, the natives will find practical solutions to their problems. However a low score can cause stress and worries. For example, the Moon in Pushya in the 10th house can cause fluctuations in career during the moon dasha, or the natives might have to travel for work. If the 10th house has good ashtakvarga points, the natives will be able to deal with the problems related to careers with a logical approach, but a low score can create anxiety. Their career will be in the field of medicine, nurturing, caring, food industry, dairy or cooking. People will see them as a very kind, gentle and loving person because they genuinely care for their wellbeing.

Wherever the moon is placed, the mind's attention is always on those areas of life. In Pushya the double effect of the moon will make the natives very sensitive towards the attributes of that house. In the 10th house moon, they will be very attached to their image in public, and their career will mean a lot to them. Opposite the 10th house is the 4th house of mother and home. Therefore, natives feel the need to secure their careers in order to stabilise their homes. Rise or fall in their profession will directly impact their emotions, happiness level and home environment.

Moon ruled Pushya natives feel very snug and comfortable at home, when they are with their family and friends, in their own community and in their home country. They are very sentimental and patriotic about helping their community. They will find great fulfilment in providing food for the hungry. To think of anyone starving brings tears to their eyes; they are most genuinely and sincerely concerned and cannot bear to see anyone suffering from hunger.

For the Pushya natives, the subjects that can bring harmony or cause tension are money, food and housing. The experience of Saturn and the wisdom that comes with time will make them handle the finances first, which can grant the security of good food and a comfortable home. They are excellent homemakers and somewhat possessive mothers or fathers.

Pushya being in the sign of Cancer, the natives are very crab-like in their behaviour. They feel the need to hold on to things and relationships because it gives them a sense of security. If they need something, they may not say it directly but build a story around it or say it through a picture, a message or a movie. Just like the crab moves sideways, they tend to say and do things in an indirect way. Their ultra sensitivity makes them keep secrets, but they don't like any secrets to be kept from them.

They are very tuned to the cycles of the moon. Like low tides on a new moon day (Amavasya), they will feel low, too. If things don't seem to be going right, it's time to nourish the body with a delicious meal, nourish the mind with good humour and nourish the emotions through music. They can get lifted out of low moods as easily as they fall into it.

Their favourite pastime will be looking through family photos and videos, admiring their baby pictures or their children or grandchildren's pictures, gardening, making flower arrangements, baking cakes, having long chats over the phone, sharing dreams, singing, listening to music, walk in a countryside or along the beach, going for holidays with the family, staying awake and making wishes under the full moon.

Whenever they create something by themselves, like a piece of art, write something new, make a new toy or a jacket for their pet, plant flowers, try a new recipe, or design a new website, their emotions will heal very quickly. They will find most fulfilment through nourishing themselves and others with genuine caring and love.

The poetic Push -ya

Push - for excellence, bring out the best,

Ya - yes, it's possible to achieve the quest.

Saturn, grants the labour of love,

Moon, the nourisher above.

Together they share, with utmost care,

The moments of joy and sorrow - so dear.

Caution and protection, a crabby vulnerability,

Nourish and provide a cow-like ability.

To care for the near and dear, a virtuous nobility.

A mother like quality, the unconditional love,

Fortunate ones, have this blessing from above.

The delight of endearment, and the pain of abandon,

Both I learn to equally relish,

For every experience is a treasure to cherish.

The past not forgotten, the future to behold,

Are precious as gold.

The cacophony of emotion and thought,

Swings the pendulum between the lost and caught.

The voiceless experience becomes a voice,

In the silent cursives of my heart's poise.

Precisely, on the stroke of a note,

The melody of life sings forth.

It's a give and take karmic transaction, so perfect,

How much you give, that much you get.

For when I give out more, that much more I receive,

When I hold back, that much I recede.

When I create, I give the gift of abundance - thrilled,

When I give, I grow - blossomed and fulfilled.

Remedies

- Das Maha Vidya -Devi Bhuvaneshwari -as described earlier.

Devi Kali - Saturn

Goddess Kali is considered the ultimate form of Brahman, who is the devourer of time. She is also seen as the divine protector and the one who bestows moksha, or liberation. The word Kal means time. In this context, Kali represents the feminine aspect of time. She is a powerful form of Shakti, a destroyer of evil forces and is worshipped as the Divine Mother or Adi Shakti (first primordial energy).

In the Sanskrit language, the word Kala represents both time and darkness. The image of Devi Kali shows her as the one who has a dark complexion, which is darker than the darkest night of the new moon. This signifies her all-encompassing quality of darkness. Just as the darkness consumes all colours in itself, she consumes all the evil and destructive forces in nature into herself. The word Kala also means time. In this context, she represents the darkness in which time itself becomes still. In other words, she represents that dimension of time in which past, present and future merge into a state of darkness. Here, the consciousness or awareness is fully alive and vibrant. Only the physical form dissolves or disappears into her.

Afflicted Saturn

Devi Kali controls the malefic effects of Saturn and represents all chronic diseases and difficult or death-like situations faced in life. Though it is easy to appease her, and she responds quickly to her devotees' prayers, but also tests them in many ways. Saturn is not placed well in the natal chart when -

- Saturn is in Leo. It is not comfortable because the Sun and Saturn are enemies, so it does not give good results.
- Mars ruled signs of Aries or Scorpio because Mars and Saturn don't get along well.
- Saturn conjunct with the Sun, Mars, Rahu or Ketu in any house.

Remedies -

- Devi Kali showers her grace and blessings when one is punctual responsible, and performs his or her duties with sincerity and dedication.
- Donate food, money or clothes on Saturdays to the physically handicapped.

- Chanting the complete Kali Mantra gives spiritual strength.
- Those who are born with their Ascendant, Sun or Moon in Pushya resonate with the energy of Devi Kali. Chanting her mantra 108 times can help to remove the negative effects of an afflicted Saturn. It is recommended to chant her mantra for 8 consecutive Saturdays for effective results.

Mantras of Devi Kali -

"Kreem Kreem Kreem Hum Hum Hreem Hreem Dakshine Kaalika Kreem Kreem Kreem Hum Hum Hreem Hreem Swaha."

Or her Beeja mantra - *"Om Kreem."*

Other remedies

- The best remedy will be to feed the hungry, donate clothes to the needy, and feed a cow on Saturdays.
- Look after a pet and nourish others through kind words.
- Make time to reflect, listen to calming music, go for long walks, moonlight drives, or spend time in nature, pray and meditate.
- Fast on Saturdays.
- Donate black colour clothes, objects made of iron, mustard oil, or black sesame seeds on Saturdays to old people.
- Wearing white and blue colours is favourable.
- Plant the flowering tree.
- Worship the peepal tree by going around it 8 times when the moon transits through Pushya.
- Worship Brihaspati for wisdom and clarity in speech.
- Worship Devi Ma in all her forms of Durga, Lakshmi and Saraswati for wellbeing.
- Worshipping Hanuman on Saturdays reduces the effects of Shani or Saturn's negative influences.
- Worshipping Shiva in the form of Mahakala and Kali, his consort, takes one beyond the fear of death by embracing both light and darkness.
- Wear 7 mukhi (7 faced) Rudraksh.
- Chant Gayatri Mantra of Saturn 108 times on a Saturday,

"Om kaak dhwajaaya vidmahe khadga hastaaya dheemahi tanno mandah prachodayaat."

- Chant the Beej Mantra of Saturn 108 times on Saturdays

"Om pram preem proum sah shanaischaraya namah."

- Chant the Pushya nakshatra mantra 108 times, regularly for 40 days, *"Om kam pushya nakshatrae namah."*

Example

Ascendent in Pushya

Wim Hof was born 20th April 1959 in Limburg, Netherlands. Time of birth not known, taken as 12 pm.

He is famously known as The Iceman for his ability to withstand freezing temperatures.

Wim has set Guinness world records for swimming under ice and prolonged full-body contact with ice and still holds the record for a barefoot half-marathon on ice and snow. He attributes these feats to his Wim Hof Method (WHM), a combination of frequent cold exposure, breathing techniques and meditation. Wim has put himself through the test of various medical parameters to show how the body-mind connection can achieve amazing fears which look superhuman, and more importantly, he has shown that this is possible for all human beings. He has trained many others who follow this amazing breath technique to become healthier and stronger in their mind and body.

Wim is one of the 9 children, and he is the 4th born. He and his brother Andre are twins. He has 6 children, 4 from his first wife Maria, who sadly died by committing suicide in 1995. A few years earlier, she was diagnosed as schizophrenic and had jumped from the 8th floor. It left him deeply hurt by the fact that he was left powerless and could not do anything to save her.

As an adolescent, when he was 17 years old, one Sunday early morning in the month of December, he felt a sudden urge to jump into the freezing cold water of the Beatrixpark canal, and since then, he has been more and more at ease in cold icy water. He says by bringing his body to the point of ultimate survival, his body chemistry changed at the core level, and he discovered the immense capabilities of the body and mind, psychology over physiology.

Wim says that the death of his first wife made him question life and seek answers within. He had felt so powerless that he had no control over life situations. He found the power within by keeping up the discipline of waking up, at 4 am every morning and connecting to himself and connecting to mother nature.

Over the years, he has developed techniques to overcome extreme temperatures, both cold and hot. His body can endure the icy cold climate and, walk barefoot in ice for many hours and walk in the Namibian desert for miles without drinking water.

He has beaten many records, which are believed to be humanly impossible. In March 2000, Wim set the Guinness World Record for farthest swim under ice, with a distance of 57.5 metres. In January 2007, Wim set a world record for the fastest half marathon barefoot on ice and snow, with a time of 2 hours 16 minutes. Wim has set the world record for the longest time in direct, full-body contact with ice 16 times, nearing 2 hours.

In 2007, Wim climbed to an altitude of 7,200 metres on Mount Everest in his shorts and shoes only. In February 2009, he reached the top of Mount Kilimanjaro in 2 days in shorts and shoes. In 2016, he reached Gilman's point on Kilimanjaro with journalist Scott Carney in 28 hours, an event later documented in the book 'What Doesn't Kill.' In September, he ran a full marathon in the Namib Desert without water under the supervision of Dr. Thijs Eijsvogels.

The Wim Hof Method (WHM), created alongside his son Enahm Hof, can be downloaded as a free app to practice this amazing breathing technique that enhances health. The method involves 3 pillars- cold therapy, breathing, and meditation. It has similarities to Tibetan Tummo meditation and pranayama, both of which employ breathing techniques.

Wim's method, as well as similar breathing practices, have shown that hyperventilating can temporarily suppress the innate immune response as well as temporarily increase heart rate and adrenaline levels.

Analysis -

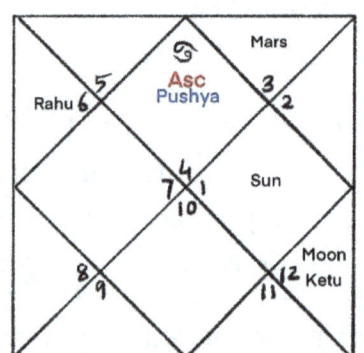

Wim Hof has his <u>Cancer Ascendant (lagna) in Pushya Pada 4.</u> Pushya Ascendent natives are very family-oriented. He often says that for him, family is everything. On being asked about his breathing method, he says just like a mother wants her child to be healthy, strong and happy, our bodies are built to be naturally healthy. Because we have forgotten how to connect to Mother Nature our bodies become weak and susceptible to disease.

<u>Moon</u>, the lord of the Cancer Ascendant, is sitting in the 9th house of Pisces with Ketu. This shows that his Mother would have been his guide and teacher, and he would have been separated from his mother for some other reason. It also shows that through his genuine care for others he would himself become a guide or a mentor. Based on his experience, he has created the - <u>Wim</u>

Hof Method (WHM), which is a breathing technique that enhances health. This is a practice that is followed by many who are inspired by his way of life.

After having lost his 1st wife, he said he had to be even stronger because he had 4 children to look after. His son is proud of his amazing feats and says Dad has always been around for us. Because of his compassion, he wants to share his breath method with everyone, so that all can enhance their health and live well. Pushya's connection to water is seen so strongly in his chart he is famously called the " Iceman."

It is interesting to see that his Sun is in Ashwini - he and his brother are identical twins. His Sun is exalted in the 10th house, which brought him fame and success. Moreover, the Sun has directional strength; the 10th house represents the south direction, and the sun shines the brightest at noon time. Here, like the king, the Sun is powerful and dominates his field of action because of his creativity, intelligence, confidence, capability and commanding presence. Sun, the lord of the 2nd house of Leo in the 10th house, gives him very strong family values and ethics. The more respect he gets from the community, the more money he makes. He gets many benefits through the government via scientific research, which has helped to spread his message and give him recognition throughout the world.

His Mars, in the 12th house in Ardra, is very strong because it's closest to the lagna degree. This makes him very brave and courageous to put his body through extreme situations that normal human beings would fear going through. Lord of Ardra is Rahu, placed in the 3rd house of heroic efforts, Mars Rahu effect gives him a daring quality and a very unconventional scientific approach. This placement made him go through extreme sadness and pain when his wife committed suicide. It had such a deep impact on him and transformed his perspective towards life.

He is like a warrior exploring the metaphysical world, keeps moving, not possessing anything, very sexual, raw and wild energy which cannot be curtailed by the domesticated civilisation. A lot of his energy goes into travelling to isolated and remote places for research and hands-on experience. He was 17 years old in 1976 when he went into the ice-cold water for the 1st time. At that time, he was running his Mars Ketu Rahu dasha. Mars is in the 12th house of Gemini (remote, isolated places), Ketu is in the 9th house of Pisces with Mercury (Guru, teacher), and Rahu is in the 3rd house of Virgo (brave heroic effort).

All these placements and the timing of the dashas culminated in the brave attempt to experience the extreme cold weather (which seems beyond human possibilities). Eventually, they helped him overcome it and gain strength from it.

Wim Hof quotes -

"I am not afraid of death, but afraid of not living fully."

"Not e-go, but we-go."

"Unless you are willing to experience new things, you will never realise your full potential."

"If we always choose comfort, we never learn the deepest capabilities of our mind or body."

"The cold is an absolute doorway to the soul."

"We are the alchemists of our own body."

"If you want conviction, dig within yourself. If you want understanding, just do it."

"Love is the greatest power of the universe."

Observations

Those who have Pushya as Ascendent, or moon in Pushya, have to set foot on snow-clad mountains at least once in their life or live in places where it snows. My sister lives in Edmonton, Canada. Her lagna is in Pushya, where it gets very cold in the winter and snows heavily. We had gone on pilgrimage to Hemkunt Sahib in the Himalayas with my mum in 1981, we had walked on snow for the last stretch of our journey. It was an adventurous trip where the thunder of the falling glaciers was heard and seen a few metres from where we were during our climb.

The chart of Iceman also shows his strong karma with snow and ice. Kishore Kumar, a famous Indian singer, has his moon in Pada 2 in Pushya in the 8th house. He had gone to perform and sing in a concert for the Indian army in the Himalayas. Where the soldiers were sitting on the snow in an open arena and he walked and sang among them to entertain and lift the spirits of brave Indian soldiers.

More research needs to be done on this in order to confirm this observation- the relationship between Pushya and snow. The cooling effect of Saturn and the moon is seen very prominently here.

<u>The effect of Saturn</u> - It took me about one month, the longest time, to finish writing about Pushya. For various reasons, I had to keep going back to edit, tidy up and put it all together so that it flowed well.

9
Ashlesha

Om kham gam Ashlesha nakshatraye namah

Zodiac degrees	16.40 - 30 deg Cancer
Ruling planet	Cancer - Moon and Ashlesha - Mercury
Sanskrit name	The word Ashlesha comes from the word Shesha, which means Shehsa nag or the king serpent/snake. It signifies coiling, serpent energy, which has the power to embrace and kill if needed.
Astronomical name	Ashlesha is seen as a ring of stars in the constellation of Zeta Hydra. They are not a very bright group of stars. The brightest among them is Zeta Hydra. They can be seen in a clear night sky. It is also called the *'clinging star'* because it's constellation image in the sky is a circular head with a long entwining tail of the hydra constellation. For this reason, its other name is - *'the one who entwines.'* Or *'the embracer.'*
Symbol	Cancer - crab and Ashlesha - Coiled snake
Element	Water
Deity	Shesha naga - the king snake.
Quality	Chara - movable and Tikshna - Sharp
Shakti	Vish Ashleshena Shakti - power to inflict poison.
Cast	Mleccha (outcast)
Gender	Female
Motivation	Moksha - liberation
Triguna	Rajas

Tridosha	Kapha
Body parts	Bone joints, nails and ears.
Direction	North, North-West and South-West
Month	January (the month of Magha)
Bird	Heron
Sound	Dee, doo, day, doh
Tree	Nag Champa
Chakras	Anhatta - Moon and Ajna - Mercury
Das Maha Vidya	Devi Bhuvaneshwari - Moon Devi Tripura Sundari - Mercury

Special degrees -

Yoga Tara	18 deg and 20.40 deg Cancer It's a point where the planet will show the strongest and sure results during its dasha.
Debilitation	28 deg Cancer- Maximum debilitation of Mars. When Mars is placed at this degree, it will feel weak and out of place, and therefore is unable to give good strong results. Especially during its dasha, it can bring situations that drain energy and make one feel weak.
Amrit nadi	29.06 - 30 deg Cancer Gives good results like the nectar that nourishes.
Visha nadi	23.46 - 24.40 deg Cancer Brings situations which one does not like dealing with.
Gandanta	29 - 30 deg Cancer The gandanta zone brings challenging situations because this is the junction point where a karmic knot is formed.

Auspicious and inauspicious table -

Auspicious	Inauspicious
Activities Good for all activities that need brave and strict measures, like - filing lawsuits, planning against opponents, dealing with chemicals, and practising yoga and meditation.	Activities Not good for travelling, initiating activities, starting new projects, business activities, borrowing or lending money, moving into a new house and for auspicious celebrations.
Days None	Days Sundays - only when it falls on the 3rd, 4th, 8th, 9th, 13th and 14th lunar day. Wednesdays - only when it falls on the 2nd, 3rd, 8th and 9th lunar day.

Compatibility table -

Ashlesha	Compatible with
Sexual compatibility Yoni animal	Ashlesha - female cat - compatible with - Male cat - Punarvasu
Sign compatibility	Cancer - Scorpio and Pisces.
Nakshatra compatibility	Jyeshta and Revati.
Lunar day compatibility	Sashti tithi -6th lunar day and Navami - 9th tithi - 9th lunar day
Day compatibility	Monday and Wednesday
Colour compatibility	White and green
Numerological compatibility	2 and 5 are all numbers that add up to make 2 and 5.
Sound compatibility	Moon - semi vowels - ya, ra, la, va, sa, sha, ssa, ha, lr, rr Mercury - lingual sounds - ta, tha, da, dha, na

Gandanta -

Ashlesha is the first junction point where water and fire meet.

Gandanta is known to be a karmic knot. In the cycle of the zodiac, there are 3 junction points between the water and fire signs where the water element transforms into the fire element.

1st gandanta zone occurs between -

Cancer Ashlesha - water	Leo Magha - fire

The transformation of water into fire happens because of the heat energy. Suppose the analogy of the water boiling and turning into steam. Water has to reach the level of heat to the boiling point to become steam. Visually, when we look at it- it is a turbulent time for water, which is needed for its transformation.

Similarly, the gandanta zone of 1 degree before and after 30 deg (29,30,1) is a turbulent zone. Anyone having their Ascendant, Sun or Moon in the last degree of Ashlesha and first degree of Magha falls into this transitional zone, which will manifest as challenging life situations during the moon or ketu dasha. It also shows deep-rooted emotional or mental blockages that have been carried on from previous life. For example, the natives may feel a deep sense of pain or detachment, attachment or anxiety, an inner calling towards a cause- for which they may not be able to find a valid reason to why they feel so. Because our profound experiences from previous lifetime do not generally find expression with clarity, but only in the form of a feeling or a strong emotion, likes and dislikes, attraction and repulsion towards someone or something.

By going through the experiences in this life, we are able to unconsciously untie these knots or we have the choice to become conscious about our inner deeper feelings through persistent practice of meditation and mindful living. Because once we become conscious of what is causing the pain, we can begin to find ways to get relief and overcome it.

Sign Lord and nakshatra lord - <u>Moon and Mercury -</u> as described earlier.

In Ashlesha, the energies of the Moon and Mercury make them very emotional and communicative about their feelings. They love to learn new things, travel and meet people. They are quick to grasp concepts, their movements are quick, and their moods can fluctuate suddenly. They will either be too quiet or too talkative, too serious or too frivolous, too attached to too detached from a situation or a relationship. They are sensitive and thoughtful and have a deeper understanding of subjects because they are able to look at them from an intellectual and intuitive perspective.

<u>Quality, element, motivation, triguna and tridosha -</u> as described earlier.

Chakras - <u>Anhatta and Ajna-</u> as described earlier.

Ashlesha is placed in the sign of Cancer, which is ruled by the moon, and Anhatta chakra resonates with the energy of the moon because it signifies the feminine and motherly qualities of love, compassion, receptivity and sensitivity. The Lord of Ashlesha is Mercury, which resonates with the energies of the Ajna chakra (third eye)-it represents the mercurian qualities of intelligence and knowledge.

When Anhatta and Ajna chakras are balanced, Ashlesha people will be compassionate, kind, curious, and quick to learn new things and gather knowledge. When the energies of these chakras are imbalanced, they will feel overly attached, possessive, emotional, sensitive, forgetful, frivolous, disoriented and unfocused.

Shakti - <u>Vish Ashleshana Shakti - power to inflict poison.</u>

Visha means poison, and Ashlesha means to burn away. Ashlesha natives have tremendous willpower to eradicate the effects of any poison. They have the quality of both inflicting poison on the negative side and getting rid of the poison on the positive side.

This quality will be more distinguished when the Ascendant, Sun or Moon are in Ashlesha. Just like the poisonous snake bites can be fatal, Ashlesha natives have the ability to inflict poison through words and deeds. But they will not do so unless they sense an imminent danger, or they are startled, provoked, or they have been cornered.

Lord Shiva drank the poison and kept it in his throat, not letting the body be affected by the poison. Ashlesha natives have an affinity towards herbs, chemicals, toxins, drugs and addictions - but they have great willpower within them to overcome these temptations or any harmful effects that can be detrimental to their physical and mental well-being. Every time they cure themselves or help others to come out of any harmful or poisonous habits, their situations in life will improve for the better.

Symbolic signification

Cancer - crab - as described earlier.

Ashlesha - snake and cat- as described earlier and a coiled snake.

In Ashlesha natives, the combination of the qualities of a snake, a cat and a crab can be seen. If pushed too far, hurt, or provoked, they can inflict the poison of words like a snake, scratch like a cat, and grab like a crab.

Snake-like qualities make them agile and cautious. They can crawl their way into and out of difficult situations through clever, ingenious plans. They are mystical, receptive, and like to keep a low profile. Just as the snakes cannot hear the external sounds, but are very good at feeling the vibrations. Ashlesha natives are very good at tuning in to their inner emotions and can feel the vibes of a place or a person without anything being said.

Crab-like qualities are seen in their emotional sensitivity and vulnerability and their need to occasionally withdraw into themselves, to heal, reflect and contemplate. A crab is very efficient at grabbing its prey. Once caught, nothing can escape its claws. Similarly, Ashlesha people are good at timing events strategically; they know how to wait attentively, and at an opportune time, they will get what they want. Just as a crab moves sideways on its legs, Ashlesha natives will not attack or reply straight on face to face. They will talk about other things, but not about the topic of concern directly. Indirectly, they will hint at it and then get back at you when you least expect it.

Cats are very independent and don't follow their master like dogs. Ashlesha natives are fiercely independent and don't like following rules by the book, their free spirit needs to go out and experience things for themselves. Cats are known to get scared easily and need more spaces to hide or escape otherwise, they will become aggressive. Similarly, Ashlesha natives need their quiet place and quiet time more often than others to heal and rejuvenate. A cat's natural instinct is to hunt their prey. Ashlesha natives find it very fulfilling to defeat their enemy. Their natural defensive instinct will be to prowl, snatch, scratch and attack like a cat.

Coiled snake -

Snakes are reptiles, like turtles and lizards. Archaeological research shows that the earliest snakes first appeared during the time of the dinosaurs. Though snakes often get a bad rap, the vast majority of species are not venomous. They also provide a valuable service by eating potential pests, like mice and slugs.

All snakes are carnivores, which means they eat meat. Their diet varies with size and species and can include insects, worms, amphibians, fish, small mammals, and occasionally birds. In fact, snakes have more to fear from us than we do from them. Sadly, many snake species have suffered from persecution and habitat loss. Nature has given them venom to hunt their prey and to defend themselves.

Snakes prefer to avoid people and will generally only bite when they are picked up, stepped on, or otherwise provoked. Though most of our snakes are harmless, several species have defensive displays, like exuding a smelly musk or rattling their tails. Snakes breed during the warmer months. Most of the species mate in the late spring and give birth to young ones in the summer. In autumn, snakes seek shelter in places like rock crevices and mammal burrows and den together in the winter to keep warm.

Interesting facts -

- During their lifespan, they never stop growing. That's why they need to shed the skin that they've outgrown. Younger snakes, which grow more quickly, may shed a few times a year, and mature snakes shed their skin less frequently.

- Snakes are ectotherms, which means that they can't regulate their body temperature from within, as humans do. That's why they need to bask in the sun to keep warm when they are cold and slip underground to cool off when they are hot.

Kundalini

In Ashlesha, the coiled snake represents the Kundalini Shakti.

The Sanskrit term Kundalini Shakti translates as Serpent Power. It is a subtle form of energy that is believed to be located at the base of the spine in the Muladhara chakra. Kundalini is described as a sleeping, dormant potential force in humans. Kundalini is described as being coiled up at the base of the spine, between the rectum and the reproductive organ. It is said to reside in the triangular sacrum bone - curled up in three and a half coils.

Shaiva tantra states that Kundalini is a form of divine feminine energy (or shakti). This energy, when cultivated and awakened through yogic practises, hatha yoga asanas, mantra chanting, pranayama and meditation, is believed to lead to spiritual liberation. Kuṇḍalinī is associated with Devi Parvati, Durga and Bhairavi. When the latent Kundalini power is awakened, it moves through the chakras in a coiled motion, rising up from the Muladhara. The experience of Kundalini awakening can happen when one is prepared or unprepared.

According to Hindu tradition, in order to be able to integrate this spiritual energy, a period of careful purification and strengthening of the body and nervous system is usually required beforehand. Yoga and Tantra propose that Kundalini can be awakened by a guru (teacher), but yogic austerities, such as pranayama, breath control, physical exercises, visualisation, and chanting, must prepare body and spirit.

Sadhguru explains that Kundalini is the fundamental life force in existence. Being alert, speaking, listening, the blossoming of a flower, or a dog barking - all these activities are Kundalini energy at play. The human system is a package of life, which is packed with layers of energy. The basic layer of life comes alive automatically and immediately because it's necessary for the survival process. The other layers of energy lie dormant unless you become aware of it and activate it consciously through regular yogic practices. This dormant energy is way bigger than the energy that is in use right now.

To live a complete physical and intellectual life, you need to activate only about 21 chakras out of 114 chakras. Less than 20 per cent of Kundalini energy is enough to lead a good, healthy life. The rest of the energy is needed only if you want to explore other dimensions of life. Even if the best things come to you when you are not ready, it can become a destructive force.

The powerful yogic practises should not be attempted without expert guidance. Without necessary focus, dedication, understanding and guidance, the life-transformative power of Kundalini can become cataclysmic. We can raise the Kundalini, either by gentle practises so that it rises slowly and changes happen slowly which can be handled easily over a period of time. The other way is by provoking it with powerful practices so that it rises quickly, but everything changes dramatically, and things can fall apart if not handled carefully.

There are 112 ways of raising the Kundalini. Out of the 7 chakras - 6 are within the body (Mooladhara to Ajna chakra), and one is outside the body (Sahasrara). From Ajna (located between the eyebrows, the 3rd eye) to Sahasrara, there is no path - you just have to jump into an abyss. To jump into a bottomless pit can happen only in madness, trust or devotion, the choice is yours. If you activate the Kundalini energy in you, the other dimensions of existence will open up for you. But are you ready for it? Kundalini yoga is the most dangerous form of yogic practice because it's the most potent. These practices must be done only under the guidance of a guru.

Inference

All human beings have the possibility of raising their Kundalini energy. However Ashlesha natives are more strongly drawn towards yogic practises that can activate this dormant energy. At some point in their life, they will follow the spiritual path and practice yoga, meditation and mantra chanting, as guided by their teacher or guru.

A coiled snake also has the power to cling and not let go until the desired goal is achieved. Ashlesha natives have this quality of determined devotion, which can go both ways - positive or negative, depending on where they apply it and in what context.

For example, Ashlesha in the 10th house will make them cling to their job, which will ultimately bring success. But what kind of means they employ to achieve this goal depends on their perspective of what their idea of success is. If they seek only their own well-being, they can use unethical ways of sticking to their position, and if they care for the wellbeing of people at large, they will focus on projects that will benefit their community, nation or the world at large.

Like a snake strikes suddenly, only when it senses danger. Ashlesha natives will strike unexpectedly, but only when hurt or provoked, for their self-defence. Just as a snake is vulnerable and sensitive to the vibration of the earth, Ashlesha natives are very sensitive to others' feelings and can sense positive or negative vibes and, therefore, feel the need to protect themselves because of their vulnerability.

Mythology -

Deity - <u>Nagas</u>

In Hindu mythology, nagas are referred to as cobras; they are unique creatures that exhibit uncanny serpentine powers. Naga, the hooded cobra, is regarded as the king of snakes (Phanindra). Nagas are the guardians of hidden treasures and are also said to possess various priceless magical gems (Naga Mani).

In the Hindu culture snakes are also associated with numerous gods and goddesses - Shiva, Vishnu, Ganapathi, Subrahmanya and Devi Kali. There are many mythical stories in India about Nagas having the magical powers of assuming various forms called <u>iccha-dhari Naga</u> or Nagin. Because of such powers, the snake is regarded with awe and veneration. The Nagas are also said to know magical spells, which they impart to the devotees or worthy recipients.

Srimad Bhagavata Purana describes the nether land known as Pātāla or <u>Nāgaloka</u>, where there are many demoniac serpents like - Śaṅkha, Kulika, Mahāśaṅkha, Sveta, Dhanañjaya, Dhritarashtra, Śaṅkhacūḍa, Kambala, Aśvatara and Devadatta. The chief among them is <u>Vāsuki</u>. These are all extremely angry species of snakes, and they have many hoods - ranging from 5 to 1000 hoods.

Their hoods are bedecked with valuable gems and there is a light emanating from the gems. There is an underground city described in the Puranas called Bhogavati, which is filled with precious gems (nagamani), jewels, gold and other treasures.

Srimad Bhagavata Purana also mentions the names of the Nagas associated with each of the months in a year.

Lunar month - Solar month	Nagas
Chaitra - March	Vasuki
Vaisakha - April	Kachnira
Jyeshtha - May	Takshaka
Ashadha - June	Shukra
Shravana - July	Elapatara
Bhadra - August	Sankhala

Magha - September	Dhanajaya
Palaguna- October	Airavata
Agrahayana - November	Mahasankha
Pausha - December	Karkotaka
Asvina - January	Kambala
Kartikeya - February	Asvatara

Lord Vishnu on Shayana -

In ancient Vedic art, Lord Vishnu is depicted as resting on a huge coiled snake with many hoods. The Anantha or the Adi-Sesha represents both the timelessness and the primal energy (mula-prakriti), reposing at rest prior to the manifestation of the created world.

Mythology of Adi Shesha Naga -

Sage Patanjali - who composed the remarkable Yoga Sutras, Balarama - the elder brother of Sri Krishna, and Lakshman- the younger brother of Sri Rama - are all revered as the incarnations of Sesha Naga.

Mahabharata connection -

In the epic of Mahabharata, it is stated that Kadru, the wife of Sage Kashyapa, becomes the mother of 1000 Nagas, who are the progenitors of the Naga race.

Pandavas are also closely associated with the nagas. The Khandava forest near Hastinapur (now called Delhi) was burnt down to construct the new capital. In this process, the Naga race was rudely dislodged. It is said that because of this, the Pandavas had to face many difficulties before getting back to their kingdom.

Lord Krishna and Kalinga -

Kalinga (Kaliya) was a dreaded poisonous snake, who had many hoods and lived in a certain part of river Yamuna. Lord Krishna, as a young boy, bravely fought Kalinga and came out victorious. While Radha, the Gopis, family, friends and many villagers waited anxiously for him at the river bank, hoping and praying that he would come out alive.

Worship of Nagas -

The nagas are both revered and dreaded because of their mystical qualities in many cultures around the world. Snake worship is a manifestation of one's devotion towards the serpent deities. The tradition is present in several ancient cultures, religions and mythologies, where the snakes are regarded as entities of strength and rejuvenation. Worship of the Naga goes back to thousands of years.

There is a belief that the snakes are associated with gods, ancestors (Pitris) and other super-beings, they are even called Deva-jana (god-people). It is believed that its destructive power is compared to that of the all-devouring fire, the Agni or Tejas. There is also a belief that through the mere fiery blast of his nostrils (Nasavata), an angry Naga can cause destruction. Such ill-wind could also pollute the air and bring about diseases (Ahi vataka roga). There is also a fear that a snake could kill merely through the power of its poisoned sight (Visha drsti). At the same time, it is believed that, by nature, the serpents are benevolent, but they can turn out to be destructive and vengeful if disrespected or not treated well.

Even today, Indian women desirous of begetting offspring worship Naga or its replica in hope and reverence. Killing or even harming a Naga (cobra) is dreaded as the deadliest of the sins. It is feared that the wrath of the serpents would haunt generation after generation. It is a traditional belief in south India that skin-related diseases happen because of the Sarpa dosha in the horoscope. The remedial rituals are quite elaborate and can be performed by a priest. Any intentional harm done to the snakes in this life can cause Kalasarpa yoga in the horoscope in the next life.

Naga Panchami -

Naga Panchami - is a traditional Hindu festival of worshipping the Nagas. It is celebrated in India on the 5th day of the bright moon phase (in some places, they celebrate during the dark moon phase) during the month of Shravana (July - August). On this day a serpent deity is made of mud, stone, wood or silver, or a picture of a naga (cobra). Milk is offered with special chants for Naga Deva.

While the Devis and Devas are worshipped in order to attain salvation (Moksha), release from ignorance and freedom from the attachments. The Nagas are worshipped for practical purposes, such as - to avoid their malevolent actions, to seek their blessings either to beget progeny or to secure health and wealth, to ward off evil effects and also for protection against drought and other natural disasters.

Inference

Ashlesha natives are highly intuitive and intelligent because they have a naga-like quality in them. The concept of energy moving through a channel signifies the serpent energy that moves in a circular motion. Ashlesha natives will have the ability to awaken their dormant Kundalini Shakti through yoga and meditation. Like a naga, they can inflict deadly poison when provoked. They can strike with venomous words if pushed too far or too often. When they are disappointed they need their quiet time to stay away from everyone and reflect on themselves.

They have an affinity towards chemicals and water-based drugs and can become very good pharmacists or herbalists. Their need to cling to something or someone is strong, and they will do anything to sustain a relationship, position, or object that matters to them. They will also have the experience of seeing a live snake or dealing with snakes.

Ashlesha padas

16.40 - 30 deg Cancer

Padas	Degrees
1	16.40 - 20 deg Cancer
2	20 - 23.20 deg Cancer
3	23.20 - 26.40 deg Cancer
4	26.40 - 30 deg Cancer

Pada 1

16.40 - 20 deg Cancer, Navamsha-Sagittarius (Lord -Jupiter)

Rashi Lord - Moon and Nakshatra Lord- Mercury

This Pada will have the energy of the Moon, Mercury and Jupiter. The natives born in this Pada will be friendly and optimistic. Since the foundation of cancer lies in the moon, they feel more connected through emotions. Mercury gives them an intellectual and hastened approach towards everything they do in life. The Jupiterian enthusiasm will drive them to aim for goals which seem expansive or larger than their estimation. The yogatara point at 18 deg falls in this Pada, any planets placed at this degree will give sure and good results during its dasha and transits over the Ascendent, natal Sun and the natal Moon.

They are soft-hearted within but tough outside. This facade protects their ultra-sensitive ego. They are acutely aware of the slightest shade of meaning, any sarcasm, any nuance or comment that makes them vulnerable to emotional hurt.

The navamsha falls in Sagittarius which makes them brutally frank and can blurt out truth that can sting even though it's unintentional. The natives will have to work hard, have a daily routine, and may have to deal with debts, disease or enemies during the Jupiter dasha because Sagittarius is 6th from Cancer. Jupiter, being a benefic, will make them go through the tests of life in a comfortable and familiar environment. Their moods tend to change with the changing phases of the moon. If born during Shukla paksha (waxing phase), their focus will be on achieving materialistic goals. In contrast, those born in Krishna paksha (waning phase) will be more inward-drawn, chasing spiritual goals.

The Jupitarian idealism makes them righteously do things and stand up for their beliefs and ideology. For example, Ashlesha Pada 1, in the 9th house, will bring opportunities for higher education and they will have the fortune of meeting the right teacher or guru who will guide them well. They will travel away from home to pursue their academic ambitions. Jupiter, being a natural teacher, will make the natives good advisors and counsellors. They love giving advice to their family, friends, colleagues, or acquaintances, even when not asked for it. In fact, it will make them feel very restless or unhappy if no one asks for their opinion. They are not good listeners but great talkers, they will always have something to say about any or every topic being discussed.

Mercury and Jupiter's influence makes them more intellectual. They like academic discussions and philosophical talks and have excellent communication skills, which makes them very social. Their idealistic approach will make them participate in social and political reform issues. Ashlesha being in the sign of cancer makes them attached to their mother and home, and they will be the first to help their family or friends in times of need. They like spending time with the family but don't like to be tied to any rules or bondage.

The Mercurian quickness and lunar emotions make them very changeable and unpredictable. They respond better spontaneously rather than planned outcomes. Staying in one place for too long will make them feel restless. Ashlesha is in the sign of Cancer which is a water sign and movable in nature. The natives will love to travel and learn about different cultures and meet people.

Being near a lake, river, sea, or ocean will give them comfort and tranquillity. They want to experience life and explore new terrains - but not alone. Ever so often, they will be planning holidays or picnics with their family or friends. But if they are chasing a certain goal, they will be willing to walk alone if needed. Lord Budha had said - *"It's better to walk alone than to walk with a fool when you are on the spiritual path."*

Careers

Counsellors, advisors, teachers, politicians, social activists, travel agents, tourist guides, chemists, ayurvedic doctors, herbalists, doctors, nurses, IT consultants, yoga teachers, snake handlers, spiritual practitioners, priests, pet owners (snakes or cats), hypnotists, psychologists, tantric and strategy consultants.

Pada 2

20 - 23.20 deg Cancer, Navamsha - Capricorn (Lord -Saturn)

Rashi Lord - Moon and Nakshatra Lord- Mercury

The qualities of the Moon, Mercury and Saturn will be seen in this Pada. Moon and mercury being quick moving planets make the natives impatient - looking for quick results. However, Saturn, being a slow, cool planet, brings delays and karmic tests. This can frustrate the natives, especially during the Saturn dasha (maha dasha or sub dashas), which can tempt the natives to resort to trickery, fraud or cheating. It will be best for natives to let the Saturn dasha pass before making any financial investments. For example, in Pada 2 in the 5th house, the natives should be careful not to invest money in speculative gains. This pada has the 2nd yoga tara point at 20.40 degrees. Planets placed at this degree will give good results.

The navamsha falls in Capricorn, which is the sign of career, public image and service to people. They are destined to serve the public through their job or business. They will be more career-oriented and will, therefore, be successful in their career later in life. Ashlesha, being the sign of cancer, makes them very possessive about their relationships and objects of material comfort. They will be very ambitious to climb the ladder of success and get to the highest position in their chosen field. Even if they have to manipulate or manoeuvre their way through to reach their desired goal, they will not hesitate to do so.

They will be very cautious and careful with financial matters because they need their security and comfort zone in order to operate efficiently. At times, they will feel that the strings of protection and safety can be binding, too, but they will never cut ties with their family, siblings, or spouse because they thrive in a familiar comfort zone. They will try their best to save their relationship, but if the situation demands separation or break, they will do so painfully and reluctantly. With time, as the wounds heal, they will form a new relationship, a new family. To float in the vast ocean without a direction is frightening for them. They prefer to anchor themselves in the safety of the shallow waters like a Cancerian crab. Ashlesha natives in this Pada often camouflage their interior empathy with a cold and unapproachable exterior to guard their vulnerability and stay focused on securing their future.

Moon represents change, movement, travel, dreams, memories, emotions, feelings, gentleness, dependency and receptivity. Saturn represents practicality, reality, steadiness, stability, caution, determination, patience, hard work and self-sufficiency. In the Zodiac chart Cancer and Capricorn are opposite to each other. These seemingly opposing qualities are actually complementary to each other and make a holistic personality when approached with a positive perspective because a harmonious home environment becomes the basis for a successful career. Their intense ambition is triggered by a need for comfort and security, which they need in great abundance. Therefore, their priority lies in securing their future and finances.

The navamsha of Capricorn gives the influence of Saturn, which can bring delays. This can frustrate the natives which can lead to making wrong choices. The natives would do well to follow the old Saturnian wisdom of experience and solve problems realistically rather than just going with their gut feeling. Saturn is a karmic planet and is pleased with discipline and hard work.

They cleverly hide their soft side with a hard exterior. They are quiet yet intense, determined, ambitious, and have a good reason to do so if they have to succeed. They cannot afford to wear their heart on their sleeve or get tangled or crushed by the surge of emotions.

It may be hard to detect behind the shy Ashlesha smile and gentle manners, but they can be snobbish about fame and prestige - the status co. They are decidedly sensitive about their public image. At home, with family and friends, they will be more relaxed in their comfort zone and drop the mask of hard-core disciplinarian once in a while. They have a strong attachment to family and relatives. They love visiting museums, ancient temples and historical landmarks with their family.

They like history and yesteryear stories. It's a personal nostalgia because they like to learn from the heroes and heroines of the past. They are also sentimental about their maternal and paternal grandparents and love to hear stories about their ancestors and their lifestyle. The mercurian influence makes them eternal students. They will be avid readers who are always curious to learn about new facets of life.

"A hundred times every day, I remind myself that my inner and outer life are based on the labours of other men, living and dead and that I must exert myself in order to give in the same measure as I have received and am still receiving." - Einstein

Careers

Managers, accountants, IT professionals, writers, librarians, office workers, pharmacists, doctors, nurses, owners of distilleries or working in one, grocery store owners- selling alcohol, yoga teachers, public service through a government job, politicians, history teachers, museum attendants or managers, archaeologists and tourist guides.

Pada 3

23. 20-26.40 deg Cancer, Navamsha - Aquarius (Lord - Saturn)

Rashi Lord - Moon and Nakshatra Lord- Mercury

The qualities of Moon, Mercury and Saturn will be there in this Pada. The sensitivity of the moon and the intelligence of Mercury combined with the service of Saturn will make them oriented towards social causes. Since the navamsa of Aquarius is 8 places away from Cancer, in their adulthood years, the Ashlesha natives will experience sudden changes and become more spiritually inclined.

Everything mystical and unknown or unknowable attracts them, which makes them more elusive and unpredictable. Like the movement of a snake, they will crawl through and steer their way towards their target, or they will wait for the target to be close enough and then grab the opportunity when it comes. Because of their effective and efficient planning, they will not miss the opportunity or strike when the time is right.

On close observation, they will see that their moods change with the changing phases of the moon. On full moon days or nights, they will feel weepy and emotional, weird and strange, spiritual and otherworldly, while on no moon nights, they will feel imaginative, restless and inwardly focused. On quarter-moon days, they might feel funny, humorous and social. While waxing moon phases will bring out more hunger and aggression, the waning moon phases can make them feel cranky or crabby, and if it's an eclipse, they will tend to brood, sulk or become reclusive.

They are capable of leaping to great heights and plunging into great depths - that can surprise others when they are least expecting it because their way of perceiving things and situations comes from the intelligence of mercury combined with an intuition of the moon. The problem is that their sensitivity easily reflects the moods of those around them, so on many occasions, they will be mirroring the emotions of others.

They are very inquisitive and are always interested in knowing what's happening in their family and friends circle, and about what's the current situation in finance and politics of the country at large. However, they will tend to be secretive and cautious about their own finances and family politics, because of the Satarian influence.

They like to set goals and work towards achieving them, and once their goal is accomplished, they will move on to the next project. Their goals could be materialistic or spiritual, social causes or uplifting the family status, personal or public agenda. Their thought process is very logical and practical, and they love to prove concepts scientifically and then use this information for the benefit of the community or for the whole of humanity. They believe in doing things the right way and prefer earning money in a justified manner because they understand that being honest is a very efficient way to lead a stress-free life.

They will get involved with large organisations and help people through charity work. Their idea of success is the progress of the whole community or society, and everyone should benefit from their project. Helping the poor or needy, participating in social welfare and social reform activities and connecting to people bring them the greatest fulfilment. They have a great talent and ability to modify things and concepts in order to make them available to all. They will, at some point in their life, work voluntarily or will have a paid job with a non-profit and charitable organisation.

They will not manipulate anyone emotionally and will make it clear right from the beginning about what their intention is, so the other person is not left in the dark. They like to do things in a straightforward, honest way, even though others may think of them as cold or cruel, but they prefer to be blunt and honest rather than sweet and hypocritical.

For example, in Ashlesha Pada 3 in the 4th house, their mother will be a social worker or will be connected to a large organisation. They will have many people coming home to ask for advice or help, in whichever job they are in, or they will be advising people over the phone. They will serve their homeland or home country in some way by serving the people. Their family members may sometimes feel that the natives care more for others than for them.

Careers

Scientists, inventors, social workers, heads of a social or charitable organisation, philanthropists, politicians, managers, IT professionals, bankers, advisors, consultants, doctors, pharmacists, nurses, astrologers, engineers, researchers, archaeologists, lawyers and librarians.

<u>Pada 4</u>

26.40- 30 deg Cancer, Navamsha - Pisces (Lord - Jupiter)

Rashi Lord - Moon and Nakshatra Lord- Mercury

This Pada will share the energies of the Moon, Mercury and Jupiter. Here, the Navamsa of Pisces makes the natives very philosophical. Since Pisces is 9 places away from the sign of Cancer, they will have a special connection with their father, teacher, guru or spiritual guide, or their father might be their guiding light. Since Pisces and Cancer are both watery signs and signify liberation, they will have a strong pull towards water - lakes, rivers, sea or ocean and they will be more introverted and spiritually inclined. Just as the tides of the ocean are affected by the moon, their moods also change according to waxing and waning lunar phases.

This Pada is the gandanta Pada marking the transiting point from the waters of the moon in Cancer - to the fire of the sun in Leo. So the natives who have Ascendent or the moon in this pada will be ultra-sensitive and can face dramatic upheavals in life, especially during the moon and mercury dasha. The effect of water getting heated up is not comfortable but transformative. It brings opportunities for a quantum leap from weakness to strength.

They have the inherent talent of connecting to people at an emotional, intellectual and psychic level. They are very intuitive and can even connect to the beings of the other dimension if they choose to do so.

As they get older, in their mid-30s, they will become more spiritually inclined. Although they are highly creative and imaginative, they will not care so much about setting targets and achieving goals. This is not because they lack the ability to do so or are too lazy to pursue them. It's because they start seeing the worthlessness of chasing materialistic goals that can keep one distracted and entangle one into the endless and vicious trap of wanting more.

On the other hand, if they choose to move towards their goals, they will do so by genuinely connecting with others. People will willingly help them with their projects because of the sincerity of their intention. They have to be emotionally connected for creativity to blossom in them.

They feel fulfilled and balanced only when they are emotionally motivated. In spite of their job, they will always find time to do some kind of creative work like - painting, drawing, singing, acting, dancing, music or writing fiction or poetry.

They will be more clingy, possessive and demanding when they are young and will try to mould others to their way of thinking or as it pleases them. Of course, they are very good at getting secrets out of others while cleverly hiding their own. They will only share their deeper feelings with a friend or family member whom they really trust and are close to. Quite often, they will find themselves complaining - *'no one understands me!'* Their need for love, a shoulder to cry on, or to listen to them is very real. It is as important as the need for food is for the survival of the body. Some of the wise Ashlesha natives born in the 4th Pada will mature into becoming good listeners as they grow older. They will realise the immensity of their capacity to share the pain of others, which in turn helps to heal their own deep-seated emotions.

They are capable of giving themselves fully to a cause and sacrificing their comforts towards a higher purpose. The natives may feel the inner struggle and dilemmas about which path to take. They are likely to face such cross-road situations in their life where they have to choose either - or they can't have both. Such scenarios may seem harsh, but they will enlighten them with the wisdom of the inner truth. They will begin to realise that there is a higher purpose to life that goes beyond the mundane, the daily routines, beyond the likes and dislikes, beyond good and bad, and beyond the pain and pleasure. They will eventually seek that eternal joy that does not diminish with difficulties or challenges faced in life. In fact, the flame of inner peace and tranquillity grows and glows more with every experience of life.

For example, Ashlesha Pada 4, in the 2nd house, will be born into a family of artists. There will be an atmosphere of creativity at home, it could be singing, dancing, acting, drawing, designing or writing. They will be well supported by their family and will have resources available to pursue their artistic talent.

"A calm and modest life brings more happiness than a pursuit of success combined with restlessness."
- Elbert Einstein

Careers-

Artists, painters, authors, actors, singers, philosophers, teachers, poets, fiction story writers, dancers, musicians, florists, YouTubers, astrologers, tarot card readers, palm readers, psychologists, psychiatrists, past life regression therapists, psychics, yoga teachers and doctors with a holistic approach to medicine.

The effect of planets

Ashlesha - Cancer	Planets that get affected
Most Benefic - Yoga karka Removes the effect of Mangal dosha.	Mars
Functional Benefic - give good results during their dasha.	Moon
Functional Malefic - can give problems during their dasha.	Mercury, Rahu and Ketu
Functional Neutral	Sun, Jupiter and Saturn
Kendra Adi Pati Dosha - can be malefic	Venus

Ashlesha Ascendant

A person born with Ascendent in Ashlesha will have an attractive physique and intense eyes and can communicate a lot by their looks, like the hypnotising gaze of the snake. They tend to be sarcastic and like to use words which have double meanings and they have a good sense of humour. They are sensitive to subtle vibrations within them and around them, which can make them overly cautious or protective. They have a very good ability to manoeuvre through situations skilfully.

Ashlesha is called the clinging star, which gives them a quality of -*'sticking it out through thick and thin and through sickness or sin.'* On the positive side, it shows their ability to endure all kinds of situations with dedication and devotion. On the negative side, they can be cruel and can inflict pain on others or themselves in the process of sticking to their beliefs or ideology. They have the power to inflict poison, and their desire is to destroy the victim. This shows that they are great friends but feared enemies. They are not aggressive or mindless in their approach but are very careful observers and know when to attack. This canny ability helps them gauge and time their encounter very precisely, and they seldom miss the target.

This is the 1st gandanta Nakshatra. Ganda means a knot, and anta means the end. This signifies the transition phase between the energy of the moon (Cancer) and the sun (Leo), from cool feminine receptivity to hot masculine dynamism. Especially for those born at 29-30 degrees of Ashlesha Ascendent will have the qualities of both moon and the sun. The gandanta point brings challenges in terms of materialistic achievements, but it also brings beautiful possibilities for spiritual progress. It has the energy of transformation.

Shiva is the deity of this nakshatra, which makes them interested in dissolving or ending things and starting fresh - a new job, a new home, or a new lifestyle. They are capable of destroying their old habits and taking on a new lifestyle which will help them enhance their growth. Ashlesha nakshatra is also closely associated with the awakening of the kundalini Shakti. The natives will like to give time and attention towards their inner wellbeing.

Just like the snake sheds its skin, Ashlesha natives will be very good at camouflaging their emotions or shedding the pain of the past and moving on. They will, at some point in their life, go through a transformation that changes their perspective of looking at life. It's like being born again as a new person. For example, if a person born with Ashlesha Ascendant has the moon placed in the 4th house, there will be psychological transformation because of their mother and home environment.

Ashlesha natives can manoeuvre their way through any system or organisation or manipulate a person or community through crafty ways to achieve their desired objective. They come across as difficult to understand because their strategies and traits are hidden, secretive, disguised or camouflaged. It is wise not to take them at face value, like a snake - they wait patiently for their prey and attack efficiently when the prey is within reach.

Snakes are carnivorous but their physiology does not allow them to chase their prey actively, but rather wait and attack with deadly accuracy when it is within reach. Just as the snake is cold-blooded, the natives can be deceptive and cold-natured.

They achieve their goals through emotional connections because of the influence of the moon and then move on to the next achievement because of the effect of mercury, which makes them interested in varied intellectual pursuits. Just as the snake wraps around its prey before gobbling it up or can shoot its poison from a distance, depending on the variety of the snake. Ashlesha natives are capable of wrapping around a person with emotional warmth that is genuine but can be suffocating at times, or they may inflict the poison of words when offended or threatened. Their intention behind their action never fails to hit its mark.

The Ashlesha Nakshatra gets activated 3 times - the 17th, 30th and 41st year of the native. The planets sitting in this nakshatra will also get activated and will give the results during these years. However, the whole chart should be considered for specific predictions. Many yogis, mystics and sadhakas who are on the spiritual path are born in this nakshatra. Lakshmana and Shatrughna, younger brothers of Lord Rama, were also born in Ashlesha.

There is a myth that says that a cobra can nurture a grudge for up to 12 years. Any harm done to the Cobra can take revenge even after a long time. Ashlesha natives will never forget any injustice done to them and can take revenge even after the person has forgotten about their misdeed. The symbol of Ashlesha is a coiled snake, just as a naga is both dreaded and revered. Ashlesha natives are respected for their tenacity of purpose, yet other people approach them cautiously when it comes to the goals that they are pursuing in their lives. The other symbol is a cat; Ashlesha natives have the cat-like qualities of being shy, elusive, and know when to pounce on the prey.

Mars is debilitated in the 4th Pada. Those who have their Ascendent in this Pada will either be very aggressive or very defensive, which makes them feel that they are in danger and need to defend or protect themselves even when there is no real threat. Their acts of bravery can sometimes be a cowardly display.

This also shows that they may face such situations where they can become the victim of others' aggression, especially during the dasha of Mars.

Ashlesha natives can become crabby, when their feelings are hurt, or they feel threatened emotionally, or don't get what they want. They will withdraw into their protective shell for many hours or days until they recover from the pain of emotional trauma. They like to be independent like the cats, who can figure out ingenious ways and paths to get out of the house and come back whenever they want to. No restrictions apply to them. They come to you when they want a cuddle and, at other times, will not be seen around the house for many hours or even days.

Ashlesha is placed in Cancer, whose element is water. This makes them very emotional and sensitive, but they are great at camouflaging their feelings because of their vulnerability to hurt.

Furthermore Cancer is a movable sign, and the added influence of the moon and mercury brings a lot of fluctuations or quick change of circumstances. However, they don't like to jump in and out of relationships thoughtlessly. They need time and space to reflect on things before making any crucial decisions.

They are deeply spiritual and religious and like to follow the rules and ethics. Ashlesha falls in the feminine sign of Cancer, which makes them very creative, artistic, emotional and caring. Being able to support or help others gives them great joy and fulfilment. They are even willing to sacrifice their happiness if it can reduce the suffering of others. Their kind nature motivates them to serve others, and they never step back whenever genuine help is needed.

Ajna chakra is associated with Ashlesha, which gives them the ability to raise their energies to this chakra if they work on themselves and spend time doing their yogic or spiritual practises.

"Realisation is not an acquisition of anything new, nor is it a new faculty. It is only the removal of all camouflage." - Ramana Maharishi

Sun in Ashlesha

Sun in Ashlesha will share the energies of Mercury and the Moon, it brings added pride, confidence and brilliance of intelligence. The fire of the Sun and water of the Moon, most often, is quite efficiently and delicately balanced by the friendly Mercury. They will have a more honest, generous and straightforward approach to life, and their motto will be - *"Be true to yourself if you want to be happy."*

Although Cancer is a feminine sign, but is also the cardinal sign of leadership. Despite the surface lunar gentleness, they want to be the boss and will resent or oppose anyone giving them orders or telling them what to do. Their focus is more on teaching others, putting their point forward, and expecting others to agree with them. They have the intelligence and confidence to carry forward their plans and achieve desired results, but listening to others is definitely not their strong point.

The goodness of the Moon and Mercury is that they are easy to get along with. They are not authoritative or fussy about anything, so the Sun in Ashlesha generally fares well. The warmth of sunshine is welcoming on the waters of the Moon as long as it doesn't overheat, which can leave the water bereft of moisture. So Ashlesha natives have to tread gently, taking care not to hurt anyone's feelings in their fire of passion or pride. On the other hand, the warmth of sunshine is a significator of life and generosity, which the over-protectiveness of the Moon should not extinguish. It's a delicate balance which is not impossible to achieve, but needs awareness.

They will often complain of not being given due credit for their work or not being respected, and the danger of becoming unmotivated and lazy is always lurking behind them, it will be sad to see their charisma being submerged into the depth of depression. They can stay strong, persevere and persist through any kind of circumstances to reach their goals.

They feel emotionally wounded if they are not appreciated for their efforts or generosity, and their proud spirit silently feels crushed, especially if they are ignored. Even a gentle nod of acknowledgement or a smile can make them happy, and that's not much to ask for what you get in return - a genuine and caring friend who will always be there for you in times of need.

Those who have Sun in Ashlesha in their birth chart are the happiest when they live life in a way that motivates and inspires others. They set a high standard for themselves - the discipline and moral code they live by, which will naturally make people look up to them for advice.

They love travelling and photography because both the luminaries - the Sun and the Moon appreciate and enjoy everything that has visual beauty, like picturesque sceneries and art work. They also love to hang on to old photographs and all articles that remind them of their wonderful or not so wonderful - but adventurous trips.

Their tenacity of purpose can help manifest at least some of their grand ideas and glorious dreams. They never say no to anyone in genuine need and are very generous with their time and money towards their family and friends. They like to buy lavish gifts, eat at good restaurants, and buy good quality clothes, but will never throw away their money in a frivolous way on gambling, unless there is an influence of the 5th house of speculation and entertainment.

Sun in Ashlesha will also give the natives a strong attachment to their dad, who will be influential and helpful in shaping their career, or their mother could take on the role of the dad and be the main earning member of the family. For example, Sun in Ashlesha in the 12th house can give a government job in a foreign country, or your dad may have to do such a job where he has to stay away from home. It also shows that natives need their own private space, their bedroom is their office, it's their kingdom, where they can do what they please and how they please. The best of their creative or ingenious ideas come when they are in their bedroom. For them to function well, their private den is an absolute need.

Moon in Ashlesha

Moon placed in Ashlesha will have the double effect of an emotional and intuitive moon with curious and friendly mercury. They will be very imaginative, moody and sensitive; they have many dreams and aspirations out of which few may manifest but most of them may be too impractical to find expression.

They have the qualities of gentleness. They are soft-spoken, friendly, chatty, love being at home, enjoy cooking, looking after the children and caring for others - these qualities will be seen in both males and females who have their moon in Ashlesha. They will be attached to their mothers and will be very motherly towards their children as well.

Water, being the element of Cancer, makes them feel the high tides of emotions especially on days when it's nearing the full moon. Just as the power and force of a flood can break all barriers and bridges, their emotional response cannot be contained in a few sobs. They can cry a bucket full of tears. They should let their emotions pour out rather than suppress them because suppressing them will cause more damage, which, over time, can lead to chronic health problems.

They don't like being direct, straight or upfront and prefer to say things or convey a message in a subtle, indirect way because of the fear of getting hurt. Keeping secrets, holding back information, or not revealing it all is their protective shield against hurt because even a mere look of disapproval can hurt their feelings. The double effect of the moon will also bring a lot of opportunities to travel. They might have to make many short journeys for work or pleasure and holidays, depending on which house moon in Ashlesha is sitting. For example, the 12th house will give foreign travel, the 3rd house can give short but regular journeys, and the 6th house can give travelling for work as a daily routine.

They are strong and resilient in tough times, but if their emotions are hurt, they crawl into their shell. They are emotionally vulnerable because of their sensitivity, and their empathy makes them feel the pain or joy of others as their own. This often gets them entangled in solving others' problems. If they get hurt, it will take time for them to heal their emotional wounds, crawl out of their protective shell and seek another friend or relationship.

Their need for emotional security makes them get married and settle quite early in life. If they are not married yet, that's because they have a mother or father who genuinely cares for them, so they don't feel the urgent need to get into any relationship. Their list of priorities is - money, food, marriage, and children - exactly in this order, the first one has to be fulfilled first for the next one to happen.

Their favourite pastimes are- watching emotional family dramas or movies on TV, listening to music, having long chats over the phone, and searching for new delicious recipes and trying them out. The influence of mercury will make them curious about everything, and they will love having discussions with their friends and family on various topics ranging from politics to gossip to science and religion.

The strong effect of the moon makes them very motherly; for them to feel fulfilled they need to have someone to care for, to nurture, to support and love and also feel loved in return. It's an absolute need - that's why many of them who have their moon placed in Ashlesha will have a pet at home- a dog, a cat, a plant, or even a snake to take care of. Of course, their home will be cosy and comfortable, with at least 2 children, 1 or 2 pets, and the smell of something delicious cooking in the kitchen. The neighbours or friends will always accompany them on the walk in the park, and their children and pets are not to be forgotten too.

Their attachment to people and things stems from the lingering fear and insecurity of losing the warmth and comfort of friendship or loss of money or resources. They dread facing any such scenarios. Therefore they unconsciously tend to cling to whatever they have and also continuously work towards having more, which gives them a great sense of security.

For example, in the moon in Ashlesha in the 10th house, their mind will always be thinking about how to secure their job. They can even be manipulative in order to get their desired position in their career. They may have more than one job to earn extra money. Most likely, they will follow their mother's career or anyone whom they look up to as a mother- and she will be very helpful and influential in helping and guiding them in their profession. They can face fluctuations in their career during the moon dasha. Their job will involve taking care of others, and they might work from home if needed.

"The meeting of two personalities is like the contact of two chemical substances. If there is any reaction, both are transformed."

- Carl Jung

Ash- Lesha, the poet

Ash - from the ashes rises the unicorn,

Lesha - noble, exalted, a quality inborn.

Moon the wondrous one, Mercury the Prince,

What a charming combo, that makes you convinced.

All is well, all is glory, all the way…

But the camouflaged ease has a price to pay.

The coiled serpent, naga disguise,

Don't be complacent, for there is a surprise!

Wait and watch, not too soon, not too fraught,

Anxiety and hope is the play of thought.

The claws of a crab, catch for good, a reward

The sideways walk, an efficient way forward,

Cat-like ways, deceptively cuddly, lovable and free,

Who can know this but only you and me.

The languishing fear, or a captivating sphere,

Both are a frontier, a boundary to clear.

Making a choice of walking the path,

Which one? Has a lesser wrath!

The material might, or the spiritual flight.

Yes- both demand a price, too, dear!

Nothing is daunting when the yearning is sincere.

So call it a day, only when the sun has set,

In the light of the romantic moon, blow the cornet.

The victorious tune, to honour the brave,

Who never gave up, amidst a stormy wave.

Enjoy the rewards, the medals of love,

In the hearts that your kindness touched.

Remedies

- <u>Das Maha Vidya -</u> as described earlier.
- The best remedy is to do hatha yoga and meditation, which will calm the agitated emotions and bring good health.
- On nag panchami, or on the day when the moon transits Ashlesha, pay reverence to the snakes by offering milk at the Shiva temple.
- Green and white colours resonate well with the energies of Ashlesha.
- Offer milk to the cat.
- Feed the cows green fodder on a Wednesday.
- Chant -'*Om Namah Shivaya.*' 108 times on Wednesday.
- Chant the Ashlesha nakshatra mantra 108 times for 45 days - '*Om Kham Gam Ashlesha Nakshatraye Namah.*'

Observations -

Among the many famous Ashlesha personalities, 2 of them are -

Mahatma Gandhi and Indira Gandhi.

Mahatma Gandhi had his Moon and Rahu in the 11th house - Moon in Ashlesha Pada 4 and Rahu in Pushya Pada 4. He was driven by the willpower to achieve his goals in a passive but determined way. Moon, sitting in his own house, is very comfortable and strong and has a Shadbala score of 466 points. Though, his strongest planet is Mercury (Lord of Ashlesha) which has a score of 495/500. This gave him the intellectual prowess and ability to articulate his thoughts very well. Moreover, his 11th house was the strongest in his birth chart, with 36 points. This brought him a lot of recognition through voluntary, social and political reform movements and rallies at the national and international level.

Indira Gandhi is an Ashlesha Ascendant Pada 4, and Saturn is sitting in the Ascendant in Ashlesha Pada 2. She was assassinated on 31st October 1984 at 9:29 am. At that time, she was running her Saturn Rahu Rahu dasha. Saturn is the Lord of the 7th and 8th house. All her life she served her country through her political guidance and leadership.

It has been very tragic to lose them. Astrologically, it is amazing to notice that they both met their end through bullet wounds and spilling of blood. Ashlesha represents all bodily fluids and is strongly associated with religion and spirituality. They were both very spiritually inclined, yet ironically, they were killed for their strong and fearless stance on faith.

Example

Moon in Ashlesha

Kalpana Chawla - First Indian woman astronaut.

Born on 17th March 1962 - 1st February 2003, sadly died on 1st February 2003 at the young age of 41.

Kalpana was born on 17th March 1962 in Karnal, India. As a child, she was fascinated by aeroplanes and flying. She used to love going to the local flying club with her father to look at the planes. She got a Bachelor's degree in Aeronautical Engineering from Punjab Engineering College, Chandigarh, India.

In 1982, she moved to the USA. Just 2 days after she had arrived in Texas, she met J P Harrison, her colleague. They found that they had a lot in common and got married in December 1983. She obtained a Master of Science degree in Aerospace Engineering from the University of Texas at Arlington in 1984. She went on to earn a 2nd Master's in 1986 and a PhD in Aerospace Engineering in 1988 from the University of Colorado Boulder.

After becoming a U.S. citizen, she applied for the NASA Astronaut Corps. She also held a Certificated Flight Instructor rating for aeroplanes, gliders and Commercial Pilot licences. In December 1994, she was selected as an astronaut on the NASA team. From 3000 applications of aspiring candidates, she was among the 6 who were selected. Her training as an astronaut started in March 1996 at Johnson Space Centre in Euston, USA. The special 2-year training prepared her for space, land and sea survival and for the intricate operations of the space shuttle.

Her 1st space mission began on 19 November 1997, as part of the 6 astronaut crew that flew the Space Shuttle Columbia flight STS-87. On her first space flight she had said, *"You are just your intelligence."*

In 2001, she was selected for her 2nd flight as part of the crew of STS-107. This mission was repeatedly delayed due to scheduling conflicts and technical problems. On 16th January 2003, Space Shuttle Columbia finally took off on the ill-fated STS-107 mission. During their space flight, the crew performed nearly 80 experiments studying Earth and space science.

At the time of launch, a piece of foam insulation had broken off from the Space Shuttle's external tank and struck the left wing of the orbiter. Previous shuttle launches had seen minor damage from foam shedding, but some engineers suspected that the damage to Columbia was more serious. NASA managers limited the investigation, reasoning that the crew could not have fixed the problem even if it had been confirmed. Tragically, Kalpana died in the Space Shuttle Columbia disaster, along with the 6 other crew members, when the Columbia disintegrated over Texas during re-entry into the Earth's atmosphere, shortly before it was scheduled to conclude its 28th mission, STS-107. On 1st February 2003, when Columbia re-entered the atmosphere of Earth, the damage allowed hot atmospheric gases to penetrate and destroy the internal wing structure, which caused the spacecraft to become unstable and break apart.

Her remains were identified along with those of the rest of the crew members and were cremated and scattered at Zion National Park in Utah in accordance with her wishes. After her death, she was awarded the Space Medal of Honour, and several streets, universities, and institutions have been named in her honour. She is regarded as a national hero in India.

Analysis -

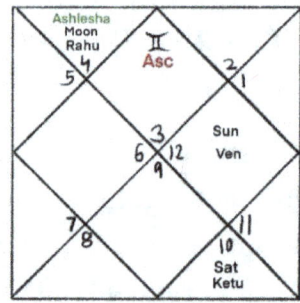

Her <u>Moon and Rahu are in the 2nd house of Cancer</u> - Moon in Ashlesha Pada 1 and Rahu in Ashlesha Pada 3. She is a Gemini Ascendent in Ardra Pada 1.

This shows that Rahu has amplified Ashlesha's qualities. Ashlesha's steely determination takes them beyond the frontiers of success. Moon Rahu's conjunction gives an abundance of emotional energy which she channelled positively. She would not feel satisfied with the ordinary. Her mind would always look for something new and challenging to do; otherwise, she would get bored easily. This gave her the ability to go for the extreme, she was very intuitive, and was not afraid of taking risks and pursued her ambitious endeavours with great faith.

Rahu also signifies a foreign element, so her mind was influenced and inspired by the advanced scientific techniques used in the USA. Rahu with the moon also makes the person use their emotions to get what they want. Ascendant Lord Rahu sitting with the moon in the 2nd house of the family resources. Saturn and ketu are in the 8th house of Capricorn. This shows that she would experience transformations, and work hard towards her goals that would take her to great heights and great depths.

The 2nd house moon Rahu placement also shows that her family supported her to pursue her ambitions and were able to provide the resources needed. Ardra Ascendant gave her a scientific and fearless perspective on life.

The nakshatra Lord Rahu sitting with the moon in the 2nd house shows the amplified effect of what the mind wants and feels, which can enhance the personality.

When the unfortunate incident of the crash happened on 1st February 2003, she was going through her Venus Ketu Saturn Moon dasha. Moon and Rahu in the 2nd house, opposite to it, in the 8th house is Saturn in Shravana, Ketu in Dhanishta, in Capricorn. Venus in Uttara Bhadrapada and Sun in Purva Bhadrapada are placed in the 10th house of Pisces.

On the day of the fatal explosion, at 8:30 am the moon was transiting over her 8th house where Saturn and Ketu are sitting. The 8th house is related to sudden events and death. Saturn was her subdasha, and the moon was her sookshma (subtle) dasha. She was also running her Sade sati period of 7 and a half years up till April 2003. In February 2003, Saturn was transiting over Gemini, her Ascendent. All these combinations confirm the unfortunate mishap that took the lives of all 7 astronauts on board.

In one of her interviews Kaplana had said- "I have always been inspired by explorers, one thing that stands out is their perseverance."

"I was not born just for one corner, the whole universe is my native land." - *Kalpana Chawla.*

Reflections -

As I was ending the writing on Ashlesha, the example that I came across was of Kalpana, who unfortunately died young. I came across this quote - *"In my beginning is my end, and in my end is my beginning."* - *T S Elliot.*

The first part of this quote is originally from the Bible. Which was taken as the opening line by T S Elliot for his poem *"Four Quarters."* *"In my end is my beginning"* - this line was found embroidered on the handkerchief of Mary, the Queen of Scotland, before she was sadly executed on 8th February 1587.

The <u>Gandanta zone</u> has culminated into an ending so appropriately! I feel that *"In these spontaneous happenings lies the hand of the divine, and in the planned activity is the working of our mind."*

10
Magha

Om gham ngam Magha nakshatraye namah

Zodiac degrees	0-13.20 deg Leo
Ruling planet	Leo - Sun and Magha - Ketu
Sanskrit name	Magha means - mighty, beneficent, and great.
Astronomical name	Alpha Leonis is the brightest star, a sickle shaped group of stars seen in front of the Leo constellation.
Symbol	Leo - Lion and Magha - Throne
Element	Fire
Deity	Pitris- ancestors
Quality	Sthira - fixed and Ugra - fierce
Shakti	Tyaga shepani shakti - power to renounce
Cast	Shudra - Worker
Gender	Male
Motivation	Dharma- righteousness
Triguna	Dharma
Tridosha	Pitta
Body parts	Nose, lips, chin and heart
Direction	East, south, northwest, southwest
Month	2nd half of Magha - February

367

Bird	Pigeon
Sound	ma, me, moo, may
Tree	Banyan tree
Chakras	Muladhara - Ketu and Manipura - Sun
Das Maha Vidya	Devi Matangi - Sun and Devi Dhumavati -Ketu

Special degrees -

Yoga Tara	6 deg Leo It's a point where the planet will show the strongest and sure results during its dasha.
Mulatrikona	4- 20 deg Leo - Mulatrikona of the Sun. When the id Sun is placed at these degrees, it will give good results because it feels comfortable in its territory.
Amrit nadi	12 - 12.53 deg Leo Gives good results, like the nectar that nourishes.
Visha nadi	6.40 - 7.33 deg Leo Brings situations which one does not like dealing with.
Gandanta	0 - 1 deg Leo The gandanta zone Pada brings challenging situations because this is the junction point where a karmic knot is formed.

Auspicious and inauspicious table -

Auspicious	Inauspicious
Activities Good for marriage and all kinds of celebrations, ceremonies, stage performances, musical shows, theatre, dance and drama performances, royal events, parades and award functions, for researching into the past - studying scriptures, religious activities, honouring the ancestors, conducting poojas, archaeological activities, past life hypnosis, and research work on genetics, taking on a new name, activities related to the government and career-related activities and doing charity work.	Activities Not good for lending money, mundane activities, planning for the future, or dealing with new technology because the energy of Ketu supports activities of the past.
Days Thursdays - only when it falls on the 4th, 5th, 7th, 9th, 13th, or 14th lunar day.	Days Mondays- only when it falls on the 6th, 7th or 11th lunar day. Fridays - only when it falls on the 2nd, 3rd, 6th, 8th, 10th or 11th lunar day.

Compatibility table -

Magha	Compatible with
Sexual compatibility Yoni animal	Magha - Male rat- compatible with- Female rat - Purva Phalguni
Sign compatibility	Leo - Pada 1 - Aries and Sagittarius.
Nakshatra compatibility	Ashwini and Mula.
Lunar day compatibility	Amavasya - no moon
Day compatibility	Sunday
Colour compatibility	Red, orange and brown
Numerological compatibility	1 all numbers that add up to make 1
Sound compatibility	Sun - all vowels - a, aa, e, ee, u, oo, ey, aye, o, ou, am, ah

Gandanta -

The gandanta zone is like an abyss which contains the energy of both water and fire, which makes it a turbulent ride. This represents transformations that happen due to challenging situations. The 1st Pada of Magha falls in the gandanta zone, which is the transition from water to fire. All ketu-ruled nakshatras have the effect of the gandanta, especially 0-1 degree of Magha - it's like a black hole zone, where the energy is very intense, and the extreme heat gobbles up or consumes everything on its path. The Cancerian water has to lose its liquid form and transcend into a gaseous form because of the fiery heat of the sun in Leo.

Amavasya, the new moon day, resonates with the energy of Magha, which shows the strong influence of the gandanta zone that is like a black hole, a gap, a dark, still and intense energy. That has the power to transform and literally does not give any other choice but to cut ties from the material and connect to the spiritual.

Transition is never easy, it's like dying to one way of living and perceiving life and being born into another. From Ashlesha to Magha, the cool waters have to bear the heat and build the passion, drive and motivation to rise above and exist as steamy clouds. Just as the rain cycle is essential for all living creatures to survive on Earth - the heat of the sun triggers the ocean and river waters to rise and become clouds. As the clouds become huge and saturated, they fall in the form of rain again - and the cycle continues. So also the soul reincarnates again and again to gather experiences that will help us to transcend and evolve into our higher self.

Sign Lord and nakshatra lord - <u>Sun and Ketu -</u> as described earlier.

In Magha, the combination of Sun and Ketu makes them intelligent, creative, confident, determined, ambitious, generous and trustworthy. At the same time, they are detached from the worldly ways of life and are spiritually inclined.

Quality, element, motivation, triguna, tridosha and chakras - as described earlier.

Since the deity of this nakshatra is the pitris, they come from the ancestral realm, and their inherent desire is to leave the body. The Lord of Leo is the Sun, which signifies the king and the soul, and Ketu, the nakshatra Lord, signifies separation or cutting the ties that bind.

The cumulative effect shows that they have the qualities of nobility, regality, pride and magnanimity. They hold their honour and pride, or of their family or community, above everything else. If, at any point in their life, they have to give it all up for a higher cause or to help their family or a dear friend, they will willingly do so.

Maybe not at a conscious level of thoughts, but at a deeper level of the soul, they know that the game of life is an illusion. Since they carry the seeds of ancestral memories within them, more strongly than any other nakshatras. The soul has come into the body, but there is a deep-rooted desire to leave the body and join the ancestors in the realms of the beyond.

Shakti - Tyaga shepani Shakti - power to renounce.

Magha natives have the power to renounce. The word tyaga means sacrifice. This shows that at some point in their lives, they will have to sacrifice their desires for the happiness of their family, spouse, or a close friend.

They are blessed with tremendous willpower to be able to make such a sacrifice. The power and energy of the sacrifice carry them through all hurdles because of their sincerity of purpose.

Symbolic signification

Leo - Lion

Magha - Throne

Lion

The lion is a well-muscled cat with a long body, large head, and shorter legs. The distinguishing feature of Male lions is their majestic mane, female lions don't have a mane. Manes may serve to intimidate rivals or impress prospective mates. The lion's skin colour ranges from yellow to brown, which is a very effective camouflage, especially in the savanna landscapes of Africa.

Lions are most active at night and live mostly in grassland, savanna, dense scrub, and open woodland. Historically, they ranged across much of Europe, Asia, India and Africa. Lions are unique among cats and live in a group or pride. A lion pride typically consists of about 15- 20 members, which has more lionesses, cubs, young growing lions and only 1 fully grown male lion, who is the head or the king of the pride.

The members of pride usually spend the day in several scattered groups. The lionesses usually hunt at night - one of the experienced lionesses initiates the hunt, and they catch the prey, which is then shared by the whole tribe, with the head lion having the 1st feed. Lionesses predominantly hunt medium- to large-sized hoofed animals like wildebeests, zebras, and antelopes. However, male lions are also adept hunters, and usually, nomadic single males have to hunt alone to secure their own food.

Lions mark their territory by roaring and scent marking by urinating in bushes and trees, which leaves a pungent smell behind. Their distinctive roar is generally delivered in the evening before a night's hunting and again before getting up at dawn. Both sexes are polygamous; females are usually restricted to 1 or 2 adult males of their pride. They usually breed once every 2 years.

Lionesses do nurse cubs other than their own. They are surprisingly inattentive mothers and often leave their cubs alone for up to 24 hours. Male cubs are expelled from the pride at about 3 years of age and become nomads until they are old enough to try to take over another pride after the age of 5. Many adult males remain nomads for life.

Mating opportunities for nomadic males are rare, and competition between male lions to defend a pride's territory and mate with the pride females is fierce. If a new cohort of males is able to take over a pride, they will seek to kill the young cubs sired by their predecessors. In the wild, lions seldom live more than 8 to 10 years, chiefly because of attacks by humans or other lions or the injuries received from kicks and gorings from intended prey animals. In captivity, they may live 25 years or more.

Interesting facts -

- When living in a pride, it's lionesses who always hunt, and the lion gets his first share. But lions, who are single nomads and not members of pride, have to hunt for their own survival.

- Lionesses can look after other cubs of the pride, even those she has not given birth to.

- Usually, young male lions get chased from the pride when they are nearing adulthood.

- If another male lion takes over the pride, he kills the young cubs of that pride, the lionesses fiercely try to protect them and are sometimes successful in saving them.

- Larger lion prides have many unrelated members, they stay together and can survive longer for many decades.

Inference

Just like a lion, Magha natives like to be the kings of their place, home, office, family and tribe. They cannot take orders from anyone, and they would rather stay alone than be subservient. For this reason, Maghas will mostly be self employed, and if they are working for someone, they will be in a position of authority. They have a medium height and strong well-built body. They take pride in their hairstyle, like the lion's mane. They are generous and like giving lavish gifts. They hold their own and their family's self-respect and prestige above everything else.

Just as the lion is the leader of his pride, Magha natives are the head of their family and are very protective of them. Even if they are the younger sibling, they like to boss around. They are also very territorial about their own space and their family's honour and prestige. They are protective about everything - their personality, beliefs, finances, children, spouse, job, business, colleagues and their position in society. They are brave and courageous and always rise up to a challenge and never back up. Although they don't like to pick fights to protect their territory, food, finance, family or friends, they are willing to face any challenge.

They need time to laze around and usually stay up late at night to finish their work. They are short-tempered and can roar like a lion when angry. They are hunters, not gatherers and will go get what they feel is rightfully theirs. They are brave to face what life throws at them, and dare to make dramatic changes that can bring them respect and success.

No matter how difficult the situation is, they take pride in standing up for their family, friends or community. That's why a group of lions is called a <u>pride </u>because they literally feel a sense of pride in looking after their loved ones.

On the other hand, they are also loners. They don't hang around for long hours chatting or partying. They prefer to be by themselves, keep their distance, relax, and work on creative projects. Their sensitive ego finds it difficult to accommodate another lion in his or her space, so they choose to be alone rather than to be among other equally influential leaders.

<u>Magha - Throne</u> - signifies a position of authority.

Magha natives have an air of royalty and regality about them, they inevitably are admired and respected for their honesty and magnanimity. They usually hold an important position in their family, at work and in their social circle. Even if they don't hold an official position of authority, they are always looked up to by their family, friends and colleagues.

They will have a particular chair or a spot where they always like to sit and hold court for their family or friends or in their office. That's when they really feel in their zone. They are very good at taking up responsibility and feel truly fulfilled when they get the opportunity to advise others, protect them, or look after them. They will always have a close connection with government officials; either they will be in a position of authority or will have good friendships with a high-ranking government officer. They love to be the centre of attraction and easily fall for praise. Their ego sensitivity is their vulnerability, and they are easily hurt when ignored.

On the positive side, they are honest and generous. On the negative side, they can be too overbearing and authoritative. The 3 things that make a Magha happy are - praise, attention and a position of power. If they use their creative potential to help and empower others, it's the greatest blessing because they have the talent and capability of becoming the king-maker and not just a king.

Mythology -

Deity - Pitris - ancestors

The 1st King - Prithu- The 1st ancestor

The Rigveda states that Prithu was - ayonija - which means the one who is not born out of a womb (yoni). Vishnu Purana narrates the story of Prithu -

Long ago, there was a King named Vena, from the lineage of the pious Dhruva, but he was an evil king who neglected Vedic rituals. Therefore, the rishis (sages) had to kill him because of his cruel anarchy. In doing so, there was no heir left to take the throne. So, the sages churned Vena's body, out of which first appeared a dark dwarf hunter. The sins of Vena had gone away with the dwarf, and the body was now pure. On further churning, Prithu emerged from the right arm of the corpse.

In the famous epic Mahabharata, it is stated that Lord Vishnu crowned Prithu as the King and then entered his body. Now, the king was endowed with Vishnu's qualities - Dharma (righteousness), Shri (goddess of wealth, beauty and good fortune) and Artha (purpose, material prosperity). All civilizations emerged in his reign.

The Atharvaveda states that he invented ploughing and started a more efficient way of farming. He also flattened the Earth's rocky surface, thus encouraging agriculture, cattle-breeding, commerce and the development of new cities on Earth. In this way, Prithu became the first true king. He granted life to the Earth and became her protector. Therefore, he came to be known as the Earth's father and she got the name of Prithvi.

Prithu's wife was called Archi, and they had 5 sons, apart from Prithvi, his 1st daughter. Archi, his wife, had also emerged from Vena's body, along with Prithu and is considered an avatar of the goddess Lakshmi, the wife of Vishnu. Prithu's son, Vijitswa, became the king and controlled the middle of the kingdom. His 4 other sons, Haryarksha, Dhumrakesha, Vrika and Dravina, ruled the east, south, west and north of the kingdom, respectively.

After acquiring many presents from the gods, Prithu conquered and ruled the earth as well as the Devas, Asuras, Yakshas, Rakshasas and Nagas in all glory. This is the time period when the Satya Yuga reached its pinnacle. Prithu liberated his father, Vena, from the hell called Pūt. After this, all sons were called Putras. Sanat Kumaras, the 4 young sages, had preached to Prithu about devotion to Vishnu.

He was also called the sage king because he was detached from material comforts and ruled according to the Vedic principles. While he was the crowned emperor of the world, many other kings were appointed by Brahma according to their special capabilities. Harivamsa Purana lists the other kings who were appointed during the ancient Vedic period.

The lineage of 26 kings -

N	King	Lord of
1	Chandra	Constellations, Yajnas - fire rituals, asceticism and plants.
2	Indra	Rain and Maruts - the storm deities.
3	Varuna	Waters- oceans and seas.
4	Kubera	Wealth
5	Agni	Pavakka- purifier, and Vasus - the wealth givers.
6	Vishnu	Adityas - the sun deities.
7	Daksha	Prajapatis - the deities
8	Shiva	Sandhyas- transition times, rudras - fierce forms, ghosts and goblins.
9	Yama	Pitris - ancestors
10	Prahlad	Daityas - demons
11	Viprachitti	Danavas, Asuras - not in harmony
12	Chitraratha	Gandharvas- celestial musicians
13	Vasuki	Nagas - snakes
14	Takshaka	Serpents and reptiles
15	Adishesha	Wild animals
16	Vayu	Disembodied beings- smell, sound and ether.
17	Uchaishravas	Horses
18	Bull	Cattle
19	Garuda	Birds
20	Tiger	Beasts
21	Airavata	Elephants
22	Himalaya	Mountains

23	Plaksha -fig tree	Trees
24	Parjanya	Rivers, lakes and streams.
25	Samvatsara	Mathematics, seasons, years, months, fortnights, weeks, and days.
26	Rakshak - guardians	Sudhanva - east, Shankapada- south, Ketuman - west and Doordarsha- north

Inference

The mythological Vedic story of King Prithu is a way of narrating the story of the evolution of a man- from a Hunter-gatherer tribes to becoming farmers and settlers. This historical past has been the way of living of all tribes that have been present on earth, in different geographical areas and in different time zones.

Magha natives are strongly connected and motivated by the past. Honouring their ancestors and accomplishing goals that the ancestors had initiated is what inspires them. Their connection to the ancestral past is so strong that a Magha native is most probably the ancestor being born again to finish off the unfinished tasks and fulfil desires that were left unfulfilled in the past life.

Magha padas

0- 13.20 degrees Leo

Padas	Degrees
1	0 - 3.20 deg Leo
2	3.20 - 6.40 deg Leo
3	6.40 - 10 deg Leo
4	10 - 13.20 deg Leo

Pada 1

0- 3.20 deg Leo, Navamsha- Aries (Lord - Mars)

Rashi Lord - Sun and Nakshatra Lord- Ketu

Pada 1 of Magha falls in the navamsa of Aries. Therefore, it carries the energies of the Sun, Ketu and Mars. This is a very fiery combination because all the 3 planets are hot and fiery in nature.

The natives will be very motivated, ambitious and self-driven. The intelligence, confidence and creativity of the Sun, the determination and courage of Mars, and the impatience and detachment of Ketu is quite a lethal combination, which can give huge success, or utter failure.

Which way the qualities will manifest, positive or negative, will have to be seen from the whole birth chart analysis and the study of dashas.

For example, the 1st Pada of Magha in the 6th house, when no other planets are sitting in it, can make the native very defensive and aggressive towards all challenges that either he or she may have to face during the Sun, Ketu or Mars dasha. The natives will have tremendous energy and willpower to overcome debts, disease, and enemies. Their daily routine will involve active involvement and hard work.

There will be a karmic ancestral connection with the mother's siblings. They will share a very strong bond with their mother's relatives. It will either be a difficult relationship between them that becomes the cause of their suffering or a loving bond that helps to eradicate or solve the impending problems. Either way they will share a special relationship with their mum's relatives. Most probably, they will get a job through them, work for them, help in their business, or carry forward a legacy left behind by their maternal relatives.

They will be very ambitious about getting a high position in their job, family or society. They want others to look up to them and acknowledge their sincere efforts. They are highly intelligent and creative, and with a patient and focused approach they can achieve a great deal and succeed in their desired goals. They also need to tread carefully because, in their enthusiasm to get things done, they could unintentionally trample over others' feelings and sensitivities. Their inherent nature is outgoing, outspoken, very dignified, regal, proud, courageous, honest, straightforward and generous (to the point of fault). They love buying lavish gifts for their family or friends.

They tend to fall for praise easily. This can become their weak point, which they need to be aware of consciously, it will help save them from falling into a trap on many vulnerable occasions. Between 0-1 deg Leo lies the gandanta zone, which can bring turbulent situations during the Sun, Ketu or Mars dasha. These upheavals will also be a conducive time for spiritual growth, a transitional time to evolve into higher possibilities.

"The judgement of the intellect is only part of the truth." - Carl Jung.

Careers

Soldiers, policemen, government officers, politicians, army officers, leaders, rotary club owners or workers, sportspeople, athletes, football players, cricket players, baseball players, hockey players, tennis players, boxers, wrestlers, swimmers, gymnasts, horse riders, business people, managers, skilled artisans, builders, taxi drivers, truck drivers, race car drivers, scientists, astrologers, mathematicians, musicians, artists, astronauts, pilots, architects, enterpruners, IT technicians, designers, electricians, engineers, road planners and workers, metal craft designers and tradesmen, industry owners or workers, doctors, surgeons, post mortem doctors, mortuary workers and coffin makers.

Pada 2

3.20 - 6.40 deg Leo, Navamsha - Taurus (Lord - Venus)

Rashi Lord - Sun and Nakshatra Lord- Ketu

The qualities of the Sun, Ketu and Venus will manifest in the 2nd Pada of Magha because it falls in the navamsa of Taurus. The natives will have the confidence of the Sun, determination of Mars and the elegance of Venus. Since the yogatara is at 6 deg Leo and it's a mulatrikona Pada for the Sun, this makes the natives very fortunate, intelligent and passionate. They will have a very graceful and attractive personality, exquisite taste and a fine sense of aesthetics. They love dressing up elegantly, literature, art and travelling. The sun feels very comfortable here and therefore gives good results during its dasha and transits.

Although Venus and the Sun are not great friends, Mars and Venus get along quite well. So, it's a neutral relationship between the planets, which means the natives will have fairly smooth sailing in terms of the house matters where it's placed. For example, in Magha 2nd Pada in the 2nd house, the natives will be born into a very prestigious family that is well respected in their social circle. They will have a good source of income and will be well supported by the family. The natives will have a charming face and an appealing personality. They will either have a government job, or their mum or dad will be working as a government official. They will be very family oriented and motivated by the desire to sustain the prestige and wellbeing of the family, to accumulate wealth and resources and will be honest and righteous in their dealings.

Since Leo and Taurus are both fixed signs, natives born in this Pada will be very set in their habits; they will be very organised and cannot work in a chaotic environment. They need to plan ahead and do things in their own habitual pattern in order to be productive and efficient.

They will also be stubborn about their beliefs, principles or habits. When they have made up their mind about doing something, they will go ahead with dogged determination and a fixed focus. It also shows that no amount of advice can convince them otherwise, and challenges cannot deter them - they will go ahead and do it anyway. All the choice that others have is to agree with them or follow them. If they disagree, they will do what they have to do - without telling them. In other words, they don't follow others, but family, friends or people have to follow them. Determined focus and endurance a needed qualities for success in any field, and they have both these qualities in abundance.

The earthy sign of Taurus also ensures a stable life routine, a steady job and a smooth flow of income and resources. There may be struggles in the early part of life, but after their middle years, they will be well settled and comfortable and will enjoy a good, respectable position in their job, family and society.

Careers

Managers, leaders, businessmen, film directors, actors, artists, fashion designers, government officials, politicians, IT professionals, graphic designers, architects, interior designers, florists, property dealers, financial advisors, bank managers, landlords, working from home, car dealers, taxi drivers, engineers and doctors.

Pada 3

6.40 - 10 deg Leo, Navamsha - Gemini (Lord - Mercury)

Rashi Lord - Sun and Nakshatra Lord- Ketu

In the 3rd Pada, navamsa is placed in Gemini, which gives the influence of the Sun, Ketu and Mercury. Since the Sun and Mercury get along well together, natives will be intelligent, confident, friendly and popular. For example, in Magha Pada 3, in the 3rd house, with no other planets sitting there, the natives will get along well with everyone. They are likely to have a past life connection with their siblings. Their younger sibling will be in a good, respectable position in a government job, or they will get a good job because of their sibling's influence. They will be very talented and enterprising. They can become popular or famous for a certain skill they have. They will have excellent communication skills and can become superb writers, speakers, IT professionals, craftsmen, artists, or designers.

They will be generous and extravagant with both words- giving compliments and money-giving gifts. They thrive on appreciation and have a very sensitive ego. They can easily be hurt if ignored and easily be won by praise or admiration. They will often deny their superiority complex and try to hide their exaggerated need for respect. They may not be outright bossy or an egotistical show-off, but they are unassumingly the master and protector of their den and their pride. The proud, generous and honest lion-like quality can be unmistakably recognised.

They will be curious about everything and impatient to know it all now. They don't lack confidence but lack patience. If they can train their active and restless minds to be more tolerant, they can achieve a lot in life. The wild and raw energy, when channelled properly, can become a great blessing and a sure recipe for success. They can become great actors, politicians, spokespersons, managers and leaders.

Leo and Gemini are both masculine signs, which shows that natives will be very structural and logical in their approach. They are more go getters, like being actively involved and being out and about. Being with the family, meeting friends, socialising and exchanging ideas gives them the greatest joy. They are very good story tellers and natural performers, that's why they become very popular in their family and friends circles.

The air of Gemini fans the fire of Leo into action. This makes them very passionately involved in everything they do, especially in creative projects. Their intelligence and unique ideas can make them reach the top of their profession. They are very good at articulation and putting their point forward, which makes them excellent diplomats and politicians.

Leo, being a fixed sign, grants stability and stubborn determination, which ensures success in the long run. The navamsa of Gemini shows that with age and experience, they will learn to diplomatically adjust and adapt well to different kinds of people and different situations as needed. The intelligence and the brilliance of the Sun help them to see things clearly and make the right decisions in life. Ketu however, will make them feel detached towards all they eventually achieve.

Careers

Actors, writers, film directors, singers, musicians, fashion designers, managers, politicians, diplomats, leaders, astrologers, IT professionals, blog writers, YouTube talkers, activists on social media, doctors, engineers, scientists, bankers, financial advisors, accountants, businessmen, lawyers, government officials, property dealers, car dealers, trip advisors, holiday planners, resort and restaurant owners or workers, hotel and motel managers, tourist planners and guides.

Pada 4

10 - 13.20 deg Leo, Navamsha - Cancer (Lord - Moon)

Rashi Lord - Sun and Nakshatra Lord- Ketu

In the 4th Pada, the navamsha lies in Cancer, and the qualities of the Sun, Ketu and Moon will be seen. The sun and moon are friends because the moon is receptive to the sun's light. In this Pada, the natives will be more emotional, kind and generous. The intelligence and confidence of the Sun and the empathy and imagination of the Moon are a wonderful combination of idealistic and humanistic qualities. Their maternal instinct will be strong, and they will find great fulfilment in caring for their loved ones and keeping them safe and protected. The best of both the luminaries grant the excellent attributes and needed ingredients for a comfortable and successful life. The fiery passion and dramatic emotions make them very sensitive about everything. Even a suggestion or a gesture can offend them or please them because they think and feel things from a deeper perspective.

However the practical realities of life are harsher than the idealistic world, and with time, Ketu makes them disillusioned and detached from the false and hypocritical lifestyles of people in general. For example, the 4th Pada of Magha is in the 7th house, with no other planets sitting there. The natives will have a past life connection with their spouse, he or she could be one of their ancestors re-incarnated. The Sun, Moon and Ketu dasha and transits will bring significant changes in their life. They might meet their spouse or get married during that time period. Their spouse will be very emotional, idealistic and intelligent. The natives will find great fulfilment and joy in helping others, protecting them and guiding them. They will be generous with their time, effort and money whenever and wherever genuine help is needed.

Turning dreams into reality will not be impossible, but not easy going either. It will need sensitive awareness and care to blend the emotional waters of cancer with the fiery passion of Leo. They will have to learn to make adjustments, let go of the possessive reflexes, and recognise their occasional moody outbursts. Suppose they learn to focus and develop on their excellent qualities of creativity, intelligence, honesty and generosity. In that case, they can confidently pave their way to a joyous, comfortable and successful life. They don't have to crush their sensitivities but recognise and acknowledge them so that they can positively channel their creative potential, which can enhance their wellbeing.

For example, spending time creating something new and innovative will be a wonderful outlet for their inner brilliance. The influence of the Sun and moon will make them shine and be recognised in their job, businesses, family, or friends circle.

Sun, as the Lord of Leo, gives the feeling of superiority, and expects an easy recognition and appreciation by family, friends and society at large. This quality can either make the natives very loud and attention-seeking or very quiet and inward-focused if the sun has a low ashtakavarga score. This can also make them doubt their talent or lack confidence. They might not get enough opportunities to express their full potential, but even the shy lions do not lose their quality of being extraordinary.

The Cancerian crab will make them grab and hold onto relationships and things, and Leo's lion will roar in defence if he or she senses any trespassers. The masculinity of Leo and the femininity of cancer give them a good balance of being able to express their artistic and imaginative abilities with confidence and grandeur. Leo is a fixed sign, and Cancer is a cardinal sign, which makes them obstinate and stubborn about leading the way, and they tend to be rather bossy. Either things get done their way, or they will walk out of the project and refuse to participate.

At their best, they can be generous, giving, honest, sincere, supportive, protective and caring. At their worst, they can be bossy, overbearing, impatient and demanding. The solar, lunar effect is not an easy one to handle. They have to tread the path of life with awareness, taking care not to hurt others' feelings in an ambitious rush to take their seat on the throne. The king and queen have their majestic presence at the top of the hierarchy. This also renders them with the huge responsibility of looking after their subjects well. To stay at an altar or a pedestal, firstly, one has to earn it and then be constantly vigilant because inevitably, there is always competition for the top position.

A lion is not afraid of challenges. In fact, fighting it out and winning gives him or her the confidence and confirmation that he or she is the ruler. They are not good losers, and 2 lions cannot stay in the same den. Sun, being the Lord of the day, and the moon, ruler of the night, both are masters of their domain.

The solar and lunar qualities give the natives the clarity of purpose and sensitivity to emotions. They can charm others with their charismatic personality, and nonchalant talk, or can unintentionally wound others with their sunny aloofness or lunar moodiness.

The sun is the life-giver, and the moon is the nourisher of life. Both are equally important and equally needed for initiating and sustaining life on Earth. Similarly, those who are born in this Pada have the talent to create things and sustain them with their intelligence and clarity. The sun shows the path, the moon cools the heat of ruthless ambition, and ketu detaches from the endless pursuit of desires. During the sun, ketu or moon dasha, this effect will be more prominent.

Careers-

Actors, film directors, artists, singers, writers, poets, IT graphic designers, government job, politicians, philanthropists, psychologists, astrologers, spiritual mediums, managers, leaders, businessmen, government employees, cooks, travel guides, doctors, nurses, scientists, self-employed and working from home.

The effect of planets

Magha - Leo	Planets that get affected
Most Benefic - Yoga karka Removes the effect of Mangal dosha.	Mars
Functional Benefic - give good results during their dasha.	Sun
Functional Malefic - can give problems during their dasha.	Moon, Rahu and Ketu
Functional Neutral	Mercury, Jupiter and Saturn
Kendra Adi Pati Dosha - can be malefic	Venus

Magha Ascendant

Those who are born with Magha Ascendent, or moon in Magha, will prominently exhibit these personality attributes. Since the sign Lord is Sun and the nakshatra Lord is Ketu, they have a full face, with high cheekbones and full lips. Their eyes will have a deep, enchanting beauty because Ketu gives a deep mysterious look to the black or dark coloured pupils. They will have large, sleepy, protruding eyes with thicker eyelids. Ketu gives the face an oblong look because of a bigger, longer or pointy chin, and their nose will have a rounded nostril space. They tend to have dark-coloured hair ranging from black to red or brown; the effect of sun and ketu makes their hairline recede with age, and they tend to become bald in the later years.

Like the radiance of the sun, their presence in a room can never be missed. When in public, they are friendly and outspoken. Inwardly, they are spiritually inclined, the effect of the sun makes them confident and generous, but ketu makes them elusive and detached. Even when no planets are sitting in Magha, in the 1st house, they will have a very strong personality. In Sanskrit, Magha means - a gift, reward, or bounty, which shows that they are generous givers. They will have a good physique, charismatic looks and an air of regality about them that cannot be ignored.

Most probably they might be one of the ancestors being born again into the same family. They will have a strong desire to carry on their family legacy, business or job, for what was left undone in a previous life, they want to accomplish it in this lifetime. The resources will become available, and the situations will be conducive for them to pursue their desire when the time is right and ripe, during their sun or ketu mahadasha, antardasha and transits.

The symbol of Magha is a throne. This shows that they strive to sit on a throne, are ambitious to attain the highest honours, and have a respectable position in society. Whether it's within the family, in their friends' circle, or in their job, they will have a favourite chair on which they sit and feel that this is where they belong. Just as a king sits on his throne and holds his council, they will be most productive and efficient when they do their job sitting in that chair. Whether it's talking, instructing, writing, planning, or IT skills, they can perform very well when sitting in their special seat because they are totally relaxed in their zone of authority and kingship.

Ketu, the Lord of Magha, sitting in the house of the Sun, gives them detachment from people in general. Just as the king talks to his close confidantes, who further administer his instructions, they prefer to keep to themselves and do what is needed. For public appearances, they present themselves well in a regal and kingly way. Therefore you will see a Magha always well dressed, smart and proper. There are the loud, bashful and flamboyant ones, and the shy and quiet ones - both types of Magha natives have an aura of dignity around them which is unmistakable.

Even if the king is going through difficult times, his sense of dignity and prestige will not let it become obvious to anyone else. Similarly, in any kind of hardship, a Magha will maintain his or her self-respect and will not ask for help but will manage with whatever resources he or she has.

The deity of Magha is the ancestors. This shows a strong ancestral bond. They may not be consciously aware of this, but in one way or another other, they will continue the legacy. It may be through business, a job or a skill that has been the family's tradition. For example, if the Lord of Magha - Ketu is sitting in the 2nd house and the Lord of Leo - Sun is placed in the 10th house, most likely the native is his own ancestor born again in the same family. He or she will move away from his or her parent's home at a young age and will rise and shine in his or her career during the sun dasha because the Sun gets directional strength in the 10th house. The native will have a respectable top executive post in his or her company or will be a highly influential government official. His or her public image will be such that he or she will be seen as a leader or a king in his field.

The nakshatra Lord is Ketu, their desire to leave the body and they have the power to renounce - all these symbolic factors will make them feel very detached, especially during the ketu dasha.

Although the position of responsibility, respect and status comes easy to them, within themselves they have an uncanny aloofness or detachment from all the worldly pursuits. At some point in their life, they will sense the illusory nature of chasing materialistic goals.

Magha has a very fiery energy, and it's in the fixed sign of Leo. This makes the natives passionate, motivated and inspired to follow their dreams with determination. They are very organised and like to plan ahead, which helps them to work towards their goals steadily. There are 2 special points in Magha where excellent results are seen - one is the Yoga Tara point at 6 degrees in the 1st Pada, and the other is the Amrit Nadi point placed in the 4th Pada at 12 degrees. 0 - 1 degrees of Leo falls in the gandanta zone, which can bring challenges.

All nakshatras placed in Leo represent the heart because just as the sun is the giver of life, the heart is a vital organ that keeps the body alive. Life starts with the rhythmic beat of the heart-right from the womb and ends when the heart stops beating at the time of death.

The quality of Magha is fierce, like the lion in the wild, and it's in the masculine sign of Leo, which makes the natives active go-getters and are not the type who will passively wait for opportunities to come to them but will actively chase their desired goals. Magha has a fierce, wild and raw energy, which helps them to chase goals actively. They are very enterprising and excellent at creating opportunities for themselves and for others. Their actions are motivated by the desire to get honour and prestige, and they like to do so in an honest and righteous way.

Sun in Magha

The sun feels very comfortable in Magha because it's the mulatrikona sign, therefore it gives good results. There will also be an influence on Ketu's quality of detachment. The double influence of the sun helps them spread their splendid sunny sunshine wherever they are, and their presence can never be ignored. For example, Sun in Magha in the 11th house, will bring tremendous gains, success, rise of position, prestige and awards through a large organisation during the dasha of Sun.

They will be very generous, proud and honest in their dealings. For them, honour and respect hold more worth than money. There are always positive and negative effects of each nakshatra energy, depending on the situations we face, the kind of people we attract into our lives and most importantly how we respond or react to them.

At their best, they are most charming, loving, affectionate, helpful, kind and generous, and at their worst, they can be self-centred, bossy, impatient, like spoiled and pampered kings who are constantly telling you what to do and how to do it. They are fiercely protective of their family clan, and their sincerity and devotion are unsurpassed. Their friendship goes beyond the ordinary ease and convenience. They truly are the most enduring friends.

They are capable of heroic sacrifice. For them, friendship and relationships work on sacred trust a persistent devotion. This honesty is their inherent quality, and they expect the same kind of sincerity from the one they love. For this reason, they can come across as snobbish and domineering. They have the potential for extreme loyalty and nobility in human relationships.

The gamekeepers who have observed the lions closely have seen that Lions and Lionesses, can walk thousands of miles to reunite with their pride. They are capable of risking great danger and enduring extreme hardship to reach the group they had been separated from. Similarly, Magha natives can make extreme sacrifices, if needed, for their loved ones, such as their level of sincerity and loyalty. The Sun Ketu effect and their power to renounce makes this quality of abandonment manifest very strongly in Magha natives. To reach their desired goal or for their loved ones, they can bear the unbearable and truly emerge as heroes.

However, if the Sun is weak and has a low shadbala score or is in a sleeping state because of low degrees, it will not be able to display courage. During challenging times, they can become arrogant irritable and have a sense of false pride. They will roar an angry warning to anyone who threatens to infringe upon their royal right to be respected or obeyed.

Lions like to laze under a shady tree to escape the afternoon heat and are more active in the coolness of the night. Similarly, Maghas like to relax in the middle of the day and prefer to work at night. When the sun is placed in Magha, it accentuates the effect of the heat, so they need to take care to keep their system cool with a pitta-pacifying diet and lifestyle.

Especially if Sun in Magha is in the 1st house, their pitta constitution will naturally make them love spicy food and a non-vegetarian diet, but they should avoid having it. All sweet and bitter-tasting fruits and vegetables are good for them because they pacify the high Pitta. During midday, when the sun is at its maximum heat they should avoid intense activity and should exercise only in the early mornings or late evenings.

Respect and honour are the name of the game for them to win over someone, or if they have to be won over, this is the currency of their happiness and contentment. " *The privilege of a lifetime is to become who you truly are.*" - *Carl Jung*

Moon in Magha

When the moon is placed in Magha, it will share the qualities of The Sun and Ketu. The receptivity of the moon, the confidence of the sun and the detachment of Ketu make the natives emotionally inclined and sensitive. The emotional and intuitive moon, sitting in the fiery, dramatic, generous and fun-loving sign of Leo, makes the Maghas passionate, expressive, creative, warm, kind and innately confident.

The waters of the moon, sitting in the fiery presence of the sun in Leo, can either gently warm the water or burn it into evaporation. This will depend on how strong the moon is - a good shadbala score of over 400 points will make the moon strong. This means the natives will be warm hearted, kind, generous, and can deal with difficult situations with sympathy and understanding. They can become excellent actors because of their creative, emotional expression and keen sense of art and drama. For example, the moon in Magha in the 10th house will have a career in a creative field of design, art, drama, theatre or films, and they get to enjoy the throne of fame and honour.

However, if the moon is weak because of the low shadbala score, it can be ultra-sensitive. Their ego would get hurt easily if they were ignored. If they are in a pleasant and conducive environment, they will be overly joyful and confident. But a challenging situation can make them lose their confidence or make them utterly miserable. They can become too bashful or show off, which helps them defend their sense of pride.

Magha is placed in the fixed sign of Leo, which makes them stubborn and set in their habits. When the moon sits here, the warmth of their emotions is seen in all their actions. The influence of Ketu, will separate them from their mother, or a motherly figure, during the Ketu dasha. It could be mum, dad or any other person whom they are attached to or look up to.

The fluctuating influence of the moon brings in a spectrum of colourful emotions - of joy and sorrow - laughter, fun, sunshine, cloudy, rain, gloom, dark and dismal. A strong and honest expression of all these and many more feelings is the true nature of Magha. Maghas who have a waxing moon will be very open and expressive about their feelings, but those who have the waning moon in their birth chart will express these quietly through writing or another form of art, like dance or drama.

Suppose life demands a sacrifice, where they have to make a choice between the materialistic comforts and the honour of the family. In that case, they will willingly forgo comforts to keep up their own and their family's dignity. The empathy and imagination of the moon, combined with the creativity and confidence of the sun, can help them achieve and realise their grand dreams. Their unerring instincts, tenacity of purpose, and single-minded determination can successfully guide them to manifest their glorious plans into reality.

"Do not compare, do not measure. No other way is like yours. All other ways deceive and tempt you. You must fulfil the way that is in you." - Carl Jung

Magha the poet

Magha, the generous one, gives not for selfish gains,

In giving, the bounty of joy he obtains.

The ancestral crown and the Game of Thrones,

Domain of the Lion's pride and the honour he owns.

To renounce the known and embrace the unknown,

Brave are the ones, who venture the path forlorn.

To reach the peak of K2, a heroic climb for sure,

Tougher than the climb of Everest, they say so.

Who else but the brave Magha, would have the resolute,

For their dauntless efforts, we all salute.

The Lion's share of life, a desirous song they sing,

For their love of giving graciously, befitting a king.

The fire that warms and protects the family,

Can become the scorching heat that burns the enemy,

A true friend, a fierce protector, an honest partner,

Spreads its shine of splendid rays ever after.

True to his word, upholds the honour,

A testing time it is, to turn the corner,

The mortal body, with immortal potential,

For those who realise the truth essential,

Through loyal bravery, earned the medals of nobility,

Deserve admiration, a heroic ability.

Remedies

The problems can manifest in areas of - loss of position, job or honour, during the Ketu dasha. These remedial measures will help to elevate the negative effects of any malefic influence of Mars, Saturn, Rahu or Ketu in Magha. Specific remedies can be done when the Moon is transiting over the natal Ketu in the birth chart.

- <u>Das Maha Vidya</u> - as described earlier.

- The best remedy is to do yogic and spiritual practices that can help to connect to the divine within.

- To respect the elders in the family and in the community.

- Wear dark colours like red, yellow, orange and gold.

- To honour the ancestors by doing shradh Pooja in the month of Magha (Middle of January to mid-February). It's called the pitru paksha (waning moon), which is done on the 13th lunar day and on the new moon day (Amavasya). It is better to ask the temple priest to conduct this Pooja.

- To worship Devi Kali and Lord Shiva.

- To chant the mantra - *"Om Gham Magha nakshatra ye Namah."* 108 times.

Example

Moon in Magha

Usha Uttap - Indian Playback singer

Born on 7th November 1947 at 12 pm in Mumbai (approximate time of birth).

Usha Uthup is an Indian pop, film, jazz, and playback singer who has sung songs in many languages since the 1960s. She studied at St. Agnes High School, Byculla. She had a very deep boyish voice, so her music teacher did not take her as a singer in the chorus but told her to play the clappers in the orchestra because she had a good sense of rhythm. She did not get any formal training in singing but grew up in an atmosphere of music. Her parents used to listen to a wide range from Western classical to Hindustani and Carnatic classical music. She used to enjoy listening to Radio Ceylon and would sing along to many songs, which gave her a good awareness of her singing talent.

Her friend Jamila, who was her next-door neighbour, encouraged her to learn Hindi and practise singing in Indian classical music. The fusion of English and Hindi language helped her to pioneer her unique brand of Indian pop in the 1970s. She is married to Jani Chacko Uthup, and they have a daughter and a son. She is currently settled in Kolkata, India.

Usha Uthup started her music career in Chennai in 1969, singing in a small nightclub called 9 Gems in the basement of a theatre complex. Her performance was so well received that the owner of the nightclub asked her to stay on for a week. After her first nightclub gig, she began singing in Calcutta at other nightclubs. She met her future husband, Uthup, in Trincas nightclub. Afterwards, she started singing at the Oberoi hotels, where Dev Anand heard her sing and asked her to sing for his film. Later, she sang many English and Hindi songs in Indian films.

She also spent some time in London during the early days of her singing career and visited Nairobi as part of an Indian festival. She was so popular that she was invited to stay on. Her talent of being able to pick up languages easily and singing in their local Swahili language made her very popular in Nairobi. The then President of Kenya, Jomo Kenyatta, was so thrilled with her singing that he made her an Honorary Citizen of Kenya. She sang the famous song "Malaika" ('Angel') with Fadhili Williams who was the original singer. Later, she produced a record, "Live in Nairobi", with a local band, Fellini 5. She is a stage performer and has given performances all over the world. And is known for her lively stage presence. She has been honoured with several awards over the years. Usha has received a lot of recognition for having a unique husky voice.

She has sung in 16 Indian languages and 9 foreign languages, including English, German, French, Swahili and others. Her husky voice is her trademark. She says, *"Singing has no barriers of cast, colour, creed. The most important thing is to sing in the language of the people."* When asked about her talent for singing comfortably in so many languages. Does she know them all? She replies *"Language is one of my strongest points. I love it and take pains to learn a new one. I know 14 Indian and 7 foreign languages but am not very fluent in all."*

Analysis

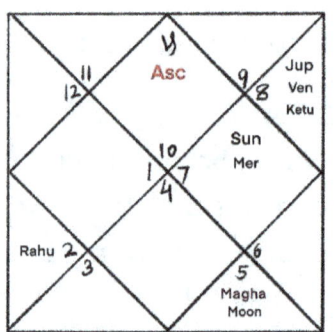

Usha has her <u>Moon in Magha Pada 4 in the 8th house of Leo.</u> The Lord of Leo is the Sun, and the Sun (in Vishakha) is sitting with Mercury (in Swati) in the 10th house of Libra.

Sun and Mercury are her strongest planets, having a high Shabala score of 450, which brought her fame and recognition from 1969 onwards after she gave her first public performance. She was running her <u>Sun-Mars Rahu</u> dasha during that time.

Which continued during the 1980s when she was running her <u>Moon maha dasha</u> from 1974 to 1984. When benefic planets are placed 4th from the moon, it forms an auspicious Gaj Keshari Yoga, which makes the person popular, he or she is polite and generous, and a leader or pioneer in his or her field, and it grants the comfort of vehicles. Usha has Jupiter, Venus and Ketu placed in the 11th house of Scorpio, which is 4th from the 8th house of Leo, where the Moon is placed in Magha.

The 11th house gives easy gains, with 2 benefits sitting there. Jupiter and Venus are conjunct in Anuradha, and Ketu is in Vishakha. The avastha (state) of Ketu is very old and awake.

Anuradha is the nakshatra of devotion, and Vishakha has an ugra (upward-moving) energy. This makes her very dedicated to her talent, but she also missed opportunities during the Sun Ketu Ketu dasha in 1973.

Although she did not originally get to sing these film songs (Mehebooba Mehabooba and Dum Maro Dum), when she sang these songs later in her public performances, they became very popular because her voice and style of singing were so in sync with the feeling of the song.

Usha is a music legend who bridges the West and the East. She is also lovingly called didi (elder sister) by many of her fans because of her caring nature. She is famous for her graceful style of dressing up in a silk saree, wearing matching bangles and having a round bindi on her forehead. When asked about her famous look, she says she loves that as much as she loves music. *"Wearing sarees and jasmine flowers on the hair has been part of our family tradition, and it will never change."* It's a very Magha-like statement and highlights the fixed quality of Leo in a graceful way.

Since her Moon in Magha is in the 8th house of occult, which directly aspects the 2nd house of speech. She started her career as a nightclub singer and went on to become the reigning queen, singing pop, jazzy spiritual, mystical and folk songs in many languages. She also has a very dignified and regal style of dressing up, which is a very Leo-like quality. Moreover, the 8th house is the house of hidden treasures, spirituality and mysticism. She has not been heavily involved in the mainstream singing of Hindi cinema but has become famous for her dance-beat rhythmic songs that are mostly sung in discos and nightclubs. When asked about what she really wishes to do in her life? She put it very simply, *"Laugh till I cry and sing till I die."*

On her unique style of singing, She says, *"I am happy that I started as a nightclub singer because, in live singing, there is no second take. If you have only one take you better be good and perfect. However, one hit Bollywood song got me 325 shows, but the magic of the stage is something totally different."*

Her first performance was at 'Trinca's nightclub,' on 1st October 1969 - She was running her Sun-Mars Rahu dasha. In her birth chart, the Sun (in Vishakha) is sitting with Mercury (in Swati) in the 10th house of Libra, which signifies a career. Rahu (in Kritika) is in the 5th house of Taurus, which signifies entertainment. Additionally, on this day, the Moon and Ascendant were also transiting over her 5th house of entertainment.

Rahu and Moon were transiting over her birth Rahu placement, which amplified the effect and catapulted her into a busy and successful phase of her singing career.

She says, *"I am a compulsive optimist and never think of the bad side at all. Trincas has changed the misconception among people about a bar, and they began expecting wonderful clean entertainment."*

11
Purva Phalguni

Om cham Purva Phalguni nakshatraye namah

Zodiac degrees	13.20 - 26.40 deg Leo
Ruling planet	Leo - Sun and Purva Phalgni - Venus
Sanskrit name	Purva means previous, former red one, or rising in the east, Phala means fruit, and guna means quality.
Astronomical name	The 2 bright stars are seen in the back of the Leo constellation.
Symbol	Leo - Lion and Purva Phalguni - hammock
Element	Fire
Deity	Bhaga
Quality	Ugrasthira -fierce and fixed.
Shakti	Prajna Shakti - to unite and procreate
Cast	Brahmin- priest
Gender	Male
Motivation	Dharma - righteousness
Triguna	Tamas
Tridosha	Pitta
Body parts	Left hand, lips, and sexual organs.
Direction	East, southeast
Month	1st half of Phalguni - Late February
Bird	Swan

Sound	mo, ta, tee, too
Tree	Flame of the forest and Plash
Chakras	Manipura - Sun and Swadhisthana - Venus
Das Maha Vidya	Devi Matangi - Sun and Devi Kamala - Venus

Special degrees -

Yoga Tara	17.30 deg Leo It's a point where the planet will show the strongest and sure results during its dasha.
Mulatrikona	4- 20 deg Leo - Mulatrikona of the Sun. When the Sun is placed in these degrees, it will give good results because it feels comfortable in its territory.
Amrit nadi	23.60 - 24 deg Leo Gives good results like the nectar that nourishes.
Pushkar Amsha	Pada 3 Planets sitting here will blossom fully and give good results during their dasha.
Visha nadi	17.46 - 18.40 deg Leo Brings situations which one does not like dealing with.
Vargottama	1st and 2nd Pada. The planets placed here will give a steady foundation and balanced results.

Auspicious and inauspicious table -

Auspicious	Inauspicious
Activities Good for marriage, romance and sexual activity, for doing all jobs related to authority and government, career-related activities, persuading others, using personal charisma, political agendas, diplomatic work, clearing long-standing disputes, relaxation and enjoyment, creative and artistic activities, and developing hobbies, buying a property and dealing with all property related matters.	Activities Not good for activities that require one to be humble or complacent. For starting new projects, intellectual or academic activities and for healing. Illness that starts at this time is hard to overcome.
Days Wednesdays- only when it falls on the 5th or 7th lunar day.	Days Saturdays - only when it falls on the 3rd, 7th, 9th or 11th lunar day.

Compatibility table -

Purva Phalguni	Compatible with
Sexual compatibility Yoni animal	Purva Phalguni - female rat. Compatible with make rat - Magha.
Sign compatibility	Leo - Pada 1 - Aries and Sagittarius.
Nakshatra compatibility	Bharani and Purva Ashadha.
Lunar day compatibility	Trayodashi - 13th Lunar day
Day compatibility	Sunday and Friday
Colour compatibility	Red, orange and all light shades.
Numerological compatibility	1 and 6 are all numbers that add up to make 1 and 6.
Sound compatibility	Sun - all vowels - a, aa, e, ee, u, oo, ey, aye, o, ou, am, ah Venus - palatal sounds - cha, ccha, ja, jha, nga

Sign Lord and nakshatra lord - Sun and Venus - as described earlier.

The influence of the Sun and Venus in Purva Phalguni makes them very creative, intelligent, confident, generous, proud and ambitious. They have a very fine sense of aesthetics and love beauty, elegance and harmony. They are very well-mannered and dignified.

Quality, element, motivation, triguna, tridosha and chakras - as described earlier.

Shakti - Prajnana Shakti - Union and procreation.

Purva Phalguni natives have the inherent quality of bearing fruit. They have the creative talent to produce a masterpiece in art, music, design or any artistic ability. They find fulfilment and feel settled only when they find their spouse and have children. Their special talent lies in their ability to procreate. Especially after they have children their conditions improve, they experience financial gains, and succeed in their endeavours.

Symbolic signification

Leo - Lion- as described earlier and Purva Phalguni - Hammock.

Hammock

Those who have their Ascendent, Sun or Moon in Purva Phalguni like an easy pace of life because a hammock signifies the time to relax. After the exhausting array of continuous responsibility of sitting on the throne and managing people and situations, in Purva Phalguni, the natives want to relax and enjoy the fruits of their hard work.

Mythology -

Deity - Bhaga

Bhaga is the presiding deity of the Purva Phalguni. He is the god of wealth, fortune, money, power and due inheritance and is described as the 'bestower' - the giver of worldly wealth, security and abundance, and the spiritual wealth of devotion. He is said to be the male counterpart of Goddess Lakshmi (the goddess of wealth). Bhanga's wife is called Sidhi (which means to gain mastery), both Bhaga and Sidhi grant the wishes of prosperity, abundance and mastery over a certain field through practice.

He is one of the 12 Adityas, the son of Aditi and Kashyapa. Since he is an Aditya, he represents an aspect of the Sun that has a bright light. Bhaga is usually invoked along with the other Adityas, and is considered in-charge of the month of March.

The word 'bhagya' means destiny, which signifies Bhaga's responsibility to make sure that people receive their share of goods in life. He is also associated with his brother, Aryaman, who gives the inherent wish for a successful marriage. In Rigveda, bhaga is an epithet of both mortals and gods who bestow wealth and prosperity. Bhaga is also described as the god of the morning and is invoked along with Indra, Varuna and Mitra.

Bhaga was blinded -

The story in the Puranas states that Bhaga was blinded by Veerabhadra, whom Lord Shiva had created to avenge the death of his first wife, Sati. Long ago, it so happened that King Daksha arranged a grand yagna but did not invite his son-in-law - Lord Shiva and his daughter Sati because, according to him, Shiva was too uncivilised. Lord Shiva was known to hang around at the cremation grounds, and with ganas, ghosts, goblins and disembodied beings, which did not fit in with the usual norms of the society. Daksha could not understand the strange and mystical ways of Shiva's life, which were too far removed from the so-called civilised way of life.

In spite of Lord Shiva's dissuasion, Sati insisted on going to the celebrations alone. At the yagna, she felt humiliated by Daksha's remarks about Lord Shiva. In her rage, she annihilated herself by jumping into the ritual fire of the yagna. On hearing this, Lord Shiva was extremely upset and sent Veerbhadra to destroy the Yagna. Bhaga was the appointed priest of the yagna, and he was blinded by Veerbhadra. Since then Bhaga is said to distribute power and wealth blindly, which means he seems to give indiscriminately whether one deserves it or not.

Inference

Those who are born with their Ascendant, Sun or Moon in Uttara Phalguni are fortunate and get to enjoy the fruits of their work or effort. Since Bhaga is the deity of prosperity and abundance, they tend to get more than expected, even with little effort. Like Bhaga, they tend to give generously when they have it.

Purva Phalguni padas

13.20 - 26.40 degrees Leo

Padas	Degrees
1	13.20 - 16.40 deg Leo
2	16.40 - 20 deg Leo
3	20- 23.20 deg Leo
4	23.20 - 26.40 deg Leo

Pada 1

13.20 - 16.40 deg Leo, Navamsha- Leo (Lord - Sun)

Rashi Lord - Sun and Nakshatra Lord- Venus

Pada 1 of Purva Phalguni falls in the navamsa of Leo; therefore, it carries the energy of the Sun and Venus. Sun has a double and strong influence in this Pada because it's the Lord of Leo which is vargottama in the navamsha.

Therefore, those who are born with the Ascendant, Sun or Moon in this Pada have a very steady flow of resources, they are fortunate and usually, their life pattern remains the same in their younger and older days.

They are confident, intelligent, creative and have very good leadership skills. They have the ability to inspire and motivate others through their creative and ingenious ideas. For example, in the 1st Pada of Purva Phalguni in the 5th house, even if there are no planets sitting there, the natives will be very talented, will succeed in the field of entertainment and will have many innovative business ideas. If they can overcome their tendency to take it easy or laze around and put in a little effort, they can achieve a great deal. Success can comparatively come easily to them because Bhaga, the ruling deity, grants them an abundance of resources.

They enjoy attention and their weak point lies in easily being flattered. It's not a negative trait on its own but it can lead to losses if combined with the natural inclination of the Purva Phalgunis to relax and take the easy option always. Not putting in enough effort can become their vice or regret in their later years of life. If they can overcome their compulsion of falling for praise and venture into the open field of reality, they can achieve phenomenal success, because they are immensely creative and intelligent.

"You are what you do, not what you say you will do." - Carl Jung.

Careers

Actors, directors, fashion designers, graphic designers, interior designers, landscape designers, farmers, artists, scientists, astrologers, musicians, astronauts, architects, photographers, entrepreneurs, IT designers, doctors, paediatricians, gynaecologists, politicians, diplomats, homemakers, restaurant owners, hotel managers, club owners and club workers.

Pada 2

16.40 - 20 deg Leo, Navamsha - Virgo (Lord - Mercury)

Rashi Lord - Sun and Nakshatra Lord - Venus

The qualities of the Sun, Mercury and Venus will manifest in the 2nd Pada of Purva Phalguni because it falls in the navamsa of Virgo. The natives will have the confidence of the Sun, the communicative skills of Mercury and the grace of Venus. The yogatara is at 17.30 deg Leo; any planets sitting at this degree will give good and strong results during its dasha. For example, Mercury at 17 deg in the 2nd house will give the natives excellent communication skills, and they will have many friends. They will be very fortunate and will have wonderful resources family support, and are well known in their social circle. They will have a very graceful and attractive personality, exquisite taste and a fine sense of aesthetics.

They will love dressing up elegantly and will love gathering information about every subject under the sky. Any work of beauty, creativity and genius attracts their attention. Sun, Mercury or Venus placed here feel very comfortable and therefore give good results during its dasha and transits. For example, Purva Phalguni in the 3rd house will show good communication skills and a lot of interaction with siblings, friends and neighbours. They will find a similar kind of scenario being repeated again, for example, if they had an elderly couple as a neighbour in their first house when they shift to another house once again, they have an elderly couple as their neighbour.

When the Ascendant, Sun or the Moon is in Purva Phalguni, the natives are very intelligent and creative. They are very family-oriented, love spending time with friends and are well-known in their social circle. Since Leo is a fire sign and Virgo is an earth sign, the natives born in this Pada will be passionate and grounded. In their adulthood, they will become more conscious about their duties and work routine and will be honest and righteous in their dealings. Their excellent communication skills help them to smooth out the difficulties with ease. The navamsha in the earthy sign of Virgo also ensures a stable life routine, a steady job and a smooth flow of income and resources. They are usually well-settled, and comfortable and are well-loved and popular in their workplace, family and society.

Careers

Businessmen, managers, accountants, politicians, film directors, actors, artists, fashion designers, government officials, IT professionals, graphic designers, architects, interior designers, florists, property dealers, financial advisors, bank managers, landlords, working from home, homemakers, club owners, club workers, engineers and doctors.

Pada 3

20 - 23.20 deg Leo, Navamsha - Libra (Lord - Venus)

Rashi Lord - Sun and Nakshatra Lord- Venus

In the 3rd Pada, navamsa is placed in Libra, which gives the influence of the Sun and double influence of Venus. The Sun and Venus are said to be enemies because it makes a hot and volatile combination. Moreover, Venus gives the Kendra Adi Pati dosha in Leo, so the placement of Venus in the natal chart and in the Navamsha should be looked at carefully. If Venus is debilitated, it can give relationship problems, and if it's exalted it will give the comforts and convenience of vehicles but can make the native very intolerant, which can create problems. This is more likely to happen during Venus or Sun dasha.

When the Ascendant, Sun or the Moon is in this Pada, the natives will be very intelligent and creative but will be short-tempered. They will not be able to take orders from anyone and will do their best by working independently. Their creativity needs to find expression, which cannot happen if they have to work according to someone else's vision. They are not made to lead the mundane life of a 5 to 9 office job like a clockwork mouse. If it comes to that, they will only do it as a part-time job, so that they have time to develop their favourite hobbies and slowly build it up to make it as a source of income.

Their sensitive ego easily feels trampled if they are not recognised or appreciated because of this, their relationships can be touchy and difficult. As they grow older they will always be trying to strike the right balance in order to create a harmonious vibration between them and their partner. Their short temper becomes another main cause of repeatedly landing them in situations which can break a relationship or a friendship.

For example, in Purva Phalguni Pada 3 in the 6th house, the natives will follow routines but can face opposition from colleagues regarding prestige and respect. They may face financial or health issues during the Sun or Venus dasha. They may get very busy during the dasha or antar dasha of these planets to make up for the financial setback, which can take a toll on their health. Consequently they may not be able to take care of their eating habits and can start neglecting physical exercise, which can lead to chronic fatigue and general weakness. Usually, the most successful time in life is also the most taxing time for the body and mind. In order to sail smoothly through this hectic time period, making time for yoga and meditation helps greatly. It will enhance the working capacity by calming the mind.

The airy Libra fans the fire of Leo and keeps him or her motivated and inspired to carry on various creative projects. Their intelligence and leadership skills easily grant the possibility of success, provided they don't fall into the lazy lion slumber for too long.

Careers

Artists, painters, actors, writers, film directors, singers, musicians, fashion designers, managers, politicians, diplomats, leaders, astrologers, IT professionals, consultants, therapists, blog writers, youtube talkers, activists on social media, doctors, bankers, businessmen, government officials, florists, trip advisors, holiday planners, resort and restaurant owners or workers, hotel and motel managers, tourist planners and guides.

Pada 4

23.20 - 26.40 deg Leo, Navamsha - Scorpio (Lord - Mars)

Rashi Lord - Sun and Nakshatra Lord - Venus

In the 4th Pada, the navamsha lies in Scorpio, and the qualities of the Sun, Venus and Mars will be seen. Sun and Mars make a good team because Mars, the commander, is quite comfortable with taking orders from Sun, the king. Mars becomes the yogakaraka for Leo. Therefore, it gives benefic results during its dasha.

The natives will be mentally strong, determined and deep thinkers. When the exuberant and confident Sun energy combines with the brave Mars energy, it makes a fearless warrior and achiever for whom nothing is impossible. The combination of Sun, Venus and Mars gives a very fiery energy. They will be very passionate and will be the go-getters who cannot sit around and wait for things to happen. They are the ones who can fearlessly activate a sleeping lion or a dormant volcano.

They will be attracted to professions like - armed or police force, stunt man or a woman, athlete, firefighter, or a lifeguard rescuer. Even if they don't work in these fields, they will have a hobby where they offer their time towards any cause that uplifts and helps others. They will not be afraid to stand up against any kind of injustice done in the society. The sheer trust and dedication towards their chosen purpose or goal opens the avenues for them.

Any planet sitting between 23 - 24 deg Leo in Purva Phalguni Pada 4 will give very good results during its dasha because it is the zone of Amrit nadi, which has a very nourishing effect. For example, Mars sitting in Purva Phalguni Pada 4 in the 11th house will give easy gains during the dasha of Mars. If the 11th house is Leo, then Mars becomes the Lord of the 2nd and 7th house, which shows that these gains will come through the family and the spouse, or after marriage, they will benefit in terms of buying a property or becoming the head of a large organisation. They will also have a karmic connection with their elder sibling or a close friend who is older than them, and the natives will feel that they share an uncanny, intuitive and telepathic bond with their older sibling.

However, the fire of the Sun and Mars makes them short-tempered. Although they don't hold a grudge for long, at the spur of the moment, they will surely pierce the opponent with a scorpion sting. They like to and also need to have quiet time in order to reflect, plan and create. It's very important for them to channel their creative energy into positive avenues like having an exercise routine, yoga and meditation, creating a piece of art or music, designing a new product or giving time towards a humanitarian cause. Otherwise, there is a danger of this tremendous potential finding release in anger and aggression.

If they set their mind to it, there is nothing that they cannot achieve. They just have to find a creative channel to harness their energy.

Careers-

Stunt actors, firefighters, life rescue guards, ambulance operators, police officers, army commanders, gym trainers, film directors, philanthropists, psychologists, astrologers, spiritual mediums, managers, leaders, businessmen, government employees, politicians, doctors, surgeons, scientists, engineers, race car drivers, athletes, football and cricket players, self-employed and working from home.

The effect of planets

Purva Phalguni - Leo	Planets that get affected
Most Benefic - Yoga karka Removes the effect of Mangal dosha.	Mars
Functional Benefic - give good results during their dasha.	Sun
Functional Malefic - can give problems during their dasha.	Moon, Rahu and Ketu
Functional Neutral	Mercury, Jupiter and Saturn
Kendra Adi Pati Dosha - can be malefic	Venus

Purva Phalguni Ascendant

Those who are born with their Ascendent in Purva Phalguni, (even if there are no planets placed in the ascendant), will have very prominent Sun-like qualities. It is so because this nakshatra is placed in the sign of Leo. They will be very intelligent, generous, creative, passionate and independent. The fiery nature of the Sun also makes them very ambitious, and their way of life can become an inspiration or motivation for others.

The special ability and power of Purva Phalguni is to procreate, plus Venus, the planet of beauty and harmony, being the nakshatra Lord, and Bhaga, the deity who is the giver of abundance, makes the natives triply more fortunate, creative and talented. The only danger is their laxity or laziness of not putting in enough effort, which can become the reason for not making it big or being successful. The astrological prediction shows a great possibility of success.

The blessings of the Deity Bhaga give them the fortune of getting to enjoy the fruit of their actions. If they work towards a certain goal, they will surely get the results and succeed in their efforts. The energy of Vishnu also gives the Purva Phalgunis an added ability and advantage to have a steady flow of resources.

The laziness stems from the symbol of a hammock, which shows their love of relaxation. They don't like putting in too much effort or going out of their comfortable den. This also shows their need to relax well before jumping into any activity or after doing any intense physical or mental activity. Since Purva Phalguni is placed in Leo, the natives are quite fixed and stubborn about their viewpoint. They like to do things in a structured way by planning them out, yet their creative intelligence allows them a lot of leeway to explore different aspects of life. For example, they will love to create new things and will have many innovative ideas but will need to plan them out before they can implement them.

Sun in Purva Phalguni

Sun and Venus are said to be anaemic towards each other, but being in the sign of Leo, the Sun feels very comfortable in Purva Phalguni; therefore, it gives good results. The presence of the Sun can never be ignored because of its brilliance, originality and creativity. For example, the Sun in Purva Phalguni in the 10th house will bring success and a rise in position and prestige during the dasha of the Sun.

When the Sun and Venus come together, their heat energy becomes explosive. This is because the Sun is the source of heat for all life, and Venus is the hottest planet because it's heat gets trapped under the acid clouds of its atmosphere.

So the cumulative effect makes the natives short-tempered, and they are more prone to pitta imbalance, which can cause skin rashes and blood pressure on the physical level and impatience, quick temperament, irritability and intolerance on the emotional level. So they have to consciously develop a sense of peace and calm their irritable nerves by doing some physical workout or listening to calming music.

For one to be successful, one has to have drive, ambition, intelligence and creativity. They have plenty and also have the talent of rubbing this enthusiasm on others. For example, Sun in Purva Phalguni, in the 4th house, will have a very ambitious and creative mum or a mother-like figure who will guide them to success. Their home atmosphere will be very dignified and artistic, or wherever they choose to settle and make their home, they will decorate it in such a way that it exudes the air of creativity.

They will be motivated by the desire to unite and create and will feel a strong need to marry, have children and settle down as a loving, happy family. They are very generous with both their gifts and words of praise, and they expect the same from others.

Appreciation is the food they thrive on, and lack of it can demotivate them. If they are not properly respected or admired, or they have been ignored, or their pride has been hurt, it can make them wear a mask of icy sarcasm, arrogance, willfulness, boredom or cool disinterest to hide their pain. Since the Sun rules the heart and digestion, over time, emotional pain can lead to chronic problems in the heart or the stomach.

Simple incidents can trigger an emotional impasse for them. For instance, forgetting to complement or carelessly spoken words of disregard can brew up a storm of harsh words. The only way out is, with experience, if they begin to realise that each individual has his or her unique way of dealing with situations, and should give them the leeway to express themselves freely. We cannot enforce our way of thinking on the other. Even though it may be the right way of doing things, each one learns from his or her own mistakes. The best we can do is to develop a sense of empathy within ourselves and learn to find goodness even in the worst of situations.

Purva Phalgunis with Sun are good motivators for others but may sometimes overlook their own shortcoming of imposing themselves on others. Just a little awareness of finding the good quality in others and appreciating it, can easily resolve and even prevent many nasty situations.

They are generally lucky and tend to be the leaders in their family, friends circle, community, nation or globally, depending on the strength of the shadbala score and the avastha (state) of the Sun. For example, if Sun has a Shabala score of more than 400, it is strong and will give good results during its dasha. However, if the avastha of the Sun is old (vridha) or dreaming (swapna), it will reduce its capacity to give results in full vigour and potential, and it will also lose the ability to do much harm because of its old and dreamy state.

"No one succeeds without effort... Those who succeed owe their success to perseverance."

— *Ramana Maharshi*

Moon in Purva Phalguni

When the moon is placed in Purva Phalguni, it will share the qualities of the Sun and Venus. The receptivity of the moon, the confidence of the sun and the refinement of Venus make the natives very creative, intelligent and imaginative. The empathy of the emotional moon, the passion of the fiery Sun and the artistic beauty of Venus give the natives a very attractive, charming, appealing and pleasing personality.

Moon is friendly with all, it brings in the imaginative, emotional and intuitive quality into the sign and nakshatra it sits in. For example, the Moon in Purva Phalguni in the 12th house will make the natives spend a lot of time on their own. They will need the 'alone time' to bring out their creativity. Life will bring them into situations where they feel isolated, but they will also prefer to keep to themselves and spend time doing something creative rather than wasting time socialising. They will like to spend time in the comfort of their bedroom. They will most likely travel away from home to a foreign country for a job and settlement, which can happen during the Moon, Sun or Venus dasha.

If Moon in Purva Phalguni is placed in the 11th house, it will be associated with a large group or organisation and will be known by many people and have a wide circle of friends. Their elder sibling or a friend will be instrumental in helping them get a job in a big, reputable company, or they might start their own business company.

An emotional and watery moon sitting in Leo will feel rather hot in the presence of the fiery Sun, and the added influence of equally active and hot Venus can make the moon feel uncomfortable in the sense that the natives will be very sensitive and edgy about what people say or don't say to them. Their emotions will quite often make them feel the roller coaster effect when others don't seem to understand or respond to their artistic and creative streak. Their actions and thoughts can seem weird or crazy to those around them, but following their heart's desire and going with the flow, being spontaneous, helps to keep them in balance because their creativity needs an outlet.

They can make great poets, artists, actors, film directors, fiction writers, and designers and will do very well in all creative fields. However they will be able to best express their creativity if they connect to something emotionally. For example, those who have their moon in Purva Phalguni can make a wonderful documentary or a film about the people or the culture where they spent their childhood.

Wherever the moon is placed, it shows the psychological makeup of the person and how one will deal with situations. Moon in Purva Phalguni makes one very generous, caring and protective towards their family, but they will also be authoritative and will expect respect and appreciation in return. They will find the greatest fulfilment in providing for the family and having a comfortable, snug home.

The poetry of Purva Phalguni

Purva Phalguni - the previous karma comes to fruitify,

Time now to enjoy the results and lay by

To unite, create and procreate,

To live, love, laugh - a bonus of fate.

Through the ravages of time immortal,

The mortal form experiences life, again in total.

Been there, done it all before,

The soul's journey - a yearning for more.

And so the cycle of birth -death - birth,

Continues the dance of creation on earth.

Remedies

- <u>Das Maha Vidya -</u> as described earlier.

- Since Venus is the Lord of Purva Phalguni, the best remedy is to create something with your personal touch, because it will activate the energies of Venus and bring abundance.

- Connect to the energy of Surya Dev (Sun God) by watching sunrise and sunset. This will bring balance and harmonise you with Mother Nature.

- All bright and light colours resonate well with Purva Phalgunis because bright colours represent the Sun and all light colours represent Venus.

- Doing yogic practices, meditation, pranayama and hatha yoga will help to calm the turbulent emotions.

- Chant the mantra - *"Om Cham Purva Phalguni nakshatra ye Namah."* 108 times, on Fridays, this will help to align with the energies of the nakshatra. Which will, in turn, bring harmony and fruitful results.

Example

<u>Moon in Purva Phalguni</u>

<u>Emma Lazarus - An American author, poet and activist for the Jewish community.</u>

Born on 22nd July 1849, New York (estimated time of birth)

Died young at 38 on 19th November 1887

Emma wrote the sonnet "The New Colossus" in 1883. Its lines appear inscribed on a bronze plaque installed in 1903 on the pedestal of the Statue of Liberty.

"Give me your tired, your poor,

Your huddled masses yearning to breathe free, The wretched refuse of your teeming shore. Send these, the homeless, tempest-tossed to me. I lift my lamp beside the golden door!"

Emma was born to Moses Lazarath and Esther. Her dad was a wealthy Jewish merchant, and she was the 4th born of 7 children.

She was educated privately by tutors from an early age and studied American and British literature as well as several languages, including German, French, and Italian. From a very young age, she started penning her thoughts and wrote her first poem when she was just 11 years old.

Sadly, she died at the very young age of 38. She had fallen seriously ill after her second trip to Europe and died 2 months later. The Poems of Emma Lazarus were published after her death.

Analysis

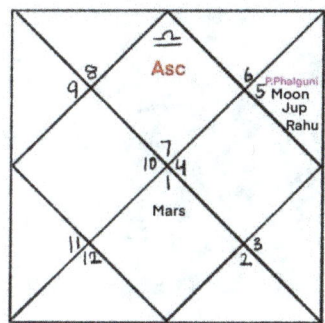 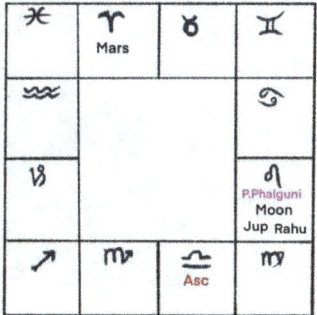

Emma has her Moon in Purva Phalguni Pada 1 in the sign of Leo in the 11th house, along with Jupiter and Rahu. Moon and Rahu, combined with Jupiter, show her intuitiveness, imagination, creativity, literary talent and an idealistic, philosophical, righteous and spiritual approach to life. Rahu amplified the effects of feelings of empathy and idealism.

The 11th house brought her everlasting gains and fame even after her death by getting her poetic words inscribed on the Statue of Liberty, which is the symbol of America's idealism and philosophy.

Sadly, when she died at a young age, on 19th November 1887, she was running her Mars Sun Mercury dasha. Her Mars is placed in the 7th house of Aries in the nakshatra of Bharani. The 7th house is also considered a Maraka house, and the Lord of Bharani is Yamraj. Moreover, for Libra Ascendants, Mars gets a Kendra Adi Pati dosha. On that day, Mars was transiting over her natal moon in Leo in the 11th house, where her Moon Rahu and Jupiter are placed.

12
Uttara Phalguni

Zodiac degrees	26.40 deg Leo - 10 deg Virgo Leo - 1st Pada and Virgo - 2nd, 3rd and 4th padas.
Ruling planet	Leo - Sun and Virgo - Mercury Uttara Phalguni - Sun
Sanskrit name	Uttara means the latter, or rising in the north, Phala means fruit, and guna means quality.
Astronomical name	A very bright star and a faint star are seen at the tail end of the Leo constellation.
Symbol	Leo - Lion, Virgo - Virgin Uttara Phalguni - back legs of the bed.
Element	Fire and Earth
Deity	Aryaman - one of the solar deities, symbolises a close friend or a companion.
Quality	Dwi - dual - Virgo Uttara Phalguni - Ugrasthira -fierce and fixed
Shakti	Chavyani Shakti - prosperity through union.
Cast	Kshatriya - warrior
Gender	Male - Leo and Female - Virgo
Motivation	Dharma - righteousness - Leo Artha - to gather resources - Virgo
Triguna	Tamas - Leo and Satwa - Virgo

Tridosha	Pitta - Leo and Kapha - Virgo
Body parts	Right hand, lips, and sexual organs.
Direction	East, north and south.
Month	March - 2nd half of Phalguni.
Bird	Peacock
Sound	Tay, to, pa, pee
Tree	Payari rose
Chakras	Manipura - Sun and Ajna - Mercury
Das Maha Vidya	Devi Matangi - Sun Devi Tripura Sundari - Mercury

Special degrees -

Yoga Tara	27.45 deg Leo It's a point where the planet will show the strongest and sure results during its dasha.
Pushkar Amsha	1st and 4th Pada Planets sitting here will blossom fully and give good results during their dasha.
Pushkar Bhaga	9 deg Virgo Planets placed here will fruitify results during its dasha, like the blossoming of a flower.
Amrit nadi	6 - 6.53 deg Virgo Gives good results like the nectar that nourishes.
Visha nadi	1 - 1.33 deg Virgo Brings situations which one does not like dealing with.
Vargottama	1st Pada The planets placed here will give a steady foundation and balanced results.

Auspicious and inauspicious table -

Auspicious	Inauspicious
Activities Good for marriage and sexual activity, for starting long-term projects - societies and organisations, doing all government-related jobs, career-related activities, dealing with official or higher authorities, political agendas, diplomatic work, administrative work, paternal activities, fatherly	Activities Not good for ending things, finishing projects, confrontations and arguments and lending money.

responsibilities, buying a property, entering a new house, inauguration ceremonies, taking oaths, making promises, performing rituals, wearing new clothes and jewellery and for giving charity.	
Days **Sundays**- only when it falls on the 1st, 4th, 6th, 7th or 12th lunar day. **Tuesdays** - only when it falls on the 1st, 3rd, 5th, 6th, 7th, 8th, 11th or 13th lunar day. **Fridays** - only when it falls on the 1st, 2nd, 6th, 7th, 11th or 12th lunar day.	**Days** **Thursdays**- only when it falls on the 6th, 8th, 9th, 12th or 13th lunar day. **Saturdays** - only when it falls on the 3rd, 7th, 9th or 11th lunar day.

Compatibility table -

Uttara Phalguni	Compatible with
Sexual compatibility Yoni animal	Uttara Phalguni - Male cow, compatible with Uttara Bhadrapada - female cow.
Sign compatibility	Leo - Pada 1 - Aries and Sagittarius. Virgo - Padas 2, 3 and 4 - Taurus and Capricorn.
Nakshatra compatibility	Kritika and Uttara Ashadha.
Lunar day compatibility	Dwadashi tithi - 12th Lunar day.
Day compatibility	Sunday and Wednesday
Colour compatibility	Red, orange and green.
Numerological compatibility	1 and 5 and all numbers that add up to make 1 and 5.
Sound compatibility	Sun - all vowels - a, aa, e, ee, u, oo, ey, aye, o, ou, am, ah Mercury - lingual sounds - ta, tha, da, dha, na

The Purva and Uttara are always a pair of nakshatras that go together in terms of their qualities, with slight variations in the sign it sits in and the nakshatra lords. Astronomically, both Purva Phalguni and Uttara Phalguni nakshatra belong to the Leo constellation. The stars of Purva are seen towards the east side of it, and the stars of Uttara are seen on the north side of it.

Sign Lord and nakshatra lord - Sun and Mercury - as described earlier.

The 1st Pada of Uttara Phalguni is in Leo, which has a strong influence on the Sun since the lord of Uttara Phalguni is also the Sun. Here, the natives will be very intelligent, creative, confident, honest, generous, proud, and intolerant of bad behaviour.

The 2nd, 3rd and 4th padas are placed in Virgo, where the influence of the Sun and Mercury makes them more grounded, friendly and communicative. Since Virgo is ruled by Mercury, they like analysing things and looking at everything in detail. The mercurian influence makes them more like young, enthusiastic students, learners who imbibe knowledge and learn eagerly from every experience of life. They are very academic and like sticking to their routines and schedules. They feel that there is no time to waste or have unrealistic dreams. It's time to work and get the job done.

Since it's an original 6th house, they have to provide their service to others and, in a way, feel forced to comply with society's rules and restrictions. Over time, they figure out that in serving others, their own needs get taken care of, or to fulfil their own needs, they need to serve others in some way. The energy of Virgo teaches that one must work for his or her money. In a way, they have to shelve their ideas and ideals and focus their attention on immediate routines. They have to keep up with the fierce competition in the business and political world. For them, learning to compete becomes both necessary and mandatory in order to survive in the fast-paced lifestyle.

Quality, element, motivation, triguna, tridosha and chakras - as described earlier.

Shakti - Chavyani Shakti - prosperity through union.

As described in Purva Phalguni, Uttara Phalguni has the same power and energy to unite, which brings prosperity. This shows that whenever they venture into joint projects with their partners, they prosper. They have the special blessing to succeed in doing things in partnership rather than alone. Whatever projects they undertake along with others as a team, they get to enjoy the fruits of it. This also shows that after they get married, they are bound to succeed in their career.

Symbolic signification

Leo - Lion - as described earlier.

Virgo -Virgin - kanya

Virgo is symbolised by a virgin, an unmarried girl. This stands for the quality of purity and perfection. Virgo's are young adults learning the skills of survival. They become more critical because of the added responsibility on their young shoulders. From teenage years to young adults is a transition phase which is both exciting, ambitious and ambiguous in terms of what lies ahead. Their young heart is pure and filled with silent hope, and their mind feels the need to discern and analyse everything that comes their way in order to gain perfection.

Here, the actions of a virgin are driven by the will to be free from the dependency of parents, and so, with dogged determination, they pursue their ambitions. They feel that they cannot dodge their duty. Here, the soul learns not to waste vital life energy but to harness it towards his or her own growth. They know how to channel their energy into excellence in work.

On the positive side, they have wonderful qualities of clarity of thought, discernment to make the right choices, service to others, gathering knowledge, intelligent analysis, perfectionist and being true to themselves. On the negative side, when the Virgo energy is out of balance, they can feel overly critical and cranky and get into hair-splitting detail - and in the process, can become pessimistic and miss the bigger picture.

Inference

Uttara Phalguni's 1st Pada is placed in Leo, so they will be more ambitious, determined, fiery, generous and confident. They are more likely to be their own bosses and run their own businesses simply because they cannot tolerate being a subordinates or taking orders from anyone. They are full of creative ideas which they need to explore and develop and do not feel that freedom if they are working for someone else. In the process of pursuing their ambition, they could intentionally hurt others' feelings because of their aloofness and pride.

The 2nd, 3rd and 4th padas of Uttara Phalguni fall in the sign of Virgo, which makes them more service-oriented. They will happily work in a 9 am to 5 pm government job and stick to routines but in a managerial position. They do find fulfilment in serving others from a position of authority. They will be more analytical and strive to do everything perfectly.

They are more likely to be involved with handling financial debts, credit card payments, confronting opponents, or some minor health issues, and can feel stressed over matters like - people not following the rules. These scenarios could come up during the Sun or Mercury dasha or of any planet sitting in this nakshatra. However, from these slight upheavals in their career, they will climb the ladder of success because of the learning experiences which will make them more wise.

Those who have their Ascendent, Sun or Moon in Uttara Phalguni earn respect in the family, friends, community, or the whole nation, where people admire them for how they handle difficult situations.

Uttara Phalguni - Back legs of a bed.

Back legs of the bed symbolise the legs and feet, which shows that they are ready to get up and take action and stand on their own feet rather than depend on someone else to do the job for them. In Uttara Phalguni it's time to get up and take charge of the situation and enjoy the fruits of their work.

Mythology -

Deity - Aryaman

The word Aryaman in Sanskrit means a close friend, partner, or a companion. He is one of the Adityas (Son of Devi Aditi and the Sun God) and is depicted as the mid-morning sun disk. He is the deity of Vedic fire rituals, customs, events, hospitality and ceremonies.

In the Rigveda, Aryaman is described as the protector of mares, and the Milky Way (aryamṇáḥ pánthāḥ) is said to be his path. Aryaman is commonly invoked together with Varuna-Mitra,

Bhaga, Bṛhaspati, and other Adityas. Rigveda states that Aryaman is a supreme deity alongside Mitra and Varuna. Even Indra, who is traditionally considered the most important deity in the Rig Veda, is asked to obtain boons and gifts from Aryaman.

The Hindu marriage oaths are administered with an invocation to Aryaman being the witness to the oaths and the special event.

Aryaman is associated with chivalry, honour and nobility that govern the rules of the society. He is the disciplinarian who orders us to do the right thing to carry out our dharma (rightful duties). The Vedas refer to him as a guard of the cosmic or sacred laws. He is also referred to as the destroyer of enemies and servant of dharma.

Inference

Uttara Phalguni natives are very good at keeping friendships, they are very social and well respected in the family, friends and community. They get invited to many social events, family functions and religious ceremonies and are often asked to participate in the traditional rituals. They like to abide by the laws and regulations of the society and the nation, and appreciate and respect those who do the same.

Uttara Phalguni padas

26.40 deg Leo - 6.40 deg Virgo

Padas	Degrees
1	26.40 - 30 deg Leo
2	0 - 3.20 deg Virgo
3	3.20 - 6.40 deg Virgo
4	6.40 - 10 deg Virgo

Pada 1

26.40 - 30 deg Leo, Navamsha- Sagittarius (Lord - Jupiter)

Rashi Lord - Sun and Nakshatra Lord- Sun

Pada 1 of Uttara Phalguni falls in the navamsha of Sagittarius. Therefore, it carries the energy of the Sun and Jupiter. Sun has a double and strong influence in this Pada because it's the Lord of Leo as well as Uttara Phalguni.

Therefore, those who are born with the Ascendant, Sun or Moon in this Pada are very honest, straightforward, idealistic, confident, intelligent, creative, courageous, generous, fiercely independent and have very good leadership skills. They like to do things on a grand scale and have the ability to inspire and motivate others.

They will be very dignified, righteous and ethical in their dealings. However, their stiff pride can sometimes prevent them from mingling freely with people. Once they learn to relax and become more tolerant of others' flaws, it becomes much easier for them and more fun for others to be around them. They can mingle more gracefully when they are not too fanatical about their religious ideologies.

When their pride has been hurt, they tend to freeze in icy dignity, but their warm-hearted nature is quick to overcome and not succumb to the fragile feelings that cause emotional pain. And when their scars are healed, they will shower their friend or loved one with a much longed for gift of honest appreciation and forthright respect. Among many others, their wonderful qualities of being a true friend, keeping their promises, and their integrity of purpose make it worth a try to win them over after any disagreement. The best way to do that is by appreciating their sincerity.

They do get approached quite often for their practical and benevolent guidance, which they love giving. Their inherent wisdom can get people out of tons of trouble. As long as it doesn't become a command, they do get appreciated for their foresight and intelligence. Their unshakable faith in the truth and righteousness is their greatest strength and an inspiration for others. They will be stubborn and set in their way of doing things. This works to their advantage in terms of being persistent and achieving the goals they set for themselves.

For example, in the 1st Pada of Uttara Phalguni in the 2nd house, the natives will be born into a well to do prestigious family who is well respected for their knowledge and talent. As they grow older, they will be very family-oriented and will make sure there are always enough resources available for the family, and they will have a good regular source of income.

Careers

Managers, leaders, co-ordinators, film directors, professors, teachers, councillors, advisors, politicians, government officers, doctors, scientists, astrologers, musicians, astronauts, architects, photographers, entrepreneurs, IT professionals, diplomats, corporate and economic and spiritual leaders.

Pada 2

0 - 3.20 deg Virgo, Navamsha - Capricorn (Lord - Saturn)

Rashi Lord - Mercury and Nakshatra Lord - Sun

The qualities of the Sun, Mercury and Saturn will manifest in the 2nd Pada of Uttara Phalguni because it falls in the navamsa of Capricorn. The natives will be more ambitious and service oriented and will be well known in their community, or the whole nation, or globally, for their respectable profession.

They will have excellent communication, leadership, managerial and IT skills. Their practical and intelligent approach to things will bring them recognition and success in their profession. They will serve the community, nation or the whole world through their chosen field of work. They will be very talented speakers and can articulate their thoughts, and put forward their plans in a very convincing way.

The restrictive nature of Saturn can bring delays and frustrations. It will not deny the success but will make the native work for it. Although the progress may seem slow or laborious, Saturn gives the assurety of results when one works sincerely for it.

Their air of confidence can quickly rub on others and motivate them into action. People around them grow to appreciate their sensible advice and instinctive wisdom. They do have a marvellous knack for turning dreams into reality. For example, in the 2nd Pada of Uttara Phalguni, in the 7th house, they tend to meet people who are ambitious and intelligent. Most likely, their partner will be doing a managerial job, and he or she will be dignified, honest and proud.

Careers

Businessmen, industrialists, managers, accountants, politicians, film directors, government officials, IT professionals, graphic designers, architects, property dealers, financial advisors, bank managers, landlords, scientists, engineers and doctors.

Pada 3

3.20 - 6.40 deg Virgo, Navamsha - Aquarius (Lord - Saturn)

Rashi Lord - Mercury and Nakshatra Lord- Sun

In the 3rd Pada, navamsa is placed in Aquarius, which gives the influence of Saturn, Sun and Mercury. The natives born in this Pada will be intelligent, creative, and will have very good communication skills. They will be associated with a large organisation. Either they will work or volunteer for one or will have their own business company.

They will be more unconventional in their approach and tend to follow an unpredictable pattern, which can keep others around them guessing continuously. Here, they are determined and anxious to pour out and share their knowledge. They do have the good fortune of gains and get to enjoy the results of their efforts, though the slowness of Saturn can make them wait for things to happen, longer than they expect.

For example, the 3rd Pada of Uttara Phalguni in the 5th house will make the natives very creative, and they will be able to gain from their talent through a well-established organisation. They may be able to establish their own company through their IT skills, but this will take time and effort. Their scientific approach, ingenious ideas, good communication skills, ability to stick to routines, meet deadlines, the box thinking - all these wonderful qualities will culminate in a successful career.

Careers

IT professionals, consultants, scientists, doctors, bankers, businessmen, government officials, managers and co-ordinators of large business or voluntary organisations, social workers, lawyers, social workers, social activists and politicians.

Pada 4

6.40 - 10 deg Virgo, Navamsha - Pisces (Lord - Jupiter)

Rashi Lord - Mercury and Nakshatra Lord- Sun

The 4th Pada, the navamsha, lies in Pisces, the qualities of Sun, Mercury and Jupiter will be seen. The navamsha of Pisces makes them more philosophical, dreamy and spiritual. Here, the Jupitarian wisdom comes from the experience of having passed through the pains and pleasures of life and hence has gained a deeper understanding of this life and the life beyond.

They are immensely intelligent, creative and idealistic, and do not see any wisdom or logic in chasing ambitions that ultimately will not bring any inner fulfilment. They would much rather sit at home and read religious scriptures, Vedas, or books on yoga, meditation, philosophy, astrology and other esoteric subjects from which they get a deeper understanding of themselves rather than chase any materialistic goals. They are happy having intellectual and philosophical discussions with their friends or partners rather than being involved in the politics of the day.

For example, in the 4th Pada of Uttara Phalguni in the 3rd house, they will love to travel to places of pilgrimage and historical significance with their friends and family. They will have a good circle of friends and will get along well with their siblings and neighbours.

Careers-

Artists, actors, poets, writers, teachers, councillors, philanthropists, psychologists, psychiatrists, astrologers, spiritual mediums, government employees, doctors, IT professionals, self-employed and working from home.

The effect of planets

Uttara Phalguni - Leo Pada 1	Planets that get affected
Most Benefic - Yoga karka Removes the effect of Mangal dosha.	Mars
Functional Benefic - give good results during their dasha.	Sun

Functional Malefic - can give problems during their dasha.	Moon, Rahu and Ketu
Functional Neutral	Mercury, Jupiter and Saturn
Kendra Adi Pati Dosha - can be malefic	Venus
Uttara Phalguni - Virgo Padas 2, 3 and 4	**Planets that get affected**
Functional Benefic - give good results during their dasha.	Mercury and Venus
Functional Malefic - can give problems during their dasha.	Mars, Rahu and Ketu
Functional Neutral	Sun, Moon and Mercury
Kendra Adi Pati Dosha - can be malefic	Jupiter

Uttara Phalguni Ascendant

Those who are born with their Ascendent in the 1st Pada of Uttara Phalguni will have a double influence of the Sun (being the sign Lord and nakshatra lord). If there is any planet sitting in the 1st house, it's influence will alter the qualities in terms of tendencies and personality of the person.

The strong influence of the Sun gives them a very regal and dignified persona. They will be very confident, honest, generous, intelligent, creative, passionate, proud and independent. The fiery nature of the Sun also makes them very ambitious, and their way of life can become an inspiration or motivation for others.

For this reason, others may perceive them as arrogant, but they are the most warm-hearted, genuine and trustworthy friends. Just as the king feels pride and honour in looking after his subjects, they love taking care of their family.

Since the 1st Pada of Uttara Phalguni falls in Leo, which is a fixed sign, they have a very set way of doing things, are very organised and like to plan everything before putting it into action. This also makes them stubborn about their likes and dislikes and determined about their ambitions. The fiery nature of the Sun gives them a very pitta-dominant physiology, which draws them towards spicy food and gives them an adventurous spirit and leadership qualities. They should try to balance the fire in them by going for a swim, taking showers, spending time by the lake or an ocean, and exercising regularly in a cool place - preferably under a shady tree.

In the 2nd, 3rd and 4th padas of Uttara Phalguni, the energies of the Sun and Mercury will be seen. The influence of Virgo makes the natives very meticulous and like to do everything perfectly. They are able to handle the nitty gritty of the detail and do the job so well that there are no flaws in it. They also have the special talent of wonderful IT skills, communication and handling accounts, therefore they make very good financial advisors and bank managers.

Since the latter 3 padas of Uttara Phalguni fall in the earthy sign of Virgo, they will be more aware of their duties and don't mind following routines because it makes them feel grounded and gives them the security of a stable foundation. Sun and Mercury are good friends, which gives them confidence, intelligence, and excellent communication skills. Therefore, they have the potential to become great managers and co-ordinators.

Aryaman is the deity of Uttara Phalguni. This gives the natives the fortune of having a good circle of friends. They are very social and like to attend family functions, weddings and religious ceremonies. The special ability of Uttara Phalguni blesses them to become prosperous through union, which means whenever they get into a business partnership, or they get married, they will succeed in their endeavours.

The triguna of tamas is predominant in the 1st Pada of Uttara Phalguni, which makes them feel more comfortable with an easy-paced life rather than running around or chasing deadlines. They like to do things well and do it in their own time. The 2nd, 3rd and 4th padas lie in Virgo, which gives a Satvic quality. The natives born in these padas will be oriented towards doing things which help them enhance their inner and outer wellbeing.

<u>William Henry Davies</u> was a Welsh poet and writer of the 19th century, and his poems, which are grounded in realism, have been very popular. Here is one of his famous poems, which I had read in school, and it's first verse has always stayed with me. This simple, yet wonderfully enchanting poem echoes the soul desire of Uttara Phalguni to enjoy the real gifts of life.

"What is this life if, full of care,

We have no time to stand and stare.

No time to stand beneath the boughs

And stare as long as sheep or cows.

No time to see, when woods we pass,

Where squirrels hide their nuts in grass.

No time to see, in broad daylight,

Streams full of stars, like skies at night.

No time to turn at Beauty's glance,

And watch her feet, how they can dance.

No time to wait till her mouth can

Enrich that smile, her eyes began.

A poor life this is if full of care,

We have no time to stand and stare.

Sun in Uttara Phalguni

When the Sun is placed in the 1st Pada of Uttara Phalguni, it's impact will be 3 times stronger because it's the lord of Leo, and the lord of Uttara Phalguni, and is placed in its own sign and nakshatra. Therefore very prominent Leo-like qualities will be present in them.

They will be very self-confident and will take pride in their individuality. They will have tremendous willpower to achieve the targets that they set for themselves. Their bright sunshine smile, their dignified manner, creative ideas, and a sense of pride cannot be missed by those around them.

Since Leo is a fixed and masculine sign, they will be good planners, will be very organised, and can be stubborn about their opinions and habits. They will love to lead and offer help to the vulnerable and will get opportunities to do so, especially during the dasha of the Sun. On the positive side, they are very generous and considerate, and on the negative side, they can be intolerant and egoistic. For example, Sun in the 1st Pada of Uttara Phalguni in the 11th house will gain from associating with large organisations or running a voluntary or a business organisation themselves.

The 2nd, 3rd and 4th padas of Uttara Phalguni are placed in Virgo, therefore it gives more grounding and an earthy effect. Since Virgo is the original 3rd house, they will serve others through a position of responsibility. Their life patterns will be woven around survival and competition. However, every time they face a challenge, they will gain in terms of becoming wiser. If the Sun has a good shadbala score of 400 or more, it will easily influence the opponent and emerge victorious. However, if the Sun has a very low degree, they can face difficulties with the authorities during the dasha of the Sun.

In these padas, the Sun will be influenced by Mercury, so the natives will be more approachable and communicative. They will be very conscious about their responsibilities and will do their duties diligently. Since the Sun and Mercury are good friends, the natives have the capability of becoming excellent managers, co-ordinators, politicians, writers and public speakers. They will have an analytical approach and will strive for perfection in everything they do. On the positive side, they will be very practical and will have clarity of thought. On the negative side, they can become overly critical. For example, Sun in the 2nd Pada of Uttara Phalguni in the 3rd house will get along very well with their siblings and neighbours and will be exceptionally good in some talent, which involves the use of their arms and hands.

Moon in Uttara Phalguni

When the Moon is placed in the 1st Pada of Uttara Phalguni, it will have a strong influence on the Sun. Here the soft feminine qualities of the moon get empowered by the blazing masculine qualities of the Sun. However, the moon is very receptive and reflects the shine of the Sun almost like a mirror. This makes the natives very emotional, imaginative, intelligent, intuitive, confident and brave. When the moon is strong with a good Shabala score, the natives will have a beautiful balance of intuition and intelligence. On the other hand, if the moon is weak, they can feel a surge of strong emotions, which might become too overwhelming for them or for others around them. They can make very good actors, artists, film directors, writers and poets - any creative field will be a wonderful outlet for their passion and deep, intense emotions, which will help to balance the coolness of the moon and the heat of the sun in a beautifully elegant way.

For example, the Moon in the 1st Pada of Uttara Phalguni in the 10th house will make them ambitious about pursuing a career in a creative field, and they will surely realise their dreams, especially in the Sun or moon dasha.

In the 2nd, 3rd and 4th padas of Uttara Phalguni, the Moon will share the qualities of the Sun and Mercury because these padas fall in Virgo. Here, the moon will reflect the qualities of the Sun and Mercury, which make them more communicative and service-oriented. They are more likely to work for someone in a creative field. When the moon is placed in the earthy sign of Virgo in the latter 3 padas of Uttara Phalguni, the natives will be more grounded, down to earth, humble and will be able to stick to routines. This will provide a good stable foundation to climb the ladder of success in the later years of life.

For example, Moon in the 2nd Pada of Uttara Phalguni in the 9th house will pursue their higher education in a creative field and will travel away from home to meet their teacher, whom they will look up to. Their teacher will guide and train them to master their creative talent and get employment in a prestigious company.

The poetry of Uttara Phalguni

Uttara Phalguni - rising from the north,

The sweet fruits of previous efforts henceforth

Through partnerships comes alive,

As the destiny unfolds the sequences of life,

The brilliance of Sun and intelligence of Mercury,

enhance the communicative skills greatly.

The fire of Leo - in the earthy Virgo gets grounded,

A new fragrant freshness surrounded.

The tree that bears the sweet fruits in plenty,

Graciously lowers its branches to share its bounty

The source of life - our fiery Sun,

Warms up Mother Earth for spring time fun.

The play of elements is ever on,

And in subtle ways reveals the grandeur.

Remedies

- <u>Das Maha Vidya</u> - as described earlier.
- A regular routine of physical exercise will help to balance the fiery heat of the Sun and Pitta dominant physiology.
- The best remedy is to do yogic and spiritual practices, which will help to balance the thoughts, emotions and actions.
- To include your partner in your plans and projects.
- To share the fruits of your hard work with family and friends.
- Green, red, orange and earthy colours resonate well with the energy of Uttara Phalguni.
- Chanting the mantra - *"Om cham jham Uttara Phalguni nakshatraye namah,"* 108 times on days when the moon is transiting Uttara Phalguni will help to connect you with your inner self, and this will help you to get deeper insights into solving any issues that might be on your mind.

Example

<u>Moon in Uttara Phalguni</u>

<u>Rajesh Khanna -</u> Popular Hindi film actor of the 1970s

Born on 29th December 1942, Amritsar, India, at 5:45 pm.

Rajesh Khanna was a famous Indian actor and a superstar romantic hero in Hindi films in the 1970s. He starred in 15 consecutive solo hit films from 1969 to 1971, a record unbroken. He did 106 solo hero films, of which 97 were released between 1967 and 2013.

Rajesh Khanna was born on 29th December 1942, in Amritsar in a Hindu family. At a young age, he was adopted and raised by Chunnilal Khanna and Leelawati Khanna, who were relatives of his biological parents. His adoptive parents belonged to a family of railway contractors who had moved from Lahore to Bombay in 1935.

Rajesh spent his early years in Mumbai and, from a young age, started taking an interest in theatre. He did many stage and theatre plays in his school and college days and won many prizes in inter-college drama competitions. His original name was Jatin Khanna, which was later changed to Rajesh Khanna when he started his career in films.

He made his debut in 1966 with Aakhri Khat, which was also India's first official Oscar Entry in 1967. He received the Filmfare Best Actor Award 3 times and the BFJA Awards for Best Actor 4 times. In 1991, he was awarded the Filmfare Special Award for completing 26 years in Hindi cinema and in 2005, he was honoured with the Filmfare Lifetime Achievement Award on the 50th Anniversary of the Filmfare Awards. He was the highest-paid Indian actor from 1970 to 1987.

He was married to Dimple Kapadia in March 1973, 8 months before her debut film Bobby was released, which was a super hit. They have 2 daughters from the marriage.

Rajesh died on 18th July 2012 after a period of illness. He has been posthumously awarded India's 3rd highest civilian honour, Padma Bhushan. He has also been honoured with a stamp and statue in his likeness and a road renamed after him by the Prime Minister of India. In 2014, his biography Rajesh Khanna - The Untold Story of India's First Superstar by Yasser Usman was published by Penguin Books. In 2018, a one-kilometre fitness trail in Lajpat Nagar National Park was named after him, which was inaugurated by his wife Dimple Kapadia.

Analysis

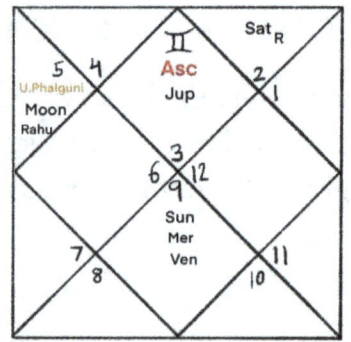

Rajesh has his <u>Moon and Rahu in Leo</u> in the 3rd house. Moon is in the 1st Pada of Uttara Phalguni. He had a very dignified and pleasing personality. Moon being in the sign and nakshatra of the Sun gave him the strong Sun-like qualities of ambition, pride, confidence, creativity, intelligence and dignity, combined with the intuitive imagination and receptivity of the moon. Moon and Rahu, sitting in the 3rd house of Leo, amplified his talent of articulation, communication, and ability to make brave decisions in his life, which could make or break his career. It also brought him a lot of travel during the course of his active film career.

Moon-Rahu conjunction in the 3rd house of Leo - brought him huge success. During the entire Mahadasha of Rahu he enjoyed an active film career and his rise to superstardom from 1965 - 1983. Sun - as the lord of the sign and the nakshatra, has a very powerful say in the birth chart. The Sun is sitting in the 7th house with Venus and Mercury in Sagittarius. Mercury is his Atma Karka, and Venus makes him very attractive to the females. The lord of the 7th house - Jupiter, is in the Ascendant, and Jupiter is his strongest planet with a shadbala score of 546 out of a total of 550.

This shows that his personality had a very powerful impact on the other person; he was blessed with good health and a pleasing personality, and he was especially attractive to the opposite sex, which gave him the superstar image as a romantic hero. In the navamsha, Sun is sitting in the 10th house of Leo in Magha Pada 2 (the 10th house is also the destiny point of the navamsha chart). This shows in his adulthood years his indisputable image as the king of his field - as a romantic superstar hero.

In 1965, Rajesh was running his - Rahu Rahu Rahu dasha.

United Producers and Filmfare had organised an all-India talent contest in 1965, for which 10,000 contestants were chosen.

Rajesh Khanna was one of the lucky 8 finalists who had won this prestigious contest. This shows the impact of Moon - Rahu conjunction in the 3rd house of communication. It amplified his artistic skill of projecting his voice very well, in all shades of human emotions. Moreover, the 3rd house is his destiny point, which means he was destined to be involved with things related to the 3rd house (communication and travel). It also shows that Rahu dasha always brings in big significant changes, which prove to be turning points in one's life, especially if Rahu is sitting with the moon or is in the ascendant. He got married to Dimple in March 1973, when he was running his Rahu Mercury Mercury Jupiter dasha -Mercury is sitting with Venus and Sun in the 7th house of Sagittarius, and the lord of Sagittarius - Jupiter is stirring in the Gemini Ascendant. So, all the planets involved were sitting in the 1st and 7th house, which brought marriage.

He made his debut in 1966 with the film Aakhri Khat, which was also India's first film to be nominated for an Oscar in 1967 as Best Foreign Language Film. His rise to superstardom came from the film Aradhana, which was released on 27th September 1969, when he was running his Rahu Jupiter Rahu dasha. Through this film, he rose to "instant national fame", and film critics referred to him as the "1st Superstar of India". In this film he was cast in a double role (father and son). After that, he gave 15 consecutive solo hit films between 1969 and 1971, which established him as a superstar and the highest-paid actor of his time.

If we look at the overall factors that contributed to his maga success, we can see that - the dasha and antar dasha of Rahu brought him stupendous fame and success. His Jupiter is sitting in Punarvasu, in the Ascendant, in the sign of Gemini. This shows his special talent in articulating his emotions, his natural ability to act and his philosophical, benevolent and gentle approach to life. It also brought him plenty of good luck, grace, goodwill and an irresistible charm during the Rahu Jupiter Rahu dasha. Moreover, the 5th house of creativity, entertainment, fans and followers has the highest ashtakavarga score of 35 points, which gave him a huge fan following in the creative field of acting, films and entertainment.

He died from Cancer on 18th July 2012, when he was running his <u>Saturn Mars Moon Rahu dasha -</u> Saturn is retrograde, sitting in the 12th house of Taurus, and Mars is in the 6th house of Scorpio. Moon and Rahu are in the 3rd house of Leo. This shows the impact of Saturn in the 12th house of hospitals, isolation and foreign places and Mars in the 6th house of debts, enemies and diseases. While the influence of Moon and Rahu shows his anxious state of mind. It was reported by social media that his last words were, *"It's time to pack up."*

13
Hasta

Om jham, nyam Hasta nakshatraye namah

Zodiac degrees	10 - 23.20 deg Virgo
Ruling planet	Virgo - Mercury and Hasta - Moon
Sanskrit name	Hasta means the hand.
Astronomical name	5 very prominent stars are seen in the constellation of Corvi (the crow), which resemble the 5 fingertips. These stars are seen just below the constellation of Virgo.
Symbol	Virgo - Virgin and Hasta - hand
Element	Earth
Deity	Savitar (one of the solar deities) symbolises the first rays of the Sun, also known as the impeller or the giver of life.
Quality	Dwi - dual - Virgo Hasta - Laghu - light and kshipra - fast
Shakti	Hasta sthapani agama Shakti - All gains placed in your hands.
Cast	Vaishya - trader
Gender	Female
Motivation	Artha- to gather resources.
Triguna	Satwa
Tridosha	Kapha
Body parts	Hands
Direction	East, north, northeast and south.
Month	Late March - first half of Chaitra month.

Bird	Crow
Sound	Pu, sha, nu, tu
Tree	Wild Mango
Chakras	Anhatta - Moon and Ajna - Mercury
Das Maha Vidya	Devi Bhuvaneshwari - Moon and Devi Tripura Sundari - Mercury

Special degrees -

Yoga Tara	2 yoga Tara points at 10 deg and 20 deg Virgo. It's a point where the planet will show the strongest and sure results during its dasha.
Exaltation and Moola trikona	Mercury is exalted at 15 deg Virgo, and Moola trikona Mercury is from 16 - 20 deg Virgo. When Mercury is placed at these degrees in Virgo, it will become very strong and will give excellent results during its dasha.
Pushkar Amsha	1st and 2nd Pada Planets sitting here will blossom fully and give good results during their dasha.
Visha nadi	14.40 - 15.33 deg Virgo Brings situations which one does not like dealing with.

Auspicious and inauspicious table -

Auspicious	Inauspicious
<u>Activities</u> Good for all types of fun activities that give joy, lots of jokes and laughter, all hobbies that involve the skilled use of hands, magic tricks, playing indoor and outdoor games that involve the use of hands, playing cards, all activities and projects that give quick results, for domestic work, studying, learning languages, astrology, art and science, for buying and selling things, for business deals in farming and textiles, holistic treatment for diseases, change of residence, travel and for marriage.	<u>Activities</u> Not good for planning long-term projects and goals, making mature or responsible decisions, inactivity or relaxation and for nighttime activities.
<u>Days</u> Sundays- only when it falls on the 1st, 4th, 5th, 6th, 7th or 12th lunar day.	<u>Days</u> Saturdays - only when it falls on the 3rd, 7th, 9th or 11th lunar day.

Compatibility table -

Hasta	Compatible with
Sexual compatibility Yoni animal	Hasta - female Buffalo Compatible with Swati - Male buffalo
Sign compatibility	Virgo - Taurus and Capricorn.
Nakshatra compatibility	Rohini and Shravana.
Lunar day compatibility	Dwadashi tithi - 12th Lunar Day.
Day compatibility	Monday and Wednesday
Colour compatibility	White and green
Numerological compatibility	2 and 5 - and all numbers that add up to make 2 and 5.
Sound compatibility	Moon - semi vowels - ya, ra, la, va, ssa, sha, sa, ha, lr, rr Mercury - lingual sounds - ta, tha, da, dha, na

Sign Lord and nakshatra lord - Mercury and Moon - as described earlier.

In Hasta, the energy of the Moon and Mercury gives it a very swift, light and elegant quality because both Moon and Mercury are quick-moving planets. On days when the Ascendant, Sun or Moon is in Hasta, things will move fast and give quick results.

Quality, element, motivation, triguna, tridosha and chakras - as described earlier.

Shakti - Hasta sthapani agama Shakti - All gains placed in your hands.

Hasta natives have a special talent and blessing of gaining profits through everything they do with their hands. They will be gifted with some extraordinary talent. The rewards they get are not only in terms of finance but also in terms of appreciation, recognition, fame and awards.

Symbolic signification

Virgo -Virgin - as described earlier, and Hasta - Hand

Hand

The word Hasta means hand, and it's derived from the root word 'has', which means laughter in Sanskrit. The lightness of this nakshatra gives them the quality of swiftness and a good sense of humour.

The symbol of the hand signifies their talent to do something creative with their hands. The Shakti of Hasta confirms their special ability to use their hands skilfully and make a profit from their inborn talent, which could be skills like - painting, drawing, designing, crafting, sculpturing, embroidery, stitching, cutting, braiding, hairstyling, knitting, crotchet, or IT typing skills.

Mythology -

Deity - Savitar

Savitr is a deity whose name primarily denotes an agent. The word Savitar in Sanskrit means impeller or rouser. This name has been given because Savitar refers to the 1st rays of the Sun, which arouse us from the night-long sleep and usher us into the activity of the day. Basically, Savitar signifies the time of sunrise.

He is venerated in the Rig Veda as a patron deity. Here is a short excerpt of hymn 35 from Rig Veda, dedicated to Savitar.

"I call on Savitar the God to lend us help, who looks on every creature.

Born in his golden chariot, he cometh, Savitar, the God from the far distance, and chases from us all distress and sorrow. The golden-handed Savitar, far-seeing, goes on his way between the earth and heaven. Drives away sickness, bids the Sun approach us, and spreads the bright sky through the dark region."

The Vedas describe him as - the one who has golden arms and is broad-handed or beautiful-handed. He is also pleasant-tongued or beautiful-tongued and is called iron-jawed. His eyes are golden as well. He is yellow-haired, an attribute shared with Agni and Indra.

He dons a tawny garb and rides a golden chariot with a golden axle, which is uniform, just as he is capable of assuming all forms. His resplendent chariot is drawn by 2 radiant white-footed stallions. Mighty splendour is attributed to Savitar, which he stretches out or diffuses. He illuminates the air, heaven and earth.

Savitar is the lord of that which is mobile and stationary. He upholds the movables and immovable, which signifies the aspect of maintenance. Savitr is a beneficent god who acts as a protector of all beings, guards the world of spirits, and is true to the Eternal Order.

His primordial pathways in the air are dustless, and he takes the departed soul to where the righteous dwell. Savitar is also said to bestow immortality on the gods and man. He is a supporter of the cosmos and holds the whole world, a role which is also assigned to Vishnu in the Vedas.

Inference

Hasta born have the energy and brilliance of the sunrise, ready to get on with the day's activity after a good night's sleep. The freshness of the morning gives them the youthfulness to get on with their daily routine with ease. The energy of Savitar renews them with solar power every morning. Just as the air lights up with the golden glow, they get energised by their inner Sun.

Hasta padas

10 - 23.20 degrees Virgo

Padas	Degrees
1	10 - 13.20 deg Leo
2	13.20 - 16.40 deg Virgo
3	16.40 - 20 deg Virgo
4	20 - 23.20 deg Virgo

Pada 1

10 - 13.20 deg Virgo, Navamsha- Aries (Lord - Mars)

Rashi Lord - Mercury and Nakshatra Lord- Moon

Pada 1 of Hasta falls in the navamsha of Aries. Therefore, it carries the energy of Mercury, Moon and Mars. The Moon and Mercury give them the quickness of movement, and Mars gives the energy, drive, determination, passion and ambition.

Those who are born with the Ascendant, Sun or Moon in this Pada will be full of energy and will be quick at analysing a situation, spot the flaws, and express them honestly. They will be very good at reaching a compromise and clearing the confusion. Hasta is placed in Virgo, which makes them very grounded and practical. They are not looking for appreciation for doing something that's so instinctive and comes naturally to them. Their language can be harsh and straightforward, cynical and critical, especially when they feel things around them are not being perfectly done. They need to consciously develop the habit of holding back sarcastic and sharp words that can injure the sensitive feelings of others and make them feel remorseful.

Mercury loves the mental gymnastics of thought analysis, the moon likes to feel through emotions, and Mars provides the drive and energy for both. Therefore, in this Pada, they will express their thoughts and emotions more freely and intensely. They will follow their ambition with more determination.

For example, the 1st Pada of Hasta in the 6th house will be very competitive, or they will always have to face competition. They will be very disciplined and punctual in their duty and, will follow routines up to perfection and will expect the same from others. They will have a responsible position at work and even at home, they will have the responsibility of someone.

Careers

Accountants, lawyers, bank workers, businessmen, IT professionals, writers, speakers, managers, actors, advisors, social workers, doctors, nurses, teachers, office workers, travel agents, travel guides and working from home.

Pada 2

13.20 - 16.40 deg Virgo, Navamsha - Taurus (Lord - Venus)

Rashi Lord - Mercury and Nakshatra Lord- Moon

The qualities of Mercury, Moon and Venus will manifest in the 2nd Pada of Hasta because it falls in the navamsa of Taurus. Since both Virgo and Taurus are earth signs, they will be very grounded, humble and family-oriented. The Venusian qualities of aesthetics, beauty and harmony will be very prominent. Their positive qualities will be steadfastness, conviction, patience, and reliability. On the negative side, they can become critical and obstinate.

They will firmly hang on to their principles, will not be frivolous about anything, and will carefully keep track of their incoming financial and outgoing expenses. They will have a wonderful sense of aesthetics and the musical talent for singing, gardening and cooking delicious recipes. For example, the 2nd Pada of Hasta in the 5th house will be very creative and will have a wonderful sense of aesthetics and can become great artists, singers, musicians, actors, writers or poets. Their children, students or followers will admire their talent.

Careers

Financial advisors, property dealers, artists, actors, singers, musicians, writers, florists, interior designers, architects, businessmen, IT professionals, graphic designers, fashion designers, architects, bank managers, landlords, doctors, nurses, cooks and working from home.

Pada 3

16.40 - 20 deg Virgo, Navamsha - Gemini (Lord - Mercury)

Rashi Lord - Mercury and Nakshatra Lord - Moon

In the 3rd Pada, navamsa is placed in Gemini, which gives the double effect of Mercury and Moon. This makes them very communicative, restless, free-spirited, friendly, and curious, and they have a great sense of humour. They love intellectual debates, analysis, arguments, reasoning, logic, contemplation and thought-provoking puzzles.

They will be swift thinkers and doers and will respond to situations with quick alertness. Their reaction usually will be like a hurricane - stirring up the tempest, carping and harping, and getting it all sorted even before others realise what the commotion is about.

They are very friendly humble, adjust to changes quickly, and are not particularly fussy about anything. Their lovely curiosity, uncommon intelligence, and charming, graceful manner allow them to skip happily through all life's situations. For example, the 3rd Pada of Hasta in the 11th house will be involved with a large organisation, either through their job or through volunteering. They will know a lot of people and have many friends.

Careers

Writers, actors, comedians, artists, IT professionals, consultants, bankers, accountants, businessmen, government officials, social workers, lawyers, social activists, politicians and working from home.

Pada 4

20 - 23.20 deg Virgo, Navamsha - Cancer (Lord - Moon)

Rashi Lord - Mercury and Nakshatra Lord- Moon

In this Pada, there will be the influence of the double moon and Mercury. They will be more emotional, dreamy, sensitive, intuitive, gentle, kind and caring. They will tend to be more crabby, attached and possessive. Their moods will seem to wane and wax with the cycles of the moon. They are shy in public and usually hide their emotions because they are very vulnerable to emotional hurt.

Their sensitive perception helps them to see both sides - the tragedy and comedy of life. They see and feel things more deeply than others, but only their close friends will know this side of their intuitive nature. As time goes by, they develop a hard-outer shell of protection against the cruel and insensitive remarks of people around them. Their positive qualities are imagination, tenacity, sensitivity, tenderness, care and caution. On the negative side, they can become stingy, clingy, possessive and moody. They find their emotional comfort at home and with their family and friends.

To give and receive love, care and kindness is a special gift they have in abundance, but their sensitivity makes them hide this side of theirs behind the moody tears and joyous laughter.

For example, the 4th Pada of Hasta in the 3rd house makes them share a special friendship with their siblings, friends or neighbours. They will like going on holidays with their family and friends and may have to do a lot of short distance travel because of family commitments, jobs or business.

Careers-

Artists, actors, poets, writers, teachers, councillors, philanthropists, psychologists, astrologers, spiritual mediums, government employees, doctors, IT professionals, self-employed and working from home.

The effect of planets

Hasta - Virgo	Planets that get affected
Functional Benefic - give good results during their dasha.	Mercury and Venus
Functional Malefic - can give problems during their dasha.	Mars, Rahu and Ketu
Functional Neutral	Sun, Moon and Mercury
Kendra Adi Pati Dosha - can be malefic	Jupiter

Hasta Ascendant

Hasta Ascendant people have the swiftness of Moon and Mercury. Their positive qualities are clarity of thought, distinction, logic, reasoning, humbleness, grounded, excellent communication, skills of the hands, following routines, kind, considerate, imaginative and caring. On the negative side, they can become overly critical about themselves and others, which can lead to chronic stress.

Virgo, being the original 6th house and an earthy sign, makes them very grounded in terms of doing their everyday chores. With experience, they discover that to receive their own needs they must serve others in some way. In the 2nd cycle of the earth element (the first earthy sign being Taurus), communication assumes great importance because Virgo is ruled by Mercury. Here, the philosophical ideas and ideals have to be shelved under the demands of work or study. They are not ideological dreamers but practical applicators who achieve goals through persistent and regular input. Their attention is focused on achieving academic and scholastic excellence because Mercury is an eternal student who is always happy to learn new things.

Since Hasta falls in the original 6th house of Virgo, this also brings in fierce competition in the business, financial, political and academic world. For them, learning to compete becomes mandatory in order to survive, to the point where survival and security can become an obsession.

When they are feeling out of sorts, the Lordship of Mercury gives them a critical and cynical approach to everything they see or hear. As they grow older it seems only more work, more study and more responsibility! This makes them look at life as realistically as possible. Slowly, over time, human flaws and imperfections assume exaggerated importance in their minds. When a favourable dasha runs for them, which brings to harvest the fruits of their labour, they begin to relax and begin to enjoy their jovial self, and the sense of good humour.

The emotions of the moon keep their hearts full of hope and purity, but the intellectual and logical side of Mercury keeps tugging at their thoughts, for them to be watchful and prepared for any unplanned events. Savitar, the deity of Hasta, brings them the blessing of fresh energy and the quality of lightness, which gives them youthful agility. Their special talent and skill of hands always bring them gains. Whenever they make something with their hands - they gain in terms of appreciation, fulfilment and financial gains.

Sun in Hasta

When the Sun is placed in Hasta, it will share the qualities of Mercury and Moon. Sun and Mercury get along well, and Moon is friendly with all. Therefore, the natives will have very good communication skills and will have the talent of expressing themselves beautifully through their writings. Apart from being wonderful writers, once they have overcome their initial shyness they can become excellent actors or public speakers as well.

They will be perfectionists and will like to get even the minutest details correct before finalising any of their work. Sun in Virgo also shows that the native will be working in a position of authority, or will be having a government job, and will be very diligent in performing his or her duties, and fulfilling his or her responsibilities.

Virgo is an earthy sign, which makes them very practical and down-to-earth. The radiance and intelligence of the Sun will shine through their work and talent. They will have wonderful handcraft skills like pottery, sculpturing, embroidery, knitting, crotchet, tailoring, painting, artwork, cutting, pasting and designing. Great dexterity of their hands can make them excellent surgeons, artists, tailors, creative designers, or IT professionals.

Their life scenarios will be tinged with competition or opposition, especially during the dasha of the Sun, Moon or Mercury. However, if the Sun is strong, with a good shadbala score of more than 400, they will overcome these challenges with much ease. For example, Sun in Hasta in the 5th house, the native will be very talented in some form of hand skill, will be a very creative writer, and will do very well in the field of academics.

Moon in Hasta

When the moon is placed in Hasta, it makes the earthy Virgo more emotional, intuitive, imaginative and receptive. Since the moon is the lord of Hasta, when placed in its own nakshatra is comfortable and gives good results. Here, the double influence of the moon combined with Mercury will give swiftness of thought and action since both the moon and Mercury move very fast.

The moon's ability to uncannily perceive everything seen and heard makes them very sensitive to the environment. Their moody and sensitive teenage soul oscillates between the rebellious spirit of an adolescent and the enticing world of freedom of adulthood. As they grow older and step into the world of grown-up people, quite often, they are faced with disappointment and get disillusioned with the ways in which society functions. The maturity into adulthood brings with it the responsibilities and a sense of duty. In the beginning, they can feel frustrated by feeling forced to comply with society's rules and restrictions, but with time, they learn how to submit gracefully with innate courtesy.

Virgo carries the energy of the original 6th house of daily routines. Their life situations will be such that they have to work to earn their money. Most likely, they will be doing a regular job where they get a monthly salary. They will be serving others in some way either via counselling, giving financial advice or teaching. For example, when the moon is placed in Hasta in the 7th house, their partner will be intelligent and academically oriented, who likes to learn new subjects and discuss and analyse things. They will love learning new subjects and skills and will enjoy having long debates and discussions with their partner.

The poetry of Hasta

Your destiny is in your hands - a phrase so true,

Hasta - the hand that holds the fate, anew.

As a new born child opens his or her fists so tiny,

Hidden are the codes that can reveal the timing.

What will be, when and how?

Slowly it unfolds, as you grow.

The finer motor skills of the hands,

When used with intelligence and wisdom of the lands.

Just as the potter shapes the pot, with calibered precision,

The skill of the hands, trained to perfection.

He is the master of his trade,

Can be said by looking at the pot made.

For, in the creation - lies the creator,

Revealing the secret of the matter.

Remedies

- Das Maha Vidya - as described earlier.
- The Vata Kapha constitution can be balanced by having a regular routine and eating warm-cooked foods.

- The yogic asanas and pranayama help to pacify the mercurian restlessness and the moon's fluctuating emotions.

- Whenever Hasta is born, people create something with their own hands, they will always gain and profit - financially, emotionally, mentally, physically and spiritually.

- Green, and white colours resonate well with the energy of Hasta.

- Chanting the mantra - "*Om jham, nyam Hasta nakshatraye namah,*" 108 times on days when the moon is transiting Hasta or on Mondays will help to connect you with your inner self, and this will help you to calm your mind and get insights into solving any issues that might be bothering you.

Example

Moon in Hasta

Doris Lessing - a British novelist who won the Nobel Prize in Literature in 2007.

Born on 22nd October 1919 in Kermanshah, Iran, at 12 pm (estimated time of birth).

Died on 17th November 2013 at the age of 94.

She was a British novelist born in Iran, where she lived until 1925. Her family then moved to Zimbabwe, where she stayed until moving to London, England, in 1949. In 2001, Doris was awarded the David Cohen Prize for a lifetime achievement in British literature. In 2008, The Times ranked her 5th on a list of 'The 50 greatest British writers since 1945.'

Her dad was in the British army, Captain Alfred Tayler, and her mum, Emily Tayler, was a nurse. Her father had lost a leg during his service in World War I and had met his future wife, a nurse, at the Royal Free Hospital in London, where he was recovering from his amputation. The couple later moved to Iran, where her dad worked at a bank. This is where Doris was born.

In 1925, the family moved to the British colony of Southern Rhodesia (now Zimbabwe) to farm maise and other crops on about 1,000 acres of bush that her dad bought. As a girl, Doris was educated at a Roman Catholic convent. She left school at the age of 13 and was self-educated from then on. She left home at 15 and worked at a lawyer's office for some time, where she started reading material that her employer gave her on politics and sociology and began writing around this time.

In 1937, Doris moved to Salisbury to work as a telephone operator, and she soon married her first husband, Frank Wisdom, with whom she had 2 children. They got divorced in 1943. Doris left the family home in 1943, leaving the 2 children with their father. After the divorce, Doris's interest was drawn to the community around the Left Book Club. It was here that she met her future 2nd husband, Gottfried Lessing.

They married shortly after she joined the group and had a child together before they divorced in 1949. She did not marry again.

She moved to London in 1949 with her younger son to pursue her writing career and socialist beliefs. She later said that at the time, she saw no choice, "for a long time, I felt I had done a very brave thing. There is nothing more boring for an intelligent woman than spending endless amounts of time with small children. I felt I wasn't the best person to bring them up. I would have ended up an alcoholic or a frustrated intellectual like my mother."

At the age of 15, she began to sell her stories to magazines. Her first novel, The Grass Is Singing, was published in 1950. The work that gained her international attention, The Golden Notebook, was published in 1962. By the time of her death, she had published more than 50 novels, some under a pseudonym. Her last novel, 'Alfred and Emily' was published in 2008. She said this book was written as a gift and a tribute to her mum and dad.

As well as campaigning against nuclear arms, she was an active opponent of apartheid, which led her to being banned from South Africa and Rhodesia in 1956 for many years. In one of her articles, she wrote that "it is our imaginations which shape us, keep us, create us – for good and for ill. It is our stories that will recreate us when we are torn, hurt, even destroyed."

In 2007, Doris was awarded the Nobel Prize in Literature. She received the prize at the age of 88 years, making her the oldest winner of the literature prize. She was out shopping for groceries when the Nobel Prize announcement came. Arriving home to a gathering of reporters, she exclaimed, "Oh Christ! I've won all the prizes in Europe, every bloody one, so I'm delighted to win them all. It's a royal flush."

During the late 1990s, Lessing suffered a stroke, which stopped her from travelling during her later years, but she was still able to attend the theatre and opera. She began to focus her mind on death, for example, asking herself if she would have time to finish a new book. She died on 17th November 2013, aged 94, at her home in London, predeceased by her 2 sons but was survived by her daughter, Jean, who lives in South Africa.

Analysis

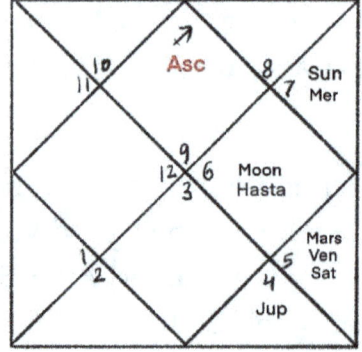

Doris has her <u>Moon in Hasta Pada 3 in the 10th house of Virgo</u>. The 10th house signifies the profession and public image. Moon, the Lord of Hasta, is sitting happily in its own nakshatra, and Mercury, the Lord of Virgo, is sitting with Sun in the 11th house of Libra. This brought her gains and fame through literary work in writing. Moreover, the Sun is the strongest planet in her chart, having the maximum shadbala score of 573 points out of 600. Her intelligence shined through her writings and she was the king in her domain as a fiction writer.

Moon in Hasta literally made her write and type a lot throughout her life (skill of the hands). It has also given her great imagination, intuitiveness, quick thinking and a wonderful sense of humour. When asked about winning the Nobel prize she answered, "They thought, better give it to her. She might pop out anytime. I am now 89, very, very old for anything really. I once won a prize which was called, 'the best milkmaid in Norway,' which was one the most charming prizes I have ever won. Winning the Nobel prize is the most glamorous one."

On 11th October 2007, when she won her Nobel prize at the age of 88, she had just started her Venus mahadasha. She was running her <u>Venus Venus Venus</u> dasha. That shows the strong influence of Venus during that time of her life. Venus, Saturn and Mars are sitting in the 9th house of Leo. Venus is in Purva Phalguni, sitting comfortably in its own nakshatra and is the Lord of the 6th house (Taurus) and of the 11th house (Libra).

The scenario of the 6th house of job (as a fiction writer) got maximum gains in terms of winning the most prestigious Nobel prize in the field of literature (the effect of the 11th house).

Her first book was titled, 'The <u>grass is singing,</u>' - it's interesting to note that she chose this name for her first book. Green is the colour associated with Mercury. This book was published in 1950 when she was running her <u>Jupiter Jupiter Moon</u> dasha. Jupiter is exalted in the 8th house of Cancer. Jupiter is the most beneficial planet for her, which is also the Lord of her Ascendant (Sagittarius), that gave her a long life. She had the talent of digging out the hidden gems of imagination and presenting them to the world through her writing.

In a 2008 interview for the BBC's Front Row, she stated that increased media interest after the award had left her without time or energy for writing. She passed away on 17th November 2013, aged 94, at her home in London. At that time, she was running her <u>Venus Mars Jupiter Rahu Mercury</u> dasha. She is a Sagittarius Ascendant, where Mercury gets the Kendra Adipati Dosha being the Lord of the 7th house - a Maraka house (Gemini) and the 10th house (Virgo). She was running the prana dasha of Mercury when she passed away.

<u>Here are some of her quotes -</u>

"There is no doubt fiction makes a better job of the truth."

"That is what learning is. You suddenly understand something you've understood all your life, but in a new way."

"Words. I play with words, hoping that some combination, even a chance combination, will say what I want."

"We are all creatures of the stars."

- Doris Lessings

14
Chitra

Om tam tham Chitra nakshatraye namah

Zodiac degrees	23.20 deg Virgo - 6.40 deg Libra Virgo - 1st and 2nd padas Libra - 3rd and 4th padas
Ruling planet	Virgo - Mercury and Libra - Venus Chitra - Mars
Sanskrit name	Chitra means as beautiful as a picture.
Astronomical name	A single star called Spica is seen near the constellation of Virgo.
Symbol	Virgo - Virgin and Libra - balancing scales Chitra - picture
Element	Earth - Virgo and Air - Libra
Deity	Vishwakarma - the celestial architect, also called Tvastar.
Quality	Virgo - Dwi - dual and Libra - Chara - movable Chitra - Mridu - gentle
Shakti	Punya chayani Shakti - Power to accumulate virtuous deeds.
Cast	Farmer
Gender	Female - Virgo and Male - Libra
Motivation	Artha - to gather resources - Virgo Kama - to fulfill desires - Libra
Triguna	Satwa - Virgo and Rajas - Libra
Tridosha	Kapha - Virgo and Vata - Libra
Body parts	Forehead and neck
Direction	West, south and southeast.
Month	April - 2nd half of Chaitra month.

Bird	Heron
Sound	Pe, po, ra, re
Tree	Biva, apple and Pear tree.
Chakras	Muladhara - Mars, Swadhisthana - Venus Ajna - Mercury
Das Maha Vidya	Devi Bagalamukhi Devi - Mars, Devi Tripura Sundari - Mercury and Devi Kamala - Venus.

Special degrees -

Yoga Tara	Yoga Tara at 29.45 deg Virgo It's a point where the planet will show the strongest and sure results during its dasha.
Vargottama	2nd and 3rd Pada. The planets placed here will give a steady foundation and balanced results.
Moola trikona	0 - 15 deg Libra - Moola trikona of Venus. When Venus is placed at these degrees in Libra, it will become very strong and will give excellent results during its dasha.
Amrit Nadi	3.60 - 4 deg Libra This brings good results, just like the nectar that nourishes.
Visha Nadi	27.46 - 28.40 deg Virgo Brings situations which one does not like dealing with.
Debilitation	27 deg Virgo - Maximum debilitation of Venus. This will bring in situations which can create misunderstandings and arguments in a relationship.

Auspicious and inauspicious table -

Auspicious	Inauspicious
<u>Activities</u> Good for all creative activities, art and craft work, designing, buying new clothes and wearing new clothes, wearing jewellery for the first time, fixing things at home, redesigning the house, putting on a new gemstone, decorative activities, for technical and mechanical activities, health and body improvement measures, for collecting herbs and preparing herbal drinks and medicines, for visualisation - guided meditations, for meeting the opposite sex, all activities that require personal charisma and giving public performances.	<u>Activities</u> Not good for all activities that require direct confrontation or an argument, for marriage, any kind of research, investigation or or trying to get to the root of any problem. Because one can get misguided by an illusionary image.

Days Mondays - only when it falls on the 2nd, 7th or 12th lunar day. Fridays - only when it falls on the 1st, 2nd, 6th, 7th, 11th or 12th lunar day.	Days Mondays - only when it falls on the 2nd lunar day.

Compatibility table -

Chitra	Compatible with
Sexual compatibility Yoni animal	Chitra - Male tiger Compatible with Vishakha - Female tiger
Sign compatibility	Virgo - Padas 1 and 2- Taurus and Capricorn. Libra - Padas 3 and 4 - Gemini and Aquarius.
Nakshatra compatibility	Mrigashira and Dhanishta.
Lunar day compatibility	Dwitiya tithi - 2nd Lunar day.
Day compatibility	Tuesday, Wednesday and Friday
Colour compatibility	Red, green and all light shades.
Numerological compatibility	5, 6 and 9 - and all numbers that add up to make 5, 6 and 9.
Sound compatibility	Mars - guttural sounds - ka, kha, ga, gha, kna Mercury - lingual sounds - ta, tha, da, dha, na Venus - palatal sounds - ch, ccha, ja, jha, nga

Sign Lord and nakshatra lord - Mercury, Venus and Mars - as described earlier.

The 1st and 2nd padas of Chitra are placed in Virgo, which makes them more set in their way of doing things. They will be more practical, grounded, and humble in their approach to life. The 3rd and 4th padas fall in Libra. They will be more creative, independent, and flexible and will have a more romantic approach to life.

Quality, element, motivation, triguna, tridosha and chakras - as described earlier.

Shakti - Punya chayani Shakti - Power to accumulate virtuous deeds.

Every time Chitra natives do something good for others, selflessly without any vested interests, it helps them to overcome their problems. Their special power to accumulate the merit of good and virtuous deeds helps them to sail through difficult situations with ease. On close introspection, they will begin to notice their special blessing and grace - every time they help another person, they automatically find solutions to their problems.

Symbolic signification

<u>Virgo -Virgin -</u> as described earlier.

<u>Libra -</u> Balancing scales and <u>Chitra</u> - Picture.

<u>Balancing scales -</u>

The scales represent the balancing aspect of Libra born people. Their senses are so finely tuned that even the slightest imbalance or disharmony can make them fall sick or give them tension and stress. They quite often find themselves in dilemmas where their choice might inevitably hurt one or the other, it shatters their conscience to be unfair, therefore decisions can be difficult and painful at times. They always try to maintain the balance between their work and family life and like to pass a fair judgment if they have to.

When faced with prejudice or intolerance, they often find themselves getting involved in long-winded debates or arguments. They are masters at persuading and yet softening their approach with their Venusian charm. Their fine sense of harmony and balance knows that it's not the might of the muscle but the artful collage of words that works, and it's a sure way to win.

<u>Picture-</u>

The literal meaning of the word Chitra is picturesque - as beautiful as a painting or a picture. Even the Vedic month of Chitra, which falls in April, refers to the start of the springtime.

When Mother Earth wakes up from her winter slumber, everything begins to blossom into the beautiful, exorbitant colours seen on the hills, valleys and grasslands. At this time of the year, wherever you look, it is most scenic and beautiful, like an artist's expression of beauty, harmony, and tranquillity captured in a painting.

<u>Inference</u>

Chitra natives have a very fine sense of aesthetics and are very good at creating and appreciating art in all forms. They will be particularly good with their gardening skills, and nurturing a beautiful garden will be one of their favourite hobbies. Whichever planet is sitting in Chitra and wherever it's placed, the native will have an artistic talent in that area of life. For example, Mercury in Chitra in the 5th house will be very talented writers, speakers or actors and will pass on this skill to their children or students.

Mythology -

Deity - <u>Vishwakarma</u>

Vishwakarma is known as the celestial architect, which means he has designed all forms seen in creation - including the stars, planets and the physical forms seen on Earth.

According to the Vedic legend, Vishwakarma's daughter - Samjna, was married to Surya (Sun god). Samjna had left her house because she could not bear the intense heat of the Sun. Vishvakarma, being his father in law, Surya had gone to him to ask for help, and he helped Surya by reducing the heat of his rays.

It is said that Vishvakarma also built various cities like Lanka, Dwarka and Indraprastha. The hymns of Rig Veda describe him as being the source of all prosperity, has swift thoughts, and is seen as a seer, and lord of speech.

According to some parts of the Rigveda, Vishwakarma was the personification of ultimate reality, the abstract creative power inherent in deities and living and non-living beings in this universe.

He is both The Architect and The Divine Engineer of The Universe from before the advent of time. In later mythology, Vishvakarman is sometimes identified with Tvastr and is a craftsman deity.

Inference

Here again, it shows the creative energy of Chitra which is - intelligent, artistic, a very fine sense of aesthetics and their ability to keep things in a harmonious balance.

Chitra padas

23.20 deg Virgo - 6.40 deg Libra

Padas	Degrees
1	23.20 - 26.40 deg Virgo
2	26.40 - 30 deg Virgo
3	0 - 3.20 deg Libra
4	3.20 - 6.40 deg Libra

Pada 1

23.20 - 26.40 deg Virgo, Navamsha- Leo (Lord - Sun)

Rashi Lord - Mercury and Nakshatra Lord- Mars

Pada 1 of Chitra falls in the navamsha of Leo. Therefore, it carries the energy of the Sun, Mercury and Mars. Sun gives them confidence, ambition and determination. Mercury gives them the quickness of movement, and Mars gives them energy, drive and ambition.

Since this Pada is placed in Virgo, the natives will be very grounded and practical, and the navamsha of Leo gives them energy and enthusiasm to do their duties well. Appreciation, compliments, recognition and rewards keep them motivated, and they will be very sensitive to what people say or don't say. Their language will usually be authoritative and analytical.

For example, the 1st Pada of Chitra in the 2nd house will be very family-oriented, generous, and will have a good steady source of income. They will be very disciplined and punctual in their routines and will expect the same from others. They will take their responsibilities seriously and will make sure there is always a good and steady stock of resources available for the family.

Careers

Politicians, government officers, accountants, managers, co-ordinators, directors, leaders, lawyers, bank workers, businessmen, IT professionals, writers, speakers, actors, advisors, social workers, doctors, nurses, teachers, office workers and working from home.

Pada 2

26.40 - 30 deg Virgo, Navamsha - Virgo (Lord - Mercury)

Rashi Lord - Mercury and Nakshatra Lord - Mars

The double effect of Mercury and Mars will manifest in the 2nd Pada of Chitra because it falls in the navamsa of Virgo. This is a vargottama Pada since the navamsha also falls in Virgo. The natives who have their Ascendant, Sun or moon placed in this Pada will be very fortunate and will never shy away from their responsibilities. Since this Pada has a strong influence of Virgo, which is an earthy sign, they will have a steady, stable job, or any other source of income. They will be very duty-bound, humble, grounded and practical.

On the positive side, they will be steadfast, patient and reliable. On the negative side, they can become overly analytical and detail-oriented. They will not be frivolous about anything and will carefully keep track of their incoming finance and outgoing expenses. For example, the 2nd Pada of Chitra in the 9th house will be very good in their studies and will travel away from home for their higher education.

Careers

Financial advisors, property dealers, businessmen, IT professionals, bank managers, accountants, lawyers, writers, speakers, YouTubers, landlords, doctors, nurses, teachers, cooks and working from home.

Pada 3

0 - 3.20 Libra, Navamsha - Libra (Lord - Venus)

Rashi Lord - Venus and Nakshatra Lord - Mars

In the 3rd Pada the navamsha is placed in Libra, which gives the double effect of Venus and Mars. They will be very passionate and determined and will have a wonderful sense of beauty, harmony, balance and aesthetics. The double effect of Venus makes them very sensitive to their inner and outer environment, if they see or feel anything which seems to be chaotic, shabby, disharmonious or out of place, it disturbs their fine sense of peace and harmony. Their choice of colours, clothes, home decor, or anything else they create or buy will be exceptionally beautiful and unique. For example, in the 3rd Pada of Chitra in the 12th house, they will like to spend a lot of time in their bedroom or study room - grooming themselves, studying, analysing, or creating something new and astounding.

The 3rd Pada placed in Libra is governed by the air element, which makes them very independent and creative. The balancing scales of Libra also make them feel the need to have harmonious relationships. They need to feel a sense of balance in everything and everyone they interact with. Therefore, having a good relationship and friendship with all whom they meet matters a lot to them. It's absolutely important for them not to stay in a toxic relationship or an unpleasant environment for longer than they can bear. Otherwise, it can destroy their inner essence of harmony up to the soul level. They should not let it come to that point where a friendship or a relationship becomes a burden and begins to take a toll on their mental, emotional or physical health. It will be wise for them to leave the scene of unpleasantness as soon as possible or to change their circumstances as much as possible.

Careers

Writers, poets, artists, actors, IT professionals, interior designers, fashion designers, architects, marriage consultants, psychologists, doctors, teachers, businessmen and working from home.

Pada 4

3.20 - 6.40 deg Libra, Navamsha - Scorpio (Lord - Mars)

Rashi Lord - Venus and Nakshatra Lord - Mars

In this Pada, there will be the influence of the double effect of Mars, and Venus. They will be determined, passionate, secretive and ambitious. Scorpio, being a water and fixed sign, gives them a very emotional and one-pointed approach to life. This can work both ways - their determined endeavours lead them to success, or their stubbornness can land them into problems. Either way, they are blessed with tremendous energy to pursue their ambitions. For example, the 4th Pada of Chitra in the 10th house will climb their way to success in their career through their persistence, hard work and determination. Mars dasha will be very supportive of them and will bring opportunities for a rise in their career.

The strong influence of Mars will make them very outspoken and straightforward, and they can use harsh words when provoked. They are not frivolous, have a high moral code of conduct and set a high standard for themselves and for those whom they love. They like to understand things from a deeper perspective and need to get to the bottom of things in order to resolve them. Unless they know a person well enough, they will not commit to any relationship. They are not the chatty types, are reserved, and take time to get into a relationship, but once they have decided or made their choice, they will stick to it through thick and thin.

For those who are Libra Ascendants in the 4th Pada of Chitra, Mars gets the Kendra Adipati dosha, being the Lord of the 2nd and 7th house (Maraka houses). During the Maha dasha or antardasha of Mars and when matched with the transits over the Ascendant or Moon some minor injuries can happen. However, the whole chart should be looked at carefully before making any decisive conclusions.

Careers

Psychologists, astrologers, spiritual mediums, doctors, IT professionals, army officers, police officers, firefighters, managers, directors, self-employed and working from home.

The effect of planets

Chitra - Virgo Padas 1 and 2	Planets that get affected
Functional Benefic - give good results during their dasha.	Mercury and Venus
Functional Malefic - can give problems during their dasha.	Mars, Rahu and Ketu
Functional Neutral	Sun, Moon and Mercury
Kendra Adi Pati Dosha - can be malefic	Jupiter
Chitra - Libra Padas 3 and 4	**Planets that get affected**
Yoga Karka - Most benefic	Saturn
Functional Benefic - give good results during their dasha.	Venus
Functional Malefic - can give problems during their dasha.	Jupiter, Rahu and Ketu
Functional Neutral	Sun, Moon and Mercury
Kendra Adi Pati Dosha - can be malefic	Mars

Chitra Ascendant

Those who are born with the Ascendent in the 1st or 2nd Pada of Chitra, they will have the influence of Mars and Mercury. This will make them very intelligent, curious, assertive, determined, and fearless in their communication. They will be very clear, precise and neat in their plans. They will have good administration skills, and have a special ability to bring calm and order to a chaotic situation. It gives them great fulfilment to be of some help or service to others, especially in demanding or emergency situations. Since the first 2 padas of Chitra lie in Virgo, the element of earth gives them stability and practicality, and they will be more grounded and humbler in their approach.

The 3rd and 4th padas of Chitra are placed in Libra. Therefore, it will carry the energies of Mars and Venus. This gives them a passionate approach to life. They will tend to be short tempered and will easily be provoked by any misconduct. They should build up a regular exercise routine which will keep them physically fit and their martian energy will be channelised positively.

For those who are born in the 3rd or 4th pada, relationships matter a lot. Any disharmony in their friendships makes them feel out of balance and anxious. They will be assertive, short tempered and can become aggressive when things are not going their way. They like to be fair in their dealings and like to ponder on the virtues and vices before making their choices. They don't like making decisions impulsively because they like to weigh the pros and cons before deciding on which option to take.

Sun in Chitra

When the Sun is placed in the 1st and 2nd padas of Chitra, it will share the influence of Mars and Mercury. Sun, Mars and Mercury get along well with each other; therefore, the energy flows with ease with this placement. The natives will be very determined, confident and communicative. They will follow their goals with dogged determination, will not waste time or shirk duty, and will always aspire to better themselves in whatever they do. Therefore, they reach the heights of excellence and success through consistent practice.

For example, Sun placed in the 1st Pada of Chitra in the 5th house. They will be very scholarly and will love to study the subjects of their interest. They can become excellent writers, managers, co-ordinators, army officers, police officers, doctors, surgeons, sportsmen or sportswomen, scientists, engineers or politicians. Their children or students will follow their guidance or profession because they will be inspired by their way of dealing with things.

In the 3rd and 4th padas of Chitra, the Sun will share the energies of Mars and Venus. Sun and Venus are not friendly to each other because they are both hot planets.

Mars gets along well with the Sun and is neutral to Venus. Therefore, when the Sun is placed in these padas, the natives will tend to be short tempered and will have a creative and aggressive approach to life. When the Sun is placed in the sign of Libra, the native will want to be fair to all and will try to balance the polarities as much as possible. For example, Sun placed in the 3rd Pada of Chitra, in the 12th house, the native will be influential and successful in a foreign land but will also incur a lot of expenses. It will be good for them to budget their expenses, otherwise their bank balance will keep going into a negative balance, or credit will easily build up. This is more likely to happen in the Sun, Mars or Venus dasha.

Moon in Chitra

When the moon is placed in Chitra in the 1st and 2nd padas in Virgo, it will share the energies of Mars and Mercury. Virgo, being an earthy sign, makes the natives practical, humble, grounded and stable. The influence of Mars makes them determined and assertive, Mercury makes them very communicative, and the energies of the moon make them imaginative, caring, emotional and receptive to others' feelings. For example, the moon in Chitra Pada 2 in the 8th house of sudden events will bring opportunities for gains from insurance, inherited property, or a secondary source of income during the dasha of the moon.

The 3rd and 4th padas of Chitra are placed in Libra, where Mars and Venus will influence the moon. This will make the natives very emotional, passionate, assertive and determined. In their endeavour to strike the right balance, they may end up hurting others' feelings through harsh language or actions. Even though they do things with good intentions, their aggressive approach can cause problems. To calm down and bring balance to their emotions, they should do some form of physical exercise. Going to the gym, cycling, running, hatha yoga and meditation will help them greatly.

In these padas, the moon is placed in the airy sign of Libra; therefore, the natives will be more creative and will have a very fine sense of aesthetics.

For example, the moon placed in the 4th Pada in the 4th house, the native's mum will be very creative and their home will be decorated very aesthetically. They will imbibe artistic talent, which will help them greatly in their chosen profession.

The poetry of Chitra

Chitra - picturesque and beautiful,

Fills the cup of life to the brimful.

A pleasure to behold, an honour to know,

A friendship that forever will blossom and grow.

The determined Mars, fearless and brave,

The mercurian curiosity tries to enslave,

A Venusian beauty - a breath of fresh air,

Though cannot be contained, to be fair.

From maiden Virgo to Libra Liberty,

Moves on to adulthood maturity.

Balancing the scales of relationships,

Partnership and friendships.

Creation of harmonious interaction,

Paints the enthralling canvas of love and affection.

Remedies

- <u>Das Maha Vidya</u> - as described earlier.

- For the Pitta Kapha constitution - a daily exercise routine will keep them in good health. They should take care not to exercise in the afternoon heat and not to eat very spicy food.

- The yogic asanas and pranayama help to pacify the excessive heat of Mars and the turbulence of disturbed Venusian relationships.

- Chitra people are naturally good at helping others. Whenever they get an opportunity to help someone in need, their circumstances improve, and problems get resolved.

- Red, green, and all pastel colours resonate well with the energy of Chitra.

- Chanting the mantra - "Om *tam tham Chitra nakshatraye namah*" 108 times on days when the moon is transiting Chitra or on Tuesdays will help to connect you with your inner self, which in turn will help you to calm your mind.

Example

<u>Moon in Chitra</u>

<u>Anu Agarwal -</u> Indian film actress and a social worker.

Born on 11th January 1969, in Delhi, India, at 12 pm (estimated time of birth).

Anu Aggarwal was born on 11 January 1969 in New Delhi. She was a gold medalist in sociology at Delhi University. Her life has been an intriguing story. A dusky model who wanted to be a social worker, she found overnight stardom with her debut film, Aashiqui, in the 90s. She was an exception in the industry, which was still ruled by the 'fair-is-beautiful' dictum in 1990. A few years later, she gave up the arc lights to follow her inner calling.

In 1997, she joined a Yoga training school in Bihar. After 2 years, she was back in Mumbai to give up films altogether and to live her life as a yoga practitioner and to serve people. In 1999, she met with a fatal car accident, which left her with a shattered body and in a coma for 29 days. The car she was driving early one morning had turned 3 somersaults during torrential rains before crashing near Mumbai's Chowpatty area.

In 2015, Anu wrote her autobiography, where she talks about her near-death experience. 'Anusual - Memoir of a Girl Who Came Back from the Dead,' in which she talked about the accident and how her life changed after that. Anusual is the story of Anu Aggarwal, the dusky Delhi girl who went to Bombay and became an international model and then a star with her very first Bollywood movie, Aashiqui, only to chuck it all up and join a yogashram. Coming back to Bombay, she was involved in a horrifying car crash that put her in a coma for 29 days.

Miraculously, the girl who broke into a million pieces recovered and put the pieces of her life back together, first taking sanyas and then returning to Bombay to teach yoga.

In one of her interviews, Anu had said, "In the year 1999, I met with an accident and slipped into a coma. I used to live in an ashram before the accident, where I had a spiritual name. After the accident, I knew nothing, but I knew my spiritual name. In 2001, I took 'sanyas (renunciation)' and kept my head shaved. I lived with a bag in one hand, in humble surroundings. Just studying the mind and human psychology,"

After that, in 2001, she became a monk. She lives in Mumbai, practices yoga and is single. From Self-made to Self-healed, currently Anu works for the upliftment of society. She is a motivational TED featured speaker, runs the Anu Aggarwal Foundation for mental health, environmental well-being, and stress relief, and is discovering joy in the challenging times of today.

Analysis

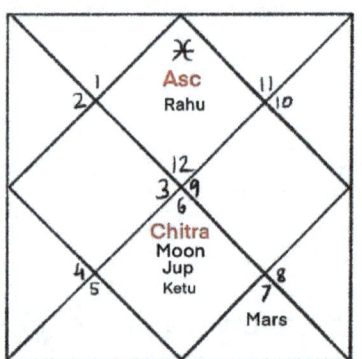

Anu has her <u>Moon in Chitra Pada 1 in the 7th house of Virgo.</u> Moon is sitting with Jupiter and Ketu in the 7th house of marriage and relationships. She is a Pisces Ascendant. Jupiter, the lord of the Ascendant, is sitting in the 7th house with Moon and Ketu. The lord of Chitra is Mars, who is sitting in the 8th house of sudden events in Libra.

In her book, 'Anusual,' she states that it was a Saturday, a day filled with heavy deluge of untimely rain, 2nd October 1999, in the early morning hours at 4 am (estimated time), when the fatal car accident happened.

She was running her <u>Jupiter Mercury Mars</u> dasha at that time.

- Jupiter and Saturn were transiting her first house, and Mercury and Mars were transiting her 7th house (Maraka house).

- On taking a closer look, in the Vimshotari dasha sequence - she was running her Jupiter Mercury Mars Saturn Mercury dasha. <u>Mercury</u> prana dasha, in a way, finalised the confirmation because, for Pisces Ascendants, Mercury becomes a functional malefic as it gets the Kendra Adi Pati Dosha, being the Lord of the 4th (Gemini) and 7th (Virgo) Kendra houses.

- Moreover, she was running her 31st year, which activated the 7th house.

- In the Chara dasha, she was running her - Cancer Pisces Pisces dasha (she is a Pisces Ascendant).

Here we can see that the placement of the planets, the 3 types of dashas and the transits confirm the event - which culminated in such circumstances (torrential tropical rain), the speed of the car, and it was nighttime, which caused the accident.

In an interview with Hindustan Times, Anu said that she has no memories of her car crash that left her in a coma for 29 days. When she regained consciousness, she was half-paralysed. "I didn't know the meaning of words and languages when I woke up... I didn't know English, though it came to me faster than Hindi did. I had lost everything. It was like landing on another planet altogether. I had no knowledge of history, geography or culture. I remembered nothing. There was a complete loss of memory," she had said.

She mentioned in one of her other interviews that after the accident, doctors had said, "She won't live. She will survive for hardly 3 years. But I was certain I could heal. Then everything I had learned I applied on myself and healed myself. Later, I started yoga therapy for slum kids and was recognised by other organisations where I gave talks."

She quoted in one of her interviews, *"To feel strong, to walk amongst humans with a tremendous feeling of confidence and superiority is not at all wrong. The sense of superiority in bodily strength is borne out of the long history of mankind paying homage in folklore, song and poetry to strong women."*

Anu is a Pisces Ascendant, where <u>Mars</u> becomes a functional benefic because it's the Lord of the 2nd house and the 9th house. The 9th house Lord is always considered a functional benefic for any birth chart because it's a house of bhagya - good fortune. Moreover, the avastha (state) of Mars is yuva (youth) so it's capable of giving strong results during its dasha and transit. The energies of Mars, the lord of Chitra in the 8th house of sudden events, brought the accident but also gave her the strength and determination to fight back and emerge as a victorious warrior.

The beneficence of Jupiter, the Ascendant lord, saved her life and gave her a positive outlook and optimism - even in the times of worst crises, she never lost hope. Anu is a brave hero who fought the inner war in order to restore and rebuild the strength of her body, her memory, and her personality. She has now become a source of motivation and inspiration for many others.

15
Swati

Om dam Swati nakshatraye namah

Zodiac degrees	6.40 - 20 deg Libra
Ruling planet	Libra - Venus and Swati - Rahu
Sanskrit name	Swati means independent and self-governing.
Astronomical name	A bright yellow star called Alpha- bootis, is seen in the constellation of Libra.
Symbol	Libra - balancing scales Swati- Pearl and a young plant blown by the wind.
Element	Air
Deity	Devi Saraswati - Goddess of music and learning. Vayu Dev
Quality	Chara - movable - Libra
Shakti	Pradhvamsha Shakti - Power to scatter like the wind, to transform.
Cast	Butcher
Gender	Male - Libra
Motivation	Kama - to fulfil desires.
Triguna	Rajas.
Tridosha	Vata
Body parts	Lungs and chest.
Direction	West, southwest and southeast.
Month	April - May, the latter half of Chaitra month.
Bird	Pigeon

Sound	Ru, re, ra, tha
Tree	Arjuna tree
Chakras	Swadhisthana - Venus and Ajna - Rahu
Das Maha Vidya	Devi Kamala - Venus and Devi Chinnamasta - Rahu

Special degrees -

Yoga Tara	0 deg Libra - Yoga Tara of Swati lies in the 3rd Pada of Chitra. It's a point where the planet will show the strongest and sure results during its dasha.
Pushkaramsha	3rd Pada The planets placed here will give good results during its dasha, like the blossoming of a flower.
Moola trikona	0 - 15 deg Libra - Mulatrikona of Venus When Venus is placed at these degrees in Libra, it will become very strong and will give excellent results during its dasha.
Amrit Nadi	15.20 - 15.26 deg Libra This brings good results, just like the nectar that nourishes.
Visha Nadi	9.46 - 10.40 deg Libra Brings situations which one does not like dealing with.
Debilitation	10 deg Libra - Maximum debilitation of the Sun. This will bring in situations which can create misunderstandings and arguments in a relationship.

Auspicious and inauspicious table -

Auspicious	Inauspicious
Activities Good for business and trade, starting any new courses, education and learning, social events, public dealings, financial transactions, buying and selling, grooming oneself, diplomatic activities, and pursuing art and music.	Activities Not good for travel and any aggressive war-like behaviour or activities, or any kind of arguments.
Days Mondays - only when it falls on the 5th or 7th lunar day. Thursdays - only when it falls on the 4th, 5th, 7th, 9th, 13th or 14th lunar day. Fridays - only when it falls on the 1st, 6th and 11th lunar day. Saturdays - only when it falls on the 2nd, 4th, 7th, 9th, 12th or 14th lunar day.	Days None

Compatibility table -

Swati	Compatible with
Sexual compatibility Yoni animal	Swati - Male buffalo Compatible with Hasta - Female buffalo
Sign compatibility	Libra - Gemini and Aquarius.
Nakshatra compatibility	Ardra and Shatbhishak.
Lunar day compatibility	Saptami tithi - 7th Lunar day.
Day compatibility	Friday
Colour compatibility	Grey and all light colours.
Numerological compatibility	6 and all numbers that add up to make 6.
Sound compatibility	Venus - palatal sounds - ch, ccha, ja, jha, nga

Sign Lord and nakshatra lord - Venus and Rahu - as described earlier.

Swati is the 2nd nakshatra ruled by Rahu. Here, the Rahu exaggerated the Venusian qualities of harmony, beauty and balance. The Libran charm of sweet words, amicable manners and a dazzling smile can easily win over many hearts. They will be very creative, will have a very good sense of dressing up, and will be exceptionally good at art, music, poetry and romance. Rahu makes them feel that there is always something more to achieve and more room for improvement, no matter how good they are at their work or how successful they become.

They like to be fair in their dealings and always see both sides of the story before making any conclusions. For them, keeping a harmonious balance in relationships and the interaction of give and take is vitally important. It can shatter their ideology and beliefs to see any kind of prejudice, intolerance or injustice being done in the society.

Quality, element, motivation, triguna, tridosha and chakras - as described earlier.

Shakti -

Pradhvamsha Shakti - Power to scatter like the wind, to transform.

Swati lies in the airy sign of Libra, which gives them a very Vata like qualities of creativity, movement and flexibility. Just as a strong wind can scatter the leaves and twigs, the plants that are strongly rooted sway in the direction of the wind but are not uprooted.

Wind is a very important natural phenomenon which helps the ecology of plants and animals. Whether it's a blowing winter gale or a soft summer breeze, the wind has the ability to help things move that otherwise couldn't. For example, seeds are dispersed by the wind, which helps the plant population to grow. Subsequently, this helps the herbivorous animals to find their food.

Research has shown that wind is very beneficial to plants because plants that begin growth in the absence of wind tend to fall over or break more easily than those grown in the presence of some wind.

Inference

Swati natives have an amazing resilience to go through tough times with a natural ease, because of their wonderful quality of being able to adjust to the change of circumstances more easily than others. In the process of doing so, they are able to discard the habits that are harming them and transform themselves by consciously developing habits that benefit their growth and success in every way. Every change they face in life brings them to a better place than before.

Symbolic signification

Libra - Balancing scales - as described earlier.

Swati - A young plant swayed by the wind and Pearl.

A young plant swayed by the wind -

Swati is placed in Libra, which is governed by the air element. The lord of Swati is Rahu, and the influence of air is stronger. The symbol of the wind and the resilience of a young plant show the strength of Swati-born natives.

Pearl -

Natural pearls are formed in the oysters under the water and can come from either salt or freshwater sources. It is formed when an irritant, like a sand grain, finds its way into a particular oyster, mussel, or clam. As a defence mechanism, the mollusc secretes a fluid to coat the irritant. Layer upon layer of this coating is deposited on the irritant until a lustrous pearl is formed.

There are essentially 3 types of pearls - natural (also called an oriental Pearl), cultured Pearl and imitation Pearl. A cultured pearl undergoes the same process. The only difference is that the irritant is a surgically implanted bead or piece of shell called Mother of Pearl. Often, these shells are ground oyster shells that are worth significant amounts of money because they are used as irritant catalysts to produce other quality pearls. The resulting core is, therefore, much larger than in a natural pearl. Yet, as long as there are enough layers of nacre (the secreted fluid covering the irritant), it results in a beautiful pearl.

Imitation pearls are a different story altogether. In most cases, a glass bead is dipped into a solution made from fish scales. This coating is thin and may eventually wear off. One can usually tell an imitation by biting on it. Fake pearls glide across your teeth, while the layers of nacre on real pearls feel gritty. The Island of Mallorca is known for its imitation pearl industry.

Inference

Those who are born with the Ascendant, Sun or Moon in Swati gain strength from every challenge they face. Just as the making of a precious pearl is initiated by an irritant and the process is slow, but in the end the refined outcome is worth every minute of the incubation time spent in the stillness of the oyster. Swati natives also pass through oyster-like situations and emerge as precious pearls with beautiful, gracious qualities. This makes them unassumingly attractive and irresistible because they have taken the time to groom and develop themselves into wholesome beings who exclude the beauty of a perfectly shaped Pearl.

Mythology -

Deity - Vayu Dev

Vayu Dev is a primary Hindu deity. He is the lord of the winds and breath. The other names of Vayu are - anila, vata, vayana, pavana and prana (the vital life force). Vayu is the root of vātāvaranam, which means atmosphere in Sanskrit.

In the Rigveda, Vayu is associated with the winds, the Maruts being described as being born from Vayu's belly. Vayu is also said to be the first god who received the soma (nectar), and then he and Indra shared their first drink. In the Vedic hymns, Vayu is described as having exceptional beauty, who is a fighter and destroyer, powerful and heroic. He is also said to be the spiritual father of Hanuman and Bhima.

The significance of Prana Vayu - the life-giving force, is beautifully highlighted in the Upanishads via a mythological story, which states that - once the deities engaged in a contest to determine who among them is the greatest. The only way to find out was by seeing how their exit would affect the human being. So, one by one, the deities took turns to leave the body- as the man or the woman grew frail and old. When the deity of vision left - the person could still continue to live as a blind person. As the deity of hearing left - one could not hear. As the deity of taste left - one could not enjoy the delicious food. As the deity of movement left - one could not walk or hold things…and so on, but still, a person could continue to live on, though impaired and health being compromised in various ways.

On the other hand, even if all the deities of vision, hearing, taste and movement stayed in their place and did not leave, the Mukhya Prāna (main life breath force) started to leave the body, all the other deities (of sight, hearing, taste, touch and movement) were inexorably pulled off their posts by force, just as a powerful horse yanks off pegs in the ground to which he is bound. This caused the other deities to realise that they could function only when empowered by Vayu and could be overpowered by him easily.

Interesting facts -

- Prana Vayu, as the life breath, is the giver and taker of life.

- Vayu is said to be the only deity not afflicted by demons of sin and disease who can attack without warning.

- It is said that if one has to know Brahman (the creator), one has to know Vayu through the mantric syllable 'OM.'

Recently, the 2nd wave of COVID in 2021 has made us all realise and become acutely aware of how vital the life breath is. The process of inhalation and exhalation marks life. It's cessation causes the death of the physical body promptly and surely.

Inference

Since Swati is placed in Libra, which is governed by air, it gives it the vital, mobile and creative qualities of the air. It also shows the flexible nature of Swati, which is heightened by the lordship of Rahu. They are extremely friendly people and know how to get along even with those who may be completely opposite to them in their likes, dislikes and behaviour.

Just as the power of the wind or air should not be underestimated or taken for granted, similarly, the power of Swati natives lies in their charm. In their quietness, they are resilient. In their fury they can come across as a tornado, destroying everything that comes in its way. But like a blade of grass, they have the endurance to withstand it not because of their pride but because of their humility. This is the most beautiful and the most charming aspect of their personality.

Devi Saraswati

Devi Saraswati is known as the goddess of knowledge, music, art, speech, wisdom, and learning. The earliest known mention of Saraswati as a goddess is in the Rigveda. Some Hindus celebrate the festival of Vasant Panchami (also called Saraswati Pooja), the 5th day of spring, in her honour. On this day, the young children are initiated into writing the letters of the alphabet, starting with the sound 'Om.'

Saraswati is a Sanskrit fusion word of saras, which means pooling water, but it also sometimes is translated as speech and the word vati means- she who possesses. The word Saraswati signifies - ponds, lakes and plenty of water. In Rig Veda, Saraswati appears both as a reference to a river on the northwestern side of India and as a significant deity in the Hindu tradition. She is described as the best of rivers, mothers, and goddesses. In some interpretations, Sara is translated as essence and Sva (the self). Thus, the name Saraswati would translate to - She who helps realise the essence of self.

She is the personification of purity and consort of Lord Brahma - the creator. She is often depicted as a beautiful woman dressed in pure white, often seated on a white lotus, which symbolises light, knowledge and truth. She not only embodies knowledge but also the experience of the highest reality. Her iconography is typically in white themes, from dresses to flowers to swans. The white colour symbolises Sattva Guna or purity, which shows the discriminating ability to recognise true knowledge from false information.

Inference

Those who are born with the Ascendant, Sun or Moon in Swati are very learned, wise and talented in creative arts, music, acting and singing. They have inherent artistic talent and can become successful in the fields of art, drawing, painting, crafts, designing, acting, singing, writing and public speaking. They always find great fulfilment in creating any work of art, making their own designs, writing their own stories and designing their own costumes.

Swati padas

6.40 - 20 deg Libra

Padas	Degrees
1	6.40 - 10 deg Libra
2	10 - 13.20 deg Libra
3	13.20 - 16.40 deg Libra
4	16.40 - 20 deg Libra

Pada 1

6.40 - 10 deg Libra, Navamsha- Sagittarius (Lord - Jupiter)

Rashi Lord - Venus and Nakshatra Lord- Rahu

Pada 1 of Swati falls in the navamsha of Sagittarius. Therefore, it carries the energy of Venus, Rahu and Jupiter. Venus and Jupiter are both Gurus in their own right and expert advisors in their own field. Rahu amplifies this quality. Therefore, those who are born in the 1st Pada will be natural advisors. They will love to counsel others - telling them what is the best thing to do, which is the best way forward, and how to solve a particular problem. They will find that somehow, people around them always end up asking them for their wise input and philosophical guidance. For example, Swati Pada 1 in the 3rd house will love to tell stories and give advice to their siblings and neighbours.

They will also be masters at exaggerating the facts and expressing the stories at a grander and bigger scale than they actually are. It's very important for them to present things in an admirable and pleasant manner, even if it means adding frills to create an inflated image. Because of this quality, they can do very well in the field of advertising.

Careers

Teachers, advisors, counsellors working in the field of advertisement, public relations co-ordinators, film directors, leaders, businessmen, IT professionals, fashion designers, writers, speakers, actors, social workers, psychologists, philosophers, religious leaders, priests, astrologers, office workers and working from home.

Pada 2

10 - 13.20 deg Libra, Navamsha - Capricorn (Lord - Saturn)

Rashi Lord - Venus and Nakshatra Lord- Rahu

In the 2nd Pada of Swati, the influence of Venus, Rahu and Saturn will be seen, which makes them feel the responsibility of relationships. Since the navamsha of this Pada lies in Capricorn, the natives will be more ambitious and service-oriented. The effect of Saturn in Libra gives slow but steady and good results because Saturn is exalted in Libra.

Navamsha represents adulthood after 30 years, which shows that as they grow older they will become more ambitious about doing something for the society, community, nation or the world. They will hold a position of responsibility where their decisions can make a difference in bringing well-being to the people around them. Their public image will be that of a responsible, hard-working person who does not rush into things but has a slow and cautious approach to life.

Careers

Managers, office workers, businessmen, IT professionals, film-makers, fashion designers, florists, farmers, gardeners, actors, musicians, astrologers, social workers, technicians, doctors, nurses, teachers, cooks, doing a regular job and working from home.

Pada 3

13.20 - 16.40 deg Libra, Navamsha - Aquarius (Lord - Saturn)

Rashi Lord - Venus and Nakshatra Lord - Rahu

The navamsha of the 3rd Pada of Swati is placed in Aquarius, which gives the effect of Venus Rahu and Saturn. Both Capricorn and Aquarius are ruled by Saturn, the difference is in the orientation. In the navamsha of Aquarius, the influence of Saturn will associate them with a large organisation, serving people through a job or through volunteering. They may even run their own organisation, which will be globally recognised. In Aquarius, Saturn expands its area of work in terms of reaching out to people, they reach a larger audience or cater to a large group of customers.

Rahu expands the effect of Venus and Saturn, which makes them artistic yet technical and scientific, so they have the intelligence to create something that looks good as well as serves the purpose very well for what the product is built. For example, Swati pada 2 in the 5th house will make them very creative and they will benefit through large organisations. Their children, followers or students are likely to follow their trade.

Careers

Engineers, scientists, architects, writers, poets, artists, actors, IT professionals, interior designers, fashion designers, doctors, teachers, and businessmen, running voluntary organisations or working for them and working from home.

Pada 4

16.40 - 20 deg Libra, Navamsha - Pisces (Lord - Jupiter)

Rashi Lord - Venus and Nakshatra Lord - Rahu

In this Pada, there will be the influence of Venus, Rahu and Jupiter.

Since the navamsha lies in Pisces- after 30 years of age, they will move to a foreign country for settlement or will have to work away from home. They will have a very dreamy and philosophical approach to life. Life's circumstances will make them reflect and introspect on human behaviour and relationships.

Jupiter gives them a very moralistic and righteous outlook on life and the reality of the world does not match their ethical standards. As they get older, they will begin to feel disillusioned with the unethical ways of society in general. For example, Swati Pada 4, in the 9th house, will travel to a foreign country or away from home for higher education. Their teacher, father, or father-like figure will be their greatest support and motivation, who will guide the native through all difficult circumstances.

Rahu amplifies the Jupitarian optimism and Venusian sense of aesthetics. This makes them lovers of beauty and harmony in all forms, and they appreciate all forms of art. Peaceful thoughts, loving emotions and creative ideas are what drive them, keep them motivated and bring fulfilment. Even if the situations are not conducive for creativity to happen, they will still find hope, beauty and harmony in the worst of circumstances. Such is the beneficence of Jupiter and Venus, who are both Gurus and have the brilliance of guiding one through all good and bad situations.

Careers-

Psychologists, philosophers, guides, gurus, astrologers, priests, teachers, advisors, counsellors, spiritual mediums, designers, artists, florists, actors, singers, musicians, writers, poets, IT professionals, self-employed and working from home.

The effect of planets

Swati -	Planets that get affected
Yoga Karka - Most benefic	Saturn
Functional Benefic - give good results during their dasha.	Venus
Functional Malefic - can give problems during their dasha.	Jupiter, Rahu and Ketu
Functional Neutral	Sun, Moon and Mercury
Kendra Adi Pati Dosha - can be malefic	Mars

Swati Ascendant

Those who are born with the Ascendant in Swati will have the exaggerated effect of Venus because the lord of Swati is Rahu. This gives them a very pleasing personality and the opposite sex finds them very attractive. Moreover, they have the knack of charming others through their handsome and beautiful looks, amicable manners, sweet speech and a dashing smile.

The air element of Libra makes them very creative, talented and intelligent. They are great at making friends when they wish to and are very flexible in their approach to life. Vata tridosha will be more predominant in them. Having a stable and regular routine will help to make them feel grounded and balanced. Having warm beverages and warm-cooked meals will suit their Vata constitution. Disruption of routine or too much travelling can also cause Vata problems like constipation and joint pains and aches, especially in old age.

Their sense of aesthetics is so finely tuned that any shabby or filthy surroundings can make them feel physically ill and out of their element. Relationships are the pivot of their joys and sorrows. A sense of peace, tranquillity, harmony and beauty is a very vital need for them. They are very good at making friends and handling public relations.

Their adaptable nature helps them to adjust to situations quickly and get on with what needs to be done. Swati-born people are usually very successful in a profession that deals with people.

Sun in Swati

When the Sun is placed in Swati, it will share the qualities of Venus and Rahu. Since the Sun and Venus are not good friends and Rahu amplifies the effect, the natives will have a very sensitive ego and are likely to be quick-tempered. They will be very creative and intelligent and will do well to explore and develop their talent independently. They can become excellent artists, writers, poets, singers, actors, film directors, designers, architects, scientists, astronomers, or astrologers. Their positive qualities will be generosity, creativity, intelligence, being fair in their dealings and a wonderful sense of aesthetics. On the negative side, they can become pompous or overly judgemental.

For example, in Sun in Hasta, in the 4th house, the natives will try to keep a balance between work and home life. Since the Sun is sitting in the sign of Libra, which is ruled by Venus (Sun and Venus are considered enemies), and Rahu exaggerates this effect - therefore the native will find that at home - discussions can easily flare up into arguments, and their mum will be a very creative person but short-tempered. This is more likely to happen during the Sun, Venus or Rahu dasha.

Moon in Swati

Moon in Swati will make the natives very emotionally attached to people who are close to them - friends and relations. They will be very intuitive, imaginative, talented, artistic and creative, and can make successful public relations managers, actors, designers, film directors, writers, singers and artists. The opposite sex finds them very attractive. They have very pleasing personalities and beautiful manners. For example, moon in Swati, in the 5th house of creativity, will be very talented and can become successful in any kind of show business of acting or advertising.

Their positive qualities are - standing up for justice, being fair in their dealings, being intelligent, charming, friendly, gentle, well-mannered, caring, loving and kind. When they are feeling out of balance, they can become indecisive, tend to procrastinate, become argumentative, lazy, pleasure seeking and temperamental.

For them, the epitome of love means mating of the hearts and the mind. Their partner has to be their good friend, too, with whom they can share their thoughts, ideas, philosophy, emotions, likes, dislikes, plans, hopes and aspirations. Together, they can build their place of tranquillity called home. Without a sense of genuine sharing, there can be no relationship for them.

The poetry of Swati

Swati - Swa - the self, Ati - the extreme.

To discover thy own enchanting self - is the theme.

Through the pearls of wisdom, untold

Through the unfolding of relationships new and old,

Through the might of winds - to cope,

The young plant survives with hope.

A touch of love - that seems like a flight of a feather so light,

A charming manner is such a delight,

With a twinkle in the eyes, and a smile so dashing,

Wins over hearts effortlessly, the attraction so smashing,

Balancing the scales of the game of life,

They become skilled masters - who learn to ride the tide.

Remedies

- <u>Das Maha Vidya</u> - as described earlier.

- For the Vata constitution - a daily exercise routine will keep them grounded and in good health. They should not do very vigorous exercises, like running or cycling in the hot sun, or tough muscle-building gym exercises for a long duration at a stretch. It will be better to listen to their body. When they feel exhausted, they must take ample rest before getting into excessive activity again.

- Planning well before travelling, taking care of your diet, and eating warm meals at regular times will help to keep the Vata in balance.

- The yogic asanas and pranayama will be particularly helpful in balancing the excessive Vata or out-of-sync feeling. The alternate nose breathing technique (alom vilom) is an excellent and quick way to pacify restlessness, calm down the mind and prepare oneself for any creative projects.

- Meditation (breath watch) is another beautiful and scientific technique for calming any agitation or stress in the body or the mind. This will help to calm the turbulence of disturbed Venusian relationships.

- Swati people will find that every time they face any challenging or difficult situation in their life, it transforms them and brings them to a better place than before.

- Grey and all pastel colours resonate well with the energy of Swati.

- Chanting the mantra - *"Om dam Swati nakshatraye namah"* 108 times on days when the moon is transiting Swati, or on Fridays, will help to connect you with your inner self, and this will help you to calm your mind.

Example

<u>Ascendant and Moon in Swati</u>

<u>George Harrison -</u> He was an English musician, singer-songwriter, and film producer who achieved international fame as the lead guitarist of the Beatles.

Born on 25th February 1943, in Liverpool, UK, at 12:10 am, died on 29th November 2001 at the age of 58, in California, USA.

George was born in Liverpool and was the youngest of 4 children of Harold Harrison and Louise. His mother was particularly supportive, "All she wanted for her children is that they should be happy, and she recognised that nothing made George quite as happy as making music." She was an enthusiastic music fan and was known among friends for her loud singing voice, which at times startled visitors by rattling the Harrisons' windows. When Louise was pregnant with George, she often listened to the weekly broadcast of Radio India. Harrison's biographer Joshua Greene wrote, "Every Sunday she tuned in to mystical sounds evoked by sitars and tablas, hoping that the exotic music would bring peace and calm to the baby in the womb."

In early 1956, he had an epiphany. While riding his bicycle, he heard Elvis Presley's "Heartbreak Hotel" playing from a nearby house, and the song piqued his interest in rock and roll. He often sat at the back of the class, drawing guitars in his school books. George later commented, "I was totally into guitars, the first person I ever saw playing a guitar was Slim Whitman, either a photo of him in a magazine or live on television. Guitars were definitely coming in."

At first, his dad was apprehensive about his son's interest in pursuing a music career. However, in 1956, he bought George a Dutch Egmond flat-top acoustic guitar, which, according to Harold, cost £3.10. One of his father's friends taught Harrison how to play "Whispering", "Sweet Sue" and "Dinah". Inspired by Donegan's music, Harrison formed a skiffle group, the Rebels, with his brother Peter and a friend, Arthur Kelly.

In 1958, George became part of the Beatles at the young age of 15, with McCartney and John Lennon when the band were still a skiffle group called the Quarrymen. In 1963, George's 1st solo writing credit for the song "Don't Bother Me" was included in the Beatles album. George embraced Indian culture and helped broaden the scope of popular music and Hindu-aligned spirituality in the Beatles' work. By 1978, George had moved away from the Beatles and started taking great interest in Indian classical music, eastern Gurus and the Sitar, and he became known as "the maharaja of raga-rock".

In June 1965, Harrison and the other Beatles were appointed Members of the Order of the British Empire (MBE). They received their insignia from the Queen at Buckingham Palace on 26 October. Rolling Stone magazine ranked him number 11 in their list of the "100 Greatest Guitarists of All Time".

His 1st marriage was to model Pattie Boyd in 1966, and ended in divorce in 1977. The following year, he married Olivia Arias, with whom he had a son, Dhani. Harrison died from lung cancer in 2001 at the age of 58, 2 years after surviving a knife attack by an intruder at his Friar Park home. His remains were cremated, and the ashes were scattered according to Hindu tradition in a private ceremony in the Ganges and Yamuna rivers in India. He left an estate of almost £100 million.

Eric Idle described George as "one of the few morally good people that rock and roll has produced." A documentary film entitled George Harrison - Living in the Material World, directed by Martin Scorsese, was released in October 2011. George was posthumously honoured with the Lifetime Achievement Award at the Grammy Awards in February 2015.

Analysis

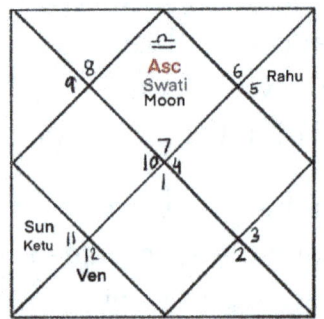

George Harrison has his <u>Ascendant in the 2nd Pada of Swati and his Moon in the 1st Pada of Swati</u>, so he is a very strong Libra personality whose approach to life was absolutely led by the creative talent of music, harmony and beauty. He is a Libra ascendant, and the moon is sitting in the 1st house, which shows that his physical personality, life events, thoughts and emotions are in sync. The kind of situations that happened around him supported him in his love for music.

He was born with the inherent gift of musical talent of playing the string instruments. It's interesting to see that his mother also had a musical inclination. When she was pregnant, she listened to a lot of Indian classical instrumental music which had the sound of the tabla and sitar.

This shows that the soul that has come into the womb influences the mother's interests. The very fact that a particular soul chooses a particular womb is based on the matching or synchronisation of their interests, likes, dislikes and tendencies.

George had a very clear path and vision of what he wanted to pursue in his life, and right from childhood, he began to show his talent for music. His documentary states that he often sat at the back of the class drawing guitars in his school books and said, "I was totally into guitars."

Rahu, being the lord of Swati, amplified the Venusian qualities of - having a fine sense of balance and rhythm, beauty and harmony, creativity and spirituality. In 1956 he got his first guitar when he was running his <u>Rahu Venus Ketu</u> dasha. This marked the beginning of the spark of music that filled his life with the sound of music.

Rahu, the lord of Swati, is in the 11th house of Leo in Magha, the house of gains, which made him the king of music. He became known as "the maharaja of raga-rock", which means the king of kings of rock music and classical music. In hindsight, we can see how befittingly perfect this title was for Rahu sitting in Magha.

Venus is the Lord of the Ascendant (Libra), exalted in the 6th house of Pisces. Which shows his job and daily routine involved music, creativity and spirituality. Moreover, Venus is in Uttara Bhadrapada, which is ruled by Saturn - he served the public through his Music.

Ketu and Sun are sitting in the 5th house of creativity in Aquarius - Sun is in Shatabhishak, which gave him technical understanding, and Ketu is in Dhanishta, which gave a wealth of music and spirituality. We can see how appropriately the role of nakshatras plays out - Ketu in Dhanishta shows a strong past life connection with music, because Dhanishta is associated with drum beats, dance and rhythm. This is confirmed by the fact that his life theme revolved around music. Right from the time of being in his Mother's womb - to the time even after his death- he was honoured with the most prestigious Grammy award in Music.

In such worldly and mystical ways, destiny unfolds and plays out the drama of life. In this context, Astrology helps us to understand life from a deeper perspective of the inner world and a wider perspective of the outer world.

16
Vishakha

Om dham nam Vishakha nakshatraye namah

Zodiac degrees	20 deg Libra - 3.20 deg Scorpio Libra - 1st, 2nd and 3rd padas and Scorpio - 4th pada
Ruling planet	Libra - Venus and Scorpio - Mars Vishakha - Jupiter
Sanskrit name	Vishakha means forked, a point where the branch splits into 2 or has a sub-branch.
Astronomical name	The 4 stars that form the shape of the hanging scale, or a forked branch, seen in the constellation of Libra.
Symbol	Libra - balancing scales and Scorpio - scorpion Vishakha - decorated arched gateway.
Element	Air - Libra and Water - Scorpio
Deity	Indra dev and Agni dev
Quality	Chara - movable - Libra and Sthira - fixed - Scorpio Vishakha - Mishra - mixed
Shakti	Vayapna Shakti - Ability to manifest. The Sanskrit word Vyapana means - to completely cover, overspread, occupy thoroughly, or pervade throughout the area.
Cast	Mleccha - outcast
Gender	Male - Libra Female - Scorpio
Motivation	Kama- to fulfil desires - Libra Moksha - liberation - Scorpio
Triguna	Rajas - Libra and Tamas - Scorpio

Tridosha	Vata - Libra and Kapha - Scorpio
Body parts	Breast and arms.
Direction	West and north
Month	May, the first half of Vishakha month.
Bird	Swan
Sound	tee, tu, tey, to
Tree	Apple tree
Chakras	Muladhara - Mars, Swathishtana - Venus and Ajna - Jupiter
Das Maha Vidya	Devi Bagalamukhi - Mars, Devi Kamala - Venus and Devi Tara - Jupiter

Special degrees -

Yoga Tara	21 deg Libra It's a point where the planet will show the strongest and sure results during its dasha.
Pushkaramsha	2nd and 4th Pada The planets placed here will give good results during its dasha, like the blossoming of a flower.
Pushkar bhaga	24 deg Libra Any planets sitting at this point will give excellent results during their dasha, like the blossoming of a flower.
Amrit Nadi	28.22 - 29.16 deg Libra This brings good results, just like the nectar that nourishes.
Visha Nadi	23.60 - 24 deg Libra Brings situations which one does not like dealing with.
Exaltation	20 deg Libra - Maximum exaltation of Saturn. When Saturn is placed at this degree, it will give excellent results during its dasha. It will be a particularly supportive period for relationships and partnerships.
Debilitation	3 deg Scorpio - Maximum debilitation of the Moon. This will bring in situations which make one feel emotionally starved or not able to express their deepest feelings, and can create misunderstandings and arguments in a relationship.

Auspicious and inauspicious table -

Auspicious	Inauspicious
<u>Activities</u> Good for all activities that require skill, ability, an	<u>Activities</u> Not good for travel, initiations, starting new

aggressive, forceful and focused approach, arguments, debates, and fighting court cases. Working towards one's goal, making resolutions, and penance, all types of ceremonies, functions, parties and awards, dressing up and decorating, for romance and sexual activities.	projects, laying foundations, marriage, and activities that require a tactful, calm and composed approach.
<u>Days</u> **Saturdays** - only when it falls on the 2nd, 4th, 7th, 9th, 12th, or 14th lunar day.	<u>Days</u> <u>Sundays</u> - only when it falls on the 3rd, 4th, 8th, 9th, 13th, or 14th lunar day. <u>Thursdays-</u> only when it falls on the 6th, 8th, 9th, 12th, or 13th lunar day. <u>Fridays</u> - only when it falls on the 2nd, 3rd, 6th, 8th, 10th, or 11th lunar day.

Compatibility table -

Vishakha	Compatible with
Sexual compatibility Yoni animal	Vishakha - Female tiger Compatible with Chitra - Male tiger.
Sign compatibility	Libra - Padas 1, 2 and 3 - Gemini and Aquarius. Scorpio - Pada 4 - Cancer and Pisces.
Nakshatra compatibility	Punarvasu and Purva Bhadrapada.
Lunar day compatibility	Sashti tithi - 6th lunar day and Saptami tithi - 7th Lunar day.
Day compatibility	Tuesday, Thursday and Friday
Colour compatibility	Grey, red and all light colours.
Numerological compatibility	3, 6 and 9 - all numbers that add up to make 3, 6 and 9.
Sound compatibility	Jupiter - dental sounds - ta, ttha, da, dha, knna Venus - palatal sounds - ch, ccha, ja, jha, nga Mars - guttural sounds - ka, kha, ga, gha, kna

Sign Lord and nakshatra lord - <u>Venus, Mars and Jupiter</u> - as described earlier.

Vishakha is the 2nd nakshatra ruled by Jupiter. Here, Jupitarian energy combines with Venus in the 1st, 2nd and 3rd padas, which makes the natives very idealistic in their approach to life. They like to do things lawfully and ethically and strive to keep the balance between worldly and spiritual endeavours. Jupiter also likes to expand its horizons. With the influence of Venus, it does so in a way that helps to harmonise and pleasantly balance situations.

Since Jupiter and Venus are both Gurus, they can bring a sense of knowing better than others. Jupiter and Venus dashas will be significant for them, which can bring success, comfort and happiness. The placement of Jupiter and Venus in the birth chart and the navamsha will reveal the areas of life in which the transformations can happen, and the dashas and transits will give a clue about the timings.

For example, Venus in the 2nd house will have good and happy relations with the family one is born into, and Jupiter in the 4th house will give the support of a very wise and learned mother or a mother-like figure. The natives themselves will be very fortunate, learned and wise, which will help them to sail through difficult situations quite effortlessly.

The 4th Pada of Vishakha lies in Scorpio, whose Lord is Mars. Those who are born with the Ascendant, Sun or Moon in this Pada will have a more determined and ambitious quality.

They would like to get to the root of the problem and study things in depth in order to gain a complete understanding. The Jupiter Mars influence will give them a very ethical approach to life. They will stick to their principles no matter what and will be brave enough to follow the path of righteousness even in adverse circumstances.

They will like to keep things to themselves and will have very few close friends with whom they can share their inner feelings. They can come across as arrogant and stubborn, but the truth is that they cannot operate frivolously. They have to know the depth of a person or a relationship before they are convinced and can commit themselves to it. Once they make their choice they follow it sincerely through thick and thin.

Quality, element, motivation, triguna, tridosha and chakras - as described earlier.

Shakti - Vayapna Shakti - Ability to manifest.

The Sanskrit word vyapak literally means all-inclusive, or as expansive as it can get, or have a wide range of influence. The energy of Vishakha is such that it has a mixed quality of endurance and stability, and of ambition and determination. Between a desire and the goal, there is a distance to cover, the distance of determination and endurance. Vishakha natives have the ability to manifest their dreams into reality because of sustained perseverance, and every time they achieve the desired result, it helps them grow and expand towards higher possibilities.

Jupiter, being the nakshatra lord, gives them a very optimistic and idealistic approach to life. Their strong belief in having a positive outcome carries them through their tough times and helps them to manifest their dreams at a much higher scale, which has the quality of influencing everyone around them.

Symbolic signification

Libra - Balancing scales - as described earlier, Scorpio - scorpion

Vishakha - the split and a decorated arched gateway.

Scorpion

The evolutionary history of scorpions goes back 435 million years. Scorpions are predatory arachnids of the order Scorpiones. Like many of the modern crabs, early scorpions were marine or amphibious. They have 8 legs and are easily recognized by a pair of grasping pincers and a narrow, segmented tail, often carried in a characteristic forward curve over the back and always ending with a stinger.

They mainly live in deserts but have adapted to a wide range of environmental conditions. Scorpions, with their powerful stingers, appear in art, folklore and mythology. A classical myth about Scorpius tells how the giant Scorpion and its enemy, Orion, became constellations on opposite sides of the sky.

There are over 2,500 described species of scorpions, which primarily prey on insects and other invertebrates. They use their pincers to restrain and kill prey. Scorpions themselves are preyed on by larger animals. They use their venomous sting both for killing prey and for defence. Owls, lizards, a few small snakes, some rodents, frogs and toads eat scorpions. Many predators are able to handle scorpions safely by biting or breaking off the scorpion's tail. While some vertebrates and arthropods are immune to the scorpion venom.

The stinging of scorpions usually results in pain, swelling, and lesions varying in severity, with only a few that can cause severe allergic or necrotizing reactions. There are 2 species of scorpions that can inflict stings which can result in death- the Palestinian deathstalker and the Brazilian yellow scorpion. However, life-saving antivenom exists for both species of scorpion stings.

Scorpions are largely nocturnal, and they hide during the day in the confines of their burrows, in natural cracks, or under rocks and bark. They become active after darkness has fallen and cease activity sometime before dawn. The vast majority of scorpions are nonsocial, solitary creatures and interact only at birth, during courtship, or for cannibalism.

Scorpions are quite adaptable in terms of ecology, behaviour and physiology. Some species can be supercooled below the freezing point for weeks yet return within hours to normal levels of activity. Others survive total immersion underwater for as long as 1 or 2 days. Desert scorpions can withstand temperatures of 47 °C which is several degrees higher than the lethal temperatures for other desert arthropods.

Interesting facts and observations -

- A Scorpio has 8 legs. - Scorpio represents the 8th sign in the original horoscope.

- Scorpios are largely nocturnal and hide during the day in the confines of their burrows. They feel safe in the darkness and, become active at night and cease their activity just before dawn in the morning. - Scorpio Ascendants tend to be more active during the night and like working on their projects in the coolness of the night.

- They have a deep and natural connection with the phases of the moon, especially with the new moon days. - Those who have their moon placed in Scorpio will feel more connected to the new moon days when the nights are absolutely dark, and the energy is more intense and inward drawn.

- Scorpios shine in the dark because of the fluorescence effect. On new moon nights, scorpions can be seen at distances of 10 metres. - Scorpio Ascendant natives like wearing fluorescent colours, or a small fluorescent design will be marked on any of the accessories they carry, especially when they are going out at night.

- A Scorpio stings suddenly without warning, both for attack and defence. - Similarly, the 8th house represents sudden events. Those who are born with Ascendant or Moon in Scorpio, when upset about something, their words can sting like venom.

- Scientists have found out that early scorpions were marine or amphibious. Their origin lies in water. - In Astrology, Scorpio is a water sign, the water of the deep wells, which is a safe haven for the Scorpios.

- Scorpios have a very strong grip that helps them to move rapidly along surfaces at any angle, even upside down. Once they grab something, they will not let go. - Those who have their Ascendant or Moon in Scorpio, even in difficult circumstances and tough terrain, have the resilience to move across fearlessly with determination.

- The fact that Scorpios have been around for 435 million years shows their great quality of endurance. Over time, Scorpios learnt to adapt and evolve to survive under extreme heat and extreme cold. - Scorpio-born natives have an amazing ability to survive under harsh circumstances, which is a very clever and heroic quality.

- Majority of scorpions are nonsocial, solitary creatures. - Those who are born in the sign of Scorpio like to have their solitary time because they are deep thinkers and need a lot of time by themselves to contemplate and figure out the root cause of any external situations they face.

Inference

The 4th Pada of Vishakha lies in Scorpio. Therefore, they have the influence of scorpion characteristics of energy, strength, depth, secrecy, research, defence, aggression, determination, resilience and survival.

Scorpios have a deep connectivity with water and moonless nights. Their deep emotional nature stems from the fact that the Scorpio is a water sign. Here the water represents the confined space of wells or ponds, where the water merges from the depth of the earth. They feel very comfortable and very much at home in dark, hidden spaces and in the coolness of the moonlight. We must understand that dark space does not have a negative connotation but signifies a dimension or an area of life that can be understood or perceived only by looking deeper. This is where one can discover a whole new world where life is throbbing with much more intensity.

They are born survivors. Their determination and grit help them overcome the toughest obstacles. Scorpions are known to be aggressive by nature. Moreover, Mars, the planet of energy and aggression, rules the sign of Scorpio.

Similarly, Scorpio-born natives have a determined and aggressive approach towards surviving through tough times and attaining their goals. They do this by going deep into the problem, understanding the situation fully and coping with it accordingly. They are very sensitive to feelings and emotions and, therefore, more vulnerable. Because of this they feel the inner need to protect and defend themselves from outside influences that can impact them negatively.

For them to connect to any person, philosophy or faith, they need to feel a deep connection at the emotional level. They are the types who give themselves totally towards a relationship or a cause or give nothing. They cannot be frivolous about anything in their lives and are very enduring friends. On the other side, they can also be deadly enemies, because when they are hurt, their sting of words or actions can wound the opponent deeply or seriously.

The split

The word Vishakha literally means - branched into 2. For a split to happen, there has to be a very forceful energy that can push through and cause a split. If we look at a junction point of a branch of a tree closely where, the branch splits into 2. It will have a slightly bulbous node, which highlights the residual effect of the concentrated and focused form of effect that caused the split to happen.

Inference

Vishakha natives have forceful energy, which can cause the split to happen, yet this outburst of energy is stable and controlled enough to hold the forked branch in place and does not let it fall off completely. Similarly, Vishakha born people have the capability of breaking through old beliefs and traditions and forming their own code of conduct, yet their branched approach is not radically different but has the essence of the mother branch in it.

They are ambitious enough to set their own goals and follow them, even though the attempt to do so may not be initially an easy change. The quality of this inherent forceful energy in them lures and helps them take this step - to branch out independently, yet stay connected at the root level.

The split also signifies a situation where they have to split their energy, time, finance or resources between 2 areas- of work or home life, between 2 people, 2 relationships, or 2 jobs. This can also bring dilemmas in their life, where they cannot decide which one to choose because both choices available look equally necessary, equally good or equally bad.

The decorated arched gateway

A decorated gateway marks the triumph, the celebrations and a happy occasion. Vishakha natives have several such occasions in their lives where they feel victorious - like having won a battle or having passed through a difficult situation and emerged a winner. Or they might get to literally pass through a decorated gateway as a very important guest invited to a function, or hosting it. Those who have their Ascendant, Sun or the Moon in Vishakha, at some point in their life will surely pass through a decorated gateway.

Mythology -

Deity - Indra Dev and Agni Dev

Indra Dev

The Vedas describe Indra as the king of heaven and the gods. He is associated with lightning, thunder, storms, rain, rivers, and war. Indra's mythology and powers are similar to other Indo-European deities such as Jupiter, Perun, Perkūnas, Zalmoxis, Taranis, Zeus, and Thor, which show a common origin of Proto-Indo-European mythology.

Indra is the most referred to deity in the Rigveda and is celebrated for his powers, and as the one who kills the great symbolic evil - malevolent type of Asuras. One of the most prominent ones was called Vritra, who obstructed human prosperity and happiness. The mythological stories state that Indra destroys Vritra and his deceiving forces, and thereby brings rain and sunshine for the good of mankind.

Indra is shown as deva holding a powerful thunderbolt weapon called Vajra and riding on a white elephant named Airavata. His heavenly abode is said to be on or near Mount Sumeru in the Himalayas of Northern India. Indra is strengthened by the elixir of immortality, the soma, which the priests offer to him in the sacrifice. Among his allies are the Rudras (or Maruts). Indra is sometimes referred to as the thousand-eyed one.

In later Hinduism, Indra is no longer worshipped but plays the important mythological roles of the god of rain, regent of the heavens, and guardian of the east. In the Mahabharata, Indra fathers the great hero Arjuna and tries in vain to prevent the god of fire - Agni, from burning a great forest. One of the mythological stories in the Puranas states that Lord Krishna persuaded the cowherds of Gokula to stop worshipping Indra. Enraged, Indra sent down torrents of rain, but Krishna lifted Mount Govardhana on his fingertip and gave the people shelter under it for 7 days until Indra relented and paid homage.

Indra also means the king of his own body and mind. The one who has over his or her senses (Indriya) or has disciplined the mind and body. The Vedic way of life guides us on how to become the master of our sense perceptions and not give in to the temptations that can bring us ill health and suffering.

The word Indriya comes from the root word Indra. In Sanskrit, the word <u>Indra</u> also signifies - will power to control the senses and thereby gain physical and mental strength, or becoming the king of your sense perceptions.

Ayurvedic texts describe Indra as -

"Indram *Atma tasya sadhanam Indriyam.*

This means - Indra is the soul (atma), and Indriya (sense organs) are a tool or an instrument (sadhan) for perception to attain knowledge.

The Vedas describe 11 Indriyas - 11 main phenomenological faculties-

Indriyas Sensory faculties	Organs	Function
5 Gnaana Indriyas Sensory faculties	Eyes - Chakshu Indriya Ears - Shrota Indriya Nose - Gandha Indriya Tongue-Rasana Indriya Skin - Sparsh Indriya	Seeing Hearing Smell Taste Touch
5 Karma Indriyas Organs of action or movement - motor organs	Tongue - Vaak Indriya Hands - Paani Indriya Feet - Pada Indriya Anus - Payu Indriya Urethra - Mootra Organ for sex - Upastha Indriya Male - Penus Female - Vagina	Speech Grasp Movement Excretion Urination For sexual intercourse
1 Ubhaya - Indriya For both sensory and motor function	Manas Indriya - Mind	Nervous system

Over time, with overuse and misuse, our sense perceptions get dulled. For example, if we listen to loud music all the time, our ears will not be able to hear the soft sounds they will be defended to subtle sounds. So, to bring back the ability to hear well and hear fully, we need to slowly train our ears to listen to music at a lower volume and practice yogic kriyas like shanmukhi mudra (closing the 6 senses of perception for a brief time), which will enhance the quality of hearing. These practices should be learnt from a trained yoga teacher.

Just as a sitar (string instrument) produces a fantastic sound when it's strings are well tuned - tightened to the right degree where they are not too lax or too tight. Similarly, when we train and fine-tune our sense receptions through yoga and meditation, our ability to perceive is enhanced phenomenally.

Agni Dev

Agni Dev is the fire god of Hinduism, second only to Indra in the Vedic mythology of ancient India. He signifies the fire of the sun, of lightning, the domestic and sacrificial fire. As the divine personification of the fire of sacrifice, he is the mouth of the gods, the carrier of the oblation, and the messenger between the human and the divine realms.

Agni is the guardian of the south-east direction. He is described in the scriptures as the one who has a reddish-orange complexion. He rides a Ram and has 2 faces — one beneficent and one malignant. He is shown with 3 or 7 tongues, hair that stands on ends like flames, 3 legs, and 7 arms. In the Rigveda, he is sometimes identified with Rudra, the forerunner for Lord Shiva. His presence is invoked in many ceremonies and fire rituals.

Inference

Those who are born with the Ascendant, Sun or Moon in Vishakha will have Indira-like qualities of having a leadership role in the family, community, nation or worldwide. They will have the ability and will love to take up the responsibility of fighting for a good cause, helping voluntarily as an advisor or a consultant. They will also have the fire and passion to work towards their goals and transform themselves for the better. Agni Dev, the god of fire, gives the ambition, fire and zeal to constantly make an effort to purify oneself and transform into a better human being.

They have the ability to train their mind and body, discipline their senses of perception and thus win over their limitations, which makes them the king of their own mind and body. The Vedic way of life guides one to become the master of their senses and not be enslaved by them. This means not falling into the temptation of those habits which harm us, cause ill health, pain or suffering. For example, overcoming the temptation of eating sweets, which can cause ill health or chronic problems in the long run. Therefore, Vishakha natives have a tremendous sense of discipline and willpower to overcome those tendencies that can hinder their growth and well-being.

Vishakha padas

20 deg Libra - 3.20 Scorpio

Padas	Degrees
1	20 - 23.20 deg Libra
2	23.20 - 26.40 deg Libra
3	26.40 - 30 deg Libra
4	0 - 3.20 deg Scorpio

Pada 1

20 - 23.20 deg Libra, Navamsha- Aries (Lord - Mars)

Rashi Lord - Venus and Nakshatra Lord- Jupiter

Pada 1 of Vishakha falls in the navamsha of Aries. Therefore, it carries the energy of Venus, Jupiter and Mars. When the energies of Venus and Mars come together, it makes the person very passionate, romantic, energetic, forceful, short-tempered and goal-driven. Jupiter is the planet of expansion and optimism. Therefore, the combined effect makes one very idealistic, and they like to do things in a grand way. They are blessed with the fortune of having a very happy and optimistic approach towards relationships and partnerships. It's a fortunate Pada because the yoga tara point is at 20 degrees, which is also the point of maximum exaltation of Saturn. So any planets sitting here, especially Saturn, will give excellent results during its dasha and transits.

For example, Vishakha Pada 1, placed in the 5th house, will be very creative and will benefit from creating something that can be useful for everyone - like having a business in the field of clothes or food. Passion and romance will be their guiding motivation in whatever they do.

Careers

Teachers, engineers, financial advisors, counsellors, property dealers working in the field of advertisement, public relations coordinators, film directors, leaders, businessmen, IT professionals, fashion designers, writers, speakers, actors, social workers, religious leaders, priests, astrologers, office workers and working from home.

Pada 2

23. 20 - 26.40 deg Libra, Navamsha - Taurus (Lord - Venus)

Rashi Lord - Venus and Nakshatra Lord- Jupiter

In the 2nd Pada of Vishakha, there will be the energy of Jupiter and the double influence of Venus. This will make the natives very receptive towards all that is as aesthetically beautiful. They will have the ability to create something beautiful, even from a piece of stone or a plane sheet of paper. Jupiter and Venus are both beneficent planets. Therefore, the dashas and transits of Venus and Jupiter will be particularly beneficial for them. However, if Venus or Jupiter have a low Shabala score, or they are afflicted by the conjunction or direct aspect of Saturn, Mars, Rahu or Ketu, it can reduce the benefits or cause delays and obstacles.

The 2nd Pada is a Pushkar bhaga and Pushkar amsha Pada, which means it's a fortunate Pada and planets sitting here give wonderful results during its dasha and transits. For example, the 2nd Pada of Vishakha in the 8th house will bring sudden gains from the insurance or inheritance.

Careers

Teachers, advisors, astrologers, consultants, IT professionals, filmmakers, fashion designers, florists, actors, artists, musicians, writers, philosophers, poets, cooks and working from home.

Pada 3

26.40 - 30 deg Libra, Navamsha - Gemini (Lord - Mercury)

Rashi Lord - Venus and Nakshatra Lord - Jupiter

The navamsha of the 3rd Pada of Vishakha is placed in Gemini, which gives the effect of Venus, Jupiter and Mercury. They will be more vocal and communicative about their ideology, faith and philosophy. Libra and Gemini are both air signs - the navamsha falls in Gemini, which shows that in their adulthood years after 30, they will maintain their friendly nature. In fact they will become more flexible in their approach to life and will adjust to situations easily. They can become excellent artists, designers, creators, writers, poets, and actors.

For example, in the 3rd Pada of Vishakha in the 10th house they will have a career where they will have to deal with a lot of people - like a public relations manager. They will have the capability and talent to create peace and harmony in relationships through interactive communication.

Careers

Philosophers, guides, gurus, teachers, astrologers, advisors, consultants, managers, public relations coordinators, writers, poets, artists, actors, film directors, IT professionals, designers, doctors, businessmen, accountants and working from home.

Pada 4

0 - 3.20 deg Scorpio, Navamsha - Cancer (Lord - Moon)

Rashi Lord - Venus and Nakshatra Lord - Jupiter

In this Pada, there will be the influence of Venus, Jupiter and Moon. The natives born in this Pada will be more emotional and will feel things more deeply. They will be very sensitive to what people say, or if they don't say what should have been said, it can make them feel hurt. They are usually not easily shaken or disturbed, but if their tolerance has been put to the test because they have been badly treated repeatedly - they will surely strike back with deadly precision. Although they will be friendly and cordial with all whom they meet, in their hearts, they hold many secrets and share them only with their closest friends.

In the 4th Pada, the moon gets debilitated at 3 degrees in Scorpio. This will bring in situations which make one feel emotionally starved or not able to express their deepest feelings, and can create misunderstandings and arguments in a relationship. For example, the 4th Pada of Vishakha in the 3rd house can bring challenging or difficult relationships with siblings or neighbours.

Careers-

Psychologists, philosophers, lawyers, detectives, spies, researchers, IT professionals, astrologers, priests, teachers, advisors, counsellors, spiritual mediums, designers, artists, actors, singers, musicians, writers, poets, self-employed and working from home.

The effect of planets

Vishakha - Libra Padas 1,2 and 3	Planets that get affected
Yoga Karka - Most benefic	Saturn
Functional Benefic - give good results during their dasha.	Venus
Functional Malefic - can give problems during their dasha.	Jupiter, Rahu and Ketu
Functional Neutral	Sun, Moon and Mercury
Kendra Adi Pati Dosha - can be malefic	Mars
Vishakha - Scorpio Pada 4	**Planets that get affected**
Functional Benefic - give good results during their dasha.	Mars, Sun and Moon
Functional Malefic - can give problems during their dasha.	Mercury, Rahu and Ketu
Functional Neutral	Jupiter and Saturn
Kendra Adi Pati Dosha - can be malefic	Venus

Vishakha Ascendant

The first 3 padas of Vishakha are placed in Libra. Therefore, those who are born with the Ascendant in the 1st, 2nd or 3rd pada will have the influence of Venus and Jupiter. This gives them a very attractive and pleasing personality. Since Jupiter and Venus are both Benefic planets and Gurus or masters in their own fields, the natives will be fortunate in the sense that even through the most difficult situations, they will come out unharmed. They will be great advisors because they have the knack of counselling others with Venusian charm and Jupitarian wisdom.

The 4th Pada of Vishakha lies in Scorpio, which gives the quality of Martian energy and Jupitarian optimism. The natives will pursue their goals with more determination and idealism. When they are faced with challenging situations or a more serious danger threatens them, the Martian energy comes to their rescue. They will not push ahead immediately, but with quiet poise and inner strength, they will achieve their goals. Just like a Scorpio's behaviour, they can sense danger from a distance and quickly charge with absolute precision.

Their determined Martian zeal has a steely willpower that helps them to make the impossible possible. They are intensely loyal and will never compromise their principles. They will never give in or admit defeat. Their brave souls, fuelled by the Martian energy, will fight on till the bitter or sweet end. The Jupitarian influence gives them a lot of wisdom and knowledge, even more than it can be sensed or defined. The Scorpion vibration also brings a burning need to discover the unknown.

Sun in Vishakha

When the Sun is placed in the 1st, 2nd and 3rd padas of Vishakha, it will share the qualities of Venus and Jupiter because these padas lie in Libra. Sun is friendly with Jupiter and enemy with Venus, therefore there will be a mixed result. The natives will be very intelligent, dignified, generous and fair in their dealings. They could come across as arrogant or aloof and will be very sensitive to what others say about them. The Libran sense of beauty, harmony and aesthetics will make them very sensitive to their immediate environment.

For example, if Sun is placed in the 2nd Pada of Vishakha in the 8th house, the natives can face difficulties regarding their vitality and health because Sun gets debilitated in Libra. This could happen during the dasha of the Sun, Venus or Jupiter.

The 4th Pada of Vishakha is placed in Scorpio. Therefore, the Sun will have the influence of Mars and Jupiter in this Pada. This placement will give good results during the dashas of the Sun, Mars or Jupiter because Sun is friendly with both Mars and Jupiter. The natives will be brave, determined, intelligent and secretive. They will be interested in everything that's mystical and mysterious. They can make great psychologists, psychiatrists, doctors, astrologers, therapists, and teachers. For example, if the Sun is placed in the 4th Pada of Vishakha in the Ascendant, the natives will be dignified, good-looking, proud and influential. They will have good support from their father and will be honoured by the authorities or the government for their particular talent or skill. They will be good motivational speakers and will love to dress up well and look presentable in public.

Moon in Vishakha

The Moon in the 1st, 2nd and 3rd padas of Vishakha lie in Libra, which will give the influence of Venus and Jupiter. Their actions and thoughts are motivated by the desire to maintain peace and harmony. The Jupitarian expansion and Venusian sense of beauty make them very creative and knowledgeable. For example, the moon in the 2nd Pada of Vishakha in the 2nd house will give a very creative and academic home environment. They will be fortunate to have the resources and ambience which support the development of their creativity and knowledge.

The 4th Pada of Vishakha lies in Scorpio, which gives it a very Martian influence mixed with the Jupitarian quality of wisdom and expansion. In the deep waters of Scorpio, the fiery Mars gains more willpower, resilience, resoluteness and determination. Scorpio is the 2nd cycle of the water element and has the influence of the night forces and feminine receptivity.

This gives them a great in-depth understanding of human emotions, and they can become excellent psychologists. Scorpio, being a fixed sign, makes them enormously capable of executing and organising events and daily routines. They are very intrigued by the mysteries of life and have a great interest in studying esoteric subjects that have a mystical dimension. All that cannot easily be seen by the eyes or comprehended by the mind attracts them, and they end up spending a great deal of time trying to discover the awesome mystery of one's mind and body.

The Martian influence in the original 8th house of Scorpio gives a deep desire to penetrate into the unknown that lies buried beneath the layers of reason and logic. Their desires are so intense that an emotion or a thought can consume their attention fully until they have fully understood the mechanics of it. For example, the 4th Pada of Vishakha in the 9th house will make them travel to far-off lands or a foreign country in search of higher knowledge, a higher degree, a learned teacher, or a spiritual guru.

A Vishakha born in the 1st pada will have the Libran influence. They will argue or debate over a topic in order to achieve peace, justice and harmony. While a Vishakha native born with the moon in the 4th Pada will have the Martian outlook in Scorpio, they may not argue to prove their point but achieve their desired goal with a quiet approach and a steel-like determination.

The poetry of Vishakha

Vishakha - the branch that forked,

As a new path, from each junction- life evolved,

And so the diversity brought richness,

The creative ways of nature's genius.

Jupiter and Venus in Libran ways,

Justice, harmony, balance and grace.

The air fires the passion to discover the depth,

Mysteries fascinate the Scorpio - beginning to end.

From the experiences - clear and unclear,

Joy, love, pain and fear,

A seeker is born - What is the truth? What is real?

Name and form - the seeming truth of the surface,

The mirage of experience - the card of ace.

The game of life - a pack of cards,

The deal of destiny - a play of sorts.

Learning to make the best of what fate has given,

Is our side of the deal - chosen.

Remedies

- <u>Das Maha Vidya</u> - as described earlier.

- Those who are born in the 1st, 2nd or 3rd pada of Vishakha will have a Vata predominant constitution - a daily exercise routine will keep them grounded and in good health. Planning well before travelling, taking care of your diet, and eating warm meals at regular times will help to keep the Vata in balance.

- The 4th Pada of Vishakha will have a Kapha predominant tridosha - for them also a daily exercise routine will keep them active and in good health. They should eat more fresh fruits and salads and avoid heavy foods like cakes, sweets and dairy products.

- The yogic asanas and pranayama will be particularly helpful in balancing the excessive Vata and Kapha. The alternate nose breathing technique (alom vilom) is an excellent and quick way to pacify restlessness and calm the mind.

- Meditation (breath watch) is another beautiful and scientific technique for calming any agitation or stress in the body or the mind.

- Every time Vishakha natives create something that can be useful for everyone, they will experience a sense of victory within themselves for having overcome their limitations or a particular weakness.

- Yellow, red and all pastel colours resonate well with the energy of Vishakha.

Chanting the mantra - "Om *dham nam Vishakha nakshatraye namah*," 108 times on days when the moon is transiting Vishakha or on Thursdays will help to connect you with your inner self.

Example

Ascendant in Vishakha

K N Rao - famous Indian Astrologer - Born on 12th October 1931, 7 54 am in Machilipatnam, India.

Kotamraju Narayana Rao is the 2nd of the 4 sons of the famous journalist of the pre-independence era, K. Rama Rao. His father was the founder and editor of the National Herald. Rao was initiated into astrology by his late mother, K. Saraswani Devi, at the age of 12 in 1943. He regards her as the best astrologer he has known in 2 areas, marriage and children and prashna (horary).

Rao was a lecturer in English before joining the government service through an all-India competition in 1957. He joined the Indian Audit and Accounts Service, from which he retired as Director General in November 1990. He was more interested in games and sports than in astrology in his youth. He won brilliant prizes in chess competitions and 2 state championships in bridge competitions.

He did his fundamental research in astrology during his career because of which he managed to collect horoscopes systematically in thousands. He has more than 50,000 horoscopes with 10 important events of each individual noted with him. It is perhaps the largest individual collection of horoscopes any astrologer has.

The strain of doing astrology as a mission and not charging any fee almost made him give up astrology many times. But in December 1981, he was forced out of his shell to participate in a 3-day seminar on astrology in Delhi. After this groundbreaking speech, there has been a persistent demand for his astrological articles. From then onwards, he has been sharing his original research, for which he has won worldwide praise. He is the Advisor of Astrology Courses in the Bharatiya Vidya Bhawan, New Delhi. The teachers on the teaching faculty of the astrology course in the Bharatiya Vidya Bhawan have, like him, never charged any fees for teaching, which they do in an honorary capacity.

Between 1993 and 1995, Rao visited the USA on 5 lecture tours. He has worked hard and has used his skills to make some very true and attractive predictions about people, which won him worldwide praise. His biggest contribution to the field of astrology was in starting the Vedic Astrology course at Bharatiya Vidya Bhavan in New Delhi.

Analysis

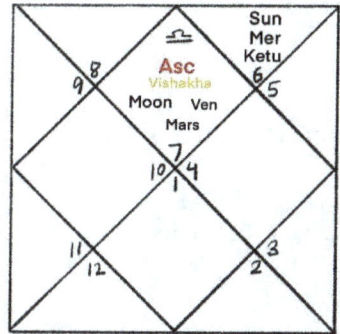 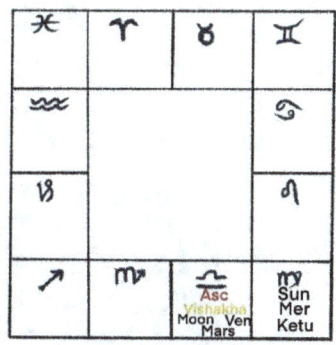

K N Rao is a <u>Vishakha Ascendant</u> in the 1st Pada. He has a strong Libra influence because he has his Moon, Venus and Mars placed in the Ascendant. Moon and Venus are in Chitra, and the Ascendant and Mars are in Vishakha.

He is a very creative person and has a very fine sense of keeping everything in balance and harmony. Like a true Vishakha native, he had the capability to break away from the malpractices of some traditional astrologers, who had fallen into the greed of making false predictions for the sake of making more money. Through his intelligence, sincerity, resilience and hard work, he opened up a new shakha (branch) of Vedic astrology with a scientific approach based on the data and research which could provide plenty of evidence for any of the techniques that had been mentioned in various old astrological texts, thus reviving the glory of Vedic astrology.

Moon is the lord of the 10th house, and Jupiter is exalted, sitting in the 10th house of Cancer. His Jyotish Guru, Yogi Bhaskarananda had told him that he would have to visit many foreign countries to bring back the honour, recognition and dignity of Vedic Astrology. On his first visit to the USA in 1993, one of the speakers at the Vedic conference had very befittingly said this about him, "Vedic astrology before Rao and after Rao".

The first time he travelled out of India (his trip to the USA) in 1993, he was running his <u>Mercury Sun Sun dasha</u>. His Mercury and Sun are sitting with Ketu in the 12th house of Virgo, which brought him foreign travel, fame and recognition. Sun is the lord of the 11th house of gains, and Mercury is the lord of the 9th house (Gemini) and the 12th house (Virgo). He has to travel abroad to give lectures on Vedic Astrology (the communication aspect of Mercury).

17
Anuradha

Om tam tham dam Anuradha nakshatraye namah

Zodiac degrees	3.20 - 16.40 deg Scorpio
Ruling planet	Scorpio - Mars and Ketu and Anuradha - Saturn
Sanskrit name	Anu means - atom, and Radha - Lord Krishna's beloved. Anuradha is the subtle form of Radha.
Astronomical name	The 3 stars in a row, which look like a staff. Seen in the constellation of Scorpio.
Symbol	Scorpio - scorpion Anuradha-staff- a long stick held by a saint or a yogi. and - a Lotus flower.
Element	Water
Deity	Mitra - a friend
Quality	Scorpio - Sthira - fixed Anuradha - Mishra - mixed and mridu - gentle
Shakti	Radhana Shakti - Power of Worship
Cast	Shudra - worker, farmer
Gender	Female
Motivation	Moksha - liberation
Triguna	Tamas
Tridosha	Kapha
Body parts	Breast, stomach, womb and bowels.
Direction	North, South and West

Month	Late May, the second half of Vishakha month.
Bird	Peacock
Sound	na, nee, noo, nay
Tree	Nagkesar tree
Chakras	Muladhara - Mars and Vishuddhi - Saturn
Das Maha Vidya	Devi Kali - Saturn and Devi Bagalamukhi - Mars

Special degrees -

Yoga Tara	10 deg Scorpio It's a point where the planet will show the strongest and sure results during its dasha.
Pushkaramsha	2nd Pada The planets placed here will give good results during its dasha, like the blossoming of a flower.
Amrit Nadi	9.33- 10.26 deg Scorpio This brings good results, just like the nectar that nourishes.
Visha Nadi	5.30- 6.26 deg Scorpio Brings situations which one does not like dealing with.
Exaltation	16 deg Scorpio - Maximum exaltation of Ketu. When Ketu is placed at this degree, it will give excellent results during its dasha. It will be particularly supportive for ending something.

Auspicious and inauspicious table -

Auspicious	**Inauspicious**
<u>Activities</u> Good for all group-related activities, research and study of occult subjects, for spending time with friends, managing things and making decisions, finance and accounts, for travel and dealing with immigration and foreign affairs, secretive activities, for reflection, meditation and healing.	<u>Activities</u> Not good for marriage, confrontations, inaugurations, beginnings and routine mundane activities.
<u>Days</u> <u>Tuesdays</u> - only when it falls on the 1st, 3rd, 6th, 8th, 11th, or 13th lunar day. <u>Wednesdays</u>- only when it falls on the 2nd, 3rd, 7th, 8th, 12th, or 13th lunar day. <u>Saturdays</u> - only when it falls on the 2nd, 4th, 7th, 9th, 12th, or 14th lunar day.	<u>Days</u> <u>Sundays</u> - only when it falls on the 3rd, 4th, 8th, 9th, 13th, or 14th lunar day. <u>Mondays</u>- only when it falls on the 6th, 7th, or 11th lunar day. <u>Thursdays</u>- only when it falls on the 6th, 8th, 9th, 12th, or 13th lunar day. <u>Fridays</u> - only when it falls on the 2nd, 3rd, 6th, 8th, 10th, or 11th lunar day.

Compatibility table -

Anuradha	Compatible with
Sexual compatibility Yoni animal	Anuradha - Female deer Compatible with Jeyshtha - Male deer.
Sign compatibility	Scorpio - Cancer and Pisces.
Nakshatra compatibility	Pushya and Shatbhishak.
Lunar day compatibility	Dwadashi tithi - 12th lunar day.
Day compatibility	Tuesday and Saturday
Colour compatibility	Red and blue.
Numerological compatibility	8 and 9 - all numbers that add up to make 8 and 9.
Sound compatibility	Saturn - labial sounds - pa, pha, ba, bha, ma Mars - guttural sounds - ka, kha, ga, gha, kna

Sign Lord and nakshatra lord - Mars and Saturn - as described earlier.

Anuradha is the 2nd nakshatra ruled by Saturn. Here Saturn's energy combines with Mars, which makes the natives very determined and practical.

It's a tough combination, considering the challenges one has to face in worldly matters. Since Saturn is the planet of discipline, restriction and caution, and Mars is the planet of aggression and determination - and both are considered malefic. As the famous saying goes - "in the tough circumstances the tough get going." Those who are born with their Ascendant, Sun or Moon in Anuradha have the dedication, devotion and ability to refine, transform and become the master of his or her skill.

Quality, element, motivation, triguna, tridosha and chakras - as described earlier.

Shakti - Aradhana Shakti - Power to worship.

Anuradha natives have power in their prayer, because of the intensity, sincerity and depth of their emotion. If they observe closely, they will notice that whenever they perform a certain puja or worship, their problems begin to get resolved in one way or another.

Devotion is a beautiful quality that Anuradha natives have. They will be devoted to some path, person, relationship, ideology, religion or faith. Just as Radha was totally devoted to Lord Krishna. Many romantic and beautiful incidents have been narrated in the Devi Bhagavata Purana about the meetings of Radhe and Lord Krishna. Radha's devotion was such that although she could not physically be with Lord Krishna, her whole being was connected with him through the purity of her love and devotion.

One such incident highlights the devotion of Radha and the Gopis towards Lord Krishna. After Krishna had left Vrindavan he never went back there again. When Lord Krishna had settled in Dwarka, he had requested Uddhava (his friend and cousin) to visit Vrindavan with a message on his behalf to the Gopis and other residents of the village because Lord Krishna knew that they were all missing him terribly.

When Uddhava reached Vrindavan, he was so overwhelmed by seeing the devotion of Radha and Gopis towards Lord Krishna. The Gopis were crying with tears of devotion, Radha was engrossed in Lord Krishna's thoughts, and saw him everywhere. He decided to stay in Vrindavan longer than he had planned in order to imbibe the quality of love and devotion from the Gopis and Radha.

Symbolic signification

Scorpio - scorpion - as described earlier.

Anuradha - staff and lotus flower.

Staff

The Sanskrit word danda means stick or a staff. It symbolises strength and spiritual prowess. In mythological iconography, many saints, seers, mystics and yogis are shown holding a staff. Since they would walk long distances and go through rough terrains of valleys, climbing hills and mountains, a stick was needed for support. The word staff also signifies strict discipline and punishment. When one chooses to walk on the spiritual path, self-discipline becomes necessary to overcome the laziness of the body and the mind.

One famous example is the Staff of Moses, which has been mentioned in the Book of Exodus when God appears to Moses in the burning bush. God asks what Moses has in his hand, and Moses answers a staff. The staff is miraculously transformed into a snake and then back into a staff. The staff is thereafter referred to as the staff of God. It has been mentioned in the Hebrew Bible that Moses used this magical staff on various occasions as and when needed. Here are some of the incidents where the magical and mystical staff has been used -

- The Lord said unto Moses in Midian, "Go, return into Egypt, for all the men are dead which sought thy life." And Moses took his wife and his sons and set them upon an ass, and he returned to the land of Egypt, and Moses took the rod of God in his hand.

- Moses and Aaron appear before the Pharaoh of the Exodus when Aaron's rod is transformed into a serpent. It is used several times on God's command to initiate the Plagues of Egypt.

- During the Exodus, Moses stretches out his hand with the staff to part the Red Sea.

- While in the wilderness after leaving Egypt, Moses strikes the rock with the rod to create a spring for the Israelites from which to drink.
- Finally, Moses uses the staff in the battle at Rephidim between the Israelites and the Amalekites. When he holds up the "rod of God," When he drops it, their enemies gain the upper hand. Aaron and Hur help him to keep the staff raised until victory is achieved.

Insight

A stick is an inert object which has a practical use, but when it's constantly in touch with an enlightened being it imbibes spiritual energy. A staff in the hand of a yogi or a saint can be used as a spiritual conductor to transmit energy which can be triggered only through the intention of the enlightened being who holds it. Another factor is the sensation of touch. The palms of our hands and the soles of our feet are richly supplied with fine nerves and are, therefore, very sensitive to tactile sensations. That's why our palms and soles of the feet can receive and transmit vibrations more easily than any other part of the skin. So, a spiritually advanced being can use a stick like a magic wand when it's backed with his energy and intention.

Lotus flower

The Lotus Flower starts its growth in the deep mud, away from the sunlight. Slowly, as it grows, it reaches the sunlight, becoming the most beautiful flower. In many Eastern traditions, it is regarded as a symbol of purity, enlightenment, self-regeneration and rebirth. The yogic way of life guides us to live our life like a lotus flower, just as a lotus grows from the depth of muddy waters but blossoms into the most beautiful flower. It grows in the murky waters but is untouched by it.

A Lotus flower, therefore, is a perfect example of how one can stay in the material world yet use every experience as a manure to blossom into an enlightened being. For this reason, the Lotus flower is considered a symbol of serenity and purity. Many male and female deities in Eastern cultures are shown holding a lotus flower or sitting on it because of its aspect purity.

Interesting facts -

- A Lotus grows in a tropical climate and needs a depth of at least 8 feet to grow and blossom fully.
- The leaves of a lotus are water-resistant.
- Lotus is hermaphroditic (both male and female) and is pollinated by insects and beetles.
- The Lotus rises from the mud to blossom but is virtually untouched by the substrate from where it grows.
- The stem of a lotus bends easily but is difficult to break.

- People in Asia have also been using the Lotus for its <u>herbal and medicinal properties</u> for centuries.

- The lotus flower can be brewed into a heart tonic.

- Lotus seeds are extremely hardy and long-lived and are used in a tonic for digestive problems and diarrhoea.

- The dried roots of Lotus, when taken internally, are traditionally believed to be effective in stopping excessive bleeding.

- Lotus roots have a delicate taste and crunchy texture. The leaves make a nutritious vegetable when young and can serve as plates or food wrappers when mature.

- Lotus seeds contain about 15 percent protein and 70 percent carbohydrate and can be popped like popcorn, ground into flour or roasted and brewed like coffee.

- Lotus petals are not particularly tasty but often serve as a garnish for soups, and the stamens sometimes serve as flavouring for tea.

Inference

Anuradha natives have a great sense of self-discipline, they have the tenacity of purpose and can work towards their goals with incredible determination. In tough circumstances, they pull through with an amazing inner strength and live their life like a lotus flower, staying in the world but untouched by it's impurities. At some point in their life, they will feel that they are living in the murky waters of difficult relationships, but they learn to find solutions to their problems through inner realisation.

Just as a lotus grows in very deep ponds, Anuradha natives' emotions run deep and they are not frivolous in friendship, relationship or anything that they do. The quality of depth of understanding is seen in every aspect of their life.

Mythology -

Deity - <u>Mitra - friend</u>

The word Mitra literally means a friend. In the Rigveda, the oldest of the Vedic texts, Mitra is mostly indistinguishable from Varuna. Together, they form a pair of Mitra-Varuna. They both essentially have the same characteristics. Mitra is associated with the light of dawn and the morning sun, while Varuna becomes associated with the evening and, ultimately, the night. In the post-Vedic texts, Mitra evolved into the patron divinity and guardian of friendship.

Mitra-Varuna is described as young. They wear glistening garments, are monarchs and guardians of the whole world, and their palace is golden, with 1000 pillars and doors. They support heaven and earth and the air between heaven and earth. They are lords of rivers and seas, and they send rain and refreshment from the sky.

They wet the pastures with dew of clarified butter, and rain abounding in heavenly water comes from them. Their domain has streams that flow with honey, and their pastures have cattle that yield refreshment.

In Rigveda, Mitra-Varuna is addressed as devas. Mitra is seen as the sustainer of mankind and of all gods and has the unique ability to bring people together. In some Vedic descriptions, Varuna is seen as the lord of the cosmic rhythm, of the sun and other celestial spheres, while Mitra brings forth the light at dawn.

Inference

Those who are born with their Ascendant, Sun or Moon in Anuradha have an inherent talent for bringing people together and working together as a team. They are very good at organising and planning functions and events on a small scale or a large scale.

The word Mitra literally means a friend. Anuradha natives make great friends. Once they have chosen, they stay committed. They prefer to have only a few close friends and are true to their friendship. They will stand by their friend through all good and bad circumstances.

Anuradha padas

3.20 - 16.40 deg Scorpio

Padas	Degrees
1	3.20 - 6.40 deg Scorpio
2	6.40 - 10 deg Scorpio
3	10 - 13.20 deg Scorpio
4	13.20 - 16.40 deg Scorpio

Pada 1

3.20 - 6.40 deg Scorpio, Navamsha- Leo (Lord - Sun)

Rashi Lord - Mars and Nakshatra Lord- Saturn

The navamsha of the 1st Pada lies in Leo. Therefore, it carries the energy of the Sun, Mars and Saturn. Sun and Saturn don't get along well, so it can bring frustrations and delays. The influence of Mars and the Sun will make them very ego-sensitive, authoritative and proud, and they will not like taking orders from anyone. Yet Saturn will cause delays and restrictions and make them work towards self-discipline if they want to succeed in life. Over time, they will learn to be more humble and accepting of others' shortcomings and will try to overcome their own limitations of comparing themselves with others or having an egoistic attitude.

For example, in the 1st Pada of Anuradha, in the 3rd house, they will not get along very well with their siblings or neighbours. The situations will be such that they do not get an opportunity to have a close friendship with them. They will have to make many short trips related to work, home or holidays.

Careers

Technicians, engineers, politicians, financial advisors, counsellors, property dealers, working in the office, leaders, managers, businessmen, IT professionals, athletes, sportsmen or sportswomen, army officers, policemen, firefighters, lifeguards and working from home.

Pada 2

6.40 - 10 deg Scorpio, Navamsha - Virgo (Lord - Mercury)

Rashi Lord - Mars and Nakshatra Lord- Saturn

In the 2nd Pada, there will be the energy of Mars, Saturn and Mercury. The natives will be more vocal about their thoughts and emotions. It's a pushkara navamsha Pada. Therefore, it will fruitify the results of any planet sitting here during its dasha and transit. Especially after the age of 30, the natives will begin to feel the positivity of this Pada. As they grow older they will be able to express themselves more freely and develop their skills of oral and written communication. They will be more academically oriented and will love to research and learn about everything that is mystical and mysterious. They will also be good with accounts and handling finance.

For example, the 2nd Pada of Anuradha in the 5th house will be very creative and intelligent and will have a deep understanding of subjects like psychology, philosophy, ayurveda, astrology, occult, Vedas, palmistry, yoga, meditation, life after death, past life regression, hypnosis, religious and spiritual subjects.

Careers

Psychiatrists, philosophers, astrologers, consultants, therapists, past life regression therapists, hypnotists, doctors, researchers, archaeologists, IT professionals, actors, filmmakers, artists, writers, and working from home.

Pada 3

10 - 13.20 deg Scorpio, Navamsha - Libra (Lord - Venus)

Rashi Lord - Mars and Nakshatra Lord - Saturn

The navamsha of the 3rd Pada is placed in Libra, which gives the effect of Mars, Saturn and Venus. The combination of Mars and Venus makes them very passionate and creative.

They will be exceptionally good in art and music, and will be more friendly and social than those born in the other padas of Anuradha. They will be romantic and will have a wonderful sense of aesthetics, and the opposite sex will find them very attractive.

For example, the 3rd Pada of Anuradha in the 7th house will bring such situations in their life where they have to deal with the opposite sex, and they get magnetically drawn towards each other. Once they choose their partner or spouse, they will be dedicated to them, and in turn, they will find a spouse who is equally committed. They will have their share of arguments, but when it comes to the crux, they will always stand by their spouse.

Careers

Artists, actors, architects, designers, decorators, astrologers, advisors, consultants, managers, public relations coordinators, writers, poets, film directors, IT professionals, doctors, businessmen and working from home.

Pada 4

13.20 - 16.40 deg Scorpio, Navamsha - Scorpio (Lord - Mars)

Rashi Lord - Mars and Nakshatra Lord- Saturn

In this Pada, there will be the influence of Saturn and the double effect of Mars. This makes them very energetic and ambitious to pursue their goals with focused determination. They will be physically and mentally strong, but if Mars is retrograde or weak with a low Shadbala score, it can bring a lack of vitality or strength. A weak Mars can make them more defensive and cowardly. If the fierce and excessive energy of Mars is not channelled into positive thoughts and actions, it can cause harm and pain to the natives. They should endeavour to have a regular gym routine or build some exercise regime which will help them maintain good physical, mental and emotional health. Practising Hatha yoga asanas will be particularly beneficial for them.

If Mars is placed in the 6th, 8th or 12th house, it can bring challenging situations during the dasha of Mars. For example, the 4th Pada placed in the 6th house will have to give their time, attention and energy towards a daily routine.

Careers-

Army officers, policemen, firefighters, sportsmen and sportswomen, athletes, race car drivers, emergency doctors, surgeons, psychologists, detectives, spies, researchers, IT professionals, businessmen, property dealers, builders, factory workers, farmers, labourers, mechanics, car dealers, garage owners, self-employed and working from home.

The effect of planets

Anuradha - Scorpio	Planets that get affected
Functional Benefic - give good results during their dasha.	Mars, Sun and Moon
Functional Malefic - can give problems during their dasha.	Mercury, Rahu and Ketu
Functional Neutral	Jupiter and Saturn
Kendra Adi Pati Dosha - can be malefic	Venus

Anuradha Ascendant

Anuradha natives are equipped with the fierce determination of Mars and the cool endurance of Saturn because they have to pass through extremely intense soil testing times in their lives. The Saturn-Mars combination gives them great intensity, determination, strength and patience to endure hardships bravely and pass through these challenges.

They will trust love and friendship only after it has been proven that the other person is worthy of their trust. But once they have chosen their friend or partner, their loyalty and devotion is unwavering. They fiercely protect their own integrity and that of their loved ones. If they feel there is any injustice done, they feel compelled to demand an eye for an eye to make sure that injuries are not repeated again.

Since Anuradha lies in the heart of the sign of Scorpio, the mystical experience of death comes to them through dreams, visions, or the death of their close friends or relatives, which transforms them in a big way. From an early age they will begin to look at life from a deeper perspective compared to those around them, and their spiritual seeking begins from a very young age.

Their positive qualities are loyalty, sincerity, endurance, devotion, determination, willpower, magnetism, gentleness, insight, intuition, and an amazing sense of self-discipline. When they are feeling out of their element, frustrated or disillusioned with life, they can become suspicious and fanatic and can seek revenge.

Sun in Anuradha

When the Sun is placed in Anuradha, it will share the energies of Mars and Saturn. Sun and Mars are friendly to each other, but Sun and Saturn don't get along well, so there will be tug of war-like situations. The influence of the Sun makes the natives want to shine and show its brilliance, but Saturn restricts and curtails the response of a determined Mars and the confident Sun. They will have a dignified personality and will be deep thinkers. Once they commit themselves to a person, relationship or cause, they sincerely follow it through with utmost devotion and integrity.

For example, in the Sun in Anuradha in the 6th house, the natives bravely face any opposition that comes their way and will be victorious over their enemies because the Sun is happily sitting in his friend's house of Scorpio, whose ruler is Mars. They will be sincere and hard-working and will do their duties with diligence.

Moon in Anuradha

When the Moon is placed in Anuradha, it will share the influence of Mars and Saturn. The Mars-Saturn vibration gives them amazing willpower, which they learn to silently and secretly use as and when needed. There is much that an Anuradha soul knows, but even more of what they can perceive or sense but cannot define or articulate.

It brings the burning need in them to penetrate the unknown and discover the mysteries of life with a calm sense of reason. When they want to know something it completely consumes their mind until they have found their answers.

They are ultra-sensitive but are able to disguise their sensitivity very effectively. They express their opinions with caution because they are wary of those who might heartlessly shred their ideology or beliefs to pieces. Each defeat or unpleasant experience sustained by them strengthens their conviction that their first loyalty lies towards their own personal integrity. They always stand true to their word because, for them - if the self is lost, then all is lost. They will never do anything that will make them feel ashamed of their own actions or thoughts. They hold a high moral code for themselves and stick to their principles even in the toughest of circumstances.

They are really intrigued by everything mystical and mysterious, and love to research and find out more about esoteric subjects of philosophy, religion, sex, astrology, yoga, meditation and spirituality. Their intense pull and passion towards exploring the silent subconscious realms of the mind makes them disinterested in worldly desires, and they begin to question the worthiness of running after materialistic goals.

They are intense lovers and intense enemies, too. When they love- they truly love, with all their heart and soul, but if a friendship becomes bitter or sour, they will stay away or walk out with equal intensity and assurity- never returning back to a toxic relationship. They learn their lessons for good and don't repeat their mistakes.

Their intensity of purpose nourishes their physical needs, their mental pursuits, emotional longings and their soul's search. For example, when the moon in Anuradha is placed in the 9th house, they will be very devoted to their teacher, Guru, or higher learning. They will be willing to take the brave step into the unknown and travel to a foreign land in order to learn and understand the deeper esoteric dimensions of life.

The poetry of Anuradha

Anuradha - Radha - Krishna's love,

The enchanting flute - a song sung

The full moon nights - romantic ecstasy,

Etched in the hearts - a living legacy.

The lotus flower - a symbol of beauty,

Grows in murk, yet untouched by the impurity.

Live in the world such a way,

Turning filth into manure - day by day.

Dedication, discipline, devotion,

Pave the path to liberation.

For in giving totally and fully,

The doors open, when humbled by your sincerity.

The coolness, the calm of the night,

The silence within can show the delight,

Unfolding the secrets within - what is it that binds?

And what liberates from the confines?

The conquest to explore - is another desire,

The ambition and passion - a burning fire,

There is no end - only an infinity

That stretches beyond the realms to eternity.

Remedies

- <u>Das Maha Vidya</u> - as described earlier.

- Kapha is the predominant tridosha of Anuradha. Consciously developing an active lifestyle and including fresh fruits and salads in your diet will be helpful. Avoid sleeping for too long, especially during the day.

- The yogic asanas, pranayama and meditation always enhance the ability to focus, which in turn improves the quality of whatever you do and brings ease into all thoughts and actions.

- Anuradha natives have a beautiful quality of devotion, whenever they pray or worship sincerely, their problems get resolved.

- Red and blue colours resonate well with the energy of Anuradha.

- Chanting the mantra - "Om *tam tham dam Anuradha nakshatraye namah,*" 108 times on days when the moon is transiting Anuradha or on Saturdays will help to connect you with your inner self, and this will help you to calm your mind and make the right choices.

Example

Moon in Anuradha

<u>Kiran Bedi - 1st Woman Police Officer in India.</u>

Born on 9th June 1949 in Amritsar, Punjab, India, at 12 pm (estimated time of birth).

Kiran is an Indian politician, social activist, retired police officer and tennis player who was the 24th Lieutenant Governor of Puducherry from 28 May 2016 to 16 February 2021. She is the 1st Indian female to become an officer in the Indian Police Service and started her service in 1972. She remained in service for 35 years before taking voluntary retirement in 2007 as Director General Bureau of Police Research and Development.

Kiran was born in Amritsar in a well-to-do Punjabi business family. She is the 2nd of the 3 daughters, born to Prakash Lal Peshawaria and Prem Lata. She started her formal studies in 1954 at the Sacred Heart Convent School in Amritsar. She participated in the National Cadet Corps (NCC), among other extra-curricular activities.

As a teenager, Kiran was crowned the national junior tennis champion in 1966. Between 1965 and 1978, she won several titles at various national and state-level championships.

She graduated in 1968 with a BA (Honours) in English from Government College for Women at Amritsar. The same year, she won the NCC Cadet Officer Award. In 1970, she obtained a master's degree in political science from Panjab University, Chandigarh. From 1970 to 1972, Bedi taught as a lecturer at Khalsa College for Women in Amritsar.

She taught courses related to political science. Later, during her career in the Indian Police Service, she also earned a law degree from the Faculty of Law, University of Delhi, in 1988 and a Ph.D. from IIT Delhi's Department of Social Sciences in 1993.

After joining the Indian police service (IPS), she served in Delhi, Goa, Chandigarh and Mizoram. She started her career as an Assistant Superintendent of Police (ASP) in the Chanakyapuri area of Delhi and won the President's Police Medal in 1979. Next, she moved to West Delhi, where she brought about a reduction in crimes against women. Subsequently, as a traffic police officer, she oversaw traffic arrangements for the 1982 Asian Games in Delhi. As Deputy Commissioner of Police of North Delhi, she launched a campaign against drug abuse, which evolved into the Navjyoti Delhi Police Foundation (renamed to Navjyoti India Foundation in 2007).

She has a lot of integrity and devotion towards serving humanity and has wonderful leadership qualities. She has the ability to bring people together and work as a team for the well-being of others. There is an amazing incident that highlights her bravery and sincerity. When she had just started her job in Delhi as a police officer.

One of her first challenging assignments was to evacuate the people who were trapped in a building that had caught fire in Delhi. When she went on the scene with a group of 12 policemen, the fire had spread up to the front entrance, and they could not access the building. They did not have the facility of the fire extinguisher truck. When she asked the police constables to get into the building no one moved. There was a hand pump in the yard, so she asked one of the policemen to pump it, she wet herself fully and went into the building and managed to safely bring out a woman and a child. Then, all her other team members followed her example and wet themselves thoroughly before going into the building that was blazing with fire - and brought out the others safely. She was hugely appreciated and recognised for her ingenuity and sincerity. This earned her a lot of respect in the community and among her colleagues and officers.

In May 1993, Kiran was posted to the Delhi Prisons as Inspector General (IG). She introduced several reforms at the Tihar Jail, which gained worldwide acclaim and won her the Ramon Magsaysay Award in 1994. In 2003, she became the first Indian and first woman to be appointed as head of the United Nations Police and Police Advisor in the United Nations Department of Peace Operations. She resigned in 2007 to focus on social activism and writing. She has written several books and runs the India Vision Foundation. During 2008–11, she hosted a court show, 'Aap Ki Kachehri' on TV. She was one of the key leaders of the 2011 Indian anti-corruption movement and joined the Bharatiya Janata Party (BJP) in January 2015.

Analysis

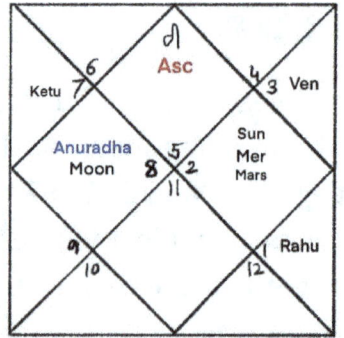 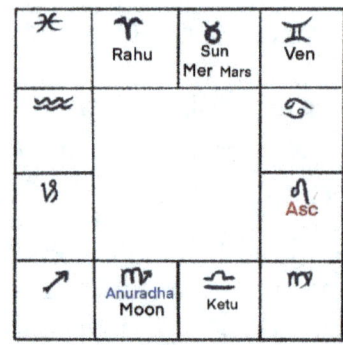

Kiran has her <u>Moon in Anuradha</u> in the 1st Pada in the 4th house of mother and home. Moon, the lord of the 12th house, is sitting in the 4th house of Scorpio. Mars, the lord of the 4th house, is sitting in the 10th house of Taurus with Sun and Mercury. Her 10th house of career and public image is very powerful, where the Sun and Mars have directional strength. The moon has directional strength in the 4th house. The conjunction of Sun and Mercury in the 10th house makes a budha Aditya yoga, which makes the native extremely intelligent and Mars sitting with them strengthens the leadership capabilities.

Out of the many brilliant things that she has done to help the people of her community and her nation. One outstanding example is that in 1979, Kiran was posted to Delhi's West District, where there were not enough officers to handle the high volume of criminal activity. To compensate, she started recruiting civilian volunteers.

Each village in the district was night patrolled by 6 local volunteers led by an armed policeman. This enabled anonymous reporting of any knowledge about crimes and helped her clamp down on bootlegging and the illicit liquor business to reduce crimes in the area.

Kiran won the President's Police Medal in 1979, she was running her <u>Mercury Rahu Mercury</u> dasha. Rahu is sitting in the 9th house of Aries, and Mars, the lord of Aries, is sitting with Mercury and Sun in the 10th house of Taurus. It makes Raj yoga - which states that the native will be very fortunate and successful in his or her professional life. Maharishi Parashara states this in Hora Shastra - that when the lord of the 9th house is placed in the 10th house, the native will be a minister or a commander, will be full of good qualities and will get great honours from the public. He or she will work for the government and will be brave and famous. We can see this prediction coming alive in Kiran's birth chart during her Mercury Mahadasha. Mercury is in the 10th house (of professional and public image) with the Sun and Mars.

Reforming Tihar jail

In May 1993, she was posted to the Delhi Prisons as inspector general (IG). Seeing the appalling conditions there, Kiran decided to turn Tihar into a model prison and introduced several reforms. She arranged separate barracks for the hardened criminals, who had been using their time in prison to recruit gang members, sell contraband and extort money. These prisoners unsuccessfully challenged Kiran in court for unfairly segregating them. For other prisoners, Kiran arranged vocational training with certificates so that they could find a job after their release.

Kiran banned smoking in the prison. This move faced a lot of resistance from the staff as well as the prisoners. She introduced yoga and Vipassana meditation classes to change the prisoners' attitudes. She organised additional activities such as sports, prayer, and festival celebrations. She also established a de-addiction centre and pulled up or imprisoned the staff members involved in drug supply. A bank was also opened inside the prison. A bakery and small manufacturing units, including carpentry and weaving units, were set up in the jail. The profits from the products sold were put into the prisoners' welfare fund.

Kiran went on daily prison tours, observing the staff, listening to prisoners' complaints, inspecting food quality and evaluating overall management. She developed a panchayat system, where prisoners who were respected for their age, education, or character represented other inmates and met every evening with senior officers to sort out problems. She also established petition boxes so that prisoners could write to the IG about any issue. As a result of her reforms, there was a drop in the fights and disturbances in the jail. Even the hardened criminals, who had been isolated in separate barracks, started behaving well. Kiran then arranged for them to attend education and meditation courses.

Kiran's reform programme at Tihar received worldwide acclaim. But it also attracted envy from her superiors, who accused her of diluting prison security for personal glory. Khushwant Singh described her transfer from Tihar as "a victory for a handful of small-minded, envious people over a gutsy woman."

She had started her job as the Inspector General of Police, in charge of the Tihar jail, in May 1993, when she was running her Venus Venus Moon Ketu dasha. Venus is sitting in the 11th house (Gemini) of gains and is the lord of the 9th and the 3rd house. Ketu is sitting in the 3rd house of Libra, the house of heroic efforts. Moon, the lord of the 12th house in the 4th house, this made her move away from her birthplace and she got transferred to many new places away from home during her career. Transfer to Tihar jail was one of her many transfers during the length of her glorious career.

She has truly done a lot of amazing transformations in the jails and for the people of her country through her brave, honest and determined efforts. She is an icon and role model for many women and symbolises the qualities of 'Mother India' in the true sense. Inspired and motivated by her, many women have now joined the Indian police service.

Here are some of Kiran Bedi's quotes -

"Empowered women who reach tough or unconventional positions make choices, not sacrifices."

"My motto in life is that nothing is impossible, no target is unachievable. One just has to try harder."

"I know how to work and how to get work done."

"No marriage is sacred if it practices violence."

"People who do not take charge of their life are lathi (a stick) charged by time."

"The focus is - what is right before you - give it your best. It shows the seeds for tomorrow."

"Believe in yourself 100%, give your 100% and you will get 100% in return."

"Once you stop fearing fear, you'll have a sense of freedom in all that you do."

18
Vishakha

Om dham nam Vishakha nakshatraye namah

Zodiac degrees	20 deg Libra - 3.20 deg Scorpio Libra - 1st, 2nd and 3rd padas and Scorpio - 4th pada
Ruling planet	Libra - Venus and Scorpio - Mars Vishakha - Jupiter
Sanskrit name	Vishakha means forked, a point where the branch splits into 2 or has a sub-branch.
Astronomical name	The 4 stars that form the shape of the hanging scale, or a forked branch, seen in the constellation of Libra.
Symbol	Libra - balancing scales and Scorpio - scorpion Vishakha - decorated arched gateway.
Element	Air - Libra and Water - Scorpio
Deity	Indra dev and Agni dev
Quality	Chara - movable - Libra and Sthira - fixed - Scorpio Vishakha - Mishra - mixed
Shakti	Vayapna Shakti - Ability to manifest. The Sanskrit word Vyapana means - to completely cover, overspread, occupy thoroughly, or pervade throughout the area.
Cast	Mleccha - outcast
Gender	Male - Libra Female - Scorpio
Motivation	Kama- to fulfil desires - Libra Moksha - liberation - Scorpio
Triguna	Rajas - Libra and Tamas - Scorpio

Tridosha	Vata - Libra and Kapha - Scorpio
Body parts	Breast and arms.
Direction	West and north
Month	May, the first half of Vishakha month.
Bird	Swan
Sound	tee, tu, tey, to
Tree	Apple tree
Chakras	Muladhara - Mars, Swathishtana - Venus and Ajna - Jupiter
Das Maha Vidya	Devi Bagalamukhi - Mars, Devi Kamala - Venus and Devi Tara - Jupiter

Special degrees -

Yoga Tara	21 deg Libra It's a point where the planet will show the strongest and sure results during its dasha.
Pushkaramsha	2nd and 4th Pada The planets placed here will give good results during its dasha, like the blossoming of a flower.
Pushkar bhaga	24 deg Libra Any planets sitting at this point will give excellent results during their dasha, like the blossoming of a flower.
Amrit Nadi	28.22 - 29.16 deg Libra This brings good results, just like the nectar that nourishes.
Visha Nadi	23.60 - 24 deg Libra Brings situations which one does not like dealing with.
Exaltation	20 deg Libra - Maximum exaltation of Saturn. When Saturn is placed at this degree, it will give excellent results during its dasha. It will be a particularly supportive period for relationships and partnerships.
Debilitation	3 deg Scorpio - Maximum debilitation of the Moon. This will bring in situations which make one feel emotionally starved or not able to express their deepest feelings, and can create misunderstandings and arguments in a relationship.

Auspicious and inauspicious table -

Auspicious	Inauspicious
Activities Good for all activities that require skill, ability, an aggressive, forceful and focused approach, arguments, debates, and fighting court cases. Working towards one's goal, making resolutions, and penance, all types of ceremonies, functions, parties and awards, dressing up and decorating, for romance and sexual activities.	Activities Not good for travel, initiations, starting new projects, laying foundations, marriage, and activities that require a tactful, calm and composed approach.
Days Saturdays - only when it falls on the 2nd, 4th, 7th, 9th, 12th, or 14th lunar day.	Days Sundays - only when it falls on the 3rd, 4th, 8th, 9th, 13th, or 14th lunar day. Thursdays - only when it falls on the 6th, 8th, 9th, 12th, or 13th lunar day. Fridays - only when it falls on the 2nd, 3rd, 6th, 8th, 10th, or 11th lunar day.

Compatibility table -

Vishakha	Compatible with
Sexual compatibility Yoni animal	Vishakha - Female tiger Compatible with Chitra - Male tiger.
Sign compatibility	Libra - Padas 1, 2 and 3 - Gemini and Aquarius. Scorpio - Pada 4 - Cancer and Pisces.
Nakshatra compatibility	Punarvasu and Purva Bhadrapada.
Lunar day compatibility	Sashti tithi - 6th lunar day and Saptami tithi - 7th Lunar day.
Day compatibility	Tuesday, Thursday and Friday
Colour compatibility	Grey, red and all light colours.
Numerological compatibility	3, 6 and 9 - all numbers that add up to make 3, 6 and 9.
Sound compatibility	Jupiter - dental sounds - ta, ttha, da, dha, knna Venus - palatal sounds - ch, ccha, ja, jha, nga Mars - guttural sounds - ka, kha, ga, gha, kna

Sign Lord and nakshatra lord - Venus, Mars and Jupiter - as described earlier.

Vishakha is the 2nd nakshatra ruled by Jupiter. Here, Jupitarian energy combines with Venus in the 1st, 2nd and 3rd padas, which makes the natives very idealistic in their approach to life. They like to do things lawfully and ethically and strive to keep the balance between worldly and spiritual endeavours. Jupiter also likes to expand its horizons. With the influence of Venus, it does so in a way that helps to harmonise and pleasantly balance situations.

Since Jupiter and Venus are both Gurus, they can bring a sense of knowing better than others. Jupiter and Venus dashas will be significant for them, which can bring success, comfort and happiness. The placement of Jupiter and Venus in the birth chart and the navamsha will reveal the areas of life in which the transformations can happen, and the dashas and transits will give a clue about the timings.

For example, Venus in the 2nd house will have good and happy relations with the family one is born into, and Jupiter in the 4th house will give the support of a very wise and learned mother or a mother-like figure. The natives themselves will be very fortunate, learned and wise, which will help them to sail through difficult situations quite effortlessly.

The 4th Pada of Vishakha lies in Scorpio, whose Lord is Mars. Those who are born with the Ascendant, Sun or Moon in this Pada will have a more determined and ambitious quality.

They would like to get to the root of the problem and study things in depth in order to gain a complete understanding. The Jupiter Mars influence will give them a very ethical approach to life. They will stick to their principles no matter what and will be brave enough to follow the path of righteousness even in adverse circumstances.

They will like to keep things to themselves and will have very few close friends with whom they can share their inner feelings. They can come across as arrogant and stubborn, but the truth is that they cannot operate frivolously. They have to know the depth of a person or a relationship before they are convinced and can commit themselves to it. Once they make their choice they follow it sincerely through thick and thin.

<u>Quality, element, motivation, triguna, tridosha and chakras -</u> as described earlier.

Shakti - <u>Vayapna Shakti - Ability to manifest.</u>

The Sanskrit word vyapak literally means all-inclusive, or as expansive as it can get, or have a wide range of influence. The energy of Vishakha is such that it has a mixed quality of endurance and stability, and of ambition and determination. Between a desire and the goal, there is a distance to cover, the distance of determination and endurance. Vishakha natives have the ability to manifest their dreams into reality because of sustained perseverance, and every time they achieve the desired result, it helps them grow and expand towards higher possibilities.

Jupiter, being the nakshatra lord, gives them a very optimistic and idealistic approach to life. Their strong belief in having a positive outcome carries them through their tough times and helps them to manifest their dreams at a much higher scale, which has the quality of influencing everyone around them.

Symbolic signification

<u>Libra - Balancing scales -</u> as described earlier, <u>Scorpio - scorpion</u>

<u>Vishakha - the split and a decorated arched gateway.</u>

<u>Scorpion</u>

The evolutionary history of scorpions goes back 435 million years. Scorpions are predatory arachnids of the order Scorpiones. Like many of the modern crabs, early scorpions were marine or amphibious. They have 8 legs and are easily recognized by a pair of grasping pincers and a narrow, segmented tail, often carried in a characteristic forward curve over the back and always ending with a stinger.

They mainly live in deserts but have adapted to a wide range of environmental conditions. Scorpions, with their powerful stingers, appear in art, folklore and mythology. A classical myth about Scorpius tells how the giant Scorpion and its enemy, Orion, became constellations on opposite sides of the sky.

There are over 2,500 described species of scorpions, which primarily prey on insects and other invertebrates. They use their pincers to restrain and kill prey. Scorpions themselves are preyed on by larger animals. They use their venomous sting both for killing prey and for defence. Owls, lizards, a few small snakes, some rodents, frogs and toads eat scorpions. Many predators are able to handle scorpions safely by biting or breaking off the scorpion's tail. While some vertebrates and arthropods are immune to the scorpion venom.

The stinging of scorpions usually results in pain, swelling, and lesions varying in severity, with only a few that can cause severe allergic or necrotizing reactions. There are 2 species of scorpions that can inflict stings which can result in death- the Palestinian deathstalker and the Brazilian yellow scorpion. However, life-saving antivenom exists for both species of scorpion stings.

Scorpions are largely nocturnal, and they hide during the day in the confines of their burrows, in natural cracks, or under rocks and bark. They become active after darkness has fallen and cease activity sometime before dawn. The vast majority of scorpions are nonsocial, solitary creatures and interact only at birth, during courtship, or for cannibalism.

Scorpions are quite adaptable in terms of ecology, behaviour and physiology. Some species can be supercooled below the freezing point for weeks yet return within hours to normal levels of activity. Others survive total immersion underwater for as long as 1 or 2 days. Desert scorpions can withstand temperatures of 47 °C which is several degrees higher than the lethal temperatures for other desert arthropods.

Interesting facts and observations -

- A Scorpio has 8 legs. - Scorpio represents the 8th sign in the original horoscope.

- Scorpios are largely nocturnal and hide during the day in the confines of their burrows. They feel safe in the darkness and, become active at night and cease their activity just before dawn in the morning. - Scorpio Ascendants tend to be more active during the night and like working on their projects in the coolness of the night.

- They have a deep and natural connection with the phases of the moon, especially with the new moon days. - Those who have their moon placed in Scorpio will feel more connected to the new moon days when the nights are absolutely dark, and the energy is more intense and inward drawn.

- Scorpios shine in the dark because of the fluorescence effect. On new moon nights, scorpions can be seen at distances of 10 metres. - Scorpio Ascendant natives like wearing fluorescent colours, or a small fluorescent design will be marked on any of the accessories they carry, especially when they are going out at night.

- A Scorpio stings suddenly without warning, both for attack and defence. - Similarly, the 8th house represents sudden events. Those who are born with Ascendant or Moon in Scorpio, when upset about something, their words can sting like venom.

- Scientists have found out that early scorpions were marine or amphibious. Their origin lies in water. - In Astrology, Scorpio is a water sign, the water of the deep wells, which is a safe haven for the Scorpios.

- Scorpios have a very strong grip that helps them to move rapidly along surfaces at any angle, even upside down. Once they grab something, they will not let go. - Those who have their Ascendant or Moon in Scorpio, even in difficult circumstances and tough terrain, have the resilience to move across fearlessly with determination.

- The fact that Scorpios have been around for 435 million years shows their great quality of endurance. Over time, Scorpios learnt to adapt and evolve to survive under extreme heat and extreme cold. - Scorpio-born natives have an amazing ability to survive under harsh circumstances, which is a very clever and heroic quality.

- Majority of scorpions are nonsocial, solitary creatures. - Those who are born in the sign of Scorpio like to have their solitary time because they are deep thinkers and need a lot of time by themselves to contemplate and figure out the root cause of any external situations they face.

Inference

The 4th Pada of Vishakha lies in Scorpio. Therefore, they have the influence of scorpion characteristics of energy, strength, depth, secrecy, research, defence, aggression, determination, resilience and survival.

Scorpios have a deep connectivity with water and moonless nights. Their deep emotional nature stems from the fact that the Scorpio is a water sign. Here the water represents the confined space of wells or ponds, where the water merges from the depth of the earth. They feel very comfortable and very much at home in dark, hidden spaces and in the coolness of the moonlight. We must understand that dark space does not have a negative connotation but signifies a dimension or an area of life that can be understood or perceived only by looking deeper. This is where one can discover a whole new world where life is throbbing with much more intensity.

They are born survivors. Their determination and grit help them overcomes the toughest obstacles. Scorpions are known to be aggressive by nature. Moreover, Mars, the planet of energy and aggression, rules the sign of Scorpio.

Similarly, Scorpio-born natives have a determined and aggressive approach towards surviving through tough times and attaining their goals. They do this by going deep into the problem, understanding the situation fully and coping with it accordingly. They are very sensitive to feelings and emotions and, therefore, more vulnerable. Because of this they feel the inner need to protect and defend themselves from outside influences that can impact them negatively.

For them to connect to any person, philosophy or faith, they need to feel a deep connection at the emotional level. They are the types who give themselves totally towards a relationship or a cause or give nothing. They cannot be frivolous about anything in their lives and are very enduring friends. On the other side, they can also be deadly enemies, because when they are hurt, their sting of words or actions can wound the opponent deeply or seriously.

The split

The word Vishakha literally means - branched into 2. For a split to happen, there has to be a very forceful energy that can push through and cause a split. If we look at a junction point of a branch of a tree closely where, the branch splits into 2. It will have a slightly bulbous node, which highlights the residual effect of the concentrated and focused form of effect that caused the split to happen.

Inference

Vishakha natives have forceful energy, which can cause the split to happen, yet this outburst of energy is stable and controlled enough to hold the forked branch in place and does not let it fall off completely. Similarly, Vishakha born people have the capability of breaking through old beliefs and traditions and forming their own code of conduct, yet their branched approach is not radically different but has the essence of the mother branch in it.

They are ambitious enough to set their own goals and follow them, even though the attempt to do so may not be initially an easy change. The quality of this inherent forceful energy in them lures and helps them take this step - to branch out independently, yet stay connected at the root level.

The split also signifies a situation where they have to split their energy, time, finance or resources between 2 areas - of work or home life, between 2 people, 2 relationships, or 2 jobs. This can also bring dilemmas in their life, where they cannot decide which one to choose because both choices available look equally necessary, equally good or equally bad.

The decorated arched gateway

A decorated gateway marks the triumph, the celebrations and a happy occasion. Vishakha natives have several such occasions in their lives where they feel victorious - like having won a battle or having passed through a difficult situation and emerged a winner. Or they might get to literally pass through a decorated gateway as a very important guest invited to a function, or hosting it. Those who have their Ascendant, Sun or the Moon in Vishakha, at some point in their life will surely pass through a decorated gateway.

Mythology -

Deity - Indra Dev and Agni Dev

Indra Dev

The Vedas describe Indra as the king of heaven and the gods. He is associated with lightning, thunder, storms, rain, rivers, and war. Indra's mythology and powers are similar to other Indo-European deities such as Jupiter, Perun, Perkūnas, Zalmoxis, Taranis, Zeus, and Thor, which show a common origin of Proto-Indo-European mythology.

Indra is the most referred to deity in the Rigveda and is celebrated for his powers, and as the one who kills the great symbolic evil - malevolent type of Asuras. One of the most prominent ones was called Vritra, who obstructed human prosperity and happiness. The mythological stories state that Indra destroys Vritra and his deceiving forces, and thereby brings rain and sunshine for the good of mankind.

Indra is shown as deva holding a powerful thunderbolt weapon called Vajra and riding on a white elephant named Airavata. His heavenly abode is said to be on or near Mount Sumeru in the Himalayas of Northern India. Indra is strengthened by the elixir of immortality, the soma, which the priests offer to him in the sacrifice. Among his allies are the Rudras (or Maruts). Indra is sometimes referred to as the thousand-eyed one.

In later Hinduism, Indra is no longer worshipped but plays the important mythological roles of the god of rain, regent of the heavens, and guardian of the east. In the Mahabharata, Indra fathers the great hero Arjuna and tries in vain to prevent the god of fire - Agni, from burning a great forest. One of the mythological stories in the Puranas states that Lord Krishna persuaded the cowherds of Gokula to stop worshipping Indra. Enraged, Indra sent down torrents of rain, but Krishna lifted Mount Govardhana on his fingertip and gave the people shelter under it for 7 days until Indra relented and paid homage.

<u>Indra also means the king of his own body and mind.</u> The one who has over his or her senses (Indriya) or has disciplined the mind and body. The Vedic way of life guides us on how to become the master of our sense perceptions and not give in to the temptations that can bring us ill health and suffering.

The word Indriya comes from the root word Indra. In Sanskrit, the word <u>Indra</u> also signifies - will power to control the senses and thereby gain physical and mental strength, or becoming the king of your sense perceptions.

Ayurvedic texts describe Indra as -

"Indram *Atma tasya sadhanam Indriyam.*

This means - Indra is the soul (atma), and Indriya (sense organs) are a tool or an instrument (sadhan) for perception to attain knowledge.

The Vedas describe 11 Indriyas - 11 main phenomenological faculties-

Indriyas Sensory faculties	Organs	Function
5 Gnaana Indriyas Sensory faculties	Eyes - Chakshu Indriya Ears - Shrota Indriya Nose - Gandha Indriya Tongue-Rasana Indriya Skin - Sparsh Indriya	Seeing Hearing Smell Taste Touch
5 Karma Indriyas Organs of action or movement - motor organs	Tongue - Vaak Indriya Hands - Paani Indriya Feet - Pada Indriya Anus - Payu Indriya Urethra - Mootra Organ for sex - Upastha Indriya Male - Penus Female - Vagina	Speech Grasp Movement Excretion Urination For sexual intercourse
1 Ubhaya - Indriya For both sensory and motor function	Manas Indriya - Mind	Nervous system

Over time, with overuse and misuse, our sense perceptions get dulled. For example, if we listen to loud music all the time, our ears will not be able to hear the soft sounds they will be defended to subtle sounds. So, to bring back the ability to hear well and hear fully, we need to slowly train our ears to listen to music at a lower volume and practice yogic kriyas like shanmukhi mudra (closing the 6 senses of perception for a brief time), which will enhance the quality of hearing. These practices should be learnt from a trained yoga teacher.

Just as a sitar (string instrument) produces a fantastic sound when its strings are well tuned - tightened to the right degree where they are not too lax or too tight. Similarly, when we train and fine-tune our sense receptions through yoga and meditation, our ability to perceive is enhanced phenomenally.

Agni Dev

Agni Dev is the fire god of Hinduism, second only to Indra in the Vedic mythology of ancient India. He signifies the fire of the sun, of lightning, the domestic and sacrificial fire. As the divine personification of the fire of sacrifice, he is the mouth of the gods, the carrier of the oblation, and the messenger between the human and the divine realms.

Agni is the guardian of the south-east direction. He is described in the scriptures as the one who has a reddish-orange complexion. He rides a Ram and has 2 faces — one beneficent and one malignant. He is shown with 3 or 7 tongues, hair that stands on ends like flames, 3 legs, and 7 arms. In the Rigveda, he is sometimes identified with Rudra, the forerunner for Lord Shiva. His presence is invoked in many ceremonies and fire rituals.

Inference

Those who are born with the Ascendant, Sun or Moon in Vishakha will have Indira-like qualities of having a leadership role in the family, community, nation or worldwide. They will have the ability and will love to take up the responsibility of fighting for a good cause, helping voluntarily as an advisor or a consultant. They will also have the fire and passion to work towards their goals and transform themselves for the better. Agni Dev, the god of fire, gives the ambition, fire and zeal to constantly make an effort to purify oneself and transform into a better human being.

They have the ability to train their mind and body, discipline their senses of perception and thus win over their limitations, which makes them the king of their own mind and body. The Vedic way of life guides one to become the master of their senses and not be enslaved by them. This means not falling into the temptation of those habits which harm us, cause ill health, pain or suffering. For example, overcoming the temptation of eating sweets, which can cause ill health or chronic problems in the long run. Therefore, Vishakha natives have a tremendous sense of discipline and willpower to overcome those tendencies that can hinder their growth and well-being.

Vishakha padas

20 deg Libra - 3.20 Scorpio

Padas	Degrees
1	20 - 23.20 deg Libra
2	23.20 - 26.40 deg Libra
3	26.40 - 30 deg Libra
4	0 - 3.20 deg Scorpio

Pada 1

20 - 23.20 deg Libra, Navamsha - Aries (Lord - Mars)

Rashi Lord - Venus and Nakshatra Lord- Jupiter

Pada 1 of Vishakha falls in the navamsha of Aries. Therefore, it carries the energy of Venus, Jupiter and Mars. When the energies of Venus and Mars come together, it makes the person very passionate, romantic, energetic, forceful, short-tempered and goal-driven. Jupiter is the planet of expansion and optimism. Therefore, the combined effect makes one very idealistic, and they like to do things in a grand way. They are blessed with the fortune of having a very happy and optimistic approach towards relationships and partnerships. It's a fortunate Pada because the yoga tara point is at 20 degrees, which is also the point of maximum exaltation of Saturn. So any planets sitting here, especially Saturn, will give excellent results during its dasha and transits.

For example, Vishakha Pada 1, placed in the 5th house, will be very creative and will benefit from creating something that can be useful for everyone - like having a business in the field of clothes or food. Passion and romance will be their guiding motivation in whatever they do.

Careers

Teachers, engineers, financial advisors, counsellors, property dealers working in the field of advertisement, public relations coordinators, film directors, leaders, businessmen, IT professionals, fashion designers, writers, speakers, actors, social workers, religious leaders, priests, astrologers, office workers and working from home.

Pada 2

23. 20 - 26.40 deg Libra, Navamsha - Taurus (Lord - Venus)

Rashi Lord - Venus and Nakshatra Lord- Jupiter

In the 2nd Pada of Vishakha, there will be the energy of Jupiter and the double influence of Venus. This will make the natives very receptive towards all that is as aesthetically beautiful. They will have the ability to create something beautiful, even from a piece of stone or a plane sheet of paper. Jupiter and Venus are both beneficent planets. Therefore, the dashas and transits of Venus and Jupiter will be particularly beneficial for them. However, if Venus or Jupiter have a low Shabala score, or they are afflicted by the conjunction or direct aspect of Saturn, Mars, Rahu or Ketu, it can reduce the benefits or cause delays and obstacles.

The 2nd Pada is a Pushkar bhaga and Pushkar amsha Pada, which means it's a fortunate Pada and planets sitting here give wonderful results during its dasha and transits. For example, the 2nd Pada of Vishakha in the 8th house will bring sudden gains from the insurance or inheritance.

Careers

Teachers, advisors, astrologers, consultants, IT professionals, filmmakers, fashion designers, florists, actors, artists, musicians, writers, philosophers, poets, cooks and working from home.

Pada 3

26.40 - 30 deg Libra, Navamsha - Gemini (Lord - Mercury)

Rashi Lord - Venus and Nakshatra Lord - Jupiter

The navamsha of the 3rd Pada of Vishakha is placed in Gemini, which gives the effect of Venus, Jupiter and Mercury. They will be more vocal and communicative about their ideology, faith and philosophy. Libra and Gemini are both air signs - the navamsha falls in Gemini, which shows that in their adulthood years after 30, they will maintain their friendly nature. In fact, they will become more flexible in their approach to life and will adjust to situations easily. They can become excellent artists, designers, creators, writers, poets, and actors.

For example, in the 3rd Pada of Vishakha in the 10th house they will have a career where they will have to deal with a lot of people - like a public relations manager. They will have the capability and talent to create peace and harmony in relationships through interactive communication.

Careers

Philosophers, guides, gurus, teachers, astrologers, advisors, consultants, managers, public relations coordinators, writers, poets, artists, actors, film directors, IT professionals, designers, doctors, businessmen, accountants and working from home.

Pada 4

0 - 3.20 deg Scorpio, Navamsha - Cancer (Lord - Moon)

Rashi Lord - Venus and Nakshatra Lord- Jupiter

In this Pada, there will be the influence of Venus, Jupiter and Moon. The natives born in this Pada will be more emotional and will feel things more deeply. They will be very sensitive to what people say, or if they don't say what should have been said, it can make them feel hurt. They are usually not easily shaken or disturbed, but if their tolerance has been put to the test because they have been badly treated repeatedly - they will surely strike back with deadly precision. Although they will be friendly and cordial with all whom they meet, in their hearts, they hold many secrets and share them only with their closest friends.

In the 4th Pada, the moon gets debilitated at 3 degrees in Scorpio. This will bring in situations which make one feel emotionally starved or not able to express their deepest feelings, and can create misunderstandings and arguments in a relationship. For example, the 4th Pada of Vishakha in the 3rd house can bring challenging or difficult relationships with siblings or neighbours.

Careers-

Psychologists, philosophers, lawyers, detectives, spies, researchers, IT professionals, astrologers, priests, teachers, advisors, counsellors, spiritual mediums, designers, artists, actors, singers, musicians, writers, poets, self-employed and working from home.

The effect of planets

Vishakha - Libra Padas 1,2 and 3	Planets that get affected
Yoga Karka - Most benefic	Saturn
Functional Benefic - give good results during their dasha.	Venus
Functional Malefic - can give problems during their dasha.	Jupiter, Rahu and Ketu
Functional Neutral	Sun, Moon and Mercury
Kendra Adi Pati Dosha - can be malefic	Mars
Vishakha - Scorpio Pada 4	Planets that get affected
Functional Benefic - give good results during their dasha.	Mars, Sun and Moon
Functional Malefic - can give problems during their dasha.	Mercury, Rahu and Ketu
Functional Neutral	Jupiter and Saturn
Kendra Adi Pati Dosha - can be malefic	Venus

Vishakha Ascendant

The first 3 padas of Vishakha are placed in Libra. Therefore, those who are born with the Ascendant in the 1st, 2nd or 3rd pada will have the influence of Venus and Jupiter. This gives them a very attractive and pleasing personality. Since Jupiter and Venus are both Benefic planets and Gurus or masters in their own fields, the natives will be fortunate in the sense that even through the most difficult situations, they will come out unharmed. They will be great advisors because they have the knack of counselling others with Venusian charm and Jupitarian wisdom.

The 4th Pada of Vishakha lies in Scorpio, which gives the quality of Martian energy and Jupitarian optimism. The natives will pursue their goals with more determination and idealism. When they are faced with challenging situations or a more serious danger threatens them, the Martian energy comes to their rescue. They will not push ahead immediately, but with quiet poise and inner strength, they will achieve their goals. Just like a Scorpio's behaviour, they can sense danger from a distance and quickly charge with absolute precision.

Their determined Martian zeal has a steely willpower that helps them to make the impossible possible. They are intensely loyal and will never compromise their principles. They will never give in or admit defeat. Their brave souls, fuelled by the Martian energy, will fight on till the bitter or sweet end. The Jupitarian influence gives them a lot of wisdom and knowledge, even more than it can be sensed or defined. The Scorpion vibration also brings a burning need to discover the unknown.

Sun in Vishakha

When the Sun is placed in the 1st, 2nd and 3rd padas of Vishakha, it will share the qualities of Venus and Jupiter because these padas lie in Libra. Sun is friendly with Jupiter and enemy with Venus, therefore there will be a mixed result. The natives will be very intelligent, dignified, generous and fair in their dealings. They could come across as arrogant or aloof and will be very sensitive to what others say about them. The Libran sense of beauty, harmony and aesthetics will make them very sensitive to their immediate environment.

For example, if Sun is placed in the 2nd Pada of Vishakha in the 8th house, the natives can face difficulties regarding their vitality and health because Sun gets debilitated in Libra. This could happen during the dasha of the Sun, Venus or Jupiter.

The 4th Pada of Vishakha is placed in Scorpio. Therefore, the Sun will have the influence of Mars and Jupiter in this Pada. This placement will give good results during the dashas of the Sun, Mars or Jupiter because Sun is friendly with both Mars and Jupiter. The natives will be brave, determined, intelligent and secretive. They will be interested in everything that's mystical and mysterious. They can make great psychologists, psychiatrists, doctors, astrologers, therapists, and teachers. For example, if the Sun is placed in the 4th Pada of Vishakha in the Ascendant, the natives will be dignified, good-looking, proud and influential. They will have good support from their father and will be honoured by the authorities or the government for their particular talent or skill. They will be good motivational speakers and will love to dress up well and look presentable in public.

Moon in Vishakha

The Moon in the 1st, 2nd and 3rd padas of Vishakha lie in Libra, which will give the influence of Venus and Jupiter. Their actions and thoughts are motivated by the desire to maintain peace and harmony. The Jupitarian expansion and Venusian sense of beauty make them very creative and knowledgeable. For example, the moon in the 2nd Pada of Vishakha in the 2nd house will give a very creative and academic home environment. They will be fortunate to have the resources and ambience which support the development of their creativity and knowledge.

The 4th Pada of Vishakha lies in Scorpio, which gives it a very Martian influence mixed with the Jupitarian quality of wisdom and expansion. In the deep waters of Scorpio, the fiery Mars gains more willpower, resilience, resoluteness and determination. Scorpio is the 2nd cycle of the water element and has the influence of the night forces and feminine receptivity.

This gives them a great in-depth understanding of human emotions, and they can become excellent psychologists. Scorpio, being a fixed sign, makes them enormously capable of executing and organising events and daily routines. They are very intrigued by the mysteries of life and have a great interest in studying esoteric subjects that have a mystical dimension. All that cannot easily be seen by the eyes or comprehended by the mind attracts them, and they end up spending a great deal of time trying to discover the awesome mystery of one's mind and body.

The Martian influence in the original 8th house of Scorpio gives a deep desire to penetrate into the unknown that lies buried beneath the layers of reason and logic. Their desires are so intense that an emotion or a thought can consume their attention fully until they have fully understood the mechanics of it. For example, the 4th Pada of Vishakha in the 9th house will make them travel to far-off lands or a foreign country in search of higher knowledge, a higher degree, a learned teacher, or a spiritual guru.

A Vishakha born in the 1st pada will have the Libran influence. They will argue or debate over a topic in order to achieve peace, justice and harmony. While a Vishakha native born with the moon in the 4th Pada will have the Martian outlook in Scorpio, they may not argue to prove their point but achieve their desired goal with a quiet approach and a steel-like determination.

The poetry of Vishakha

Vishakha - the branch that forked,

As a new path, from each junction - life evolved,

And so, the diversity brought richness,

The creative ways of nature's genius.

Jupiter and Venus in Libran ways,

Justice, harmony, balance and grace.

The air fires the passion to discover the depth,

Mysteries fascinate the Scorpio - beginning to end.

From the experiences - clear and unclear,

Joy, love, pain and fear,

A seeker is born - What is the truth? What is real?

Name and form - the seeming truth of the surface,

The mirage of experience - the card of ace.

The game of life - a pack of cards,

The deal of destiny - a play of sorts.

Learning to make the best of what fate has given,

Is our side of the deal - chosen?

Remedies

- <u>Das Maha Vidya</u> - as described earlier.

- Those who are born in the 1st, 2nd or 3rd pada of Vishakha will have a Vata predominant constitution - a daily exercise routine will keep them grounded and in good health. Planning well before travelling, taking care of your diet, and eating warm meals at regular times will help to keep the Vata in balance.

- The 4th Pada of Vishakha will have a Kapha predominant tridosha - for them also a daily exercise routine will keep them active and in good health. They should eat more fresh fruits and salads and avoid heavy foods like cakes, sweets and dairy products.

- The yogic asanas and pranayama will be particularly helpful in balancing the excessive Vata and Kapha. The alternate nose breathing technique (alom vilom) is an excellent and quick way to pacify restlessness and calm the mind.

- Meditation (breath watch) is another beautiful and scientific technique for calming any agitation or stress in the body or the mind.

- Every time Vishakha natives create something that can be useful for everyone, they will experience a sense of victory within themselves for having overcome their limitations or a particular weakness.

- Yellow, red and all pastel colours resonate well with the energy of Vishakha.

Chanting the mantra - "Om *dham nam Vishakha nakshatraye namah,*" 108 times on days when the moon is transiting Vishakha or on Thursdays will help to connect you with your inner self.

Example

Ascendant in Vishakha

K N Rao - famous Indian Astrologer - Born on 12th October 1931, 7 54 am in Machilipatnam, India.

Kotamraju Narayana Rao is the 2nd of the 4 sons of the famous journalist of the pre-independence era, K. Rama Rao. His father was the founder and editor of the National Herald. Rao was initiated into astrology by his late mother, K. Saraswani Devi, at the age of 12 in 1943. He regards her as the best astrologer he has known in 2 areas, marriage and children and prashna (horary).

Rao was a lecturer in English before joining the government service through an all-India competition in 1957. He joined the Indian Audit and Accounts Service, from which he retired as Director General in November 1990. He was more interested in games and sports than in astrology in his youth. He won brilliant prizes in chess competitions and 2 state championships in bridge competitions.

He did his fundamental research in astrology during his career because of which he managed to collect horoscopes systematically in thousands. He has more than 50,000 horoscopes with 10 important events of each individual noted with him. It is perhaps the largest individual collection of horoscopes any astrologer has.

The strain of doing astrology as a mission and not charging any fee almost made him give up astrology many times. But in December 1981, he was forced out of his shell to participate in a 3-day seminar on astrology in Delhi. After this groundbreaking speech, there has been a persistent demand for his astrological articles. From then onwards, he has been sharing his original research, for which he has won worldwide praise. He is the Advisor of Astrology Courses in the Bharatiya Vidya Bhawan, New Delhi. The teachers on the teaching faculty of the astrology course in the Bharatiya Vidya Bhawan have, like him, never charged any fees for teaching, which they do in an honorary capacity.

Between 1993 and 1995, Rao visited the USA on 5 lecture tours. He has worked hard and has used his skills to make some very true and attractive predictions about people, which won him worldwide praise. His biggest contribution to the field of astrology was in starting the Vedic Astrology course at Bharatiya Vidya Bhavan in New Delhi.

Analysis

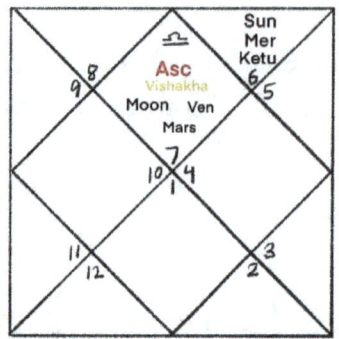 

K N Rao is a Vishakha Ascendant in the 1st Pada. He has a strong Libra influence because he has his Moon, Venus and Mars placed in the Ascendant. Moon and Venus are in Chitra, and the Ascendant and Mars are in Vishakha.

He is a very creative person and has a very fine sense of keeping everything in balance and harmony. Like a true Vishakha native, he had the capability to break away from the malpractices of some traditional astrologers, who had fallen into the greed of making false predictions for the sake of making more money. Through his intelligence, sincerity, resilience and hard work, he opened up a new shakha (branch) of Vedic astrology with a scientific approach based on the data and research which could provide plenty of evidence for any of the techniques that had been mentioned in various old astrological texts, thus reviving the glory of Vedic astrology.

Moon is the lord of the 10th house, and Jupiter is exalted, sitting in the 10th house of Cancer. His Jyotish Guru, Yogi Bhaskarananda had told him that he would have to visit many foreign countries to bring back the honour, recognition and dignity of Vedic Astrology. On his first visit to the USA in 1993, one of the speakers at the Vedic conference had very befittingly said this about him, "Vedic astrology before Rao and after Rao".

The first time he travelled out of India (his trip to the USA) in 1993, he was running his Mercury Sun Sun dasha. His Mercury and Sun are sitting with Ketu in the 12th house of Virgo, which brought him foreign travel, fame and recognition. Sun is the lord of the 11th house of gains, and Mercury is the lord of the 9th house (Gemini) and the 12th house (Virgo). He has to travel abroad to give lectures on Vedic Astrology (the communication aspect of Mercury).

19
Anuradha

Om tam tham dam Anuradha nakshatraye namah

Zodiac degrees	3.20 - 16.40 deg Scorpio
Ruling planet	Scorpio - Mars and Ketu and Anuradha - Saturn
Sanskrit name	Anu means - atom, and Radha - Lord Krishna's beloved. Anuradha is the subtle form of Radha.
Astronomical name	The 3 stars in a row, which look like a staff. Seen in the constellation of Scorpio.
Symbol	Scorpio - scorpion Anuradha-staff- a long stick held by a saint or a yogi. and - a Lotus flower.
Element	Water
Deity	Mitra - a friend
Quality	Scorpio - Sthira - fixed Anuradha - Mishra - mixed and mridu - gentle
Shakti	Radhana Shakti - Power of Worship
Cast	Shudra - worker, farmer
Gender	Female
Motivation	Moksha - liberation
Triguna	Tamas
Tridosha	Kapha
Body parts	Breast, stomach, womb and bowels.
Direction	North, South and West

Month	Late May, the second half of Vishakha month.
Bird	Peacock
Sound	na, nee, noo, nay
Tree	Nagkesar tree
Chakras	Muladhara - Mars and Vishuddhi - Saturn
Das Maha Vidya	Devi Kali - Saturn and Devi Bagalamukhi - Mars

Special degrees -

Yoga Tara	10 deg Scorpio It's a point where the planet will show the strongest and sure results during its dasha.
Pushkaramsha	2nd Pada The planets placed here will give good results during its dasha, like the blossoming of a flower.
Amrit Nadi	9.33- 10.26 deg Scorpio This brings good results, just like the nectar that nourishes.
Visha Nadi	5.30- 6.26 deg Scorpio Brings situations which one does not like dealing with.
Exaltation	16 deg Scorpio - Maximum exaltation of Ketu. When Ketu is placed at this degree, it will give excellent results during its dasha. It will be particularly supportive for ending something.

Auspicious and inauspicious table -

Auspicious	Inauspicious
Activities Good for all group-related activities, research and study of occult subjects, for spending time with friends, managing things and making decisions, finance and accounts, for travel and dealing with immigration and foreign affairs, secretive activities, for reflection, meditation and healing.	Activities Not good for marriage, confrontations, inaugurations, beginnings and routine mundane activities.
Days Tuesdays - only when it falls on the 1st, 3rd, 6th, 8th, 11th, or 13th lunar day. Wednesdays- only when it falls on the 2nd, 3rd, 7th, 8th, 12th, or 13th lunar day. Saturdays - only when it falls on the 2nd, 4th, 7th, 9th, 12th, or 14th lunar day.	Days Sundays - only when it falls on the 3rd, 4th, 8th, 9th, 13th, or 14th lunar day. Mondays - only when it falls on the 6th, 7th, or 11th lunar day. Thursdays - only when it falls on the 6th, 8th, 9th, 12th, or 13th lunar day. Fridays - only when it falls on the 2nd, 3rd, 6th, 8th, 10th, or 11th lunar day.

Compatibility table -

Anuradha	Compatible with
Sexual compatibility Yoni animal	Anuradha - Female deer Compatible with Jeyshtha - Male deer.
Sign compatibility	Scorpio - Cancer and Pisces.
Nakshatra compatibility	Pushya and Shatbhishak.
Lunar day compatibility	Dwadashi tithi - 12th lunar day.
Day compatibility	Tuesday and Saturday
Colour compatibility	Red and blue.
Numerological compatibility	8 and 9 - all numbers that add up to make 8 and 9.
Sound compatibility	Saturn - labial sounds - pa, pha, ba, bha, ma Mars - guttural sounds - ka, kha, ga, gha, kna

Sign Lord and nakshatra lord - Mars and Saturn - as described earlier.

Anuradha is the 2nd nakshatra ruled by Saturn. Here Saturn's energy combines with Mars, which makes the natives very determined and practical.

It's a tough combination, considering the challenges one has to face in worldly matters. Since Saturn is the planet of discipline, restriction and caution, and Mars is the planet of aggression and determination - and both are considered malefic. As the famous saying goes - "in the tough circumstances the tough get going." Those who are born with their Ascendant, Sun or Moon in Anuradha have the dedication, devotion and ability to refine, transform and become the master of his or her skill.

Quality, element, motivation, triguna, tridosha and chakras - as described earlier.

Shakti - Aradhana Shakti - Power to worship.

Anuradha natives have power in their prayer, because of the intensity, sincerity and depth of their emotion. If they observe closely, they will notice that whenever they perform a certain puja or worship, their problems begin to get resolved in one way or another.

Devotion is a beautiful quality that Anuradha natives have. They will be devoted to some path, person, relationship, ideology, religion or faith. Just as Radha was totally devoted to Lord Krishna. Many romantic and beautiful incidents have been narrated in the Devi Bhagavata Purana about the meetings of Radhe and Lord Krishna. Radha's devotion was such that although she could not physically be with Lord Krishna, her whole being was connected with him through the purity of her love and devotion.

One such incident highlights the devotion of Radha and the Gopis towards Lord Krishna. After Krishna had left Vrindavan he never went back there again. When Lord Krishna had settled in Dwarka, he had requested Uddhava (his friend and cousin) to visit Vrindavan with a message on his behalf to the Gopis and other residents of the village because Lord Krishna knew that they were all missing him terribly.

When Uddhava reached Vrindavan, he was so overwhelmed by seeing the devotion of Radha and Gopis towards Lord Krishna. The Gopis were crying with tears of devotion, Radha was engrossed in Lord Krishna's thoughts, and saw him everywhere. He decided to stay in Vrindavan longer than he had planned in order to imbibe the quality of love and devotion from the Gopis and Radha.

Symbolic signification

Scorpio - scorpion - as described earlier.

Anuradha - staff and lotus flower.

Staff

The Sanskrit word danda means stick or a staff. It symbolises strength and spiritual prowess. In mythological iconography, many saints, seers, mystics and yogis are shown holding a staff. Since they would walk long distances and go through rough terrains of valleys, climbing hills and mountains, a stick was needed for support. The word staff also signifies strict discipline and punishment. When one chooses to walk on the spiritual path, self-discipline becomes necessary to overcome the laziness of the body and the mind.

One famous example is the Staff of Moses, which has been mentioned in the Book of Exodus when God appears to Moses in the burning bush. God asks what Moses has in his hand, and Moses answers a staff. The staff is miraculously transformed into a snake and then back into a staff. The staff is thereafter referred to as the staff of God. It has been mentioned in the Hebrew Bible that Moses used this magical staff on various occasions as and when needed. Here are some of the incidents where the magical and mystical staff has been used -

- The Lord said unto Moses in Midian, "Go, return into Egypt, for all the men are dead which sought thy life." And Moses took his wife and his sons and set them upon an ass, and he returned to the land of Egypt, and Moses took the rod of God in his hand.

- Moses and Aaron appear before the Pharaoh of the Exodus when Aaron's rod is transformed into a serpent. It is used several times on God's command to initiate the Plagues of Egypt.

- During the Exodus, Moses stretches out his hand with the staff to part the Red Sea.

- While in the wilderness after leaving Egypt, Moses strikes the rock with the rod to create a spring for the Israelites from which to drink.

- Finally, Moses uses the staff in the battle at Rephidim between the Israelites and the Amalekites. When he holds up the "rod of God," When he drops it, their enemies gain the upper hand. Aaron and Hur help him to keep the staff raised until victory is achieved.

Insight

A stick is an inert object which has a practical use, but when it's constantly in touch with an enlightened being it imbibes spiritual energy. A staff in the hand of a yogi or a saint can be used as a spiritual conductor to transmit energy which can be triggered only through the intention of the enlightened being who holds it. Another factor is the sensation of touch. The palms of our hands and the soles of our feet are richly supplied with fine nerves and are, therefore, very sensitive to tactile sensations. That's why our palms and soles of the feet can receive and transmit vibrations more easily than any other part of the skin. So, a spiritually advanced being can use a stick like a magic wand when it's backed with his energy and intention.

Lotus flower

The Lotus Flower starts its growth in the deep mud, away from the sunlight. Slowly, as it grows, it reaches the sunlight, becoming the most beautiful flower. In many Eastern traditions, it is regarded as a symbol of purity, enlightenment, self-regeneration and rebirth. The yogic way of life guides us to live our life like a lotus flower, just as a lotus grows from the depth of muddy waters but blossoms into the most beautiful flower. It grows in the murky waters but is untouched by it.

A Lotus flower, therefore, is a perfect example of how one can stay in the material world yet use every experience as a manure to blossom into an enlightened being. For this reason, the Lotus flower is considered a symbol of serenity and purity. Many male and female deities in Eastern cultures are shown holding a lotus flower or sitting on it because of its aspect purity.

Interesting facts -

- A Lotus grows in a tropical climate and needs a depth of at least 8 feet to grow and blossom fully.

- The leaves of a lotus are water-resistant.

- Lotus is hermaphroditic (both male and female) and is pollinated by insects and beetles.

- The Lotus rises from the mud to blossom but is virtually untouched by the substrate from where it grows.

- The stem of a lotus bends easily but is difficult to break.

- People in Asia have also been using the Lotus for its <u>herbal and medicinal properties</u> for centuries.

- The lotus flower can be brewed into a heart tonic.

- Lotus seeds are extremely hardy and long-lived and are used in a tonic for digestive problems and diarrhoea.

- The dried roots of Lotus, when taken internally, are traditionally believed to be effective in stopping excessive bleeding.

- Lotus roots have a delicate taste and crunchy texture. The leaves make a nutritious vegetable when young and can serve as plates or food wrappers when mature.

- Lotus seeds contain about 15 percent protein and 70 percent carbohydrate and can be popped like popcorn, ground into flour or roasted and brewed like coffee.

- Lotus petals are not particularly tasty but often serve as a garnish for soups, and the stamens sometimes serve as flavouring for tea.

<u>Inference</u>

Anuradha natives have a great sense of self-discipline, they have the tenacity of purpose and can work towards their goals with incredible determination. In tough circumstances, they pull through with an amazing inner strength and live their life like a lotus flower, staying in the world but untouched by its impurities. At some point in their life, they will feel that they are living in the murky waters of difficult relationships, but they learn to find solutions to their problems through inner realisation.

Just as a lotus grows in very deep ponds, Anuradha natives' emotions run deep and they are not frivolous in friendship, relationship or anything that they do. The quality of depth of understanding is seen in every aspect of their life.

Mythology -

Deity - <u>Mitra - friend</u>

The word Mitra literally means a friend. In the Rigveda, the oldest of the Vedic texts, Mitra is mostly indistinguishable from Varuna. Together, they form a pair of Mitra-Varuna. They both essentially have the same characteristics. Mitra is associated with the light of dawn and the morning sun, while Varuna becomes associated with the evening and, ultimately, the night. In the post-Vedic texts, Mitra evolved into the patron divinity and guardian of friendship.

Mitra-Varuna is described as young. They wear glistening garments, are monarchs and guardians of the whole world, and their palace is golden, with 1000 pillars and doors. They support heaven and earth and the air between heaven and earth. They are lords of rivers and seas, and they send rain and refreshment from the sky.

They wet the pastures with dew of clarified butter, and rain abounding in heavenly water comes from them. Their domain has streams that flow with honey, and their pastures have cattle that yield refreshment.

In Rigveda, Mitra-Varuna is addressed as devas. Mitra is seen as the sustainer of mankind and of all gods and has the unique ability to bring people together. In some Vedic descriptions, Varuna is seen as the lord of the cosmic rhythm, of the sun and other celestial spheres, while Mitra brings forth the light at dawn.

Inference

Those who are born with their Ascendant, Sun or Moon in Anuradha have an inherent talent for bringing people together and working together as a team. They are very good at organising and planning functions and events on a small scale or a large scale.

The word Mitra literally means a friend. Anuradha natives make great friends. Once they have chosen, they stay committed. They prefer to have only a few close friends and are true to their friendship. They will stand by their friend through all good and bad circumstances.

Anuradha padas

3.20 - 16.40 deg Scorpio

Padas	Degrees
1	3.20 - 6.40 deg Scorpio
2	6.40 - 10 deg Scorpio
3	10 - 13.20 deg Scorpio
4	13.20 - 16.40 deg Scorpio

Pada 1

3.20 - 6.40 deg Scorpio, Navamsha - Leo (Lord - Sun)

Rashi Lord - Mars and Nakshatra Lord - Saturn

The navamsha of the 1st Pada lies in Leo. Therefore, it carries the energy of the Sun, Mars and Saturn. Sun and Saturn don't get along well, so it can bring frustrations and delays. The influence of Mars and the Sun will make them very ego-sensitive, authoritative and proud, and they will not like taking orders from anyone. Yet Saturn will cause delays and restrictions and make them work towards self-discipline if they want to succeed in life. Over time, they will learn to be more humble and accepting of others' shortcomings and will try to overcome their own limitations of comparing themselves with others or having an egoistic attitude.

For example, in the 1st Pada of Anuradha, in the 3rd house, they will not get along very well with their siblings or neighbours. The situations will be such that they do not get an opportunity to have a close friendship with them. They will have to make many short trips related to work, home or holidays.

Careers

Technicians, engineers, politicians, financial advisors, counsellors, property dealers, working in the office, leaders, managers, businessmen, IT professionals, athletes, sportsmen or sportswomen, army officers, policemen, firefighters, lifeguards and working from home.

Pada 2

6.40 - 10 deg Scorpio, Navamsha - Virgo (Lord - Mercury)

Rashi Lord - Mars and Nakshatra Lord- Saturn

In the 2nd Pada, there will be the energy of Mars, Saturn and Mercury. The natives will be more vocal about their thoughts and emotions. It's a pushkara navamsha Pada. Therefore, it will fruitify the results of any planet sitting here during its dasha and transit. Especially after the age of 30, the natives will begin to feel the positivity of this Pada. As they grow older they will be able to express themselves more freely and develop their skills of oral and written communication. They will be more academically oriented and will love to research and learn about everything that is mystical and mysterious. They will also be good with accounts and handling finance.

For example, the 2nd Pada of Anuradha in the 5th house will be very creative and intelligent and will have a deep understanding of subjects like psychology, philosophy, ayurveda, astrology, occult, Vedas, palmistry, yoga, meditation, life after death, past life regression, hypnosis, religious and spiritual subjects.

Careers

Psychiatrists, philosophers, astrologers, consultants, therapists, past life regression therapists, hypnotists, doctors, researchers, archaeologists, IT professionals, actors, filmmakers, artists, writers, and working from home.

Pada 3

10 - 13.20 deg Scorpio, Navamsha - Libra (Lord - Venus)

Rashi Lord - Mars and Nakshatra Lord - Saturn

The navamsha of the 3rd Pada is placed in Libra, which gives the effect of Mars, Saturn and Venus. The combination of Mars and Venus makes them very passionate and creative.

They will be exceptionally good in art and music, and will be more friendly and social than those born in the other padas of Anuradha. They will be romantic and will have a wonderful sense of aesthetics, and the opposite sex will find them very attractive.

For example, the 3rd Pada of Anuradha in the 7th house will bring such situations in their life where they have to deal with the opposite sex, and they get magnetically drawn towards each other. Once they choose their partner or spouse, they will be dedicated to them, and in turn, they will find a spouse who is equally committed. They will have their share of arguments, but when it comes to the crux, they will always stand by their spouse.

Careers

Artists, actors, architects, designers, decorators, astrologers, advisors, consultants, managers, public relations coordinators, writers, poets, film directors, IT professionals, doctors, businessmen and working from home.

Pada 4

13.20 - 16.40 deg Scorpio, Navamsha - Scorpio (Lord - Mars)

Rashi Lord - Mars and Nakshatra Lord- Saturn

In this Pada, there will be the influence of Saturn and the double effect of Mars. This makes them very energetic and ambitious to pursue their goals with focused determination. They will be physically and mentally strong, but if Mars is retrograde or weak with a low Shadbala score, it can bring a lack of vitality or strength. A weak Mars can make them more defensive and cowardly. If the fierce and excessive energy of Mars is not channelled into positive thoughts and actions, it can cause harm and pain to the natives. They should endeavour to have a regular gym routine or build some exercise regime which will help them maintain good physical, mental and emotional health. Practising Hatha yoga asanas will be particularly beneficial for them.

If Mars is placed in the 6th, 8th or 12th house, it can bring challenging situations during the dasha of Mars. For example, the 4th Pada placed in the 6th house will have to give their time, attention and energy towards a daily routine.

Careers-

Army officers, policemen, firefighters, sportsmen and sportswomen, athletes, race car drivers, emergency doctors, surgeons, psychologists, detectives, spies, researchers, IT professionals, businessmen, property dealers, builders, factory workers, farmers, labourers, mechanics, car dealers, garage owners, self-employed and working from home.

The effect of planets

Anuradha - Scorpio	Planets that get affected
Functional Benefic - give good results during their dasha.	Mars, Sun and Moon
Functional Malefic - can give problems during their dasha.	Mercury, Rahu and Ketu
Functional Neutral	Jupiter and Saturn
Kendra Adi Pati Dosha - can be malefic	Venus

Anuradha Ascendant

Anuradha natives are equipped with the fierce determination of Mars and the cool endurance of Saturn because they have to pass through extremely intense soil testing times in their lives. The Saturn-Mars combination gives them great intensity, determination, strength and patience to endure hardships bravely and pass through these challenges.

They will trust love and friendship only after it has been proven that the other person is worthy of their trust. But once they have chosen their friend or partner, their loyalty and devotion is unwavering. They fiercely protect their own integrity and that of their loved ones. If they feel there is any injustice done, they feel compelled to demand an eye for an eye to make sure that injuries are not repeated again.

Since Anuradha lies in the heart of the sign of Scorpio, the mystical experience of death comes to them through dreams, visions, or the death of their close friends or relatives, which transforms them in a big way. From an early age they will begin to look at life from a deeper perspective compared to those around them, and their spiritual seeking begins from a very young age.

Their positive qualities are loyalty, sincerity, endurance, devotion, determination, willpower, magnetism, gentleness, insight, intuition, and an amazing sense of self-discipline. When they are feeling out of their element, frustrated or disillusioned with life, they can become suspicious and fanatic and can seek revenge.

Sun in Anuradha

When the Sun is placed in Anuradha, it will share the energies of Mars and Saturn. Sun and Mars are friendly to each other, but Sun and Saturn don't get along well, so there will be tug of war-like situations. The influence of the Sun makes the natives want to shine and show its brilliance, but Saturn restricts and curtails the response of a determined Mars and the confident Sun. They will have a dignified personality and will be deep thinkers. Once they commit themselves to a person, relationship or cause, they sincerely follow it through with utmost devotion and integrity.

For example, in the Sun in Anuradha in the 6th house, the natives bravely face any opposition that comes their way and will be victorious over their enemies because the Sun is happily sitting in his friend's house of Scorpio, whose ruler is Mars. They will be sincere and hard-working and will do their duties with diligence.

Moon in Anuradha

When the Moon is placed in Anuradha, it will share the influence of Mars and Saturn. The Mars-Saturn vibration gives them amazing willpower, which they learn to silently and secretly use as and when needed. There is much that an Anuradha soul knows, but even more of what they can perceive or sense but cannot define or articulate.

It brings the burning need in them to penetrate the unknown and discover the mysteries of life with a calm sense of reason. When they want to know something it completely consumes their mind until they have found their answers.

They are ultra-sensitive but are able to disguise their sensitivity very effectively. They express their opinions with caution because they are wary of those who might heartlessly shred their ideology or beliefs to pieces. Each defeat or unpleasant experience sustained by them strengthens their conviction that their first loyalty lies towards their own personal integrity. They always stand true to their word because, for them - if the self is lost, then all is lost. They will never do anything that will make them feel ashamed of their own actions or thoughts. They hold a high moral code for themselves and stick to their principles even in the toughest of circumstances.

They are really intrigued by everything mystical and mysterious, and love to research and find out more about esoteric subjects of philosophy, religion, sex, astrology, yoga, meditation and spirituality. Their intense pull and passion towards exploring the silent subconscious realms of the mind makes them disinterested in worldly desires, and they begin to question the worthiness of running after materialistic goals.

They are intense lovers and intense enemies, too. When they love - they truly love, with all their heart and soul, but if a friendship becomes bitter or sour, they will stay away or walk out with equal intensity and assurity- never returning back to a toxic relationship. They learn their lessons for good and don't repeat their mistakes.

Their intensity of purpose nourishes their physical needs, their mental pursuits, emotional longings and their soul's search. For example, when the moon in Anuradha is placed in the 9th house, they will be very devoted to their teacher, Guru, or higher learning. They will be willing to take the brave step into the unknown and travel to a foreign land in order to learn and understand the deeper esoteric dimensions of life.

The poetry of Anuradha

Anuradha - Radha - Krishna's love,

The enchanting flute - a song sung

The full moon nights - romantic ecstasy,

Etched in the hearts - a living legacy.

The lotus flower - a symbol of beauty,

Grows in murk, yet untouched by the impurity.

Live in the world such a way,

Turning filth into manure - day by day.

Dedication, discipline, devotion,

Pave the path to liberation.

For in giving totally and fully,

The doors open, when humbled by your sincerity.

The coolness, the calm of the night,

The silence within can show the delight,

Unfolding the secrets within - what is it that binds?

And what liberates from the confines?

The conquest to explore - is another desire,

The ambition and passion - a burning fire,

There is no end - only an infinity

That stretches beyond the realms to eternity.

Remedies

- <u>Das Maha Vidya</u> - as described earlier.

- Kapha is the predominant tridosha of Anuradha. Consciously developing an active lifestyle and including fresh fruits and salads in your diet will be helpful. Avoid sleeping for too long, especially during the day.

- The yogic asanas, pranayama and meditation always enhance the ability to focus, which in turn improves the quality of whatever you do and brings ease into all thoughts and actions.

- Anuradha natives have a beautiful quality of devotion, whenever they pray or worship sincerely, their problems get resolved.

- Red and blue colours resonate well with the energy of Anuradha.

- Chanting the mantra - "Om *tam tham dam Anuradha nakshatraye namah,*" 108 times on days when the moon is transiting Anuradha or on Saturdays will help to connect you with your inner self, and this will help you to calm your mind and make the right choices.

Example

<u>Moon in Anuradha</u>

<u>Kiran Bedi - 1st Woman Police Officer in India.</u>

Born on 9th June 1949 in Amritsar, Punjab, India, at 12 pm (estimated time of birth).

Kiran is an Indian politician, social activist, retired police officer and tennis player who was the 24th Lieutenant Governor of Puducherry from 28 May 2016 to 16 February 2021. She is the 1st Indian female to become an officer in the Indian Police Service and started her service in 1972. She remained in service for 35 years before taking voluntary retirement in 2007 as Director General Bureau of Police Research and Development.

Kiran was born in Amritsar in a well-to-do Punjabi business family. She is the 2nd of the 3 daughters, born to Prakash Lal Peshawaria and Prem Lata. She started her formal studies in 1954 at the Sacred Heart Convent School in Amritsar. She participated in the National Cadet Corps (NCC), among other extra-curricular activities.

As a teenager, Kiran was crowned the national junior tennis champion in 1966. Between 1965 and 1978, she won several titles at various national and state-level championships.

She graduated in 1968 with a BA (Honours) in English from Government College for Women at Amritsar. The same year, she won the NCC Cadet Officer Award. In 1970, she obtained a master's degree in political science from Panjab University, Chandigarh. From 1970 to 1972, Bedi taught as a lecturer at Khalsa College for Women in Amritsar.

She taught courses related to political science. Later, during her career in the Indian Police Service, she also earned a law degree from the Faculty of Law, University of Delhi, in 1988 and a Ph.D. from IIT Delhi's Department of Social Sciences in 1993.

After joining the Indian police service (IPS), she served in Delhi, Goa, Chandigarh and Mizoram. She started her career as an Assistant Superintendent of Police (ASP) in the Chanakyapuri area of Delhi and won the President's Police Medal in 1979. Next, she moved to West Delhi, where she brought about a reduction in crimes against women. Subsequently, as a traffic police officer, she oversaw traffic arrangements for the 1982 Asian Games in Delhi. As Deputy Commissioner of Police of North Delhi, she launched a campaign against drug abuse, which evolved into the Navjyoti Delhi Police Foundation (renamed to Navjyoti India Foundation in 2007).

She has a lot of integrity and devotion towards serving humanity and has wonderful leadership qualities. She has the ability to bring people together and work as a team for the well-being of others. There is an amazing incident that highlights her bravery and sincerity. When she had just started her job in Delhi as a police officer.

One of her first challenging assignments was to evacuate the people who were trapped in a building that had caught fire in Delhi. When she went on the scene with a group of 12 policemen, the fire had spread up to the front entrance, and they could not access the building. They did not have the facility of the fire extinguisher truck. When she asked the police constables to get into the building no one moved. There was a hand pump in the yard, so she asked one of the policemen to pump it, she wet herself fully and went into the building and managed to safely bring out a woman and a child. Then, all her other team members followed her example and wet themselves thoroughly before going into the building that was blazing with fire - and brought out the others safely. She was hugely appreciated and recognised for her ingenuity and sincerity. This earned her a lot of respect in the community and among her colleagues and officers.

In May 1993, Kiran was posted to the Delhi Prisons as Inspector General (IG). She introduced several reforms at the Tihar Jail, which gained worldwide acclaim and won her the Ramon Magsaysay Award in 1994. In 2003, she became the first Indian and first woman to be appointed as head of the United Nations Police and Police Advisor in the United Nations Department of Peace Operations. She resigned in 2007 to focus on social activism and writing. She has written several books and runs the India Vision Foundation. During 2008-11, she hosted a court show, 'Aap Ki Kachehri' on TV. She was one of the key leaders of the 2011 Indian anti-corruption movement and joined the Bharatiya Janata Party (BJP) in January 2015.

Analysis

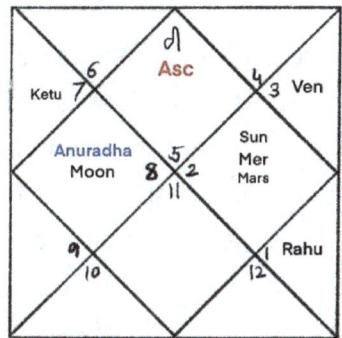

Kiran has her <u>Moon in Anuradha</u> in the 1st Pada in the 4th house of mother and home. Moon, the lord of the 12th house, is sitting in the 4th house of Scorpio. Mars, the lord of the 4th house, is sitting in the 10th house of Taurus with Sun and Mercury. Her 10th house of career and public image is very powerful, where the Sun and Mars have directional strength. The moon has directional strength in the 4th house. The conjunction of Sun and Mercury in the 10th house makes a budha Aditya yoga, which makes the native extremely intelligent and Mars sitting with them strengthens the leadership capabilities.

Out of the many brilliant things that she has done to help the people of her community and her nation. One outstanding example is that in 1979, Kiran was posted to Delhi's West District, where there were not enough officers to handle the high volume of criminal activity. To compensate, she started recruiting civilian volunteers.

Each village in the district was night patrolled by 6 local volunteers led by an armed policeman. This enabled anonymous reporting of any knowledge about crimes and helped her clamp down on bootlegging and the illicit liquor business to reduce crimes in the area.

Kiran won the President's Police Medal in 1979, she was running her <u>Mercury Rahu Mercury</u> dasha. Rahu is sitting in the 9th house of Aries, and Mars, the lord of Aries, is sitting with Mercury and Sun in the 10th house of Taurus. It makes Raj yoga - which states that the native will be very fortunate and successful in his or her professional life. Maharishi Parashara states this in Hora Shastra - that when the lord of the 9th house is placed in the 10th house, the native will be a minister or a commander, will be full of good qualities and will get great honours from the public. He or she will work for the government and will be brave and famous. We can see this prediction coming alive in Kiran's birth chart during her Mercury Mahadasha. Mercury is in the 10th house (of professional and public image) with the Sun and Mars.

Reforming Tihar jail

In May 1993, she was posted to the Delhi Prisons as inspector general (IG). Seeing the appalling conditions there, Kiran decided to turn Tihar into a model prison and introduced several reforms. She arranged separate barracks for the hardened criminals, who had been using their time in prison to recruit gang members, sell contraband and extort money. These prisoners unsuccessfully challenged Kiran in court for unfairly segregating them. For other prisoners, Kiran arranged vocational training with certificates so that they could find a job after their release.

Kiran banned smoking in the prison. This move faced a lot of resistance from the staff as well as the prisoners. She introduced yoga and Vipassana meditation classes to change the prisoners' attitudes. She organised additional activities such as sports, prayer, and festival celebrations. She also established a de-addiction centre and pulled up or imprisoned the staff members involved in drug supply. A bank was also opened inside the prison. A bakery and small manufacturing units, including carpentry and weaving units, were set up in the jail. The profits from the products sold were put into the prisoners' welfare fund.

Kiran went on daily prison tours, observing the staff, listening to prisoners' complaints, inspecting food quality and evaluating overall management. She developed a panchayat system, where prisoners who were respected for their age, education, or character represented other inmates and met every evening with senior officers to sort out problems. She also established petition boxes so that prisoners could write to the IG about any issue. As a result of her reforms, there was a drop in the fights and disturbances in the jail. Even the hardened criminals, who had been isolated in separate barracks, started behaving well. Kiran then arranged for them to attend education and meditation courses.

Kiran's reform programme at Tihar received worldwide acclaim. But it also attracted envy from her superiors, who accused her of diluting prison security for personal glory. Khushwant Singh described her transfer from Tihar as "a victory for a handful of small-minded, envious people over a gutsy woman."

She had started her job as the Inspector General of Police, in charge of the Tihar jail, in <u>May 1993,</u> when she was running her <u>Venus Venus Moon Ketu dasha.</u> Venus is sitting in the 11th house (Gemini) of gains and is the lord of the 9th and the 3rd house. Ketu is sitting in the 3rd house of Libra, the house of heroic efforts. Moon, the lord of the 12th house in the 4th house, this made her move away from her birthplace and she got transferred to many new places away from home during her career. Transfer to Tihar jail was one of her many transfers during the length of her glorious career.

She has truly done a lot of amazing transformations in the jails and for the people of her country through her brave, honest and determined efforts. She is an icon and role model for many women and symbolises the qualities of 'Mother India' in the true sense. Inspired and motivated by her, many women have now joined the Indian police service.

<u>Here are some of Kiran Bedi's quotes -</u>

"Empowered women who reach tough or unconventional positions make choices, not sacrifices."

"My motto in life is that nothing is impossible, no target is unachievable. One just has to try harder."

"I know how to work and how to get work done."

"No marriage is sacred if it practices violence."

"People who do not take charge of their life are lathi (a stick) charged by time."

"The focus is - what is right before you - give it your best. It shows the seeds for tomorrow."

"Believe in yourself 100%, give your 100% and you will get 100% in return."

"Once you stop fearing fear, you'll have a sense of freedom in all that you do."

20
Jyeshtha

Om dham Jyeshtha nakshatraye namah

Zodiac degrees	16.40 - 30 deg Scorpio
Ruling planet	Scorpio - Mars and Ketu and Jyeshtha - Mercury
Sanskrit name	Jyeshtha means - the eldest.
Astronomical name	The 3 stars that are seen in the shape of an earring in the constellation of Scorpio. Jyeshtha is a splendid red star - Antares. This star dwells at the core of Scorpio and is bigger than our own Sun.
Symbol	Scorpio - scorpion Jyeshtha - An umbrella and a circular talisman - a symbol of divine protection and authority.
Element	Water
Deity	Indra Dev
Quality	Sthira - fixed - Scorpio Jyeshtha - Tikshna - sharp
Shakti	Arohana Shakti - courage in battle and power to conquer.
Cast	Farmer
Gender	Female
Motivation	Moksha - liberation.
Triguna	Tamas
Tridosha	Kapha
Body parts	Neck and right side of the body.
Direction	North and South

Month	Late May, the second half of Vishakha month.
Bird	Eagle and crow
Sound	na, ya, yee, yu
Tree	Pine tree
Chakras	Muladhara - Mars and Ajna - Mercury
Das Maha Vidya	Devi Bagalamukhi - Mars and Devi Tripura Sundari - Mercury.

Special degrees -

Yoga Tara	16 deg Scorpio - Yoga Tara of Jyeshtha lies in the 4th Pada of Anuradha. It's a point where the planet will show the strongest and sure results during its dasha.
Amrit Nadi	25.20 - 25.56 deg Scorpio This brings good results, just like the nectar that nourishes.
Visha Nadi	19.46 - 20.40 deg Scorpio Brings situations which one does not like dealing with.
Gandanta	29 - 30 deg Scorpio The gandanta zone brings challenging situations because this is the junction point where a karmic knot is formed.

Auspicious and inauspicious table -

Auspicious	**Inauspicious**
Activities Good for harsh activities - spying, plotting, scheming, passing judgements, getting even, confronting, taking decisions, putting your foot down, taking control, being authoritative, taking responsibility, taking care of family matters, planning, having discussions, solving serious issues. Good for occult activities, administration, managing, monitoring, policing, for caretaking activities, taking care of the elderly, for penance, restraint and self-discipline.	Activities Not good for marriage, healing, travelling, for self-pity, feeling depressed, for selfish or self-centred activities, or taking advantage of others, rest or recreation, diplomacy, gentle or sensitive activities.
Days None	Days Sundays - only when it falls on the 3rd, 4th, 8th, 9th, 13th, or 14th lunar day. Tuesdays - only when it falls on the 1st, 2nd, 7th, 8th, 10th, or full moon day - purnima tithi. Fridays - only when it falls on the 2nd, 3rd, 6th, 8th, 10th, or 11th lunar day.

Compatibility table -

Jyeshtha	Compatible with
Sexual compatibility Yoni animal	Jeyshtha - Male deer. Compatible with Anuradha - Female deer
Sign compatibility	Scorpio - Cancer and Pisces.
Nakshatra compatibility	Ashlesha and Revati.
Lunar day compatibility	Saptami tithi - 7th lunar day and Chaturdashi tithi - 14th lunar day.
Day compatibility	Tuesday and Wednesday
Colour compatibility	Red and green
Numerological compatibility	5 and 9 - all numbers that add up to make 5 and 9.
Sound compatibility	Mars - guttural sounds - ka, kha, ga, gha, kna Mercury - lingual sounds - ta, tha, da, dha, na

Initially, there were only 18 nakshatras mapped in the sky as seen by the ancient sages, and Jyeshtha was the final nakshatra. This is why it was given the name Jyeshtha, which means the eldest one.

Sign Lord and nakshatra lord - Mars and Mercury - as described earlier.

Jyeshtha is the 2nd nakshatra ruled by Mercury. Here, the influence of Mercury and Mars makes them very ambitious and determined to achieve their goals. They have the capability of leading and protecting their family, community or the whole of humanity. Mercury gives them intellectual prowess, and Mars gives them the abundance of energy and will power, which makes them capable of taking up responsibility and living up to their commitments.

Quality, element, motivation, triguna, tridosha and chakras - as described earlier.

Shakti - Arohana: Shakti - courage in battle and power to conquer.

In the context of Indian classical music, the word Arohana means the ascending scale of notes in a raga. The pitch increases as we go up from shadja Sa is the 1st note, to Sa teevra, which is the last note on the 1st set of the scale.

SA. RE. GA. MA. PA. DHA. NEE. SA ↑

It signifies the upward-moving energy. Since Jyeshtha lies in the sign of Scorpio, whose Lord is Mars, it gives them tremendous Martian energy, courage, drive and motivation to win and conquer. Especially in challenging and battle-like situations, they do very well, because it leaves them with no choice but to fight it out and in doing so, they discover their hidden capabilities, which bring out the best in them.

On close observation, they will see that every time they pass through a difficult situation and brave it out, life opens new doors of success for them. Or in other words, before reaching their desired goal, they have to brave through some hurdles. Once they surpass it, which they always do, with Mercurian skill and Martian grit, they achieve their goals with honour, respect and glory, which is well earned and well deserved.

Symbolic signification

<u>Scorpio - scorpion -</u> as described earlier.

<u>Jyeshtha</u> - <u>An umbrella and a circular talisman</u> - a symbol of divine protection and authority.

<u>Talisman</u>

The word talisman comes from the Arabic word tilism, which comes from the ancient Greek word telesma, which means completion or religious rites. A talisman is any object infused with mystical or magical energy intended to protect or heal any person for whom it has been made.

They have been used in many civilisations throughout history, with connections to astrological, scientific, and religious practices. Since ancient times, talismans have been used for protection, aiding fertility, and helping crop production.

There are many types of natural talismans, made of precious stones, metals, teeth and claws of animals, bones, wood and plants. Man-made talismans are equally varied, which have religious carvings and engravings of icons and mantras. Among believers, Talismans are thought to derive power from their connection with natural forces, from religious associations, or from being made ritually at a favourable time.

In the Middle Ages, Christian talismans included the traditional relics of saints and letters said to have been sent from heaven. Among Jews, the preparation of Talismans became a rabbinic function. Muslims today often carry verses from the Quran, the names of God, or sacred numbers, which they carry in small satchels.

<u>Umbrella</u>

The Sanskrit word Chattra means an auspicious umbrella. From ancient times in India, an honorary umbrella was held on top of a king or a sage as a mark of respect. According to Hindu mythology, it is the emblem of Varuna and is also considered an embodiment of kingship. Many deities are depicted with a chhatra on top of their head to show their kingship, like Surya, Vishnu, Indra, and many sages and seers.

<u>Inference</u>

Those who have their Ascendant, Sun or Moon in Jyeshtha will be attracted to talismans and amulets, and at some point in their lives, they will wear or possess one. This gives them protection in many unexplained mystical ways.

Jyeshtha natives get honoured for their sincere efforts and excellence in their chosen field at some point in their lives. They earn their respect through a sustained practice of self-discipline and thereby master their skills. Through their capabilities and leadership skills, they are able to help many people.

Secrecy -

The quality of all aspects that are hidden, mysterious, not easy to understand, or are usually kept as a closely guarded secret is associated with the 8th house and the sign of Scorpio. In Jyeshtha, this aspect of keeping things secret becomes a need and a blessing.

If we look at the top and bottom ends of any aspect of life, things are kept secret, and they need to be kept so for various reasons. For example, those who are in a high position in any government job or in any globally reputable companies have to keep some vital information secret for the protection and maintenance of that organisation. On the other hand, those who are involved in any illegal or unethical activities also need to keep things hidden for fear of being caught. However, the intention behind keeping something secret is entirely different for different people and different situations.

Mythology -

Deity - Indra Dev - as described earlier.

Jyeshtha people are very intelligent and have great mental prowess. They have an amazing sense of self-discipline and can work towards their goals with consistency. Jyeshtha lies in Scorpio, which is the sign of all that is hidden and mysterious; therefore, they have an intrinsic understanding and interest in occult, astrology, philosophy, spirituality, religion and rituals.

The 8th house also represents sudden events and transformations. When looked at in a positive context, pain, suffering, challenges, and difficulties help us to grow, evolve, and realise our deeper inner strengths and give us inner wisdom. Jyeshtha natives understand life from a deeper perspective and are therefore able to deal with difficult situations with greater insight.

Indra Dev had to always fight against those who were trying to take over the kingship. He had to constantly plan strategies and keep secrets in order to safeguard himself, his people and his kingdom. Jyeshta natives must take care to keep secrets and not to carelessly reveal their plans or financial assets. Otherwise, they could be attracting opponents who are waiting in the wings to grab any opportunity to take over their hard-earned assets or status.

Jyeshtha padas

16.40 - 30 deg Scorpio

Padas	Degrees
1	16.40 - 20 deg Scorpio
2	20 - 23.30 deg Scorpio
3	23.20 - 26.40 deg Scorpio
4	26.40 - 30 deg Scorpio

Pada 1

16.40 - 20 deg Scorpio, Navamsha- Sagittarius (Lord - Jupiter)

Rashi Lord - Mars and Nakshatra Lord- Mercury

The navamsha of the 1st Pada lies in Sagittarius, therefore it carries the energy of Mars, Mercury and Jupiter. They will have a more idealistic and philosophical approach to life. They will do things directly and honestly without mincing words or beating about the bush. They might say things abruptly, which can pierce and hurt like the arrows of truth, though they never intentionally do so. With time and experience, they will learn to curb their urge to give their honest opinion, where it's best left unsaid.

They will be an excellent guide, consultant or an advisor on many aspects of life. Their family and friends will always come up to them and seek their wise counsel whenever any crucial decisions have to be made. This is because they have the capability of looking at things from a depth and understanding the consequences in a broader perspective. Because of their idealism, they will take a long time to choose and settle down into the job that's right for them. They can make excellent teachers and councillors.

Especially after the age of 30, they will start feeling that the reality of the world is such that ethics or morality are sacrificed for the greed of money or power. They will be better off working independently or working at a managerial position where they can keep up and uphold the ethical standards of the company and of humanity. They would rather leave the job and start their own business than succumb to the pressure of doing anything that is morally wrong or against the voice of their conscience.

For example, the 1st Pada of Jyestha in the 2nd house will make them very responsible towards their family, the resources, financial assets and the income. They will lead and guide their family into having a comfortable home and a comfortable bank balance.

Careers

Teachers, philosophers, psychologists, counsellors, advisors, coordinators, leaders, film directors, managers, astrologers, doctors, scientists, researchers, psychiatrists, politicians, financial advisors, entrepreneurs, businessmen, writers, IT professionals, athletes, gym trainers, sportsmen or sports women and working from home.

Pada 2

20 - 23.20 deg Scorpio, Navamsha - Capricorn (Lord - Saturn)

Rashi Lord - Mars and Nakshatra Lord - Mercury

In the 2nd Pada, there will be the energy of Mars, Saturn and Mercury. The navamsha of Capricorn gives them a more practical approach. They will be ambitious and will be able to set targets and work towards their planned goals. They will be very authoritative and clear about what they want to achieve in life. Others may perceive them as insensitive, stingy, selfish or vengeful.

But the truth is that they are sincerely trying to work towards their desired goal. Once they have achieved their desired position, they are more relaxed and at ease with themselves and with others around them.

They are blessed with tremendous patience and are capable of enduring difficulties, going through long periods of penance and ultimately achieving their goals. They may seem to progress slowly because they are very cautious, but the secret of their success is their formidable sense of endurance. For example, the 2nd Pada of Jyeshta in the 4th house, their mum will be very disciplined and hardworking. This sense of perseverance comes into them too, and they ultimately have a comfortable home and a stable platform where they can relax and plan their future endeavours.

Careers

Managers, consultants, property dealers, financial advisors, doctors, scientists, engineers, bank managers, psychiatrists, therapists, researchers, archaeologists, writers, businessmen or business women, IT professionals and working from home.

Pada 3

20 - 23,20 deg Scorpio, Navamsha - Aquarius (Lord - Saturn)

Rashi Lord - Mars and Nakshatra Lord - Mercury

The navamsha of the 3rd Pada is placed in Aquarius, which gives the effect of Mars, Saturn and Mercury. In Aquarius, Saturn begins to broaden its horizons and expands its desire to help not just the immediate family or community, but to help the whole of humanity. In their adulthood, after 30 years of age, they will either start their own company, which will have a wide impact locally or worldwide, or they will work for a very large organisation. They will be well known in their circle for the good work they do for humanity.

Their elder sibling or a friend will be influential in motivating them to volunteer or work for a large organisation where they can reach out to a larger group of people. They will most likely be in a managerial position where their decisions can make a difference and have an impact. They will work towards improving the working conditions of people around them, and will be willing to help others whenever they genuinely need it.

For example, the 3rd Pada of Jyeshta in the 5th house, they will be very creative and intelligent, and they will have children, students or followers who will always look up to them for advice and guidance. They will be recognised and appreciated for their wisdom and helpful nature.

Careers

Running a volunteer organisation or managing one, philanthropists, astrologers, advisors, consultants, managers, public relations coordinators, film directors, writers, IT professionals, doctors, businessmen and working from home.

Pada 4

26.40 - 30 deg Scorpio, Navamsha - Pisces (Lord - Jupiter)

Rashi Lord - Mars and Nakshatra Lord- Mercury

In this Pada, there will be the influence of Mars, Mercury and Jupiter.

The navamsha of Pisces will make them more philosophical as they get older. They will be more dreamy, emotional and sensitive. They tend to get carried away and are often called gullible by those who know them closely. If life becomes too difficult or unbearable, they can seek escapism in their own fantasy land.

They can channel their creativity into a positive expression of writing fiction stories, poetry, art, music, acting or singing. Or there is also a danger of drowning oneself in some kind of compulsive indulgence. Just as Indra Dev, they have an extreme sense of self-discipline and have the ability to pull themselves out of any doldrums. In its highest expression, they have an amazing resilience that can take them from untruth to truth and from darkness to enlightenment. On the negative side, they can get into some kind of addiction, which can be detrimental to their health.

For example, the 4th Pada of Jyeshtha in the 6th house will make the natives feel very responsible towards their daily duties. They may face difficulties in finance, from maternal relatives, or in terms of health during the dasha of Mars or Mercury. But they will sail through this tough period through their sense of discipline.

They gave the intelligence to make the right choices and do what is needed for their own well-being and that of those around them.

Careers-

Teachers, philosophers, psychologists, counsellors, advisors, astrologers, doctors, scientists, researchers, psychiatrists, writers, poets, artists, actors, singers, business men and business women, IT professionals and working from home.

The effect of planets

Jyeshtha - Scorpio	Planets that get affected
Functional Benefic - gives good results during their dasha.	Mars, Sun and Moon
Functional Malefic - can give problems during their dasha.	Mercury, Rahu and Ketu
Functional Neutral	Jupiter and Saturn
Kendra Adi Pati Dosha - can be malefic	Venus

Jyeshtha Ascendant

When the Ascendant is in Jyeshtha, it has the influence of Mars and Mercury. This makes the natives very communicative and determined. Their passion and ambition are like a flame that consumes their attention fully. When they do something, they do it wholeheartedly. The Martian rashness and directness can upset people, but the Mercurian tact can handle situations and keep things in balance.

In the sign of Aries, the Martian energy innocently and enthusiastically jumps into things with great enthusiasm, but does not have the patience and maturity to see it all the way through. Whereas in Scorpio, the Martian energy has learnt the lessons of life and through the richness of experience, the soul is now more capable of handling even the toughest of situations with more ease and grace.

Their positive qualities are dedication, magnetism, intelligence, insight, depth, amazing will power and an incredible sense of self-discipline. On the negative side, when they are hurt, they can become revengeful, fanatic and suspicious.

They are very responsible and feel protective towards their family and community. Even though they may not be the 1st born in the family, their advice and guidance will be sought. They will be considered the wise ones and will earn the respect of their family or community. This is because they genuinely care and take the responsibility of their loved ones and excel in taking care of family, community and all humanitarian matters.

Wherever Mars (the Lord of Scorpio) is placed, that's where they will spend their energy and attention. For example, if Mars is sitting in the 10th house, their focus, attention, energy and ambition will be towards building a successful career or their own business. If Mercury, the nakshatra lord, is sitting in the 11th house, they will gain through association with large organisations. They will get many opportunities to interact with those who run these organisations and will have very good relations with them. Their ability to express and articulate their thoughts very well will put them in leadership roles.

"We cannot solve problems with the same thinking we used when we created them." - Einstein.

Sun in Jyeshtha

When the Sun is placed in Jyeshtha, it will have the influence of Mars and Mercury. Both Mars and Mercury are friendly with the Sun; therefore, it's a comfortable placement for the Sun. They will have a very dignified personality and can be very influential writers, speakers and motivators. On the positive side, they will be dedicated, sincere, straightforward and hard working; on the negative side, they can be short-tempered, jealous and secretive. They will be quick in their thinking and will have an aggressive and determined approach to life.

For example, Sun is in Jyeshtha in the 9th house, the natives will be intelligent and will pursue their higher education with academic excellence. They will be religiously or spiritually inclined and will follow their father's profession, or their father will be influential in helping them choose their career.

To look further into the possible inferences. For a Pisces Ascendant, the 9th house will be Scorpio, and the Sun will be the lord of the 6th house of Leo. Therefore, the native may face some challenges or opposition from the government, authorities or their father, regarding his or her higher education (the 6th house significations), but they will emerge victorious over their enemies. This can happen during the dasha of the Sun, Mars or Mercury, if the Sun is weak with a low degree. From the 9th house Sun directly aspects the 3rd house of siblings; therefore, they can have some differences of opinion with their brothers or sisters. But these are not major hurdles; the radiance and intelligence of the Sun and the energy of Mars help them to sail through any difficulties that they might face.

Moon in Jyeshtha

When the Moon is placed in Jyeshtha, it will share the influence of Mars and Mercury. This will make them more emotional, passionate and communicative about their feelings. They will be very intuitive, imaginative and intelligent. They will be driven by the desire to explore the mysterious, to understand the deeper meaning of life and to gain knowledge.

For example, moon in Jyeshtha in the 9th house, they will have a great interest in esoteric subjects like - occult, rituals and other religious practices, astrology, palmistry, ayurveda, meditation, yoga, and past life hypnosis, and will want to research and find out more about ancient knowledge of the scriptures. They will find an excellent teacher or a Guru who will guide them. They may have to travel to a foreign country or stay away from home in order to pursue higher education.

They have the knack of digging into your secrets but not revealing their own, because this is their armour of defence and needed protection. They are very loyal towards their loved ones and towards the goals they set for themselves, and will not hesitate to openly show their scorn if anyone threatens to stand in their way. The sheer intensity of their emotion and sincerity of purpose slowly begins to pave the path and opens the doors for them. For them, love and commitment are all the way or not at all; they cannot think, feel or act frivolously about anything in their life.

Their personality is an intriguing mix of intense colours -determined, cool, calm, quiet, mysterious and feminine all at the same time. Their Mercurian curiosity can make them plunge into the depths of the mind and soul of their own self, or of the other person if they so wish to, in order to find answers to the many mysteries of human nature. They are capable of doing all kinds of strange, wonderful or weird things in their quest to know the unknown, which can be both pleasant and unpleasant surprises.

Their reaction to hurt is more inward drawn; they will not say much but go into an icy, stony silence. Their aloofness is a warning sign about something that has hurt them a lot; they simply tend to turn off, looking uninterested and detached. This is their way of concealing their emotional hurt and protecting themselves from further pain or damage. Once they choose to be your friend or partner, they are extremely loyal and committed and expect the same from the other.

"Your visions will become clear only when you look into your own heart. Who looks outside, dreams; who looks inside, awakens." *Carl Jung*

The poetry of Jyeshtha

Jyeshtha - The eldest, who takes on responsibility,

Capable of guiding effectively.

Indra, who won over the compulsions of the sense perceptions,

Tough is the path of self-discipline and overcoming temptations.

Rewards of brave efforts are many, and respect is well earned.

Some was worth it and some was not, through lessons learned.

The intrigue and wonder never cease,

With life's experience, the game eases.

The actions performed in thought, feeling, word and deed,

A vicious circle indeed.

The magical talisman of luck - a karmic play,

Master the skills - if you may.

How, then, to break the cycle of birth and death?

The answers lie in the inner depths.

To live a life beyond suffering and pain,

Beyond the joys of gain.

Remedies

<u>Das Maha Vidya</u> - as described earlier.

Kapha is the predominant tridosha of Jyeshtha. Consciously developing an active lifestyle and including fresh fruits and salads in your diet will be helpful. Avoid sleeping for too long, especially during the day.

The yogic asanas, pranayama and meditation always enhance the ability to focus, which in turn improves the quality of whatever you do and brings ease into all thoughts and actions.

Jyeshtha natives have a tremendous inner strength to fight the challenges and emerge victorious. '*Arohana Shakti*' gives them the power and energy to keep moving forward. With every difficult situation, they grow into a stronger person and better human beings. Every test they pass, they gain financially, intellectually or emotionally.

Red and green colours resonate well with the energy of Jyeshtha.

Chanting the mantra -"*Om dham Jyeshtha nakshatraye namah.*" 108 times on days when the moon is transiting Jyeshtha, or on Wednesdays, will help to connect you with your inner self and calm your mind.

Example

<u>Moon in Jyeshtha</u>

<u>Albert Einstein - world-renowned scientist.</u>

Born on Friday, 14th March 1879, Ulm, Germany, at 11.30 am.

Einstein needs no introduction, he is one of the most brilliant and genius minds of our century. He has been the man who shaped our knowledge of the world, and the most famous physicist of all time. He gave us the theory of relativity, which changed the course of scientific perspective. The famous equation E= mc square is the heart of all scientific investigations and research.

Einstein's father, Hermann, was an engineer and a salesman. They moved to Munich when Einstein was 1 year old and his dad established an electric company with his uncle Jacob, where they manufactured electrical light bulbs using direct current. As a child, Einstein went to a catholic school in Ulm in Germany, and his family stayed there until he was 8 years old. After this, they moved to Munich in Italy. In 1894, they had to close down the factory because they did not have the finances to convert their machinery to an updated and efficient way of using alternative current to make light bulbs. Einstein's family then moved to a smaller town called Pavia in Italy, but Einstein stayed in Munich till he was 15 years old to finish his studies.

In December 1984, Einstein left school and went to join his family in Pavia, where he wrote a short essay titled, 'The investigation of the state of ether in a magnetic field.' He was very brilliant with maths and physics. When he was only 12 years old, he had taught himself algebra and geometry over the summer holidays, where he discovered his own original proof of the Pythagoras theorem. He had mastered integral and differential calculus by the time he was 14 years old.

He was therefore convinced that the functioning of nature could be understood through mathematical calculations.

During this time, he also became interested in philosophy and music, and one of his favourite books was Kant's Critique of Pure Reason.

When he was 13 years old, he discovered the violin sonatas of Mozart and taught himself to play the violin. Music played a pivotal and permanent role in his life. In one of his famous quotes, he says-

"If I were not a physicist, I would probably be a musician. I often think in music, I live my daydreams in music, I see my life in terms of music, I get most joy in life out of music." - Einstein.

In 1986, he was 16 years old when he finished his secondary schooling in Aarau in Switzerland. That year, he also gave up his German citizenship to avoid being forced into military service. While staying in Aaru, he fell in love with Marie, the daughter of the professor with whom he was lodging.

At 17, he enrolled for a 4 year teaching course to teach mathematics and physics in Olsberg in Switzerland. Marie, who was a year older than him, also joined him there on a teaching post. Later, Einstein married Marie, who was from Serbia; she was the only female student among the class of 6 students doing the teaching diploma course with him.

In 1900, he graduated but could not find a suitable teaching job. He started working in a patent office as an assistant examiner. Marie and Einstein got married in 1903 and had 2 sons. They divorced in 1919 because Einstein was involved with his cousin Elsa and married her later.

In 1908, he was recognised by a leading scientist and was appointed as a lecturer at the University of Bern. He became a full professor in 1911 at the German Charles University in Prague and accepted Austrian citizenship. Here he wrote 11 scientific papers.

In 1914, he joined Berlin University, and Einstein became the director of the German Physical Society.

The days of struggle

Einstein's young years were not a success story. He dropped out of high school in Munich and failed to pass the entrance examination at the Polytechnikum Zürich. After he graduated as a teacher for mathematics and physics in Zurich, he repeatedly applied for academic assistant positions without success. He went through tough days of having to make a living as a temporary teacher and tutor.

Einstein worked at the Swiss Patent Office for 7 years. Today, he is regarded as the most famous of all patent examiners. In 1909, he finally received an extraordinary professorship for theoretical physics at the University of Zurich and was able to devote himself exclusively to science. But perhaps his most important work came about during his time as a patent examiner.

From 23rd June 1902, Einstein worked as a technical expert and examined patent applications in the mechanical field. He saw his work as a patent examiner as a bread-and-butter profession, which did not fully satisfy him. In his spare time, he devoted himself to theoretical physics and worked on his doctoral thesis.

When his probationary period ended in 1904, he was employed on a permanent basis. At first, a promotion was postponed because the director of the patent office thought that Einstein had to become better acquainted with mechanical engineering.

Special theory of relativity

In 1905, Einstein published some of his most important works, including the treatise on the photoelectric effect, for which he later received the Nobel Prize. The special theory of relativity, with the famous formula $E = mc^2$, was also propounded during this year. It was an explosion of genius.

He had successfully submitted his doctoral thesis in 1905, but his habilitation was initially rejected by the University of Bern in 1907. Only one year later, he was successful and was now able to work as a part-time private lecturer. He gave his lectures before or after his working hours at the patent office. In the first semester, he is said to have had only three listeners, including two colleagues from the Patent Office.

The most fertile years

In the peace and tranquillity of his office, a flash of inspiration came to him in 1907, which he later described as *"the happiest thought of my life."* I was sitting on my armchair in the Bern Patent Office, when suddenly the following thought occurred to me - If a person is in free fall, he does not feel his own weight. I was amazed. This simple thought made a deep impression on me. It drove me in the direction of a "*theory of gravity*" - and thus on the way to the general theory of relativity."

General theory of relativity

The main headline of the newspapers read - Revolution in science, where Einstein's paper was published, which was based on the calculations done in 1911. In this paper, he explained how light from another star should be bent by the sun's gravity. This theoretical calculation was confirmed by Sir Arthur Eddington during the solar eclipse of 29th May 1919. After which, his theory of relativity made him world-famous. In 1921, he was awarded the Nobel Prize in physics.

Meeting of the 2 geniuses -

Einstein and Charlie Chaplin.

When Einstein met Charlie Chaplin at a film premiere in 1931, this is what they said to each other-

Einstein - *"What I admire most about your art is its universality. You don't say a word, but the whole world understands you!"*

Chaplin - *"Right. But your art is even greater! The whole world admires you, even if nobody understands a word of what you say."*

Einstein and Rabindranath Tagore

Rabindranath Tagore went to visit Einstein at his house in Caputh, near Berlin, on 14th July, 1930. Here are some excerpts of what they talked about -

Tagore - *"You have been busy, hunting down the mathematics of the 2 ancient entities, time and space, while I have been lecturing in this country on the eternal world of man, the universe of reality."*

Einstein - *"Do you believe in the divine being isolated from the world?"*

Tagore - *"What we call truth lies in the rational harmony between the subjective and objective aspects of reality, both of which belong to the superpersonal man."*

Einstein - *"We do things with our mind, even in our everyday life, for which we are not responsible. The mind acknowledges realities outside of it, independent of it. For instance, nobody may be in this house, yet that table remains where it is."*

In 1933, he settled in the USA, took citizenship in 1940, and was affiliated with the Institute for Advanced Studies. He was working on unified field theory and accepted interpretation of quantum physics, until his death on 17th April 1955, at Princeton Hospital early morning at the age of 76.

He had refused surgery, saying, *"I want to go when I want, it's tasteless to prolong life artificially. I have done my share, it's time to go, I will do it elegantly."*

In a memorial speech, J Roberts, the head of nuclear physics at UNESCO, had said, "Einstein was almost wholly without sophistication and worldliness. There was always with him a wonderful purity at once childlike and profoundly stubborn."

Analysis-

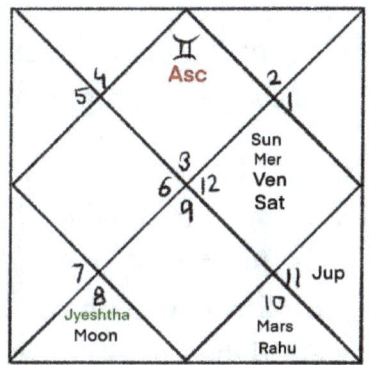

Einstein's <u>Moon is placed in Jyeshtha</u> in the 2nd pada in the 6th house of Scorpio. Mars, the lord of Scorpio, lies in the 8th house of Capricorn, conjunct with Rahu.

The placement of the Moon in the 6th house of Scorpio in Jyeshtha brought struggle in the initial days. When he was in school, his genius was not recognised. His dad wanted him to get a degree in electrical engineering, but Einstein did not like the teaching method and resented the school regimen. *"The spirit of learning and creative thought was lost in strict rote learning."* - Einstein.

Even in his early adulthood years, he had to face difficulties in terms of finding a job that was suitable or befitting of his calibre and genius. Mars (Lord of Scorpio) and Rahu in the 8th house emphasise that his energy, attention, effort and focus were to be on digging into the mysteries of life. Einstein was always fascinated with the concept of light, time and space.

As a child, he grew up seeing his dad manufacturing electrical light bulbs in his factory. Einstein had worked at the Swiss patent office for 7 years, where much of his groundwork was done. His thought experiments led him to radical conclusions about the nature of light and the fundamental connection between space and time. During this time, he also started small discussion groups where they would talk about science and philosophy and published 4 groundbreaking research papers while working at the patent office.

These 7 years from 1902 to 1909 were the most difficult years in terms of worldly hardships, but the most fruitful years in terms of insightful realisations. In June 1902, he had started his <u>Venus, Mars, Jupiter dasha.</u> Mars is an important planet in his chart because it is the lord of Scorpio, where his moon is placed. It gives an indication of where his thoughts will be focused and what will consume his attention and energy. Mars, the lord of the 6th and 11th houses, is sitting with Rahu in the 8th house of research and exploration. The 6th house is the house of routine job, and the 11th house is the house of gains.

The nature of his job at the patent office was such that it allowed him a lot of free time, which was his gain in terms of utilising this free time towards exploring the secrets of the physical laws of nature, concerning light, time and space. During this time, he did most of his scientific work quietly and secretly (a very Jyeshtha-like quality), researching and formulating mathematical formulas which eventually made him the master physicist.

His academic genius provided logical answers and scientific proof, which literally made him Jyeshtha (the eldest). Throughout the world, he was respected and recognised for his exceptional intelligence and wisdom.

In 1907, in a tranquil moment, a flash of inspiration came to him, which he later described as *"the happiest thought of my life."* He was running his <u>Venus, Jupiter, Mercury dasha</u> at that time. It was the most inspirational and enlightening moment of his life that set him on the path of scientific exploration. Venus, the lord of the 5th house of creativity and the 12th house of isolation, is exalted in the 10th house of Pisces. He spent many long hours by himself contemplating the laws of natural sciences.

Jupiter is sitting in the 9th house of Aquarius, which is the house of higher learning. He wrote his scientific research papers during this time. Mercury is sitting with Venus, Sun and Saturn in the 10th house of career. Mercury is the lord of the Ascendant - Gemini and the 4th house - Virgo. The ascendant lord sitting in the 10th house shows that his destiny would inevitably make him a well-known personality. The 4th house of home and mother shows that his career would, in turn, influence the people of his homeland. In his childhood days, his mother would have been a very positive influence in encouraging his scientific interests.

The genius of Einstein and his life situations was the cumulative effect of the combination of all the planets in his birth chart. His <u>Sun, Saturn, Mercury and Venus are placed in the 10th house of Pisces</u>, which brought him worldwide fame. The navamsha of the 2nd Pada of Jyeshtha lies in Capricorn. Saturn is the lord of the 8th house of Capricorn and the 9th house of Aquarius, sitting in the 10th house. Whenever more than 3 planets are sitting in one house, it's a clear mark of greatness in that area of life. Their life events will be focused on bringing that aspect of life to light again and again.

He was awarded the Nobel Prize for his discovery of the law of photoelectric effect, during <u>Sun Sun-Venus Venus dasha</u>. Venus is exalted in the 10th house of Pisces, which brought worldwide fame and recognition during its dasha and transit over the 10th house. Sun and Mercury together form 'Budha Aditya yoga' in the 10th house, which is a Kendra house and the house of career and public image.

He had an extraordinary intelligence, and the timing of dasha and transits won him recognition and awards. The Sun is the lord of the 3rd house of Leo, which is the house of brave efforts. The 3rd house is also the Bhavat Bhavam of the 8th house (8th from 8th), which makes it the higher octave of the 8th house of transformations. Although he was awarded the Nobel Prize in 1921, he actually received it in 1922, one year later. Saturn sitting in the 10th house brought delays.

The American magazine, Time, voted Einstein as the Person of the Century in 1999. Here are some of the famous quotes by Einstein -

"The really important things are learned differently than by words."

"Be a loner, that gives you time to wonder."

"The only thing that interferes with my learning is my education."

"Two things are infinite - the universe and human stupidity, I am not sure about the former."

"Anyone who has never made a mistake has never tried anything new."

"Unthinking respect for authority is the greatest enemy of truth."

"A ship is always safe at the shore, but that's not what it was built for."

"If you want to live a happy life, tie it to a goal, not to people or things."

"If people are good only because they fear punishment, and hope for reward, then we are a sorry lot indeed."

"I never think of the future, it comes soon enough."

21
Mula

Om nam pam pham Mula nakshatraye namah

Zodiac degrees	0 - 13.20 deg Sagittarius
Ruling planet	Sagittarius - Jupiter and Mula - Ketu
Sanskrit name	Mula means - the root, foundation, core, centre.
Astronomical name	Mula is a group of 9 stars, which form the shape of a lion's tail, and are seen at the end of the Scorpio constellation. In the night sky, these stars can be seen stretched towards the centre of the Milky Way galaxy.
Symbol	Sagittarius- Archer and Centaur - a horse with a man's torso and head. Mula - roots and a lion's tail.
Element	Fire
Deity	Niritti Devi - the Goddess of dissolution and destruction.
Quality	Sagittarius - Dwi - dual Mula - Tikshna - sharp
Shakti	Brahana Shakti - power to destroy.
Cast	Butcher
Gender	Male
Motivation	Dharma - righteousness
Triguna	Satwa
Tridosha	Pitta
Body parts	Feet and the left side of the body.
Direction	East, north east, north west and south west.

Month	June, the second half of Jyeshtha month.
Bird	Heron
Sound	ye, yo, bha, bhee
Tree	Anjan sarjaka and black dammer tree
Chakras	Muladhara - Ketu and Ajna - Jupiter
Das Maha Vidya	Devi Dhumavati Devi - Ketu and Devi Tara - Jupiter

Special degrees -

Yoga Tara	28.50 deg Scorpio - Yoga Tara of Mula lies in the 4th Pada of Jyeshtha. It's a point where the planet will show the strongest and surest results during its dasha.
Mulatrikona	0 - 10 deg Sagitarius - Mulatrikona of Jupiter. When Jupiter is placed at these degrees in Sagittarius, it will become very strong and will give excellent results during its dasha.
Amrit Nadi	9.46 - 10.40 deg Sagittarius. This brings good results, just like the nectar that nourishes.
Visha Nadi	4.26 - 5.20 deg Sagittarius. Brings situations which one does not like dealing with.
Gandanta	0 - 1 deg Sagittarius. The gandanta zone brings challenging situations because this is the junction point where a karmic knot is formed.

Auspicious and inauspicious table -

Auspicious	Inauspicious
Activities Good for getting to the root of the matter, for gathering knowledge, gathering people, singing and all oratory activities, all adventurous activities that require self assertion or dynamism, administering herbs and medicines, planting, gardening and agricultural activities, for laying foundations of houses and buildings, buying or selling houses, for self exploration, contemplation, yoga, meditation, occult, astrology, initiations and spiritual pursuits.	**Activities** Especially not good for any financial transactions, borrowing or lending money, for any diplomatic, harmonious, peaceful and gentle activities that need to be handled with care and delicacy, for starting anything new for materialistic gains. and for any marital ceremonies.
Days Sundays - only when it falls on the 1st, 4th, 5th, 6th, 7th or 12th lunar day. Tuesdays - only when it falls on the 1st, 3rd, 6th, 8th, 11th or 13th lunar day.	**Days** Wednesdays- only when it falls on the 2nd, 3rd, 8th or 9th lunar day.

Compatibility table -

Mula	Compatible with
Sexual compatibility Yoni animal	Male - Female dog Compatible with Ardra - Male dog
Sign compatibility	Sagittarius - Aries and Leo.
Nakshatra compatibility	Ashwini and Magha.
Lunar day compatibility	Pratipad tithi - 1st lunar day and Chaturthi tithi - 4th lunar day.
Day compatibility	Thursday
Colour compatibility	Yellow and brown
Numerological compatibility	3 - all numbers that add up to make 3.
Sound compatibility	Jupiter - dental sounds - ta, ttha, da, dha, knna

Sign Lord and nakshatra lord - <u>Jupiter and Ketu</u>- as described earlier.

Jupiter has the quality of air and expansion, and Ketu is the fire. Just as the air fans the fire and the fire in turn warms and expands the air around it. Both these elements support and complement each other. Mula natives will be very spiritually inclined and aware that everything in life is transitory. Mula is the 3rd nakshatra ruled by Ketu. Here, the energy and motivation become more sattvic. The influence of Jupiter and Ketu makes them very philosophical and spiritual.

<u>Quality, element, motivation, triguna, tridosha and chakras -</u> as described earlier.

Shakti - <u>Brahana Shakti - power to destroy.</u>

Since Mula lies near the galactic centre, it has an energy like the power of a black hole, which can dissolve everything within its powerful gravitational pull towards the core. Similarly, Mula natives will have such transformative situations in their lives where the old is destroyed, and there is a new beginning for them. Every time life makes them go through such drastic changes, it brings them to a better place. Their challenges bring an opportunity for growth, to look at life from a different perspective, and their failures are a stepping stone to success.

Symbolic signification

<u>Sagitarius-</u> Archer and Centaur - a horse with a man's torso and head. <u>Mula</u> - roots and a lion's tail.

Archer -

An archer is a person who has the skill of shooting a target at long range using a bow and arrow. Only a person who has the ability to focus, to concentrate on a single point, has the discipline to go through the training, has strength in his or her arms and has good eyesight can be a good archer.

Those who are born with their Ascendant, Sun or Moon in Mula have the tenacity and talent of staying focused on the job at hand and achieving their targets.

Centaur -

A centaur is a creature from Greek mythology with the upper body of a human and the lower body and legs of a horse. They symbolise wild and untamed horses. The centaur's half-human, half-horse composition has led many writers to treat them as liminal beings, caught between the two natures; they are the embodiment of untamed nature. The centaurs were usually said to have been born of Ixion and Nephele. As the story goes, Nephele was a cloud made in the likeness of Hera in a plot to trick Ixion into revealing his lust for Hera to Zeus. Ixion seduced Nephele, and from that relationship, centaurs were created. The Centaurs are best known for their fight with the Lapiths, who, according to one original myth, would have been cousins to the centaurs.

Mula natives have the raw, untamed centaur-like energy, which can be used towards positive or negative thoughts and actions depending on their perspective and outlook.

Roots -

The word Mula literally means roots. It has been named so because of it's location near the galactic centre, which is the core of our Milky Way galaxy. This makes it powerful and vulnerable at the same time, because any kind of power carries both possibilities - of destruction and creation.

Those who have their Ascendant, Sun or Moon in Mula like to stay connected to their roots and love researching ancient artefacts, archeology and historical information about the culture and tradition they are born into. They also inevitably have to go through such situations in their life where they feel uprooted from their roots and have to start life afresh. This becomes a very intense and transformative experience for them. Since Mula has the energy of Jupiter and Ketu, they will always seek answers in religion, spirituality and philosophy. The Jupiterian optimism keeps them positive and hopeful even in the most dire circumstances.

Lion's tail -

The lion's tail is also a symbolic representation of the shape of the constellation as seen in the night sky. Mula is a group of 9 stars, which form the shape of a lion's tail, and are seen at the end of the Scorpio constellation. It also signifies the quality of fearlessness.

Mula natives have the fearless spirit of a lion and are very adventurous. They love to explore new terrains, new cultures, visit new places and talk to people from different cultures and backgrounds. They are also very independent and cannot be confined to a small space of 4 walls; they need to be out and about. Their sole desire is to experience life to the fullest without any inhibitions.

Inference

Mula natives have an amazing quality of being able to focus completely on their target and hit the bull's eye. Like a skilled archer, their arrows never fail to miss the target or their desired goal. They also have the incredible strength of a centaur, which helps them to gallop at a fast speed and still keep their focus. Only those who have mastered their skill through practice can achieve such incredible feats of absolute precision, speed and strength. Mula natives have it in them to achieve what they set out for.

On the positive side, their straightforward and direct manner is very motivating and enthusing. However, on the negative side, it can become too overbearing or hurtful because they become oblivious to others' pain when they are too focused on what they want.

Mythology -

Deity - <u>Nirriti Dev -</u> The Goddess of destruction.

The Vedas describe Nirriti as the Goddess of destruction and darkness. She is associated with pain, misfortune and death, and is much feared because of these qualities. She is the guardian of the South-West direction.

Nirriti is often linked to Devi Kaali, Alakshmi, Jyeshtha or Dhumavati. While some texts suggest that she is the goddess of misfortune and also the remover of misfortunes. In the sense that she represents a destructive force that indiscriminately has the power to destroy good and bad, auspicious and inauspicious, fortune and misfortune. Generally, Nirrti is associated with calamity, misfortune, poverty, infertility and death (particularly death and endings).

The story of Nirriti

In the epic of Mahabharata, Nirriti is mentioned as the wife of Adharma - unrighteousness, and she has 3 sons - Bhaya - fear, Maha-Bhaya - great fear and Mrityu - death. Another version says that she is the daughter of Adharma and Himsa - violence or injury. Shree Bhagwatam states that she is, however, one of the necessary creations of Brahma.

Interesting mythological references -

Nirritti is described as a female deity in the earlier texts. Interestingly, in later texts, Nirriti seems to change sex, and he is described as a god who has a dark green hue, seated on a horse holding a sword.

The association of owls and Nirrti - the owl becomes the vehicle of Lakshmi (goddess of wealth and abundance). This might signify that an owl-like wisdom can change misfortune to fortune.

A verse in the Rig Veda describes the realm of Nirriti as an endless pit without light or warmth – a place reserved for those who do evil deeds. Which is synonymous with the qualities of a black hole.

Inference -

Mula-born people have a powerful energy that has the power to dissolve and annihilate. They have to pass through circumstances that leave them with no choice but to discard or destroy everything that is old, or end things that have been familiar to them and start anew. They also face situations where they have to deal with the death of their family member or their friend.

These are very difficult and transformative situations which need a lot of courage and wisdom to deal with. Each one of us is given the karmic quota of what we can handle. If one is destined to deal with tough situations, they are also blessed with extraordinary strength to overcome those challenges. After having passed through such profound experiences, Mula natives become very philosophical about life. Their sharp arrows of curiosity pierce through the veil of Maya (illusion) and reveal the truth to them.

Mula padas

0 - 13.20 deg Sagitarius

Padas	Degrees
1	0 - 3.20 deg Sagitarius
2	3.20 - 6.40 deg Sagitarius
3	6.40 - 10 deg Sagitarius
4	10 - 13.20 deg Sagitarius

Pada 1

0 - 3.20 deg Sagitarius, Navamsha- Aries (Lord - Mars)

Rashi Lord - Jupiter and Nakshatra Lord- Ketu

The navamsha of the 1st Pada lies in Aries, therefore it carries the energy of Mars, Jupiter and Ketu. This will give them a more childlike and impatient approach to life. They will enthusiastically jump into things but may not have the patience to finish the project.

They feel that they don't have much time on hand, and need to rush ahead and find answers to the profound questions - before life is over. For example, the 1st Pada of Moola in the 3rd house will bring a lot of opportunities to interact with siblings, friends and neighbours. They may face some difficult situations, like the loss of a sibling or a friend, which will make them seek the profound truths of life.

They seek their soulmate with optimism of finding their true love. In a way, love's idealism and their anxious quest blinds them - but in the end, after having faced the realities and challenges, they realise that the search for love was not somewhere outside, but true love was within them - hidden in their own heart. The sweetness of emotion, when expanded, can be projected to any living being, and they begin to find fulfilment in all that comes their way.

Careers

Teachers, philosophers, psychologists, counsellors, advisors,

coordinators, leaders, social activists, film directors, managers, astrologers, doctors, scientists, researchers, psychiatrists, businessmen, writers, IT professionals, athletes, yoga teachers and working from home.

Pada 2

3.20 - 6.40 deg Sagitarius, Navamsha - Taurus (Lord - Venus)

Rashi Lord - Jupiter and Nakshatra Lord- Ketu

In the 2nd Pada, there will be the energy of Jupiter, Venus and Ketu. The navamsha of Taurus gives them a more practical approach.

They will be more creative and artistic and will love spending time with their family and friends, and will be more grounded and determined to achieve their goals.

The Jupiterian wisdom makes them seem deceptively quiet, but they are intelligent, funny, clumsy, frank and very idealistic. The Venusian sense of balance makes them very sensitive to their environment. They are inspired researchers, scientists and authors who drive their friends, relatives and friends crazy with weird answers to simple questions.

In their attempt to find the right balance, they can argue over every word you speak and drive you into a frenzy. They also have the ability to charm you with their motivational speeches and logical inferences.

For example, the 2nd Pada of Moola in the 4th house, their mother will be a great influence in their lives. They will love spending time at home, but their job might be such that they have to stay away from home intermittently.

Careers

Managers, consultants, financial advisors, actors, artists, doctors, scientists, bank managers, psychiatrists, therapists, researchers, archaeologists, writers, businessmen or business women, IT professionals, astrologers and those working from home.

Pada 3

6.40 - 10 deg Sagitarius, Navamsha - Gemini (Lord - Mercury)

Rashi Lord - Jupiter and Nakshatra Lord - Ketu

The navamsha of the 3rd Pada is placed in Gemini, which gives the effect of Mercury, Jupiter and Ketu. In this Pada, they become like a sceptical philosopher and a reluctant prophet who is still unsure about the final answers to the riddle of life. The archer in them probes into the profound questions of life through reason and logic. They seem to do nothing at all except read and think. The curiosity and intelligence of Mercury, combined with the Jupitarian wisdom, keep them motivated to explore and learn more.

They can be embarrassingly curious, because their exploration is not limited to the realm of human behaviour and planet Earth alone; it extends up to space and beyond. Their mentally agility and verbal dexterity blend very well with quiet moments of reflection and being talkative. They are capable of being absolutely charming conversationalists or utterly quiet thinkers. They get bored easily and need mental stimulation and would much rather wander around in nature, pondering on nature's bounty, rather than be stuck with mundane responsibilities at home or in the office.

For example, the 3rd Pada of Moola in the 5th house, they will be very creative, intelligent and studious. They will love spending time reading and gathering knowledge. They have the potential to become great artists, actors, singers, musicians or writers.

Careers

Managers, consultants, financial advisors, actors, artists, fashion designers, film directors, doctors, scientists, bank managers, psychiatrists, therapists, researchers, archaeologists, writers, businessmen or businesswomen, IT professionals, astrologers, public relations coordinators, and those working from home.

Pada 4

10 - 13.20 deg Sagitarius, Navamsha - Cancer (Lord - Moon)

Rashi Lord - Jupiter and Nakshatra Lord- Ketu

In this Pada, there will be the influence of the Moon, Jupiter and Ketu. The navamsha of Cancer will make them very kind-hearted, generous, dreamy, emotional, philosophical and sensitive. The Jupiterian optimism and receptivity of the moon are a very pleasant and auspicious combination. In a way, the cooling effect of lunar waters on the fiery heat of Ketu is quite comforting.

They have a wonderful knack of comforting and paying flattering attention when it's needed. This is because they sense vibrations of joy or pain and respond accordingly. However, when they feel exhausted or frustrated with life in general, they tend to go into long periods of silence and reflection. This helps them to restore their depleted energies and rejuvenate.

For them, physical love is only one superficial level of a relationship. True love has a deeper and more profound element of trust, sharing, giving and receiving at the intellectual and emotional level. For example, the 4th Pada of Moola in the 7th house, their spouse or partner will be very knowledgeable, kind and spiritual. They will come across people who, like them, are intellectual and love philosophical discussions, because their soul resonates with these qualities, as seekers of truth.

Careers-

Teachers, philosophers, psychologists, counsellors, therapists, advisors, astrologers, doctors, scientists, researchers, psychiatrists, writers, poets, artists, actors, singers, business men and business women, IT professionals and working from home.

The effect of planets

Mula - Sagitarius	Planets that get affected
Functional Benefic - gives good results during their dasha.	Sun, Mars, Jupiter and Venus
Functional Malefic - can give problems during their dasha.	Rahu and Ketu
Functional Neutral	Moon, Mars and Saturn
Kendra Adi Pati Dosha - can be malefic	Mercury

Mula Ascendant

When the Ascendant is in Mula, it has the influence of Jupiter and Ketu. The Jupiterian idealism and detachment of Ketu make them search for truth, which can take them through a maze of religious concepts veering from stark atheism to fanaticism. They will have blind faith or will reject religious dogma totally.

The piercing energy of Mula is such that it makes them restless as if they are in constant search of something. Their dual quality helps them enact both the roles simultaneously - a serious thinker and a clown, the actor. This enables them to entertain themselves amidst the harsh realities of everyday living and to explore the idiosyncrasies of human behaviour.

They are willing to walk a thousand miles or travel a long distance for any humanitarian cause, simply because they cannot bear to stand by without trying to save the situation, a person or an animal. It's also their intrigue and curiosity to know the deeper realities that attract them towards such situations.

Since Sagitarians are symbolised by a centaur, who is half horse and half man, and an archer, they tend to be a little clumsy because it's not easy to balance the personality of half human and half animal, nor is it easy to balance the half philosopher and half clown in them. The abundance of Jupiterian idealism makes them shoot their arrows towards some undiscovered and unseen galaxy from planet Earth. Although it's not an easy task, because the arrows of the archer invariably get stuck in the cloudy atmosphere of not-so-enthusiastic people. Their good intentions have the possibility of becoming a reality because of their determined faith. In one way or another, even if it's through fictitious storytelling, via the medium of creative cinema, they will manage to tell their tale.

They love to travel and study about different cultures, meet different people and interact with life at every level. Their positive qualities are optimism, cheerfulness, logic, honesty, enthusiasm and daring. On the negative side, when feeling frustrated, they can become reckless, careless, confused, lack tact and be rude.

Sun in Mula

When the Sun is placed in Mula, it will carry the energies of Jupiter and Ketu. Sun and Jupiter are good friends, so it's a comfortable placement for the Sun and gives fortune and success during the dasha of Sun or Jupiter. The effect of Ketu brings separation or detachment from the father or teacher in some way. The natives will be religious and spiritually inclined, and will be honest, knowledgeable, talented, and good-looking. They can become influential and motivational speakers, and will be helpful and good-natured.

or example, Sun is in Mula in the 2nd house, the natives will be born into a family which has a good source of income, and they will have a comfortable home. They will have their father's support and can do well in business.

However, if there are any malefic aspects from Saturn, Rahu or Ketu, or the Sun has a very low degree (0-1), there could be some problems or issues with their father. During the dasha of Sun or Jupiter, they could receive rewards, honour or recognition from the government or authorities in their home country. They are fortunate and do well in their chosen area of profession, because the Sun gives them the intelligence and confidence to deal with situations as needed, and the beneficence of Jupiter provides a comfortable source of income.

Moon in Mula

When the Moon is placed in Mula, it will share the influence of Jupiter and Ketu. The influence of the moon makes them very friendly, and helping others gives them great joy. They will feel a compelling urge to explore the human mind and unravel the secrets of human behaviour. They will be drawn towards philosophy, religion, spirituality and higher learning. Their philosophical way of thinking is high above and beyond their peers.

There is always something that keeps them interested and fascinated, some riddle that they have to solve keeps them thoroughly engaged and busy. For example, Moon in Mula in the 9th house will be interested in learning about their ancestral legacy, the ancient wisdom, and the mysterious and spiritual side of life. They will find a mentor or a teacher who will inspire them towards attaining higher education in philosophy, psychology, religion, astronomy, astrology, or to know the secrets of the galaxies.

Since Sagittarius is the original 9th house of fortune (bhagya), they are blessed with the Jupitarian luck, and are startlingly fortunate, in the sense that opportunities fall into their lap at the right time, they are in the right place, and everything falls in place for them to pursue their ambitions. They seem to get dual benefits from life - both spiritual and material. Ketu, being the nakshatra lord, has an uncanny way of knowing what it is that they really need to do, not at the level of the mind, but by responding to the needs of their body, or by going with their gut feeling.

They are active, ambitious, motivated, outspoken and dislike taking orders from anyone. The human side of dualistic Sagitarian Centaur can accept things cheerfully and philosophically, but the horse side of them will rear their equestrian legs to show their annoyance. They are bright, clever, studious, intellectual, and optimistically philosophical, but can be equally stubborn, unpredictable, contrary and difficult to handle like a wild horse. They can kick dangerously when their freedom is threatened, and are also amazingly swift at racing out of their problems.

Jupiter's benign and benevolent good humour gives them the beautiful quality of being able to laugh over their own clumsiness and their shortcomings. They have the ability to recognise their limitations, they do not polish or glorify their faults, but try to overcome them, and this is not a small feat. It's an important and significant step towards realising our true self.

Quotes of Carl Jung -

"*The judgment of the intellect is only part of the truth.*"

"*In all chaos there is a cosmos, in all disorder a secret order.*"

"*The shoe that fits one person pinches another, there is no recipe for living that suits all cases.*"

"*I am not what happened to me, I am what I choose to become.*"

'*Where love rules, there is no will to power, and where power predominates, love is lacking. One is the shadow of the other.*"

The poetry of Mula

Mula - The root - galactic centre of our Milky Way,

Like a whirlpool of energy - sucking away,

Demolishing and destroying - the false illusion,

To reveal the truth and clear the confusion.

The centaur - a mythical being

Half man - half horse - has anyone seen!

A glorious stride - an intelligent synergy,

A fictitious character - to enlighten the dreams.

The bows of the archer - the arrows to truth - sought,

The bull's eye- at times on target, and sometimes not.

Jupiter's wisdom and Ketu's detachment,

Life and death - both an enchantment.

Remedies

<u>Das Maha Vidya</u> - as described earlier.

Pitta is the predominant tridosha of Mula, and a regular routine of physical exercise will help to balance the fiery heat of Ketu. Avoid exercising in the afternoon as it can aggravate pitta.

Pranayama and meditation will be particularly helpful to calm the restlessness of the mind and bring clarity to thought.

Avoid eating spicy foods and having too many stimulants like caffeine-rich coffee.

The yogic asanas always enhance the ability to focus, which in turn improves the quality of whatever you do and brings ease into all thoughts and actions.

Yellow and brown colours resonate well with the energy of Mula.

Chanting the mantra -"*Om nam pam pham Mula nakshatraye namah.*" 108 times on days when the moon is transiting Mula, or on Thursdays, will help to connect you with your inner self, and this will help you to calm your mind.

Example

<u>Ascendant in Mula</u>

<u>Kishore Kumar</u> - The legendary playback Hindi film singer and actor. Born on 4th August 1929, at 4pm in Khandwa, India- died on 13th October 1987 in Mumbai at the age of 58.

He was multi-talented - a singer, actor, music director, lyricist, writer, director, producer and screenwriter. He won 8 Filmfare Awards for Best Male Playback Singer. In 1997, the Government initiated an award called the "Kishore Kumar Award" for his contributions to Hindi cinema.

Kishore Kumar was born in a Bengali family in Khandwa. His father, Kunjalal Ganguly, was a lawyer, and his mother, Gouri Devi, was a homemaker. Kishore was the youngest of 4 siblings; they were 3 brothers and 1 sister. While Kishore was still a child, his brother Ashok became a Bollywood actor. Later, Anoop, his other brother, also went to the cinema with Ashok's help. Kishore graduated from Christian College, Indore. After his eldest brother became a successful star in Hindi films, Kishore also started his career in Hindi cinema as a chorus singer at Bombay Talkies. He was a very talented singer and very good at acting comedy, too. During 1970 - 1980, he became a very successful singer and sang many playback songs for star film actors.

Kishore had married 4 times. His first wife was a Bengali singer and actress, Ruma Gosh; their marriage lasted for 8 years. His 2nd wife was the beautiful actress Madhubala, who had worked with him in many films. When Kishore had proposed to her, she was not well and was planning to go to London for treatment. She had a ventricular septal defect (hole in the heart). They got married in 1960, and after their marriage, they travelled to London, UK, to get treatment for her heart condition. Unfortunately, in those days, they did not have the advanced technology to fix her pathological heart deformation. Sadly, Madhubala died on 23rd February 1969 at a young age of 36.

Kishore's 3rd marriage was to Yogeeta Bali, which lasted only for 2 years- from 1976 to 1978. He married for the 4th time to Leena Chandavarkar (an Indian film actress) in 1980. This marriage lasted until his death. He had 2 sons, Amit Kumar with Ruma (his 1st wife) and Sumit Kumar with Leena (his 4th wife).

Kishore said he preferred talking to the trees in his garden, who were his closest friends, instead of talking to false human friends. He was planning to retire in September 1987 because he was not happy with the kind of songs the music directors were offering him. So he was preparing to leave Mumbai and go and stay at his birthplace in Khandwa. After attending his elder brother, Ashok Kumar's birthday party, he passed away on 13th October 1987 at 4:45 pm in Mumbai, because of a heart attack.

Analysis -

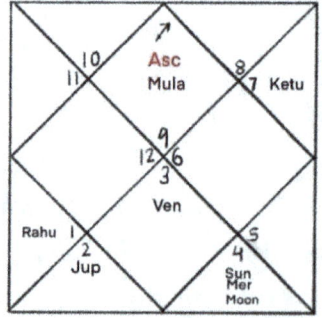

Kishore is a <u>Sagitarian Ascendant, Mula Pada 2</u>. The lord of Sagittarius, Jupiter, is in Rohini in Taurus in the 6th house. Ketu, the Lord of Mula, is in Libra in Vishakha in the 11th house. Jupiter, the Lord of the Ascendant (Sagittarius) and 4th house (Pisces), is sitting in the 6th house of debt, diseases, enemies and competition. This brought him many struggles and also gave him great skill in guiding and counselling others on these matters.

Being a Mula Ascendant, he had to pass through the painful experience of 2 divorces (with 1st and 3rd wife) and the death of his 2nd wife, which led him towards an inner transformation. His struggles were more personal and in his married life. <u>Venus</u> represents females in a male's horoscope; it's sitting in the 7th house (Gemini) of marriage and is the lord of the 6th house (Taurus) of competitions and the 11th house (Libra) of gains. His 1st wife, Ruma, was a very good singer. They got divorced because of ego clashes between the couple, because at that time she had more singing assignments than him. He had to pass through situations where he faced opposition and separation from his spouse, but it also brought him gains in terms of his popularity and income.

It's interesting to note that his Venus is placed in Mrigashira. He was searching for his soul mate, or he was being searched by the females who came into his life to fulfil the karma. Because Saturn, the Karma karka, is sitting in the Ascendant (in Mula) aspecting the 7th house of marriage directly. This also highlights the fact that his life was spent serving the public by entertaining them through his singing and acting.

Sadly, when his 2nd wife, Madhubala, died on 23rd February 1969. Kishore was running his <u>Venus Sun Mercury dasha</u>. His Venus is placed in the 7th house of Gemini, which is the house of the spouse. Sun, Mercury and Moon are in the 8th house (Cancer) of sudden events. Moreover, <u>Mercury</u> gets the Kendra Adi Pati dosha, being the Lord of the 7th house (Maraka house) and 10th house (career). Mercury sitting in the 8th house with Sun and Moon brought many upheavals in his married and professional life. Sun and Moon together have an intense effect; he was born on Amavasya (new moon day). He was born on a Sunday, which shows the significant effect of the Sun in his life. His talent made him shine like a bright Sun among the other stars in his field of Cinema and entertainment.

Apart from many of his early days of struggle, even at the peak of his singing career, his songs were once banned from being played on All India Radio in 1975 for nearly 20 months, during the time of emergency, because he had refused to sing at a political rally in Mumbai.

Like the dual nature of Sagittarius - there were 2 sides to him - a happy face and clownish acting for the world, and an inner serious thinker and philosopher, which he preferred to keep hidden from the public. He was well known for his eccentric behaviour and a great sense of humour - among many weird and funny things that he did, one of them was - he had put a sign on his door which read - <u>'Be aware of Kishore.'</u> It reflects the funny and serious side of the Sagittarian Centaur like nature.

His Rahu is placed in the 5th house of creativity in Bharani, and Ketu is placed in the 11th house of Libra in Vishakha. The 5th house Rahu made him highly talented and a genius in the creative field of singing and entertainment. He was especially good at acting comedy roles; his great sense of humour and his ability to make people laugh were extraordinary. His clownish and clumsy ways were a cover for his deeper understanding of the illusionary ways of the world. He was deeply philosophical and religious. He especially became famous for his philosophical songs sung for the screen presence of Rajesh Khanna. The dual nature of Sagittarius stands out in one of his comedy performances, where he sang a Hindi song in both male and female voices, which was a masterpiece.

The 11th house Ketu detached him from the gains. There were instances when he had to chase people for his payment that was due to him. He had his own unique ways of dealing with difficult situations or problems in his life. Kishore was very particular about his payments being done on time. During recordings, he would sing only after his secretary confirmed that the producer had made the payment. He was very hilarious and had a fantastic sense of humour. On one such occasion, when he found that his payment was not done fully, he appeared on set with make-up done only on one side of his face. When the director questioned him, he replied, "Aadha paisa to aadha make-up." Half make-up for half payment."

Sun and Moon effect -

There are 3 planets placed in the 8th house - Sun, Moon and Mercury. This gives a very strong influence on the 8th house - we can see that the 8th house scenarios were very dominant in his life. He had to face many life-transforming situations in his life. His mother passed away when he was young, and he had to marry 4 times because of divorce or the death of his previous wife. His elder brother's wife (his bhabhi) was a motherly figure in his life, who sadly passed away just about 4 months before he himself passed away. It shows how strongly the 8th house theme and karmic connections played in his life.

He was born on Amavasya (new moon day) on a Sunday. This placed both his Sun and Moon in the same house. Sun and Moon are placed in the 8th house of Cancer. The Sun is strong at 18 degrees; moreover, he was born on a Sunday, which makes the influence of the Sun very significant in his birth chart. On 13th October 1987, when he passed away, he was running his Sun mahadasha. The Sun is considered mildly cruel and can give separation.

His Moon is placed in Pushya, and the Sun and Mercury are in Ashlesha. This gave him strong Cancerian qualities of - being generous - where he felt an emotional connection, caring, emotional, imaginative, intelligent, intuitive and creative. His Moon is happily and comfortably sitting in his own house in Cancer, which nourished his thoughts and emotions beautifully, and the Sun gave him confidence and determination.

His kind and sensitive nature is a wonderful Cancerian quality that can be seen in many of his actions. Those who were close to him knew his sensitivity, kindness and generosity. Kishore had his own unique sense of generosity and helped his friends where he thought was needed. In spite of his "no money, no work" principle, he would sometimes record for free even when the producers were willing to pay. On another occasion, he helped producer Bipin Gupta with Rs 20,000 for making his film. When another actor, Arun Kumar Mukherjee, passed away, he regularly sent money to support his bereaved family in Bhagalpur, because Mukherjee was the 1st person to appreciate his singing talent, and he never forgot the kind gesture of his friend, which had touched him deeply. To show his gratitude and appreciation, he supported his friend's family in whichever way he could.

Jupiter, the lord of his Ascendant (Sagitarius), is placed in the 6th house of Taurus. It can be noticed that the 6th and 8th house scenarios were predominant in his life. He faced struggles, competition and disease, and sadly died at a relatively young age from a heart attack, which happened suddenly, because he was planning to retire in his hometown, Khandwa.

We can also see that number 4 was very significant in his life. Kishore was born on 4th August at 4pm. They were 4 siblings, and he was the youngest, 4th born in the family. As fate would have it, he married 4 times, and his 4th marriage was longer-lasting and stable. His 3rd wife, Yogeeta, had walked out on him on 4th August 1978, on his 49th birthday. (4+9=13 and 1+3=4). He passed away on 13th October 1987 at 4:45 pm (4+4+5=13), in Mumbai at the age of 58 (5+8=13).

Quotes of Kishore Kumar -

"I hate my life as much as a mother loves her child."

"Film people bore me, that's why I prefer talking to my trees."

"If you want something you've never had, you have to do something you've never done."

"Every place in the world is beautiful in the light of love."

"Love is the name of a thing that teaches a person how to sacrifice."

"Love doesn't have a single destination."

"The difference between poor and rich is not only of status, but also of the heart."

"I don't believe you have to be better than anybody else, you have to be better than you ever thought you could be."

22
Purva Ashadha

Om bam Purva Ashadha nakshatraye namah

Zodiac degrees	13.20 - 26.40 deg Sagittarius
Ruling planet	Sagittarius - Jupiter and Purva Ashadha - Venus
Sanskrit name	Purva means - the previous, the first, the former or seen in the east. Ashadha is also called Aprajita - which means undefeated, invincible, unconquered. Ashadha is the name of the month - June, when it's the peak of the summer season in India. It signifies the extreme heat-like quality of Venus.
Astronomical name	Purva Ashadha are the 3 bright stars seen in the constellation of Sagittarius. They form the shape of a handheld fan and are located close to the Milky Way galaxy.
Symbol	Sagittarius- Archer and Centaur - a horse with a man's torso and head. Purva Ashadha - hand fan and winnowing basket.
Element	Fire
Deity	Apah - water (consort of Varuna)
Quality	Sagittarius - Dwi - dual Purva Ashadha - Ugra- fierce
Shakti	Varcha grahana Shakti - power to invigorate.
Cast	Brahmin-priest
Gender	Male
Motivation	Dharma - righteousness
Triguna	Satwa
Tridosha	Pitta

Body parts	Thighs and back
Direction	East, north east and south west.
Month	Later half of June- Ashadha month.
Bird	Pigeon
Sound	bu, dah, bha, dha
Tree	Ashoka tree and Guduchi
Chakras	Swadhisthana - Venus and Ajna - Jupiter
Das Maha Vidya	Devi Kamala - Venus and Devi Tara - Jupiter

Special degrees -

Yoga Tara	10.40 deg Sagittarius - Yoga Tara of Purva Ashadha lies in Mula. 21.30 deg Sagitarius - Yoga Tara of Abhijeet. It's a point where the planet will show the strongest and sure results during its dasha.
Pushkar bhaga	23 deg Sagittarius. Any planets sitting at this point will give excellent results during their dasha, like the blossoming of a flower.
Pushkar amsha	3rd Pada The planets placed here will give good results during their dasha, like the blossoming of a flower.
Amrit Nadi	24 - 24.53 deg Sagitarius This brings good results, just like the nectar that nourishes.
Visha Nadi	18.40 - 19.33 deg Sagitarius Brings situations which one does not like dealing with.

Auspicious and inauspicious table -

Auspicious	Inauspicious
Activities Good for marriage and sexual activities, for activities that require courage, opposition, confronting enemies, going to war, motivating others into action, giving up bad habits, for reconciliation, forgiveness, settling debts, for revitalisation, achieving goals, adventure, exploration, playing sports, for boosting confidence, brave heroic acts, pioneering activities, for traveling over water, sailing, for equine activities, water sports and all activities related to water, artistic activities, decorating, agricultural activities, visiting historical sites, for worshiping female deities, for spiritual and occult practices.	Activities Not good for activities that need tact and diplomacy, for calm reflections, endings and for land journeys.

Days Wednesdays - only when it falls on the 5th or 7th lunar day. Thursdays - only when it falls on the 4th, 5th, 7th, 9th, 13th or 14th lunar day. Fridays - only when it falls on the 1st, 2nd, 6th, 7th, 11th or 12th lunar day.	Days Mondays- only when it falls on the 6th, 7th or 11th lunar day. Tuesdays- only when it falls on the 1st, 2nd, 7th, 8th, 10th or Purnima (full moon day). Saturdays- only when it falls on the 3rd, 7th, 9th or 11th lunar day.

Compatibility table -

Purva Ashadha	Compatible with
Sexual compatibility Yoni animal	Male - Monkey Compatible with Shravana - Female Monkey
Sign compatibility	Sagittarius - Aries and Leo.
Nakshatra compatibility	Bharani and Purva Phalguni.
Lunar day compatibility	Trayodashi tithi - 13th lunar day
Day compatibility	Thursday and Friday.
Colour compatibility	Yellow and all pastel colours.
Numerological compatibility	3 and 6 - all numbers that add up to make 3 and 6.
Sound compatibility	Jupiter - dental sounds - ta, ttha, da, dha, knna Venus - palatal sounds - cha, ccha, ja, jha, nga

Sign Lord and nakshatra lord - <u>Jupiter and Venus</u> - as described earlier.

Purva Ashadha is the 3rd of the Venus-ruled nakshatras; it symbolises the peak of Venusian energy. The optimism and expansive nature of Jupiter is heightened here; they like to do things on a grand scale and are very motivated. Even in the worst of circumstances, they know in their hearts that this phase shall pass and everything will be ok. In fact, they take it as a blessing, a learning experience from which they gain profound understanding. The Venusian qualities of creativity, beauty, harmony, aesthetic sense and trying to keep everything in balance are also felt very prominently in this nakshatra.

Since Jupiter is the guru of the Devas and Venus is the guru of the Daityas, this gives them an all-inclusive quality. They understand both sides of the picture, try to reason out and come to logical conclusions. They will be very idealistic, intelligent, creative, optimistic, motivated, wise and capable.

<u>Quality, element, motivation, triguna, tridosha and chakras -</u> as described earlier.

Shakti - <u>Varcha grahana Shakti - power to invigorate.</u>

The word Varcha comes from the root word varsha, which means rain and grahana means to absorb, to consume fully, to be satiated. Only a dry land which feels parched with the blazing heat of the sun will feel the hunger and intense need for water to rejuvenate it. And when the much-awaited rain comes and pours in abundance; the land is able to absorb it all and feel rejuvenated. Moreover, during the month of Ashadha (June), the heat is at its maximum in the tropical climate of India. That's why the ancient sages named this month Ashadha and associated it with the energy of Varcha grahana, which literally means the power to absorb the rain water. This is the month when the dry land is eagerly waiting for the monsoon rains to arrive.

Inference

Purva Ashadha natives have to pass through such challenging situations where they feel dry and bereft of all vital nourishment. It could be the physical hunger, emotional, intellectual or hunger to create something spectacular. Only after passing through this dry and testing phase in their life are they blessed with the opportunities that will truly invigorate, fulfil and satisfy them.

Symbolic signification

Sagitarius- Archer and Centaur, as described earlier.

Purva Ashadha - hand held fan and a winnowing basket.

Hand fan -

The hand fan symbolises the impact of the extreme heat one has to face in this month. Similarly, the Purva Ashadha natives have the fire of passion and ambition. They are very motivated to create something truly beautiful that will have value in both material and spiritual planes.

They will need to cool down the heat of their desires and learn to gracefully wait for the nourishment of rain to come forth. When the time is right, their plans will materialise.

Winnowing basket-

A winnowing basket is used to separate the chaff (the outer covering of the grain) from the inner grain. Similarly, Purva Ashadha natives have the capability of distinguishing the truth from lies and differentiating between honesty and hypocrisy. In public, they may not always be able to shoot the arrows of truth or express their opinion, but in their hearts, they will very clearly be able to separate the good from the bad and evil from virtue.

Just as the process of winnowing involves throwing the mixture into the air so that the wind blows away the lighter chaff, while the heavier grains fall back for recovery. Purva Ashadha natives go through such situations in their lives where they feel thrown from one end to the other. It could happen in terms of a hectic travel schedule, a demanding job, or trying to juggle time constraints to meet deadlines. Life puts one through such rigmarole in order to realise - what is it that we are truly seeking? Ultimately, with time and experience, when the chaff of illusion is removed, one can begin to see things clearly, as truly they are.

Mythology

Deity - <u>Apah</u> - Water

Ap or Apas is the Vedic Sanskrit term for water. In the Rigveda, several hymns are dedicated to the waters, Apas. In the oldest of these, the waters are connected with the drought of Indra. Agni, the god of fire, has a close association with water and is often referred to as Apām Napāt - offspring of the waters. In Hindu philosophy, the term refers to water as an element, one of the Panchamahabhuta, or five great elements. It is also the name of the Varuna Dev, who is the personification of water in the form of the ocean.

<u>Inference -</u>

The waters of Bharani flow as a river or a stream, the waters of Purva Phalguni flow as a lake or a sea, and the waters of Purva Ashadha expand into the vastness of the ocean. That's why Apah (water) is the deity of this nakshatra. The impact of the ocean tides is much stronger, and there is more biodiversity of creatures that live under the oceans, ranging from small fish to large blue whales.

Purva Ashadha natives have reached maturity and balance in the 3rd cycle of the Venus-ruled nakshatras. Here, they have the experience of having passed through the rajasic (active) stage and the tamasic (inertia) stage. The soul is now ready for the Satwic (balance) stage of life. The transformational energy of fire and the powerful chemistry of water sets a conducive ambience for life to thrive in the vast expanse of high and low oceanic tides.

Purva Ashadha natives pass through such experiences where they get a lot of opportunity to meet and interact with people from different cultures, visit many far-off places, see diverse landscapes, and enjoy the diversity of life on planet earth. They will have a special connection to water, and will get to spend a lot of time doing water-related activities, near the ocean, lakes or rivers. This will be a deeply fulfilling experience for them.

Purva Ashadha padas

13.20 - 26.40 deg Sagitarius

Padas	Degrees
1	13.20 - 16.40 deg Sagitarius
2	16.40 - 20 deg Sagitarius
3	20 - 23.20 deg Sagitarius
4	23.20 - 26.40 deg Sagitarius

<u>Pada 1</u>

13.20 - 16.40 deg Sagitarius, Navamsha- Leo (Lord - Sun)

Rashi Lord - Jupiter and Nakshatra Lord- Venus

The navamsha of the 1st Pada lies in Leo, therefore it carries the energy of Jupiter, Venus and Sun. The navamsha of the Sun will give them a lot of fire, drive, ambition and confidence, especially after the age of 30. The influence of Jupiter and Venus gives them the wisdom, intelligence, creativity and optimism to pursue their desires. The beneficence of Jupiter and Venus brings a lot of wonderful opportunities during their dasha periods.

For example, the 1st pada of Purva Ashadha in the 2nd house, they will be very motivated and ambitious about having a secure family base with an abundance of resources. They will be born into a family that is into politics or immediate family members who have high-ranking government positions.

It's a fortunate Pada, where they get opportunities to achieve their desired goals. However, they must take care not to get carried away or become arrogant about their success. They tend to be short-tempered and can end up hurting others' feelings unintentionally.

Careers

Politicians, managers, actors, directors, fashion designers, graphic designers, interior designers, landscape designers, farmers, artists, scientists, astrologers, musicians, astronauts, architects, photographers, entrepreneurs, IT designers, doctors, diplomats, homemakers, restaurant owners, hotel managers and club owners.

Pada 2

16.40 - 20 deg Sagitarius, Navamsha - Virgo (Lord - Mercury)

Rashi Lord - Jupiter and Nakshatra Lord- Venus

In the 2nd Pada, there will be the energy of Jupiter, Venus and Mercury. The navamsha of Virgo gives them a more practical approach. They will like to do things perfectly, and will be very analytical, intelligent and creative. After the age of 30, they will become more methodical, meticulous and critical.

Mercury gets the Kendra Adi Pati dosha for Sagittarius Ascendants only. For instance, the native is Purva Ashadha Ascendant in the 2nd Pada - the placement of Mercury should be looked at in the birth chart and the navamsha chart to see how life situations may pan out. For example, a debilitated Mercury sitting in Pisces can bring disruptions in academic progress in early life. However, suppose Mercury is placed in Aquarius in the navamsha. In that case, it shows that the condition of Mercury has improved, because Mercury and Saturn (the Lord of Aquarius) are neutral to each other. This signifies that the native will get better opportunities to pursue any academic courses in his or her adult life.

They will have a very good sense of aesthetics and will like dressing up elegantly. They will love gathering information about various topics that interest them. Any work of beauty, creativity and genius will attract their attention. For example, the 2nd Pada of Purva Ashadha placed in the 3rd house will show good communication skills and karma related to the siblings, friends and neighbours. They will be very enterprising and have the capability of achieving success through their own efforts.

Careers

Business men, managers, accountants, politicians, film directors, actors, artists, fashion designers, government officials, IT professionals, graphic designers, architects, interior designers, florists, property dealers, financial advisors, bank managers, land lords, working from home, home makers, club owners, club workers, engineers and doctors.

Pada 3

20 - 23.20 deg Sagitarius, Navamsha - Libra (Lord - Venus)

Rashi Lord - Jupiter and Nakshatra Lord - Venus

The navamsha of the 3rd Pada is placed in Libra, which gives the effect of Jupiter and double influence of Venus. In this Pada, they will be very intelligent and creative, but will also be short-tempered, because of the double influence of Venus. They will be very independent and will not be able to take orders from anyone. Their creativity can find expression only if they work according to their vision.

For example, the 3rd Pada of Purva Ashadha in the 5th house, the natives will be very talented in the field of entertainment, and can achieve success during the Venus and Jupiter dashas. They will be attracted to the field of entertainment and speculation.

Jupiter and Venus, being the gurus, have sensitive egos because of which their relationships can be touchy and difficult. As they grow older, they will always be trying to strike the right balance in order to create a harmonious vibration between them and their partner. Their short temper becomes another main cause of repeatedly landing them in situations which can break a relationship or a friendship.

Careers

Artists, painters, actors, writers, film directors, singers, musicians, fashion designers, managers, politicians, diplomats, leaders, astrologers, IT professionals, consultants, therapists, blog writers, you tube talkers, activists on social media, doctors, bankers, businessmen, government officials, florists, trip advisors, holiday planners, resort and restaurant owners or workers, hotel and motel managers, tourist planners and guides.

Pada 4

23.20 - 26.40 deg Sagitarius, Navamsha - Scorpio (Lord - Mars)

Rashi Lord - Jupiter and Nakshatra Lord- Venus

In this Pada, there will be the influence of Jupiter, Venus and Mars. The navamsha of Scorpio will make them very determined and deep thinkers, and they will be very strong mentally. The combination of Venus and Mars gives a very fiery energy, expanded by the optimism of Jupiter. They will be very passionate and will be the go-getters, and will not wait around for things to happen. They are the ones who can fearlessly bell the cat or activate a sleeping lion.

The sheer trust and dedication towards their chosen purpose or goal open the avenues for them. For example, the 4th Pada of Purva Ashadha in the 10th house will give them success in their career during the dasha of Jupiter, Venus or Mars, especially after the age of 30. However, the fire of Mars makes them short-tempered.

Although they don't hold a grudge for long, at the spur of the moment, the sharp arrows of an archer will surely pierce the opponent.

It's very important for them to channel their creative energy into positive avenues like having an exercise routine, yoga and meditation, creating a piece of art or music, designing a new product or giving time towards a humanitarian cause, otherwise there is a danger of this tremendous potential finding release in anger and aggression.

Careers-

Stunt actors, fire fighters, life rescue guards, ambulance operators, police officers, army commanders, gym trainers, film directors, philanthropists, psychologists, astrologers, spiritual mediums, managers, leaders, business men, government employees, doctors, surgeons, scientists, engineers, race car drivers, athletes, football and cricket players, self-employed and working from home.

The effect of planets

Purva Ashadha - Sagitarius	Planets that get affected
Functional Benefic - give good results during their dasha.	Sun, Jupiter and Venus
Functional Malefic - can give problems during their dasha.	Rahu and Ketu
Functional Neutral	Moon, Mars and Saturn
Kendra Adi Pati Dosha - can be malefic	Mercury

Purva Ashadha Ascendant

When the Ascendant is in Purva Ashadha, it has the influence of Jupiter and Venus. The Jupitarian idealism and Venusian sense of harmony give them a very Satwic approach to life. Their optimism is such that they can pass through any kind of difficulties with ease.

They are multi-talented and versatile, and many go through a variety of careers in their quest for truth and self-knowledge. They are attracted to art, music, drama, acting, sports, teaching, stock market, advertising, Internet research, IT technology, writing, publishing, politics, religion, astronomy, spirituality, yoga, meditation, legal, business, scientific, and medical professions.

Since it's a dual sign, there is always something perplexing or contradictory about their nature. On some occasions, they can be playful, happy-go-lucky people, and at other times, they are studious, serious thinkers or philosophers. Both bouncy extroverts and extremely quiet introverts, Purva Ashadhas, can be seen. They always express their opinions and ideas in a very creative Venusian way; whatever they create has to be aesthetically appealing.

Purva Ashadha lies in Sagittarius, which is the original 9th house of dharma, righteousness, teacher, guru and father. They will gain a lot of knowledge and wisdom from their father or mentor. First, trying to search the truth, then recognise it, and finally express it openly is a Jupiterian pattern. In some way, they will carry on the legacy of their teacher or father.

With the intensity of the fire, they chase their dreams, their honesty and optimism help them sail through obstacles, but can also at times keep them eluded from reality. Through failures, they learn their lessons- to balance the 2 sides of life - the practical and essential with ethical and moral. Those who mature and gain deeper insight realise the truth of existence - that nothing is contradictory in nature, everything complements everything else. The contradictions exist only in our minds, in our thoughts and emotions.

Apah - water being the deity of Purva Ashadha, makes them very sensitive and vulnerable to the high and low tides of their emotions.

They need to consciously practise being aware of their strong emotions, especially anger, and look at what triggers them. Once they figure out the cause, the solutions will come easy.

Sun in Purva Ashadha

When the Sun is placed in Purva Ashadha, it will share the qualities of Jupiter and Venus. Sun and Jupiter get along well, but Sun and Venus are considered enemies; therefore, there will be a mixed effect. The natives will be very talented, creative, intelligent and learned, but will tend to be short-tempered and could face some minor health problems like headaches or high blood pressure. They could face some challenges in their relationships during the dasha of the Sun or Venus. They can become excellent managers, coordinators, politicians and leaders. The influence of the Sun gives them confidence, Venus gives creativity, and Jupiter gives optimism and foresight.

For example, Sun is placed in Purva Ashadha in the 5th house, the natives will be very intelligent, will be scholarly and influential in their speech and writing. Their children or students will bring them happiness and fulfilment, in the sense that they will feel proud of their achievements. They will be spiritually inclined and can be great visionaries and inspirational teachers. For a Leo Ascendant, when Sun, the lord of the Ascendant, is placed in the 5th house of Sagittarius, it's a fortunate placement and the natives will get opportunities of being recognised, getting awards, or becoming successful during the dasha of Sun or Jupiter. They will also tend to be proud and impatient.

Moon in Purva Ashadha

When the Moon is placed in Purva Ashadha, it will share the influence of Jupiter and Venus. They will feel strongly about religion, spirituality, righteousness, ethics, morals, philosophies, faith and beliefs. With the strength of their faith, even the impossible becomes possible.

They will love to interact with people from varied backgrounds and explore different cultures, and will get many opportunities to do so. For them, travelling, going for vacations and exploring nature is a magical solution for everything. Especially travelling by boat or a ship makes them feel very connected to their soul. All activities related to water, like swimming, fishing, surfing, and canoeing, will attract them immensely and will be beneficial for them.

Just as the winnowing basket separates the chaff from the grains, they will have the ability to distinguish the truth from untruth. They will also face such situations where they feel they have to make a choice between 2 aspects of their life, they could face such dilemmas - how to balance their work and family life? The dual nature of Sagittarius helps them to integrate both roles with ease and choose a middle ground of working from home. Or giving genuine time to their family when they go on family holidays.

The Jupiterian idealism and optimism help them sail through all difficulties quite effortlessly. The beneficence of Jupiter does not mean that there will be no obstacles, but they will be able to overcome the challenges with wisdom and understanding.

For example, Moon in Purva Ashadha in the 6th house, they can face financial debts, minor health problems, or some confrontation with their colleagues or staff members during the dasha of Jupiter or Venus. The Jupiterian frankness and the sharp arrows of truth can sometimes ignite blazing fires and cause breakups or arguments, but the air can be cleared up because there is no element of deliberate deception. They will be able to deal with it effectively because of the Jupitarian foresight. The Jupitarian luck will always bring a new opportunity for them as and when needed.

The poetry of Purva Ashadha

Purva Ashadha - the first undefeatable one.

In the winnowing basket - the pods were swung,

Separating the chaff from the grain,

The sane from insane.

Both exist in me - from time to time,

Again, and again.

Travel and explore - people and places - to what end?

Only to find myself - in them

Apah - the water is my solace,

Food for the soul - a deity of grace.

The heat of June - as the hand fan sways,

Cools the emotions - strong tidal waves.

Jupitarian idealism and Venusian harmony,

Can conquer frontiers - one and many.

Remedies

- <u>Das Maha Vidya</u> - as described earlier.

- Pitta is the predominant tridosha of Purva Ashadha; a regular routine of physical exercise will help to balance the fiery heat.

- Pranayama and meditation will be particularly helpful to calm the restlessness of the mind and bring clarity to thought.

- The yogic asanas always enhance the ability to focus, which in turn improves the quality of whatever you do and brings ease into all thoughts and actions.

- Yellow and all pastel colours resonate well with the energy of Purva Ashadha.

- Chanting the mantra - *"Om bam Purva Ashadha nakshatraye namah."* 108 times on days when the moon is transiting Purva Ashadha, or on Thursdays or Fridays, will help to connect you with your inner self, and this will help you to calm your mind.

Example

Ascendant in Purva Ashadha

Hema Malini - Famous Indian film actress.

Born on 16th October 1948, 12 pm, Tamil Nadu, India (estimated time of birth).

She is a Bharatnatyam dancer and an actress, and has been the top actress of the 1970s - 1980s. Even now, she is active in politics. Hema Malini is an Indian actress, writer, director, producer, dancer and politician. She is primarily known for her work in Hindi films. Hema made her acting debut in 1963 with the Tamil film Idhu Sathiyam. She first acted in a lead role in Sapno Ka Saudagar in 1968 and went on to feature in numerous Bollywood films. She has been one of the highest-paid Indian actresses from 1976 to 1980.

Hema Malini was born in a Tamil Iyengar Brahmin family to Jaya Lakshmi and Chakravarti Iyengar in Srirangam. She attended the Andhra Mahila Sabha school in Chennai and later studied at Mandir Marg until the 11th Standard, after which she pursued her acting career.

Her first film with Dharmendra was Tum Haseen Main Jawaan in 1970. The two got married in 1980. Dharmendra was already married at the time, and so he converted to Islam to marry Hema Malini. Dharmendra already had 2 sons and 2 daughters with his first wife. Hema and Dharmendra have 2 daughters.

During her career, she received 11 nominations for the Filmfare Award for Best Actress. She won the first Best Actress award in 1973. In 2000, she won the Filmfare Lifetime Achievement Award and in 2019 Filmfare Special Award for 50 Years of Outstanding Contribution to Cinema. She has also been honoured with the Padma Shri, which is the 4th highest civilian honour awarded by the Government of India.

From 2003 to 2009, she was elected to the Rajya Sabha, the upper House of parliament, as a representative of the Bharatiya Janata Party. In 2014, she was elected to the Lok Sabha. She has also been actively involved with charitable and social organisations. Currently, she is a life member of the International Society for Krishna Consciousness - ISKCON.

As of June 2021, 3 biographical books about Hema have been published - Hema Malini Diva Unveiled in 2005, Hema Malini The Authorised Biography in 2007 and Beyond the Dream Girl in 2017. In her 3rd autobiography, she says, "At this age it's not appropriate to call me a dream girl, but I have had a dream life."

<u>Analysis -</u>

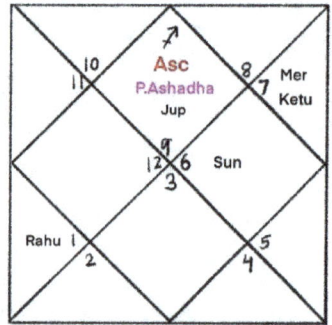

We have studied her example briefly while looking at the significance of atmakaraka. She is a <u>Sagittarius Ascendant - Purva Ashadha 3rd Pada.</u> Jupiter, the lord of Sagittarius, is sitting in the Ascendant, which makes her Ascendant very stable, powerful and capable of fruitifying the desires. The beneficence of Jupiter and the beauty of Venus literally made her the screen goddess- *'dream girl'* of Hindi cinema in the 1970s-1980s. Her beautiful face was seen on many Indian wall calendars, and people began to personify beauty with Hema Malini.

The film *'Johny Mera Naam'* was released in 1970, which became a huge success and was the highest-grossing film of that year. Hema Malini became a superstar heroine after this film. She was running her <u>Mercury Rahu Sun dasha</u> during that time. The Sun is placed in the 10th house of career in Virgo-Chitra. Sun is her atmakaraka and is very well placed, and gets directional strength in the 10th house.

Mercury is sitting with Ketu in the 11th house in Libra - Swati, the house of gains and fulfilment of desires. Rahu is sitting in the 5th house of Aries - Ashwini, the house of creativity and entertainment.

After this, her career took off full-fledged, powered by the horsepower energy of Ashwini, amplified by Rahu.

23
Uttara Ashadha

Om bham Uttara Ashadha nakshatraye namah

Zodiac degrees	26.40 deg Sagittarius - 10 deg Capricorn Sagittarius - 1st Pada Capricorn - 2nd, 3rd and 4th padas. Abhijeet - 6.40 - 10.53 deg Capricorn
Ruling planet	Sagittarius - Jupiter and Capricorn - Saturn Uttara Ashadha - Sun
Sanskrit name	Uttara means - the latter or rising in the North. Ashadha is also called Aprajita, which means undefeated, invincible, unconquered, or the final victory.
Astronomical name	Uttara Ashadha is represented by 4 bright stars seen in the constellation of Sagittarius, which resemble the shape of an elephant's tusks.
Symbol	Sagitarius- Archer and Centaur - a horse with a man's torso and head. Capricorn - Mountain goat and alligator Uttara Ashadha - elephant tusk
Element	Fire - Sagittarius and Earth - Capricorn
Deity	The 10 Vishwa Devas and Ganesha Abhijeet - Vishnu
Quality	Dwi - dual - Sagittarius Chara -movable- Capricorn
Shakti	Apra adrishya Shakti - ability to see the unseen and attain the unattainable.
Cast	Kshatriya - warrior
Gender	Male - Sagittarius Female - Capricorn

Motivation	Dharma - righteousness - Sagittarius Artha - to gather resources - Capricorn
Triguna	Satwa - Sagittarius and Rajas - Capricorn
Tridosha	Pitta - Sagittarius and Kapha - Capricorn
Body parts	Waist and thighs
Direction	South, west, east, north and northeast.
Month	July - the 2nd half of Ashadha month.
Bird	Swan
Sound	bay, bo, ja, jee
Tree	Jackfruit tree
Chakras	Manipura - Sun, Vishuddhi - Saturn and Ajna - Jupiter
Das Maha Vidya	Devi Matangi - Sun, Devi Kali - Saturn, and Devi Tara - Jupiter

Special degrees -

Yoga Tara	18.30 deg and 19.40 deg Sagittarius - There are 2 Yoga Tara points for Uttara Ashadha, which lie in Purva Ashadha. 21.30 deg Sagittarius - Yoga Tara of Abhijeet. It's a point where the planet will show the strongest and sure results during its dasha.
Pushkar amsha	1st Pada The planets placed here will give good results during their dasha, like the blossoming of a flower.
Debilitation	5 deg Capricorn - Maximum debilitation of Jupiter. This will bring in situations which can create misunderstandings and arguments in a relationship.
Amrit Nadi	6.26 - 7.20 deg Capricorn This brings good results, just like the nectar that nourishes.
Visha Nadi	18.40 - 19.33 deg Sagittarius Brings situations which one does not like dealing with.

Auspicious and inauspicious table -

Auspicious	Inauspicious
Activities Generally good for everything, for new beginnings, initiations, planning new projects, laying foundations, for business deals, signing contracts, for promotions, management, for	Activities Not good for travel, for endings, or for any unethical or unlawful activities.

marriage and sexual activities, for entering a new house, government related activities, political and legal affairs, discernment, judgement, getting things in order, for creative and artistic activities, spiritual and religious activities.	
Days Sundays - only when it falls on the 1st, 4th, 6th, 7th or 12th lunar day. Tuesdays - only when it falls on the 5th or 7th lunar day. Wednesdays - only when it falls on the 2nd, 3rd, 7th, 8th, 12th or 13th lunar day.	Days Mondays - only when it falls on the 6th, 7th or 11th lunar day. Tuesdays - only when it falls on the 1st, 2nd, 8th, 10th or Purnima (full moon day). Saturdays - only when it falls on the 3rd, 7th, 9th or 11th lunar day.

Compatibility table -

Uttara Ashadha	Compatible with
Sexual compatibility Yoni animal	Uttara Ashadha - Mongoose No counterpart
Sign compatibility	Sagittarius - Aries and Leo. Capricorn, Taurus and Virgo.
Nakshatra compatibility	Kritika and Uttara Phalguni.
Lunar day compatibility	Purnima tithi - full moon day
Day compatibility	Sunday, Thursday and Saturday.
Colour compatibility	Yellow, orange and blue.
Numerological compatibility	1, 3 and 8- all numbers that add up to make 1,3 and 8.
Sound compatibility	Sun - all vowels - a, aa, e, ee, u, oo, ey, aye, o, ou, am, ah Jupiter - dental sounds - ta, ttha, da, dha, knna Saturn - labial sounds - pa, pha, ba, bha, ma

Sign Lord and nakshatra lord - <u>Jupiter, Saturn and Sun</u> - as described earlier.

Uttara Ashadha is the 3rd of the Sun ruled nakshatras; here the quality is more satvik, therefore the natives will be more religious and spiritual. The 1st Pada of Uttara Ashadha lies in Sagittarius and therefore shares the energy of Jupiter and Sun, which makes them very idealistic and confident. The 2nd, 3rd and 4th padas of Uttara Ashadha are placed in Capricorn and have the influence of Saturn and Sun, which makes them more ambitious, determined, grounded and practical.

Abhijeet -

The word Abhijeet means - invincible victory, or undefeatable.

The mythological story in the Vedas states that Daksha Prajapathi and Panchajani had 27 daughters and only one son called Abhijeet. Chandra Dev, the moon god, had married the 27 daughters, who were named as the 27 nakshatras (constellations). The 28th Nakshatra, which is not visible but has a significant effect, is called Abhijeet.

This nakshatra is only used in muhurats, in terms of looking at the auspicious time for doing certain activities. It is not counted as a separate nakshatra while preparing the birth chart. While reading the birth chart, some interpretations are done with the 28-nakshatra system, where Abhijeet is considered.

For example, while reading the Prashna chart, which is the chart of that current moment, one can use the 28 nakshatra system because it will give a complete analysis of the predictions, or the auspicious and inauspicious times.

In Bhagavad Gita, Lord Krishna says that - He was Shiva among Rudras, He was Arjuna among Pandavas, and He was Abhijeet among Nakshatras.

<u>Quality, element, motivation, triguna, tridosha and chakras -</u> as described earlier.

Shakti - <u>Apra adrishiya Shakti</u> - ability to see the unseen and attain the unattainable.

The word <u>Apra</u> in Sanskrit means - to fulfil one's desire, to accomplish, to achieve, able to reach, busy, active, or zealous. And the word <u>Adrishya</u> means - to become invisible, not seen, or unperceivable.

In Vedic texts, there are certain mantras and yogic practices that can give one the ability to become invisible at will. These are called siddhis (supernatural powers). There are ashta siddhis - 8 kinds of supernatural powers that one can attain through dedicated yogic practices, and the ability to become invisible is one of them. These unusual abilities can be used for defence or protection if they're genuinely needed. However, the misuse of these supernatural powers takes away these subtle and powerful capabilities and also incurs a huge karmic debt. And there is a great danger for spiritual aspirants or seekers of truth to get distracted, attached or entertained by these extraordinary human capabilities, which can become an impediment towards realising the ultimate truth or enlightenment. The ashta siddhis are-

N	Siddhi - supernatural power	Meaning
1	Anima	To reduce one's body to a very small size.
2	Mahima	To expand one's body to a very large size.
3	Garima	To become very heavy, so that one's body cannot be moved.
4	Laghima	To become very lightweight - the ability to float in the air.

5	Praptika	To have unrestricted access to all places by becoming invisible.
6	Prakamya	To materialise one's desires - manifesting things from thin air.
7	Ishtiva	To become the absolute master or lord of whatever one desires to achieve.
8	Vastiva	To have absolute control or power over all situations as desired.

Inference

Uttara Ashadha natives are blessed with tremendous possibilities of achieving the impossible. All those capabilities which seem not to be humanly possible, they can achieve if they choose to dedicate their time and energy towards it. This doesn't mean they will desire to achieve these supernatural powers, but whatever they need to do in a worldly context, they will be able to achieve it. The kind of success they are blessed with is like an undefeatable victory in that area of life. Even after they retire or after they have passed away, they leave a legacy behind that continues to inspire and motivate others to follow their extraordinary example.

Their total attention and energy are focused on achieving their goal. For this reason, Uttara Ashadha is the only nakshatra whose Yoni animal is a Mongoose, and does not have a counterpart. They cannot afford to get distracted by easy comforts and pleasures of life. If one wants to master a particular skill, one has to give all of oneself with absolute focus.

Some interesting facts about the Mongoose -

- Mongooses are long, furry creatures with a pointed face and a bushy tail. They are members of the Herpestidae family, which also includes civets and meerkats.

- Some species of mongoose are very social and live in large groups called colonies. Colonies can have as many as 50 members. Other species of mongoose like to live alone.

- Mongoose colonies live, travel and fight together as a team. They stay in one area for around a week, then move in a wave to another location.

- Mongooses are active during the day and sleep at night. Throughout the day, they chatter incessantly to each other, and combine discrete units of sound somewhat like human speech, using vowel and syllable combinations to possibly coordinate group movements, foraging information and other important messages.

- Mongooses are omnivores, which means they eat both meat and vegetation. Typically, they prefer to eat small animals such as birds, reptiles, fish, snakes, crabs, rodents, frogs, insects and worms.

<u>Inference</u>

Uttara Ashadha natives have the ability to manage and lead large groups of people and organise huge events. Mongoose is the only animal that can efficiently kill snakes. This highlights their great skill and precision in dealing with potentially dangerous situations and emerging victorious. They are blessed with the power of invincible victory - the final victory.

Symbolic signification

<u>Sagitarius-</u> Archer and Centaur - a horse with a man's torso and head - as described in Mula.

<u>Capricorn -</u> Mountain goat and crocodile.

<u>Uttara Ashadha -</u> hand held fan and a winnowing basket.

<u>Mountain goat -</u>

A mountain goat is a sure-footed and confident mountain climber. Their feet are well-suited for climbing steep, rocky slopes because their inner pads provide traction and cloven hooves that can spread apart.

The tips of their feet have sharp dewclaws that keep them from slipping. They also have powerful shoulder and neck muscles that help propel them up steep slopes.

Both male and female mountain goats have beards, short tails, and long black horns, which contain yearly growth rings. They are protected from the elements by their woolly white double coats. They moult in spring by rubbing against rocks and trees, shedding their extra wool. Their coats help them to withstand winter temperatures as low as −46 °C and winds of up to 160 kilometres per hour.

They are the largest mammals found in their high-altitude habitats, which can exceed elevations of 13,000 ft. They sometimes descend to sea level in coastal areas to lick the minerals and get nourishment. They are herbivores and spend most of their time grazing. In the wild, mountain goats usually live 12 to 15 years, with their lifespans limited by the wearing down of their teeth. In zoos, they can live for 16 to 20 years.

They can be very competitive and protective of their space and food sources. They fight with one another for dominance. These conflicts can occasionally lead to injury or death, but are usually harmless. To avoid fighting, an animal may show a posture of nonaggression by stretching low to the ground.

In regions below the tree line, they use their fighting abilities to protect themselves and their offspring from predators, which include eagles, wolves and bears. The mountain lion is perhaps the primary predator, being powerful enough to overwhelm the largest adults and uniquely nimble enough to navigate the rocky ecosystem of the goats.

Interesting facts -

- Mountain goats are natural mountaineers and may be considered the world's best climbers. These sure-footed and agile creatures are most at home on rocky ridges and make treacherous climbing look easy.

- They are equipped with hard hooves and flexible pads for traction on rocky cliffs.

- They can jump up to 12 feet in one leap.

- They can become aggressive and protective of their space and food sources.

- They are wild animals, and they can be unpredictable. Give them space and admire them from a distance.

- If you do see a mountain goat up close, give it the respect that it deserves and steer clear.

Alligator -

In Vedic astrology, the sign of Capricorn is called Makara rashi, which means an alligator.

An alligator belongs to the crocodile family. The word alligator comes from the Spanish el lagarto, which means a lizard.

Adult alligators are black or dark olive-brown with white undersides, which provides them camouflage amongst reeds and wetland grasses.

Alligators are carnivorous. They have very strong jaws that can crack a turtle's shell. They eat fish, snails, birds, frogs and mammals that come to the water's edge. They use their sharp teeth to seize and hold prey. They swallow small prey whole. If it is very large, they will bite it, then spin on the long axis of their bodies to tear it off into easily swallowable pieces.

Both males and females have an armoured body with a muscular, flat tail. They have four short legs; the front legs have five toes, while the back legs have only four toes. Alligators have a long, rounded snout that has upward-facing nostrils at the end, which allows breathing to occur while the rest of the body is underwater. The young have bright yellow stripes on the tail, and the adults have dark stripes on the tail.

Females aggressively defend their young during their first few years of growth. Crocodilians are one of the only orders of reptiles that offer maternal care to their young. The juveniles grow about a foot a year. An adult alligator grows up to 4 feet in length.

One interesting aspect of alligator biology is that even though they do not hibernate, they undergo periods of dormancy when the weather becomes cold. They excavate a depression called a gator hole along a waterway to be used when the seasonal temperature falls.

In areas where the water level fluctuates, alligators dig themselves into hollows in the mud, which fill with water. Many other animals also use these burrows after their builder abandons them. Alligators can live up to 50 years in the wild.

Interesting facts

- Alligators have a very powerful gripping bite. Once they have their prey between their teeth, it seldom escapes their grip.

- They can consume almost a quarter of their body weight in one meal.

- They can eat their young ones. When alligators are born, they're small enough to be light snacks for the older alligators.

- Their stomachs can dissolve bones. An alligator's stomach is a hostile environment. Their stomach acids have a pH of less than 2, in the range of lemon juice and vinegar, and most soft-bodied prey is totally digested in two to three days.

- They have an antibiotic blood. They are tough not just because of the bony armour in their skin. The serum in the alligator blood is incredibly effective at combating bacteria and viruses. If a crocodile gets injured in mucky swamps, they often don't get infected.

- They are not strict carnivores, but also eat fruit when they get the chance, and might be important seed-dispersers.

- They can climb trees.

- Alligators lure waterbirds by placing sticks and twigs across their snouts while they remain submerged. When the birds go to pick up the twigs for nesting material, they chomp them.

- Alligators have no vocal cords, despite this they make sounds by sucking in and then expelling air to defend their territory, call to mates or their young, or fight off competitors.

Inference

Uttara Ashadha's determined and powerful energy is associated with animals like - mongoose, the mountain goat and the crocodile. This shows their immense capability of achieving their desired target. The quality of these animals signifies their incredible agility, sharpness, precision, determination, confidence and capability of striking at the right time and grabbing the opportunity. If they set their mind on it, there is nothing they cannot achieve. The impossible becomes possible for them.

Mythology -

Deity -

The deities associated with Uttara Ashadha are - the 10 Vishwa Devas, Lord Ganesha and Lord Vishnu.

10 Vishwa Devas

Vishwa Devas- in Sanskrit, means all gods. The word Vishva means the whole world, and Devas means gods. These deities are also called the Gana devatas. Though many devas are named in the Rig Veda, only 33 devas are counted as significant - 11 each for earth, space and heaven. According to the Vishnu Purana, out of these 33 gods, Vishva and Dharma had 10 sons who were called Vishwa Devas; they were named -

N	Vishwa Devas	Represents
1	Vasu	Goodness
2	Satya	Truth
3	Kratu	Willpower
4	Daksha	Skill
5	Kala	Time
6	Kama	Desires
7	Dhriti	Firmness - the ability to endure with patience.
8	Kuru	Ancestors
9	Puru ravas	Brightness and abundance
10	Mad ravas	Peak of intelligence, creativity and joy.

Inference

All these universal gods are benevolent and represent virtuous qualities. Uttara Ashadha natives have the potential of all these qualities of goodness within them. They have a lot of integrity in them; they keep their promises, and their actions match their thoughts and words. They are genuine speakers; if they commit to something, they will carry it out.

They are patient and can endure hardships with grace, inner strength and discipline. They have a very honest approach to life and will always stand up for a humanitarian cause.

They have a wonderful ability of being able to focus absolutely. They can understand things at a deeper level, can solve problems and can unravel the mysteries, with much ease, when they choose to pay attention to it. They can become great leaders and visionaries who can bring people together and work towards the well-being of all humanity.

Ganesha

Ganesha is one of the most worshipped deities among Hindu gods. He is the giver of wisdom and remover of obstacles. He signifies peaceful, calm and intelligent ways of dealing with all kinds of situations. The other name for Ganesha is Ganapati, which means leader of the Ganas (his people).

Ganesha is the eldest son of Goddess Parvati and Lord Shiva. Shiva Purana narrates the story of his birth, as Lord Shiva would often go away for many months, lost in his ecstatic state of being. Devi Parvati would feel alone at home. On one such occasion, when she was at the lake preparing for her bath, she took the turmeric paste which she had rubbed on her body, mixed it with mud and sculpted a human figure. She created her own toy to play with. Through her yogic practices, she had acquired some siddhis - supernatural powers, so she breathed life into the mud doll that she had sculptured with love and care. The mud doll came to life as a little boy. She spent many joyful moments and happy days with her young son.

One day, she asked her son to stand guard at the door because she was going to take a bath. Meanwhile, Lord Shiva, after many years, returned home, oblivious to the fact that Devi Parvati now had a son. Looking forward to meeting his wife, Parvati, Shiva eagerly walked towards the entrance. To his utter surprise and dismay, the young boy at the door would not let him enter his own house. In his anger, Shiva cut off the little boy's head. When Parvati saw this, she was heartbroken and ferocious and asked Shiva to bring the little boy back to life.

Shiva asked the Ganas (his companions) to get the head of the first animal they saw and come back quickly. So, they brought the head of a baby elephant, which was put in the body of the young boy, and thereafter he was called - Ganesha - the one who has an elephant head. Although Sadhguru says that it's not the head of an elephant but one of the ganas that was used to revive Ganesha, that's why he is named Ganapati. If he had an elephant's head, he would be called Gajapati (Gaja - means an elephant).

There are numerous stories of Ganesha's quick wittedness. One of the stories, as told in the Vedas, narrates this interesting incident that happened between Ganesha and Sage Vyasa. The author of the famous epic of the Mahabharata is Sage Ved Vyasa. When Sage Vyasa was planning to write the long story of the Mahabharata, he had approached Ganesha to become the scribe. Ganesha had agreed to write only if there were no breaks in his narration. To which Sage Vyasa replied - that Ganesha should not write anything that he does not understand.

Ganesha's wisdom and intelligent choices made him worthy of being the head of the Ganas, and he was appointed as the initiator of everything. Therefore, on all religious celebrations and auspicious occasions, Ganesha is honoured first. It is considered auspicious and mandatory to receive his blessings for all new beginnings.

Lord Vishnu

Lord Vishnu is also most often called Narayana, which means an exceptional human being. In the trinity of Brahma, Vishnu and Shiva, Lord Vishnu is known as the maintainer or the preserver. He is the supreme being, and his consort is Devi Lakshmi, the goddess of wealth and abundance. Vishnu Sahasranama lists 1000 names of Lord Vishnu. Each name describes a quality, attribute, or aspect of God - being omnipresent is one of his many qualities.

He is depicted as an omniscient lord sleeping on the coils of the serpent Adishesha (who represents time), floating in the primaeval ocean of milk called Kshira Sagara with his consort Devi Lakshmi. Whenever the world is threatened with evil, chaos, and destructive forces, Lord Vishnu descends in the form of an avatar (incarnation) to restore the cosmic order and protect Dharma. Here is the list of Dashavatara are the 10 primary avatars (incarnations) of Lord Vishnu.

N	Avatars of Lord Vishnu
1	Matsya - the fish
2	Kurma - the tortoise
3	Varaha - the boar
4	Narsimha - man - lion
5	Vamana - the dwarf
6	Parasurama - the angry man
7	Lord Rama - the perfect man
8	Lord Krishna - the divine statesman
9	Balarama - Lord Krishna's elder brother
10	Kalki - the mighty warrior

Inference

Just as Lord Ganesha has the wisdom and intelligence to deal with problems very effectively, not through braun but through the brain.

Uttara Ashadha natives are blessed with an exceptional sense of integrity, sincerity, intelligence, creativity, wisdom and determination. All these qualities give them the capability of winning over all kinds of difficult and easy situations, the inner turmoils and outer challenges. Lord Vishnu, being the deity, blesses them with the fortune of being able to maintain and sustain the respect and honour they earn through their hard work, integrity and good will.

Any planets sitting in the Abhijeet degrees of Uttara Ashadha (6.40 - 10.53 deg Capricorn) give fantastic and sure results during their dasha and transits. The wonderful humanistic qualities become the basis of their success. For them, success is not measured by their bank balance, but by the respect they earn in society because of their genuine efforts and selfless caring.

Uttara Ashadha padas

26.40 deg Sagitarius - 10 deg Capricorn

Padas	Degrees
1	26.40 - 30 deg Sagitarius
2	0 - 3.20 deg Capricorn
3	3.20 - 6.40 deg Capricorn
4	6.40 - 10 deg Capricorn

Pada 1

26.40 - 30 deg Sagitarius, Navamsha- Sagittarius (Lord - Jupiter)

Rashi Lord - Jupiter and Nakshatra Lord- Sun

The navamsha of the 1st Pada lies in Sagittarius; therefore, it carries the energy of the Sun and the double effect of Jupiter. This gives them very strong Sagittarian traits. Since it remains in the same sign in navamsha, it's a vargottama Pada. The lord of the sign - Jupiter and lord of the nakshatra - Sun, gives excellent results during their dashas. For example, Uttara Ashadha 1st Pada in the Ascendant will give good stability, and the natives will not have to face drastic transformative changes or challenges in their lives. Any planets sitting in this Pada will also give good, steady results during their dasha when matched with their transits.

Those who are born with their Ascendant, Sun or Moon in the 1st Pada will be very confident, creative, idealistic, righteous, arrogant and generous. The fire of the Sun and the expansiveness of Jupiter make them aspire for humongous goals; they think in global terms and are capable of achieving the targets they set for themselves through dedicated effort. Even if they don't endeavour to do anything substantial in the world, they will be the boss at home and in their workplace. In the sense that friends and family members will turn to them for advice, and they will be admired and respected for their exceptional courage and integrity.

Careers-

All positions of authority - managers, leaders, consultants, politicians, preachers, gurus, teachers, mentors, advisors, judges, doctors, scientists, astrologers, computer experts, businessmen, managers of temples and running volunteer organisations.

Pada 2

0 - 3.20 deg Capricorn Navamsha - Capricorn (Lord - Saturn)

Rashi Lord - Saturn and Nakshatra Lord- Sun

In the 2nd Pada, there will be the energy of the Sun and double Saturn. The navamsha of Capricorn gives them a very practical outlook on life. Especially after the age of 30, they will become more ambitious and service-oriented. They will make slow but steady progress in that area of life, where this Pada is placed.

For example, the 2nd Pada of Uttara Ashadha in the 2nd house will make them very ambitious about having a good flow of resources and backup of financial assets. But their progress will be slow, and it will take them longer than they expected to build up their bank balance. Though they tend to face delays and restrictions, they are blessed with incredible endurance, which gives them the ability to pass through all challenges with grit and patience.

Careers-

Consultants, managers, social workers, government jobs, lawyers, doctors, engineers, scientists, astrologers, builders, IT professionals, running recruitment agencies, factory owners and factory workers, property dealers, financial advisors, doctors, scientists, engineers, bank man, businessmen or businesswomen and working from home.

Pada 3

3.20 - 6.40 deg Capricorn, Navamsha - Aquarius (Lord - Saturn)

Rashi Lord - Saturn and Nakshatra Lord - Sun

The navamsha of the 3rd Pada is placed in Aquarius, which gives the effect of the Sun and double influence of Saturn. In this Pada, the natives will be more community-oriented. They would like to do things on a bigger scale, which can help them reach out to more people. They will be ambitious about accumulating more knowledge, resources and material assets as needed for their personal and family's use, for their job, or business enterprise.

For example, the 3rd Pada of Uttara Ashadha in the 6th house, they will be employed by a huge organisation, which will have a global reach. They will get the opportunity to serve many people through their job, or they might run or manage a huge organisation themselves.

Careers

Managers or an employee of a large company, entrepreneurs, engineers, doctors, scientists, running a Social service or working on one, running a volunteer organisation or managing one, philanthropists, astrologers, advisors, consultants, managers, public relations coordinators, film directors, writers, IT professionals, businessmen and working from home.

Pada 4

6.40 - 19 deg Capricorn, Navamsha - Pisces (Lord - Jupiter)

Rashi Lord - Saturn and Nakshatra Lord- Sun

Abhijeet - 6.40 - 10.53 deg Capricorn.

In this Pada, there will be the influence of Jupiter, Saturn and Sun. The navamsha of Pisces will give them a more spiritual approach to life. They are likely to face moral or ethical dilemmas where they have to make a choice between what is ethically correct and what is more practical or profitable in financial or worldly terms.

For example, the 4th Pada of Uttara Ashadha in the 8th house, they will face transformational situations, where their perspective of life changes from being more materialistic to more spiritual. They are likely to gain benefits through insurance or inheritance.

Abhijeet - The end of the 4th Pada is overlapped by Abhijeet, which is considered the most auspicious point in terms of achieving the final victory. In the epic of the Mahabharata, when Lord Krishna is describing his qualities to Arjuna, he says, "among the Nakshatras he is Abhijeet," which highlights the auspiciousness of this Nakshatra.

Any planets placed in this portion of Capricorn (6.40 - 10.53 deg) will give sure and fruitful results during their dasha. Here, the term victory does not necessarily mean winning over someone, but rather overcoming our own limitations or mastering a certain skill.

Careers

Teachers, philosophers, psychologists, counsellors, advisors, astrologers, doctors, scientists, researchers, psychiatrists, writers, poets, artists, actors, singers, dancers, musicians, business men and business women, advisors, consultants, psychics, priests, astrologers, mediums, tarot card readers, yoga and meditation practitioners or teachers, doctors, IT designers, illustrators, fashion or interior designers, IT professionals and working from home.

The effect of planets

Uttara Ashadha - Sagitarius	Planets that get affected
Functional Benefic - gives good results during their dasha.	Sun, Jupiter and Venus
Functional Malefic - can give problems during their dasha.	Rahu and Ketu
Functional Neutral	Moon, Mars and Saturn
Kendra Adi Pati Dosha - can be malefic	Mercury

Uttara Ashadha - Capricorn	Planets that get affected
Yoga Karka - most benefic	Venus
Functional Benefic - gives good results during their dasha.	Saturn
Functional Malefic - can give problems during their dasha.	Sun, Jupiter, Rahu and Ketu
Functional Neutral	Moon, Mars and Mercury
Kendra Adi Pati Dosha - can be malefic	Waning Moon

Uttara Ashadha Ascendant

When the Ascendant is in the 1st Pada of Uttara Ashadha, it has the influence of Jupiter and Sun. The natives will be more confident, determined, optimistic and idealistic. On the positive side, they are very honest, sincere and are genuinely willing to work towards those goals which will bring well-being to all. On the negative side, there is a danger of not having a realistic understanding of the given situation. They can feel that they are born to lead and not serve. There is no denying that they have great managerial and leadership qualities in them, because of which they can also come across as being too pompous or arrogant.

If at any time in their life they feel overcome by the feeling of arrogance, they just need to remind themselves that a leader is not the one who stands first in the line, but is willing to stand last in the line when needed - to support and guide his or her team in every way.

Their pure-hearted approach and determination bless them with much grace and abundance, because of which they are able to achieve the impossible. Through dedication, hard work and sincerity, they are capable of leading by example and not by force. Their way of life can become an inspiration for others, which can motivate many more.

The 2nd, 3rd and 4th padas of Uttara Ashadha lie in Capricorn, they will have the influence of Sun and Saturn. Those who have their Ascendant in these padas will have a more practical and grounded approach to life. Since these padas fall in Capricorn, the natives are more mature, understanding and calm. Although they are enormously capable, they don't feel the need to display or flaunt their talent for adulation. Through experience, they have learnt that true leadership also brings added responsibilities. They are capable of handling their duties with care and dedication. Because of these wonderful qualities, they have the ability to achieve success in whatever they choose to do in life.

Sun in Uttara Ashadha

When the Sun is placed in the 1st Pada of Uttara Ashadha, it will share the quality of the Sun and Jupiter. It's a fortunate placement because Sun and Jupiter are good friends, and the influence of the Sun is doubled by being placed in its own nakshatra. The natives will be confident, learned, wise, intelligent and proud, and will have a very dignified personality. For example, Sun is placed in the 1st Pada of Uttara Ashadha in the 11th house, the natives will benefit from doing business with a large organisation, or running an organisation themselves. They are likely to be successful during the dasha of the Sun or Jupiter.

The 2nd, 3rd, or 4th padas of Uttara Ashadha lie in Capricorn; if the Sun is placed in any of these padas, it will be influenced by the energy of Saturn. Since Sun and Saturn don't get along well, the native will feel the frustration, delays and obstacles in that area of life where it's placed.

For example, Sun is placed in the 10th house of career in the 2nd Pada of Uttara Ashadha, the native can experience initial delays in the start of his or her career, especially during the dasha of Sun or Saturn. They are likely to face some challenges in their profession from the authorities, the government or their father.

Moon in Uttara Ashadha

When the Moon is placed in the 1st Pada of Uttara Ashadha, it will share the influence of Jupiter and the Sun. Those who have moon in Uttara Ashadha in the 1st Pada will be confident, courageous, generous, honest, enthusiastic, idealistic and optimistic. They will be more extroverted and like to be active, both mentally and physically. They will love to travel and meet people from different cultures. They are spontaneous and honest in their approach to life and are very appreciative of those who are straightforward and not hypocritical. For example, the moon in the 1st Pada of Uttara Ashadha placed in the 10th house, they will choose a career in teaching or will do a government job. People will usually come up to them to ask for advice in their field of expertise. They will not like to take orders from anyone and will be happier doing their own business or employed in a managerial position.

The Moon in the 2nd, 3rd or 4th padas of Uttara Ashadha is placed in Capricorn. In these padas, the Moon will have the influence of the Sun and Saturn. They will be more ambitious, practical, grounded and usually hold positions of responsibility. The stability of the earth element gives them the patience to deal with all kinds of difficult situations. On the positive side, they are wise and dependable, and on the negative side, they can become ruthlessly ambitious. They have a serious and unyielding side to them, and also a more liberal and humorous side to them. Their subtle jokes are often tinged with the irony of life because of their hard-earned Saturnian wisdom. For example, the 2nd Pada of Uttara Ashadha, placed in the 11th house, they will gain from associating with large organisations. Whatever they choose to do in life can have a global reach.

The poetry of Uttara Ashadha

Uttara Ashadha - the latter undefeatable one - the final victory.

Has the capability to make history, to leave a legacy.

The intelligence shines forth like the radiance of midday sun.

The Jupitarian optimism fans the confidence.

Nothing is impossible when the goals are clear,

The determination to achieve is not far, but near.

How far can one go, how much can be done?

There is no limit when the sails are swung.

Far into the oceans of life's experience,

Enriching is the thrill of adventurous genius.

Remedies

- <u>Das Maha Vidya</u> - as described earlier.

- Pitta is the predominant tridosha of Uttara Ashadha; a regular routine of physical exercise will help to balance the fiery heat.

- Pranayama and meditation will be particularly helpful to calm the restlessness of the mind and bring clarity to thought.

- The yogic asanas always enhance the ability to focus, which in turn improves the quality of whatever you do and brings ease into all thoughts and actions.

- Yellow, orange and blue resonate well with the energy of Purva Ashadha.

- Chanting the mantra -*"Om bham Uttara Ashadha nakshatraye namah."* 108 times on days when the moon is transiting Uttara Ashadha, or on Sundays, Thursdays or Saturdays, will help to connect you with your inner self, and calm your mind.

Example

<u>Ascendant in Uttara Ashadha</u>

<u>Nadia Comaneci - Famous Olympic gymnast</u>

Born on 12th November 1961 in Onesti, Romania at 12 pm (estimated time of birth), currently 60 years old in 2021.

Nadia Elena Comaneci is a Romanian retired gymnast and a 5-time Olympic gold medalist. In 1976, at the young age of 14, she was the first gymnast to be awarded a perfect score of 10 at the Olympic Games. At the same Games (1976 Summer Olympics in Montreal), she received 6 more perfect 10s for events en route to winning 3 gold medals. At the 1980 Summer Olympics in Moscow, Nadia won 2 more gold medals and attained two more perfect 10s. During her career, she has won 9 Olympic medals and 4 World Artistic Gymnastics Championship medals. It's such an extraordinary feat that no gymnast has been able to achieve a perfect 10 in so many events till now.

Nadia was born in a small town in the Carpathian Mountains, in Romania. She was born to Gheorghe and Stefania Comaneci, and has a younger brother. Her parents separated in the 1970s. Nadia's mother, Stefania, said that she enrolled her daughter on gymnastics classes because she was a child who was so full of energy and active that she was difficult to manage.

At the age of 7, she had started getting trained for gymnastics and within 2 years began competing as a member of her hometown team and by the age of 9, she became the youngest gymnast ever to win the Romanian Nationals. At the age of 11, in 1973, she won the all-around gold, as well as the vault and uneven bars titles, at the Junior Friendship Tournament (Druzhba), an important international meet for junior gymnasts.

On 18th July 1976, Nadia made history at the Montreal Olympics. During the team compulsory portion of the competition, she was awarded the first perfect 10 in Olympic gymnastics for her routine on the uneven bars. Omega SA, the official Olympics scoreboard manufacturer, had been led to believe that competitors could not receive a perfect ten, and had not programmed the scoreboard to display this score.

Her perfect 10 thus appeared as "1.00," the only means by which the judges could indicate that she had received a 10. During the remainder of the Montreal Games, she earned 6 additional "10s".

She was the 1st Romanian gymnast to win the Olympic all-around title. She also holds the record as the youngest ever Olympic gymnastics all-around champion. The sport has revised its age-eligibility requirements. Gymnasts must be at least 16 in the same calendar year of the Olympics in order to compete during the Games. When Nadia competed in 1976, gymnasts had to be only 14 by the first day of the competition. As a result of changes to age eligibility, Nadia's record cannot be broken.

She was ranked as the "Female Athlete of the Year" by the BBC for the year 1976. Back home in Romania, Nadia was awarded the Sickle and Hammer Gold Medal for her success, and she was named a Hero of Socialist Labour. She was the youngest Romanian to receive such recognition. As of the 2020 Summer Games, she is the only gymnast to defend her Olympic gold medal in the balance beam apparatus.

Nadia is one of the world's best-known gymnasts and is credited with popularising the sport around the globe. In 2000, she was named as one of the most outstanding athletes of the 20th Century by the Laureus World Sports Academy. She has lived in the United States since 1989. She later married Bart Conner, who is also an Olympic gold medal gymnast. They have set up their own gymnast school. In 2001, she became a naturalised United States citizen and is also maintaining her Romanian citizenship. In 2006, the couple's son Dylan was born.

Nadia is a well-known figure in the world of gymnastics. She is the sports ambassador of Romania and a member of the International Gymnastics Federation Foundation. In addition, Nadia is highly involved in fundraising for a number of charities. She personally funded the construction and operation of the Nadia Comaneci Children's Clinic in Bucharest which provides low-cost and free medical and social support to Romanian children.

Analysis

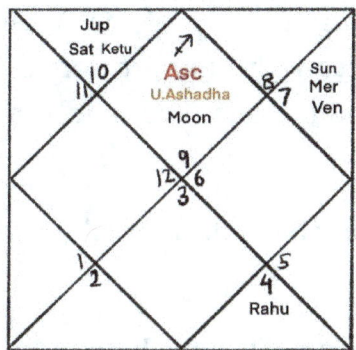
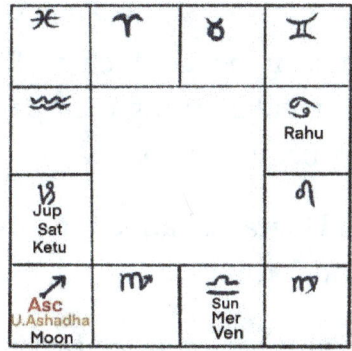

Nadia is a very strong Sagittarian personality because she is a Sagittarius Ascendant and her Moon is placed in the Ascendant.

Her <u>Ascendant is in 1st Pada of Uttara Ashadha,</u> and her Moon is placed in the 1st Pada of Purva Ashadha. Jupiter, the lord of the Ascendant, is sitting in the 2nd house of Capricorn with Saturn and Ketu. Sun, the lord of Uttara Ashadha, is sitting in the 11th house of Libra with Mercury and Venus.

As an Uttara Ashadha person, she is very talented, creative, confident and determined. The exuberance of the sun shines forth beautifully and fully in her extraordinary skill of gymnastics, and the beneficence of Jupiter has blessed her with the fortune of resources and timely training for her to explore the full potential of her talent and show her brilliance. Her achievements have made history and have set a landmark in the field of gymnastics for other gymnasts to follow. An undefeatable victory has clearly manifested in her life.

Her chart has a lot of fortunate placements where the lords of the houses are sitting happily in their own houses and are bound to give fantastic results during their dashas and transits.

- Saturn is sitting in his own house of Capricorn in the 2nd house of family assets, resources and income. Saturn is sitting with Jupiter and Ketu.

- Venus is in its own house of Libra in the 11th house of gains. Venus is sitting with the Sun and Mercury.

- Mars is sitting in his own house in Scorpio in the 12th house of long travel and foreign lands.

- Moon is very healthy and happy at 16 degrees sitting in the Ascendant.

- The Ascendant at 28 degrees is very strong, confident and mature.

- Rahu is in the 8th house of Cancer, which signifies sudden events.

- Sun is her atmakaraka at 26 degrees, sitting in the 11th house of gains, with Venus and Mercury.

- Sun (lord of the Ascendant nakshatra) and Jupiter (lord of the Ascendant) are the most significant planets in her birth chart. Both Sun and Jupiter are very strong and capable of giving fantastic results during their dashas and transits. The shadbala score for her Sun is 456, and Jupiter has a score of 452.

- The 1st Pada of Uttara Ashadha is a pushkar amsha Pada, as an Ascendant, it brought a lot of good luck and fortune.

- Her Ashtakvarga score for all houses is very good - 20 is the lowest score for the 5th house, the Ascendant has 28 points, and 38 is the highest score for the 9th house (she had a very good mentor). The 6th house (competitions) and 11th house (gains) have 32 points, and the 10th house (public image) has a score of 30.

All the above factors contributed towards her stupendous success on many occasions between 1973 to 1976. She was running her Venus mahadasha during that period. Venus, Sun and Jupiter become functional benefics for Sagittarius Ascendants - all these 3 planets are very well placed in her birth chart. In the Chara dasha system, she was running the Mahadasha of Libra, whose ruler is Venus, and it's sitting in the 11th house of gains.

In her personal dasha, she was in her 15th year, which shows that her 3rd house of heroic feats was activated. The 3rd house is the Bhavat Bhavam of the 8th house and signifies the higher values of skills and talents one polishes through effort and determination. The 3rd house also particularly represents shoulders and arms. She won her perfect 10 score for her excellence at the uneven bars, which involved the use of arms. Therefore, we can see how each of the 3 dashas in a way showed the indicators of her extraordinary success.

At the Montreal Olympics on 18th July 1976, she made history on that fortunate day, when her skill, talent, the hard work put into the training, the timing, alignment of the dashas and transits - everything fell in place for her. She was running her Venus Ketu Rahu Rahu Venus dasha at that time. Venus is sitting in the 11th house (Libra) with Sun and Mercury - this is the house of fulfilment of desires and gains. Ketu is sitting in the 2nd house (Capricorn) with Jupiter and Saturn - the effect of Ketu took her away from home and family. Rahu is sitting in the 8th house

(Cancer), which brought sudden success and amplified it beyond all expectations - even the score board was not designed to show the score of a full 10!

In a documentary made on her - 'Legend lives on' - Nadia says, "I was only 14 at that time and did not realise the impact of it." At the end of the documentary, she adds - *"When* I started, I just went to play in a gym, because it was cool to do flips, and because I could do things that my mum wouldn't let me do at home. Just finding a place to expend my energy, I ended up going to 2 Olympic Games and scoring the first perfect 10. That was not in the script for me, it just happened."

Her statement reflects the effect of sudden pleasant surprises and an unbelievable success or gains that the 8th house can bring, which can transform one's life in a huge way and in a positive way.

Here are some of her quotes -

"Gymnastics was a way for me to lead a different life."

"Wherever I go, my name connects to the sport, Nadia - gymnastics and Romania."

24
Shravana

Om mam Shravana nakshatraye namah

Zodiac degrees	10 - 23.20 deg Capricorn
Ruling planet	Capricorn - Saturn and Shravana - Moon
Sanskrit name	Shravana means to hear; it also means the rainy season, when one can hear the sound of the rain showers.
Astronomical name	Shravana is represented as 3 stars seen near the constellation of Capricorn. One of them is the brightest star in the night sky; therefore, it's easy to spot Shravana. The Vedas interpret these 3 stars as the 3 steps of the Vamana avatar, who was the incarnation of Lord Vishnu.
Symbol	Capricorn - Mountain goat and alligator Shravana - Ear and the 3 steps.
Element	Earth and water
Deity	Lord Vishnu, as Vamana avatar and Devi Saraswati
Quality	Chara -movable
Shakti	Samhana Shakti - ability to connect.
Cast	Mleccha - outcast
Gender	Female
Motivation	Artha - to gather resources
Triguna	Rajas
Tridosha	Kapha
Body parts	Ears
Direction	South and northwest

Month	August - 1st half of the Shravana month.
Bird	Peacock
Sound	ju, jay, jo, gha
Tree	Peepal tree and arka - the milkweed.
Chakras	Anhatta - Moon and Vishuddhi - Saturn
Das Maha Vidya	Devi Bhuveneshwari - Moon and Devi Kali - Saturn

Special degrees -

Yoga Tara	8 deg Capricorn - the yoga tara of Shravana lies in Uttara Ashadha. It's a point where the planet will show the strongest and sure results during its dasha.
Pushkar bhaga	14 deg Capricorn Any planets sitting at this point will give excellent results during their dasha, like the blossoming of a flower.
Pushkar amsha	2nd Pada The planets placed here will give good results during their dasha, like the blossoming of a flower.
Amrit Nadi	17.33 - 18.26 deg Capricorn This brings good results, just like the nectar that nourishes.
Visha Nadi	12.13 - 13.60 deg Capricorn Brings situations which one does not like dealing with.

Auspicious and inauspicious table -

Auspicious	Inauspicious
Activities Good for listening to advice, receiving or giving counselling and making phone calls, for traveling, especially towards the south and north west direction, for education - reading, writing, learning, music, philosophy, studying languages, culture and traditions, for religious activities and rituals, especially good for worshiping Lord Vishnu and Devi Saraswati, for initiations, taking a new name, spiritual and yogic practices and meditation, for starting new projects and organising things, for buying a property, buying new clothes, new equipment, new furniture, or entering a new house, for all medical activities, healings, remedies, preparing herbal medicines and taking them, all activities done as preventive measures, humanitarian, social and political activities, for sexual activities and for making peace.	Activities Not good for lawsuits, arguments, war, risky or aggressive activities, for physically hard manual work, for giving money, taking oaths or making promises, for endings or demolishing buildings, for worshiping fierce deities like Devi Kali, Lord Shiva in his Rudra form and Kala Bhairava, for marriage and for adopting children.

Days	Days
Sundays - only when it falls on the 1st, 4th, 6th, 7th or 12th lunar day. Mondays - only when it falls on the 2nd, 5th, 7th or 12th lunar day.	Tuesdays - only when it falls on the 1st, 2nd, 7th, 8th, 10th or Purnima (full moon day). Fridays - only when it falls on the 2nd, 3rd, 6th, 8th, 10th or 11th lunar day. Saturdays - only when it falls on the 3rd, 7th, 9th or 11th lunar day.

Compatibility table -

Shravana	Compatible with
Sexual compatibility Yoni animal	Shravana - Female monkey Purva Ashadha - Male monkey
Sign compatibility	Capricorn - Taurus and Virgo.
Nakshatra compatibility	Rohini and Hasta
Lunar day compatibility	Tritiya tithi - 3rd lunar day
Day compatibility	Monday and Saturday.
Colour compatibility	White and blue.
Numerological compatibility	2 and 8 - all numbers that add up to make 2 and 8.
Sound compatibility	Moon - semi vowels - ya, ra, la, va, ssa, sha, sa, ha, lr, rr Saturn - labial sounds - pa, pha, ba, bha, ma

Sign Lord and nakshatra lord - Saturn and Moon - as described earlier.

Shravana is the 3rd of the Moon-ruled nakshatras, where the energy of Saturn and Moon has matured and evolved into a higher and deeper level of understanding. The Saturn moon combination gives psychic abilities which can have both the effect of fear and of deeper spiritual experiences.

This is because the Moon is our emotions, and Saturn is restrictions which can cause fear and anxiety. Moreover, Saturn, being a karmic planet, when associated with the moon, influences the mind with the transparency of karmic patterns of this life or the previous life. This can give one the ability to have psychic intuitions, which are not normally perceivable by the conscious mind.

Quality, element, motivation, triguna, tridosha and chakras - as described earlier.

Shakti - Samhana shakti - ability to connect.

The word Shravana literally means to listen. Listen to what?

Listen to their inner voice, listen to the sounds of nature, listen to the silence and listen to the cosmic presence. Through listening, they learn how to truly connect.

The ancient sages named the month of monsoons as Shravana. It is the month when heavy rains pour in the tropical climate of India.

It is also a nakshatra which has the qualities of water and earth. Without the fluidity and lubrication of water, no chemical connection is possible. Water nourishes the earth and makes it possible for the roots to connect to the soil and get nourishment.

Water is the basis of our feelings and emotional connections, too. The phrase, 'our chemistry matches,' comes from how one feels when they come in contact with certain individuals. Sadhguru explains that for every thought and feeling there is a corresponding chemical reaction in our body, which instigates action. In turn, every action triggers a chemical reaction which influences our thoughts, feelings and emotions. It's a feedback loop which continues to happen within us unconsciously.

Unless we turn our attention inwards and look at the pattern of our thoughts and feelings closely, we assume everything to be happening automatically. When we begin to realise that everything that happens within and outside, we are responsible for it, we cannot unfold or understand the intricate workings of our own thoughts and emotions. And when we understand the deeper inferences of how each emotion affects us, we can take charge of our well-being consciously with full awareness of the consequences.

Inference

Those who are born with their Ascendent, Sun or Moon in Shravana have a very keen sense of hearing, not just at the level of audible sound waves, but they can feel the inaudible sound frequencies - the subsonic waves, if they pay attention to their inner spiritual side.

Shravana natives are blessed with the ability to pay attention, hear and understand the deeper implications of everything that happens within them and around them. Whenever they genuinely take time to listen to others and be by their side at the time of need, it miraculously heals their own emotions too. They have the gift of truly listening and thereby understanding the pain or joy of others. They have a wonderful knack of clearing any misunderstandings between 2 friends and help them reunite.

Symbolic signification

Capricorn - as described earlier.

Shravana - The 3 steps of Vamana avatar and the ear.

The 3 steps -

The Vedas describe Vamana avatar as the dwarf god, who was the 5th avatar of Lord Vishnu. The story narrated in the Puranas states that - long ago, there lived King Bali who was the King of the asuras and had defeated Indra (the king of heaven) in a fierce battle between the suras (the ones who live in harmony) and asuras (the ones who create havoc and destruction). So, Indra and the suras ultimately went to seek help from Lord Vishnu, who agreed to restore Indra to power.

To do so, Vishnu incarnated as the dwarf-Brahmin, Vamana. King Bali used to conduct various sacrifices and fire rituals to establish his victory among other kingdoms. One of these ceremonies was attended by Vamana. According to the tradition in those days, the one who conducted the yagna (fire ritual) had to offer a donation to the Brahmin who attended the yagna. When asked by King Bali, Vamana requested only 3 steps of land. Bali agreed to do so, despite being warned by his guru Shukracharya about Vamana's true nature and purpose. When the time to donate came, Vamana expanded his size. In his 1st step, he covered the whole earth, in his 2nd step, he covered the whole sky, and there was no space left for him to place his 3rd step. At that point, Vamana asked Bali, Where can he place his 3rd step, Bali offered his head and said, "You can place your 3rd step on my head." This is how the 3 worlds were restored to Indra, and Bali and the asuras were banished to the netherworlds.

The Vedas describe the 3 steps of Vamana as - "Vishnu strides over this and all that exists. Thrice he plants his foot, on earth, in the intermediate space, and in heaven," says Sakamuni. "On the mountain of sunrise, on the meridian, and on the mountain of sunset," says Aurnavabha. It is said that Lord Vishnu incarnated as Vamana to protect the righteous and destroy the wicked, and to establish dharma in a peaceful way without having to fight a battle.

Inference

Shravana natives are apt at solving even war-like situations and challenging problems in a peaceful manner. One should not underestimate their capability because of their quiet way of doing things. They believe in peaceful solutions rather than violent, aggressive or forced ways of dealing with things.

Mythology -

Deity - Lord Vishnu and Devi Saraswati

Lord Vishnu - as the Vamana avatar

Lord Vishnu, in his 5th incarnation, had come as a dwarf in the form of Vamana, the Brahmin, to establish dharma - righteousness (as described above).

Devi Saraswati

The word Saraswati appears both as a reference to a river and as a significant deity in the Rigveda. In some interpretations, the word Sara is referred to as sva, which means the true self. Therefore, the name Saraswati would translate to - She who helps us realise our true self.

Saraswati is a Sanskrit fusion word of saras, which means pooling water, but also sometimes is translated as speech, and vati- means she who possesses. It is also a composite word of surasa-vati, which means the one with plenty of water.

Saraswati is also the name of the mighty river that flowed during the era of the Harappa and Mohenjo-Daro civilisations in India. The archeological findings suggest that around 4000 years ago, River Saraswati flowed in its full might and glory along the plains of the Indus region. Which is the present-day region of India and Pakistan stretching from the Himalayas in the north to the Bay of Kutch in Gujarat in the south. Over time, the river Saraswati dried up, and the Indus Valley Civilisation declined into smaller agricultural communities.

The Sarasvati River is mentioned in the Rig Veda, which shows that it played an important role in the Vedic religion. As a physical river, in the oldest texts of the Rig Veda, she is described as a "great and holy river in north-western India." She is also described as a powerful river and a mighty flood. The Sarasvati is also considered by Hindus to exist in a metaphysical form, in which it forms a confluence with the sacred rivers Ganges and Yamuna, at the Triveni Sangam. The Sarasvati river is considered the heavenly river Milky Way, which is seen as "a road to immortality and heavenly after-life."

Saraswati is also the Hindu goddess of knowledge, melody, language, eloquence, creativity, music, art, speech, wisdom and learning. She is a part of the trinity (Tridevi) of Saraswati, Lakshmi, and Parvati. All 3 forms of the feminine unite with the trinity of Brahma, Vishnu, and Shiva to create, maintain, destroy and regenerate the Universe.

She is generally shown to have 4 arms, holding a book, a rosary, a water pot and a musical instrument called Veena. Some Hindus celebrate the festival of Vasant Panchami, the 5th day of spring, known as Saraswati Puja or Saraswati Jayanti in many parts of India, in her honour. They mark the day by helping young children learn how to write the letters of the alphabet on that day.

She represents - waters that purify, vach (speech) that purifies and knowledge that purifies. She is the goddess whose flow purifies the self of a person. Saraswati is invoked to remind us to meditate, to focus on virtues and on the essence of one's activity.

The hymns of the Rig Veda describe her as -

"Ambitmay naditmay devitmay Saraswati."

Meaning - Best of mothers, the best of rivers, best of goddesses, Saraswati.

<u>Inference</u>

Shravana natives are very good at maintaining, planning and organising things. Their calm approach to life makes them wonderful managers and administrators. They love to learn, they are very talented in all forms of music and art and can become excellent singers and musicians.

Ultimately, through all their pursuits of worldly activities, they seek to know the essence of their true self.

Shravana padas

10 - 23.20 deg Capricorn

Padas	Degrees
1	10 - 13.20 deg Capricorn
2	13.20 - 16.40 deg Capricorn
3	16.40 - 20 deg Capricorn
4	20 - 23.20 deg Capricorn

<u>Pada 1</u>

10 - 13.20 deg Capricorn, Navamsha- Aries (Lord - Mars)

Rashi Lord - Saturn and Nakshatra Lord- Moon

The navamsha of the 1st Pada lies in Aries, therefore it carries the energy of the Moon, Saturn and Mars. In this Pada, the natives will be more energetic, determined, enthusiastic and ambitious about achieving their goals. Saturn gives discipline, Mars gives motivation and drive, and the Moon gives imagination. They will love to initiate new projects and be the pioneers in their field.

For example, the 1st Pada of Shravana in the 4th house will make them ambitious about having a comfortable home, with all the necessary facilities. They are most likely to have an interest and a career which deals with buying or selling properties. Their mother will be a very spiritual or religious person and will be a wonderful listener.

<u>Careers</u>

Farmers, botanists, herbalists, doctors, pharmacists and nurses, engineers, bankers, accountants, musicians, artists, actors, industrialists, factory owners, grocery store owners, professions connected to food industry, hotel managers, shipping business, sports careers, interior decorators, architects, designers, jewellers, business, property dealers, IT professionals and builders

<u>Pada 2</u>

13.20 - 16.40 deg Capricorn, Navamsha - Taurus (Lord - Venus)

Rashi Lord - Saturn and Nakshatra Lord- Moon

In the 2nd Pada, there will be the energy of the Moon, Saturn and Venus. The navamsha of Taurus gives them more grounding and stability. It's a pushkar amsha Pada, which highlights the fortunate aspect of this Pada. Venus is the yoga Karka for Capricorn Ascendants only. It will give wonderful results during its dasha, especially after the age of 30, the natives will have good success in their career and happiness and comfort in their family life. Wherever Venus is placed in the birth chart will show the area of life that they will benefit from most.

For example, the 2nd Pada of Shravana in the 2nd house, they will be born into a family that has all the comforts and resources that can provide a good start to life. Especially after the age of 30, they will have a good, steady source of income. If Venus, the lord of Taurus, is placed in the 10th house, their career will pick up after marriage. Their spouse or partner will prove very lucky for them.

Careers

Businessmen, artists, actors, singers, dancers, musicians, designers, florists, beauticians, wedding planners, party venue hirers, gardners, farmers, dairy owners, hotel managers, cooks, restaurant owners, writers, poets, leaders, gurus, mystics, saints, IT professionals, salesmen, journalists, lawyers, consultants, teachers, doctors, pharmacist, nurses, psychologists, yoga teachers, ayurveda doctors, architects, interior decorators, priests, astrologers, accountants and bankers.

Pada 3

16.40 - 20 deg Capricorn, Navamsha - Gemini (Lord - Mercury)

Rashi Lord - Saturn and Nakshatra Lord - Moon

The navamsha of the 3rd Pada is placed in Gemini, which gives the effect of the Moon, Saturn and Mercury. In this Pada, the natives will be more communicative and flexible about their approach to life. The effect of the moon and Mercury (especially if Mercury is retrograde, or afflicted with Rahu or Ketu) can make them very quick in their movements and in their style of talking. They will tend to be impatient with those who seem to move slowly or do things slowly. They will be quick-witted and can make excellent actors, lawyers, salesmen or saleswomen, businessmen or businesswomen. They will be curious about everything and will love to learn about and latest IT technology.

For example, the 3rd Pada of Shravana in the 3rd house, they will love to travel and will have many friends. They will get along well with their neighbours and siblings.

Careers

All careers that require creativity, art, IT professionals, writers, poets, businessmen, lawyers, artists, actors, singers, dancers, musicians, designers, florists, beauticians, wedding planners, party venue hirers, gardners, farmers, dairy owners, hotel managers, cooks, restaurant owners, writers, poets, leaders, gurus, mystics, saints, salesmen, journalists, consultants, teachers, doctors, pharmacist, nurses, psychologists, yoga teachers, ayurveda doctors, architects, interior decorators, priests, astrologers, accountants and bankers.

Pada 4

20 - 23.20 deg Capricorn, Navamsha - Cancer (Lord - Moon)

Rashi Lord - Saturn and Nakshatra Lord- Moon

In this Pada, there will be the influence of the double moon and Saturn. The navamsha of Cancer will make them more emotional, especially as they grow older. After the age of 30, they will become more sensitive to people's remarks. They will be imaginative and intuitive and can make excellent writers, astrologers, tarot card readers or psychics.

For example, the 4th Pada of Shravana in the 7th house, they will be attracted to people who are on the spiritual path. Their partner will be religiously and spiritually inclined. Their career will involve talking to people and listening to their complaints. They will be good at understanding the problems of others from a deeper perspective; therefore, they can make very good advisors and counsellors.

Careers

Insurance consultants, counsellors, advisors, hotel managers, cooks, restaurant owners, dietitian, cake and sweet shop owners, grocery store owners, working at a clothes shop - salesman or saleswoman, accountants, bankers, child care takers, nursery owners, writers, poets, businessmen, artists, singers, dancers, musicians, designers, florists, beauticians, gardners, farmers, dairy owners, journalists, architects, interior decorators, priests, astrologers, doctors, pharmacist, nurses, psychologists, yoga teachers and ayurvedic doctors.

The effect of planets

Shravana - Capricorn	Planets that get affected
Yoga Karka - most benefic	Venus
Functional Benefic - gives good results during their dasha.	Saturn
Functional Malefic - can give problems during their dasha.	Sun, Jupiter, Rahu and Ketu
Functional Neutral	Moon, Mars and Mercury
Kendra Adi Pati Dosha - can be malefic	Waning Moon

Shravana Ascendant

Shravana Ascendant natives will be calm, composed, stable, wise, dependable and determined. They are soft spoken and like to do things in a methodical way. They are very conscious of their duties and have excellent counselling skills. The Satarian wisdom knows that sheer idealism is impractical, that spontaneous enthusiasm can only initiate things, but does not have the endurance to see it through. It takes the tenacity of experience, patience and dedication to manifest dreams into reality. They are willing to impart their hard-earned wisdom, only when asked to do so, because they know that one learns best from his or own experience.

The stability of the earth and the nourishment of water give them a wonderful sense of grounding, humility and practicality. They have the enduring quality of working steadily towards their goals. On the negative side, they can become ruthless, selfish, narrow-minded, rigid, fearful, lonely and depressed.

They learn a lot through listening and have a wonderful ability to stay focused for long periods. Their success comes from their resilience and patience to follow their plans and projects to completion.

Like a mountain goat, they are sure-footed and comfortable at heights. They climb the ladder of success in their career through their own determined effort.

Sun in Shravana

When the Sun is placed in Shravana, it will share the qualities of Saturn and the Moon. Since Saturn and the Sun are enemies, but the moon is friendly with everyone, it will soften the effect of feeling frustrated because of the delays. The natives will be calmer and mature, and will know how to wait for things to fall into place. The warmth and confidence of the Sun will give them hope, the Saturnian wisdom will bring caution, and the friendly Moon will bring in the spiritual and psychic gift. This beautiful combination will help the natives sail through any kind of difficult situation and emerge victorious.

For example, if the Sun in Shravana is placed in the 7th house, the natives will face some problems with business partnerships, relationships, or with their spouse, during the dasha of Sun, Saturn or Moon. The placement of Saturn and the Moon can show the causes and effects of the possible problems. The best remedy for them will be to give more time and attention to others (who matter to them) and listen to their opinions, problems or suggestions.

Moon in Shravana

When the Moon is placed in Shravana, it brings great love for learning music and art. In Shravana, the moon reaches the highest point of lunar energy. They are very loving, caring and emotional. They are great listeners and imbibe knowledge easily. They will be fortunate in terms of earning a good, steady income through their skill and knowledge. They often travel to foreign lands to learn new skills or pursue higher education.

They are selfless and like to help people without any ulterior motive or expectation. They will be interested in learning about herbs, ayurveda and pharmaceutical medicines and will have a very good understanding of these subjects. They will be spiritually and religiously inclined because they are very sensitive to feeling subtle vibrational changes within themselves and in the environment around them.

For example, if the moon is in Shravana in the 9th house, they will travel away from home, or to a foreign country for higher education. They have the capability of becoming an excellent teacher in subjects related to medicine, herbs, chemistry, spirituality, religion, psychology and astrology. Their profession can involve dealing with water or fluids in some way, or their father will have a career in one of these fields, and they will follow that profession.

The poetry of Shravana

Shravana - the gift of listening,

The showers of rain bring forth the nurturing.

The tranquil calm after the rain,

Returns the smile on faces again.

Goals are reached in steps three,

An ambition that binds, but longs to be free.

Responsibilities and duties - grind the mill,

The will power fuels - to have its fill.

By serving others - I listen and learn,

The respect and love - I earn.

Love - a universal connection,

Fills my heart with joy - an act of devotion.

Remedies

- <u>Das Maha Vidya</u> **-** as described earlier.
- Taking time to listen to others, rather than imposing your decision or opinion on them, will work as a great remedy. Just by being a good listener, they will earn many friends and their good wishes.

- Whenever they get an opportunity, a wonderful remedy for them will be to help their friends or relatives to clear any misunderstandings between them. Being the middle person who helps to bring 2 people closer and improve their relationship will always benefit them in terms of their problems getting solved in unexpected ways.

- Kapha is the predominant tridosha of Shravana. Consciously developing an active lifestyle and including fresh fruits and salads in your diet will be helpful. Avoid sleeping for too long, especially during the day.

- The yogic asanas, pranayama and meditation always enhance the ability to focus, which in turn improves the quality of whatever you do and brings ease into all thoughts and actions.

- White and blue colours resonate well with the energy of Shravana.

- Chanting the mantra - *"Om mam Shravana nakshatraye namah."* 108 times on days when the moon is transiting Uttara Ashadha, or on Sundays, Thursdays or Saturdays, will help to connect you with your inner self.

Example

Moon in Shravana

Swami Ram Dev - Yoga teacher and co-founder of Patanjali Ayurveda and yoga centre.

Born on 25th December 1965, 8:24 pm, Mahendragarh, India.

Ram Kisan Yadav, now known as Baba Ramdev, is primarily known for popularising Yoga and Ayurveda in India. He has been organising and conducting large yoga camps since 2002, broadcasting his yoga classes on various TV channels. He co-founded Patanjali Ayurved Ltd with his colleague Balkrishna.

Ramdev was born in a Hindu family in 1965 to Ramniwas Yadav and Gulabo Devi at Saiyad Pur village of Mahendragarh district, Haryana. Both of his parents were farmers. He comes from the tradition of the Arya Samaj. At a young age, he was profoundly affected by Satyarth Prakash, a Hindi book written by Maharishi Dayanand Saraswati, who was a renowned religious and social reformer and was the founder of the monotheistic Arya Samaj movement.

Ram Dev fled from home and ardently began to study Indian scriptures, Yoga and Sanskrit in various Gurukul schools. At Arsh Gurukul Khanpur, he met his life-long associate Balkrishna. Here, he and Balkrishna spent 3 years together, developing their friendship as they studied.

At the age of 25, Ram Dev adopted sannyasa and took the name Baba Ramdev. He spent the next 3 years in the Himalayas, near Gangotri, in search of moksha. While living in Kalwa Arsh Gurukul in Jind district, Haryana, Ramdev offered free yoga training to villagers. Then he moved to Haridwar in Uttarakhand, where he practised self-discipline and meditation, and spent some more years studying the ancient Indian scriptures.

Towards the end of the 1990s, farming conditions in his native village worsened due to the region's depleting water table, which prompted Ramdev's move to Haridwar. Subsequently, he called his family to Haridwar. Ramdev's family members have played different roles in his ayurveda ventures depending on their capabilities. His father oversees activities in Patanjali Ayurveda, and his brother Rambharat looks after the company's finances.

Ramdev's main yoga centre, called 'Yog Gram,' is based in Haridwar, where he practices and teaches yoga in the mornings and evenings in an auditorium, which is also broadcast on TV channels. In 1995, Ramdev founded the Divya Yog Mandir Trust. In 2003, Aastha TV began featuring him in its morning yoga slot and gained a large following. A large number of people, including some celebrities from India and abroad, have attended his Yoga camps. He also has students in some foreign countries, including the United Kingdom, the United States, and Japan. He has also addressed Muslim clerics at their seminary in Deoband, Uttar Pradesh.

Patanjali Ayurved is a consumer-packaged goods company, based in Haridwar, that was started by Ramdev and Balkrishna in 2006. According to a company official, sales as of early March 2016 were Rs 4,500 crore. Balkrishna remains the CEO of Patanjali Ayurved with 94% shareholding and supervises its day-to-day activities, while Ramdev remains the face of the company and makes most of the business decisions.

Over a 20-year career, he became the face of Patanjali Ayurved. Patanjali went on to become one of the highest-grossing companies in India. In 2012, Ramdev established the Divya Yog Pharmacy at Kankhal in Haridwar.

In June 2020, Patanjali Ayurved announced a drug named Coronil for COVID-19 treatment. Ramdev, by organising a press conference regarding the same matter, had claimed that Coronil has cured Covid-19 patients. The Indian government has allowed Patanjali Ayurved to market Coronil as an immunity booster but not a cure.

Analysis -

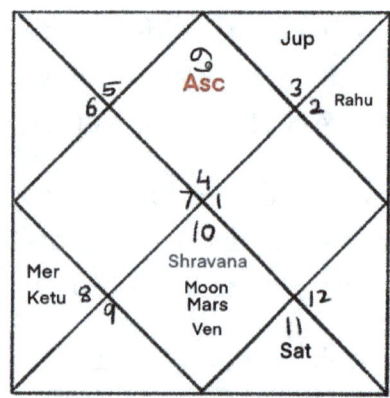

His <u>Moon is in the 1st Pada of Shravana</u> in the 7th house of Capricorn. The Moon is sitting with Mars and Venus in the 7th house of partnerships. He is a Cancer Ascendant, Moon, the lord of the Ascendant, is sitting in the 7th house in the nakshatra of the Moon (Shravana). This shows that the Moon has a strong influence on his birth chart. The shadbala score of 537 confirms that the moon has a very nourishing and positive effect in his horoscope. This also gives him a very caring nature, who genuinely cares for the well-being of the other person.

Moon in Shravana has given him a spiritual inclination and an inherent knowledge about Ayurveda, herbs and yoga. Moon, Venus and Mars placed in the 7th house have given him great strength, determination, resilience, ambition, passion and motivation to spread the knowledge of yoga and ayurveda to as many people as possible. Capricorn, being his 7th house, shows that his career and public image will involve serving the public in some way.

Venus is also sitting in the 7th house, which is the lord of the 11th house of gains and the 4th house of home and mother. All his thoughts, feelings and actions are devoted towards his home country and his people. Rahu is sitting in the 11th house of gains, which amplifies the effect. Patanjali Ayurveda, as a business, became a huge success and is known globally.

Saturn, the lord of the 7th house of Capricorn, is sitting in the 8th house of Aquarius, which is placed 2nd from the moon. The 8th house brings sudden events and gains from incomes other than regular income. This placement becomes the gain of the previous house and forms a sunapha yoga, which gives him a dignified personality, a kingly presence, wealth, intelligence and good reputation.

Patanjali is an Indian multinational company that sells ayurvedic products, based in Haridwar, India. It was founded by Baba Ramdev and Acharya Balkrishna in the year 2006. He was running his <u>Jupiter Mercury Mars dasha</u> at that time. Jupiter, the lord of the 6th house and 9th house, is sitting in the 12th house of Gemini. Mercury is sitting with Ketu in the 5th house of Scorpio. Mercury is the lord of the 3rd house and the 12th house. Mars is sitting in the 7th house of Capricorn with the Moon and Venus. Mars is the lord of the 10th house and the 5th house. Jupiter gave the beneficence, Mercury gave the intelligence, and Mars gave the energy and drive to fruitify the efforts.

25
Dhanishta

Om yam ram Dhanishta nakshatraye namah

Zodiac degrees	23.20 deg Capricorn - 6.40 deg Aquarius Capricorn - 1st and 2nd Pada Aquarius - 3rd and 4th Pada
Ruling planet	Capricorn and Aquarius - Saturn Dhanishta - Mars
Sanskrit name	Dhanishta means the wealthiest, the most beneficent, the most heard of, the most famous.
Astronomical name	Dhanishta is represented by 4 stars seen just above the constellations of Capricorn and Aquarius. These stars were seen in the shape of a rhombus - a drum, by the ancient sages.
Symbol	Capricorn - Mountain goat and alligator Aquarius - water bearer Dhanishta - A musical drum - a damru - mridangam
Element	Earth - Capricorn and Air - Aquarius
Deity	Ashta Vasus - the guardians of the 8 directions
Quality	Chara -movable - Capricorn Fixed - sthira - Aquarius
Shakti	Khyapaytri Shakti - Fame and abundance, and to bring Poe and please together.
Cast	Kshatriya - warrior
Gender	Female - Capricorn and Male - Aquarius
Motivation	Artha - to gather resources - Capricorn Kama - to fulfil desires - Aquarius
Triguna	Rajas - Capricorn and Tamas - Aquarius

Tridosha	Kapha - Capricorn and Vata - Aquarius
Body parts	Back and anus
Direction	West, South, Southeast, East and South West
Month	August - Shravana month.
Bird	Crow
Sound	ga, gee, gu, gay
Tree	Khejri tree - Indian Mesquite
Chakras	Muladhara - Mars and Vishuddhi - Saturn
Das Maha Vidya	Devi Bagalamukhi - Mars and Devi Kali - Saturn

Special degrees -

Yoga Tara	2 yoga tara points - 22.30 Capricorn in Shravana and 24 deg Capricorn in Dhanishta. It's a point where the planet will show the strongest and sure results during its dasha.
Exaltation	28 deg Capricorn - Maximum exaltation of Mars. When Ketu is placed at this degree, it will give excellent results during its dasha. It will be particularly supportive for ending something.
Mulatrikona	0 - 20 deg Aquarius - Mukatrikona of Saturn. When Saturn is placed at these degrees in Aquarius, it will become very strong and will give excellent results during its dasha.
Amrit Nadi	0.53 - 1.46 deg Aquarius This brings good results, just like the nectar that nourishes.
Visha Nadi	25.33 - 26.25 deg Capricorn Brings situations which one does not like dealing with.

Auspicious and inauspicious table -

Auspicious	Inauspicious
Activities Good for creative activities, especially music and dance, for all group activities, mega celebrations and concerts, for buying movable and immovable properties, buying new clothes, jewellery and gemstones, for lending money and all financial transactions, learning IT skills, using weapons, and educational pursuits, for career related activities, for fame and recognition, for travelling, for interactive and energetic activities, religious activities and rituals, for meditation and yogic practices, for gardening and for treating diseases.	Activities Not good for marriage and sexual activities or new partnerships, for activities that restrict, endings, or giving up old habits, for quiet, homely activities and for diplomatic or gentle activities.

Days	Days
Mondays - only when it falls on the 2nd, 7th or 12th lunar day.	Sundays - only when it falls on the 3rd, 4th, 8th, 9th, 13th or 14th lunar day.
Tuesdays - only when it falls on the 3rd, 6th, 11th or 13th lunar day.	Tuesdays - only when it falls on the 1st, 2nd, 7th, 8th, 10th or Purnima (full moon day).
Saturdays - only when it falls on the 2nd, 4th, 7th, 9th, 12th or 14th lunar day.	Wednesdays - only when it falls on the 2nd, 3rd, 8th or 9th lunar day.
	Fridays - only when it falls on the 2nd, 3rd, 6th, 8th, 10th or 11th lunar day.

Compatibility table -

Dhanishta	Compatible with
Sexual compatibility Yoni animal	Dhanishta - Male Lion Purva Purva Bhadrapada - Female Lioness
Sign compatibility	Capricorn - Taurus and Virgo Aquarius - Gemini and Libra
Nakshatra compatibility	Mrigashira and Chitra
Lunar day compatibility	Ashtami tithi - 8th lunar day
Day compatibility	Tuesday and Saturday.
Colour compatibility	Red and blue.
Numerological compatibility	8 and 9 - all numbers that add up to make 8 and 9.
Sound compatibility	Mars - guttural sounds - ka, kha, ga, gha, kna Saturn - labial sounds - pa, pha, ba, bha, ma

Sign Lord and nakshatra lord - Saturn and Mars - as described earlier.

Dhanishta is the 3rd of the Mars-ruled nakshatras, where the energy of Saturn and Mars has expanded into becoming all-inclusive. They are very community-oriented. They like to do things, plan projects and offer help that can benefit a lot of people. Rahu is the co - lord of Aquarius, which amplifies all these qualities. Moreover, Aquarius is the highest of the Kama houses, which gives many desires and also has the capacity to fulfil them.

Quality, element, motivation, triguna, tridosha and chakras - as described earlier.

Shakti - Khyapaytri Shakti - Fame and abundance, and to bring people together.

Those who are born with their Ascendant, Sun or Moon in Dhanishta have the ability to organise events, bring people together and arrange huge functions. The first 2 padas of Dhanishta lie in Capricorn, so the natives will like to stick to the traditional way of doing things, but in the later 2 padas, they will like to try new ways, use the latest technology and expand their reach globally to as many people as possible.

They are blessed with the gift of abundance in terms of reaching out and serving as many people as possible, not in terms of hoarding things that are not needed. The more they share, the more they receive, the less they give, the less is the abundance. They feel an inner fulfilment when they share their wealth, resources, time, knowledge, art or skills for the benefit of humanity.

Symbolic signification

Capricorn - as described earlier, Aquarius - water bearer, and

Dhanishta - The drum

Water bearer

In olden days, when the only source of drinking water was wells and rivers. There was a profession of water bearers, who would have a sack full of water on their back (which was made from animal skin) and would go around giving water to the thirsty and needy.

Story of Bhai Kanhaiya -

There is a beautiful incident that happened in the year 1704. Bhai Kanhaiya (1648–1718) was a devoted Sikh disciple of the 9th and the 10th Sikh Guru. He became famous for offering water indiscriminately to all wounded soldiers on the battlefield, irrespective of the fact that they belonged to the enemy camp.

He was often seen carrying a mashak (a pouch made of goat's skin that was used to carry water from one place to another), to serve water to anyone who was thirsty.

He took on the task of quenching the thirst of the wounded soldiers in the battle of Anandpur Sahib in 1704. He did this sewa (voluntary service) with love, without any discrimination between the Guru's Sikh soldiers and the Mughal armies' soldiers. His act of compassion stirred up stern criticism amongst his fellow Sikhs, who complained to Guru Gobind Singh Ji, pointing out that Bhai Kanhaiya was serving water to the wounded soldiers from the enemy camp. They were especially annoyed because the Mughals had surrounded the city and stopped all their food supplies, and here was Bhai Kanhaiya sharing with them what little water they had.

Guru Gobind Singh summoned Bhai Kanhaiya and said, "These brave Sikhs are saying that you go and give water to the enemy, it quenches their thirst and they recover to fight again – Is this true?" Bhai Kanhaiya replied, "Yes, my Guru, what they say is true. But I saw no Mughal or Sikh on the battlefield. I only saw human beings." Guru Ji smiled and blessed Bhai Kanhaiya and said, "Bhai Kanhaiya Ji, you have understood the true message of Gurbani." Guruji also gave him a balm and said, "From now on, you should also put this balm on their wounds when needed."

Bhai Kanhaiya died in 1718 after retiring in his village, Sodhara. His life has been an inspiring example of selfless service to humanity, which becomes possible only when we see divinity in all beings.

Inference

The latter 2 padas of Dhanishta are placed in Aquarius, the sign of the water bearer. The natives will be more inclined to do some kind of voluntary work and help humanity. They will either be involved in working for a voluntary organisation or running their own. Or they will have a quiet routine of going and serving in the temple, or as a philanthropist giving financial help, donations, or charity wherever needed.

The musical drum

Dhanishta is symbolised by a musical drum - mridangam. This signifies that they have a great sense of rhythm and music. They can become excellent musicians, dancers and singers. In olden days, the drum was also used to make community announcements. Those who are born with their Ascendant of the moon in Dhanishta are good at spreading information or advertising for a particular product or an event.

It does not mean they will go around making announcements, but through writing or through their excellence of work, the word will spread.

Mythology -

Deity - Ashta Vasudevas

The Vedas describe a group of 8 deities, known as Ashta-Dikpala, which literally means guardians of the 8 directions. Each deity rules a specific direction. This table shows the directions, the Sanskrit names and the ruling deities.

N	Direction	Sanskrit name	Ruling deity
1	North	Uttara	Kubera
2	South	Dakshina	Yama
3	East	Purab	Indra
4	West	Paschim	Varuna
5	North east		Ishana
6	South east		Agni
7	North west		Vayu
8	South west		Niritti

Besides the 8 guardians, these 2 directions are added for the top and bottom, Brahma - Zenith is the farthest up from the gravitational force and Vishnu - Nadir - the direction in which gravity pulls. These are called the Dasa Dikpalas - the guardians of the 10 directions.

The 8 Vasus are also called the elemental gods, where their qualities are described according to the element they represent. The earlier Vedic texts refer to the Vasus as the attendant deities of Lord Vishnu - they were then called Vasubandhu's (friends of Vasudeva - the lord of the universe), later they came to be known as Vasus.

These 8 Vasus were said to be wealthy and very good dancers and singers. Here is the list of the Ashta Vasus and their elemental qualities.

N	Ashta Vasus	Qualities
1	Apa	Water - the water goddess of Purva Ashadha.
2	Dhruva	The fixed pole stars.
3	Dhara	Stream of water - as a water bearer pouring water from a container, the symbol of Aquarius.
4	Anila	Wind - Vayu - the deity of Swati.
5	Soma	The Moon - the deity of Mrigashira.
6	Anala	Fire - Agni - the deity of Kritika.
7	Pratyusha	Dawn - sunrise
8	Prabhasa	Light - the morning light.

Inference

The deity of the nakshatra always gives a good insight into the nature of that nakshatra. Ashta Vasus, as the guardians of direction, give Dhanishta natives a very good sense of navigation and direction. They are good at giving directions and remembering travel routes.

We can see that on the whole, it's a very fortunate nakshatra that has immense possibilities of fulfilling desires. Moreover, the word Dhan literally means wealth. It means both - the one who is attracted to wealth and the one who attracts wealth to them (spiritual and worldly). Aquarius, being the original 11th house, provides the resources in abundance to fulfil desires.

Dhanishta padas

23.20 deg Capricorn - 6.40 Aquarius

Padas	Degrees
1	23.20 - 26.40 deg Capricorn
2	26.40 - 30 deg Capricorn
3	0 - 3.20 deg Aquarius
4	3.20 - 6.40 deg Aquarius

Pada 1

23.20 - 26.40 deg Capricorn, Navamsha- Leo (Lord - Sun)

Rashi Lord - Saturn and Nakshatra Lord- Mars

The navamsha of the 1st Pada lies in Leo, therefore it carries the energy of the Sun, Saturn and Mars. In this Pada, the natives will be very determined and resolute. Since Sun and Saturn don't get along well, they can feel an inner struggle, frustration, impatience and dilemma about making choices in life. For example, they can get caught in the confusion - whether to rebel against the authorities, or follow the tradition, or leave quietly. And if they are in charge of the situation, everybody may not agree with their decisions, which can cause surface tension.

Since the 1st pada is placed in Capricorn, the natives will be more career-oriented. The effect of Mars and Sun gives them a very pitta predominant constitution; they are ambitious and motivated to do something unique and extraordinary. They should develop a routine of doing some physical exercise, or hatha yoga and pranayama, which will help to calm their restlessness.

The navamsha of Leo gives them a very dignified personality; they are very generous with their compliments and expect others to appreciate their efforts too. They have good organisational skills and like to do things methodically. As they grow older, they will become more fixed in their habits and will like to do things in a particular way only.

For example, the 1st Pada of Dhanishta in the 5th house, they will be very creative and intelligent and will do exceptionally well in the field of entertainment, music, dance and singing. They will be well known for their talent and their unique style of music, singing or dancing. The more they reach out to people, the more there will be a flow of resources and finances as needed.

Careers

Politicians, accountants, managers, coordinators, directors, leaders, builders, architects, bank workers, businessmen, IT professionals, singers, actors, dancers, musicians, advisors, social workers, doctors, nurses, teachers, office workers and those working from home.

Pada 2

26.40 - 30 deg Capricorn, Navamsha - Virgo (Lord - Mercury)

Rashi Lord - Saturn and Nakshatra Lord- Mars

In the 2nd Pada, there will be the energy of Mercury, Saturn and Mars. The navamsha of Virgo gives them a very analytical approach to life. They have to analyse carefully, logically and practically before making their choices. They will have wonderful IT skills and will be very good speakers and writers.

Mars reaches maximum exaltation at 28 deg in this Pada. The placement of Mars will show where the energy and effort will be spent. For example, if Mars is placed in the 9th house, they will have to spend time, effort and energy into higher education. The natives will have tremendous willpower and energy to follow their dreams and ambitions and will not be disheartened by any difficulties or challenges they might face in the pursuit of their careers.

Since the navamsha falls in Virgo, which is the original 6th house of service, they will serve the community through their job. Especially as they get older and have the wealth of experience with them, they will be able to offer their service through their written or spoken words. They will be very duty-conscious and punctual.

For example, the 2nd Pada of Dhanishta in the 7th house, their partner or spouse will be very academic and will love to study and learn more about their chosen profession. The natives themselves will love to read books and learn about various subjects of interest through the internet.

Careers

Financial advisors, property dealers, businessmen, IT professionals, bank managers, accountants, lawyers, writers, speakers, YouTubers, landlords, doctors, nurses, teachers and working from home.

Pada 3

0 - 3.20 deg Aquarius, Navamsha - Libra (Lord - Venus)

Rashi Lord - Saturn and Nakshatra Lord - Mars

The navamsha of the 3rd Pada is placed in Libra, which gives the effect of Venus, Saturn and Mars. In this Pada, the natives will have a very fine sense of aesthetics and will look for harmony and balance in everything. The 3rd Pada falls in Aquarius, so the natives will be more community-oriented and will be more of a people's person. They are most likely to serve the community, the nation, or internationally through their talent.

The combination of Venus and Mars will make them very passionate, motivated and enthusiastic about everything they do in life. Mars gives energy and drive, Venus provides creativity and beauty, and Saturn brings calm and wisdom. They have the talent and capability of becoming excellent musicians, artists, actors, dancers or singers.

For example, the 3rd Pada of Dhanishta in the 3rd house, they can become the master of their skill and talent with dedicated practice. They are capable of putting in sincere effort into their chosen profession and bringing out the best in themselves.

Careers

Writers, poets, artists, actors, IT professionals, interior designers, fashion designers, architects, marriage consultants, psychologists, doctors, teachers, businessmen, running a voluntary organisation or working for one and working from home.

Pada 4

3.20 - 6.40 deg Aquarius, Navamsha - Scorpio (Lord - Mars)

Rashi Lord - Saturn and Nakshatra Lord - Mars

In this Pada, there will be the influence of double Mars and Saturn. The navamsha of Scorpio will make them very determined and inwardly drawn. They will have great intensity of purpose in them and will have the grit and sincerity to follow their dreams. They are also blessed with an exceptional ability to focus and understand things from a deeper perspective. They can become excellent psychologists, psychiatrists, astrologers, police officers, army officers, emergency doctors, surgeons and detectives.

The double influence of Mars also gives them a very aggressive approach and a forceful way of doing things. It is a good quality when used positively to break through one's own shortcomings and limitations. On the negative side, it can make them impatient, short-tempered, secretive and revengeful.

For example, the 4th Pada of Dhanishta in the 2nd house, they will put their energy into having enough resources and financial security for the family. They will be secretive about their sources of income and about how much they earn, and about their savings.

Careers-

Psychologists, psychiatrists, astrologers, spiritual mediums, emergency doctors, surgeons, IT professionals, army officers, police officers, detectives, fire fighters, managers, directors, self-employed and working from home.

The effect of planets

Dhanishta - Capricorn	Planets that get affected
Yoga Karka - most benefic	Venus
Functional Benefic - gives good results during their dasha.	Saturn
Functional Malefic - can give problems during their dasha.	Sun, Jupiter, Rahu and Ketu
Functional Neutral	Moon, Mars and Mercury
Kendra Adi Pati Dosha - can be malefic	Waning Moon

Dhanishta - Aquarius	Planets that get affected
Yoga Karka - most benefic	Venus
Functional Benefic - gives good results during their dasha.	Mars, Sun and Jupiter
Functional Malefic - can give problems during their dasha.	Moon, Rahu and Ketu
Functional Neutral	Mercury and Saturn

Dhanishta Ascendant

Those who have their Ascendant in the 1st and 2nd padas of Dhanishta will have a more calm and traditional approach to life. They have a marvellous ability to face the facts and come up with practical solutions as needed. Like a mountain goat, they are tough climbers and their destination is to reach the top. They are not immune to making mistakes, but have an earthy, steady and patient way of dealing with situations.

In the 3rd and 4th padas of Dhanishta, the natives will have more Aquarian qualities of fulfilling desires and being in touch with people. Like a water bearer, they are determined to pour out their knowledge and skills and share it with as many people as possible.

They are more open to trying new innovative ways of doing things and using the latest IT technology to spread their business. Since Aquarius is a fixed sign, they are very organised and like to plan things ahead of time. They have their own peculiar wisdom behind doing things in a certain way, which works wonderfully for them.

They are not afraid to revolt against the rigid rules of society if they feel their freedom of expression is being strangled. They will always stand up for what is correct and ethical in terms of humanity at large and not just for one sect of society, because they look at life from the larger perspective, which includes all beings.

Their positive qualities are far-sighted vision, originality, tolerance, friendliness, ingenious, inventive ideas and genius. On the negative side, when they are feeling frustrated, they can become eccentric, detached, absent-minded, non-cooperative and rebellious.

Sun in Dhanishta

When the Sun is placed in the 1st or 2nd pada of Dhanishta, it will share the influence of Mars and Saturn. Sun is friendly with Mars but an enemy with Saturn, therefore it will give a mixed effect. This will make the natives feel the restrictions of delays and obstacles, especially during the dasha of the Sun or Saturn. In Capricorn, the Sun feels ambitious and Mars is happy, because it gets exalted in Capricorn, but the wisdom of Saturn makes them move cautiously.

For example, Sun in the 1st Pada of Dhanishta in the 3rd house, the native may have some disagreements between his or her siblings during the dasha of Sun, Mars or Saturn. They are intelligent, brave and not afraid of facing obstacles.

The 3rd and 4th padas of Dhanishta are placed in Aquarius, when the Sun is placed in these padas, it will be influenced by Mars, Saturn and Rahu. Sun and Mars get along well, but Sun and Saturn are enemies with each other, and Rahu amplifies the effect. The natives will be practical in their approach and will be more scientifically oriented.

For example, if the Sun is placed in the 4th Pada of Dhanishta in the 4th house, the native may have some problems at home, and a clash of opinions with his or her mother can happen during the dasha of Sun, Saturn or Rahu. The natives will have a comfortable home and will love to work from home, and do research on the topics of their interest.

Moon in Dhanishta

When the Moon is placed in the 1st and 2nd padas of Dhanishta, it shares the qualities of Saturn in Capricorn. Saturn brings caution and respect for authority, because they see law and tradition as necessary ingredients for a civilised society and can understand the wisdom behind certain traditions. They revere achievement, hard work, dedication, discipline, patience and success. The Satarian wisdom knows the value of being resourceful and practical.

For example, the Moon in the 1st Pada of Dhanishta, in the 5th house, the native will be very creative, intelligent and enterprising. They will be happy and satisfied with the work of their children, students or followers. It's a fortunate placement, which brings the possibility of good luck, wealth and success during the dasha of the Moon, Mars or Saturn. Because if the Moon is placed in the 5th house of Capricorn, then the native will be a Taurus Ascendant, and for them, Saturn becomes a yoga karka (the most benefic planet), and Moon and Mars give neutral results.

In the 3rd and 4th padas of Dhanishta, the moon is influenced by the qualities of Saturn in Aquarius. They are amazingly intuitive and can come up with workable solutions without any trace of logical steps. They have an unprejudiced approach to life. They look at every human being as a fellow citizen and don't judge or label them for whatever their personal values may be.

Their myriad range of interests can make them come across as unpredictable at times, because they intuitively and suddenly might have a great idea which they want to explore. Their long-term plan is to someday integrate all of these fantastic ideas into a wholesome business or organisation. The Saturn moon combination gives them a slower but steady progress towards achieving their aspirations.

Since the co-ruler of Aquarius is Rahu, an endless string of desires entangles them more and more as they get older, because the fulfilment of one desire gives rise to many more. The cassandra of desires can weave an enchanting web of marvellous illusion, from which a Dhanishta may never be able to escape.

For example, Moon in the 3rd Pada of Dhanishta, in the 10th house, will give them a career that deals with serving humanity. They will either be managing a huge organisation or will have their own. Moon in the 10th house will also bring fluctuations in their job or business; however, every time they choose to make some changes in their career, it will bring them to a better place, which will become a stepping stone for their success.

The poetry of Dhanishta

Dhanishta - the wealthy and famous,

The wealth of knowledge and skills - genius.

If not shared - among all

Will be a burden for the soul.

While Satarian caution holds the calm,

The Martian spirit moves on,

To weave the web and catch the dreams,

Of many a lifetime - in a moment serene.

Like a water bearer who readily pours,

The wisdom of this world and many more.

Expand the horizons as far as the eye can see,

Include all humanity, all creatures, all beings - you and me.

Remedies

- <u>Das Maha Vidya</u> - as described earlier.

- Organising events, bringing people together, doing voluntary work - all these activities bring them great fulfilment, and they will find that whenever they involve themselves selflessly, their problems get solved miraculously.

- Dhanishta natives will have a Kapha Vata constitution - a daily exercise routine will help to maintain good health. It will be better to listen to their body. When they feel exhausted, they must take ample rest before getting into activity again.

- Red and blue colours resonate well with the energy of Dhanishta.

- Chanting the mantra - *"Om yam ram Dhanishta nakshatraye namah."* 108 times on days when the moon is transiting Dhanishta, or on Tuesdays or Saturdays, will help to connect you with your inner self.

Example

<u>Ascendant in Dhanishta</u>

<u>Amitabh Bachan-</u> Famous Hindi film actor of the 1980s.

Born on 11th October 1942, 4 pm, Prayagraj, India.

Amitabh Bachchan is an Indian film actor, film producer, television host, occasional playback singer and former politician. He is regarded as one of the greatest and most influential actors in the history of Indian cinema. During the 1970s–1980s, he was the most dominant actor in Indian movies.

Amitabh was born in Allahabad to the Hindi poet Harivansh Rai Bachchan and his wife, the social activist Teji Bachchan. He was educated at Sherwood College in Nainital and later at the University of Delhi. His film career started in 1969 as a voice narrator in Mrinal Sen's film Bhuvan Shome. He first gained popularity in the early 1970s for films such as Zanjeer, Deewaar and Sholay, and was famously called India's angry young man for his on-screen roles in Hindi films. He has been popularly called the star of the Millennium, or Big B, and has since appeared in over 200 Indian films in a career spanning more than 5 decades.

He has won numerous accolades in his career, including 4 National Film Awards as Best Actor, Dadasaheb Phalke Award as lifetime achievement award and many other awards at international film festivals and award ceremonies. He has won 16 Filmfare Awards and is the most-nominated performer in any major acting category at Filmfare. In addition to acting, he has worked as a playback singer, film producer and television presenter. He has hosted several seasons of the game show Kaun Banega Crorepati, India's version of the game show franchise, Who Wants to Be a Millionaire? He also entered politics for some time in the 1980s.

He was struggling in his early days of his film career and was seen as a failed newcomer. By the age of 30, he had 12 flops and only 2 hits (as a lead in Bombay to Goa and supporting role in Anand). He was soon discovered by screenwriter duo Salim–Javed, consisting of Salim Khan and Javed Akhtar. Salim Khan wrote the story, screenplay and script of Zanjeer (1973), and conceived the angry young man persona of the lead role. The film was a huge success and one of the highest-grossing films of that year. Subsequently, scripts were written with Amitabh in mind for the lead role. Deewaar (1975) and Sholay (1975) were the first of the many blockbuster hit films that followed. Eventually, he became one of the most successful leading men of the film industry. In 1973, he married Jaya, who was his co-star in Zanjeer (his first hit film), and they later appeared in several films together. He rose to superstardom in the years 1975 - 1988.

On 26 July 1982, while filming a fight scene with co-actor Puneet for Coolie, he suffered a near-fatal intestinal injury. He was performing his own stunts in the film, and one scene required him to fall onto a table and then onto the ground. However, as he jumped towards the table, the corner of the table hit his abdomen, resulting in a splenic rupture from which he lost a significant amount of blood. He required an emergency splenectomy and remained critically ill in the hospital for many months, at times close to death. There were long queues of well-wishing fans outside the hospital where he was recuperating. The public response included prayers in temples and offers to sacrifice limbs to save him. Nevertheless, he resumed filming later that year after a long period of recuperation. The director, Manmohan Desai, altered the ending of Coolie. His character was originally intended to have been killed, but later the character lived till the end.

Desai felt it would have been inappropriate for the man who had just fended off death in real life to be killed on screen. The footage of the fight scene is frozen at the critical moment, and a caption appears onscreen marking it as the instant of the actor's injury. The film was released in 1983, and due to his accident, the film was a box office success and the top-grossing film of that year.

Apart from industry awards won for his performances throughout the years, Bachchan has received several honours for his achievements in the Indian film industry. In 1991, he became the first artist to receive the Filmfare Lifetime Achievement Award, which was established in the name of Raj Kapoor. Bachchan was crowned as Superstar of the Millennium in 2000 at the Filmfare Awards. In June 2000, he became the first living Asian to be modelled in wax at London's Madame Tussauds Wax Museum. Another statue was installed in New York in 2009, Hong Kong and Bangkok in 2011, Washington, DC in 2012, and Delhi in 2017.

In 2020, Bachchan was helping the Government of India promote its public health message concerning COVID-19 before he and some members of his family themselves became infected. He was hospitalised with reported mild symptoms of the disease on 11th July and was discharged from the hospital on 2nd August 2020.

<u>Analysis</u> -

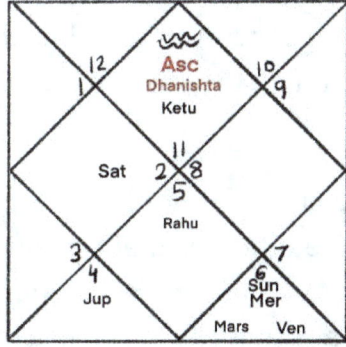

Amitabh is an <u>Aquarius Ascendant,</u> in Dhanishta Pada 3, and Ketu is sitting in the Ascendant. His life has been a path of service to entertain people through the world of cinema. He has abundance and wealth, financially and in the field of acting. As a talented actor, he has brought him worldwide fame.

Saturn, the lord of the Ascendant, is sitting in the 4th house of Taurus. This makes a mahapurush Sasha yoga with Saturn sitting alone in the Kendra house. This gave him the blessing of serving and entertaining the public. His home atmosphere has been very disciplined, and he has great financial wisdom, which has given him unbridled success.

He also has the fortune of Gajakeshari yoga because Jupiter is exalted in the 6th house (Cancer), which is Kendra (10th) from the moon in the 9th house. This brought him comfort and the luxury of vehicles, wealth, position, recognition and abundance of fixed assets.

Raj yoga - another auspicious yoga for wealth, fame and abundance is formed in his birth chart. The lords of the 9th and 10th houses are associated. Venus, the lord of the 9th house of Taurus and Mars, the lord of the 10th house of Scorpio, are sitting in the 8th house of Virgo along with Mercury and Sun. Mars is also the lord of his Ascendant nakshatra, which brought him recognition during its dasha. The dasha of these planets brought him much wealth and success. He rose to stardom (1973-1974) in his Saturn-Mars dasha.

Venus becomes the yogakaraka for an Aquarius Ascendant. After his marriage to Jaya in 1973, he reached the height of superstardom (1975-1988), when all his films were proving to be big hits one after the other.

Ketu sitting in the Ascendant also brought the near fatal intestinal injury in his abdomen on 26th July 1982, while filming a fight scene for his film Coolie. He was running his Saturn Sun Ketu dasha. On that day, Saturn was transiting over his 8th house of Virgo, which signifies sudden events (moreover, the transiting Saturn was in Hasta).

The fight scene that was being enacted involved a fake punch with the hand, to which Amitabh had to respond by falling onto a table. The corner of the table had caused that fatal wound. The Sun was transiting in Cancer, over his 6th house, which signifies duties, job, and daily routines. He got injured while acting, which is his job (the 6th house represents daily routines). Ketu was transiting Sagittarius over his 11th house - the house of gains and fulfilment of desires. Although the injury was serious and took him many months to recover, Jupiter's beneficence saved his life (Jupiter, the lord of the 11th house of Sagittarius, is sitting in the 6th house of Cancer and is exalted in his birth chart).

Sage Bhrigu has mentioned that Jupiter shows our curses, or faults. One cannot remember the karmic debts or blessings from previous lives, but the effect of them prevails in this life. Since Karma is the principle of cause and effect, one tends to be in a certain situation at a certain time and therefore enjoy the benefits or face the consequences, which cannot be escaped. In this sense, Jupiter, the guru, teaches us life's lessons as a teacher would teach a student, in order to improve his performance and make him bring out the best in him. But we must remember that no matter what situations we face in life, how we handle them and how we respond is entirely in our hands, because the karma of this moment is always in our hands and is our choice.

26
Shatabhishak

Om lam Shatbhishak nakshatraye namah

Zodiac degrees	6.40 - 20 deg Aquarius
Ruling planet	Aquarius - Saturn and Shatabhishak - Rahu
Sanskrit name	Shatabhishak - shata means 100 and bhishaj means a doctor. So the word Shatbhishak signifies 100 doctors, 100 medicines or 100 healers.
Astronomical name	Shatabhishak is represented by a faint group of about 100 stars in the constellation of Aquarius. These stars are seen as - forming a circle with an empty space in the centre.
Symbol	Aquarius - water bearer Shatabhishak - an empty circle
Element	Air
Deity	Varuna
Quality	Fixed - sthira
Shakti	Bheshaja Shakti - Power to heal and support.
Cast	Butcher
Gender	Male
Motivation	Kama - to fulfil desires
Triguna	Tamas
Tridosha	Vata
Body parts	Jaw, chin and right thigh.
Direction	South east and South west
Month	August - later half of Shravana month.

Bird	Heron
Sound	go, sa, see, su
Tree	Kadamba tree
Chakras	Vishuddhi - Saturn and Rahu - Ajna
Das Maha Vidya	Devi Kali - Saturn and Devi Chinnamasta - Rahu

Special degrees -

Yoga Tara	17.45 deg Aquarius It's a point where the planet will show the strongest and sure results during its dasha.
Pushkar bhaga	19 deg Aquarius Any planets sitting at this point will give excellent results during their dasha, like the blossoming of a flower.
Mulatrikona	0 - 20 deg Aquarius - Mukatrikona of Saturn. When Saturn is placed at these degrees in Aquarius, it will become very strong and will give excellent results during its dasha.
Amrit Nadi	16 - 16.53 deg Aquarius This brings good results, just like the nectar that nourishes.
Visha Nadi	10.40 - 11.33 deg Capricorn Brings situations which one does not like dealing with.

Auspicious and inauspicious table -

Auspicious	Inauspicious
Activities Good for taking medicine, therapies and rejuvenation, for business deals, signing contracts, making land, house and property deals, for education and learning medicine, astrology and astronomy, for travel, especially over water, for getting new vehicles, bike rides, for media and technology related activities, recreation, especially near lakes, rivers or oceans, for sexual activities, meditation and yoga.	Activities Not good for any new beginnings, marriage, childbirth and fertility treatments, lawsuits and arguments, for any unethical activities, for socialising and financial activities, buying new clothes or jewellery, and for quiet domestic activities.
Days Mondays - only when it falls on the 2nd, 7th or 12th lunar day. Fridays - only when it falls on the 1st, 6th or 11th lunar day. Saturdays - only when it falls on the 2nd, 4th, 7th, 9th, 12th or 14th lunar day.	Days Tuesdays - only when it falls on the 1st, 2nd, 7th, 8th, 10th or Purnima (full moon day). Thursdays - only when it falls on the 6th, 8th, 9th, 12th or 13th lunar day.

Compatibility table -

Shatabhishak	Compatible with
Sexual compatibility Yoni animal	Shatbhishak - Female Horse Ashwini - Male horse
Sign compatibility	Aquarius - Gemini and Libra
Nakshatra compatibility	Ardra and Swati
Lunar day compatibility	Chaturdashi tithi - 14th lunar day
Day compatibility	Saturday
Colour compatibility	Blue and grey
Numerological compatibility	8 - all numbers that add up to make 8.
Sound compatibility	Saturn - labial sounds - pa, pha, ba, bha, ma

Sign Lord and nakshatra lord - Saturn and Rahu - as described earlier.

Shatabhishak is the 3rd of the Rahu-ruled nakshatras, where the energy of Saturn and Rahu has expanded into becoming all-inclusive. Rahu is the co - lord of Aquarius, which amplifies the karmic quality of Saturn. Aquarius, the original 11th house, is also the highest of the Kama houses, which gives many desires, entanglements, and also has the capacity to fulfil them.

Aquarius being a fixed sign and Saturn and Rahu being the lords, highlights the fact that any planets placed here represent the karma that cannot be escaped. Life will bring such situations - both good and bad - through which one has to experience extreme rise or extreme fall, extreme joys and extreme sorrows.

Aquarius is also a sign of science and new age technology, because of the influence of Rahu. They will be very apt in using the latest IT gadgets for learning and enhancing their skills.

Quality, element, motivation, triguna, tridosha and chakras - as described earlier.

Shakti - Bheshaja Shakti - Power to heal and support.

Those who are born with their Ascendant, Sun, or Moon in Shatabhishak have a special blessing where their wisdom and advice can show others the path of healing. Even if they are not professional doctors, they will inherently know which herb, which medication or which concoction can cure a certain disease. Or they might face an ailment where they have to consult many doctors, because it may not be easily cured.

They will surely have a close connection with healing, either they will themselves be in the medical profession or someone close to them in their family or friends will be a doctor, physician, therapist or healer.

Symbolic signification

<u>Aquarius -</u> as described earlier, and <u>Shatabhishak</u> - an empty circle.

<u>An empty circle - What is emptiness?</u>

The scientific perspective

Among the latest discoveries done in the world of science, many experiments have been conducted to see if there truly exists such a thing as - empty space. Modern physics is now converging on a surprising answer to the question - What is nothing?

Imagine a round container, with no air inside, all the molecules are sucked out of it, what's left in the container? Our instant reply will be - vacuum or nothing. But is it truly nothing?

Between 2 asteroids in space, what really creates a distance between them, or keeps them apart. From this, the physicists infer that there must be a frictionless medium permeating the whole space, what we call as ether. The scientists have now conferred that empty space in the container actually contains energy.

This energy has been measured in experiments and has been called the ' Casimir effect.' In the universe, they call this mysterious dark space the dark energy. So, new age scientists confirm that there is no such thing as absolute emptiness or absolute nothingness.

The spiritual perspective

Shoonya

There is a spiritual practice called shoonya meditation. The word Shoonya means - zero, nothing, or emptiness. In the state of shoonya, the activity of the conscious mind gradually lessens and slowly one begins to experience the emptiness of thoughts - a state of pure awareness.

This meditative state is also called nirvana or freedom from the bondage of the mind, because in this state (however brief or prolonged it is) the activity of the mind - the thoughts, emotions and feelings come to pause. It is the state of purity and clarity one can begin to experience - a space that is not distracted or contaminated by any thoughts.

Sadhguru explains that 12 - 18 minutes of shoonya meditation can bring you to such a relaxed, clear and fresh state of mind, which you would get only after 8 - 10 hours of good, sound sleep. One has to be initiated into this practice by a Guru or a teacher who is himself or herself established in this state of shoonya, and who has been authorised to initiate others. Sadhguru also mentioned that Lord Budha used to offer shoonya meditation to very few close disciples. Otherwise, to most of the spiritual aspirants who came to him, he used to offer Vipassana meditation (breath watch).

Shoonya meditation is considered as one of the most important practices for those who are genuine seekers on the spiritual path and want to experience deeper states of meditativeness. With regular practice, one can be in the state of pure awareness for longer periods of time, even amidst doing daily activities.

Tantric practices -

Therefore, an empty space offers a very powerful possibility of experiencing and knowing the source of creation from within. There are some tantric practices where they chant a mantra and draw a circle to invite disembodied beings for their own selfish gains or to help someone.

These are dangerous realms and should not be explored for spiritual entertainment or for any other purpose. The laws of nature are like the laws of science, and they work for whoever knows the technique or knows the code of opening mystical doors. That's why in the Hindu tradition and in other ancient traditions, these codes and mantras have been kept secret, only the rightful and responsible people would be told about them or given access to it. The wise sages and seers would impart their knowledge only to the worthy disciples after putting them through a severe penance or a tough test, in order to make sure these seemingly and deceptively simple but powerful techniques don't fall into the wrong hands.

Inference

Shatabhishak natives have tremendous capability of exploring the mystical realms in a scientific context. They can bring home the ancient knowledge and put it across in the modern context, in a language that today's generation can understand and relate to.

They may experience such situations in their life, where they feel like being caught up in a situation and there is no way out of it, even if they try their best. This shows the fixed side of Aquarius and the karmic side of Saturn, and the only choice one has is to go through that experience, lie low, or let that situation pass, and with time, things will get better. The phrase that is used quite often when one is in distress literally stands true for them in their difficult times: *'Time is a great healer.'*

Their challenging time in a way, forces them to look inwards for answers, which helps them to progress speedily on their spiritual path.

Mythology -

Deity - Varuna

The word Varuna comes from the verbal root vṛ -, which means to surround, to cover, to restrain or bind. The suffix -uṇa means he who covers or binds. The Vedas refer to the cosmological ocean or waters encircling the land.

The Vedas associated Varuna with the sky, later with the seas as well as justice and truth. He is said to be the son of Sage Kashyapa - one of the 7 ancient sages, the saptarishis. In the Hindu Puranas, Varuna is the god of oceans, his vehicle is a Makara (crocodile) and his weapon is a Pasha (noose, rope loop). He is the guardian deity of the western direction. In some texts, he is said to be the father of the Vedic sage Vasishtha.

It is also inferred that Varuna binds the wicked or our wicked thoughts or acts. In the earliest of the Rigveda texts, Varuna is described as the guardian of moral law; he punishes those who sin without remorse and forgives those who err with remorse. Varuna and Mitra are often mentioned together and seen as twin deities. They are responsible for societal affairs, including taking oaths. Varuna is also called the patron deity of physicians, one who has 100 and 1000 remedies.

In the epic of Ramayana, it is said that Varuna (the lord of the oceans) had promised to remain calm while Lord Rama and his army built a path of stones across the waters to reach the island of Sri Lanka.

Inference

Shatabhishak natives have an affinity with water and water-based herbal concoctions. They can become excellent pharmacists, doctors, ayurvedic doctors or chemists. They have an inherent knowledge about the herbal properties of plants and the chemistry of medicines. If they choose to study these subjects, they can become masters of their profession.

Varuna also has a restrictive nature, but in a good way. It stops us from doing anything unethical or unlawful. Therefore, those who are born with their Ascendant, Sun or Moon in Shatabhishak will find that if they try to cut corners, or do anything which might be a quick fix, or false, they never succeed in the long run. On the other hand, when they do things honestly, according to the rules, or laws of nature, they don't fail others or themselves.

Shatabhishak padas

6.40 - 20 degree Aquarius

Padas	Degrees
1	6.40 - 10 deg Aquarius
2	10 - 13.20 deg Aquarius
3	13.20 - 16.40 deg Aquarius
4	16.40 - 20 deg Aquarius

Pada 1

6.40 - 10 deg Aquarius, Navamsha- Sagittarius (Lord - Jupiter)

Rashi Lord - Saturn and Nakshatra Lord- Rahu

The 1st Pada will have the energy of Saturn, Rahu and Jupiter. The navamsha of Sagittarius gives them a very optimistic approach to life. Saturn and Jupiter are very spiritual planets; when amplified by the influence of Rahu, it makes the natives very idealistic and religious. They will love to give charity and donate wherever it's genuinely needed. They will be involved in philanthropic work and large organisations, which will help them to reach the maximum number of people.

For example, the 1st Pada of Shatabhishak in the 10th house, they will either run a large organisation or manage one. Through their organisation, they will be able to help a lot of people financially or through their advice and connections.

Careers

Teachers, advisors, counsellors, astrologers, priests, doctors, herbalists, pharmacists, horse keepers, coordinators, directors, leaders, business men, IT professionals, writers, speakers, social workers, psychologists, philosophers, religious leaders, office workers and working from home.

Pada 2

10 - 13.20 deg Aquarius, Navamsha - Capricorn (Lord - Saturn)

Rashi Lord - Saturn and Nakshatra Lord- Rahu

In the 2nd Pada, there will be double energy of Saturn and Rahu, which will amplify the Saturnian qualities of caution, slowness and restriction. The navamsha of Capricorn will give them a very practical and organised approach to life. They will have great resilience and discipline and will have the tenacity to steadily work towards their goals and rise in their career. Since Capricorn is the original 10th house of career and public image, they will achieve success after the age of 30.

For example, the 2nd Pada of Shatabhishak in the 8th house, the family of their spouse will be influential in some way to establish their career. They will face sudden events that will become a turning point in their career, they may seem challenging at that moment, but in the long run, it will prove to be a blessing. This is more likely to happen in Rahu or Saturn dasha.

Careers

Managers, office workers, social workers, businessmen, IT professionals, astrologers, technicians, doctors, nurses, pharmacists, herbalists, teachers, cooks, doing a regular job, and working from home.

Pada 3

13.20 - 16.40 deg Aquarius, Navamsha - Aquarius (Lord - Saturn)

Rashi Lord - Saturn and Nakshatra Lord - Rahu

The navamsha of the 3rd Pada is placed in Aquarius, which gives a strong effect of Saturn and Rahu. In this Pada, the natives will be more community-oriented. They will get involved in some kind of voluntary work where they can help the community or the nation at large, or even globally. Any planets placed in this Pada will give wonderful results during their dashas and bring success, because it's a vargottama Pada. In the birth chart and the navamsha chart, the sign of Aquarius remains the same, which gives the stability and assurance of things moving smoothly, without having to face any drastic changes in later life.

For example, the 3rd Pada of Shatabhishak in the 4th house, they will have good support from their family, especially from their mother, to get involved in voluntary projects and help people as much as possible.

Careers

Engineers, scientists, architects, writers, IT professionals, astrologers, philanthropists, doctors, herbalists, pharmacists, teachers, businessmen, running voluntary organisations or working for them, and working from home.

Pada 4

16.40 - 20 deg Aquarius, Navamsha - Pisces (Lord - Jupiter)

Rashi Lord - Saturn and Nakshatra Lord- Rahu

In this Pada, there will be the influence of Saturn, Rahu and Jupiter. The navamsha of Pisces gives them great intuitive abilities and they can become excellent healers, psychologists, doctors, astrologers, herbalists, therapists and pharmacists. However, in Pisces, one does not have much of the worldly ambition to pursue any materialistic goals. In spite of having the talent and capability, they might not choose to make a career or a living out of it, because they feel anything that takes them away from their inner world of imagination, dreams, spirituality, religion or philosophy is not worth making an effort for.

For example, the 4th Pada of Shatabhishak in the 9th house, they will be very devoted to learning the higher philosophy of life, about spirituality, religion, yoga and meditation. After the age of 30, they will find a mentor, teacher or a guru who can guide them. They will be instrumental in spreading the word and teachings of their guru.

Careers-

Psychologists, philosophers, guides, gurus, astrologers, priests, teachers, advisors, counsellors, spiritual mediums, designers, artists, film directors, actors, singers, musicians, writers, poets, IT professionals, doctors, herbalists, pharmacists, self-employed and working from home.

The effect of planets

Shatbhishak - Aquarius	Planets that get affected
Yoga Karka - most benefic	Venus
Functional Benefic - give good results during their dasha.	Mars, Sun and Jupiter
Functional Malefic - can give problems during their dasha.	Moon, Rahu and Ketu
Functional Neutral	Mercury and Saturn

Shatabhishak Ascendant

Those who have their Ascendant in Shatabhishak will have the influence of Saturn and Rahu. In Aquarius, the Saturnian quality of serving or helping others is amplified and expanded. They feel great satisfaction and fulfilment in connecting to people and reaching out to them when needed. The fixed nature of Aquarius makes them firmly set in their ethics. Their principles or philosophies may seem peculiar to others, but they are not selfish, because they have great feelings for humanity.

Whichever profession they choose, it will be associated with dealing with a lot of people. Shatabhishak natives will be well-known members of their community because of their friendly and helpful nature. Because of the airy nature of Shatabhishak, they can feel restless and get bored easily, and constantly seek to do something that is mentally exciting, intriguing and worthwhile.

They have a very good business and financial sense because of the cool and cautious approach of Saturn. Their practical and logical approach, at times, makes them come across as heartless or lacking in emotion. They are more interested in permanent solutions rather than quick fixes. Rahu represents the latest technology, science, astronomy, electricity, the Internet and communication. The influence of Rahu makes them think and envision things way ahead of their times.

Sun in Shatabhishak

When the Sun is placed in Shatabhishak, it will share the qualities of Saturn and Rahu. Sun and Saturn don't get along well and Rahu amplifies the effect. The natives will have a dignified personality, will be intelligent and proud. They will have the confidence and talent of addressing a large audience and will not be stage shy. They will like to do everything on a bigger scale.

Whatever business or job they choose to do, they would like to reach out to as many people as possible, and will always endeavour to have the impact of their organisation (they work for), or their own business on a global scale. They will be people's person and can become excellent managers, coordinators and leaders.

For example, Sun in Shatabhishak in the 9th house, the natives will be academically minded and will be ambitious about pursuing their higher education and mastering the subject of their interest, even if they have to travel away from home or go abroad. They are likely to face delays during the dasha of Sun, Saturn or Rahu and could have some problems with their father, government or the authorities. However, their confidence and capability will eventually help them achieve their goals.

Moon in Shatbhishak

When the Moon is placed in Shatabhishak, it shares the qualities of Saturn and Rahu. Because of their intuitive nature, very little comes as a surprise to a Shatabhishak person. They are interested in everybody and have no prejudices. They adapt smoothly to change whenever it's needed, despite their fixed personal habits. Shatabhishak lies in the sign of Aquarius, which is governed by the air element. It is hard to define or pinpoint, but there is something unique, mystical and delightfully vague about their personality.

Being at the seaside, lakeside or near the ocean is always the most enchanting moment for them. This is where they can sit for hours and bask in the openness and expansive quality of water. There is a curious absentmindedness and detachment about them. Others may interpret it as daydreaming, but their minds are probably busy gathering wool and planning on their next ingenious idea or project.

The influence of Rahu gives them driving ambition and profusion of desires which shoot like comets in the farthest realms of the airy Saturnian environment. They readily embrace the latest IT technology in order to manifest their ingenious ideas. The Shatabhishak way of doing things might seem crazy at times, but it's in tune with their vision, which is way ahead of current times. Their greatest virtue will be patience and their greatest limitation will be fear or anxiety of the unknown.

For example, Moon in Shatabhishak in the 2nd house, the native will be born into a family that greatly sup port the work of charity, giving donations, and helping people. From their source of income, they will contribute to humanitarian causes whenever possible. They will know many people, will have an extended family and relatives who will influence and shape their beliefs and ideology in their younger years of growing up.

The poetry of Shatabhishak

Shatabhishak - the 100 healers,

Find the perfect cure for seekers.

Varuna the lord of the west,

Brings forth the knowledge from the oceanic depths.

The water bearer - who pours the water,

To quench the thirst now and after.

The selfless service in times of need,

A gracious act indeed.

Saturn, the karmic lord - lays the plot,

The game of dice - enjoyed or not.

Rahu - the bodiless serpent with only a head,

No matter what has been read or said.

Cause and effect - the formula grand,

Has deeper implications - for those who understand.

The experience the soul gathers within,

Marks the track for the next round to begin.

And so the journey shall continue,

After a pause of death and life anew...

Remedies

- <u>Das Maha Vidya</u> - as described earlier.
- Whenever they help those who are not well, they miraculously recover from their ailments as well.

- For the Vata constitution - a daily exercise routine will keep them grounded and in good health. They should not do very vigorous exercises, like running or cycling in the hot sun, or tough muscle building gym exercises for a long duration at a stretch. It will be better to listen to their body, when they feel exhausted, they must take ample rest, before getting into excessive activity again.

- The yogic asanas, pranayama and meditation always enhances the ability to focus, which in turn improves the quality of whatever you do and brings ease into all thoughts and actions.

- Blue and grey colours resonate well with the energy of Shatabhishak.

- Chanting the mantra - "Om *lam Shatabhishak nakshatraye namah.*" 108 times on days when the moon is transiting Shatabhishak or on Saturdays, will help to connect you with your inner self.

Example

Moon in Shatabhishak

Satyajit Ray - Renowned Indian art film director

Born on 2nd May 1921 in Calcutta, India, at 12 pm (estimated time of birth).

Satyajit was an Indian film director, scriptwriter, author, lyricist, illustrator and music composer. He is widely considered to have been one of the greatest filmmakers.

Satyajit Ray was born to Sukumar and Suprabha Ray in Kolkata. His father, Sukumar Ray, was an illustrator, critic, and a pioneering Bengali writer of nonsense rhyme (Abol Tabol) and children's literature. His father died when he was barely 3 years old, and the family survived on Suprabha Ray's meagre income. Ray studied at Ballygunge Government High School in Calcutta and completed his BA in economics at Presidency College, Calcutta.

In 1940, his mother insisted that he should study at Vishva Bharati University in Shantiniketan, founded by Rabindranath Tagore. Ray was initially reluctant to go, due to his fondness for Calcutta. In Santiniketan, he came to appreciate Oriental art. His visits to Ajanta, Ellora, and Elephanta caves stimulated his admiration for Indian art.

In 1943, Ray started working at a British advertising agency as a junior visualiser, earning 80 rupees a month. Although he liked visual design (graphic design) and was mostly treated well, there was always an underlying tension between the British and Indian employees of the firm. The British were better paid, and Ray felt that "the clients were generally stupid." Later, he worked for the Signet Press, where he was given complete artistic freedom to create book cover designs for the company. He designed covers for many famous books, including Jawaharlal Nehru's Discovery of India.

In 1949, he married Bijoya Das, his first cousin and long-time sweetheart. The couple had a son, Sandip Ray, who also directs films. In the same year, French director Jean Renoir came to Calcutta to shoot his film, 'The River.' Ray helped him find locations in the countryside. He told Renoir about his idea of filming Pather Panchali, which had long been on his mind, and Renoir encouraged him. In 1950, D.J. Keymer sent Ray to London to work at the headquarters. During his 6 months in London, Ray watched 99 films. Among these was the neorealist film Ladri di biciclette (Bicycle Thieves) (1948) by Vittorio De Sica, which had a profound impact on him. Ray later said that he walked out of the theatre determined to become a filmmaker.

He was "deeply moved" by Pather Panchali, the 1928 classic of Bengali literature, and he decided to adapt it for his first film. Pather Panchali is a semi-autobiographical novel describing the maturation of Apu, a small boy in a Bengal village.

He started working on this concept in 1952 and finished making the film in 1955. 1959 -1964, Ray made films about the British Raj period, a documentary on Tagore, and a series of films that are considered by critics among the most deeply felt portrayals of Indian women on screen.

In 1964, Ray directed Charulata (The Lonely Wife), one of Ray's favourite films, which was regarded by many critics as his most accomplished film. Based on Tagore's short story, Nastanirh (Broken Nest), the film tells of a lonely wife, Charu, in 19th-century Bengal. In 1992, the Government of India honoured him with the Bharat Ratna, its highest civilian award. Ray had received many noticeable awards and gained a prestigious position over his lifetime. Ray's work has been described as full of humanism and universality, and of a deceptive simplicity with deep underlying complexity. Ray is a cultural icon in India and in Bengali communities worldwide.

For his first film, Pather Panchali (1955), he won 11 international prizes, including the inaugural Best Human Document award at the 1956 Cannes Film Festival.

A heavy smoker but non-drinker, Ray valued work more than anything else. He would work 12 hours a day and would go to bed at 2 o'clock in the morning. He also enjoyed collecting antiques, manuscripts, rare gramophone records, paintings, and rare books. In 1992, Ray's health deteriorated due to heart complications. He was admitted to a hospital but never recovered. 24 days before his death, Ray was presented with an Honorary Academy Award by Audrey Hepburn via video-link. He was in a gravely ill condition, but gave an acceptance speech, calling it the "best achievement of his movie-making career." As of 2020, Ray is the first and only Indian to have received the award. He died on 23rd April 1992, 9 days before his 71st birthday.

Analysis -

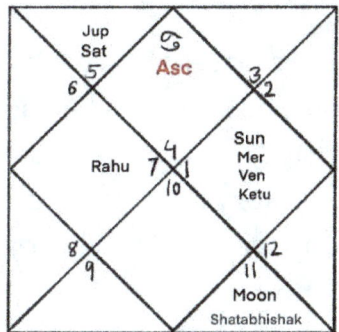

He is a Cancer Ascendant, and it's Lord moon, is in the 8th house of Aquarius in the 2nd Pada of Shatabhishak. This shows that he is very sensitive to the outer and inner environment of the human psyche, yet he is a very practical and scientific thinker. The 8th house is connected with exploring the deeper and profound aspects of life. His personality was influenced by ancient Indian art, philosophy, and literature. He was a master of his art of depicting the simple yet profound human emotions and portraying the character on screen, without saying it in too many words. The purity of the emotions stood out in its simplicity.

Moon is in the 8th house of Aquarius, which signifies a source of income other than the regular job. The lords of Shatabhishak, Saturn and Rahu - Saturn is in the 2nd house sitting with Jupiter in Leo, and Rahu is sitting in the 4th house of Libra, which signifies home and mother. The 4th house is aspected by the 10th house of Aries, where Venus, Mercury, Sun, and Ketu are sitting.

Rahu in the 4th house shows that his mother was influential in his creative genius. He left home at an early age of 19, in 1940, on the instance of his mother. Which became the foundation of his art and creativity in the later years of filmmaking. In 1940, when he left home, he was running his Jupiter Ketu Saturn dasha. Jupiter and Saturn are in the 2nd house of family, and Ketu is in the 10th house of career, sitting with Venus, Mercury and Sun. This shows that he had to leave home to pursue his future career.

He is a Cancer Ascendant in the 4th Pada of Ashlesha, it's Lord Mercury is in Ashwini in the 10th house of Aries with Sun, Venus and Ketu. This placement brought him world-renowned fame in his creative work of art, storytelling and filmmaking. He has been a pioneer in the field of Indian Cinema in making realistic art movies.

He started working on his first film, Pather Panchali, in 1952 during the Saturn Mercury Ketu dasha. Mercury and Ketu are sitting in the 10th house with Venus and Sun. He was running his 32nd year in 1952, which represents the 8th house. Which means his 8th house was activated that year, and 8th house scenarios would play out that year. He went into the depths of creative expression, combined with the struggles of meagre finance, for the next 3 years. It took him 3 years to complete his first film. His moon is sitting in the 8th house of Aquarius in Shatabhishak.

So 1952 proved to be a breakthrough year for him in terms of initiating his dream project - Pather Panchali. For which he won the national film award for best feature film in 1956.

The 10th house signifies the public image and career. Saturn is with Jupiter in the 2nd house of resources. Ray had mentioned in his interview about the struggles he had to face in the making of his first film. He had shown his illustrations of the story to a few producers, but they said they would produce it only if he made some changes to his story as they suggested. But Ray was not willing to compromise his storyline or characters in any way. So in the end, he decided to finance the movie himself.

Although he did not have enough money and resources, he had tremendous faith in his talent. So he started shooting the film only on weekends, because during the weekdays he used to do a regular job. Every month, he used nearly all his salary towards the making of this film. Those were his struggling days, but he had the fulfillment of being able to express his creativity most beautifully through the world of cinema. Saturn brought the delays and restrictions, but Jupiter helped to carry on the project, gave a very idealistic and optimistic approach, and did not let him abandon his dream project.

<u>Here are some of Satyjit Ray's quotes -</u>

"The director is the only person who knows what the film is about."

"Cinema's characteristic forte is its ability to capture and communicate the intimacies of the human mind."

"The only solutions that are ever worth anything are the solutions that people find themselves."

"Dominus Omnium Magister. It means God is the master of all things."

27
Purva Bhadrapada

Om vam sham Purva Bhadrapada nakshatraye namah

Zodiac degrees	20 deg Aquarius - 3.20 deg Pisces Aquarius - 1st, 2nd and 3rd padas Pisces - 4th Pada
Ruling planet	Aquarius - Saturn and Pisces - Jupiter Purva Bhadrapada - Jupiter
Sanskrit name	Purva Bhadrapada - Purva means the former, or rising from the east, and Bhadra means excellent, blessed, pleasant, fortunate, auspicious, fair, or prosperous. The Vedas also describe Bhadra as the Goddess of hunting and one of Shiva's servants. Bhadra was also the name of Lord Krishna's 8th queen. Purva Bhadrapada means the former one whose feet are auspicious.
Astronomical name	Purva Bhadrapada is represented by 2 bright stars seen in the constellation of Pegasus.
Symbol	Aquarius - water bearer Pisces - 2 fish moving towards each other. Purva Bhadrapada - front legs of a funeral cot.
Element	Air - Aquarius and Water - Pisces
Deity	Aja Ekapada - the one-footed goat or the unborn one.
Quality	Fierce - Ugra - Purva Bhadrapada Fixed - sthira - Aquarius and Dual - Dwi - Pisces
Shakti	Yajamana Udyamana Shakti - The power of fire worship and to rise and support people and devas.
Cast	Brahmin-priest
Gender	Male - Aquarius and Female - Pisces
Motivation	Kama - to fulfil desires - Aquarius

	Moksha - liberation - Pisces
Triguna	Tamas - Aquarius and Satwa - Pisces
Tridosha	Vata - Aquarius and Kapha - Pisces
Body parts	Lateral sides of the body
Direction	West and Southeast
Month	September - the first half of the Bhadrapada month.
Bird	Pigeon
Sound	say, so, the, dee
Tree	Mango tree
Chakras	Vishuddhi - Saturn and Jupiter - Ajna
Das Maha Vidya	Devi Kali - Saturn and Devi Tara - Jupiter

Special degrees -

Yoga Tara	29.30 deg Aquarius It's a point where the planet will show the strongest and confirm results during its dasha.
Pushkar amsha	2nd Pada Any planets sitting at this point will give excellent results during their dasha, like the blossoming of a flower.
Mulatrikona	0 - 20 deg Aquarius - Mukatrikona of Saturn. When Saturn is placed at these degrees in Aquarius, it will become very strong and will give excellent results during its dasha.
Amrit Nadi	28.53 - 29.46 deg Aquarius This brings good results, just like the nectar that nourishes.
Visha Nadi	23.33 - 24.26 deg Aquarius Brings situations that one does not like dealing with.

Auspicious and inauspicious table -

Auspicious	Inauspicious
Activities Good for all dangerous, uncertain, and adventurous activities, mechanical and technical activities, endings and funerals, for agricultural activities, and water-based activities like sailing or swimming.	Activities Not good for most activities, especially not good for new beginnings, for traveling, marriage, sexual activities, dealing with the government or authorities. Activities done on the days when the Ascendant, Sun, or Moon is in Purva Bhadrapada can cause pain, suffering, anxiety, regret, sorrow, or some difficulty.

Days	Days
<u>Mondays</u> - only when it falls on the 2nd, 7th, or 12th lunar day. <u>Tuesdays</u>- only when it falls on the 1st, 3rd, 5th, 6th, 7th, 8th, 11th, or 13th lunar day. <u>Wednesdays</u> - only when it falls on the 5th or 7th lunar day. <u>Thursdays</u> - only when it falls on the 4th, 5th, 7th, 9th, 13th, or 14th lunar day.	<u>Wednesdays</u>- only when it falls on the 2nd, 3rd, 8th or 9th lunar day.

Compatibility table -

Purva Bhadrapada	Compatible with
Sexual compatibility Yoni animal	Purva Bhadrapada - Female Lioness Dhanishta - Male Lion
Sign compatibility	Aquarius - Gemini and Libra Pisces - Cancer and Scorpio
Nakshatra compatibility	Punarvasu and Vishakha
Lunar day compatibility	Chaturdashi tithi - 14th lunar day
Day compatibility	Thursday and Saturday
Colour compatibility	Blue and yellow
Numerological compatibility	3 and 8 - all numbers that add up to make 3 and 8.
Sound compatibility	Saturn - labial sounds - pa, pha, ba, bha, ma Jupiter - dental sounds - ta, ttha, da, dha, knna

Sign Lord and nakshatra lord - <u>Saturn and Jupiter</u> - as described earlier.

The word Bhadra means auspicious; this highlights the beneficence of Jupiter. Purva Bhadrapada marks the culmination of Jupitarian energy. Jupiter is considered the most beneficent planet, which brings much fortune, grace, honour, respect, and grants the quality of positive thinking and optimism. They have a very righteous approach to life and like to do things lawfully and ethically.

It has a fierce energy, which shows that they will have their share of challenges and tests; however, they will be able to overcome the difficulties with the grace and blessing of positive thinking.

The 1st, 2nd, and 3rd padas of Purva Bhadrapada lie in Aquarius. Here, the quality of Saturn and Jupiter will give them a more practical approach. The 4th Pada of Purva Bhadrapada is placed in Pisces. This Pada has a very strong and pure Jupitarian energy. This makes the natives very idealistic and spiritually inclined.

<u>Quality, element, motivation, triguna, tridosha, and chakras -</u> as described earlier.

Shakti - <u>Yajamana Udyamana Shakti</u> - The power of fire worship and to rise and support people and devas.

They have the special blessing of being able to harness the auspicious energy of mantras when used in the presence of fire. It creates a certain etheric space of purity that acts like an invitation to divine energy. Through the blessing and grace of divine beings, a field of positiveness is created. Not at the level of thoughts or feelings, but at a deeper subconscious level, it enhances our well-being, and problems get resolved.

Those who are born with the Ascendent, Sun or Moon in Purva Bhadrapada will find that whenever they light a candle, or a lamp, or perform a fire ritual, and pray or worship sincerely, not only theirs, but the problems of those whom they think of also get resolved.

This is the power of positive thinking and sending thoughts and feelings of love and harmony to all whom one cares for.

Symbolic signification

<u>Aquarius</u> - as described earlier, <u>Pisces</u> - 2 fish moving towards each other, and <u>PurvaBhadrapada</u> - front legs of a funeral cot.

2 fish, moving towards each other

The sign of Pisces is symbolised by 2 fish who are moving towards each other. This shows opposing thoughts or feelings that counter each other, which can create confusion or make it difficult for one to decide which path to take.

It also highlights the dual nature of Pisces; they can comfortably handle playing 2 roles in one. They are very flexible and can easily adjust to situations or escape them when needed. Just as water is the basis of the existence of fish, emotional connection is the basis of joy and fulfilment for Pisces natives. For them, life becomes meaningless without love or empathy.

The funeral cot

Purva Bhadrapada is symbolised by the front legs of a funeral cot.

This again signifies their spiritual inclination. Pisces, being the last sign of the zodiac wheel, are highly evolved souls because they have gone through the entire gamut of the zodiac cycle and experienced the joys and sorrows of each sign. Their inherent wisdom of taking it easy and being more inward drawn and spiritual comes from a very deep understanding. They don't believe in wasting time, energy, and effort in pursuing worldly ambitions; they would rather be by themselves and give time to discovering their true nature of who they are.

They are very aware of the mortal nature of the physical body, and they look at death as the journey of the soul to move onto the next dimension.

Sadhguru's quotes on death

"Death is a function of the unaware. There is only life, life and life alone, moving from one dimension to another."

"Death is a cosmic joke. If you get the joke, falling on the other side will be wonderful."

"Life and death are like inhalation and exhalation. They always exist together."

"Life and death are not different."

Mythology -

Deity - <u>Aja Ekapada</u> - the one-footed goat or the unborn one.

The word Aja has many varied meanings in Sanskrit - it means a driver, mover, instigator, leader, goat, and not born - name of the unmanifest being. The Vedas also refer to Aja Ekapada as - one of the names of Lord Vishnu, one of the 11 Rudras, one of the Maruts (wind god), or as the vehicle of Agni (fire god).

As the unmanifest and unborn one, it signifies the external nature of existence, which is never born and can never die. As a one-footed goat, it shows the unique strength of a goat; it is a very resilient eater, and has the unique ability of eating a variety of plants and digesting them well.

Aja Ekapada is sometimes depicted as Lord Shiva in his Rudra form, when he is in severe penance, and is shown standing on one leg, which emphasises his ascetic nature. Standing on one foot has been one of the yogic practices, which has been practised by the sages and yogis since Vedic times. Among other austerities, some of the hatha yogis practised standing on one foot for long periods to gain mastery over their body and mind. Standing on 2 feet is a naturally balanced posture of the human body, but to stand on one foot and still maintain perfect balance cannot come without practice and will power. This asana (yogic posture) helps to improve balance, strength, and concentration. It also gives emotional stability, increased body and mind coordination, inner determination, resolute confidence, and spiritual enhancement.

Slowly, with regular practice, it helps one bring the body and mind to such a level of ease that they are comfortable and free in all kinds of situations.

This question can boggle the mind - Why would anyone choose to leave the easy comforts of life and put their body and mind through such difficult and harsh practices? Surely there might be something more enduring, more real, more captivating, more pleasurable, or more joyful that attracts them. Or is it just to explore the depth and dimension of their own intrinsic nature?

Sadhguru explains that true competence means blossoming into a full-fledged human being. To build a body and mind in such a way that it can be used to the fullest extent. Excellence is never in comparison, but to function at your own best, with utmost balance, ease, clarity, and focus. Over time, with regular yogic practices, the body and mind come to utmost ease.

This is the path of a true yogi and a true sage - they are truly free and beyond the fear of suffering, and the temptations of bodily pleasures. Because of this, they become hugely capable of handling situations and solving problems as it is needed according to the current situation.

Inference

Purva Bhadrapada natives are very spiritually inclined and are capable of enduring austerities like fasting, praying, worshipping, performing fire rituals or yajnas, mantra chanting, practising hatha yoga asanas, pranayama, and meditation.

Their fierce determination and willpower help them endure pain, hunger, thirst, or any extreme circumstances. On the other hand, if their mind gets tempted into bodily pleasures, they also have tremendous tenacity, stability, and willpower to overcome any alluring temptations, if they choose to do so.

Purva Bhadrapada padas

20 deg Aquarius - 3.20 deg Pisces

Padas	Degrees
1	20 - 23.20 deg Aquarius
2	23.20 - 26.40 deg Aquarius
3	26.40 - 30 deg Aquarius
4	0 - 3.20 deg Pisces

Pada 1

20 - 23.20 deg Aquarius, Navamsha- Aries (Lord - Mars)

Rashi Lord - Saturn and Nakshatra Lord- Jupiter

The 1st Pada will have the energy of Saturn, Jupiter, and Mars. The navamsha of Aries gives them a lot of energy, drive, and motivation. On the positive side, they will be very brave, honest, and adventurous. On the negative side, they can become short-tempered, aggressive, and impatient. Regular physical exercise, hatha yoga practices, pranayama, and meditation will be a great asset for them. This will help them positively channelise their energy.

For example, the 1st Pada of Purva Bhadrapada in the 5th house, they will be very energetic, determined, enterprising, helpful, spontaneous, generous and ambitious, and will be learned and well educated. Their children, students, or followers will look up to them for advice.

Careers

Teachers, engineers, builders, athletes, sportsmen and sportswomen, army officers, police officers, financial advisors, counsellors, property dealers, working in the field of advertisement, public relations coordinators, film directors, leaders, business men, IT professionals, designers, writers, speakers, social workers, religious leaders, priests, astrologers, office workers and working from home.

Pada 2

23.20 - 26.40 deg Aquarius, Navamsha - Taurus (Lord - Venus)

Rashi Lord - Saturn and Nakshatra Lord - Jupiter

In the 2nd Pada, there will be the energy of Saturn, Jupiter, and Venus, which will provide a good source of income and a good bank balance. Especially after the age of 30, or after marriage, they will have a steady job and a comfortable home. Relationships will matter a lot to them. They will be very well mannered and will be quite apt at being diplomatic or use sweet talk where needed, and will be religiously inclined.

Mostly, they will try to budget and control their expenses, but occasionally, they might give in to the temptation of shopping sprees, because of their sense of aesthetics and wanting to do things in a grand way. They usually enjoy their life, their routine, and their lifestyle.

For example, the 2nd Pada of Purva Bhadrapada is in the Ascendant. Venus, being the yoga Karka, becomes the most beneficent planet for Aquarius Ascendants. Therefore, they have the fortune of steady income, a good job, and a comfortable home. Depending on where Venus is placed, that area of life will be particularly beneficial during the dasha of Venus. If Venus is in the 5th house, they will enjoy good education and the joy of marriage and children.

Careers

Teachers, advisors, astrologers, consultants, IT professionals, film makers, fashion designers, florists, actors, artists, musicians, writers, philosophers, poets, cooks, and working from home.

Pada 3

26.40 - 30 deg Aquarius, Navamsha - Gemini (Lord - Mercury)

Rashi Lord - Saturn and Nakshatra Lord - Jupiter

The navamsha of the 3rd Pada is placed in Gemini, which gives the influence of Saturn, Jupiter, and Mercury. In this Pada, the natives will be intelligent and well informed, they will be very skilled in using computers, and will be eloquent speakers and wonderful writers.

Their curiosity will motivate them to constantly learn new things, and they will be especially interested in and exploring esoteric subjects like astrology, mythical stories, ancient texts, religious philosophies, and scriptures.

For example, the 3rd Pada of Purva Bhadrapada in the 3rd house, they will be very friendly and will get along well with their siblings and neighbours. They will love to travel, read, meet people, research on the internet and find out more about subjects that interest them.

Careers

Philosophers, guides, gurus, teachers, astrologers, advisors, consultants, managers, public relations coordinators, writers, poets, artists, actors, film directors, IT professionals, designers, doctors, businessmen and working from home.

Pada 4

0 - 3.20 deg Pisces, Navamsha - Cancer (Lord - Moon)

Rashi Lord - Jupiter and Nakshatra Lord- Jupiter

In this Pada, there will be a double influence of Jupiter and the Moon. The combination of Jupiter and the Moon is very beneficial and auspicious. They will be fortunate and will not have to work hard for worldly comforts. Their interest will lie in studying scriptures and exploring the inner realms. The gentle nature of both planets can make them utterly submissive or extremely imaginative and illusionary. They can come across as dreamy or disinterested in the mundane activities of life. The navamsha of Cancer makes them more intuitive, imaginative, emotional, loving, kind, and caring as they grow older, especially after the age of 30.

For example, the 4th Pada of Purva Bhadrapada in the 11th house, they will be associated with a large religious or spiritual organisation and will be well known for their kindness and empathy. Offering voluntary help in spiritual or religious endeavours will give them great fulfilment and joy.

Careers-

Psychologists, philosophers, researchers, IT professionals, astrologers, priests, teachers, advisors, counsellors, spiritual mediums, designers, artists, actors, singers, musicians, writers, poets, self-employed, and working from home.

The effect of planets

Purva Bhadrapada - Aquarius	Planets that get affected
Yoga Karka - most benefic	Venus
Functional Benefic - give good results during their dasha.	Mars, Sun and Jupiter

Functional Malefic - can give problems during their dasha.	Moon, Rahu and Ketu
Functional Neutral	Mercury and Saturn
Purva Bhadrapada - Pisces	**Planets that get affected**
Functional Benefic - give good results during their dasha.	Jupiter, Mercury, Mars and Moon
Functional Malefic - can give problems during their dasha.	Sun, Rahu and Ketu
Functional Neutral	Venus and Saturn
Kendra Adi Pati Dosha - can be malefic	Mercury

Purva Bhadrapada Ascendant

Those who have their Ascendant in 1st, 2nd, and 3rd padas of Purva Bhadrapada will have the influence of Saturn and Jupiter. These padas are placed in Aquarius, which is ruled by the air element and has a fixed quality. Therefore, they are very adaptable, but also very organised. Saturn, being the farthest planet with an attractive blue hue, gives it a quality of being elusive and attractive at the same time.

The influence of Saturn makes them rebellious, but for a good reason, a good cause, and not for any selfish motives. For them, the well-being of the whole community is their well-being. Because of this, they end up joining an organisation or offering voluntary help wherever needed.

In the 4th Pada of Purva Bhadrapada, there will be a strong influence of Jupiter. This is a very fortunate Pada, in the sense that things come easy to them, the only danger is that they become too complacent or lazy to work towards and worldly ambitions. Their gentle and gracious nature creates an ambience of peace, love, and harmony; they usually don't have to face any violent or aggressive situations or people. Because the way we are within ourselves, that's the kind of life we attract to ourselves.

Sun in Purva Bhadrapada

When the Sun is placed in the 1st, 2nd and 3rd padas of Purva Bhadrapada, it will have the influence of Saturn and Jupiter. Sun and Jupiter get along well, but Sun and Saturn are enemies, so there will be a mixed effect of positive and negative vibes. The natives will be intelligent, confident, wise, and learned. The influence of Saturn can bring frustration and delays during the dasha of the Sun or Saturn. For example, Sun in the 2nd Pada of Purva Bhadrapada in the 2nd house, the native will like to live life in a grand style. Whatever he or she earns will be spent quite easily and will not be able to save much. There could be frustration or restriction felt on the home front, especially during the dasha of Saturn. From the 2nd house Sun aspects the 8th house of Leo (his own house) directly; therefore, the native benefits from sudden gains through government policies, insurance, or ancestral property.

The 4th Pada of Purva Bhadrapada lies in Pisces; when the Sun is placed here, it will share the qualities of Jupiter. Sun and Jupiter are friends; therefore, it's a good placement. The natives will have the intelligence and confidence of the Sun, and the wisdom and optimism of Jupiter, which can make them wonderful writers, speakers, actors, teachers, or philosophers. For example, Sun is placed in the 4th Pada of Purva Bhadrapada in the 10th house, the native's father will be a great support, and he or she will follow the father's profession or take his legacy forward. He or she will achieve honour, recognition and success during the dasha of the Sun or Jupiter.

Since the Sun is the lord of the 3rd house of Leo sitting in the 10th house of public image, the native will be appreciated for his or her sincere and brave effort towards his or her career.

Moon in Purva Bhadrapada

When the Moon is placed in the 1st, 2nd, and 3rd padas of Purva Bhadrapada, it will have the influence of Saturn and Jupiter. The energies of Jupiter and Saturn vibrate well at one level, because they are both outer planets, farthest away from Earth and are gaseous in nature. At another level, they have opposing qualities because Jupiter is considered benefic and Saturn is considered malefic. The beneficence of Jupiter reduces the malefic quality of Saturn and helps it to embrace all and include all in its well-being. Therefore, the natives' thoughts and actions are always motivated by the desire to help and serve the people in some way.

For example, if the moon is in Purva Bhadrapada in the 7th house, their spouse or partner will be very community-oriented. After marriage, the native will also get more opportunities to get involved in serving the public in some way.

When the Moon is placed in the 4th Pada of Purva Bhadrapada, it will share the qualities of Jupiter. The combination of Jupiter and the Moon is always auspicious. The natives will be gentle, kind, and caring and will like to do things righteously.

Their way of coping with disappointments, hurt, pain, or injury is by turning inwards, turning to God, and seeking spiritual guidance. It works wonders for them, because at the subconscious level, the soul has gained much experience and wisdom to know that ultimately, one has to turn to the source to find workable solutions. They naturally feel more inclined towards inner wisdom and understanding. For example, if Moon is in Purva Bhadrapada in the 9th house, the native will be very religious or spiritually inclined. He or she will be devoted to his or her father, a father-like figure, a teacher, or a guru, and will travel away from home for his or her higher education.

The poetry of Purva Bhadrapada

Purva Bhadrapada - the former one with auspicious feet,

Aja Ekapada - balanced on one foot - a tremendous feat.

The resolute to continue and not cease,

The dedicated effort and austerities,

Brought the body to perfect ease.

The yogic strength - of sages and seers,

An ultimate freedom from one's own fears.

The karmic play of Saturn - a silent saga,

Jupiterian goodness - the final bhava.

The test of time and the rest of phase,

Before the next one we embrace.

Aquarius - the pot that pours water,

To Pisces - the oceanic beauty draws her.

The happy fish - a peaceful serenity,

The end of the zodiacal extremity.

Remedies

- <u>Das Maha Vidya</u> - as described earlier.

- Whenever they light a lamp or a candle, or perform any fire rituals (yajna), their problems begin to ease out and they find answers to questions they were seeking.

- For those who are born in the 1st, 2nd or 3rd padas of Purva Bhadrapada, their predominant tridosha will be Vata, so a daily exercise routine will keep them grounded and in good health. They should not do very vigorous exercises, like running or cycling in the hot sun, or tough muscle-building gym exercises for a long duration at a stretch. It will be better to listen to their body. When they feel exhausted, they must take ample rest before getting into excessive activity again.

- Those who are born in the 4th Pada of Purva Bhadrapada will have a more Kapha predominant constitution. So, for them, consciously developing an active lifestyle and including fresh fruits and salads in their diet will be helpful. Avoid sleeping for too long, especially during the day.

- The yogic asanas, pranayama, and meditation always enhance the ability to focus, which in turn improves the quality of whatever you do and brings ease into all thoughts and actions.

- Blue and yellow colours resonate well with the energy of Purva Bhadrapada.

- Chanting the mantra - *"Om vam sham Purva Bhadrapada nakshatraye namah."* 108 times on days when the moon is transiting Purva Bhadrapada or on Thursdays will help to connect you with your inner self.

Example

Ascendant in Purva Bhadrapada

Deepak Chopra - an Endocrinologist Doctor, promotes Ayurveda and Vedic lifestyle, and has written many books on spirituality, and is a well-known public speaker.

Born on 22nd October 1947, 3:45 pm, Delhi, India.

Deepak is an Indian-American author and alternative medicine advocate. He is a prominent figure in the New Age movement; his books and videos have made him one of the best-known and wealthiest figures in alternative medicine.

Deepak was born in New Delhi, British India, to Krishan Lal Chopra and Pushpa Chopra. His paternal grandfather was a sergeant in the British Indian Army. His father was a prominent cardiologist, head of the department of medicine and cardiology at New Delhi's Moolchand Khairati Ram Hospital for over 25 years, and was also a lieutenant in the British army, serving as an army doctor at the front in Burma and acting as a medical adviser to Lord Mountbatten, viceroy of India.

He completed his primary education at St. Columba's School in New Delhi and graduated from the All India Institute of Medical Sciences in 1969. He spent his first months as a doctor working in rural India, including, he writes, 6 months in a village where the lights went out whenever it rained. It was during his early career that he was drawn to study endocrinology, particularly neuroendocrinology, to find a biological basis for the influence of thoughts and emotions.

He married in India in 1970 before emigrating, with his wife, to the United States that same year. The Indian government had banned its doctors from sitting for the exam needed to practice in the US; consequently, he had to travel to Sri Lanka to take it. After passing, he arrived in the

United States to take up a clinical internship at Muhlenberg Hospital in Plainfield, New Jersey, where doctors from overseas were being recruited to replace those serving in Vietnam.

He earned his license to practice medicine in the state of Massachusetts in 1973, becoming board certified in internal medicine, specialising in endocrinology. He taught at the medical schools of Tufts University, Boston University, and Harvard University before establishing a private practice in Boston in endocrinology.

Maharishi Mahesh Yogi was an influence on Deepak in the 1980s.

While visiting New Delhi in 1981, he met the Ayurvedic physician Brihaspati Dev Triguna, head of the Indian Council for Ayurvedic Medicine, whose advice prompted him to begin investigating Ayurvedic practices.

His involvement with TM led to a meeting in 1985 with the leader of the TM movement, Maharishi Mahesh Yogi, who asked him to establish an Ayurvedic health centre. He left his position at the NEMH. Deepak said that one of the reasons he left was his disenchantment at having to prescribe too many drugs, "When all you do is prescribe medication, you start to feel like a legalised drug pusher. That doesn't mean that all prescriptions are useless, but it is true that 80 % of all drugs prescribed today are of optional or marginal benefit."

He became the founding president of the American Association of Ayurvedic Medicine. That year, Chopra's Quantum Healing book - Exploring the Frontiers of Mind-Body Medicine was published, followed by a book on Perfect Health - The Complete Mind-Body Guide in 1990.

In January 1993, he left the Transcendental Meditation movement and moved to California. In 1995, he founded the 'Chopra Centre for Well-being' in Carlsbad, California. Which is now called - 'Chopra Well.' He is the owner and supervisor of the Mind-Body Medical Group within the Chopra Centre, which, in addition to standard medical treatment, offers personalised advice about nutrition, sleep-wake cycles, and stress management based on mainstream medicine and Ayurveda.

His book, Ageless Body, Timeless Mind - The Quantum Alternative to Growing Old, was published in 1993. The book and his friendship with Michael Jackson gained him an interview on 12th July that year on Oprah. Paul Offit writes that within 24 hours, Chopra had sold 137,000 copies of his book and 400,000 by the end of the week. Chopra and his wife have, as of 2013, 2 adult children (Gotham Chopra and Mallika Chopra) and 3 grandchildren. As of 2019, Deepak lives in a health-centric condominium in Manhattan.

In 2016, Chopra was promoted from voluntary assistant clinical professor to voluntary full clinical professor at the University of California, San Diego, in their Department of Family Medicine and Public Health. Chopra and physicians at the Chopra Centre practise integrative medicine, combining the medical model of conventional Western medicine with alternative therapies such as yoga, mindfulness meditation, and Ayurveda.

He coined the term quantum healing to invoke the idea of a process whereby a person's health imbalance is corrected by quantum mechanical means. He said that quantum phenomena are responsible for health and well-being. He has attempted to integrate Ayurveda, a traditional Indian system of medicine, with quantum mechanics in order to justify his teachings.

He has been described as America's most prominent spokesman for Ayurveda. His treatments benefit from the placebo response. Chopra states - The placebo effect is real medicine, because it triggers the body's healing system.

Analysis -

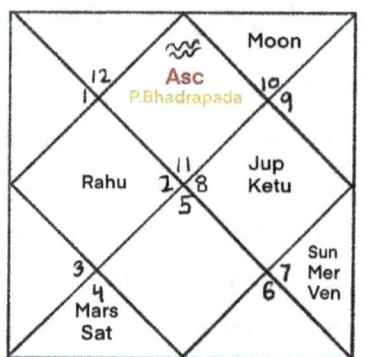

His <u>Ascendant is in Aquarius in Purva Bhadrapada 2nd Pada</u>. Saturn, the lord of Aquarius, is sitting in the 6th house of Cancer along with Mars. Jupiter, the lord of Purva Bhadrapada, is sitting in the 10th house of Scorpio along with Ketu.

Jupiter, being the nakshatra Lord sitting in the 10th house of career, made him a well-known and well-respected public figure. However, Jupiter sitting with Ketu has brought many controversies about his philosophy on a holistic approach to medicine. On the other hand, Ketu detaches him from his persona as a well-known public face and public speaker.

The Aquarius Ascendant made him expand his horizons and include everyone in their plan of wellbeing. Jupiter, the Ascendant nakshatra lord, gives him beneficence, expansion, and growth. His interest in philosophy, spirituality, and inner understanding and knowledge comes from the benefic nature of Jupiter. Saturn, the lord of Aquarius, is the karmic planet and the planet of service. The events and situations that have happened in his life have all been geared towards preparing him to understand and master the skill of holistic medicine and self-healing, and in turn, be able to serve humanity through his knowledge and wisdom.

Saturn is the lord of the Ascendant and the 12th house, which made him settle in a foreign country after starting his job and after marriage. In 1969, after graduating, he spent his first months as a doctor working in rural India. In 1969, he was running his Rahu Jupiter Moon dasha. Rahu is in the 4th house, Jupiter is in the 10th house, and the Moon is in the 12th house. So he had to move away from home for his job. Moreover, he was in his 33rd year in 1969, which activated the 9th house of long travel and higher education.

He married in India in 1970 before emigrating with his wife to the United States. In 1970, he was running his <u>Rahu Ketu Venus</u> dasha.

Rahu is in the 4th house of home - he settled in a foreign land with foreign people. Ketu is sitting with Jupiter in the 10th house of career - he had to change his residence and move to a foreign land because of better career prospects. Venus is sitting with Sun and Mercury in the 9th house - he moved to a foreign country after marriage. The 9th house signifies higher education. He continued his higher education in a foreign land and completed a residency in internal medicine and a fellowship in endocrinology. He was in his 34th year in 1970, which activated the 10th house of career.

He has got 3 planets sitting in the 9th house of fortune - Sun, Venus, and Mercury. The 9th house lord, Venus, is sitting in his own house of Libra. Sun is the lord of the 7th house of Leo. Mercury is the lord of the 5th house, which is a trikona house. The connection between Kendra and trikona houses makes a very powerful Raj yoga, which gives a kingly status. It promises wealth, abundance, prestige, status, comforts, and joys of family life - wife and children, an excellent career, and the grace and blessing of the ancestors, father and teachers.

During the 16 years of Jupiter's mahadasha from 1983 to 1999, his perspective changed from worldly to spiritual. This is the time in his life when he started practising meditation and writing books on spirituality and holistic medicine.

Saturn and Mars being in the 6th house of debts, disease, or enemies, brought him a lot of controversies. He has been criticised for his frequent references to the relationship of quantum mechanics to healing processes, a connection that has drawn scepticism from some physicists who say it creates confusion. However, malefic planets in the 6th house do very well because they give the strength, energy, determination, and discipline to stand up against any opposition and overcome difficulties.

Not just the challenges that we face in the outer world, but it's a real test to recognise our flaws and then try to overcome them. Deepak was drinking black coffee by the hour and smoking at least a pack of cigarettes a day. He took up Transcendental Meditation to help him stop, and as of 2006, he continues to meditate for 2 hours every morning and half an hour in the evening.

It's interesting to note that he named his organisation '<u>Chopra Well</u>'. Scorpio is in his 10th house, which represents public image. The sign of Scorpio signifies the deep waters of a well. Very appropriately, his company is called - 'Chopra Well.' In 1995, he founded the - 'Chopra Centre for Wellbeing in Carlsbad, California. Which is now called - 'Chopra Well.'

Deepak Chopra Quotes -

"You must find the place inside yourself where nothing is impossible."

"The use of love is to heal. When it flows without effort from the depth of self, love creates health."

"Be happy for no reason like a child. If you are happy for a reason, you are in trouble, because that reason can be taken from you."

28
Uttara Bhadrapada

Om sham sam ham Uttara Bhadrapada nakshatraye namah

Zodiac degrees	3.20 deg - 16.40 Pisces
Ruling planet	Pisces - Jupiter and Uttara Bhadrapada - Saturn
Sanskrit name	Uttara Bhadrapada - Uttara means the latter, or rising in the north and Bhadra means excellent, blessed, pleasant, fortunate, auspicious, fair or prosperous. Uttara Bhadrapada means the latter one whose feet are auspicious.
Astronomical name	Uttara Bhadrapada is represented by 2 bright stars seen in the constellation of Pegasus.
Symbol	Pisces - 2 fish moving towards each other. Uttara Bhadrapada - back legs of a funeral cot.
Element	Water
Deity	Ahirbudhnya - the serpent of the deep waters
Quality	Mridu - gentle and Dual - Dwi
Shakti	Varshodyamana Shakti - The power to bring rain, growth and stability.
Cast	Kshatriya - warrior
Gender	Female
Motivation	Moksha - liberation
Triguna	Satwa
Tridosha	Kapha
Body parts	Lateral sides of the body
Direction	North and West
Month	September - later half of Bhadrapada month.

Bird	Pigeon
Sound	du, tha, jha, na
Tree	Neem tree
Chakras	Vishuddhi - Saturn and Jupiter - Ajna
Das Maha Vidya	Devi Kali - Saturn and Devi Tara - Jupiter

Special degrees -

Yoga Tara	15 deg Pisces It's a point where the planet will show the strongest and sure results during its dasha.
Pushkar amsha	2nd Pada Any planets sitting at this point will give excellent results during their dasha, like the blossoming of a flower.
Debilitation	15 deg Pisces - Maximum debilitation of Mercury. This will bring in situations which can create misunderstandings and arguments in a relationship.
Amrit Nadi	14 - 14.53 deg Pisces This brings good results just like the nectar that nourishes.
Visha Nadi	8.40 - 9.33 deg Pisces Brings situations which one does not like dealing with.

Auspicious and inauspicious table -

Auspicious	Inauspicious
Activities Good for all peaceful and artistic activities, research work, for prayers, worship, spiritual practices and meditation, for making promises and taking oaths, marriage, for new beginnings and starting constructions, entering a new home, naming a child, for making financial deals, getting help and support, treatment of diseases, sexual activities, planting and gardening.	Activities Not good for traveling, dealing with legal activities, dealing with opposition, speculation, gambling, activities that require quick action, not good for lending money, physically strenuous activities.
Days Sundays - only when it falls on the 1st, 4th, 6th, 7th or 12th lunar day. Tuesdays- only when it falls on the 5th or 7th lunar day.	Days Mondays- only when it falls on the 6th, 7th or 11th lunar day.

Compatibility table -

Uttara Bhadrapada	Compatible with
Sexual compatibility Yoni animal	Uttara Bhadrapada - Female Cow Uttara Phalguni - Male Cow
Sign compatibility	Cancer and Scorpio
Nakshatra compatibility	Pushya and Anuradha
Lunar day compatibility	Navami tithi - 9th lunar day
Day compatibility	Thursday and Saturday
Colour compatibility	Blue and yellow
Numerological compatibility	3 and 8 - all numbers that add up to make 3 and 8.
Sound compatibility	Saturn - labial sounds - pa, pha, ba, bha, ma Jupiter - dental sounds - ta, ttha, da, dha, knna

Sign Lord and nakshatra lord - <u>Saturn and Jupiter</u> - as described earlier.

The word Bhadra means auspicious; this highlights the beneficence of Jupiter. Uttara Bhadrapada is the 3rd of the Saturn-ruled nakshatras and marks the apex of Saturnian energy. Saturn, the karma karka, when combined with the beneficence of Jupiter, makes it expand its horizons and wants to reach out and help people as much as possible.

Both Purva Bhadrapada and Uttara Bhadrapada carry the energy of Jupiter and Saturn. The only significant difference is that Purva Bhadrapada has a fierce rising energy, and Uttara Bhadrapada has a calm and gentle energy. Just as the eruption of a volcano needs the push of a rising force, after the eruption, it still carries the intensity of fire, but now the lava flows with more ease.

Uttara Bhadrapada natives don't care much for worldly achievements; their thoughts and actions are oriented more towards realising their true self. Everything mystical, spiritual, religious, esoteric and philosophical attracts them.

Since Pisces is the last sign of the zodiac, the soul has passed through the experience of all previous zodiacs, starting from Ashwini. This is the final excursion into the sensitive water element and the feminine energy. Just as the soul is born into the innocent, carefree nature of Aries, it symbolically dies or leaves the interest of earthly desires in the sign of Pisces.

In the last sign, the soul enters into an empathetic humility because it begins to become aware of dimensions that exist beyond the physical planes. The natives born in Uttara Bhadrapada begin to get glimpses of the eternal nature of truth, of time and space - that always exists. In a way, at an unconscious level, the soul has attained spiritual enlightenment after having gone through the long journey of the preceding 11 signs.

Quality, element, motivation, triguna, tridosha and chakras - as described earlier.

Shakti - Varshodyamana Shakti - The power to bring rain, growth and stability.

Those who are born with their Ascendent, Sun or Moon in Uttara Bhadrapada have a special affinity with water, because it's placed in the water ruled sign of Pisces. They have a special blessing of nurturing others through their kind words, which fall like refreshing raindrops on a dry, parched land that was yearning for the wetness of water.

They will notice that rainfall is an auspicious sign for them. If they are going for some important job, or preparing for some major event, or doing something that means a lot to them, and if it rains at that time, they usually get good results.

Symbolic signification

Pisces - as described earlier.

Uttara Bhadrapada - back legs of the funeral cot.

Uttara Bhadrapada represents the back legs of a funeral cot, which signifies the movement of energy towards its culmination, or the end point. The quality of Pisces is more of a mystical nature that deals with the dimensions of the beyond.

Mythology -

Deity - Ahirbudhnya - the serpent of the deep waters.

The Sanskrit word Ahirbudhnya is the combination of 2 words - Ahi means a serpent, and Budhna means the foundation of the world. Ahirbhudnya refers to the Shesha naga or Ananta naga- a 1000-headed serpent. Vishnu Purana, the ancient Hindu text, mentions that AhirBudhnya is the greatest devotee of Lord Vishnu, because he offers his body as a bed for Lord Vishnu. Lord Vishnu is often shown lying down in a relaxed posture on the coils of Shesha naga, and Goddess Lakshmi is sitting near his feet.

Ahirbudhnya is a water serpent or dragon of the deep seas. The Vedic texts have also described him as the god of fertility. He represents the kundalini energy, feels comfortable in the depths and has a special need for seclusion. He is considered to be one of the 11 Rudras and is the Son of Viswakarma, the Celestial Architect.

Inference

Those who are born with their Ascendant, Sun or Moon in Uttara Bhadrapada, like Ahirbhudnya, have a beautiful quality of devotion. They will be devoted to someone, or some ideology, philosophy, faith, religion, or some form of spiritual practices that will help them enhance their inner and outer wellbeing. Because of their total dedication, they always have the blessings of Lord Vishnu and Goddess Lakshmi. They will also be very good at maintaining and sustaining things.

Uttara Bhadrapada natives feel the need to be alone and spend time by themselves. The ones who are genuine spiritual seekers need a lot of time on their own to contemplate their true nature, meditate, pray and do their spiritual practices. Just as a student who aims to achieve a higher degree, or anyone who is trying to master a certain skill, needs to spend a lot of time by himself or herself in order to perfect their practice.

Uttara Bhadrapada padas

3.20 - 16.40 deg Pisces

Padas	Degrees
1	3.20 - 6.40 deg Pisces
2	6.40 - 10 deg Pisces
3	10 - 13.20 deg Pisces
4	13.20 - 16.40 deg Pisces

Pada 1

3.20 - 6.40 deg Pisces, Navamsha- Leo (Lord - Sun)

Rashi Lord - Jupiter and Nakshatra Lord- Saturn

The 1st Pada of Uttara Bhadrapada will have the energy of Jupiter, Saturn and Sun. The navamsha of Leo gives them a very dignified personality. They will be very honest, generous, straightforward, intelligent and creative. After the age of 30, they will become more confident about themselves and will be able to express their opinions and thoughts more openly and freely. They are likely to face delays or some frustrations during the dasha of Saturn.

For example, the 1st Pada of Uttara Bhadrapada in the 5th house, they will be very intelligent, creative, well educated, learned and will take pride in their work. Their children or students will look up to them for advice.

Careers

Teachers, politicians, advisors, counsellors, psychologists, psychiatrists, managers, businessmen, IT professionals, doctors, nurses, astrologers, therapists, healers and working from home.

Pada 2

6.40 - 10 deg Pisces, Navamsha - Virgo (Lord - Mercury)

Rashi Lord - Jupiter and Nakshatra Lord - Saturn

In the 2nd Pada of Uttara Bhadrapada, there will be the energy of Jupiter, Saturn and Mercury, which will make them more detail-oriented and analytical. They will be perfectionists and will want to do things exactly as they are supposed to be done, following the minutest details. They will be very good at handling finance, accounts and will have wonderful IT skills. They will be very communicative about their feelings and will be great listeners and advisors too. Since Uttara Bhadrapada lies in the watery sign of Pisces, they are naturally sensitive, feminine and receptive to others' feelings and needs.

For example, the 2nd Pada of Uttara Bhadrapada, placed in the 3rd house, they will have a very good relationship with their siblings. They will be very friendly and very apt at giving sensible advice to their friends, family and neighbours. They will love travelling to places which are near water.

Mercury has the Kendra Adapati dosha and can become malefic for those who have Pisces - Uttara Bhadrapada as their Ascendant. This can manifest in problems with education or misunderstandings in communication that can come up during the dasha of Mercury.

Careers

Psychiatrists, philosophers, astrologers, consultants, therapists, past life regression therapists, hypnotists, doctors, researchers, IT professionals, actors, film makers, artists, writers, and working from home.

Pada 3

10 - 13.20 deg Pisces, Navamsha - Libra (Lord - Venus)

Rashi Lord - Jupiter and Nakshatra Lord - Saturn

The navamsha of the 3rd Pada of Uttara Bhadrapada is placed in Libra, which gives the influence of Jupiter, Saturn and Venus. In this Pada, the natives will have a very fine sense of aesthetics, balance and harmony. They will be very sensitive to their surroundings, and any shabby environment can make them feel stressed. If they end up in such a situation, they will need to tidy up the place, redecorate, or find another place to live.

They are very creative and can make great actors, artists, poets and fiction writers. Since Venus gets exalted in Pisces, especially during the Venus dasha, and after the age of 30, they will have the comfort of a well-decorated home and good vehicles. Depending on where Venus is placed, they will be very creative in that area of life. For instance, if Venus is placed in the 6th house, they will have a job where they get to use their artistic talent, or they might run their own business where they get to express their creativity.

For example, in the 3rd Pada of Uttara Bhadrapada in the 4th house, their mother will be a very creative person. Their home will be very well decorated and well-kept. The native will imbibe all these wonderful qualities and will be a very creative person himself or herself.

Careers

Artists, actors, architects, designers, decorators, astrologers, advisors, consultants, managers, public relations coordinators, writers, poets, film directors, IT professionals, doctors, businessmen and working from home.

Pada 4

13.20 - 16.40 deg Pisces, Navamsha - Scorpio (Lord - Mars)

Rashi Lord - Jupiter and Nakshatra Lord- Saturn

In the 4th Pada of Uttara Bhadrapada, there will be the influence of Jupiter, Mars and Saturn. Mars becomes a functional benefic for Pisces Ascendants only and will give good results during its dasha. For example, the 4th Pada of Uttara Bhadrapada, placed in the Ascendant, and Mars is placed in the 6th house of Leo. The natives are likely to face opposition during the dasha of Mars, but they will be able to win over their opponents through their determination and faith. In Fact, any confrontations that they might face, they will benefit from it, in the sense that it will open up new avenues for them, which they would otherwise not have paid attention to.

They will be more inward drawn and will be happy to do their own research and find answers to many mystical questions that intrigue them. Especially after the age of 30, they will become more determined about following their ambition. For example, in the 4th Pada of Uttara Bhadrapada in the 2nd house, the natives will be very devoted to providing a stable income source for their family.

Especially during the dasha of Mars, they will have a good, steady income. They will benefit or gain from another source apart from their regular income, like insurance or ancestral property.

Careers-

Astrologers, archaeologists, sportsmen and sportswomen, athletes, doctors, nurses, psychologists, detectives, spies, researchers, IT professionals, businessmen, property dealers, builders, farmers, gardeners, self-employed and working from home.

The effect of planets

Uttara Bhadrapada - Pisces	Planets that get affected
Functional Benefic - gives good results during their dasha.	Jupiter, Mercury, Mars and Moon
Functional Malefic - can give problems during their dasha.	Sun, Rahu and Ketu
Functional Neutral	Venus and Saturn
Kendra Adi Pati Dosha - can be malefic	Mercury

Uttara Bhadrapada Ascendant

Those who have their Ascendant in Uttara Bhadrapada will have the influence of Jupiter and Saturn. Jupiter gives optimism, expansion, knowledge and beneficence, and Saturn gives the slow, cautious approach, wisdom and restriction.

Pisces is the last of the zodiac signs and the most difficult one to comprehend, because the 12th house signifies everything that is unknown - alien, foreign, mysterious and mystical. It also signifies isolation and loss. When seen from the material perspective, it seems to be daunting, scary and petrifying.

But when looked at from the spiritual, religious or divine perspective, being alone is a blessing, because one needs to spend a lot of time by himself or herself if one has to realise their true self. When a spiritual seeker is genuinely on the path, there is nothing that is boring, because he or she realises that there is so much to be explored - it's a limitless dimension, so there is no time left for boredom. Since one can never fully fathom, but only dissolve into the source and become that.

The Vedas describe our true nature as - *'Aham Brahmasmi,'* which literally means - I am Brahman. It expresses the fact that our individual self (jiva Atma) appears to be separate from the universal consciousness (param Atma), but the truth is that we are all a part of the whole (Brahman) and therefore that which has been created has the same attributes as the creator (Brahman).

Those who are born with the Pisces Ascendant are old souls and have been through the rigmarole of life many times over and in many lifetimes. So this time around, in this lifetime, the soul has chosen to be born with the intention to finish off the pending karma and move into the other mystical realms and not come back to the earthly realm once again. Therefore, Uttara Bhadrapada natives seem to be unassuming and unambitious from the worldly perspective, but are very ambitious spiritually and therefore more inwardly drawn.

There is a very interesting connection which often gets overlooked. The Roman mythology has emphasised the goodness of Saturn, which can be observed in the astrological readings as well. Saturn, the lord of Uttara Bhadrapada, is named after the Roman god of agriculture and wealth, who is also said to have been the father of Jupiter. Saturn was also known as the god of time. In this context, those who have their Ascendant in Uttara Bhadrapada will be connected to land, farm, agriculture, or gardening in some way. It also signifies that connecting to Mother Earth in some way will bring them much abundance and grace.

Sun in Uttara Bhadrapada

When the Sun is placed in Uttara Bhadrapada, it will share the energies of Jupiter and Saturn. Sun and Jupiter get along well, but Sun and Saturn are not comfortable together. Therefore, there will be a mixed influence of the brilliance of the Sun, Jupiterian optimism and Satarian caution. The natives will have a very positive approach towards life, but will feel restricted, especially during the dasha of Saturn.

Sun is considered to be a functional malefic for a Pisces Ascendant. For example, suppose the 1st Pada of Uttara Bhadrapada is placed in the 1st house. In that case, the natives will feel the confusion between whether they should be assertive or submissive in certain demanding situations. They will feel caught up in these ethical dilemmas, especially in their younger years; later, as they grow older, they will become clearer about what choices they should make. Sun being the lord of the 6th house placed in the Ascendant, the natives can face some minor problems with their finances, health, or some kind of opposition. Or some difficulty could come up regarding their father, boss, teacher, government or authorities during the dasha of the Sun.

Moon in Uttara Bhadrapada

When the Moon is placed in Uttara Bhadrapada, it will have the influence of Jupiter and Saturn. Jupiterian idealism and Saturnian coolness make a very spiritual and religious combination. The natives' thoughts, emotions and feelings will be inspired and motivated by the ancient scriptures, religious texts, and biographies of saints, mystics and yogis. They tend to seek escapism or isolation, not in a negative way, but to reflect, contemplate, understand and liberate themselves from the very cause that triggers any negativity. They will be very good at expressing their joys or sorrows, or something that touches them deeply through writing, poetry, art, drawing, painting or acting.

When a person is born with their Moon placed in Pisces - Uttara Bhadrapada, they feel a new urgency, a new vulnerability to finish off the pending karma and attain moksha - liberation. This is so because subconsciously they are searching for the truth that is all-pervading, all-inclusive and eternal. They are seeking something that does not die when the body dies, that is not forgotten or lost when the mind shuts down.

Their sensitive and peace-loving nature makes them tread carefully, especially in terms of choosing friends. They are intensely loyal - when they give themselves to some person, relationship, or cause, they do so completely. For them, emotional connection, dedication and devotion are very important. For example, Moon in Uttara Bhadrapada in the 4th house they will be emotionally connected to their mother and will be devoted to their home. Their home will have a peaceful ambience. The natives will love spending time at home with their family, or by themselves - creating a piece of art, reflecting, contemplating, meditating or doing their spiritual practices.

The poetry of Uttara Bhadrapada

Uttara Bhadrapada - the latter one with auspicious feet,

Ahirbudhnya from the depths of calm retreat.

The coiled bed of his body - a devotional frame,

Lord Vishnu and Goddess Lakshmi relax and sustain.

The exalted Venus - an ultimate ecstacy,

For each one - their own fantasy.

Seems to be simple - yet hard to comprehend,

Human effort - a worthwhile trend.

The care and gentle sensitivity,

Living the dream - we call life - with empathy.

The raindrops that nourish the soil and plants,

Can fulfil the thirst of the mind and beyond.

The last sign of the of the zodiac wheel,

Carries the wisdom of previous yields.

Pursue that which is worth pursuing,

Not lost, not forgotten and has no ending.

Remedies

- <u>Das Maha Vidya</u> - as described earlier.
- Rain is an auspicious sign for them.

- They have a Kapha predominant constitution. So for them, consciously developing an active lifestyle and including fresh fruits and salads in your diet will be helpful. Avoid sleeping for too long, especially during the day.

- The yogic asanas, pranayama and meditation always enhances the ability to focus, which in turn improves the quality of whatever you do and brings ease into all thoughts and actions.

- Blue and yellow colours resonate well with the energy of Purva Bhadrapada.

- Chanting the mantra -" *Om sham sam ham Uttara Bhadrapada nakshatraye namah.*" 108 times on days when the moon is transiting Uttara Bhadrapada or on Thursdays or Saturdays, will help to connect you with your inner self.

Example

Ascendant in Uttara Bhadrapada

Ramanujan - A Renowned Indian Mathematician.

Born on 22nd December 1887 and died on 26th April 1920, at a young age of 32. Born in Erode, Madras, India, estimated time of birth 12 pm.

Ramanujan was an Indian mathematician who made substantial contributions to mathematical analysis. He was born to a Tamil Brahmin Iyengar family at the residence of his maternal grandparents. His father, Srinivasa Iyengar, worked as a clerk in a sari shop, and his mother, Komalatammal, was a housewife and sang at a local temple. The family home is now a museum.

Since Ramanujan's father was at work most of the day, he was very close to his mother. From her, he learned about tradition and puranas, to sing religious songs, to attend pujas at the temple, and to maintain particular eating habits, all part of Brahmin culture. At Kangayan Primary School, Ramanujan performed well. He was good in his studies, and when he started his secondary school, he got greatly interested in mathematics.

He was deeply religious and credited his substantial mathematical capacities to divinity, and said the mathematical knowledge he displayed was revealed to him by his family goddess Namagiri Thayar - one of the forms of Devi Mahalakshmi. He once said, "An equation for me has no meaning unless it expresses a thought of God."

On 14th July 1909, Ramanujan married Janaki, a girl his mother had selected for him. In 1912, she and Ramanujan's mother joined him in Madras. He departed from Madras aboard the ship S.S. Nevasa on 17th March 1914. On reaching London, Ramanujan immediately began his work with Littlewood and Hardy, who had already received 120 theorems from Ramanujan earlier in his letters. But there were many more results and theorems in his notebooks. Hardy saw that some were wrong, others had already been discovered, and the rest were new breakthroughs.

Ramanujan was plagued by health problems throughout his life. His health worsened in England, possibly because he was also less resilient due to the difficulty of keeping to the strict dietary requirements of his religion there and because of wartime rationing in 1914-18. He was diagnosed with tuberculosis and a severe vitamin deficiency and confined to a sanatorium. In 1919, ill health compelled Ramanujan's return to India, where he died in 1920 at the age of 32. After his death, his brother compiled Ramanujan's remaining handwritten notes, consisting of formulae on singular moduli, hypergeometric series and continued fractions.

His last letters to Hardy, written in January 1920, show that he was still continuing to produce new mathematical ideas and theorems. His lost notebook containing discoveries from the last year of his life caused great excitement among mathematicians when it was rediscovered in 1976.

During his short life, Ramanujan independently compiled nearly 3,900 identities and equations. Nearly all his claims have now been proven correct. As late as 2012, researchers continued to discover that mere comments in his writings about simple properties and similar outputs for certain findings were themselves profound. In 2015, a biographical film was made on his life, which was based on Kanigel's book, "Man Who Knew Infinity." British actor Dev Patel portrays Ramanujan in this film.

Analysis -

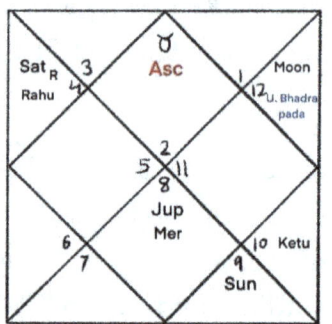

He is a Taurus (Rohini) Ascendant. Moon, the lord of Rohini, is in the 2nd Pada of Uttara Bhadrapada, placed in the 11th house of Pisces. It gave him incredible intuitive abilities, logic, reason, and mathematical genius. The 11th house is the house of gains, fulfilment of desires, and it's the highest of the trik houses. He did not use his intelligence or wisdom towards any materialistic gains, but was deeply devoted to the spiritual possibility. He found his inspiration in Namagiri Thayar (Goddess Mahalakshmi) and said that he sees visions of scrolls of complex mathematical content unfolding before his eyes. He often said, "*An equation for me has no meaning unless it expresses a thought of God.*"

Jupiter, the lord of the 11th house of Pisces, is sitting in the 7th house of Scorpio with Mercury. He brought the hidden and mystical knowledge of the cosmos and wrote it down in the form of mathematical formulas. Saturn, the lord of Uttara Bhadrapada, is sitting in the 3rd house of Cancer with Rahu. Saturn is retrograde, which shows he put tremendous and heroic effort towards unfolding his genius and towards the love of his life - which was mathematics.

Moon being in Pisces, made him spend a lot of time by himself, in isolation, working out many mathematical formulas, and decoding these formulas gave him immense joy.

<u>Venus, the lord of the Taurus Ascendant, is in the 6th house of Libra.</u> The 6th house signifies debts, disease and enemies. Moreover, Venus is placed 8 houses away from the moon. This brought him recurring problems of ill health. The circumstances of life were such that his vegetarian diet was not easily available in a foreign land; hence, over time, it took a toll on his health. Sadly, he died at a very young age of 32.

Jupiter, the lord of the 11th house of Pisces and the 8th house of Sagittarius, is sitting in the 7th house of Scorpio. He died on 26th April 1920, he was running his <u>Ketu Sun Rahu dasha,</u> and his 8th house was activated (he was in his 32nd year). Ketu is sitting in the 9th house of Capricorn, directly aspected by Saturn and Rahu in the 3rd house of Cancer. Sun is sitting in the 8th house of Sagittarius, which represents sudden events, and Rahu is sitting with retrograde Saturn in the 3rd house of Cancer, whose lord, Moon, is in the 11th house of Pisces. This strong influence of the 8th house unfortunately culminated into death on 26th April 1920.

The number 26 also adds up to make the number 8. Therefore, we can see the scenario of the 8th house was very prominent in his life. He was born on 22nd December, which adds up to make the number 4. Both the numbers 4 and 8 are very mystical numbers, which usually bring substantial difficulties on the materialistic level, but many gains on the spiritual path.

29
Revati

Om lam ksham am aam Revati nakshatraye namah

Zodiac degrees	16.40 - 30 deg Pisces
Ruling planet	Pisces - Jupiter and Revati - Mercury
Sanskrit name	Revati - means wealthy.
Astronomical name	Revati is represented by 3 stars seen in the constellation of Pisces. The ancient sages saw these 3 stars in the shape of a musical drum - Dhol
Symbol	Pisces - 2 fish moving towards each other. Revati - drum beat on the path.
Element	Water
Deity	Pushan - the solar deity who lights up all paths.
Quality	Mridu - gentle and Dual - Dwi
Shakti	Kshira dyapani Shakti - The power to foster, nourish and protect.
Cast	Shudra - worker
Gender	Female
Motivation	Moksha - liberation
Triguna	Satwa
Tridosha	Kapha
Body parts	Armpits, abdomen, groin and feet
Direction	North and North east
Month	September - later half of Bhadrapada month.
Bird	Pigeon

Sound	the, tho, cha, chee
Tree	Mahua, honey tree and butter tree.
Chakras	Ajna - Jupiter and Mercury
Das Maha Vidya	Devi Kali - Saturn and Devi Tripura Sundari- Mercury

Special degrees -

Yoga Tara	26 deg Pisces It's a point where the planet will show the strongest and sure results during its dasha.
Exaltation	27 deg Pisces - Maximum exaltation of Venus. When Venus is placed at this degree, it will give excellent results during its dasha. It will be a particularly supportive period for relationships and partnerships.
Amrit Nadi	28.40 - 29.33 deg Pisces This brings good results, just like the nectar that nourishes.
Visha Nadi	23.20 - 24.13 deg Pisces Brings situations which one does not like dealing with.
Gandanta	29 - 30 deg Pisces The Gandanta zone Pada brings challenging situations because this is the junction point where a karmic knot is formed. This gandanta is between water of Pisces and fire of Aries. Any planets sitting in the last degree of Pisces can bring difficulties during their dasha.

Auspicious and inauspicious table -

Auspicious	Inauspicious
Activities Good for all positive activities, for marriage, sexual activity, religious rituals, business, financial dealings, exchanging goods, traveling, dealing with gemstones - putting them on for the first time, buying a vehicle, home, or valuable goods, creative activities, music, drama, for charity, peaceful activities, completions, learning, spirituality, occult, healing, treatment of diseases, rest, relaxation, gardening and leisure.	Activities Not good for harsh or bold activities, over challenges, overcoming difficulties, obstruction, arguments, confrontations, surgery, negative actions, aggression, adventurous strenuous activities and mountain climbing. The 3rd and 4th padas should be avoided for any new beginnings, because they fall in the gandanta zone.
Days Thursdays - only when it falls on the 4th, 5th, 7th, 13th or 14th lunar day. Fridays- only when it falls on the 1st, 2nd, 6th, 7th, 11th or 12th lunar day.	Days Saturdays- only when it falls on the 8th lunar day.

Compatibility table -

Revati	Compatible with
Sexual compatibility Yoni animal	Revati - Male elephant Bharani - Female elephant
Sign compatibility	Cancer and Scorpio
Nakshatra compatibility	Ashlesha and Jyeshta
Lunar day compatibility	Purnima tithi - full moon day
Day compatibility	Wednesday and Thursday
Colour compatibility	Green and yellow
Numerological compatibility	5 and 8 - all numbers that add up to make 5 and 8.
Sound compatibility	Jupiter - dental sounds - ta, ttha, da, dha, knna Mercury - lingual sounds - ta, tha, da, dha, na

Sign Lord and nakshatra lord - Jupiter and Mercury - as described earlier.

Pisces is the last sign and Revati is the last Pada in the zodiacal wheel. This is the 3rd nakshatra ruled by Mercury and represents the culmination of Murcarian and Jupitarian energy. Jupiter and Mercury are both intellectual planets and are geared towards supporting higher cognitive skills of logic, analysis, wisdom, learning and knowledge.

Through a long, winding road of experience, Pisces has gathered the precious wisdom and inherently knows that there is a way to live a fulfilled life. Both sadness and joy have a certain beauty of truth about them when experienced profoundly.

Revati, being the last nakshatra, is like a death initiation - death of the human ego and the death of materialistic desires. They become more forgiving, more gentle, more compassionate and are better able to understand their true relationship between the creation and the creator.

Quality, element, motivation, triguna, tridosha and chakras - as described earlier.

Shakti - Kshira dyapani Shakti - The power to foster, nourish and protect.

Those who are born with their Ascendent, Sun or Moon in Revati have a special blessing to support and help others through their kind words, empathy and understanding. They will notice that every time they help others in some way, their own problems miraculously get resolved. They find their greatest joy and fulfilment in helping others, giving advice and guiding them wherever necessary, or when asked.

Symbolic signification

Pisces - as described earlier, and Revati - drum beat on the path.

Drum beat

Not long ago, till late 1900s in small towns and villages in India, to give a general message to the public, a man would walk around the streets beating the drum and shouting the message. Now, the world of advertisement has become a huge industry by itself, and the practice of 'beating the drum' to spread a message is no longer needed and has become rudimentary.

Inference

Revati natives beat the drum to spread the word by giving advice, spiritual guidance and philosophical talk to anyone who seeks it. They love to offer guidance or take guidance from any spiritual masters or scriptures they might look up to. They are not really interested in becoming the drum beaters for any worldly pursuits.

Mythology -

Deity - Pushan - the solar deity who lights up all paths.

The word Pushan is derived from the Sanskrit word Pushyati, which means to cause to thrive. Pushan is a Vedic solar deity and one of the Adityas. He is considered to be the god of meeting and is responsible for marriages, journeys, roads, and the feeding of cattle. He was seen as a soul guide, conducting souls to the other world after death. He protected travellers from bandits and wild beasts, and protected men from being exploited by other men. He is seen as a supportive guide who can show the path towards rich pastures and wealth.

Rig Veda describes Pushan as driving the Sun in its course across the sky. He seems to represent the sun as a guardian of flocks and herds. He is a knower of paths and a guardian of roads. In this role, he protects people from various dangers on the roads, such as wolves and ambushers. He is also associated with divine paths and is familiar with the path between earth and heaven, which allows him to lead souls to heaven. He is invoked to guard cattle, horses, and sheep, and is asked to find those cattle that have been lost.

Inference

Pushan is the driver of the Sun God's chariot. Therefore, he is a good navigator and knower of all paths on earth, and the paths that lie beyond the earthly realms.

Those who are born with their Ascendant, Sun or Moon in Revati have the blessing of Pushan and are always protected and looked after when they are travelling. In turn, when they help some fellow travellers to find the path, they get the blessings of Pushan. Having gone through the entire zodiacal experience, Revati is the light on the spiritual path. They have the blessing and possibility of realising their true self by walking the path of the divine.

Revati padas

16.40 - 30 deg Pisces

Padas	Degrees
1	16.40 - 20 deg Pisces
2	20 - 23.20 deg Pisces
3	23.20 - 26.40 deg Pisces
4	26.40 - 30 deg Pisces

Pada 1

16.40 - 20 deg Pisces, Navamsha- Sagittarius (Lord - Jupiter)

Rashi Lord - Jupiter and Nakshatra Lord- Mercury

The 1st Pada of Revati will have the double energy of Jupiter and Mercury. The navamsha of Sagittarius gives them a very honest, philosophical, optimistic and straightforward approach to life. They will be very spiritually and religiously inclined and will be very firm believers. Others may see them as fanatics because they will love to talk about and propagate the ideology or faith they follow.

The double effect of Jupiter makes them very fortunate, and things will come easy to them. They will not have to struggle hard to accomplish their goals. The influence of Mercury makes them very communicative, vocal and friendly. They can become excellent psychiatrists, philosophers, writers and counsellors.

For example, the 1st Pada of Revati, in the 11th house, the natives will be involved with a large organisation, or will run a volunteer organisation. They will be great advisors, guides and consultants, and will do a lot of philanthropic work and give to charities wherever needed.

Careers

Counsellors, advisors, teachers, priests, astrologers, social activists, travel agents, tourist guides, ayurvedic doctors, herbalists, doctors, nurses, IT consultants, yoga teachers, spiritual practitioners, psychologists and strategy consultants.

Pada 2

20 - 23.20 deg Pisces, Navamsha - Capricorn (Lord - Saturn)

Rashi Lord - Jupiter and Nakshatra Lord- Mercury

In the 2nd Pada of Revati, there will be the energy of Jupiter, Saturn and Mercury, which will give them the Jupitarian knowledge, Satarian caution and Mercurian intelligence. The navamsha of Capricorn will make them more ambitious, they are more likely to pursue their worldly g after the age of 30. They will have a very practical approach and will be great organisers. They more realistic and don't have a dreamy, unrealistic or idealistic outlook on life.

For example, the 2nd Pada of Revati in the 10th house. They will pursue their ambition and get success in their career after the age of 30. They will make excellent managers, advisors and consultants.

Careers

Managers, accountants, consultants, advisors, IT professionals, writers, librarians, office workers, doctors, nurses, yoga teachers, teachers, priests, psychiatrists, psychologists, healers and therapists.

Pada 3

23.20 - 26.40 deg Pisces, Navamsha - Aquarius (Lord - Saturn)

Rashi Lord - Jupiter and Nakshatra Lord - Mercury

The navamsha of the 3rd Pada of Uttara Bhadrapada is placed in Aquarius, which gives the influence of Jupiter, Saturn and Mercury. In this Pada, the natives will be more community-oriented and will contribute towards humanitarian causes. They will help people through voluntary work or manage a voluntary organisation. They will genuinely feel for those who need help and will do a lot of charity and philanthropy work.

For example, the 3rd Pada of Revati in the 6th house, they will work for a large organisation, or manage or run it. Their organisation will be actively involved in giving donations and charities for humanitarian causes. Even in their daily routine, they will never say no to anyone who needs their help or guidance.

Careers

Teachers, preachers, scientists, inventors, social workers, heads of a social or charitable organisation, managers, IT professionals, advisors, consultants, doctors, astrologers, psychologists, psychiatrists, healers and therapists.

Pada 4

26.40 - 30 deg Pisces, Navamsha - Pisces (Lord - Jupiter)

Rashi Lord - Jupiter and Nakshatra Lord- Mercury

In the 4th Pada of Revati, there will be the influence of double Jupiter and Mercury. This makes them very spiritually inclined and more optimistic than realistic. They are very sensitive and easily tend to drift into escapism and dreamland. They have a wonderful sense of intuition and can become excellent healers, therapists, astrologers, psychic mediums, spiritual teachers and yoga teachers. However, they might not feel motivated enough to follow a worldly ambition and prefer to silently progress on the spiritual path that leads them to liberation and enlightenment.

For example, the 4th Pada of Revati in the 5th house, they will be very creative and intelligent and will be well learned. Their children, followers or students will look up to them for advice. They will seek spiritual inspiration through biographies of saints and mystics.

Careers

Consultants, advisors, therapists, healers, teachers, artists, painters, authors, actors, singers, philosophers, poets, fiction story writers, dancers, musicians, florists, youtubers, astrologers, tarot card readers, palm readers, psychologists, psychiatrists, past life regression therapists, psychics, yoga teachers and doctors with a holistic approach to medicine.

The effect of planets

Revati - Pisces	Planets that get affected
Functional Benefic - gives good results during their dasha.	Jupiter, Mercury, Mars and Moon
Functional Malefic - can give problems during their dasha.	Sun, Rahu and Ketu
Functional Neutral	Venus and Saturn
Kendra Adi Pati Dosha - can be malefic	Mercury

Revati Ascendant

Those who have their Ascendant in Revati will have the influence of Jupiter and Mercury. Through the Mercurian intelligence and Jupitarian knowledge, they are able to fathom many mysteries and explore the path of self-realisation. Since Revati is the nakshatra of wealth, they will have a comfortable life where all the basic needs are met with ease, and they don't have to struggle much in terms of working hard physically.

In Revati, the inherent desire of the soul is to focus on spiritual pursuits, rather than spending time and effort on physical survival. Therefore, life's situations happen in such a way that their physical needs are taken care of, not necessarily in a luxurious way, but in a comfortable way. Revati people come with the desire to focus on their spiritual progress. For a Pisces Ascendant, their 9th house of Guru is Scorpio (which is the original 8th house of sudden events). This shows their life will pass through such life-transforming situations where they are left with no choice but to turn inwards, or turn to God. The lessons that they learn through difficult situations are their real Guru, which guides them towards their self-realisation.

Initially, they will want to turn away from troubles, worries and apprehensions of others because they want to stay away from sticky entanglements. Only when they find enough courage to face their own problems with much spiritual wisdom are they ready to advise or guide others.

They can become excellent teachers, advisors, monks, nuns, mystics, artists, musicians, actors, intuitive astrologers or tarot card readers, healers and therapists. Or they may choose to swim down the murky waters of alcohol or drugs. Their sensitivity makes it difficult for them to bear the harshness and negativity of the world around them.

They have the capability of realising the full glory of truth and love. Because they can choose to draw in from the experience of - innocence, and spontaneous enthusiasm of Aries, the patience and stability of Taurus, the awareness and intelligence of Gemini, the perception and care of Cancer, the nobility and confidence of Leo, the discrimination and perfection of Virgo, the judgement, harmony and balance of Libra, the depth, devotion and penetration of Scorpio, the honesty and straightforwardness of Sagittarius, the wisdom and ambition of Capricorn, and the humanitarianism and all-inclusiveness of Aquarius. But at times, such a huge storehouse of experience and information only serves to confuse them even more, and they choose to take the easier path of passive non-resistance.

There is great wisdom in letting it be, because they know that time is a great teacher and a great healer, and in time, everything falls in place. Moreover, when the time is right, situations become conducive and fortune begins to unfold. Their positive qualities are - humility, compassion, sensitivity, spiritual awareness, psychic comprehension, philosophical insight and a healing potential. On the negative side, they can become timid, apprehensive, idle, lazy and lack willpower.

Sun in Revati

When the Sun is placed in Revati, it will share the influence of Jupiter and Mercury. Sun and Jupiter are friends, but Jupiter and Mercury don't feel comfortable around each other; therefore, there will be some resistance felt in terms of communication.

The natives will be sensitive, creative, intelligent, curious and philosophical. The confidence of the Sun, the optimism of Jupiter and the communicative talent of Mercury can make them excellent advisors, consultants, teachers, psychologists, astrologers, writers and speakers.

For example, Sun is placed in Revati in the 11th house, the natives will have the fortune of easy gains and will always donate or volunteer towards humanitarian causes. Since the Sun directly aspects the 5th house (Virgo) of creativity and children, the natives will be intelligent, learned, and wise, and will be appreciated by their children, students or followers.

Moon in Revati

When the Moon is placed in Revati, it will have the influence of Jupiter and Mercury. They will be very sensitive, intuitive, imaginative, intelligent, spiritual, philosophical and learned. For example, Moon is in Revati in the 7th house, their partner or spouse will be very spiritually inclined. They will be drawn to people who are genuine spiritual seekers and are on the path of self-realisation.

Because they have been through it all at a subconscious level, they have a natural compassion for the troubles of those around them. They are intimately familiar with life's virtues and vices and understand the weaknesses and strengths of human nature. That's why they are great keepers of secrets and become trustworthy friends, because they are not going to judge you, but comfort you in times of need.

It is a realm of spiritual grace and supports all efforts made towards self-realisation. On the material plane, it can bring difficulties of not being understood or feeling isolated. Their vulnerability lies in their sensitivity, because they comprehend situations and people from a deeper perspective and a subtler level. This brings an urge to retreat from any negative vibrations, so they always avoid confrontations and tension. They prefer to find an escape route through religion, philosophy, meditation, prayers, art, music or writing.

They can become a romantic recluse, because the Piscean fish tries to escape the danger of being hooked by a deep or permanent emotional commitment. However, with experience, this wisdom dawns on some of them that - resisting the pain of love and being tempted only towards the pleasures of love is an unhealthy and impossible desire.

Venus being exalted in Pisces entices them to seek and experience the true beauty of love. For the fortunate ones who choose to explore the nature of human consciousness and the meaning of love, they are richly rewarded by the experience of inner ecstasy. The high possibility of understanding the final mystery of love lies in the last sign of the zodiac.

Their love is unselfish, and they have the ability to submit because they don't have a huge ego. Their desire to become complete and whole by giving, nourishing and supporting the other. They feel happier and fulfilled in giving rather than receiving, in serving rather than being served.

Revati natives have the capacity and possibility of getting a glimpse of the soul's long weary journey and to experience the true passion of blending the trinity of the mind, body and soul. Which results in rare physical ecstasy - the ultimate Piscean fulfilment of love's long-promised springtime miracle - which began in Aries.

The poetry of Revati

Revati - material and spiritual wealth,

To ease the path of travellers and to protect.

Revati in Pisces - the last of the signs,

Journey of the zodiac and planets 9.

Jupiterian knowledge and Mercurian intelligence,

With the blossoming of Venusian fragrance.

Culminates into an idealistic fantasy,

Or is it possible to experience ecstasy?

All is there in the subconscious -

The innocence of Aries and stability of Taurus,

Intelligence of Gemini and Care of Cancer,

Nobility of Leo and discretion of Virgo,

Balance of Libra and devotion of Scorpio,

Honesty of Sagittarius and ambition of Capricorn,

Humanitarian Aquarius and spiritual Pisces.

- *An experiential wisdom that rises.*

Remedies

- <u>Das Maha Vidya</u> - as described earlier.
- Whenever they help or nurture others in some way, their problems get resolved too.
- They have a Kapha predominant constitution. So, for them, consciously developing an active lifestyle and including fresh fruits and salads in their diet will be helpful. Avoid sleeping for too long, especially during the day.
- The yogic asanas, pranayama and meditation always enhance the ability to focus, which in turn improves the quality of whatever you do and brings ease into all thoughts and actions.
- Blue and green colours resonate well with the energy of Revati.
- Chanting the mantra -"Om *lam, ksham, am, aam Revati nakshatraye namah.*" 108 times on days when the moon is transiting Revati or on Wednesdays or Thursdays, will help to connect you with your inner self.

Example

Ascendant in Revati

Liam - Born on 7th January 1978, Jalandhar, Punjab, India, at 12 pm. Currently, he is 43 years old in 2021. (This example has been given by his permission.)

We had started with the example of Luke in Ashwini, who is the younger twin brother of Liam. They were born half an hour apart, and the Ascendant changed from Pisces (Revati) to Aries (Ashwini). They both have their moon in Scorpio in Jyeshtha. For the younger twin moon is in the 8th house, and for the elder twin moon is in the 9th house.

Currently, Liam is self-employed and is working as a builder in Scotland. He got married on 31st March 2001 and joined his wife in Scotland in September 2001. They have 3 lovely daughters and are well settled. He worked as a bus driver for many years, but after the COVID pandemic, he started working independently as a builder. Sadly, he and his wife separated on 1st November 2019, and officially got divorced on 15th June 2021. His younger daughter has chosen to stay with him. Both brothers had faced struggles in their younger days, but are now well settled in the UK.

Analysis -

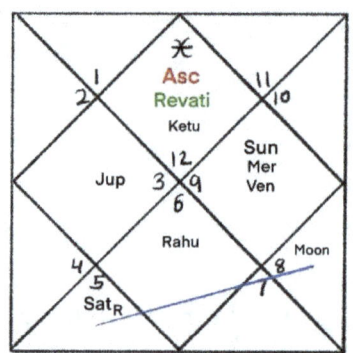

He is a <u>Pisces Ascendant, in the 2nd Pada of Revati</u>. Ketu is sitting in the Ascendant, which makes him a very humble and detached personality. His elder brother is more jovial, but he is more sensitive, serious and quiet.

Jupiter, the lord of Pisces, is sitting in the 4th house of Gemini and Mercury, the lord of Revati, is sitting in the 10th house (Sagittarius) with Venus and Sun. Rahu is sitting in the 7th house of marriage, and he got the opportunity to settle in a foreign country through marriage.

He got married in his <u>Venus, Jupiter, Mercury</u> dasha. Venus is sitting in the 10th house of Sagittarius with Mercury and Sun. After marriage, when he came to Scotland, within a few months, he got a good job with the Arriva bus company. Jupiter sitting in the 4th house is aspecting the 10th house directly, so its beneficent aspect is fully seen on the 10th house of career. He was running his 24th year and 12th house of foreign lands, and long-distance travel was activated.

He got divorced after 20 years of marriage on 15th June 2021, he was running his Moon, Saturn, Rahu dasha. Moon is in the 9th house of Scorpio, Saturn is in the 6th house of Leo - Saturn's 3rd aspect is on the Moon sitting in the 9th house. And Rahu is sitting in the 7th house of a spouse or partner, which has amplified small irritations into huge issues that come to the painful point of divorce. Currently, he is in his 44th year, and his 8th house of sudden events is activated.

In July 2010, when he was running his Sun Moon Jupiter dasha, he had met his childhood friend, who was a devout Sikh. After meeting him, his perspective towards life changed quite dramatically, and he became more spiritually inclined. Moon is in the 9th house of Guru, and Sun is in the 10th house of public image with Venus and Mercury. Jupiter is in the 4th house of the home. He is now a deeply religious person, and because of his devotion, his younger brother and his mum and dad have become more devout Sikhs and regularly follow the routine of morning and evening prayers. Moreover, in 2010, he was in his 33rd year, and his 9th house was activated.

We can see how the play of the planets is enacted through their placement in the birth chart and the timing of the dashas. The situations are not entirely in our hands, but how we deal with them is our choice.

Part 3
Application of the Nakshatras

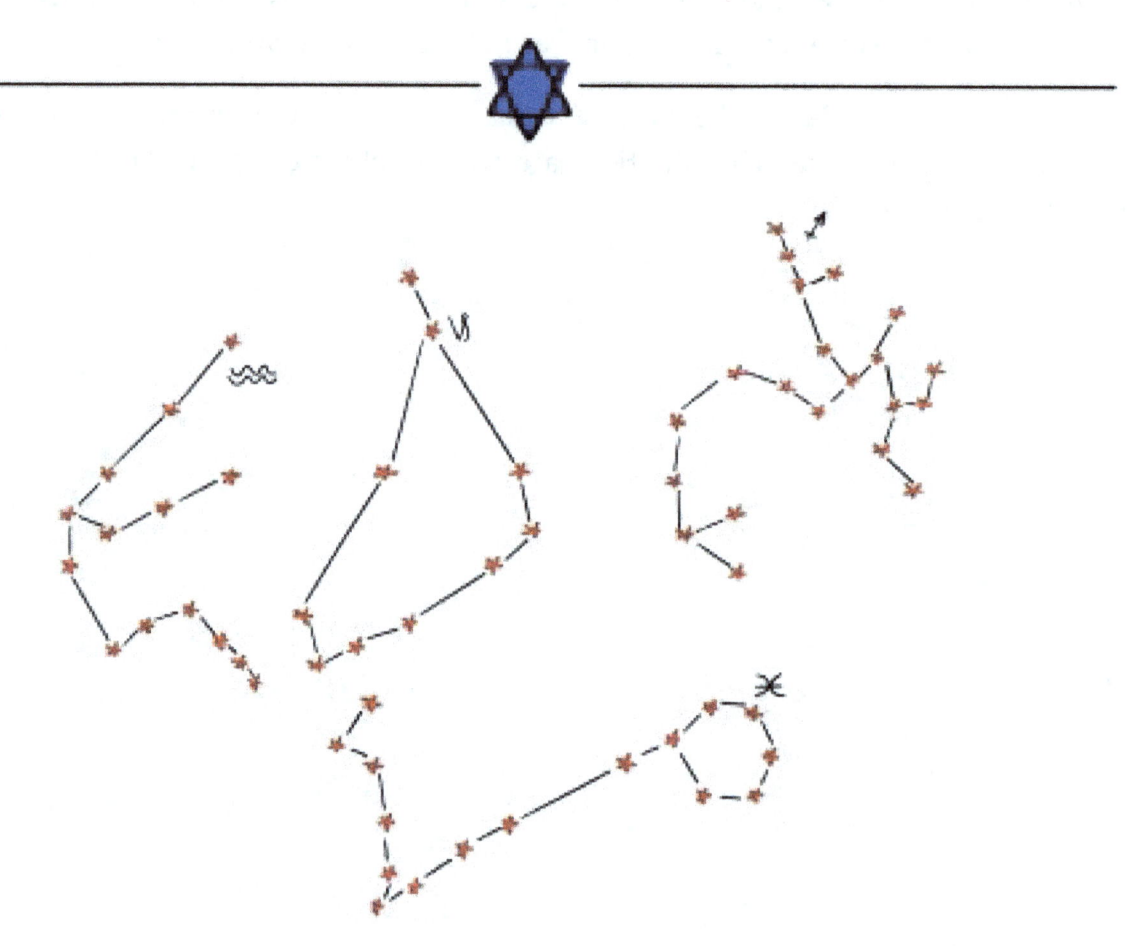

Nakshatra Application

In the last chapter, we will look at how to apply the knowledge of Nakshatras in the birth chart analysis. Please note - I use the Cosmic Insights App for all my astrological readings because of its convenience - it can be accessed from iPad and iPhone. Moreover, it gives all the needed info, which is mostly based on the Vedic astrology system.

Case study

Before we delve into our case study, let's remind ourselves of lordships of the nakshatras and their trine groups, which will make it easier to understand the contextual references.

Planet - Nakshatras

Ketu - Ashwani, Magha, Mula

Venus - Bharani, Purva Phalguni, Purva Ashadha

Sun - Kritika, Uttara Phalguni, Uttara Ashadha

Moon - Rohini, Hasta, Shravana

Mars - Mrigashira, Chitra, Dhanishta

Rahu - Ardra, Swati, Shatabhishak

Jupiter - Punarvasu, Vishakha, Purva Bhadrapada

Saturn - Pushya, Anuradha, Uttara Bhadrapada

Mercury - Ashlesha, Jeyshtha, Revati

When we look at all the nakshatras in a particular sequence, we can make certain inferences based on their chronological number sequence. Here is a table of that sequential order based on the 27 nakshatra system.

The nakshatra connectivity -

As we have followed the journey of 27 nakshatras from celestial to the practical aspects, let's put it all together and understand the connectivity of the nakshatras with each other, based on an individual horoscope.

Nava Tara nakshatras

Nava means 9, and tara means a star. These are the group of 3 nakshatras ruled by the same planet, and they show the positive or negative influence of nakshatras when seen in relation to each other. The Janma (birth nakshatra) is the first nakshatra which can be chosen based on the

Ascendant, placement of the Sun or the Moon. For example, if the Ascendant is in Revati, then the Nakshatra sequence will start from Revati, taken as Janma Nakshatra. Nava taras are the 9 sensitive points of the horoscope. Whenever transits are happening over these nakshatras, or these nakshatras are being influenced positively or negatively through aspects, along with the timing of the dasha, it will trigger certain events.

Nadi nakshatras -

The word Nadi means pulse. This sequencing of nakshatras gives vital clues to the birth chart analysis, because it senses the pulse of the whole horoscope. The nadi nakshatras are more commonly used from the Moon nakshatra. For example, if the Moon is in Jyeshtha, then Jyeshta will be taken as the birth (janma) nakshatra or the 1st nakshatra and 4th from Jyeshta - will be Uttara Ashadha nakshatra, which will signify the Jati - lineage. Here is the sequence of the navtara and nadi nakshatras.

Navtara Nakshatras - Meaning

1. Janma - The Ascendant nakshatra - birth nakshatra.
2. Sampat - Resources, wealth and nourishment.
3. Vipat - Danger and challenges.
4. Kshema - Comfort and happiness.
5. Pratyak - Struggles and opposition.
6. Sadhana - Dedication and hard work.
7. Naidhana - Poverty and end.
8. Mitram - Friends and supporters.
9. Param Mitram - Best friend and protector.

Nadi Nakshatras - Significance

1. Jati - The 4th from the birth (janma) nakshatra shows the family lineage, traditions and future of the family.
2. Matru - The 8th from the janma nakshatra shows the relationship with the mother.
3. Karma - The 10th from the birth nakshatra shows the profession or career.
4. Sanghatika - The 16th from the birth nakshatra shows the close associations that can be challenging or cause pain.
5. Samudyaka - The 16th from the birth nakshatra shows the close associations that can be

challenging or can cause pain.

6. Adhana - The 19th from the birth nakshatra shows creativity, shows the starting point of how and where new ideas and projects are conceived.

7. Vinashika - The 23rd from the birth nakshatra shows the destruction. Starting anything new when the moon is transiting this nakshatra will not be beneficial.

8. Manasa - The 25th from the birth nakshatra shows the working of the mind. It's an important nakshatra to pay attention to.

9. Abhisheka - The 27th from the birth nakshatra shows the achievements. Any planets placed here give positive support and power. Planets transiting through this nakshatra bring gains and good opportunities.

Example

Now let's understand the application of this nakshatra sequence through our case study.

Liam - Born on 7th January 1978, Jalandhar, Punjab, India, at 12 pm. Currently, he is 43 years old in 2021. His younger twin brother, Luke, who was born in Ashwini nakshatra at 12:30 pm, ½ an hour after him.

Here is Liam's birth chart in North Indian and South Indian format.

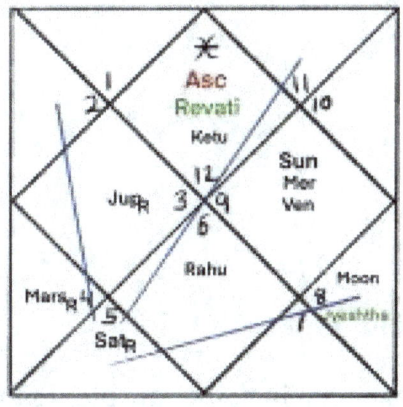
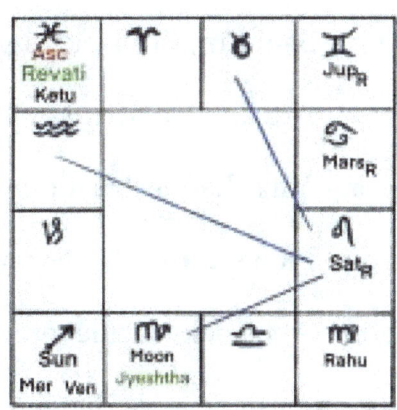

The placement of each nakshatra in the birth chart gives us vital clues about the possible events, their impact on the native and remedies, if possible. In our example, we will look at the nakshatras starting from the Ascendant (Lagna) because it is the pivotal point of the horoscope, which sets the tone for all life's events. Here is the sequential relationship of nakshatras as seen from the Ascendant.

Nava Tara Nakshatras - Lord - Sequence

1. Janma - Mercury - Revati, Ashlesha, Jyeshtha

2. Sampat - Ketu - Ashwini, Magha, Mula

3. Vipat - Venus - Bharani, Purva Phalguni, Purva Ashadha

4. Kshema - Sun - Kritika, Uttara Phalguni, Uttarta Ashadha

5. Pratyak - Moon - Rohini, Hasta, Shravana

6. Sadhana - Mars - Mrigashira, Chitra, Dhanishta

7. Naidhana - Rahu - Ardra, Swati, Shatabhishak

8. Mitram - Jupiter - Punar Vasu, Vishakha, Purva Bhadrapada

9. Param Mitram - Saturn - Pushya, Anuradha, Uttara Bhadrapada

The nadi nakshatras will tell us about Liam's state of mind, his perspective and possible remedies.

Nadi Nakshatras - when Moon is in Jyeshtha

4th from moon - Jati (lineage) - Uttara Ashadha

8th from moon - Matru (mother) - Purva Bhadrapada

10th from moon - Karma (work) - Revati

16th from Moon - Sanghatika (challenges) - Ardra

18th from Moon - Samudaya (auspicious) - Pushya

19th from Moon - Adhana (creative) - Ashlesha

23rd from Moon - Vinasha (destruction) - Hasta

25th from Moon - Manasa (mind) - Swati

27th from Moon - Abhisheka (achievement) - Anuradha

The Janma nakshatra can be looked at from all 3 aspects, in our example, Liam has his -

Ascendant in Pisces in Revati, so there is an influence of Jupiter and Mercury. The wisdom of Jupiter combined with the intellectual prowess of Mercury makes him a go-to person for advice, among those who know him. However, Jupiter and Mercury don't get along well, so it brings situations of disagreements and conflicts of interest.

The Sun is in Sagittarius (ruled by Jupiter), in Purva Ashadha (ruled by Venus), sitting in the 10th house with Venus and Mercury. Venus (19 degrees) is sitting very close to the Sun (23 degrees) - only 4 degrees apart and is therefore combust, it's being burnt by the proximity of the Sun. This has brought discontentment for him in the area of marriage. Mercury is at 0 degrees and therefore is not able to give full benefits. This placement shows that his planets are very well placed in the 10th house, which would normally bring fame and success, but their degrees do not allow the full benefits.

Moon is in Scorpio in Jyeshtha, in the 10th house of bhagya - fortune, father and guru. The Moon has the influence of Mars and Mercury. The Janma nakshatra, when seen from the moon, tells us how the native's mind works, how he perceives things and handles the situations. Moon being his atma karaka shows his inherent kind nature, but also brings a lot of fluctuations, and things move at a rapid pace in his life. In the sense that he has passed through many challenging and life-transforming situations in his life.

Moon in Jyeshtha gives him a deeper perspective on life. He is more inclined to the spiritual side of life rather than the material gains. Since Jyeshtha is ruled by Mercury, it gives him an interest in learning new things, new concepts, communication, meeting people, learning, and gathering information on topics of his interest. The influence of Mars in Scorpio gives him intensity and depth to probe deep into the spiritual and religious philosophies in search of the inner truth. It also helps him to keep up the discipline of his practices on the path of the Divine, or the search for inner truth. It has also given him great support from his mother and father.

Here is the sequence of Nakshatras starting with Revati - the Janma Nakshatra.

Ascendant in Revati

Nakshatras sequence - Planets and Houses

1. Revati - Janma (birth)- Ascendant
2. Ashwini - Sampat (wealth)
3. Bharani - Vipat (danger)
4. Kritika - Jati (lineage) and Kshema (happiness)
5. Rohini - Pratyak (obstacles) - Jupiter retrograde in the 4th house.
6. Mrigashira -Sadhana (achievement through hard work).
7. Ardra - Naidhana (poverty)
8. Punarvasu-Matru (mother)and Mitra (friend) -Mars in the 5th house.
9. Pushya - Param Mitra (great friend)
10. Ashlesha - Karma (work) and Janma (birth).
11. Magha - Sampat (wealth), Saturn retrograde in the 6th house.
12. Purva Phalguni - Vipat (danger)

13. Uttara Phalguni - Kshema (happiness)

14. Hasta - Pratyak (obstacles), Rahu in the 7th house.

15. Chitra -Sadhana (achievement through hard work).

16. Swati -Naidhana (poverty)

17. Vishakha -Matru (mother)and Mitra (friend)

18. Anuradha -Param Mitra (great friend) and Samudaya (auspicious).

19. Jyeshtha -Janma (birth), Adhana (creativity), Moon in the 9th house.

20. Mula -Sampat (wealth), Mercury in the 10th house.

21. Purva Ashadha -Vipat (danger), Sun and Venus are combust in the 10th house.

22. Uttara Ashadha -Kshema (happiness)

23. Shravana -Pratyak (obstacles)

24. Dhanishta -Sadhana (achievement through hard work)

25. Shatabhishak -Naidhana (poverty) and Manasa (mind)

26. Purva Bhadrapada -Mitra (friend)

27. Uttara Bhadrapada -Param Mitra (great friend), Abhisheka (beginning something good and auspicious), Ketu in the Ascendant.

For easy reference, let's place the nakshatras and the needed information of the Panchanga in the Sarvato Bhadra Pada Chart (SB chakra).

Sarvato Bhadra Chakra

In Vedic astrology SB chakra is a unique technique for prediction based on the Nakshatras. Sarva means– all, and Bhadra means – good or auspicious, which means this chart shows the birds-eye view of overall auspiciousness.

SB chakra is usually used in Prashna to determine an auspicious muhurat to ensure success in undertakings. All possible queries can be answered quite precisely using this chart. For a deeper analysis from the nakshatra perspective, at a glance, the SB chakra is a great help. It is an inclusive representation of many important and needed aspects of Vedic astrology. It includes many details of signs, nakshatras, sounds and tithis and Vedha aspects. However, in our example, we will not look at the complete format of the SB chakra and will only fill in the needed information for our case study.

It is drawn as a square which has 9x9 = 81 sections. If one stands facing the east - the direction of the sunrise, then the top left corner is the North East direction called Ishana, which is an auspicious starting point. The nakshatras are placed in the clockwise direction in the outer square of the SB chakra. The 1st nakshatra to be placed in the direction of Ishana will be Kritika because it's the 1st nakshatra of the Sun, followed by Rohini and so on.

Next, add the natal planetary positions onto the nakshatras and their sensitive points.

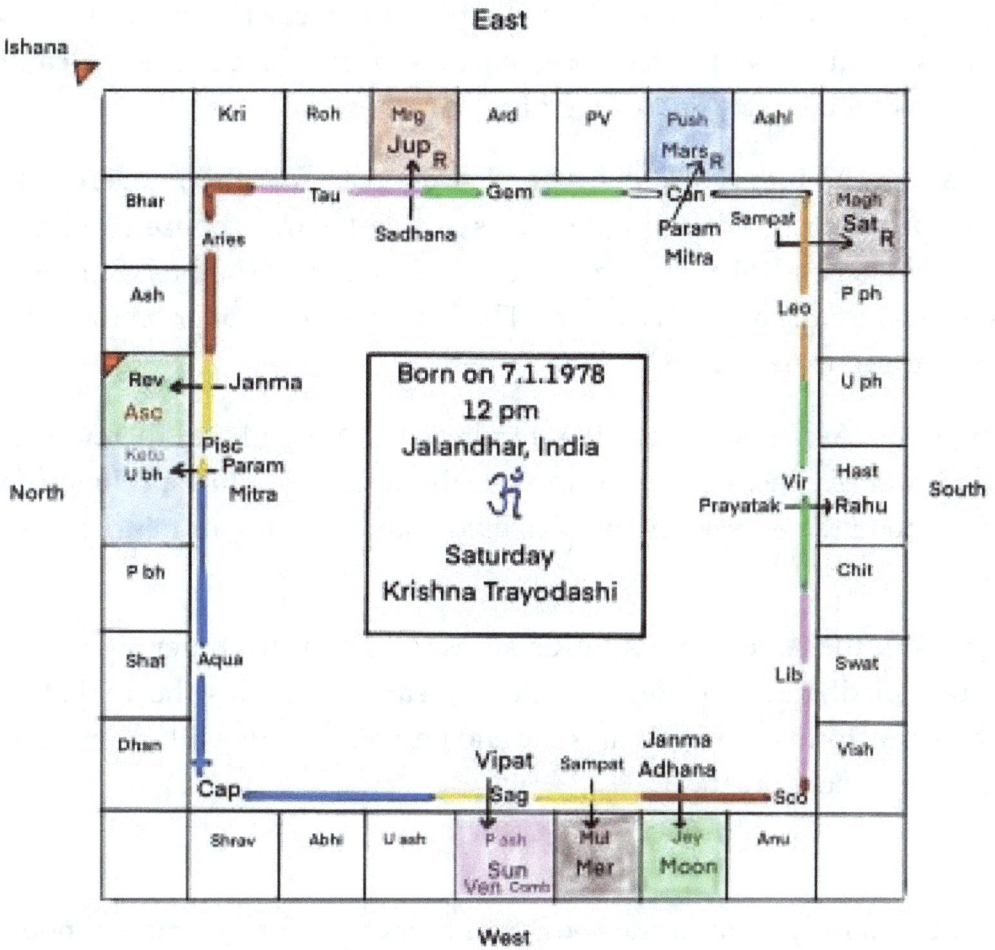

From the SB chakra, it can be seen that his benefic planets are Jupiter and Mars. Jupiter is a very important planet in his chart because it's the lord of the Ascendant, and its placement shows the soul's desire and purpose for this lifetime. Jupiter is retrograde, sitting in the 4th house of Gemini in Mrigashira.

This makes the influence of Jupiter more intense; moreover, it's sitting in the house of his enemy - Mercury, so it's not a comfortable position for Jupiter. The 4th house represents home and mother, which shows that his mother is his greatest support, teacher and guide. The influence of benefic Jupiter gave protection, but its retrograde effect and sitting in the enemy sign brought financial hardships, quarrels at home and a change of residence during his childhood.

Jupiter is sitting in Mrigashira, which represents Sadhana. He has worked hard to build his house in India and also in the UK, where he settled after marriage. Through his dedicated effort, he has learnt the skills of building a house and is now an independent builder by profession. As a Mrigashira, his soul seeks a perfect home. Similarly, other planetary positions can be looked at in detail according to the type of question asked by the client.

Ascendant

Studying the Ascendant helps to know the kind of trajectory the native's life will take. Liam is a Pisces Ascendant in Revati, and Ketu is sitting in the Ascendant. As seen above, Jupiter, the lord of the Ascendant, is in the 4th house aspecting the 8th house (Libra), 10th house (Sagitarius) and the 12th house (Aquarius). Jupiter's 5th benefic aspect on the 8th house can bring sudden gains through ancestral property and a long life span.

The 7th aspect on the 10th house gives good support from father, government, authorities, and good career prospects - because Jupiter is aspecting his own house (Sagitarius). In Liam's 10th house, Sun, Venus and Mercury are sitting. Venus is in a combust Sun, which shows no support from the spouse regarding his career. The 9th aspect of Jupiter on the 12th house shows anxiety about increased expenditure.

Ketu, sitting in his Ascendant, is his param mitra - best friend and therefore enhances his spiritual growth, and disillusions him from worldly desires. He has a religious and serious outlook on life. Ketu in the Ascendant has also given him some minor injuries while doing his building projects.

In his birth chart, the Ascendant is in Revati, which is in the water sign of Pisces and has moved to Uttara Ashadha in Capricorn, which is an earth sign. This shows that after the age of 30, there will be a transformation in his lifestyle and personality. He will become more ambitious, more responsible and more practical.

Mars

Mars retrograde is his param mitra - best friend. It is the lord of the 9th house of Scorpio sitting in the 5th house of Cancer. And the lord of Cancer (Moon) is sitting in the house of Mars (Scorpio). This makes a parivartan yoga, where the lords have exchanged houses with each other. Here, Mars will benefit Scorpio, and Moon will benefit Cancer, so it's a very positive support for the entire horoscope and helps to reduce or nullify other malefic effects of retrograde or malefic planets. The 9th house is considered the bhagya - the house of fortune. If it's strong, it lifts the whole birth chart and helps the native to sail through any difficulties in life. The trine of 1,5,9 supports the Ascendant beautifully. This blessed him with a long life in spite of many hardships.

Mars is also the lord of the 2nd house of family, resources, input and food. The sarvashtakavarga score shows that the 2nd house of Aries has the highest score of 37 points. This ensures a good backing from his family. He has spent a lot of energy, attention, desire and time on ensuring a good steady inflow of resources for both families - his parents and for his wife and children.

Saturn

Saturn retrograde in the 6th house of Leo in Magha brings confrontations and oppositions. He will have to spend money on litigation or sickness. However, malefic planets do well in the 6th house - it gives him the steadfast determination and power to overcome his weaknesses. Sage Bhrigu says that such a person will always gain from disputes, because the 3rd aspect of Saturn is on the 8th house of Libra (which is the exaltation sign for Saturn), and it also gives him a longer life span. The 7th aspect of Saturn is in the 12th house, which brings a lot of expenses, but also gives gains in a foreign land.

The 10th aspect of Saturn falls on the 3rd house of Taurus, which brings some differences of opinion with the siblings, duty and responsibility towards them, and gives courage and ability to make heroic efforts. He and his twin brother are very close to each other, and they share their joys and sorrows.

Rahu

Rahu is in the 7th house of Virgo in Hasta, which is a difficult position because it's in the Prayatak nakshatra, which signifies obstacles. This shows that Rahu will bring such situations with the spouse where interests collide, there can be an element of deceit or lies, and there will be disagreements and arguments. Rahu can exaggerate and make mountains out of molehills. Rahu, sitting in the house of Mercury in Hasta, amplifies the quality of analytical thinking and quick wittedness.

Mercury

Mercury, being the lord of the 4th (Gemini) and the 7th house (Virgo), in a way damaged both the houses because of Kendra Adi Pati dosha. The 7th house of partnerships and marriage suffers more because of the malefic influence of Rahu. Mercury, being his Sampat (wealth) nakshatra, brought financial hardships in his younger days and even in adulthood, he has to budget carefully to meet all expenses.

Dashas and Transits

Studying the dashas and transits from the SB chakra will help with the 3rd layer of analysis.

Liam got married on 31st March 2001, and they have 3 lovely daughters. At that time, he was running his Venus, Jupiter, Mercury dasha. Venus represents the wife in a man's chart, Jupiter is his Ascendant lord (Pisces), and Mercury is his Ascendant nakshatra lord (Revati). He was in his 24th year, which had activated his 12th house of foreign travel. After marriage, he travelled to settle in the UK.

Sadly, on 1st November 2019, he got separated after 18 years of marriage. It was a Friday, when the tension built up to such a point that it led to an unpleasant turn of events that triggered the separation. Friday is the day of Venus, and Venus is combust. Moreover, Sun and Venus are in the Vipat nakshatra, which signifies difficulties.

In November 2019, he was running his Moon Rahu Mars dasha. His Moon is in Scorpio in Jyeshta in the 9th house. It is debilitated in the 9th house of Scorpio. This makes him very puritanical, analytical, secretive (for his own protection), sensitive, protective about his family and community at large, and does not express his emotions freely. This placement of the moon also gives a very serious and one-pointed outlook to life and a great sense of devotion towards one's belief or faith. All these attributes can cause problems in relationships, partnerships or marriage.

To use the Nava tara nakshatras, the dasha has to be divided into 3 parts, which can help us to discern the effect of a specific nakshatra at the start of the dasha, during the middle and at the end of the dasha.

Dasha -

Currently, he is running his Moon mahadasha, which is from Jan 2016 to Jan 2026. Moon mahadasha (according to the Vimshotari dasha system) is of 10 years - when divided into 3 parts, each period will be 3 years and 3 months long. The 1st 3 years and 3 months period is called - adi, the middle years are called madhya, and the last part of the dasha is called - antya. The time period of the Moon mahadasha and the effect of the nakshatras can be seen as :

Moon dasha 10 years (Jan 2016 - Jan 2026)

Adi- start of the dasha - January 2016 - April 2019 - was influenced by Revati

Madhya - middle of the dahsa - April 2019 - July 2022 - was influenced by Ashlesha.

Antya - end of the dasha - July 2022 - Jan 2026 - will be influenced by Jyeshtha.

In the Bhrigu Samhita, Sage Bhrigu has mentioned that, when the Moon is in the 9th house of Scorpio, for a Pisces Ascendant, the native will face some obstacles in life, in terms of performing his dharma (duties). The native will not be able to pursue higher education and will not be able to experience the joy of being with the children or getting happiness through them. The mind is mostly anxious or worried about one or the other problem.

The 7th aspect of the moon is on the 3rd house of Taurus, whose Lord is Venus. Therefore, the native gets strength and support from his siblings. He and his twin brother are very close to each other and share all their joys and sorrows, although his younger brother is settled in London, away from him. As the native gets older, he will become more courageous and will be able to withstand life's challenges. Such a person is very hard-working, brave and has great resilience, willpower and patience.

In 2019, Liam was running his 42nd year, which activated his 6th house of debts, disease and confrontations. It also activated his Ashlesha nakshatra (middle of the Moon Maha dasha). Ashlesha is his karma nakshatra - his duties and responsibilities. Which lies in his 5th house of Cancer. This shows the problems that he would have to face in terms of fulfilling his responsibility towards his children. His children may not agree with his beliefs or his opinions, especially during the middle part of the Moon dasha from 2019 to 2022.

The dasha of Moon, Rahu Mars - activated the effect of these 3 planets - Moon debilitated in the 9th house caused misunderstandings, Rahu exaggerated the malefic effect, and Mars gave the fire of a heated argument, which led to separation. Liam said, "*It was inevitable, I packed my bag and left the house on 1st November 2019.*"

Transits -

When reading a birth chart, there are 2 aspects to it - 1st is the birth chart and the placement of planets. The 2nd part is the dasha and transits, which help us to time the events and accordingly suggest remedies if asked or needed.

Let's look at the transits of the dasha planets Moon, Rahu Mars. On 1st November 2019, Moon was transiting over his natal Mercury in Sagittarius in Mula (10th house), his Sampat (wealth) nakshatra. Financial matters of the family, his job, his public image, and his earnings were the cause of the argument, which literally uprooted the family tree from its roots.

Rahu was transiting Gemini in Ardra (ruled by Rahu), his 4th house of home. Ardra is his naidhana nakshatra, which signifies poverty. Rahu amplified the argument and brought it to a point of separation. The effect of Ardra literally made it a night of intense pain, tears and heartbreak. On that day, he had to leave all his possessions, assets, comforts and family- and walk out of the house just with a suitcase. He had to start his life from scratch again.

Mars was transiting Chitra in Virgo, over his 7th house of marriage and partnerships. His natal Rahu is sitting in the Virgo, the 7th house, which shows that there has been a factor of deceit and lies in their marital partnership. Chitra is ruled by Mars, which could also indicate aggressiveness. Chitra has a very tamasic, gross and grounding energy, and it's also his Sadhana nakshatra. This is the area of life where he has to learn his lessons. He has to put in dedicated effort towards his marriage and relationships if he wants them to work.

He was running his Moon Saturn Rahu dasha on the day he got divorced on 15th June 2021, Ketu was transiting over his moon in Scorpio, which cut off the marriage ties (the partnership). Rahu and Mercury retrograde were transiting his 3rd house of Taurus (whose lord is Venus - and Venus is the significator of relationships). Moreover, Mercury becomes malefic for a Pisces Ascendant (Revati), on that day Mercury was retrograde in his 3rd house of courage. He said, "*I am now more happy and at peace after the divorce has been finalised.*"

He got separated and divorced in the middle part of the Moon mahadasha, which was influenced by Ashlesha, his Karma nakshatra. All these life-transforming situations have happened during the mahadasha of Moon, which is his Atmakaraka. This shows how the soul has chosen to reap the fruits of what was sown previously in a different lifetime. The mind does not have any conscious memory of it (for a good reason), but the soul plays out the karmic imprints.

The last part of the moon mahadasha will be influenced by Jyeshtha, which is the Adhana nakshatra and represents creativity. Therefore, the time period from July 2022 - January 2026 will facilitate opportunities where he will be able to master his skills. It will bring out the best of his talent in the skill of building and renovations, and he will enjoy spending his time, energy and effort towards creating something useful and beautiful. He will also become very spiritually inclined and devoted to his faith, because Jyeshtha is placed in Scorpio, in the 9th house of Guru.

Navamsha

Navamsha chart is given great importance in Vedic Astrology, after the birth chart, it's considered the most important chart. Especially if you are looking at how marriage will pan out. The D9 chart shows the change of planetary influence in adulthood. In this chart, each zodiac sign of 30 degree span is divided into 9 divisions, and each division covers the span of 3.20 degrees, which is the same as the length of each Pada of the nakshatras.

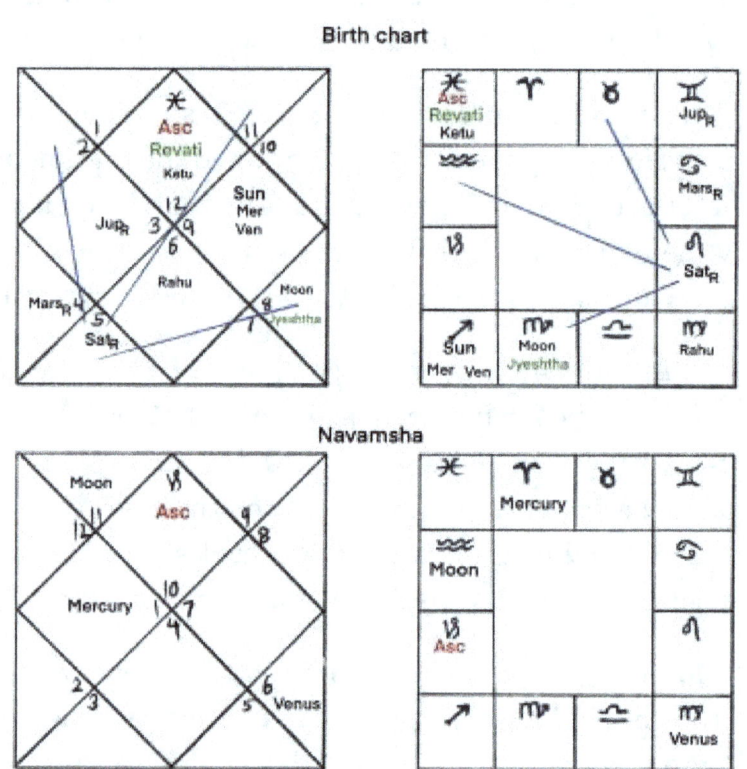

In our example, it's important to look at the lord of the 7th house of marriage, since we are looking at how the marriage would pan out for him.

In the birth chart, Rahu is sitting in the 7th house of Virgo in Hasta, and Mercury, the lord of

Virgo, is sitting in the 10th house of Sagittarius in Mula.

In Navamsha, Mercury has moved to the 4th house of Aries in Ashwini. His Sampat nakshatra is Ashwini, which made him earn a good income and quickly climb the property ladder after marriage. If Aries is the 4th house, then the Navamsha Ascendant is Capricorn, and Mercury becomes the lord of the 6th house of Gemini and the 9th house of Virgo. As the lord of the 6th house of debts, disease or enemies sitting in the 4th house of home, it brings some problems in home life in terms of communication, arguments or misunderstandings. As the lord of the 9th house, it becomes favourable and gives good results.

In Navamsha, Venus is sitting in the 9th house of Virgo in Chitra. Venus gets debilitated in Virgo, which shows that they will face struggles after marriage because of some differences of opinion with their spouse, which can impact their relationship. Venus is placed in Chitra, which is his Sadhana nakshatra. This shows that only through dedicated effort will the relationship with the spouse work.

Also, check the lord of the 7th house in Navamsha. His 7th house is Cancer, the lord Moon is sitting in the 2nd house of Aquarius in Purva Bhadrapada. Purva Bhadrapada is his Mitra nakshatra, therefore, he was able to pass through difficult circumstances with equanimity. However, Venus in the 9th house is 8 places away from the Moon, which is a challenging placement for Venus. This brought difficulties in relationships with the spouse.

This is how precisely and how closely we can study the birth chart by looking only at the Nava Tara and Nadi nakshatras.

The study of Astrology (Jyotish) is a vast subject, humongous as the ocean, and one cannot fully grasp it. However, it can be studied in bits and understood through practice. This case study highlights only one small aspect of it - the effect of planets as the base layer. The impact of the planets on the zodiac signs, nakshatras and houses, and the timing of events through dashas and transits. The mixed concoction of all these influences creates a unique, tailor-made situation for each individual, which sets a perfect ambience for the karmic patterns to play out.

"Be a loner, that gives you time to wonder, to search for the truth. Have a holy curiosity, make your life worth living." - Einstein

"The most beautiful experience we can have is the mysterious. It is the fundamental emotion that stands at the cradle of true art and true science." - Einstein.

An Afterthought

As you might have seen, through the course of reading this book, astrology is a mix-and-match tapestry of planets. The zodiac signs and the nakshatras (constellations) are all described and studied by understanding the quality and nature of the planets. When placed in the field or mandala of 12 houses - bhavas of the horoscope, an interesting, most creative and tailor-made design emerges, which we call destiny.

The play of words -

Graha

Here is an interesting insight about the play of words, which are so appropriately named, hidden in these sounds is the philosophy of life. The foundation layer of astrology is the planets called grahas in Vedic astrology. The root word Graha means - to grasp, to take in, to stay in, to ingest, to experience.

Planet

The word planet - plan-it, literally gives us our plan, a blueprint for this lifetime.

Bhava

The 12 houses are the 12 bhavas of the horoscope. The word bhava means emotion or feeling. This shows that the reason for our repeated incarnations is our emotions; this is the glue of life that keeps us in the body and is a needed desire for the soul to take on a new body after leaving the old one.

My writing experience -

Through the course of writing this book, and rattling the brain with endless logic, trying to reason out and decode every symbol associated with each nakshatra, it has naturally culminated into poetry. Because poetry, I feel, is the only medium through which one can try to express an illogical dimension logically.

Sharing the essence of my understanding is no way complete, but the beginning of a profound understanding that no matter how much the brain can comprehend, it's always limited. By the very nature of things, what we can perceive is always limited, and what we cannot perceive is unlimited. It is this boundless dimension we come from and ultimately merge into.

"Nanak jis te upjaya, tis hi maye samaye" - *Guru Nanak*

Meaning-

From where we have manifested, ultimately, we merge into that.

Writing prose is of the mind, but pouring out poetry is of the heart.

Here is a humble attempt-

The cosmic poem

The Cos-mic union of Nara and Nari-

Masc-u-line with Fem-i-9

The elemental 5, and the play of trine

Initiate divine

In the wake of Nakshatras, Graha's come alive.

Plan-it is the blueprint,

written from the ink of Eastern hori-zon

Forming the zod-iac uni-que,

for each personification of the divine.

Giving the hints for the path of the soul in this lifetime.

Read if you must - for the curiosity of the mind.

Beware though, what you consume with senses 5,

Consumes you

END SO THE CYCLE OF KARMA

With Guru's grace de-vine

Un-tangle

The karmic play of entangling vine.

I feel that in a way desire is our bondage and contentment is our liberation. It seems appropriate to end this book with a chant from the Vedas which describes the nature of Karma beautifully.

Karma

"Karma Mula Tatwam, bhautika jeevan asya.

Karma bhandanam, asya astitva asya.

Karma nahin kasya mitram, karma nahin kasya vairie.

Karma na didati harsham, karma na didati kashtam.

Karma nahin priya priyam, karma na to paap punyam.

Karma naiva purna shuklam, karma naiva purna krishnam.

Guruve swa arpanam, karma dahana suvidhi.

Guruve swa arpanam, nirvana margam.

Guruve swa arpanam, karma grahana mukti."

Meaning -

Karma - The fundamental element of physical life, becomes the basic cause of the soul being born on earth.

Karma - The bondage of this existence becomes our identity, our personality.

Karma - not a friend, not an enemy.

Karma - not the giver of joy or misery.

Karma - is neither to be liked or disliked, nor is it a sin or virtue.

Karma - is neither white (good) nor black (bad).

When one offers oneself to the Guru - it is a good and efficient way to burn one's karma.

When one offers oneself to the Guru - it is the way to ultimate freedom.

When one offers oneself to the Guru - it is a way to earn liberation from all the accumulated karma.

"Where Astrology tries to tell you how the cycles of planets and stars bind you, the spiritual process tells you how to go beyond that." - Sadhguru

Bibliography

- The book of Nakshatras by Prash Trivedi.
- Research on Nakshatras by Dr Arjun Pai.
- Linda Goodman's love signs.
- Cheiro's book of numbers.
- Bhrigu Samhita - Phalit Prakash. Hindi edition - by V S publishers.
- Brihat Parashara Hora Shastra vol 1 and 2 - by Girish Chand Sharma, Sagar publications.
- Four Vedas- Rig, Yajur, Sam and Atharva. English translations by Ralph TH Griffith, through ebook.
- Mahurta Yogas by Ernst Wilhelm.
- Sat-Chakra-Nirupana.
- Online research.
- Documentary - Hunting the hidden dimension by Nova.
- Sadhguru's talks.
- Astrology App used - Cosmic Insights

Courses

- Vedic astrology courses- done with Kapiel Raaj and Achala Sylwia Mihajlovic.
- In person Ayurveda workshop done with Dr Vasant Lad.
- Online course on Ayurveda done with Dr David Frawley.
- Spiritual yogic courses done with Sadhguru - from Inner engineering to Samyama.

www.ingramcontent.com/pod-product-compliance
Lightning Source LLC
Chambersburg PA
CBHW051349070526
44584CB00025B/3695